The Concise Oxford Dictionary of
Linguistics

SECOND EDITION

W9-BON-352

Peter Matthews is Emeritus Professor of Linguistics
at Cambridge University and a Fellow of St John's
College, Cambridge. His many publications in the
field of Linguistics include *Inflectional Morphology*
(1972), *Morphology* (2nd edn., 1991), *Generative
Grammar and Linguistic Competence* (1979), *Syntax*
(1981), *Grammatical Theory in the United States
from Bloomfield to Chomsky* (1993), *A Short History of
Structural Linguistics* (2001), *Syntactic Relations* (2007),
and (with Oxford University Press) *Linguistics: A Very
Short Introduction* (2003).

...most authoritative and up-to-date reference books for both students and the general reader.

Oxford Paperback Reference

The Concise
Oxford Dictionary of

Linguistics

SECOND EDITION

P. H. MATTHEWS

OXFORD
UNIVERSITY PRESS

Great Clarendon Street, Oxford OX2 6DP

Oxford University Press is a department of the University of Oxford.
It furthers the University's objective of excellence in research, scholarship,
and education by publishing worldwide in

Oxford New York

Auckland Cape Town Dar es Salaam Hong Kong Karachi Kuala Lumpur
Madrid Melbourne Mexico City Nairobi New Delhi Shanghai Taipei Toronto

With offices in

Argentina Austria Brazil Chile Czech Republic France Greece
Guatemala Hungary Italy Japan Poland Portugal
Singapore South Korea Switzerland Thailand Turkey Ukraine Vietnam

Oxford is a registered trademark of Oxford University Press
in the UK and in certain other countries

British Library Cataloguing in Publication Data

Data available

Library of Congress Cataloging in Publication Data

Data available

ISBN 978-0-19-920272-0

1

Typeset by SPI Publisher Services, Pondicherry, India

Printed in Great Britain by Clays Ltd, St Ives plc

Contents

Introduction

This is a 'concise dictionary' and it is 'of linguistics'. What should such a book be like and what should it include?

Linguistics is defined in general dictionaries as 'the science of language' or 'the scientific study of language'. In the more cautious wording of *The New Shorter Oxford English Dictionary*, it is 'the branch of knowledge that deals with language'. But although it is the only academic discipline that deals with language alone, and there are aspects of language that it alone is concerned with, its practitioners cannot claim a monopoly of the whole of their subject matter. A range of other disciplines, from the study of literature to computer science, deal with language in one way or another, and the boundaries between them and linguistics are not fixed. It would indeed be a pity if they were. How far into these should the entries in this dictionary go?

Let us start from the centre and work outwards. Everyone will agree that grammar, in a wider or narrower sense, is part of linguistics: in its widest sense, it includes both the study of the structure of words and of syntactic constructions, and that of sound systems. In the second half of the twentieth century these fields have seen an explosive development of technical theory, and a great deal of this dictionary is taken up with it. Everyone will agree that linguistics is concerned with the lexical and grammatical categories of individual languages, with differences between one type of language and another, and with historical relations within families of languages. These are potentially bottomless pits, and strict limitations are needed to avoid falling into them; but I hope I have included what users will judge to be important. Many languages are both spoken and written, and although the nature and history of writing systems are not always covered in university courses in linguistics, it is hard to see in what other dictionary one might expect to look them up. Apart from the details of individual systems and the technicalities of their description, there are also issues of general theory that belong to linguistics alone: that of change in language is one of them. But beyond this there are problems, and it has to be acknowledged that in a number of cases, involving both single entries and classes of entry, I could have decided differently.

Should I, for example, have included entries for parsing strategies in computational linguistics? The name of this field suggests that it is a branch of linguistics and certainly, once upon a time, it was. But it has increasingly become a part of computer science, addressing problems of its own that do not bear, and quite properly are no longer claimed to bear, on the nature of language as such. I have therefore asked myself whether someone whose interests are centred on the topics that linguists must know about is any poorer, as a linguist, for not

knowing this field as well, and, after some soul-searching, have drawn
in my net accordingly. The same test has been applied to other aspects
of language or speech processing, and to much of, for example, the
traditional terminology of rhetoric. It also applies to the study
of methods in language teaching, which, as part of what is
conventionally called 'applied linguistics', again appears, at first sight,
to belong to our subject. But we are past the days when this was seen
as literally an application of linguistics, and linguists in general do not
still expect to gain many insights from it. A further test was whether,
in drafting an entry, the terms on which a definition would rest are
themselves terms in linguistics or in a field that is clearly separate.
A dictionary of linguistics cannot systematically include things that
belong to computer science in general, or to acoustics, or to anatomy
or physiology, or to general psychology or the social sciences, even
when, as terms in neighbouring subjects, they are used by linguists in
some branches of their own. But it would frustrate the reader if other
entries were then to take them for granted. In some cases this has
forced me to cut corners: something must be in and, even if its
explanation has to be less precise than a technical definition would be,
it may at least be possible for readers who need the relevant entry to
get some help from it. In other cases even circumlocution has failed
and, where the term is marginal, I have judged it safer to leave it out.

The need to cut corners was most pressing in some areas of
phonetics and of semantics. Acoustics is not in general part of
linguistics; nor, at least as I conceive it, are topics such as the anatomy
of the larynx. But some specific terms in acoustics are, and the
distinctions between different types of phonation, which is a hard
enough topic in our present state of knowledge, might be made more
precise if anatomical detail could be assumed. Philosophy and logic
are not part of linguistics either, but the literature on semantics is full
of terms that derive from them. Many have a long history and are not
univocal; sometimes their use by linguists reflects this only in part;
sometimes, as linguists have borrowed them, their senses have slid yet
further. But since they do belong to another discipline, a dictionary of
linguistics sometimes cannot do more than pick up a fag end. It is
perhaps in this area that I feel least happy with the solutions I have at
times been driven to.

In the centre of the subject it is, of course, much easier both to lay
down principles and to apply them. Since this is a dictionary, it does
not include entries that are purely encyclopaedic. Since it is a concise
dictionary, my aim has been to explain as many things as possible
and as briefly as possible, not, as might be done in another kind of
dictionary, to cover less but cover it more expansively. But some things
have to be left out. There must, for example, be entries for some
individual languages: those that have speakers safely into the millions,
those that are important in the history of scholarship, those that,
quite simply, the majority of those who will buy this book will feel

they should be able to look up. But most languages meet none of these criteria and, however one counts, they are well in the thousands. There should, I believe, be notes on individual scholars, some of them still living. But which? I have tried to limit such entries to people who are cited for their contribution to general linguistics, as opposed to the study of a particular language or family. But if I had relaxed that test the list could have gone on and on. There must also be entries for schools, or for the competing models of syntax, phonology, and so on that tend to define schools. Where these are more than one-man bands they are, I hope, in. But both schools and individual scholars also tend to develop specialized terminology, both new terms and altered senses of old ones. These sometimes pass into general currency and then, of course, they must be included. But where they remain peculiar to a specific model, and are not needed in the entry that explains the model itself, I have had to leave them out. If I had not, the dictionary would again have been much larger.

There must also be limits on what certain classes of entry contain. Under the headings for individual languages, I have said at the least where they are spoken and what family, if any, they are known to belong to. But I have not in general said how many people speak them, and in most cases I do not think this information can be given without reference to surveys at specific dates and the specific evidence and criteria that they used. That is more than a concise dictionary can or should do. I have also refrained from saying anything about their structure: it would, for a start, take more space than can be spared. In the entries for grammatical categories, I have given concrete illustrations where they can be drawn from languages with which a substantial body of readers will be familiar. These naturally tend to be European. Where this cannot be done the illustrations are schematic. I had not at first intended that they should be and, in failing to decorate some entries in this way, I still feel rather as my wife would if she were forced to go to town without make-up. But decoration is, in reality, all it would be. A monograph or textbook must, of course, supply specific evidence that a category exists. But a dictionary need not and cannot. Its job is simply to make clear how the term is used, and a concrete illustration will at best get in the way if it comes from a language which few readers know and whose general structure is unfamiliar. At worst, there was a danger that I would misunderstand my source or use one that was itself wrong and, without references, no one might know what it was. I would like to feel that, if there are mistakes, they are unequivocally my own.

The rest is mainly a matter of style. In line with other Oxford dictionaries, I have used an asterisk to point to related entries: although its uses in linguistics are for other purposes, I do not think that, in practice, this will cause confusion. Where I refer to scholars for whom there are also entries, I have used their surname without initials, with a first name in brackets where necessary: thus 'Chomsky'

or '(Daniel) Jones'. Where an abbreviation is common I have given an
entry for it, unless it immediately precedes the term it abbreviates:
thus '**ABS** = absolutive'. The abbreviation '*cf.*' means, as usual,
'compare'; I have also used an *ad hoc* abbreviation 'opp.' to indicate a
term which is the opposite of the one defined: thus '**bound** . . . Opp.
free'. Where a term is used in two or more related senses I have
distinguished them within an entry: thus '**substratum 1.** . . . **2.** . . .'. But
where senses are effectively unrelated I have separated the entries:
thus '**head (1)**' and '**head (2)**'. When a definition begins with words in
round brackets, they generally indicate what an adjective or the like
is used of: thus '**consecutive** (Clause etc.) indicating . . .'. In giving
examples, I have indicated stress or emphasis, where necessary, by
putting a syllable in small capitals: thus '*I need the* HAMM*mer*' (not e.g. the
screwdriver). These are often preceded by an accent which gives a
rough indication of the intonation: thus '*He's* `co*ming*' (with the pitch
falling from 'co' onwards), '*He's not* ´co*ming*' (with the pitch rising),
'*Is he* ˇco*ming?*' (fall followed by a rise). Other conventions, e.g. in the
use of italics, follow what is now general practice.

Finally, I have included pronunciations (in the IPA transcription
used in *The New Shorter Oxford English Dictionary*) only when I thought
that readers might be in doubt. For a dictionary of this kind to include
them throughout did seem otiose.

Acknowledgements

A book like this can only be written by one person. If I had had to plan
it as an editor, I would have allotted too much space to some entries
and too little to others, and individual contributors might in any case
have overshot my instructions, even when I was right. But one person
cannot be a specialist in the whole of linguistics and, in the fields one
thinks one knows, one can make strange mistakes. I am therefore
very grateful to all those who have helped me: in particular, at the
beginning of the project, to Francis Nolan, Stephen Levinson, and
Nigel Vincent, who vetted my original list of headwords, and, at the
very end, to Nigel Vincent once more and to Jim McCawley, who read
through a complete draft. McCawley especially supplied comments
and corrections with a thoroughness and understanding quite beyond
the call of duty.

   I am grateful to Angus Phillips of the Oxford University Press, for
his advice and patience. I have also been fortunate in my copy-editor,
Margaret Aherne, who has done extremely well a job that requires
many kinds of vigilance simultaneously. My wife, Lucienne Schleich,
has commented from a user's viewpoint on the wording of many
entries, and has helped me very much to develop the right style. She
has also had to put up with my tantrums when, at times, the project
has been driving me round the bend: without her love and
encouragement I would not have finished it.

P.H.M.

December 1996

Note on the Second Edition

This new edition basically updates the first and corrects some errors, of omission not least. In improving its coverage I have been helped a great deal by more helpful indexing and the appearance of specialized glossaries, in sociolinguistics in particular.

A colleague who was invited by the Press to comment on the first edition assumed that its 'compilers' (plural) would seek the advice of specialists as to what, for example, should be included. I have already made clear that the author has, in my view, to be singular. But I also dispute that the process is indeed one of compiling. If Avestan and Etruscan are in, why not e.g. Sogdian or Sabellian? If 'linking r' (in English), why not perhaps 'mimation' (in Semitic)? Why not get rid of old terms such as 'crasis' or 'hyperbaton', if they no longer appear in general textbooks? Why not indeed include more new creations, such as 'ambiclipping' or 'depidginization'? What about such general terms as 'class' or 'culture', which are a subject of disagreement in neighbouring disciplines? I have consulted experts from time to time, and I am particularly grateful to a group of fellow members of the 'Linguistics and Philology' section of the British Academy, who listened to a short talk on the problem last spring. But the headwords themselves are already a product of judgement, not of accumulation.

P.H.M.

January 2007

Directory of Symbols

Symbols and other forms of notation are explained in entries headed by their names: for example, for the uses of '[ ]', see the entry for 'square brackets'. The complete list is as follows.

A 1. = adjective. **2.** = agent (2); *cf.* P, S (3). **3.** = argument, as *A-bound, *A-movement.

AAVE = African American Vernacular English.

abbreviated clause = reduced clause.

abbreviation *See* acronym; blend; clipping.

abbreviatory convention Any convention that allowed a *generative grammar to be shortened by collapsing two or more rules into one. E.g. a phrase-structure rule A′ → A + Comp (a constituent within an adjective phrase can consist of an adjective plus a complement) can be combined with a rule A′ → A into the single expression 'A′ → A (Comp). By the relevant convention 'A (Comp)' is understood as 'either A or A + Comp'.

abduction Applied in historical linguistics to the process of reasoning by which, e.g. from 'All dogs bark' and 'This animal barks', one draws the conclusion 'This animal is a dog'.

   Central, in one view, when people develop their native language. E.g. they may learn that if a noun has the ending *-s* it is plural: so, as one premiss, 'All noun forms in *-s* are plural'. They may then want to use some noun in the plural. Call the form required *f*: so, as a second premiss, '*f* is plural'. By abduction, the conclusion will be '*f* is a form in *-s*': therefore, all else being equal, a form in *-s* is what they will use. In this process of reasoning the conclusion does not necessarily follow: thus the noun in question might have a plural that does not end in *-s*. But as the result of it the language may change, with *-s* generalized to nouns that did not previously have it.

   Abductive change is change due, it is claimed, to abduction. The term as such was borrowed from *Peirce, but in this sense is specific to linguistics.

abessive *Case indicating that someone or something is absent: e.g. schematically, *I came money*-ABESS 'I came without money'. From Latin *abesse* 'to be away, be absent'.

abjad From the first four letters of the Arabic writing system, as 'alphabet' from 'alpha' plus 'beta'. Thence applied to *consonantal alphabets in general.

Abkhaz North West *Caucasian language, spoken between the west end of the Caucasus Mountains and the coast of the Black Sea.

ablative (ABL) *Case whose basic role, or one of whose basic roles, is to indicate movement away from some location: thus Latin *cedit Romā* ('departed Rome-ABL.SG') 'He left Rome'.

ablative absolute *Absolute construction in Latin in which a participle and its subject are in the ablative case and are subordinated, with no other mark of linkage, to the rest of the sentence: e.g. in the sentence *urbe capta* '(the) city-ABL.SG having-been-taken-ABL.SG' *Caesar recessit* 'Caesar withdrew'.

ablaut Morphological variation, in Germanic and other *Indo-European languages, of a root vowel. E.g. in Ancient Greek the root of the verb 'to leave' appeared in three forms: *leip-* in the present; *loip-*, in the perfect or in the adjective *loipós* 'left over'; *lip-*, in the aorist or as the first member of compounds. This illustrates the three original '**grades**' of ablaut: the *e* grade, the *o* grade, and the zero or reduced grade, with neither *e* nor *o*.

Similarly, in English, of vowel variations in *strong verbs (e.g. *drive, drove, driven*) or between verbs and nouns (*sing, song*), whether or not they derive directly from the Indo-European system.

A-bound *Bound (2) by a unit in a position which is typically that of a subject, hence more generally by an *argument of, a verb. E.g. in *I saw myself*, the reflexive *myself* is A-bound by its antecedent *I*.

A unit bound by another that is not in an argument- or **A-position** was defined in *Government and Binding Theory as '**A′-bound**'. *Cf.* A-movement.

abrupt *Distinctive feature in the scheme proposed by *Jakobson. Characterized acoustically by 'a spread of energy over a wide frequency region': thus, in particular, a feature of oral stops as opposed to fricatives. Also called 'discontinuous' or 'interrupted': opp. continuant.

ABS = absolutive.

absolute 1. (Syntactic element) not accompanied by an element to which one might expect it to be linked. E.g. in *This is bigger, bigger* is an **absolute comparative**, not linked, as other comparatives are, to a standard of comparison (*bigger than* . . .); in *His is bigger, his* is similarly an **absolute possessive**, not linked, as possessives in general are, to a noun (*his garden, his kitchen*, . . .). **2.** (Form of word) that has no inflection. Thus an **absolute case**, e.g. in Turkish, is so called because it is realized by a root alone, with no affix.

An **absolute construction** is one in which a subordinate element is not linked by a conjunction or in any other specific way to the rest of a sentence. E.g. in *We left, the wine having run out*, the last five words stand in an absolute relation to *we left*: cf. *We left because the wine had run out* (with the conjunction *because*), or *We left, having finished the wine* (with a direct relation between *having* and *we*).

From Latin *absolutus* 'freed from linkage'.

absolute adjective One whose sense might be expected to exclude a comparative or superlative. E.g. *equal*, used as if it were gradable in *Some animals are more equal than others*.

absolute neutralization Term in *Generative Phonology for the suppression in all contexts of an underlying difference between elements. E.g. in a language with *vowel harmony, a single open vowel might relate sometimes to front vowels and sometimes to back vowels: a distinction might therefore be established between an underlying front 'a' and back 'ɑ', which undergoes absolute neutralization after the rules for harmony have applied.

absolute synonymy *See* synonymy.

'absolute universal' A *linguistic universal that is genuinely universal: i.e. that holds for all languages, without exception. Opp. relative universal, statistical universal.

absolutive (ABS) *Case which identifies both the *patient in a basic transitive construction and a single argument or valent in an intransitive. E.g. schematically, *men bread-*ABS *ate* 'The men ate the bread'; *bread-*ABS *disappeared* 'The bread disappeared'. The *agent in the transitive construction will then be *ergative: *bread-*ABS *ate men-*ERG. The case is called 'absolutive' because, in many languages, it is distinguished by the absence of an affix.

Thence in general of syntactic elements that unite the same roles, whether or not the language has cases.

'absorption' 1. Used variously of phonological changes or processes in which one element is seen as incorporated in another. Thus '**tonal absorption**' is a process in some languages of West Africa by which the ending of a *contour tone (rising ˇ, falling ˆ) is 'absorbed' by a following syllable whose tone is at the same level: rising ˇ plus high ´ → low ` plus high ´; falling ˆ plus low ` → high ´ plus low `. *Cf.* fusion. **2.** Process in which a case or case role is assigned to one element in a construction and can then no longer be assigned to another.

'Abstand' language One whose perceived distinction from others rests on intrinsic differences between its system and theirs. Thus French as distinct from English, German etc. Opposed in that sense to an *'Ausbau' language. From a German word for 'distance'.

abstract (Structure, representation) which differs from that which is most transparent. E.g. the representation of *righteous* as 'rixt-i-ɔs', proposed at an underlying level in *Generative Phonology at the end of the 1960s, is more abstract than one which corresponds closely to a phonetic transcription [rʌɪtʃəs]. Similarly, a representation of the syntax of a sentence is more abstract the more the order in which the words are arranged and the units and categories to which they are assigned differ from their order and potential grouping in speech.

Since the end of the 1960s most linguists have tried to put restrictions on the degree of abstractness that their models will permit: e.g. to exclude representations such as 'rixt-i-ɔs'. But it has been hard to propose firm limits that all will accept; hence in phonology a long-standing **abstractness** controversy.

'abstract case' *See* case.

abstract noun One which denotes an abstract state, property, etc.: e.g. *love*, *happiness*. Opp. concrete.

abugida Neologism, parallel to *abjad, for a writing system that is *alpha-syllabic.

ACC = accusative.

Accadian = Akkadian.

accent (1) A phonological unit realized by auditory prominence, especially within a word. E.g. in *morning* the first syllable is perceived as more prominent than the second: in phonetic transcription, ['mɔːnɪŋ]. This distinguishes it as the **accented** syllable, or the one that 'carries the accent'. Originally of *pitch accents in Ancient Greek; thence of *stress accents, e.g. in English; thence also applied to peaks of prominence in larger units, such as sentences. E.g. in *He'll talk to ´*ME ('to me, not someone else'), the 'sentence accent', or *sentence stress, falls on *me*.

The accents in writing, as in French *père*, *bête*, *céder*, originally distinguished pitches in Greek, the acute a high pitch, the circumflex a falling pitch, the grave a low pitch. But they have since been used for many other purposes, to distinguish length or quality of vowels, different consonants, homonyms, and so on, with others added in the spelling of various languages.

accent (2) A variety of speech differing phonetically from other varieties: thus, as in ordinary usage, 'a Southern accent', 'Scottish accents'. Normally restricted by linguists to cases where the differences are at most in phonology: further differences, e.g. in syntax, are said to be between *dialects.

acceptable (Sentence, etc.) which native speakers will not see as contrary to usage. Often = grammatical (2), but many scholars insist on a distinction, drawn by Chomsky in the 1960s, between the acceptability of a sentence, taken as a datum, and its conformity to the rules of a specific grammar. Thus a sentence like *The man the girl your son knew saw arrived* may be unacceptable to speakers. But its structure conforms to general rules that may be posited for *relative clauses: *the man* ₛ[*the girl* ₛ[*your son knew*] *saw*] . . . So, by hypothesis, it is grammatical, and its unacceptability must be explained by other factors, such as the difficulty of keeping track of it in short-term memory.

accessibility scale A scale of elements or categories in order of diminishing applicability of some type or types of process. E.g. in English, a direct object (DO) can generally be made the subject of a passive: *Harry saw them* → *They were seen by Harry*. So can an indirect object (IO), but with more restrictions and exclusions. So too a locative

(Loc), but with even more restrictions and exclusions. These elements can thus be said to form a scale: DO > IO > Loc, where x > y means that x is more open to the process.

Similar scales are often formulated across languages: e.g. the *NP accessibility hierarchy.

'accident' Ancient term for a variable property of words belonging to a specific *part of speech. Accidents included categories of inflection: e.g. *number and *case as variable features of nouns. They also included any other feature that might vary: e.g. the 'quality' of nouns (lit. their 'what-sort-ness') was an accident initially distinguishing *proper nouns from *common nouns.

Later used especially of categories of inflection: hence '**accidence**' is in effect an older term for *inflectional morphology.

accommodation General term for ways in which the speech of individuals is adjusted, e.g. in intonation, in phonetic detail, in timing, in accordance with or in response to that of others with whom they are speaking. '**Accommodation Theory**' is the name for a branch of *sociolinguistics concerned with such adjustments.

accomplishment *See Aktionsart.*

accusative (ACC) *Case whose basic role, or one of whose basic roles, is to mark a *direct object. E.g. in Latin *vidi Caesarem* 'I-saw Caesar', the object *Caesarem* has the accusative singular ending *-(e)m*.

The term derives from a mistranslation into Latin of a Greek term that was already obscure. There is and was no connection with accusing.

accusative and infinitive Construction in Latin in which an indirect statement was marked by a verb in the infinitive whose subject was in the accusative: e.g. in *Dixit Caesarem venisse* 'he-said Caesar-ACC.SG had-come-INF' ('He said that Caesar had come'). Extended to formally similar constructions in other languages: e.g. in English (*He told*) *me to come*.

'accusative language' One which has a *nominative and an *accusative case, or which distinguishes subjects and objects in an equivalent way. E.g. English: thus, in *The boy saw her* and *The boy smiled*, the role of *the boy* as subject is distinguished by its position from its role as object in *She saw the boy*.

Coined in opposition to 'ergative language': *see also* active language.

achievement Basically of an event by which an entity comes into a certain state. Hence of verbs etc. that describe such events: e.g. *die,* or the progressive form of *die,* is an 'achievement verb' in *They are dying. Cf. Aktionsart.*

Achinese *Austronesian language spoken at the northern end of Sumatra. Also '**Achehnese**'.

'acoustic image' *See* linguistic sign.

acoustic phonetics The study of the physical properties of the sounds produced in speech. Opp. articulatory phonetics.

'acquired' (Speech disorder) resulting from disease or injury to the brain, in someone who did not show it before. Thus *aphasia is by definition 'acquired'; *dyslexia, as usually defined, is not 'acquired'.

acrolect Variety of a language which, of a series of varieties spoken predominantly at different social levels, has the highest prestige or is closest to a standard form. Especially in studies of *creoles: e.g. of the varieties spoken in Jamaica the acrolect has the fewest creole features and is thus most similar to standard English elsewhere. Opp. basilect; mesolect.

acronym A word formed from the initial letters of two or more successive words: e.g. *ASH*, phonetically [aʃ], from '*A*ction on *S*moking and *H*ealth'. Sometimes taken to include abbreviations where the letters are spelled out: e.g. *EU*, pronounced [iː juː].

'across the board' (Syntactic process) applying to all members of a coordination, not some members only. E.g. that of relative clauses: thus *the ones who came and left* vs. *the ones who came and they left*. Abbreviated 'ATB'.

ACT = active.

actants Originally in French, and thence in English, for the elements in a clause that identify the participants in a process etc. referred to by a verb. Proposed by L. Tesnière in application to a subject, direct object, and indirect object.

action noun A derived noun whose formation has the general meaning 'act or process of . . . ': e.g. *construction* (from *construct* + *-ion*), with the basic meaning 'process of constructing'. *Cf.* agent noun.

active (1) (ACT) (Construction, sentence) in which a verb has a *subject which is characteristically the role filled by an *agent rather than a *patient. Thus the agent *my wife* is the subject in the active sentence *My wife cut the grass*. Also (and more traditionally) of the form of verb in such a construction. Thus *cut* is an active verb and, in e.g. *the woman cutting the grass*, *cutting* is an active participle.

  Opp. passive (1). In older usage verbs were 'active' only if they had a corresponding passive. Thus *cut* would be active since there is a passive in e.g. *The grass was cut*. If a verb was active in form but had no corresponding passive it was called 'neuter'. Thus a verb like *appear* is traditionally neuter.

active (2) (Vocabulary) that a speaker uses, as opposed to **passive vocabulary**, that is known but not used. Likewise **active knowledge** of a language is knowledge that enables one to speak it, as opposed to **passive knowledge**, which enables one to understand it.

active articulator *See* articulator.

'active language' One which has two basic *intransitive constructions. In the first the noun is identified by its case or otherwise with the *agent in a *transitive construction: this might be so, in particular, when it is itself notionally an agent. In the second it is identified with the *patient in a transitive construction. Thus, in the transitive, the agent and patient might be marked as nominative vs. accusative: schematically, *Mary*-NOM *kissed Sarah*-ACC 'Mary kissed Sarah'. An intransitive would then have variously the nominative or the accusative: e.g. *Mary*-NOM *left*, where *Mary* is an agent or is relatively animate in terms of an *animacy hierarchy, but *The tree*-ACC *fell*, where *the tree* is not an agent or is minimally animate.

Also called 'split intransitive'. Distinguished from an *ergative language, in which the noun in the intransitive is identified throughout with a patient in the transitive construction, and an *accusative language, in which it is identified throughout with an agent.

activity *See* Aktionsart.

actor Sometimes in a sense equivalent to *agent (1). Alternatively, agents as linguistic elements may be distinguished from 'actors' as the individuals in the world that they refer to.

'actualization' = realization.

actuation The way in which changes in a language are initiated. The '**actuation problem**' is accordingly that of explaining why a specific change began in a specific language or dialect at a specific time, and as such is distinguished, in many theories, from the problem of 'implementation', or transmission of the change across a community of speakers.

acute 1. Diacritic (´) originally and still used, in descriptions of *tone languages, to represent a high pitch: *see* accent (1). Also, in accounts of intonation, to represent a rise in pitch. **2.** *Distinctive feature of both consonants and vowels proposed by *Jakobson in the 1950s: e.g. in English front vowels are acute, as are dental and alveolar consonants. Defined acoustically by a relative concentration of energy in higher frequencies. Opp. grave; *see also* compact.

adaptation The process by which *loan words are changed to fit the sound patterns of the language into which they are borrowed. Often progressive or otherwise a matter of degree: e.g. of the several pronunciations of *garage*, [gəˈrɑːʒ] is least adapted from its source in French, while [ˈgarɪdʒ] is fully adapted.

'additive bilingualism' *Bilingualism in which a *second language is acquired without detriment to the first. Used e.g. of the learning of French by English speakers in Canada: that of German and French by speakers of Luxembourgish or of standard German by speakers of Swiss German also seems to fit the definition. Contrasted with *subtractive bilingualism.

address *See* forms of address.

addressee The normal term for a person to whom someone else (the speaker) speaks or 'addresses' an *utterance. *Cf.* hearer.

addressee-controlled honorific *See* honorific; polite form.

Adelung, Johann Christoph (1732–1806) Student of German, important in the history of general linguistics for his last project, *Mithridates*, which compiled information, including versions of the Lord's Prayer, on all languages then known to European scholarship. Published by Adelung and J. S. Vater in four volumes (1806–17), with the contents arranged geographically: the final survey of its kind in the period before the triumph of *comparative linguistics.

adequacy *See* levels of adequacy.

adessive *Case indicating position adjacent to an object etc. E.g. schematically, *Book-ADESS red cover* 'The book has (i.e. has adjacent to it) a red cover'.

'ad hoc' Latin for 'to this'. Common from the 1960s onwards as a term of criticism or abuse. E.g. a proposed rule could be dismissed as 'ad hoc' if it covers only some of the data that a critic sees as relevant.

adhortative = exhortative.

Adj = adjective.

adjacency The usual term in linguistics for 'position next to'. Thus various forms of '**adjacency principle**' are principles by which elements that are syntactically related cannot be, or tend not to be, separated.

adjacency pair Two successive utterances by different speakers, where the second is of a type required or expected by the first. E.g. a question followed by an answer; a greeting followed by a greeting in return.

adjective A word of a class whose most characteristic role is as the modifier of a noun: e.g. in *tall men*, *tall* is an adjective modifying *men*. Hence typically understood as referring to properties (thus in this case that of being tall) not essential to whatever is denoted (in this case all possible men) by the noun. Adjectives were seen in antiquity as a distinct subclass of nouns, added or adjoined to ('ad-') others; as such they were sometimes said to have a role parallel to that of adverbs in their relation to verbs. They were distinguished as a separate *part of speech ('noun adjective' vs. 'noun *substantive') in the later Middle Ages, and are often, in the modern period, seen either as sharing properties with verbs or as intermediate between verbs and nouns.

An **adjectival** element is one either associated with or having the role of adjectives: e.g. -*less* in *clueless* is an adjectival affix; English *participial adjectives in -*ed*, such as *interested* in *very interested*, are sometimes called 'adjectival passives'.

adjective clause = relative clause: i.e. its role in a noun phrase, like that of adjectives, is as a modifier of the noun.

adjective phrase A *phrase (1) whose *head (1) is an adjective: e.g. *very tall* in [*very tall*] *men*, whose head is the adjective *tall*.

adjunct 1. Any element in the structure of a clause which is not part of its *nucleus (1) or core. E.g. in *I will bring it on my bike tomorrow*, the nucleus of the clause is *I will bring it*; the adjuncts are *on my bike* and *tomorrow*. Distinguished as such from, in one account, both *I* and *you* as *complements (1). **2.** The position or role, in one variant of *X-bar syntax, of a unit that is neither a *Complement (Comp) nor a *Specifier (Spec). E.g., in *a book on syntax in paperback*, a head *book*, which is an N, might form an N′ with a Complement *on syntax*. This N′ might in turn combine with an adjunct, *in paperback*, to form a larger N′, which would combine with a Specifier to form an NP. **3.** Specifically, in Quirk *et al.*, *CGE*, of a range of *adverbials including those of manner, place, and time: e.g. *carelessly, in the dustbin*, and *yesterday* are adjuncts, in one case obligatory, in *I put it carelessly in the dustbin yesterday*. Distinguished as such from *conjuncts, *disjuncts, and *subjuncts.

The term was originally introduced by Jespersen, for the *secondary element in a *junction (1). But it is no longer in general use in that sense.

adjunction 1. Any operation, especially in syntax, by which an element is added next to another. E.g. in *Who have you met?*, *who* is sometimes seen as **adjoined**, by *wh*-movement, to the remainder of the sentence: [*who* [*have you met*]]. **2.** Specifically, in terms of *X-bar syntax, of an operation by which, when A is adjoined to B, the two together form a unit whose category is in turn that of B. E.g. if B is a *CP, the adjunction of A will form a larger unit, [A [B]], which is also a CP. Adjunction in this sense is allowed in *Government and Binding Theory only when B is a *maximal projection (in this case of C); the structure that results is an **adjunction structure**.

*Chomsky-adjunction and *sister-adjunction are types distinguished in earlier transformational grammars.

admixture The transfer of any part of the structure of one language into that of another. Hence, in particular, *borrowing; but *cf.* interference.

adnominal (Word etc.) directly depending on a noun. Thus, in *the girl singing*, the participle *singing* depends on *girl*; a participle is accordingly, in some accounts, an adnominal form of a verb.

adposition Cover term for *prepositions and *postpositions. The sense is that of an element positioned 'next to' ('ad-'), whether before ('pre-') or after ('post-').

adstratum A language which has influenced one spoken by a neighbouring population. Thus in the modern period French has been an adstratum in the development of English. *Cf.* substratum; superstratum.

Adv = adverb.

Advanced RP *See* 'Received Pronunciation'.

Advanced Tongue Root A distinctive feature of vowels e.g. in many West African languages. Abbreviated [± ATR]: in the production of vowels that are [+ ATR] the tongue is drawn forward so that the space between the tongue root and the back of the throat is widened; in vowels that are [– ATR] the tongue is retracted so that this space is narrowed.

Often described as 'tense' vs. 'lax' before the nature of the distinction was made clear.

advancement = promotion.

'advantage' *See* dative of advantage.

adverb A word of a class whose most characteristic role is traditionally that of modifying a verb or verb phrase: e.g. *badly* in *He wrote it badly*, where (in different accounts) it modifies either *wrote* or the phrase *wrote it*.

One of the *parts of speech established in antiquity. In the grammar of English and many similar languages, an adverb is effectively a word that modifies anything other than a noun. Thus *badly* as above; *certainly* in *Certainly I'll come*, where it modifies *I'll come*; *highly* in *highly inflammatory*, where it modifies *inflammatory*; *nearly* in *nearly there*, where it modifies another adverb *there*. The reasons for lumping these roles together are (*a*) that they are often served by words of the same form (e.g. words in *-ly*), (*b*) that the same words often serve two or more of them.

adverbial (Syntactic element) whose role is one served by adverbs. Thus *on Monday* is an **adverbial phrase**, or an **adverbial**, in *I'll do it on Monday*: compare *I'll do it tomorrow,* with the single adverb *tomorrow*. Likewise *when I'm ready* is an **adverbial clause** in *I'll do it when I'm ready*.

adverb phrase A *phrase (2) whose *head (1) is an adverb: e.g. *very badly*, headed by *badly*, in *I sing very badly*.

adversative Usually of a form or construction marking an
*antithesis: e.g. *but* is an adversative conjunction in *I'll try, but it may
not work*.

aerometry The measurement of air flow, e.g. in the production of
speech. The techniques used in phonetics involve the insertion at
appropriate places in the vocal tract of instruments which measure a
drop in air pressure across a resistance, which is directly related to the
rate of flow.

affected object The *direct object of a verb denoting an action etc.
which affects individuals or things already in existence. Thus *the silver*
is an affected object in *I polished the silver*, since silver exists before it is
polished. Opp. effected object.

'affection' Older term for the effect of one sound on another that
precedes or follows: *cf.* assimilation (1); coarticulation.

affective (Function, meaning) having to do with a speaker's feelings.
E.g. one might say, as a neutral statement, 'I have finished it'; or one
might say, with triumph or amazement, 'I have ´ACTUALLY ´FInished
it'. What is said is in other respects the same, but the utterances differ
in affective meaning. Likewise intonations or words like *actually* have,
or have at times, an affective function.

   Also called 'emotive', 'expressive'. Opposed variously to *cognitive
meaning, *propositional meaning, or to the representational or
referential *function of language.

affirmative (Sentence, form, construction) by which one asserts
what is, as opposed to what is not, the case. Opp. negative; also,
implicitly, to e.g. interrogative, imperative.

affix Any element in the morphological structure of a word other
than a *root (1). E.g. *unkinder* consists of the root *kind* plus the affixes
un- and *-er*. Hence **affixation**, for the process of adding an affix. Also
affixal: thus *un-* in *unkind* is an affixal element, and the formation of
unkind is that of an 'affixal negative'.

   Affixes are traditionally divided into *prefixes, which come before
the form to which they are joined; *suffixes, which come after; and
*infixes, which are inserted within it. Others commonly distinguished
are *circumfixes and *superfixes.

'affix hopping' Rule posited in *transformational grammar in the
1950s by which elements realized by affixes of verbs in English are
placed in affixal position. E.g. *Jim left* is assigned an underlying
structure *Jim* PAST *leave*, where PAST is syntactically an auxiliary. To
derive the actual or surface structure, PAST 'hops over' *leave* and is
attached as a suffix to it: *Jim leave-*PAST.

affricate A *stop consonant released with a *fricative at the same
place of articulation: e.g. [tʃ] (written *ch*) in *chip*.

African American Vernacular English Variety of English
identified as that of urban communities especially in the USA whose
members are historically of African descent. Abbreviated AAVE.
Formerly called '**Black English Vernacular**' (abbreviated BEV);
renamed in deference to changes in political correctness.

The non-technical term '**Ebonics**' was originally proposed for
features said to characterize more generally the English of descendants
of the victims of the slave trade, in the USA and in the Caribbean.

African languages Currently classified, for convenience or as a
working hypothesis, into four main groups. *Afro-Asiatic, across North
Africa, the Sahara, and the adjacent Near East, includes, as its largest
member, *Arabic. A *Khoisan group consists of a minority towards the
southern tip of the continent. '**Nilo-Saharan**' represents a speculative
attempt to group together *Nilotic languages with others spoken between
the upper Nile and the Congo. '**Niger-Congo**' lumps together all the
remainder, including *Bantu and most of the languages of West Africa.

The classification derives in part from an application of *mass
comparison by Greenberg in the early 1960s.

Afrikaans *Germanic, derivative from Dutch, spoken in South Africa
and elsewhere in Africa by emigration. Sometimes claimed to
be a Dutch-based *creole, a claim also strongly resisted.

Afro-Asiatic Family of languages, in part well-established, which
includes *Semitic and *Cushitic; also *Berber, *Egyptian, and the
*Chadic languages in sub-Saharan Africa. Previously called '**Hamito-
Semitic**', on the assumption that Semitic forms one major branch and
the others thought to belong to it form another, called '**Hamitic**'.

age-grading Variation in speech that is correlated with the age of
speakers, but does not reflect a change in progress. E.g. certain forms of
slang may at any time be commoner in schoolchildren than in adults.

agent 1. Phrase etc. identifying an actor or actors performing some
action. E.g. *Mary* is an agent in *Mary went out* or *Mary made it*.
2. A syntactic category which is characteristically that of agents as
opposed to *patients. Thus the subject of a transitive construction in
English has the role of agent (A) in opposition to an object as patient:
Mary (A) *shut the door* (P). **3.** The element in a passive sentence which
would correspond to a subject in the active, e.g. *by Mary* in *The car
was driven by Mary*: cf. active *Mary drove the car*.

agentive 1. Having the semantic role of an *agent (1): e.g. *I* is
agentive in *I did it*. **2.** (Case) = ergative. **3.** (Noun) = agent noun: also of
a process or affix by which such nouns are formed.

agentless passive A passive without an *agent (3): e.g. *She was
promoted*, as compared with *She was promoted by her company*, with agent
by her company. *Cf*. reduced passive.

agent noun A derived noun whose formation has the general meaning 'someone who does . . .': e.g. *builder*, from *build* + *-er*, meaning 'someone who builds'. *Cf.* action noun.

agglutinating (Language, formation) in which words are easily divided into separate segments with separate grammatical functions. E.g. in Turkish, *dişçilerimin* 'of my dentists' is transparently made up of a root (*diş* 'tooth') and four suffixes: *-çi* (agentive), *-ler* (plural), *-im* 'my', and *-in* (genitive).
Opp. inflecting; isolating. **Agglutination** is likewise the process by which such structures or this type of structure is formed.

AGR ['agə] For 'Agreement'. A syntactic category in *Principles and Parameters Theory since the 1980s, which originally distinguished features of verbs traditionally relevant to agreement, such as number, from the remainder.
Hence a subdivision of, in the earliest notation, *INFL. Itself divided in turn into e.g. Agr$_S$ and Agr$_O$ (where S, O correspond to 'subject' and 'object'), seen as *heads (1) of successive levels of '**agreement phrases**', on the lines of Agr$_S$P and Agr$_O$P, overt or *null as necessary.

agrammatism Form of *aphasia in which grammatical elements are lost. The resulting speech is often described as 'telegraphic', consisting mainly of lexical items and fixed expressions; also slow and hesitant.

agreement Syntactic relation between words and phrases which are compatible, in a given construction, by virtue of inflections carried by at least one of them. E.g. *these* and *carrots* are compatible, in the construction of *these carrots*, because both are inflected as plural. Likewise, in the Italian sentence *Maria e Luisa sono arrivate* 'Mary and Louise have arrived', *sono* (lit. 'be-3PL') agrees in respect of plural number with *arrivate* ('arrived-FEM.PL') and both, or *sono arrivate* as a whole, agree with a subject, *Maria e Luisa*, which refers to more than one woman.
Also called **concord**. Distinctions are drawn between *grammatical agreement and *notional agreement; also between agreement and some similar relations of compatibility, such as the *government (2) of cases by prepositions. But the last of these is often at best imprecise.

agreement phrase *See* AGR.

AGT = agent, agentive.

airstream mechanism Any system by which a flow of air is generated in the production of speech. Types of mechanism are distinguished by two criteria: (*a*) as egressive or ingressive, according to the direction of flow; (*b*) as *pulmonic, *glottalic, or *velaric, according to the way in which the flow is initiated.

The main mechanism, and in many languages the only one that is normally employed, is breathing out. This is (*a*) egressive, in that air flows outwards, and (*b*) pulmonic, in that air is pushed out from the lungs as their volume is reduced by the contraction of the chest muscles. For other mechanisms of particular importance in speech *see* click; ejective; implosive.

Akan Group of dialects or closely related languages, spoken mainly in Ghana: separately named Asante, Fante, and Akuapem (or Twi).

Akkadian *Semitic language spoken especially, in varying forms, in ancient Babylonia and Assyria. Written in *cuneiform from about 2500 BC and by the middle of the next millennium an international language throughout the Near East. It has no modern descendant.
Also spelled '**Accadian**'.

Aktionsart The lexical class to which a verb belongs by virtue of the type of process, state, etc. that it denotes. E.g. walking is an activity; therefore *walk* is an '**activity** verb'. Knowing something is a state of mind; therefore *know* is lexically *stative.
The German term means 'kind of action'; sometimes replaced in English by '**aspectual character**', 'aspectual value', or 'semantic value'. Terms like 'activity' tend to be used indiscriminately, both of types of *situation and of verbs or *aspects etc. by which they are referred to. Thus an activity is also what is represented by the progressive in *He is crossing the road,* as opposed to an '**accomplishment**', represented by the perfect in *He has crossed the road.*

Albanian Attested from the 15th century AD, now spoken throughout Albania, in most of Kosovo, and in parts of Macedonia; also in pockets in Greece and southern Italy. *Indo-European, forming a separate branch within the family.

alethic [əˈliːθɪk] (*Modality) opposing in particular what must logically be true to what may be true in specific circumstances. Distinguished by logicians from *epistemic modality; but not usually, if ever, a distinct category in languages.
From the Greek word for 'true'.

Alexandrians School of scholars and scientists associated with the library of Alexandria from the early 3rd century BC. Aristarchus (*c*.217–145 BC) is especially important in the history of literary and textual scholarship, and it is within this tradition that earlier analyses of language, by the *Stoics especially, developed into the discipline of grammar as it has been understood from the 1st century BC onwards. The details are uncertain, a particular problem being the authenticity of the grammar attributed to Aristarchus' pupil *Dionysius Thrax.

alexia Loss of a previously acquired ability to read in consequence of disease or injury to the brain. Distinguished as such from *dyslexia.

Algonquian Family of languages spoken or once spoken over a large part of North America, in Canada and in the USA, especially in the Great Lakes region and the eastern seaboard. Varieties of *Cree and *Ojibwa now have the greatest numbers of speakers.

Also spelled '**Algonkian**'. Included in a larger family, **Algic**, with *Yurok and another Californian language.

algorithm *See* heuristic.

alienable possession Possessive construction in which the thing possessed is not an inherent part of the possessor: e.g. that of *Bill's house*, since a house exists independently of its owner. Opp. inalienable possession.

alignment Relation between the boundaries assigned to a unit at different levels of representation. E.g. those of a *phonological word may or may not correspond to, and thus 'be aligned with', those of a word as represented in morphology or ayntax. Hence processes of 'realignment', or 'alignment constraints' in e.g. *Optimality Theory.

allative (ALL) *Case whose basic role is to indicate movement to or towards some location: e.g. schematically, *I-walked shop*-ALL 'I walked to the shop'.

allegro form A form as modified phonetically in rapid speech. E.g. *I can't see him* has, as one possible allegro form, [əkãˈsɪːm]. Likewise rapid speech is sometimes called **allegro speech.**

allo- Prefix used for variant forms of any linguistic unit. Thus in general 'X-emes', e.g. *phonemes or *morphemes, are invariants, abstracted from and realized by alternative 'allo-Xes', e.g. *allophones or *allomorphs.

allograph A variant form of a *grapheme: i.e. of a letter in writing seen as analogous to a *phoneme.

allomorph One of a set of forms which realize a morpheme: *cf.* morpheme (3). E.g. -[ən] in *taken* and -[d] in *removed* are among the allomorphs of the 'past participle' morpheme.

allomorphy *Alternation in the forms that realize morphological or lexical units. E.g. in Latin *rēgis* 'king-GEN.SG' vs. *domini* 'master-GEN.SG' there is allomorphy of the genitive singular ending (*-is*/*-i*); in *ferō* 'I carry' vs. *tulī* 'I carried' there is allomorphy in the root (*fer-*/*tul-*).

allophone An audibly distinct variant of a *phoneme. E.g. the [d] and [ð] of Spanish [ˈdeðo] 'finger' are allophones of the same phoneme, written *d* in the spelling *dedo*.

Thence **allophonic**, as in 'allophonic variation', i.e. variation among allophones.

alpha (α) *See* Greek letter variables; for Move α *see* movement.

alphabet A writing system, strictly one in which consonants and vowels are represented equally by separate letters. Hence especially the *Greek alphabet and its *Roman and other derivatives; but also of *consonantal alphabets of the *Semitic type.

alpha-syllabic (Writing system) in which successive characters sometimes represent a single consonant or vowel, as in an *alphabet, and sometimes a syllable, as in a *syllabary. The type is characteristic of systems in or derived from India, such as *Devanagari.

Altaic A proposed family of languages, conservatively including *Turkic, *Mongolian, and *Tungusic in east Siberia.

Alternating Stress Rule A rule of English phonology proposed by Chomsky and Halle, *SPE which assigns stress e.g. to the first syllable of *hurricane*. By the 'Main Stress Rule', which applies first, 'primary stress' is assigned to the final syllable: *hurricáne*. By the Alternating Stress Rule, the second syllable before a primary stress also receives primary stress: *húrricáne*. Then, by a rule applying later, that of the final syllable is reduced.

alternation Variation in the forms that *realize linguistic units; hence often = allomorphy. Also a specific instance of such variation: e.g. in *taken* vs. *removed* there is an alternation in the past participle ending.

Hence **alternant**, one of the forms that enter into an alternation.

alveolar Articulated with the *tip or *blade of the tongue against or approximated to the ridge behind the upper teeth: e.g. [t] and [d] are normally alveolar in English. The ridge is called the **alveolar ridge** from the 'alveoli' or sockets for the teeth contained in it.

alveolo-palatal A consonant articulated like a *palatal consonant but in a more forward position.

ambient *it* The *it* of e.g. *It is snowing*, where the sentence refers to no individual but simply to a state of the world of which this might be said.

ambiguous (Sentence etc.) having two or more meanings. Thus *I filled the pen* is ambiguous, since *the pen* might refer to a writing instrument or an enclosure for animals. Most accounts distinguish **lexical ambiguity**, as in this example, from **grammatical** or **syntactic ambiguity**. Cf. e.g. *I like good food and wine*, where *good* might bear a syntactic relation to both *food* and *wine* ('good food and good wine') or to *food* alone ('good food and any wine').

Many linguists will talk of ambiguity only when they see it as a property of *sentences as opposed to *utterances or as explained, as in these examples, by the *language system. But such criteria are problematic as these notions are problematic.

'ambilingual' *Bilingual who has equally mastered both languages.

ambisyllabic Belonging to two syllables. E.g. single intervocalic consonants form a syllable, in one view, with the following and with the preceding vowel.

ameliorative (Change) by which a word develops a more favourable sense. E.g. in the meaning of *nice*, originally borrowed from Old French in the 13th century with the meaning 'foolish, stupid'; or that of *minister*, as in *Prime Minister*, originally meaning 'servant'. Also called **meliorative**: opp. pejorative.

American Sign Language *See* sign language.

'American structuralism' The school or theory of linguistics dominant in the USA from the 1920s or 1930s until the end of the 1950s: especially, therefore, that of *Bloomfield and the *Post-Bloomfieldians.

'Amerind' Conjectural *phylum or grouping of families comprising all the indigenous languages of the Americas other than *Eskimo-Aleut and *Na-Dené. Proposed by Greenberg on the basis of *mass comparison; hence valid or purely speculative, depending on one's assessment of his methods.

Amerindian Cover term for the indigenous languages of the Americas. *See* Central American languages; North American languages; South American languages.

Ameslan *See* sign language.

Amharic South *Semitic, the official language of Ethiopia and a second language, there and in Sudan, for many for whom it is not native. Written in a South Semitic script, technically *alpha-syllabic, distinctive to it and neighbouring languages, such as *Tigrinya.

A-movement *Movement to a position which is typically that of a subject, hence more generally an *argument of a verb: *cf.* A-bound. Movement within a larger unit was defined in *Government and Binding Theory as Aʹ-movement: thus in particular, from the mid-1980s, to a position with a *complementizer phrase, or CP.

amplifier *See* intensifying.

anacoluthon [anəkɒˈluːθən] A sentence etc. which switches from one construction to another. E.g. in *He told me that he was desperate and could I please help,* the interrogative *could I please help* does not construe with the *that* of *that he was desperate*. From Greek, with the meaning 'not following'.

analogists vs. anomalists Controversy regarding the basis for correct language, said by *Varro to have raged in the 2nd to 1st centuries BC. One side argued that irregular inflections should be regularized, as far as was reasonable, by a principle of *analogy: this view is also known from other sources. The other argued that 'anomalies', in the sense of inflectional irregularities, should be retained: for that sense Varro, and others following him, are our only testimony.

analogy Process by which a form *a* is either changed or created in such a way that its relation to another form *b* is like that of other pairs of forms whose relationship is similar in meaning. E.g. if a speaker says *contácted* instead of *cóntacted*, it is possibly **by analogy with** other verbs whose stress is on that syllable. Thus *contáct* (verb) is to *cóntact* (noun) as *impórt* is to *ímport, dispúte* to (for many speakers) *díspute*, and so on. If a speaker were to invent a verb 'locketize' (meaning to enclose in a locket) it might be by analogy with other formations in *-ize*: *locketize* is to *locket* as *palletize* is to *pallet*, and so on.

Thence generally of any changes in which similarity in meaning leads to formal similarity. E.g. in the history of English *cows* (plural) may be said to have replaced *kine* by a process in which a form analogous to that of other plurals (*cow* + *-s*) has replaced one which was irregular. But analogy is logically distinct from processes of regularization. E.g. in some dialects regular *dived* has been replaced by irregular *dove,* by analogy especially with *drove* vs. *drive*.

Thence **analogical change**, change explained by analogy.

analphabetic notation *Phonetic notation in which segments are represented not by single letters but by arrays of symbols that refer to individual *articulators. E.g. one devised by *Jespersen in the late 19th century, for which the term was invented.

'analysis by synthesis' Any strategy in *speech processing in which, given a set of rules that generate a set of speech forms, the structure of an input form is determined by the rules applied in a successful attempt to synthesize it. Proposed in the 1960s in the context of phonetics and phonology.

analytic (1) (Form, language) in which separate words realize grammatical distinctions that in other languages may be realized by inflections. Opp. synthetic (1).

Thus the perfect is realized analytically in English (*has come*) but by an inflection in e.g. Latin (*veni* 'I have come'). Likewise constructions with prepositions are analytic, as opposed to case forms.

analytic (2) (Proposition) which by definition cannot but be true. E.g. spinsters are by definition unmarried: therefore 'If Jane is a spinster, Jane is not married' is analytic or **analytically** true. Opp. synthetic (2). **Analyticity** is similarly the property of being analytic.

'analytic compound' = root compound; i.e. not a *synthetic compound.

anaphor [ˈanəfɔː] **1.** A pronoun or similar element that must be understood in relation to an *antecedent. Thus the *reflexive in *They helped themselves* is understood in relation to *they*, and could not be understood e.g. in *Please help themselves*, where no antecedent is present. In *Government and Binding Theory, anaphors were classed as [+ anaphoric] and [– pronominal] while pronouns such as *he* were [– anaphoric] and [+ pronominal]. **2.** Any element standing in a relation of *anaphora.

anaphora [əˈnafərə] The relation between a pronoun and another unit, in the same or in an earlier sentence, that supplies its referent. E.g. in *Mary disguised herself*, the reflexive pronoun *herself* is understood as **anaphoric** [anəˈfɒrɪk] to *Mary*: that is, it refers to whoever *Mary* refers to. Likewise, e.g. in conversation, across sentence boundaries. Thus if A asks 'Where's Mary?' and B says 'She's in the garden', *she* in the sentence B utters is to be understood as anaphoric to earlier *Mary*.

   Thence of similar relations involving units other than pronouns: e.g. *the idiot* is anaphoric to *John* in *I asked John but the idiot wouldn't tell me*; *do so* is anaphoric to *help* in *I wanted to help but I couldn't do so*. Also of '**anticipatory anaphora**': compare *When she read it Mary was delighted*, where *she* stands in a relation alternatively called *cataphora to a unit that follows. An **anaphoric chain** is formed by two or more successive units each linked anaphorically to the one preceding.

anaptyxis [anəˈptɪksɪs] Process or change in which successive consonants are separated by a vowel. E.g. the word for 'milk' has developed an **anaptyctic** vowel in Luxembourgish (*mellëch*) and some other Germanic dialects. The Greek term means 'unfolding'.

anastrophe [əˈnastrəfi] Term in rhetoric for a *figure of speech which departs from the usual order of words or other syntactic units.

Anatolian Branch of *Indo-European, including *Hittite and other languages attested in what is now Turkey in the 2nd to 1st millennia BC. Of the others Luwian is also early and is known from various sites in the west and south of the region.

ancestor language An earlier language from which one or more later languages are descended: e.g. Proto-Germanic as the posited ancestor of the modern Germanic languages. The converse term is 'daughter language'.

anchor Huddleston and Pullum's term, in *CGEL, for a unit to which a *supplement is related: e.g. *John* in *John—can you believe it?—was there*, as supplemented by *can you believe it*?

'androcentric' 'Male-centred'. E.g. English *he*, as used of people generally and not men in particular, is for students of sexism in language an 'androcentric generic'.

angled brackets < > Used: **1.** To distinguish orthographic units and forms written in them. E.g. orthographic <ph> is one way of writing [f]. **2.** By Chomsky and Halle, *SPE* in an abbreviatory convention by which, e.g. A <B> C <D> conflates a sequence AC, in which neither B nor D is present, with ABCD, where both are present. *See* tailless arrow for < or > used separately.

Anglo-Frisian Traditional division of *West Germanic which includes English and *Frisian.

Anglo-Saxon = Old English.

'animacy hierarchy' A proposed hierarchical ordering of noun phrases etc. ranging from personal pronouns such as *I* as maximally 'animate' to forms referring to lifeless objects as minimally 'animate'. Those at one end of the scale may differ in syntax from those at the other: e.g. the construction characteristic of an *accusative language may be found with those that are maximally animate, that of an *ergative language with the remainder.

The scale more clearly reflects degrees of *empathy: thus people empathize most with themselves and then with other people, least with stones, etc.

animate 1. (Noun) denoting entities that can act, or are perceived as acting, of their own will: e.g. *man, horse.* Hence a feature involved in collocational or 'selectional' restrictions: e.g. a verb such as *die* typically takes an animate subject. **2.** (*Gender, *noun class) characterized by nouns which are animate in that sense. Thus in the older Indo-European languages there are traces of a system in which nouns were initially classed as animate or inanimate. The inanimates are those described as *neuter, and the animates were secondarily divided into *masculine and *feminine.

Annamite An older name for *Vietnamese.

'anomalist' *See* analogists vs. anomalists.

anomia Impaired ability to name things. Sometimes the main feature of *aphasia, in which case called **anomic aphasia**.

antecedent A phrase etc. which supplies the interpretation of an *anaphoric element. E.g. in *Bill promised he would come,* the referent of *he* is supplied, in one interpretation, by the antecedent *Bill*: accordingly *he* in turn refers to 'Bill'.

A *relative pronoun is described in the classical tradition as anaphoric to a noun preceding it. Thus, in *the people who came, people* would be the antecedent of *who*.

antepenultimate Third from the end: thus the accent of *háppily* is on the antepenultimate syllable, or **antepenult**.

anterior Articulated by obstructing the airflow in a position forward from that of e.g. English [ʃ]. English [p], [t], and [s] are therefore among the consonants so classed. A distinctive feature in the scheme of Chomsky and Halle, *SPE: opp. non-anterior.

anthropological linguistics Often simply of the study of lesser-known languages through field work. Also, more generally, of any work on language from an anthropological viewpoint: of the use of language in ritual, of vocabulary in relation to the use made of material objects, and so on.

anthroponym A personal name: e.g. *Bill* or *Walker*.

anti- Used in terms for categories, constructions, etc. which are in some precise or looser sense the opposites of others. Modelled on *antipassive.

anticipatory anaphora = cataphora.

anticipatory assimilation = regressive assimilation.

anticipatory coarticulation *Coarticulation in which the production of a following unit accompanies or affects that of the unit preceding: e.g. that resulting in a rounded [s] in *sweet*, where it is followed by [w].

anticipatory subject An *empty element that occupies the syntactic position of a subject when the subject itself is in a later position. E.g. *what he does* is the subject in *What he does matters*. It has the same role in relation to *matters* in *It matters what he does*; but in this construction it comes after the verb and the subject position is occupied by anticipatory *it*.

'antilanguage' Any language or form of language, argot, slang, etc. used by a group of speakers wishing not to be understood by, and thus to exclude, others.

antipassive (ANTIPASS) (Construction) which stands to the basic transitive construction in an *ergative language in a relation which is the reverse of that of a passive construction to a basic active.

In the basic construction, a patient is 'absolutive' and an agent is 'ergative': thus schematically, with the verb as the initial element, *kissed Jack-ABS Jill-ERG* 'Jill (agent) kissed Jack (patient)'. In the corresponding antipassive, it is the agent that is absolutive, the verb is in a form that is also called 'antipassive', and the patient, if indicated, is marked otherwise: schematically, *kissed-ANTIPASS Jill-ABS (Jack-x)*. In this schema, 'x' might again be the ergative.

Thus, if we take the antipassive as a derived construction, Verb Patient-ABS Agent-ERG → Verb-ANTIPASS Agent-ABS (Patient-x). By contrast, if the relation of active to passive is represented at a similar level of abstraction, Verb Agent-NOM Patient-ACC → Verb-PASS Patient-NOM (Agent-x).

antithesis The relation between successive units that are put in contrast; e.g. between *me* and *you* in *It wasn't* ME; *it was* YOU, or between the clauses that contain them.

antonymy Relation in the lexicon between words that have opposite meanings; e.g. *tall* is in its basic sense an **antonym** of *short*. For types of oppositeness, which may or may not be classed as antonymy in particular treatments, *see* complementarity; converse terms; gradable antonymy.

aorist [ˈeɪərɪst] [ˈɛːrɪst] *Aspect e.g. in Ancient Greek, used to refer to events that have taken place, without regard to their extension over time or to the state resulting from them. E.g. *apéthane* 'he died', 'his death (whether long drawn out or sudden) happened'.
  The Greek term meant 'indefinite', 'not delimited'.

'A-over-A condition' An *island condition proposed in the 1960s, by which a constituent of class *A*, if part of a larger constituent also of class *A*, could not be involved in operations which crossed the boundaries of that larger unit. A precursor of the principle later called *subjacency.

Apachean A group of *Athabaskan languages, including *Navajo and those of the Apache themselves, spoken in the American Southwest and the extreme north of Mexico.

aperiodic Not *periodic (1).

aperture Usually of the degree to which the mouth is open in the production of vowels; hence equivalent to *tongue height. Occasionally = stricture.

aphaeresis [əˈfɪərəsɪs] [əˈfɛrɪsɪs] The loss of a vowel or syllable at the beginning of a word. The usual case is that of *aphesis. Also, by extension, of the loss of an initial consonant, e.g. earlier [k] in *knee*. The Greek term means 'taking away'.

aphasia Loss or impairment of speech resulting from brain disease or physical damage to the brain. The term is used generally for both partial and complete loss; it also covers an impaired ability to understand speech, not just to produce it. Hence **aphasic**, suffering from aphasia.

aphesis [ˈafɪsɪs] The loss of an initial unstressed vowel: e.g. *squire* is an **aphetic** form of *esquire*, from Old French *esquier*. *Cf.* aphaeresis.

apical Articulated with the tip of the tongue. Likewise **apico**-: thus an **apico-alveolar** stop is one articulated with the tip of the tongue against the alveolar ridge.

apocope [ə'pɒkəpi] The loss of a sound or sounds at the end of a word; e.g. that of [d], in some forms of English, after a nasal: [sen] (*send*). The Greek term means 'cutting off'.

apodosis [ə'pɒdəsɪs] The main clause in a *conditional sentence: e.g. *I will* in *If she comes, I will*. The Greek term has the sense of a 'response to' the *protasis or 'premiss'.

apo koinou ['apəʊ 'kɔɪnuː] Construction in which the same element is described as having a role in both a preceding and a following clause: e.g. in *There's a man wants you on the telephone*, it might be argued that *a man* is related both to *there's* (ₛ[*there's a man*]) and to *wants you on the telephone* (ₛ[*a man wants . . .*]). Greek term meaning 'from a common (element)'.

Apollonius Dyscolus Greek grammarian, working in Alexandria in the 2nd century AD. Three works survive in more than fragments, among them most of his treatment of syntax (in Latin *De Constructione*). This meant in antiquity the syntax of the individual *parts of speech; hence, in particular, an account of *solecism, or ungrammaticality, as arising from a mismatch in the semantic properties of individual words. Of the grammarians whose thought we can assess directly, Apollonius is the earliest in the west whose preoccupations were those of a linguist in the present-day sense, and the nature of some important categories, such as infinitives, seems to have been first clarified by him.

apophony [ə'pɒfəni] = ablaut.

aposiopesis [apəsʌɪə'piːsɪs] Lapse into silence before the construction of a sentence is completed: 'And suppose that they . . . ?' (understood 'don't agree', 'declare war on us', or whatever).

'apparent time' An interval between different age-groups, seen as corresponding to an interval in real time. Thus it has been argued by Labov and others that if the speech of younger members of a community differs from that of older members, this is possibly evidence of a 'change in progress' between earlier and later states of the language. *Cf.* age-grading.

appellative = common noun. The ancient term, now rare.

applicative Construction in which an *oblique element is *promoted to the role of an object, with the verb inflected to show that it has that status. Also such an inflection.

   Thus, schematically, *I made it for Mary* or *I made it with a hammer* → *I made-APPL Mary it, I made-APPL a hammer it*. The role of *Mary* or *a hammer* is then that of an object: hence, e.g. they may be further promoted to the subject of a passive. The applicative inflection (APPL) might be the same whatever element is promoted, or it might distinguish them e.g. as beneficiary ('for' Mary), instrumental ('with' a hammer), and so on.

Coined with reference especially to *Bantu languages, where verbs with an applicative inflection are often called 'applied' or 'prepositional'.

applied linguistics Strictly any application of linguistics. But often in practice of a discipline which applies the findings of linguistics, among others, in education: e.g. or especially to teaching English as a foreign or *second language.

apposition A syntactic relation in which an element is juxtaposed to another element of the same kind. Especially between noun phrases that do not have distinct referents: e.g. *Lucienne* is in apposition to *my wife* in *Do you know my wife Lucienne?* Thence of other cases where elements are seen as parallel but do not have distinct roles in a larger construction: e.g. *Smith* is seen as apposed to *Captain* in *Do you know Captain Smith?*

Cf. supplement. Distinguished from *modification (1) (or attribution) in that there is no clear tendency for either element to qualify the other.

appositional 1. Standing in a relation of *apposition: e.g. *the first president* and *George Washington* are appositional noun phrases in *the first president, George Washington.* **2.** Having a role like that of an element in apposition. Thus an **appositional relative clause** is one whose role is not as a qualifier: i.e. = non-restrictive relative clause.

appositive = appositional.

apprehensional (Clause etc.) with the meaning 'for fear that, lest that (such or such a thing should happen)'.

approximant A speech sound whose function is that of a consonant but which is produced with *open approximation of the relevant articulators: e.g. [r] in most pronunciations of *red*, [w] in *wet*. Opp. vowel, stop, fricative; *cf.* semivowel.

approximation *See* close approximation; open approximation; *also* *n*th-order approximation.

'aptote' Obsolete term for a noun which, unlike others in the relevant language, is not inflected for case.

Arabic *Semitic language first attested by inscriptions in the Arabian peninsula from about the 5th century BC. Carried by the expansion of Islam in the 7th and 8th centuries AD to a large area across the southern Mediterranean and the Middle East, and thence, as a language of religion especially, much wider. Written in a North

*Semitic alphabet, in origin purely *consonantal, but with marks for vowels added in the 8th century.

The language of the Koran is **Classical Arabic**, and modern Arabic-speaking communities are in the main *diglossic, with a range of variation between 'Modern Standard Arabic', a form of Classical Arabic with a modernized vocabulary, and one of many national or local 'dialects'. At sufficient distances these dialects are mutually unintelligible.

Aramaic [arəˈmeɪɪk] Branch of *Semitic attested from the 10th century BC, including languages in widespread use throughout the Middle East from around 700 BC, until progressively supplanted by *Arabic after the expansion of Islam. 'Middle Aramaic' includes the spoken language of Palestine at the time of the New Testament; 'Late Aramaic' includes, in particular, *Syriac.

Araucanian *See* South American languages.

Arawak(an) Family of languages spoken or formerly spoken in widely scattered parts of South and Central America, from the upper Paraná northwards, across Amazonia, to the coast of the Guyanas and westwards to Honduras and Guatemala; also in the Caribbean at the time of the European invasion. A member spoken on the Guajira Peninsula, on the boundary of Colombia with Venezuela, now has the largest number of speakers.

arbitrariness The property of language by which there is in general no natural relation between the form of a simple lexical unit and the things etc. that it denotes. E.g. there is nothing in the nature of the sounds and meanings to explain why *cat* is the word for a cat and not, for example, a dog or a pencil, or why cats should not be referred to by, say, *dog* instead.

Thence of any similar features of or differences between languages. Thus the system of colour terms in English differs arbitrarily from that of Welsh, not just in the forms but also in the way the spectrum, e.g. in the region of blue and green, is divided. Opp. iconicity; motivation. *Cf.* naturalness.

arbitrary (control, reference). *See* control.

arc A line connecting two nodes in a graph: e.g. in a *tree diagram.

archaism Form or use of a form which is obsolete or belongs recognizably to an older stage of a language: e.g. the syntax of *God Save the Queen!* or the use of words like *hereafter* in legal documents.

archi- Prefix used for units of any kind whose features are common to a set of more specific units. E.g. *animal* is in some accounts an '**archilexeme**', since its semantic features are those in common to all the more specific lexical units (*rabbit*, *horse*, etc.) in a *semantic field that it defines.

archiphoneme A phonological unit characterized by the *distinctive features which are common to two or more *phonemes whose opposition is *neutralized. Thus in English there is no opposition e.g. between [t] and [d] after an initial [s]: the unit written *t* in e.g. *stop* may therefore be identified as an archiphoneme which is neither specifically voiceless nor specifically voiced, but has only the features that these consonants share.

Arc Pair Grammar System of formal syntax derived from *Relational Grammar and published by D. E. Johnson and P. M. Postal in 1980. Sentences are represented by 'network graphs' in which e.g. the relation 'subject of' is shown by an arc connecting a noun or nominal node to a clause node, and arcs are in turn related especially to show relations at different levels.

areal linguistics Any branch of linguistics that studies the geographical distribution of variables. A term sometimes applied to *dialect geography; also to the study of 'linguistic areas' (*see Sprachbund*) involving several languages.

argot [ˈɑːɡəʊ] Special vocabulary used e.g. by criminals which is designedly unintelligible to outsiders. Thus one form of *antilanguage.

argument Any syntactic element seen as required by a verb: e.g. *love* takes two arguments, represented by *she* and *me* in *She loves me*. Thence generally of elements required by words of other categories: e.g. the adjective *happy* has the argument *she* in *She is happy*.
    The term is borrowed from mathematical logic: e.g. in the expression P (x, y), the variables x and y are the arguments of a two-place *predicate P. The **argument structure** of a verb or other lexical unit is the range of arguments that it may or must take: *cf.* valency.

arhyzotonic Having the accent elsewhere than on the root.

Aristarchus *See* Alexandrians.

Aristotle (384–322 BC) Greek philosopher, important in the early history of western linguistics both for his general contributions to logic, rhetoric, and poetics and for a specific classification of speech units. These included minimal sounds and syllables, both distinguished as units that do not in themselves have meanings; the sentence as a unit which is meaningful and has parts that are also meaningful; and the beginnings, though in a form hard to interpret, of the system of *parts of speech developed later by the Stoics and others.
    Many of the terms that are later used in grammars are in Aristotle's work, though not necessarily with the same sense. A specific analysis,

which recurs at intervals throughout the history of logic and linguistics, is that of a finite verb, such as *walks*, into a participle linked to its subject by a *copula: 'is (in a state of) walking'.

Armenian First known from texts of the 5th century AD, though surviving in later copies; now spoken throughout Armenia, in Turkey, and by a diaspora in many countries. *Indo-European, forming a branch distinct from Greek, *Indo-Iranian, etc. Written from the outset in a distinct alphabet devised primarily by St Mesrop and St Sahak.

arrow (→) 1. Used in linguistics for a synchronic process or operation; e.g. $s \rightarrow z$ indicates a change of s to z. To be distinguished from the tailless arrow (>), used for a historical process. **2.** *See* implication.

The use of the arrow in the notation of phrase structure rules derives from Chomsky's initial formulation in the 1950s, in which they were seen as *rewrite rules.

ars The Latin word for *an* 'art' or 'skill'; used in the title of grammars (*ars grammatica* or 'art of grammar'); hence often alone, e.g. in translation into other modern languages, in that sense.

article A *determiner whose basic role is to mark noun phrases as either *definite or *indefinite: e.g. definite *the* in *the girl*, indefinite *a* in *a girl*.

Articles are distinguished from other determiners for two reasons. Firstly, they cannot form phrases on their own: compare e.g. the demonstrative *this* in *This is my sister*. Secondly, the distinction they mark is obligatory. Delete, for example, *the* in *I am looking for the girls*; the object *girls* is then specifically indefinite, like the singular *a girl* in *I am looking for a girl*, and does not merely cease to be specifically definite.

articular Formed with an article. Thus the construction e.g. in Greek of an article with an infinitive forms an articular infinitive.

articulation 1. The production of speech sounds: thus *manner of articulation, *place of articulation. **2.** The property of being analysable into *discrete units standing in specific relationships: thus *double articulation (1).

Sense 2 is the older. Thus in the classical tradition speech was distinguished as 'articulate' (lit. 'jointed') from cries etc. that were 'inarticulate'.

articulator Any vocal organ used to form specific speech sounds: e.g. the upper and lower lips, in the production of [p] in *pit*, or the blade of the tongue and the ridge behind the teeth, in that of [t] (*t*). *Places of articulation are defined by the raising of a movable or **active articulator**, e.g. a part of the tongue, towards a fixed or **passive**

articulator, e.g. a part of the roof of the mouth. For example, the *labiodental place of articulation, as of *f* in *fish*, is defined by the placing of the lower lip ('labio-') in contact with the upper teeth ('dental').

articulatory gesture *See* gesture.

articulatory phonetics The study of the production of speech sounds. Opp. acoustic phonetics.

Articulatory Phonology Model developed by C. P. Browman and L. Goldstein from the mid-1980s in which an utterance is represented at the phonological level by a temporally coordinated series of articulatory *gestures. These form a 'gestural score', from which the actual movements of articulators are derived.

Compared by its authors to *Autosegmental Phonology, in that gestures which are physically independent characterize different *tiers of representation. But the units in Autosegmental Phonology are features, not gestures; and tiers in Autosegmental Phonology are defined by structural domains, which do not flow from the nature of the units themselves.

articulatory setting A medium- to long-term disposition of the vocal tract, underlying the articulation of successive units. When permanent or virtually permanent, settings may identify the voice of an individual: e.g. that of some speakers is characteristically nasalized. They may also be characteristic of particular languages or accents; in the shorter term they may carry *affective meaning, and so on.

articulatory target *See* target.

'artificial language' Any invented 'language', whether an *auxiliary language such as *Esperanto, or a formal system used e.g. in logic or in computer programming.

'artificial underlying form' A *basic form of a morpheme which is not identical to any of those by which it is realized. For 'artificial' *cf*. abstract.

'Aryan' *See* Indo-Aryan. 'Aryan' was sometimes used in the late 19th century in the sense of *Indo-European.

ascension = raising (2).

ascriptive (Sentence) which ascribes a property to some entity. E.g. in *Zoe is beautiful,* Zoe is ascribed the property of beauty, in *Zoe is an undergraduate* that of being an undergraduate. Also of the construction of such a sentence, if distinct from others. *Cf*. equational.

'ash' The digraph 'æ', devised originally in the spelling of Old English, for a vowel that was phonetically [a] or [æ].

ASL *See* sign language.

aspect General term, originally of specialists in Slavic languages, for verbal categories that distinguish the status of events, etc. in relation to specific periods of time, as opposed to their simple location in the present, past, or future. E.g. *I am reading your paper* means that the reading is in progress over a period that includes the moment of speaking: *am reading* is therefore present in *tense but *progressive (or continuous) in aspect. *I have read your paper* means that, at the moment of speaking, the reading has been completed: it is therefore present in tense but *perfect in aspect.

Aspectual categories are very varied, and since both tense and aspect are defined by reference to time, a clear distinction, where it exists, will usually be drawn by formal criteria. It is also hard to separate aspects marked by inflections or auxiliaries from the *Aktionsart* or inherent lexical properties of verbs. Hence the term is commonly extended to include these and, effectively, any distinction that does not clearly fall under tense or mood.

For other individual aspects *see* aorist; durative; habitual; imperfective; inchoative; iterative; punctual.

aspectual character *See Aktionsart.*

aspirated (Plosive) whose release is followed audibly by a short period in which the vocal cords are not vibrating. Thus the *t* of English *tea* is usually aspirated: in phonetic notation [tʰiː] or [tʻiː]. For 'voiced aspirates' *see* murmured.

Assamese *Indo-Aryan language of the Brahmaputra valley in north-east India; grouped with *Bengali in all attempts to subdivide the family. Spoken in the Indian state of Assam and in Bangladesh.

assertive (Mood, verb, particle) by which speakers commit themselves, to a greater or lesser degree, to what they are saying. E.g. *assure* is an assertive verb in *I assure you he is coming*; *indicatives are assertive in opposition to *subjunctives.

assibilation Change into a *sibilant. Thus of a sound change in Old English by which e.g. *fetjan > fe[tʃ]an* 'to fetch'.

assimilation (1) Sound change or process by which features of one element change to match those of another that precedes or follows. E.g. Italian *scritto* 'written' derives from Latin *scriptu(m)* by the assimilation of a bilabial (*p*) to a following dental (*t*); English *cats* is described synchronically as deriving from an underlying [kat] + [z] by the assimilation of voiced [z] to voiceless [t].

Divided into *progressive assimilation and *regressive assimilation. *Cf.* coarticulation.

assimilation (2) In an ordinary sense as e.g. in the politics of integration. Thus a government might adopt a policy of '**linguistic assimilation**', as opposed to 'linguistic pluralism', in encouraging or trying to force all citizens to speak the same language.

association line A line drawn to represent a relation between elements at different levels or *tiers of phonological representation. Originally from *Autosegmental Phonology: thus, in the illustration, a low tone (L) is an autosegment associated with one syllable on a *skeletal or 'CV' tier; a high tone (H) with two successive syllables, of which the first might then have a rising contour.

autosegmental tier   L   H

skeletal tier   C V C V

association lines

associative (Affix etc.) With the meaning 'and others associated with X'. Thus, schematically, *John*-ASSOC might be translated 'John and his lot'.

'associative relation' Saussure's term for any relation between linguistic units which is not *syntagmatic; e.g. between phonemes or words that can be substituted one for another, between forms of a word with different inflections, between words formed in the same way or with a sequence of sounds in common. Relations of the first type are those distinguished later (by Hjelmslev and Jakobson) as *paradigmatic relations.

Assyria(n) *See* Akkadian.

asterisk (*) Used: **1.** In historical linguistics, to mark forms that are *reconstructed, not directly attested: e.g. Germanic **kuninga-* (> English *king*, German *könig*, etc.). **2.** In work on syntax since the 1950s, to mark forms judged to be ungrammatical: e.g. **I yesterday did it*, as opposed to *I did it yesterday*. **3.** In the notation for a *starred tone.

An **asterisked form** (or **starred form**) is one marked, in historical linguistics especially, with an asterisk.

asyndeton [əˈsɪndɪtən] The joining together of syntactic units without a conjunction: e.g. in *I'm tired, I'm hungry*, or *I'm exhausted, I've walked twenty miles*. A sentence etc. which has such a structure is **asyndetic** [asɪnˈdɛtɪk]: the Greek term means 'not bound together'.

ATB = 'across the board'.

atelic (Aspect etc.) that is not *telic. E.g. in *I am carrying it outside,* as representing an activity in progress, not something already accomplished.

Athabaskan Family of languages in the American South-west and in western Canada and Alaska; another group were formerly spoken on the Pacific coast, north and south of the border between California and Oregon. *Navajo has by far the greatest number of speakers. Also spelled **Athapaskan**, **Athabascan**.

athematic Not having a *thematic vowel. E.g. Latin *fertis* 'you are carrying' is a relic of an athematic formation in Indo-European, in which the inflection (*-tis*) is added directly to the root (*fer-*).

Atlantic creoles Cover term for *creoles based on European languages in the Caribbean and coastal West Africa; historically, that is, with an origin in the slave trade.

Atlantic languages *See* West Atlantic languages.

atonic (Word, syllable, vowel) not accented.

ATR = Advanced Tongue Root.

attested form One for which there is direct evidence. Thus especially, in historical linguistics, an earlier form established by written record, as opposed to *reconstructed forms marked with an asterisk.
   Likewise of any form or usage that has actually been found or observed, e.g. in compiling a dictionary or a *corpus.

attraction Agreement of a word with an adjacent element to which it does not bear a direct syntactic relation. E.g. in *Nobody but grammarians say that,* the subject of *say* is or is headed by the singular *nobody*; but the verb agrees with the plural *grammarians. See also* case attraction.

attribution = modification (1); likewise **attribute** = modifier. An **attributive adjective** is one which modifies the head of a noun phrase, as opposed to one which is *predicative.

'audience design' The behaviour of speakers in adjusting their style of speaking to the nature of whoever they may be addressing.

auditory Having to do with hearing. Thus **auditory phonetics** is concerned with the perception of speech sounds; *pitch is one of the auditory properties of sound.

augment A verbal prefix (reconstructed *e-) in Indo-European, marking finite forms with past time reference. E.g. in Greek *é-graph-on* 'I was writing'; compare *gráph-ō* 'I am writing'.

augmentative (Affix etc.) primarily indicating large or larger size. E.g. Italian *cassone* 'large case, chest, etc.' is an augmentative form of *cassa* 'box, case', with the augmentative ending -*one*. Opp. diminutive.

augmented Increased by one or more. Hence in accounts of *person: thus an augmented *inclusive, as opposed to a minimal inclusive, refers to a speaker and addressee plus at least one other.

'Ausbau' language One whose identity rests on the role it plays or the status it has acquired in a society or nation, irrespective of how far its system is intrinsically distinct from others. E.g. 'Bosnian' if seen as a language separate, within *Serbo-Croat, from Croatian and Serbian.

Opp. 'Abstand' language; the German word has the meaning 'development' among others.

Austin, John Langshaw (1911–60) British philosopher, important in linguistics as the originator, in the 1950s, of the distinction between *constative and *performative utterances, and the definition of *felicity as the requirement that the latter must meet. *How to Do Things with Words* (edited posthumously, 1962) is the first attempt to develop a general theory of *speech acts, distinguishing in particular the *locutionary, *illocutionary, and *perlocutionary aspects of utterances.

Australian languages Estimated to have been about 200 before the British invasion. Languages in an area covering most of the continent are classed as 'Pama-Nyungan' on grounds of structural similarities; the name derives from the word for 'man' at the north-east and south-west extremes. Hence persisting arguments that they are a family. Those not assigned to this group are or were spoken in the north of Western Australia and the Northern Territory, and are grouped as 'Non-Pama-Nyungan'.

A handful still have over 1,000 speakers.

Austro-Asiatic Proposed family of languages with *Mon-Khmer and *Munda as its main branches.

Austronesian Family of languages distributed over a large area, mainly islands, from Madagascar in the west to Hawaii and Easter Island. It includes the indigenous languages of Taiwan, of the Philippines, of Micronesia and Polynesia, and most of those in Indonesia, Malaysia, and Melanesia.

The name is from the words for 'south' in Latin (*austro-*) and 'island' in Greek (*nes-*). The major subdivisions of the family are still partly in dispute, and with them the routes that led to much of this distribution.

auto- From the Ancient Greek form for '-self'. Hence, e.g., a word is an **'autohyponym'** if it has two senses one of which is included in the other. *Cf.* hyponymy.

automatic alternation An *alternation in morphology to which
there are no exceptions. E.g. the regular plural suffix is always [ɪz] after
sibilants (*fish-es*), [s] after other voiceless consonants (*cat-s*), and [z]
elsewhere (*dog-s, cow-s*).

'autonomous' 1. (Linguistics, syntax, etc.) viewed as a discipline or
object of study independent of others. Thus linguistics as separate
from, or as a separate part within, e.g. psychology; syntax as a level or
component of language separate from semantics. **2.** (Form of speech)
perceived as independent of others, not as a dialect of some larger
language. *Cf.* heteronomous.

autosegment *See* Autosegmental Phonology.

Autosegmental Phonology Model of *non-linear phonology
developed in the 1970s by J. Goldsmith. The basic insight is that
certain phonological features, such as *tones or those involved in
*vowel harmony, may be realized variously in a single vowel or
consonant, or in two or more such units, or, in effect, in only part of
one. Thus, in Turkish *eller* 'hand-PL', the vowel of the plural suffix (*-ler*)
is front in harmony with that of *el* 'hand': it cannot be otherwise, and
we may therefore speak of just one feature, 'front' or [+ front], which is
realized in both syllables. In the case of tones, successive high and low
tones might be realized sometimes on two separate syllables (CV́CV̀)
and sometimes on a single syllable. The tone on that syllable will then
be phonetically falling (CV̂). Features like these are described as
autosegments, and are represented at a structural level which is
higher than that of the individual vowel or consonant segments. The
ways in which they are realized in particular forms are then shown by
*association lines which relate the units at each structural level, or
*tier, to what is, in developed versions, no more than a CV skeleton
(called the *skeletal tier or CV tier).

AUX [ɔːks] A syntactic unit proposed by Chomsky in the 1950s,
basically comprising the inflections of a main verb with any
*auxiliaries accompanying it. E.g. in *He left*, the AUX consists of the
past-tense inflection (*-t*); in *He may be leaving*, of the auxiliaries *may*
and *be* plus the inflection of the participle (*-ing*). *Cf.* I (INFL).

auxiliary (Aux) A verb belonging to a small class which
syntactically accompanies other verbs: opp. lexical verb, full verb.
E.g. *could* and *have* are auxiliaries in *He could have done it*. The first
belongs to a class of *modal verbs used only with other verbs or in
elliptical sentences where a verb is understood. The second is an
auxiliary related to the past participle (*done*); distinguished as such
from *have* as a full verb, e.g. in *I have the answer*.

Auxiliaries typically mark *modality, *tense, or *aspect: e.g. the
construction of *have* with a past participle marks the *perfect. Hence

the same term has been used of other *grammatical words that mark such categories, whether or not they are verbs.

auxiliary language A language such as *Esperanto, invented as a subsidiary means of communication among people with different native languages.

aversive (*Case) indicating someone or something feared or avoided. Characteristic of Australian languages: e.g. in Yidiny (north Queensland), ('He hid') *bama-yida* 'from, to avoid being seen by, the people', the aversive is marked by *-yida*.

Avestan Ancient *Iranian language known from texts of uncertain date, but similar in form to those in *Vedic. These are the oldest part of the Zoroastrian scriptures called the *Avesta*, compiled when the language was no longer spoken.

avoidance style Style of speech that has to be used, in some communities, in talking in the presence of someone with whom close social contact is taboo. Widespread in Australian languages, where a part or almost the whole of the vocabulary must be replaced by special avoidance terms in the presence of certain relatives. Often called 'mother-in-law language', this relative being typically or specially taboo.

'axis' Bloomfield's term for an element *governed by a verb or preposition. E.g. *me* is the 'axis' in the construction of *to me* or *saw me*.

Aymará Spoken mainly in Bolivia, on the plateau south of Lake Titicaca. The main member of the **Jaqí** family, conjecturally but not securely related to *Quechuan, spoken to the north and south.

Azerbaijani *Turkic language, closely related to *Turkish, spoken mainly in Azerbaijan and, by a greater number, in the neighbouring provinces of Iran.

Both the speakers and the language are also called **Azeri**.

Aztec *See* Nahuatl.

B

babbling The vocal sounds of infants, especially involving repeated syllable-like forms, before the development of anything recognizable as speech.

Babylonian *See* Akkadian.

'baby talk' Either the utterances of very young children or *motherese as typically addressed to them.

'Bach–Peters sentence' One in which each of two noun phrases includes a pronoun anaphoric to the other: e.g. in *The girl who won it really deserves the prize she won*, the first pronoun (*it*) might have the same referent as *the prize she won*, the second (*she*) the same referent as *the girl who won it*.

back (Vowel) articulated with the highest point of the tongue towards the back of the mouth. E.g. [uː] in *moon*. Opp. front; *cf.* central.

In the scheme of Chomsky and Halle, *SPE* [± back] is a distinctive feature of consonants as well as vowels. Of the consonants, *velars, *uvulars, and *pharyngeals are [+ back]; *palatals are [– back].

'back-channelling' The use of any channel of communication seen as subsidiary to a main channel. Hence in particular, in analyses of conversation, of any communication from a listener, who does not currently 'have the *floor', to the speaker whose turn is in progress. E.g. while A is speaking, B may express surprise, or grunt in agreement. But this does not count as a turn by B as, technically, a speaker. Instead it is treated as back-channelling, with B as a **'back-channeller'**.

back-formation The formation of a simple or simpler word from one understood as derived, e.g. *gruntled* from *disgruntled*.

'backgrounded' Treated, presented, or marked as subsidiary. E.g. in a narrative, events are backgrounded if they are subsidiary to the main story; in the structure of a sentence subordinate clauses are backgrounded, or tend to present backgrounded information; and so on. By analogy with 'foregrounded'.

'background knowledge' Knowledge of the world in general, or of the life of their specific society, that people can be assumed to share as a framework for talking to one another. E.g. if someone says 'His dog kept me awake', the person spoken to will share the knowledge that people own dogs, that dogs make a noise by barking, and so on. *Cf.* common ground; encyclopaedic knowledge; mutual knowledge.

backshifting Change of tenses e.g. in *indirect speech. Thus someone called Emma might say 'I am busy'; this might later be reported by *Emma said she was busy*, with the verb (*was*) backshifted into the past tense. Contrast *Emma said she is busy*, without backshifting.

backward anaphora = cataphora. Likewise 'backward *pronominalization'.

Bahasa Indonesia *See* Malay-Indonesian.

bahuvrihi Sanskrit term for compounds such as *whitethroat*, meaning not 'throat which is white' but 'something having a white throat'. Also called **possessive** or *exocentric compounds.

Named after a representative of the type, *bahuvrīhi* '(having) much-rice'.

'balanced bilingual' *See* bilingual.

Balinese Spoken mainly in Bali; *Austronesian, of the same branch as e.g. Javanese.

'Balkan languages' Various languages of the Balkans, especially Albanian, Bulgarian, Greek, Macedonian, Rumanian, Serbo-Croat, and more peripherally Turkish, seen as a classic instance of a 'linguistic area' or *Sprachbund.

ballistic In the sense of 'broadly parabolic'. Thus a syllable may be seen as produced by a ballistic gesture of the vocal organs, whose peak corresponds to its vowel or nucleus.

Baltic Branch of *Indo-European, of which *Latvian and *Lithuanian are the surviving representatives. Closer to *Slavic than to any other; hence *Balto-Slavic.

Balto-Slavic Hypothetical branch of *Indo-European, subsuming *Baltic and *Slavic. Widely though not universally accepted.

Baluchi *Iranian language spoken mainly in the Baluchistan and neighbouring Sind provinces of Pakistan and in neighbouring parts of Afghanistan and south-eastern Iran.

Bambara *See* Mande.

Bantoid Term covering a large group of African languages which includes *Bantu and others broadly from the Nigeria–Cameroon border eastwards.

Bantu Family of languages covering most of southern Africa, broadly south of a line crossing Cameroon, northern Congo, Uganda, and Kenya, a few degrees north of the equator. Its members are similar in structure, and in large areas form *dialect continua, with many local varieties. The divisions between languages are in places conventional, and there is no single, universally accepted scheme of classification within the family.

The most important is *Swahili; for the location of some others with speakers in the millions, either as a native language or as a lingua franca, *see* Bemba, Kikuyu, Kongo, Lingala, Luba, Luganda, Makua,

Mbundu, Nyanja, Rwanda-Rundi, Shona, Sotho, Swati, Tsonga, Tswana, Xhosa, and Zulu.

bar (⁻) **1.** As a mark of negation: thus x̄ = 'not x'. **2.** As a *macron, indicating a long vowel. **3.** *See* X-bar syntax.

barbarism The ancient term for an error in an individual word. Distinguished as such from a *solecism, which involved a combination of words.

'bare infinitive' An *infinitive in English without *to*: e.g. *jump* in *That made him jump*.

bare noun phrase Used e.g. by Huddleston and Pullum, *CGEL*, of a phrase in which a noun is not accompanied by an article or other *determiner: e.g. *large houses* as a complete noun phrase in *Large houses are expensive*. Opp. determined noun phrase.

bare phrase structure A representation of the structure of phrases in which syntactic units are not explicitly assigned to categories.

A natural development of *X-bar syntax as reformulated, with varied motives, in Chomsky's *minimalist programme. Assume that all syntactic structures are of *phrases (2) and all relations within and among phrases conform to a fixed template. There is then no need to make explicit that a *projection of a head X is an X´ or an XP.

barrier Applied in *Government and Binding Theory to a boundary, or the category defining a boundary, across which *government (3) could not operate.

barytone A word, originally one in Ancient Greek, that is not accented (and therefore had in ancient terms a low-pitched or 'grave' accent) on the final syllable. *Cf.* oxytone.

base Any form to which a process applies. Especially in morphology: thus a singular noun in English (*man, horse*) is traditionally the base for the formation of the plural (→ *men, horses*). Where processes apply to units smaller than words, 'base' is sometimes used equivalently to *root or *stem.

base component A component of a *generative grammar which assigned an initial representation to each of a set of sentences. From this other representations might be derived by other components.

The term belongs particularly to the period 1965–75, when the level of structure to be represented by a base component was a central issue.

base-generated (Element, construction) forming part of the structure assigned by the *base component of a generative grammar. Thus it was an issue at one stage whether pronouns should be base-generated or derived by later rules of *pronominalization.

base language The language from which a *pidgin or *creole has drawn the bulk of its vocabulary: e.g. the creole of Haiti is 'French-based'. Also called the '**lexifier**' or 'lexical source language'.

Basic English A reduced English vocabulary devised by C. K. Ogden in the 1930s, with the intention that it should be used internationally.

basic form A form of an affix or other morphological unit from which a range of alternating realizations is derived. Thus in most accounts the regular English plural ending has the basic form [z]. This is unchanged in *ties* or *dogs*; but it changes to [ɪz] in words like *horses* or *houses*, where the preceding forms themselves end in [s] or [z], and changes to [s] in words like *cats*, where the form which precedes it ends in a voiceless consonant.

   Cf. underlying form.

basic-level terms Lexical units belonging to a neutral level in a taxonomy. E.g. if one runs over a dog one will say 'I have run over a dog', not usually, unless perhaps one fails to recognize it as a dog, 'I have run over an animal', nor, unless perhaps one is collecting the names of breeds that one hits, 'I have run over a labrador'. In that sense *dog* belongs, with *cat*, *horse*, and others, to a neutral or basic level in comparison both with *animal*, which is more general, and with *labrador*, *poodle*, etc., which are more specific.

basic vocabulary Any set of words or concepts assumed to be central: e.g. that which was taken as the basis for *glottochronology.

basic word order An order of words or phrases which is distinguished as the commonest, or because it is in other respects *unmarked, or because others are derived, or seen as derived, from it. Thus in English the order adjective + noun is basic (*a red book*); in French it is the opposite (*un livre rouge*).

basilect The variety of a language which, of a series predominantly spoken at different social levels, has the lowest prestige or is most distant from a standard form. Especially in studies of *creoles, where the basilect is the variety with the most creole features. Opp. acrolect; mesolect.

Basque Language of the western Pyrenees, spoken by bilingual communities in Spain and France. The only language indigenous to western Europe that is not *Indo-European; nor related plausibly to any other family.

Baudouin de Courtenay, Jan (1845–1929) Polish linguist, whose contribution to phonology, originally in collaboration with his shorter-lived pupil Mikołai Kruszewski (1850–87), was fundamental to the development of structural linguistics in Europe, especially by Saussure and in the work of the *Prague School in the 1930s. The earliest to distinguish clearly between a *phoneme, seen as the psychological equivalent of a speech sound and a unit of what he called 'psychophonetics', and the speech sound itself; also remarkable for his study of *alternations, and of the changes of status that an alternation may undergo from one stage of a language to another, which are the foundation for what was later called *morphophonology.

Professor at Kazan' in Russia 1875–83; hence the leader of what is called the Kazan' School.

'Beach-la-Mar' *See* Bislama.

beat = ictus.

'Behaghel's Law' Name sometimes given to the general principle, ascribed to work by O. Behaghel in the 1930s, by which syntactic elements that are closely related in meaning also tend to be next to each other in the sentence. *Cf.* iconicity.

behaviourism Movement in psychology which sought to eliminate all reference to subjective concepts or experience. The data were accordingly restricted to the observable reactions of subjects to observable stimuli. Inaugurated by the American psychologist J. B. Watson just before the First World War; also developed by A. P. Weiss and, through him, a major influence on *Bloomfield from the 1920s onwards. Developed further after the Second World War, especially by B. F. Skinner; arguably still, through Bloomfield, an influence on the *Post-Bloomfieldians, but rapidly abandoned, in both psychology and linguistics, in the early 1960s.

Associated with the heyday of *positivism in philosophy over the same period.

Belorussian East *Slavic, closely related to Russian, from which it has diverged only since the late Middle Ages.

Bemba *Bantu language spoken mainly in the north and in the Copperbelt region of Zambia.

benefactive *Case or *case role of units that refer to individuals with an interest in an action etc. who are not directly part of it. E.g. *for the Red Cross* is benefactive in *They were collecting money for the Red Cross*. The case role is also described as that of a **beneficiary**.

Bengali *Indo-Aryan, the national language of Bangladesh, with half as many speakers in the Indian state of West Bengal. Also spoken widely, through emigration, in Britain and elsewhere. Attested by texts from the early Middle Ages onwards; written in an *Indian script that it shares with *Assamese, to which it is also closely related within Indo-Aryan.

Benue-Congo Label applied to a vast group of African languages, including *Bantu and most of those to the south of *Chadic in eastern West Africa.

Benveniste, Émile (1902–76) Indo-Europeanist and general linguist whose works on Indo-European include an elegant theory of the structure of the root (1935), a subsequent account of agentive nouns and action nouns (1948), and two brilliant volumes (1969) on the nature of Indo-European society as revealed by inherited vocabulary, together with a long series of monographs and articles on Iranian languages especially. His contributions to general linguistics are reprinted in two collections (1966, 1974), and include important essays on the nature of communication and the act of utterance, on subjectivity in language, on *deixis and the system of persons and tenses. Many of his ideas, especially on the centrality of the speaker ('sujet parlant'), have been as influential outside linguistics as within.

Berber Generic name for a group of languages in North Africa and across the Saharan region, generally where Arabic is also spoken. Most speakers are in the north-west, in Morocco especially. Grouped with *Semitic and others within *Afro-Asiatic.

BEV *See* African American Vernacular English.

Bhojpuri *Indo-Aryan language spoken in the east of Uttar Pradesh and in west Bihar, including Varanasi (Benares). Largely unwritten.

bi- From a Latin prefix related to the word for 'two'. Thus a sentence is **biclausal** if it contains two clauses; a syllable is **bimoraic** if it counts as two *morae; processes etc. are **bidirectional** if they operate in both directions. *Cf.* di-.

bidental (Consonant) produced by air passing through the closed front teeth.

bidialectal (Person, community) using two distinct dialects. Thence **bidialectalism**: *cf.* bilingual.

Bihari Proposed branch of *Indo-Aryan, including *Maithili and Magahi (in Bihar to the south of the Ganges); also *Bhojpuri and others.

bilabial Articulated with the lower lip against or approximated to the upper lip. E.g. *p* in *pit* [p] is a bilabial stop.

bilateral **1.** (Opposition) between terms distinguished by a single feature. Especially in phonology: e.g. [iː] in *feel* and [uː] in *fool* are distinguished by a single feature ([± front] or front vs. back). Opp. multilateral opposition. **2.** Two-sided: e.g. a dependency is bilateral if *a* depends on *b* and *b* also depends on *a*. Opp. unilateral.

bilingual Traditionally of someone with a native or native-like control of two languages. Thus a minority of people in Wales are bilingual in Welsh and English; many in England are bilingual in English and e.g. Punjabi. A **bilingual community**, as in Welsh-speaking parts of Wales, is one in which bilingualism is normal.

Thence more generally, in current accounts, of people or communities speaking two or more different languages, or different dialects of the same language, whether or not they are controlled equally and whether or not more than one is native. Bilinguals in the traditional sense must then be qualified as '**balanced bilinguals**'; as 'ambilingual' or 'equilingual'; or as 'full', 'true', 'ideal' bilinguals.

binarism Tendency in many schools of structural linguistics to reduce relations to binary distinctions. Thus the relations between three levels of vowel height (close, mid, open) are commonly analysed into *binary features: [+ close, – open], [– close, – open], [– close, + open]. Similarly, the relations between three elements that make up a syllable (onset, nucleus, coda) are reduced to a pattern of *binary branching: [onset [nucleus coda]].

Jakobson was the earliest and most doctrinaire exponent; through his influence, directly or indirectly, such analyses were established in the 1960s at all levels of *generative grammar, in *Generative Phonology especially.

binary (Feature etc.) with two values. Usually of one whose values are positive and negative: e.g. [± voice] has the values [+ voice] (voiced) and [– voice] (voiceless), [± animate] the values [+ animate] (animate) and [– animate] (inanimate). Opp. multivalued.

Elements distinguished only by a binary feature are in a **binary opposition** (or **binary contrast**): e.g. [t] and [d], distinguished by the feature [+ voice], in English.

binary branching Any configuration in a *phrase structure tree in which a node is connected directly to two, and only two, lower nodes. Opp. multiple branching, which has often, as in *X-bar syntax, been explicitly excluded.

binding Relation in which an element is *bound (2) by an *antecedent. E.g. in *They helped each other*, the subject *They* binds *each other*. Hence '**Binding Theory**', of a part of *Principles and Parameters Theory concerned with this relation.

binomial A pair of words linked by a conjunction such as *and*. Called 'irreversible' when their order is fixed: e.g. (*I'll put it in*) *black and white*, not *white and black*.

binyan Term in Hebrew grammar for a pattern of stem formation, characteristically involving the addition of vowels to a consonantal root, of the kind general in Semitic languages. *Cf.* pattern.

'bioprogram' A set of genetically inherited rules of language for which, according to a hypothesis advanced by D. Bickerton in 1981, there is evidence e.g. when *creoles develop rapidly from *pidgins without influence from other languages.

Bislama Creole based historically on English, spoken widely in Vanuatu, mainly as a second language. The name reflects that of a trade language, 'Beach-la-Mar', developed through the trade in sea-slugs (French *bêche-de-mer*).

biuniqueness Principle by which two representations or two different aspects of a unit each correspond uniquely to the other. Thus especially of a constraint in phonology by which a phonetic representation of a form determines its phonological representation, as well as the opposite. Identified by critics as a restriction implicit in the theory of the *phoneme current in the USA in the 1940s and 1950s.

bivalent (Verb) having two *valents. Thus, in particular, a *transitive verb such as *love* or *drink*, whose valents are a subject and object.

'Black English Vernacular' *See* African American Vernacular English.

blade The upper surface of the tongue immediately behind the tip: e.g. in the articulation of [l] in *leaf* the blade is against the teeth ridge. Distinguished as an *articulator from the tip and the *dorsum: hence **laminal** or **lamino-** ('with the blade') vs. apical or apico- ('with the tip') or dorsal ('with the dorsum').

'bleaching' Change by which the meaning of a word becomes increasingly unspecific. Typically, therefore, in instances of *grammaticalization (2): e.g. the meaning of French *pas* (from Latin *passus* 'step, pace') was 'bleached' as it developed into a mark of negation: (*ne* . . .) *pas* 'not'.

bleeding Relation between rules which are *ordered in such a way that the application of the earlier rule restricts the set of forms that the later will apply to. Especially in classic *Generative Phonology: e.g. a rule by which vowels are deleted in unstressed syllables **bleeds** a later rule by which medial consonants are voiced when a vowel follows.

Opp. feeding; *cf.* counter-bleeding, counter-feeding.

blend Word formed by joining the beginning of one form to the end of another. E.g. *smog*, formed in 1905 from *smoke* and *fog*.

blocking The barring of a process. E.g. one of word-formation: thus the formation of a noun *kingess*, on the lines of *princess*, *countess*, etc. is seen as blocked by the existing word *queen*.

block language The form of language used in newspaper headlines, in cables, in notices, on labels of products, and so on. Distinguished by specific rules or patterns, which have developed in part independently of those in ordinary language.

Bloomfield, Leonard (1887–1949) American linguist and one of the most influential of the 20th century. Originally a Germanist, but famous for his general theory and for comparative and descriptive studies of *Algonquian languages, especially Menomini. His first general work, *An Introduction to the Study of Language* (1914), was influenced by the psychology of W. Wundt; from the 1920s, however, he was committed to a 'physicalist' philosophy of science in which all scientific statements are reducible to accounts of observable phenomena, and in his great work *Language* (1933) he sought to establish the foundations of linguistics, as an autonomous science, in a way that would be compatible with this view and specifically with *behaviourism in psychology. This led, in particular, to an account of meaning in terms of the 'practical events' accompanying a speech signal, in which the meaning of a word, for example, is constituted by features of such 'events', including events within a speaker's body, common to all the occasions on which it is uttered. Bloomfield's work was continued, partly in a new direction, by the *Post-Bloomfieldians and still, in part, by their successors. Many ideas now current, especially in the theory of grammar, are therefore his in origin.

Boas, Franz (1858–1942) American anthropologist, the teacher of Sapir and other eminent scholars in both linguistics and anthropology and, more than any other before or since, the founder and organizer of linguistic field-work in the USA. His most important general contribution is his introduction to the *Handbook of American Indian Languages* (1911), which emphasizes, in particular, the structural diversity of languages and the need to describe them in terms independent, where necessary, of the grammatical categories inherited in the European tradition.

'body language' Popular term which lumps together some conventional forms of *non-verbal communication with other states or dispositions of a human body, voluntary or involuntary, identifiable as some kind of 'sign' to other people.

Bokmål *See* Norwegian.

borrowing Conventional term for the introduction into language *a* of specific words, constructions, or morphological elements of language *b*. Thus *table* and *marble* are among the many *loan words **borrowed** into English from Old French in the period after the Norman conquest. '**Dialect borrowing**' is a similar transference of features from one dialect to another, often posited to explain the lack of consistent divisions between them.

bottom-up (Procedure) which determines the structure of a sentence etc. by working from smaller units to larger. Opp. top-down, e.g. as alternative strategies in *parsing.

bound (1) (*Morpheme) which cannot stand as a word on its own. Thus *un-* in *unkind* is a **bound form**, since there is no word '*un*'. Opp. free (1): *cf.* minimal free form.

bound (2) (Pronoun etc.) linked syntactically to an *antecedent. E.g. in *He saw himself*, the reflexive *himself* would (according to most views of the scope of syntax) be '**bound by**' *he*. The syntactic relation between such an element and its antecedent is one of **bound *anaphora**.
  Opp. free (2). The sense is derived from use in logic, where a variable is 'bound' if it is within the scope of an operator and therefore does not need to be assigned a value for the expression to be meaningful.

boundary marker Any unit or feature of speech which is associated with a boundary between larger units. E.g. a glottal stop in German appears when a word begins with a vowel, and is therefore said to mark the boundary between that word and the one preceding. Translation of German 'Grenzsignal'.

boundary symbols Symbols representing the boundaries between different kinds of unit. E.g. in # the # govern + ment #, '#' is used for a boundary between words, '+' for one within words.

   Cf. juncture.

boundary tone 1. A *tone, of any kind, that serves as a *boundary marker. **2.** A tone established, in one analysis of intonation, at the beginning or end of an *intonational phrase or tone group. Distinguished as such from a *starred tone and others associated with a position of prominence.

bounded (Rule, relation) restricted to a specific syntactic domain. Opp. unbounded; *cf.* local.

'Bounding Theory' Part of *Government and Binding Theory specifying the boundaries of units within which syntactic operations applied. *Cf.* subjacency.

boustrophedon A way of writing, especially in early Greek, in which alternant lines are from left to right and from right to left. From an adverb meaning 'like an ox turning': i.e. as a field is ploughed.

braces { } Mainly used to conflate rules and examples that are partly identical. E.g. the rules s → z / V–V (s is voiced between vowels) and s → h /—# (s becomes h at the end of a word) may be conflated thus:

$$s \rightarrow \begin{cases} z / V - V \\ h / - \# \end{cases}$$

Similarly, the examples *She likes him* and **She likes himself* may be displayed thus:

$$\text{She likes} \begin{cases} \text{him} \\ \text{*himself} \end{cases}$$

   Also used at one time in representing *morphemes (3): e.g. *children* as a sequence of morphemes {child} + {plural}. Also, as in mathematics, to list the members of a set: e.g. {a, b, c} is the set whose members are a, b, and c.

'bracketing paradox' Applied to various cases in which a *constituent structure suggested by formal criteria is at variance with that suggested by meaning. E.g. in *hundred and eleventh*, the suffix *-th* is formally attached to *eleven*: thus [hundred and [eleventh]]. But in meaning it goes with the whole: [[hundred and eleven] th].

brackets *See* angled brackets, round brackets, square brackets; also braces (= 'curly brackets').

Brahmi Script developed in India by the middle of the 1st millennium BC, and attested widely from the 3rd century; the direct or indirect source, from the early 1st millennium AD, of later *Indian scripts, including those of *Thai and other languages in South-east Asia. Supposedly modelled on a *Semitic alphabet, but no precise source is certain.

branch 1. A group of languages within a language *family that are more closely related among themselves than to any others. E.g. the *Indo-Aryan languages form a branch of *Indo-Iranian, which is in turn one of the main branches of the *Indo-European family. **2.** A branch in any form of *tree diagram.

branching node A *node in a *phrase structure tree which is connected directly to two or more lower nodes.

'breaking' A sound change in the development of Old English by which front vowels were diphthongized by the addition of a close back vowel when they were followed by a velar or velarized consonant. E.g. in *feohtan* 'to fight' < **fehtan*, where *h* = [x]. Also used more generally by some specialists in Germanic, in referring to other specific cases of diphthongization.

Bréal, Michel (1832–1915) A pioneer of comparative linguistics in France, whose *Essai de sémantique* (1897) is a general introduction to grammatical and lexical theory, influential, in particular, for its treatment of changes in the meanings of words. The term 'semantics' ('sémantique') was coined by Bréal in opposition to 'phonetics' ('phonétique'), and defined, more widely than in usage since the mid-20th century, as a science concerned with the nature and relations of all meaningful units, as opposed to a science, again in the most general sense, of sounds.

breath group A unit defined by points at which speakers take in breath. Hence of an *intonational phrase or tone group, seen as a unit before or after which they tend to do so.

breathy voice *See* murmured.

Breton *Celtic language introduced into Brittany in France by emigration from south-west Britain in the 5th century AD. Increasingly restricted to the west of the province, to speakers who are bilingual in Breton and French.

breve (˘) Normally used to indicate that a vowel is short: e.g. Latin *brĕvis* 'short', phonetically [brɛwɪs].

'brightening' Used of sound changes in *Germanic languages by which back vowels become front.

Brittonic = Brythonic.

Broad Romic *See* Sweet.

broad transcription A phonetic transcription omitting details that are judged to be inessential; hence identical with, or close to, a representation of *phonemes. Opp. narrow transcription.

'Broca's area' A part of the brain included in a massive area of damage suffered by an aphasic patient of P. Broca in the mid-19th century. 'Broca's aphasia' is a form characterized by *agrammatism and associated in clinical lore with lesions in this area.

'broken plural' Term in Arabic grammar for a plural formed by a pattern of vowels which is different from that of the singular, as opposed to one formed by suffixation. E.g. (Egyptian) [ʔaswa:q] 'market-PL' vs. [su:q] 'market-SG', [kuba:r] 'big-PL' vs. [kibi:r] 'big-SG'.

Brugmann, Karl (1849–1919) Indo-Europeanist and one of the founders of the *Neogrammarian movement. His great work is a handbook of Indo-European comparative linguistics (*Grundriss der vergleichenden Grammatik der indogermanischen Sprachen*), 1st edn. (5 volumes) 1886–93.

Brythonic Branch of *Celtic which includes *Welsh, *Cornish, and *Breton. Also spelled '**Brittonic**'.

BSL *See* sign language.

Bühler, Karl (1879–1963) Psychologist, professor at the University of Vienna 1922–38, where his views influenced the thinking of Trubetzkoy and other members of the *Prague School. His *Sprachtheorie* (1934) presented a sign theory with particular emphasis on the *functions of language, and a distinction between two 'fields' which form the context in which a sign is used. The 'symbolic field' (*Symbolfeld*) is formed by the other signs that make up an utterance; the 'deictic field' (*Zeigfeld*) is formed by the context in which it is uttered and is the origin of modern conceptions of *deixis.

Bühler emigrated to the USA in 1939, practising as a clinical psychologist from 1945.

Bulgarian South *Slavic, the official language of Bulgaria, where it is mainly spoken: written in *Cyrillic. '**Old Bulgarian**' = Old Church Slavonic.

bunched Articulated with the tongue tip drawn back into the body of the tongue. Used e.g. of a bunched continuant 'ɹ' in some forms of American English.

'bundle' *See* feature; isogloss.

Burmese The official language of Myanmar (Burma), and native to about two-thirds of its people: the standard form is that of the valley of the Irrawaddy. Attested by inscriptions from the 11th century AD; written in an *Indian script adapted from that of the Mons, whom the Burmese had conquered. *Sino-Tibetan, of the *Lolo-Burmese branch of *Tibeto-Burman.

by-form Any form of a word etc. not seen as primary.

C

C = complementizer.

CA = componential analysis; Conversation Analysis.

cacuminal An old term for *retroflex.

Caddoan Family of languages in North America, spoken or formerly spoken in part of the central plains in the USA.

caesura [sɪˈzjʊərə] A metrical division in a line of verse. Hence available as a term for similar rhythmical or intonational divisions in speech.

calque A word or expression which has been formed by translation of a corresponding word or expression in another language. E.g. French *gratte-ciel* 'skyscraper' (lit. 'scratch-sky') is a calque on English *skyscraper*. Also called a **loan translation**.

Cambodian = Khmer.

Canaanite Branch of West *Semitic that included *Phoenician and *Hebrew. Also a *Semitic alphabet in which e.g. Hebrew was at one time written.

cancellable (inference) *See* defeasible.

canonical Typical or characteristic; thence also basic, most straightforward. Thus a **canonical form** of e.g. words or syllables is a phonological pattern to which they characteristically conform, in some particular language, family, part of the world, etc. *Cf.* template.

A **canonical clause**, in Huddleston and Pullum, *CGEL, is declarative and active, as opposed to 'non-canonical' interrogatives or passives.

Cantonese *See* Chinese.

cardinal numeral One which indicates the number of individuals in a set, e.g. *three*, as opposed to an *ordinal numeral, e.g. *third*.

cardinal vowels A set of vowels established and recorded by (Daniel) Jones, to serve as fixed reference points for the description of vowels in any language. Together they define the limits of a space within which vowels can be articulated, and within which a phonetician who has been trained to do so can place any particular vowel that is heard.

The space is represented as a quadrilateral, shown in the illustration overleaf in its most schematic form. Of the vowels that delimit it, cardinal 1 (in phonetic notation [i]) is articulated with the tongue as far forward and as high in the mouth as is possible without audible friction; cardinal 5 ([ɑ]) is articulated with the tongue as far back and as low in the mouth as possible. Cardinals 2, 3, and 4 ([e, ɛ, a]) are *front vowels on the limits of the space and auditorily equidistant between 1 and 5; cardinals 6, 7, and 8 ([ɔ, o, u]) correspondingly define the limits of the space for *back vowels.

Other points of reference are defined by relation to these. In particular, the **secondary** cardinal vowels are articulated in the same way as the **primary** except that rounding or spreading of the lips is reversed. E.g. to primary [i], in which in addition the lips are spread, corresponds secondary [y], with lips rounded; to primary [u], with lips rounded, secondary [ɯ], with lips spread.

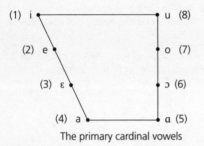

(1) i   u (8)

(2) e   o (7)

(3) ɛ   ɔ (6)

(4) a   ɑ (5)

The primary cardinal vowels

'caretaker speech' = motherese but with recognition that not only mothers use it. Also '**caregiver speech**'.

Carib(an) Family of languages in the northern part of South America, represented at intervals mainly from the mouth of the Amazon across to northern Colombia.

'Cartesian linguistics' The study of grammar in the tradition of *Port Royal, interpreted by Chomsky in a book with that title (1966) as specifically in the spirit of the 17th-century philosopher Descartes.

case Inflectional category, basically of nouns, which typically marks their role in relation to other parts of the sentence. E.g. in Latin *vidi puellam* 'I saw a girl', *puellam* '(a) girl' has the ending of the *accusative case (*puella-m*) and this marks it as the object of the verb (*vidi* 'I-saw').

Thence of various more abstract constructs. Thus, in English, *girl* in *I saw the girl* has the same form that it has in e.g. *A girl saw me*. But in many accounts *the girl* is as a whole 'accusative', this property being realized by the position of the phrase within the sentence. In Chomsky's *Principles and Parameters Theory, 'Case' is elevated to a category of *Universal Grammar, subject e.g. to the mechanism of *checking, or earlier, in *Government and Binding Theory, to principles of *government.

Also, as in *Case Grammar, of specific *case roles.

case attraction Agreement of a relative pronoun with the case of the noun on which its clause depends. Common especially in Ancient Greek. E.g. in *tôn póleōn hôn ékhei* 'of the cities which he holds', the relative pronoun is the object of its clause. Therefore one might expect it to be accusative: *hâs ékhei* 'which-ACC.PL he-holds'. But the noun to which it relates is genitive: *tôn póleōn* 'the-GEN.PL city-GEN.PL'. Hence, by attraction, it too is genitive: *hôn* 'which-GEN.PL'.

Also called '**case assimilation**'.

Case Filter *See* Case Theory.

'case frame' *See* Case Grammar.

Case Grammar Variant of *transformational grammar developed by C. J. Fillmore in the late 1960s. The central idea was that in any clause each noun phrase has, as one element at an underlying level, a 'case' which represents its semantic role or *case role. E.g. in *I opened the door with the key*, the cases of *I, the door*, and *with the key* were respectively *agent, *patient, and *instrumental. An underlying case may correspond to varying roles or forms in *surface structure: e.g. instrumental corresponds in this example to an adverbial, and is marked by *with*. But in *The key opened the door* the same element is represented by the subject (*the key*).

In the lexicon, verbs were classed by '**case frames**': that is, by the arrays of underlying 'cases' with which each can be combined. E.g. *open* can combine with an agent, a patient, and an instrumental; also with a patient alone (*The door opened*); also with a patient and an instrumental (*The key opened the door*, or *The door opened with the key*).

case role A semantic role of the kind that in many languages is marked by *cases. E.g. in *Open it with the knife*, *it* has the role of *goal in relation to *open* and *with the knife* the role of *instrumental. In English these are marked by the order of words and the use of the preposition *with*; but in Latin, for example, both would be marked by case endings.

For partial analyses of case roles *see* Case Grammar; concrete case; grammatical case; localism; theta roles.

case stacking Pattern in which a single word has two or more successive *case inflections. E.g. in Australian languages: thus, schematically, in *Bill*-GEN-DAT *wife*-DAT 'to Bill's wife', the dependent noun (*Bill*) is marked as genitive through its relation to the head noun *wife*, and also as dative in agreement with it.

Hence '**double case**', referring to instances in which, as here, two cases are so 'stacked'.

case syncretism Strictly, of the *syncretism, in some paradigms or at some points in a paradigm, of *cases distinguished elsewhere. E.g. in Latin and other older Indo-European languages, a distinction between nominative and accusative was drawn in masculines and feminines but syncretized in neuters.

Also, loosely or more generally, of the realization by the same case of two or more different *case roles. E.g. the semantic role of 'movement from' is conflated, in the Latin *ablative, with that of an *instrumental: *Roma* ('Rome-ABL.SG') 'from Rome'; *hasta* ('spear-ABL.SG') 'with a spear'.

'Case Theory' Part of *Government and Binding Theory concerned with abstract *cases. Thus including in particular a '**Case Filter**', by which such a case had to be assigned to any non-empty noun phrase: i.e. to any which was not an *'empty category'.

Cassubian *See* Polish.

Castilian *See* Spanish.

catachresis [katəˈkriːsɪs] Ancient term for the incorrect use of words: e.g. the use of the term 'universal' is **catachrestic** when it refers to features of language known not to be universal. From Greek: 'abuse' and 'abusive' are from the corresponding terms in Latin.

Catalan *Romance language spoken in an area of north-east Spain, including Barcelona. The language of medieval Aragon, with its earliest literature of that period.

cataphora [kəˈtafərə] The relation between a pronoun and a unit later in a sentence that supplies its referent. Thus *he* might or might not be understood as **cataphoric** to *Jones* in *When he had finished, Jones was exhausted*; i.e. the person it refers to might or might not be Jones.

Also called 'anticipatory', as opposed to retrospective, *anaphora. But 'anaphora' is in origin a term for a relation 'up' (Greek *aná*); hence 'cataphora' for a relation 'down' (*katá*).

categorial component The *base component of a *transformational grammar: i.e. one whose rules, called '**categorial rules**', dealt with relations of constituency among syntactic categories.

categorial grammar A type of formal grammar, originally devised by the logician K. Ajdukiewicz in the 1930s. Its basis is a lexicon, in which words are assigned to categories of greater or lesser complexity: if a string of words is well-formed, these will combine, by a repeated operation of cancellation, to a designated simple category. E.g. *run* is a word with which a preceding noun (N) can form a sentence (S): *men run*. So, assign *run* to a complex category N\S, indicating precisely that. By the operation of cancellation, X followed by X\Y reduces to Y; hence N (*men*) plus N\S (*run*) reduces to, and is thus assigned as a whole to, a sentence category S. An adjective such as *young* can combine similarly, but in the opposite order, with a following noun. So, assign *young* to a

complex category N/N. By the operation of cancellation, Y/X followed
by X also reduces to Y. So, for the string *young men run*, the reduction
will be in two stages. First, N/N (*young*) plus N (*men*) reduces to N: i.e.
the form as a whole is also of this category. Then N (*young men*) plus
N\S (*run*) will again reduce to S.

   Categorial grammars have the same *weak generative capacity as
*context-free phrase structure grammars. For the operation of
cancellation compare later concepts of *unification.

'categorical rule' *See* rule.

category Any class or system of grammatical or lexical units
distinguished at some level in the structure of a language. 'Noun
phrase' and 'noun', for example, are *syntactic categories. 'Case' and
'tense' are inflectional or *morphosyntactic categories. Colour terms
or terms for kinship form a semantic or, in the broadest sense, a
'lexical' category; and so on.

category-neutral (Rule, principle, etc.) which applies regardless of
the category to which a unit is assigned: thus regardless, especially, of
any of the syntactic categories noun, verb, etc.

catenative (Verb, construction) as in e.g. *I need to stop*, where *I* is
seen as linked, by *need*, to a following infinitive (*to stop*). Named from
the Latin word for 'chain' (*catena*): thus in *I would like to promise to stop*
a longer chain is formed by the successive catenatives *like* and *promise*.

Caucasian Cover term for languages whose families are indigenous
to the Caucasus. South Caucasian ('Kartvelian') includes *Georgian,
and is for many though not all scholars a family with no plausible
relationship to the others. North West Caucasian includes *Abkhaz,
West Circassian (Adyghe), and East Circassian (Kabardian), and is
separated by Ossetic, which is *Iranian, from North Central Caucasian
(*Chechén, Ingush) and North East Caucasian (in terms of geography,
east), of which Avar (north-east Dagestan) and Lezgi (south Dagestan
and north Azerbaijan) are the largest. The North Central and North
East groups arguably represent a larger family, possibly with the North
West also.

CAUS = causative.

causal (Clause etc.) indicating a cause or reason; e.g. *because I am busy*
in *I can't see you because I am busy*. The subordinator *because* is in turn a
causal conjunction.

causative (CAUS) (Construction, verb, affix) used in saying who or
what causes something to happen. Thus of an affix in, schematically,
I eat-CAUS-PAST the baby 'I fed the baby': i.e. 'I caused the baby to eat'.

   Similarly of *make* as a causative verb, e.g. in *I made the baby eat.*
Thence extensions of the term in many cases where the subject of a

transitive verb can be understood as responsible for something that happens. E.g. *I dropped the glass* has a construction often described as 'causative', with the speaker understood as 'causer', as opposed to one that in some accounts is 'inchoative', as in the intransitive *The glass dropped*.

cavity *See* nasal, oral. **Cavity features**, in the scheme of Chomsky and Halle, **SPE*, are ones involving primary and secondary *places of articulation.

c-command A relation of *command (2), variously defined in detail, which obtains e.g. between the subject of a sentence and an anaphoric element in its predicate. For example, in *John's father hurt himself*, the reflexive *himself* is c-commanded by its antecedent *John's father*. But it is not c-commanded by *John*, and it is for that reason, in one account, that this cannot mean 'John's father hurt John'.

Crucial to the definition of *government (3) in Government and Binding Theory.

CD *See* Functional Sentence Perspective.

Cebuano A language of the Philippines, spoken in Negros and other smaller islands and in parts of Mindanao. *Austronesian, of the same branch as *Tagalog.

Celtiberian *See* Celtic.

Celtic Branch of *Indo-European, conventionally divided into 'Continental Celtic', extinct by or soon after AD 500, and 'Insular Celtic', spoken in (or in the case of *Breton originating in) the British Isles. Continental Celtic is attested only by inscriptions and place-names, and by references in Latin authors, but forms of it were spoken widely in the area of north Italy (Lepontic), France (Gaulish), and parts of Spain (Celtiberian) before the Roman expansion; also in ancient Galatia (now part of Turkey). Insular Celtic is divided into Brythonic or Brittonic (Welsh, Breton, Cornish) and Goidelic (Gaelic).

Within Indo-European, Celtic shares features with *Italic especially: hence an old conjecture, never generally accepted, that they might at a higher level form a single '**Italo-Celtic**' branch.

ceneme Hjelmslev's term for a unit of *expression. A **cenemic** system of writing is one which represents phonological units as opposed to units of the lexicon or grammar: i.e. an *alphabet or *alpha-syllabic system or a *syllabary.

From the Greek word for 'empty': opp. plereme, pleremic.

central (Vowel) intermediate between *front and *back. For example, [ə] in [bʌtə] (*butter*) is a mid central vowel; *u* in Welsh *du* 'black' is a close central vowel ([ɨ]) in northern dialects.

Central American languages The indigenous languages of the geographical area, now dominated in most parts by Spanish. Those described as **Meso-American** form a linguistic area or *Sprachbund*, broadly between a line across the centre of Mexico (from the state of Nayarit to northern Veracruz) and another east of Guatemala: they include, in particular, the *Mayan family to the east, with the *Oto-Manguean and languages of the Nahuan or Aztecan branch of *Uto-Aztecan to the west; also smaller families (Mixe-Zoquean, centred on the Tehuantepec Isthmus, and Totonacan, in the north-east of the area), and individual languages, especially Tarascan (in the state of Michoacán), Huave, and Tequistlatec (both in Oaxaca), not belonging to any of these. Oaxaca and adjacent parts of neighbouring states form the region of greatest linguistic diversity.

Outside the Meso-American area, languages of the Sonoran branch of Uto-Aztecan are spoken in north-west Mexico; to the east of the area, mostly ones of families also represented in South America.

centralized 1. (Vowel) whose quality is more central than that of one of the *cardinal vowels: e.g. [ä], as one both closer and more back than cardinal [a]. **2.** (Vowel) resulting from a sound change or other process by which its quality becomes central or more central.

centre (of phrase) *See* ultimate head.

centre-embedding The inclusion of a syntactic unit in the middle of another which is of the same category. E.g. in *the girl* ₐ[*who the man* ᵦ[*who you met*] *liked*] the smaller relative clause (b) is included in this way within the larger (a).

Distinguished, in accounts of *recursive processes in *phrase structure grammar, from *left-branching and *right-branching.

centrifugal vs. centripetal (Languages) in which *heads (1) come before vs. after their dependents: i.e. the movement in the phrase is, respectively, 'away from' or 'towards' its syntactic centre. Distinguished by L. Tesnière in the 1950s and divided further into languages markedly of one type or the other ('accusées') vs. those less markedly so ('mitigées'). *Cf.* Head Parameter.

'centum language' *Indo-European language of any branch in which a velar stop, as in Latin *centum* 'hundred', did not change to a sibilant fricative or affricate. Opp. '*satəm* language'.

Cercle Linguistique de Prague *See* Prague School.

cerebral An old term for *retroflex.

CF For 'context-free'. Thus CF-grammar or CF-PSG = context-free (phrase structure) grammar.

CGE = *A Comprehensive Grammar of the English Language*, by R. Quirk, S. Greenbaum, G. Leech, and J. Svartvik (1985).

CGEL = *The Cambridge Grammar of the English Language*, by
R. D. Huddleston, G. K. Pullum, and others (2002).

Chadic Family of languages in sub-Saharan Africa, spoken to the east,
south, and west of Lake Chad: *Hausa is by far the largest. Grouped
with others in *Afro-Asiatic.

chain 1. Relation between units realized successively in speech and
writing: *cf.* syntagmatic. **2.** *See* anaphora; movement.

chain shift A series of two or more sound changes, by which sound
a > sound *b*, sound *b* > sound *c*, and so on. E.g. in the Greek dialect of
ancient Athens, by which [uː] > [yː] and [oː] in turn > [uː]. Divided in
principle into **drag chains** and **push chains**. E.g. in the example cited
the fronting of [uː] might be seen as having 'dragged' [oː] after it into
the phonetic space so vacated; alternatively, the raising of [oː] to [uː]
might have 'pushed' the existing [uː] out of it.

change Any change that takes place, for whatever reason or at
whatever level, in the history of a language. Thus **phonological
change** is change in *phonology, **morphological change** change in
*morphology, **syntactic change** change in *syntax, and so on.
    '**Change from above**' is distinguished by Labov as originating in
the speech of dominant social classes and developing 'with social
awareness'. '**Change from below**' is said to originate 'in the
vernacular' and to be 'below the level of social awareness'.

'change in progress' *See* apparent time.

'charm' *See* Government Phonology.

Chechén North Central *Caucasian language, spoken north of the
Caucasus Mountains, with Ingush, in the provinces of Russia named
after them.

checked Feature distinguishing glottalized consonants (= ejectives) in
*Jakobson's system. A **checked tone** is a *tone whose realization ends
in a *glottal stop.

checking Mechanism in Chomsky's *Principles and Parameters
Theory for inspecting e.g. the arguments of verbs to ensure that they
are in appropriate abstract 'Cases'.
    A reformulation in essentials of a principle familiar since antiquity,
that if a unit *X* requires the presence of other units with specific
grammatical properties, a sentence which includes *X* is grammatical
only if these requirements are met. E.g. a verb such as *needs* requires,
among other things, a subject which is traditionally third person,
singular, and nominative. Check, in the structure of *She needs help*, that
she has each of these properties, and, in that respect at least, it passes.
Check for the same properties in *I needs help* or *Them needs help,* and they

would be excluded. The same verb also requires an object, traditionally accusative. Check for this in the structures of *She needs* or *She needs they*, and they too are excluded.

Hence '**Checking Theory**', as one topic in Chomsky's programme.

chereme *See* -eme.

Cherokee Iroquoian, spoken in an area in the south-east USA, until displaced to Oklahoma by ethnic cleansing in the mid-19th century.

Commonly written, from the 1820s onwards, in a *syllabary devised by Sequoyah, a native speaker in N. Carolina.

chest (voice, register) *See* phonation.

chiasmus *Figure of speech in which the order of elements in one clause or sentence is reversed in one which follows. E.g. *if I see her I am a fool* (conditional clause + main clause) *and I am a worse fool if I don't* (main clause + conditional clause).

Chibchan Group of languages spoken in scattered places mainly in Colombia and neighbouring parts of Venezuela, and westwards in Panama and Costa Rica.

Chichewa = Nyanja.

Chinese Branch of *Sino-Tibetan. The most important member (conventionally 'dialect') is **Mandarin**, native in most of China roughly north and west of a line from south Jiangsu to west Guangxi; the regional variety of Beijing is the basis for Chinese as an official language in China, Taiwan, and (with others) Singapore. Other major 'dialects', running broadly from north to south and east to west, are: Wu (Zhejiang and to the north, including Shanghai); Northern Min (north Fujian to south of the River Min); southern Min or **Hokkien** (south Fujian and the coast southwards, also in Taiwan and Hainan); Kejia or Hakka (mainly north-east Guangdong); Xiang or Hunanese (in Hunan); Yue or **Cantonese** (most of Guangdong, including Hong Kong, and most of Guangxi). Of these, Cantonese and Hokkien especially are widely spoken through emigration in many other countries.

'**Old Chinese**' is the form spoken from the 5th century BC to the end of the Han dynasty in the 3rd century AD, and the form from which **Classical Chinese**, as a written language, derives. The *Chinese writing system is attested earlier, from the second half of the 2nd millennium BC. *Pinyin is now the standard Roman spelling.

Chinese writing system Developed, independently on all available evidence, in at the latest the first half of the 2nd millennium BC. First attested by inscriptions on bone and tortoiseshell used in divination ('oracle bones') dating from the 14th century. The characters now used developed essentially from the late 3rd century BC (Qin and Han dynasties).

Each character represents a minimal grammatical element or *morpheme, realized phonetically by a single syllable. Some characters are simple, often pictographic in origin: e.g. the precursor of the one which represents the morpheme meaning 'water' was made up of wavy lines. But the vast majority are 'compound' characters, in which, in particular, a character taken to represent a syllable as a phonetic unit has been combined with one which represents a morpheme with a related meaning. E.g. the compound character for a morpheme meaning 'sea' has as its 'semantic' element the radical of the character for the 'water' morpheme, and, as its 'phonetic' element, one which also represents a homonymous form for 'sheep' (*yáng*).

Characters of Chinese origin are used for *Japanese, partly in a very different way; also in writing *Korean.

Chinook Family of languages historically spoken along the lower Columbia River in the north-west USA.

Choctaw *See* Muskogean.

choice vs. chain Effectively = paradigmatic (1) vs. syntagmatic. In the terminology of Halliday especially, there is 'choice' among the alternatives which form a *system; a 'chain' is formed by elements in a *structure.

chômeur An element in *Relational Grammar that has been 'demoted', by a syntactic operation, from the *nucleus of a clause to its *periphery. Thus in the passive construction an *agent (3) would be a chômeur demoted from the nuclear role of subject: ~nucleus~[*a wall blocked my path*] → ~nucleus~[*my path was blocked*] *by a wall*.

From the French word for 'unemployed'.

Chomsky, Avram Noam (1928–) American linguist whose theories revolutionized much of the subject in the second half of the 20th century. In *Syntactic Structures* (1957), his first book and for many still his most important single work, he overturned the strategy of analysis developed by the *Post-Bloomfieldians and replaced it with a formal theory of *generative grammars and the concept of an *evaluation procedure as a means of justifying them. In his next major book, *Aspects of the Theory of Syntax* (1965), he proposed a theory of *levels which included, in particular, the distinction between *deep structure and *surface structure; he also introduced the notion, in the long run far more important, that much of the structure of language in general is 'innate' or genetically inherited. From the end of the 1960s Chomsky's work has been directed above all to the development of a theory of *Universal Grammar, conceived as an account of what is so inherited and, by implication, to confirming that a Universal Grammar exists. A succession of works in the 1970s led by the end of the decade to what became known as a *Principles and Parameters Theory: see in particular *Reflections on Language* (1975), *Lectures on Government and Binding* (1981), *Knowledge of Language* (1986), and, at a more popular level,

Language and Problems of Knowledge (1988). His latest formulations form part of the *minimalist programme initiated in the early 1990s: see in particular *The Minimalist Program* (1995).

'Chomsky-adjunction' Any operation on a *phrase structure tree in which an element is added to a constituent of a category A in such a way that both become part of a larger constituent, also of the category A. E.g. if *horse* has the structure ₙ[*horse*], the addition of -*s* by Chomsky-adjunction would yield the structure ₙ[ₙ[*horse*] *s*]. *Cf.* sister-adjunction.

'Chomsky-hierarchy' A ranking of *finite state grammars, *context-free and *context-sensitive phrase structure grammars, and *unrestricted rewrite systems, in respect of increasing *power or *weak generative capacity. The term refers to work by Chomsky in the mid-1950s.

'chroneme' (Daniel) Jones's term for a phonological unit of duration: e.g. long and short as chronemes distinguishing vowels in some forms of English. Likewise '**chrone**', for any phonetic degree of duration.

Chrysippus *See* Stoics.

Chukotko-Kamchatkan Small family of languages, of which **Chukchi** is the most important, spoken on the Chukotka and Kamchatka Peninsulas in Siberia.

Circassian Alternative name of two North West *Caucasian languages, Adyghe (West Circassian) and Kabardian or Kabardo-Cherkess (East Circassian).

circumfix A combined *prefix and *suffix, treated as a single unit. E.g. in German *gefragt* 'asked', the forms which mark the participle, *ge-* and *-t*, might be seen as a circumfix (*ge . . . t*) enclosing the root *frag-*. *Cf.* parasynthetic (2).

circumflex (^) In origin a sign invented for Ancient Greek to represent an *accent (1) realized by a falling pitch. Used in linguistics either for a falling *tone in tone languages or for a rise followed by a fall in intonation.

circumstantial (Adverb, adverbial) which indicates the external setting, in space and time especially, of an event etc. E.g. both *in Chicago* and *yesterday* are circumstantial elements in *We met her in Chicago yesterday*. From French, where 'circonstant' or 'complément circonstanciel' would be variously applied to these and other *adjuncts (1) forming the *periphery (1) of a clause.

citation form The form used to refer to a lexical unit. The choice is a matter of convenience and is often arbitrary. E.g. in French a verb is referred to by the infinitive: *manger* 'to eat'. But in Latin it is referred to by the first-person singular of the present indicative: *edo* 'I eat'.

classeme A semantic feature characterizing a class of lexical units, similar in grammar as well as meaning, which cuts across the organization of the lexicon into semantic fields: e.g. animate vs. inanimate. More usual in French or German accounts of word meaning ('classème', 'Klassem') than in English-speaking countries.

'classical language' = learned language. From the status of Latin and Ancient Greek as 'classical' in the Western European system of education.

classificatory verb Verb, e.g. in *Athabaskan languages, whose form varies with the physical or other character of an object referred to. Similar in that respect to *classifiers or *class prefixes.

classifier Used, in accounts of Chinese especially, of a form which marks a noun of a specific semantic class and which has to accompany e.g. a numeral. Thus in Chinese *yí-ge rén* 'one man' *ge* is a classifier, originally from a word for 'bamboo stalk', which has to follow the numeral (*yí* 'one') when it modifies any of a large class of nouns, including *rén* 'man'. Often called a '**numeral classifier**', though e.g. a classifier is also required in Chinese by a demonstrative (schematically 'that-*ge* man').

class prefix Any of a series of prefixes in *Bantu languages that vary according to *noun class.

clause Any syntactic unit whose structure is, or is seen as reduced from, that of a sentence. Thus, in particular, one which includes a verb and the elements that accompany it.

The smaller unit *who you introduced me to* is accordingly a clause in *I liked the girl who you introduced me to*. So, in many accounts, is *meeting her* in *I liked meeting her* or *to meet her* in *I want to meet her*, or even, in some, a single word or phrase like *in his cups* in *He sang hymns* (sc. *when he was*) *in his cups*. So, in current usage, is each of these sentences as a whole.

clause chaining Used of a variety of constructions in which clauses or elements seen as clauses are linked in ways unlike those characteristic of European languages. Hence, in particular, of constructions with *switch-reference; also, in some accounts, of *serial verb constructions; also of ones in which only one verb in the sequence has a full set of inflections; also of ones in which relations between clauses are marked by verb endings and not by conjunctions.

clausemate The relation between two syntactic elements that are part of a single clause. E.g. in *Jane promised* [*she would visit her*], *she* and *her* are clausemates; therefore, by a rule which distinguishes them as such, they must be understood to refer to different people.

clause union Syntactic process, distinguished by this term in
*Relational Grammar, by which a main clause and a subordinate
clause become one. Applied especially to constructions with an
infinitive in Romance languages: e.g. in Italian, *La farò venire* (lit. 'her
I-will-make to-come') is treated as a single clause derived from a main
clause with a causative verb ('I will make') with, at an underlying level,
a second clause as its complement ('she to come').

'clear *l*' *See* 'dark l'.

cleft (Construction) of e.g. *It was my sister (who/that) he married*. In cleft
sentences the copula (*was*) is preceded by *it* and followed by a noun
phrase (*my sister*) and a relative clause: distinguished as such from
*pseudo-clefts (e.g. *what he did was marry my sister*).

cliché In the ordinary sense: hence some *idioms and fixed
*expressions are clichés; also some other expressions involving
habitual *collocations.

click Sound produced by suction of the tongue against the roof of the
mouth. A body of air is trapped between the back of the tongue, which
is in contact with the velum, and a second closure further forward.
The space enclosed is then enlarged, the air within it is rarefied, the
second closure is released, and air flows inwards.

    Clicks are an important part of the consonant system in *Khoisan
and neighbouring *Bantu languages in South Africa; elsewhere mainly
in sounds outside the system of phonemes, e.g. the one written 'tut!
tut!' in English. Defined by phoneticians as a sound produced by an
ingressive velaric *airstream mechanism. But this is perhaps
misleading, since the movement of air is not in reality initiated by the
velum.

cline = gradience.

clipping Process of word-formation in which an existing form is
abbreviated. E.g. *fan* 'devotee, enthusiast' was formed in the late 19th
century by shortening *fanatic*, *hi-fi* in the mid-20th century by
shortening *high fidelity*.

clitic Any grammatical unit that is not straightforwardly either an
affix or a word on its own. E.g. in Ancient Greek *nêsós tis* 'a (certain)
island', the clitic *tis* is not an affix since, among other things, it is itself
inflected as nominative singular. Neither, as a word, is it entirely
independent, since it forms a single accentual unit with the preceding
word for 'island' (basically *nêsos*).

    From the Greek word for 'leaning': thus unaccented *tis* 'leans on'
nêsos. 'Enclitics' are clitics linked phonologically, as here, to the
word preceding, *proclitics those linked to the word following.
The distinction between clitics and *affixes is naturally fluid:
e.g. English *-n't* in *haven't* or *aren't* is a clitic by some criteria but has

been claimed as an affix by others. So too is the boundary between clitics and full words: e.g. unstressed *to* is a clitic, by some relevant criteria, in *I have to* [haftə] *go*.

clitic climbing Syntactic process, e.g. in Italian, in which a *clitic pronoun or another similar element forms a unit not with the verb to which it bears a direct syntactic relation but with one to which that verb is subordinate. E.g. in *lo faccio venire* 'I make him come', *lo* 'him' is the subject of the infinitive *venire* 'to come', but 'climbs' to form a unit with *faccio* 'make'. *Cf.* raising (2); also described in terms of *clause union.

'clitic doubling' The use of a *clitic pronoun with the same referent and in the same syntactic function as another element in its clause. E.g. in Spanish *le vi a Juan* 'I saw John', *le* 'him' is a clitic parallel to *a Juan* '(to) John'. One case of what Bloomfield called *cross-reference.

cliticization Syntactic process or historical change by which a word becomes a *clitic.

clitic pronoun A pronoun which is a *clitic: e.g. in Modern Greek *ton simpathí* (lit. 'him likes') the verb has as its object a clitic (hence unaccented) pronoun *ton*. Such pronouns are often seen as moved from a basic position of an object or other element; hence **'clitic movement'**.

close (Vowel) produced with the body of the tongue close to the roof of the mouth: e.g. those of *heat* or *hoot*. 'Close' is opposed to 'open' in the classification of *cardinal vowels; in other schemes close vowels are 'high'.

close approximation Narrowing of the space between *articulators sufficient to cause turbulence in a flow of air: e.g. of the lower lip and upper teeth in the articulation of [f] or [v]. Distinguished as a degree of stricture from *open approximation and *closure.

closed class A class of words or morphemes whose membership is fixed and can be listed. E.g. there is a closed class of determiners (*the*, *this*, etc.). Opp. open class.

closed interrogative Huddleston and Pullum's term, in *CGEL*, for an *interrogative 'with a closed set of answers': e.g. *Has she arrived?* (answer yes or no). Also subordinate: e.g. in *They asked if she had arrived.* Opp. open interrogative; *cf.* polar interrogative.

closed syllable One which ends in a consonant: e.g. the first syllable, [as], of *aster*. Opp. open syllable.

close juncture The normal linkage between successive sounds within a word. *Cf.* juncture.

close-mid (vowel) = half-close.

close transition Linkage between sounds characterized by
*coarticulation. Opp. open transition: *cf*. close vs. open juncture.

closing diphthong One which changes from relatively open to
relatively close: e.g. [aʊ] in *how*.

closure Contact between *articulators by which a flow of air is
completely blocked: e.g. between the lips in the articulation of [p] or
[m]. Distinguished as a degree of stricture from *close approximation
and *open approximation.

cloze test A test in which pupils or subjects are instructed to supply
words etc. that are missing from text presented to them.

cluster A sequence of consonants before, after, or between vowels.
E.g. [str] is a medial consonant cluster in words like *astray*.

co- In the usual sense of 'jointly', 'together'. E.g. *hyponyms of the
same word, at the same level, are **co-hyponyms**; units linked by
subscript *indices are **co-indexed**; units that go together may be seen
as **co-selected**; and so on.

coalescence = fusion.

coarticulation The simultaneous or overlapping articulation of two
successive phonological units. E.g. in a normal pronunciation of *sweet*
[swiːt] the lips are rounded in the articulation of [s]; i.e. there is
coarticulation of [s] and the [w] which follows. In one normal
pronunciation of [kp] in *duckpond* [ɪdʌkpɒnd], the contact of the back of
the tongue with the soft palate (for [k]) does not end before the closure
of the lips (for [p]): i.e. there is a period of coarticulation of both
consonants.
    To be distinguished from *double articulation (2) in that the
sounds are separate phonological units. Coarticulation is classed as
anticipatory, where the articulation of a following unit is anticipated,
vs. perseverative, where that of a preceding unit continues. Compare
the distinction between *regressive (= anticipatory) and *progressive
(= perseverative) assimilation.

coda The part of a *syllable, if any, that comes after the *nucleus (2);
e.g. [st] in [bɛst] (*best*).

code mixing Sometimes distinguished, though not always in the
same way, from *code switching. E.g. where a speaker switches at
frequent intervals from one language etc. to another, for no
discoverable external reason.

code switching Switching in speech between different languages,
dialects, etc. E.g. two business associates meet and chat in one

language; the meeting becomes formal and they switch to another. Often analysed into subtypes, e.g. as occurring within sentences or at sentence boundaries; sometimes distinguished from *code mixing, or from *borrowing, sometimes not; and so on.

The term '**code**' is loosely used of any language or distinct variety of a language, whether or not it is actually thought of as a code (like the Morse code or a legal code) in any illuminating sense.

codify To make subject to rules. Hence e.g. in forming *standard languages, as in the codification of English in the early modern period.

cognate (Languages, words, etc.) that have developed from a common ancestor. E.g. English is cognate with German; likewise English *beam* is cognate with German *Baum* 'tree'.

cognate object An object in syntax whose head noun parallels and repeats the meaning of the verb. E.g. *life* parallels *lived* in *She lived her life in Berlin*, or *She lived a full life*.

Cognitive Linguistics Movement in linguistics since the late 1980s, whose defining slogan is that the ability to speak and understand a language is continuous with other mental, or in a broad sense 'cognitive', abilities. Opposed especially to the view of Chomsky and his followers that knowledge of language forms an independent mental system interfacing with others. Characterized in practice by a range of favoured types of investigation, including *Frame Semantics, the study of *prototypes and the conceptual representation of meanings, and *Construction Grammar.

Leading proponents have included R. W. Langacker and G. P. Lakoff, both advocates, in their early careers, of *Generative Semantics.

'cognitive meaning' The meaning of a sentence considered in abstraction from *affective or emotive meaning, stylistic nuances, the meaning of word order in specific contexts, and whatever else is deemed or assumed to be irrelevant to it. E.g. *Harry kissed her* (in an amazed whisper) might be said to have the same cognitive meaning as *Harry* KISSED *her* (shouted at the top of one's voice), or HARry *kissed her*, or *She was kissed by Harry*, and so on. Often therefore, in practice, what is said to be preserved in paraphrase.

coherence Used semi-technically of the way in which the content of connected speech or text hangs together, or is interpreted as hanging together, as distinct from that of random assemblages of sentences. Especially in studies of conversation: e.g. it is by a principle of coherence that, if one speaker asks a question, the other is expected to answer. *Cf*. cohesion.

cohesion 1. The connection between successive sentences in texts, conversations, etc., in so far as it can be described in terms of specific syntactic units. E.g. A says 'Peter came' and B replies 'But he was very late': in this interchange the role of *but* as a conjunction and the link between the pronoun *he* and its antecedent *Peter* are both aspects of cohesion. **2.** The property of syntactic units which are not interrupted by elements that do not belong to them. Thus words are generally cohesive: i.e. they are not interrupted by other words or elements that belong to other words.

cohort model Model for the perception of spoken words proposed by W. Marslen-Wilson in the mid-1980s. It assumes a 'recognition lexicon' in which each word is represented by a full and independent 'recognition element'. When the system receives the beginning of a relevant acoustic signal, all elements matching it are fully activated, and, as more of the signal is received, the system tries to match it independently with each of them. Wherever it fails the element is deactivated; this process continues until only one remains active.

co-hyponym *See* hyponymy.

co-indexing *See* indices.

collective Referring to individuals as a group: e.g. *clergy* is a **collective noun** with the meaning 'clergymen in general'. Also of affixes: e.g., schematically, *sheep*-COLL 'flock of sheep'. Thence of a noun or form of a noun which distinguishes a kind from individuals of that kind: e.g. in Egyptian Arabic, [xoːx] 'peaches as a kind' in opposition to [xoːxa] (an individual peach) or the plural [xoːxat] (three or more individual peaches).

colligation Firth's term for the general relation between elements in a construction, as opposed to a *collocation or relation between individual words. Thus the collocation e.g. of *heavy* and *smoker* in *She's a heavy smoker* instances the colligation of an adjective with an agent noun, or with a noun generally.

collocation A relation within a syntactic unit between individual lexical elements; e.g. *computer* collocates with *hate* in *My computer hates me*. Used especially where words specifically or habitually go together: e.g. *blond* collocates with *hair* in *blond hair* or *Their hair is blond*; *drunk* with *lord* in *as drunk as a lord*; *run* with *riot* in *run riot*. Hence of *idioms: e.g. *blow* and *top* are part of a 'special collocation' in *She blew her top*.

A **collocational restriction** is any restriction on the collocability of one individual word with another. *Cf.* selectional restriction (1).

combinatory variants Variant realizations, especially of a phoneme, which are in *complementary distribution.

combining form A form of a word, or a form related to or in meaning like a word, used only as an element in compounds: e.g. *Anglo-* in *Anglo-American* or *socio-* in *socio-economic*; *retro-* in *retrovirus* or *bio-* in *biotechnology*. Common in English, where in some putative compounds, such as *autocrat* or *technocrat*, both members would be combining forms.

comitative *Case or *case role with the meaning 'together with, accompanied by': e.g. *with my husband*, or the preposition *with*, is comitative in *He went to town with my husband*. Also called 'sociative'.

command (1) An utterance which constitutes an order: e.g. 'Get out!' as an order to someone to leave the room. An **indirect command** is a clause representing a command in *indirect speech: e.g. in *I ordered [it to be sold]* or *We directed [that they should be rewarded]*. *Cf.* imperative.

command (2) Cover term for various relations defined over *nodes in a *phrase structure tree. In the most general case, a node A on one branch 'commands' a node B on another branch if (*a*) both are *dominated by the same node C and (*b*) C is the lowest *branching node that dominates A.

The relation most widely invoked has been *c-command, where C, as above, may be any branching node. In others C has been restricted further, e.g. to a *maximal projection of some category ('m-command'), or to a cyclic node as defined by a principle of *subjacency ('k-command').

comment A syntactic element which forms a basic sentence construction with a *topic (3). Hence the equivalent, in such a 'topic–comment' construction, of the *predicate (1) in a subject–predicate construction.

Also, more generally, of the parts of a sentence other than a topic, whether or not they are seen as forming a single syntactic unit. E.g. in *The beer you can, of course, drink*, the comment is everything after the topic *the beer*.

comment clause Used by Quirk *et al.*, *CGE* to cover various clauses seen as expressing a comment etc. which is in meaning, at least, parenthetical. E.g. ones like *I think* in *Nothing, I think, happened* or *as you know* in *As you know, nothing happened*; also, e.g. one like *what is odd* in *What is odd, she had her husband with her*.

commissive A type of *speech act by which speakers e.g. commit themselves to doing something: thus especially a promise.

commitment In the ordinary sense: e.g. *I think John did it* indicates less '**propositional commitment**', or commitment to the truth of the proposition that John did it, than *I know John did it*.

'common core' The core of a language as defined by units, constructions, etc. that distinguish all its dialects. Thus the order of subject and verb might belong to a common core of English; the inflection e.g. of the verb 'to be' does not.

common gender 1. Traditionally of the gender of nouns with which either masculine or feminine forms can agree: e.g. in French *le ministre* 'the-MASC minister', *la ministre* 'the-FEM minister'. *Cf.* epicene. **2.** Also of the use of a masculine, as a neutral gender, when reference is indifferently to male and female.

'common ground' Whatever knowledge of the world is shared, in the context of an utterance, by a speaker and addressee. *Cf.* background knowledge; encyclopaedic knowledge.

common noun One whose application is not restricted to arbitrarily distinguished members of a class. E.g. *girl* is a common noun that may be used in reference to any individual characterizable in general as a girl. Opp. proper noun.

communicative competence A speaker's knowledge of the total set of rules, conventions, etc. governing the skilled use of language in a society. Distinguished by D. Hymes in the late 1960s from Chomsky's concept of *competence, in the restricted sense of knowledge of a grammar.

communicative dynamism *See* Functional Sentence Perspective.

communicative language teaching Method of teaching a foreign language which aims to develop *communicative competence, as opposed to simple knowledge of grammatical and similar structures.

community *See* speech community. Also, loosely, of any definable set of individuals whose use of language is investigated, whether or not a community in any true sense.

commutation test *Hjelmslev's term for the basic test which distinguishes one unit of a language from another. Strictly, the replacement of one unit by another on the level of *expression (crudely a change in form) must entail a replacement at the level of *content (crudely a change in meaning) and vice versa. But often, especially in practice or in later usage, of a test involving the exchange of expression units only.

Comp *See* Complement; complementizer.

COMP *See* complementizer.

compact *Distinctive feature in the scheme proposed by *Jakobson. Characterized acoustically by a concentration of energy in a narrow part of the spectrum: thus with reference to, in particular, the *formants (1) of *open vowels. Opp. diffuse.
    The opposition of compact and diffuse is one of two that were taken by Jakobson to define both a triangle of vowels and a triangle of consonants parallel to it. In the accompanying illustration, [a] is maximally compact, [p] and [t] are maximally diffuse; on the horizontal

axis, [p] is maximally *grave and [t] is maximally *acute. This scheme was abandoned by Chomsky and Halle in *SPE*, but remains the most important achievement of Jakobson's binary method.

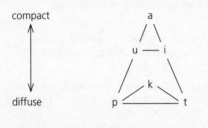

Jakobson's vowel and consonant triangles

comparative (Construction, inflection, etc.) by which individuals etc. are compared, in respect of some property, with others. Originally of inflected forms with the meaning 'more (than)': e.g. *taller*, with a comparative suffix *-er*, in *He is taller than me*. As such a term in the category of degree or grade. Thence of constructions, whether or not they are marked by inflections: e.g. in *He is more fortunate than me*; also, with *less . . . than*, in *He is less fortunate than me*.

Cf. equative; superlative.

comparative linguistics 1. The comparison of languages by the *comparative method. **2.** The comparison of languages for whatever purpose, whether e.g. for *genetic classification or for *typological classification.

comparative method The method of comparing languages to determine whether and how they have developed from a common ancestor. The items compared are lexical and grammatical units, and the aim is to discover correspondences relating sounds in two or more different languages, which are so numerous and so regular, across sets of units with similar meanings, that no other explanation is reasonable.

Three points are worth underlining. (*a*) The argument does not rest on mere similarities. Since sounds change over time, the older the ancestor the more likely it is that correspondences will be between sounds that are not similar: e.g. initial *k-* in one language might correspond to *v-* in another and to *s-* in a third. Likewise the greater the danger that similarities as such will be misleading. (*b*) The argument cannot safely rest on two or more correspondences. E.g. an *s* in language A might correspond quite frequently to an *s* in language B, not because the words in question have been inherited from a common ancestor but because they have been *borrowed, e.g. from B into A, in the not too distant past. (*c*) It is a matter of judgement how far other explanations, such as borrowing or chance, can be excluded. But the more remote the postulated ancestor the more likely it is that judgement will have to be suspended, and the hypothesis will remain a conjecture.

comparative philology The study of a *family of languages, especially the *Indo-European family, by the *comparative method.

compensatory lengthening Any change or process by which a vowel or consonant is lengthened as an element is lost: e.g. that in morphology by which Ancient Greek *melan-* 'black' + *-s* (NOM.SG) resulted in *melās*.

competence Chomsky's term in the 1960s for a 'speaker-hearer's knowledge of his language', as represented by a *generative grammar. Opp. performance: *cf.* I-language; *also* communicative competence.

complement A syntactic unit seen historically as 'completing' the construction of a word or other element. Thus, in particular: **1.** Of units within the *valency of a verb or other lexical unit. E.g. in *He put it on the floor*, the complements of *put* might be *he*, *it*, and *on the floor* and, within *on the floor*, *the floor* would be a complement of *on*. **2.** Of a *Complement (Comp) in X-bar syntax, as distinguished from a *Specifier and, in some accounts, an *adjunct. Also in specific uses: **3.** Of complements in sense 1 when they are clauses: thus *that he came* is a complement clause in *They said that he came* or *the news that he came*. **4.** Of *subject complements and *object complements: e.g. *happy* in *He seems happy* or *That will make him happy*.

The term is originally from French ('complément'). But French and English usage no longer match: in particular, the 'compléments' of a verb include all other elements of a *predicate (1), whether or not they are complements in any of the senses above.

Complement (Comp) The position in *X-bar syntax of a unit that forms an X´. Distinguished in some treatments from an *adjunct (2), which also forms an X´, but at a higher level.

complementarity Relation between lexical units whose meanings are mutually exclusive. E.g. between *male* and *female*: what is male is thereby not female, and vice versa. Words which stand in such a relation are **complementary terms** (or **complementaries**).

Distinguished in typologies of *sense relations from other relations broadly between opposites: *cf.* gradable antonymy especially.

complementary distribution Relation between sounds or forms whose *distributions do not overlap. Thus in southern British English (*RP), an unaspirated [p] appears after an initial [s], e.g. in [spɪn] (*spin*); an aspirated [pʰ] e.g. initially in [pʰɪn]; but there is no context in which both would be normal. Therefore they are in complementary distribution, and therefore, in part, they are described as *allophones of the same *phoneme.

Cf. contrast for 'contrastive distribution'; *also* free variation.

complementation 1. A set or series of *complements that a verb etc. may or must take. E.g. the complementation of verbs such as *read* includes a direct object (*I read a newspaper*); that of *put* includes both a direct object and a locative (*I put it on the floor*); that of *be*, if described in a similar way, includes a predicative adjective (*I am cold*), noun phrase (*I am a nervous wreck*), or locative (*I am in the kitchen*). Especially of complements within the *predicate (1); equivalent in that case to *valency (or *argument structure) minus the subject. **2.** The general relation in which complements stand: thus distinguished, in particular, from that of *modification (1).

complementizer (C) A word etc. originally seen as marking a *complement clause: e.g. *that* in *She said* [*that she would*].

Seen widely, since the 1980s, as *head (1) of a clause. Thus, in the same example, the subordinate clause would be a **complementizer phrase** (or CP) whose head C would be *that*; the main clause, in turn, would be a larger CP whose head C would be *null. The abbreviation 'COMP' or 'Comp' was used at one time for the position in a clause that complementizers occupy.

complete reduplication *See* reduplication.

complete sentence One in which no element in its construction requires another element that is missing. *Cf.* ellipsis: thus *I can't help* is one of many complete sentences that would correspond to an elliptical *I can't*.

Traditionally one which, in particular, lacks neither a subject nor a predicate: hence one said to express a 'complete thought'.

completive (Verb, form of verb) used of completed actions or processes. Hence often = perfective.

complex 1. (Sentence, clause, noun phrase) which includes one or more *subordinate clauses: e.g. *I know* [*he is there*] or *the fact* [*that he is there*]. **2.** (Preposition, subordinator, etc.) which consists of more than one word: e.g. *on top of* or *provided that*, seen as having the same syntax as *above* or *if*. Distinguished from *compounds (e.g. *throughout* or *whenever*) in that the words remain separate. **3.** (Word) whose form is derived by the addition of a *derivational affix: e.g. *maker*, derived by the addition of *-er* to *make*. **4.** (Coordination) in which the forms that are joined are not single syntactic units, e.g. in [[*I was*] *and* [*she wasn't*] *coming*]: cf. *I* [*was coming*], *She* [*wasn't coming*].

complex intransitive (Verb, construction) relating a subject to a *subject complement. E.g. in *They grew old*, where *they* is related to a complement *old*. *Cf.* complex transitive.

complex NP constraint Proposed principle by which an element in a clause which is in turn an element in a noun phrase cannot be related to a unit in any larger construction. Designed to exclude e.g. *What did you appreciate the fact that he had done?*, with *what* construed as the object of a verb (*had done*) whose clause is within the noun phrase *the fact that he had done*.

Cf. island. Formulated in the late 1960s as a constraint on movement: thus *what* could not be extracted by *wh*-movement from its position in *you appreciated [the fact [that he had done what]]*. Subsumed in the 1970s under a principle of *subjacency.

complex nucleus A nucleus of a *syllable which includes more than one unit: e.g. [baʊn] in *bounty* has a complex nucleus [aʊ].

'complex symbol' Chomsky's term in the mid-1960s for the syntactic class of a word as represented by a set of component features.

complex tone An intonational contour in which the pitch changes in two or more successive directions on a single *tonic syllable. E.g. the fall–rise (ˇ) in southern British English: *When will he be ˇcoming?*

complex transitive (Verb, construction) in which an object is related to an *object complement: e.g. in *That drove him mad, They made him their leader, I heard him singing*, or *They put him at the end*, where, in one analysis, *him* as object is related to the object complements *mad, their leader, singing, at the end*. Established by Quirk *et al., *CGE*, as a form of *complementation distinct from *monotransitive; *ditransitive.

component 1. A semantic feature: *see* componential analysis. **2.** A subset of rules within a *generative grammar, which is distinguished either by assigning a specific kind of representation to sentences, or by relating one such representation to another. E.g. the *base component of a classic transformational grammar, which assigned the representations called deep structures, or the transformational component, which related deep structures to surface structures.

componential analysis A treatment of lexical meaning in which the sense of each unit is distinguished from those of others by a set of semantic features or components. E.g. the basic sense of *bull* might be analysed into three components: 'bovine', distinguishing it from those of *stallion, ram*, etc.; 'fully adult', distinguishing it from that of *calf* or *bullock*; and 'specifically male', distinguishing it from that of *cow*.

Several versions of componential analysis were developed independently from the 1930s onwards. In English-speaking countries the best known was that of J. J. Katz and J. A. Fodor, proposed in 1963 within the framework of a generative grammar. This assumed, in addition, that components such as 'bovine' (or [+ bovine]), 'adult' ([+ adult]), or 'male' ([+ male]) were *substantive universals.

composition The process of forming *compounds.

compositional meaning The meaning of a syntactic unit seen as derivable from those of the smaller units of which it is composed and the constructions in which they stand: e.g. that of *tall girls* as derived from the meanings of *tall* as one lexical unit, of *girls* as the plural of another lexical unit, and of a syntactic construction in which *girls* is head and *tall* a modifier.

According to the **principle of compositionality** the meanings of sentences are compositional, either hypothetically or by definition, if considered in abstraction from particular occasions on which they are uttered. Hence accounts distinguishing semantics, as a study of such meanings, from *pragmatics.

compound A word formed from two or more units that are themselves words or forms of words: e.g. *blackboard* from *black* and *board*, or German *Schreibmaschine* 'typewriter' from *schreiben* 'write' and *Maschine* 'machine'. **Compounding** and **composition** are alternative terms for the process of forming compounds.

compound bilingualism Bilingualism in which the speaker's knowledge of the structure of one language is hypothetically integrated with that of the other. Opp. coordinate bilingualism.

compound letter Two or more successive letters which represent a single phonological unit: e.g. *sh* in English or *sch* in German, both representing [ʃ]. *Cf.* digraph. Likewise a **compound logogram** (or 'ideogram') is a *logogram which represents a single lexical or grammatical unit but can be analysed into parts that correspond to other separate logograms.

compound sentence One formed by the *coordination of two or more smaller sentences: e.g. *He sat down and she moved over*.

'compound stress' Stress in English on the first member of a compound: e.g. in *bláckbird* as opposed to *(a) black bírd*. Common and taken by some as a defining feature. The '**compound rule**', or 'Compound Stress Rule', is the one in Chomsky and Halle, *SPE*, which places stress in that position.

compound tense A form with an *auxiliary seen as forming part of the system of tenses. From French: e.g. the compound past ('passé composé'), as *(j')ai tué* 'I killed'.

compound tone A unit of *intonation in which two successive *tones are prominent in a single *intonational phrase or tone group: e.g. a 'fall-plus-rise' (falling tone followed by rising tone) in *I `THINK it may ´SNOW*.

conative (*Function of language) in trying to get an addressee to do, think, etc. what the speaker wishes. From the Latin word for 'to try' (infinitive *conari*); defined by Jakobson in 1960 in terms of orientation towards an addressee, as opposed to orientation towards the world (the *referential function) or orientation towards the speaker (the *emotive function).

Also of verb inflections with the meaning 'try to'.

concatenation The mathematical operation of juxtaposing units to form *strings.

concept A mental construct seen as mediating between a word and whatever it denotes or is used to refer to. Thus a concept 'dog' would be seen as mediating between *dog* and the set of animals denoted by it; this concept might be seen as common to both *dog* and e.g. *chien* in French; and so on.

'**Conceptualist**' accounts of meaning relate words etc. to concepts, not directly to, e.g., things. *Cf.* semantic triangle.

conceptual field *See* semantic field.

concessive (Clause etc.) indicating something conceded but not detracting from what is said: e.g. the clause introduced by *although*, and *although* as the subordinator, in *Although I am old, I am not stupid*.

concord = agreement.

concrete case A *case whose main role is to distinguish different meanings of adverbials. E.g. an *instrumental or a *locative: schematically, *cut knife-*INSTR *kitchen-*LOC 'cut with a knife in the kitchen'. Opp. grammatical case.

concrete noun One denoting a range of concrete objects or individuals: e.g. *cat*, *table*. Opp. abstract.

condition 1. = constraint. **2.** A specific part of a *rule (2) which indicates where it, or some subrule, applies. Thus a rule for German might introduce a glottal stop under the 'condition' # − V: i.e. at the beginning of a word (# −) before a vowel (− V).

conditional (*Mood) characteristically marking either a *conditional clause or, as implied by the use of the term in accounts of French and other Romance languages, a main clause accompanied by one.

conditional clause One which expresses a condition: e.g. *provided he is sober, if he can stay sober, unless he is drunk*. For types *see* remote.

conditional sentence One which consists of a main clause and a *conditional clause. The conditional clause is traditionally the *protasis, the main clause the *apodosis: e.g. *If you can come* (protasis) *I would be delighted* (apodosis).

conditioned (Sound change) explained by the phonetic context or the position in a word in which it takes place: e.g. the voicing of consonants between vowels, or a reduction of vowels in unstressed syllables. Opp. spontaneous; unconditioned.

conditioned variation Variation in the realization of a unit under specific conditions. Especially of units in phonology: thus the [ŋ] of *comfort* can be described as a **conditioned variant**, in the position before a labiodental fricative, of the unit realized by another variant, [m], e.g. in *bumper*.

'configurational language' One in which syntactic units stand in a *fixed (2) order. Effectively one, like English, for which it is easy to draw *phrase structure trees, in which 'configurations' of categories form '**configurational structures**'. Opp. non-configurational.

confirmative (Particle etc.) indicating that a statement is about something directly witnessed.

congruence The property by which words come together in a construction. E.g. *these* is a demonstrative and can combine with a following noun; *people* is a noun; in addition, both are plural. As such, they are congruent in the sense required to form a larger unit *these people*.

An ancient concept, going back at least to *Apollonius Dyscolus, and central, whatever the term used for it, in any theory in which the combinability of units is primary: *see especially* unification; Word Grammar.

conjoin Used by Quirk *et al.*, *CGE*, for a phrase etc. linked to another by *coordination: i.e. what other grammarians call a *conjunct.

conjugation The inflection of verbs; also a class of verbs which share a pattern of inflection. Thus verbs of the 'first conjugation' in Latin followed a pattern which differed in various ways from those of the 'second conjugation'. They had an *-a-* in most forms where those of the second conjugation had an *-e-*: e.g. *am-a-re* 'to love' (first) but *mon-e-re* 'to advise' (second). They also had e.g. a present subjunctive in *-e-* (third singular *am-e-t*) where the second and other conjugations had *-a-*.

A **conjugation marker** is a form which simply distinguishes one conjugation from another: thus the *-a-* and *-e-* of *amare* vs. *monere* are **conjugation vowels**, with no specific grammatical meaning.

conjunct 1. Any phrase etc. linked to another by *coordination: *cf.* conjunction (2). **2.** Used by Quirk *et al.*, *CGE*, of an adverbial indicating a connection between its clause or sentence and what precedes: e.g. *however* in *We, however, could not*, or *then* in *If not, then burn it. Cf.* adjunct; disjunct; subjunct.

conjunction (1) A word etc. which joins two syntactic units. Especially in *coordination: e.g. *and* and *but* are conjunctions in

[*He did*] *and* [*he didn't*] or *He* [[*came*] *but* [*didn't stay*]]. But also, especially in older uses, of words like *when* in *He arrived when I left*, or *that* in *He said that he did*, seen as linking the *subordinate clause to the unit it is subordinate to. Hence a distinction between **subordinating conjunctions** (= subordinators) and **coordinating conjunctions** (= coordinators).

Distinguished as a *part of speech since antiquity.

conjunction (2) Logicians' term for a proposition of the form *p* & *q* which is true if and only if both *p* is true and *q* is true. Hence of *coordination with e.g. English *and*; thence, in some usage, other cases of coordination.

'**Conjunction reduction**' is or was a rule of transformational grammar by which 'conjoined' phrases, such as *you and your sister* in *I saw you and your sister*, are reduced from conjoined sentences: in this case, from *I saw you and I saw your sister*.

conjunctive The ancient term for *subjunctive, as German 'Konjunktiv'.

conjunctive order Relation between *ordered rules each of which can apply, in sequence, to the same form. Opp. disjunctive order.

conjunctive pronoun Term for unstressed or *clitic pronouns in the Romance languages: e.g. Italian *lo* in *lo mangio* ('it eat-1SG') 'I am eating it'. Opp. disjunctive pronoun.

connected speech Speech in the ordinary sense, as distinguished by sociolinguists from words uttered separately, e.g. as elicited in a *sociolinguistic interview.

connectionism Model of mental processing inspired by the physical connections among brain cells, in which operations of different kinds are carried out in parallel by a network of different processing units, linked in such a way that each can either excite or inhibit others. Also described as a model of **Parallel Distributed Processing** (or **PDP**), and contrasted with that of serial processing, in which operations of different kinds are carried out in sequence, each having access only to the results of those that have gone before.

connective (Adverb etc.) linking a clause or sentence to whatever precedes it. E.g. *therefore* in *It was small and therefore cost less.*

connotation Used variously to refer to differences in meaning that cannot be reduced to differences in *denotation. E.g. *queer*, when applied to male homosexuals, has a connotation different from those of *gay* or *homosexual*. The usual implication is that denotations are primary and connotations secondary.

consecutive (Clause etc.) indicating a consequence or result: e.g. the *that*-clause in *I was so tired* [*that I slept for ten hours*].

consistent (Language) seen as conforming in every respect to a proposed structural *type. Thus a 'consistent' *VO language would have all the properties associated, in a specific theory of types, with verb–object order.

consonant Originally a sound or *letter that had to be accompanied by a vowel: hence the term (Latin *consonans* 'sounding with'). Now generally of phonological units which form parts of a syllable other than its *nucleus (2), or whose primary role, at least, is to do so. E.g. [n] is a consonant in English, whose primary roles are as the onset of a *syllable (e.g. in *no*) or as its coda (e.g. in *on*): its role as a nucleus (e.g. in *ridden* ['rɪdṇ]) can be seen as secondary.

In phonetic terms, most consonants are sounds in whose production the flow of air is obstructed at some point in the mouth, throat, or larynx, at least sufficiently to cause audible friction: i.e. they are produced with a degree of *stricture greater than *open approximation. But no phonetic definition will quite match the phonology of all languages; hence a distinction, in many accounts, between consonants as units in phonology, and *contoids.

consonantal *Distinctive feature in the schemes of *Jakobson and of Chomsky and Halle, *SPE*. That of all consonants except *glides, which are defined as both non-consonantal and non-*vocalic.

consonantal alphabet One in which the characters represent consonants, with vowels either not indicated or indicated by subsidiary marks. The original North *Semitic alphabet was purely consonantal; in later derivatives marks for vowels may remain optional.

consonant cluster *See* cluster.

consonant harmony Agreement in respect of one or more features between consonants that are not adjacent to one another: *cf.* vowel harmony, which is more varied and more widespread.

'conspiracy' Used in *Generative Phonology in the early 1970s, to refer to rules which the model required one to formulate separately, but which in effect contributed to a single pattern. E.g. a pattern in which all syllables were open (CV) might be achieved by rules which 'conspired' variously to delete consonants (CVCCV → CVCV) or insert vowels (CVCCV → CVCVCV).

constant opposition An opposition between phonemes that is not subject to *neutralization.

constative An utterance by which a speaker expresses a proposition which may be true or false. Opp. performative.

constituency Relation, especially in syntax, between a unit which is part of a larger unit and the whole of which it is part. E.g. the adjective phrase *very friendly* is a **constituent** of the noun phrase *very friendly people*. The **immediate constituents** of a unit are the largest such parts. E.g. the immediate constituents of *meeting very friendly people* are *meeting* and *very friendly people*; those of this second constituent are in turn *very friendly* and *people*. Constituency is usually shown by a *tree diagram or by square brackets: thus [*meeting* [[*very friendly*] *people*]].

The analysis of sentences into constituents is 'immediate constituent analysis' (or **IC analysis**): developed especially by the *Post-Bloomfieldians, whose underlying aim was to establish divisions that would allow the simplest account of the *distributions of units.

constituent sentence *See* embedded.

constituent structure A representation of relations of *constituency: thus a *phrase structure tree is, alternatively, a 'constituent structure tree'.

constraint 1. A general principle restricting the application of rules or processes. E.g., if *Which have you seen?* is derived, by a rule of *wh-movement, from *You have seen which?*, a corresponding process could be subject to a constraint, hypothetically of *Universal Grammar, that would prevent the derivation of e.g. *Which were you always asleep when you have seen?* from *You were always asleep when you have seen which?* **2.** A specific restriction on the form of *representations. Thus in the first example the position of *which* could instead be determined by constraints on word order, that would allow *Which have you seen?* while excluding e.g. *Have you seen which?*

Constraints in sense (2), as opposed to processes of derivation, are central to *Optimality Theory.

constructio ad sensum Process by which word *a* is taken to be syntactically related to word *b* supposedly 'by meaning' (Latin *ad sensum*) although they do not conform to some proposed rule. E.g. *notional agreement, if seen in this way.

construction 1. Any pattern, at whatever level of generality, in which units are connected in syntax. E.g., in *His family hunts*, either *family* or *his family* are related to *hunts* in what is traditionally a subject–predicate construction. The construction of *his family* is in turn that of a noun as *head (1) to a *modifier, more specifically a possessive modifier; and so on. **2.** Any combination of units seen as instancing a construction. E.g. *I know his family hunts* includes a construction *his family hunts*, which in turn includes the smaller construction *his family*.

Constructions as units are central to some models of syntax. Thus, in particular, that of Bloomfield, who included them in his concept of a *tagmeme: *see also* Construction Grammar.

constructional homonymy Chomsky's term in the 1950s for a syntactic unit to which a generative grammar, justified in abstraction from the meanings of sentences, assigned two or more different structures. 'Constructional homonymy' was then found to correspond, in many instances, to *grammatical or 'structural' ambiguity.

Construction Grammar Any of a range of similar accounts of syntax and the lexicon, formulated in the spirit of *Cognitive Linguistics, for which a notion of *constructions (1) is central. Distinguished from earlier formulations by, in particular, the level of detail at which constructions may be identified. Thus *She can't come, though* might be said to have a specific '*though*-construction', in which the role of *though* as a *connective would distinguish it from that of the *subordinator in *Though she can't come, I will*; its position from that of *but* in *But she can't come*; details of its uses from that of *however* in *She can't come, however*; and so on.

Developed historically in the early 1990s from an analysis of idioms by C. J. Fillmore and others. Hence in particular an insistence on a sign-like relation between meanings of whatever kind associated with constructions as wholes, and all relevant formal features: of word order, intonation, phonetics of individual words, etc.

construct state Used in accounts of *Semitic languages for the form taken by a noun that is modified by another noun. Thus, in a phrase which means '(a) man's coat', the relation between the nouns for 'man' and 'coat' is marked on the latter: schematically, *man coat*-CONSTR. Opp. absolute state.

construe To determine what word etc. is syntactically related to what. Hence of the relation between such units: e.g. in *I'll try it on next week*, *on* '**construes with**' *try* and not directly with either of the units (*it, next week*) adjacent to it.

No longer usual in technical accounts of syntax. But in Chomsky's terminology, rules e.g. for *control or *binding were called '**rules of construal**' at one stage in the 1970s.

consuetudinal = habitual.

consultant = informant.

contact language Any language used systematically in contacts between speakers whose native languages are different. This could be a language native to one participant: e.g. French might be described as a 'contact language' for speakers of English after the Norman conquest; also for a linguist in the 20th century, either French-speaking or not, beginning an investigation e.g. of an African language.

Likewise '**contact dialect**'.

contamination The influence of one form on the historical development of another form to which it is related in meaning.

E.g. Old French *femelle*, borrowed into English in the 14th century, > *female* by contamination from *male*.

content Level in *Hjelmslev's model of language whose *substance is that of meaning. Defined formally by its opposition to the level of *expression.

content word A word with *lexical meaning: hence = lexical word. Also called '(a) **contentive**'.

context Any relevant features of the setting in which a form appears or might appear. Suppose, e.g. that one person shouts to another 'Let's get out of here!' Within the sentence uttered, *get* is in a 'context' formed by the surrounding words *Let's — out of here!* The surroundings in which it was uttered might, e.g. have been in a room full of noisy machinery: that is an aspect of the 'context' that explains why it was shouted. Of its elements, *let's* is appropriate to a 'context' in which one person proposes joint action to another; the place referred to by *here* is identified in the 'context' of where they are situated; and so on.

The term *co-text is sometimes used of linguistic context as distinct from the wider setting. Hence distinguished from e.g. a '**social context**' which would involve the social status of a speaker and an addressee, the social setting in which speech takes place, etc.

context-free grammar A form of *phrase structure grammar in which each rule holds for a specific category regardless of context: hence, more fully, **context-free phrase structure grammar**.

As originally formulated in the 1950s, a phrase structure rule was a *rewrite rule by which a single element in a string (A) is replaced by a string of one or more elements (Z). Each rule had in general the form XAY → XZY, where X and Y are further strings of elements, and the form of grammar was context-free if it met the restriction that, in any such rule, both X and Y are null: i.e. the replacement of A with Z applies regardless of context. A form of grammar not subject to this restriction was defined as **context-sensitive**.

A '**context-free language**' is a *formal language that can be generated by a context-free grammar.

context of situation Used by Firth to cover all the relevant circumstances in which a specific act of speech takes place. E.g. when a specific person says on a specific occasion 'Well played!', it might be part of the context of situation that the speaker is sitting, with others, watching a cricket match, that a batsman has driven for four through covers, that the speaker is from a certain social background, and so on. In the analysis of a language, features recurring in individual utterances (considered again as specific acts of speech) will be related to specific types of situation and to specific features in them.

The term was originally that of the anthropologist B. Malinowski.

context-sensitive grammar A form of *phrase structure grammar which is not subject to the restriction that defines a *context-free grammar: hence, more fully, **context-sensitive phrase structure grammar**. A **context-sensitive language** is a *formal language that can be generated by a context-sensitive grammar.

'contextualize' To put a sentence etc. into a context in which it might be said: e.g. *My sister will be a dormouse* can be contextualized in a conversation about a dramatic performance of *Alice in Wonderland*.

continuant (Consonant) that can be articulated continuously: thus the *r* in many forms of English is described as a **frictionless continuant**. Also a *distinctive feature in the scheme proposed by *Jakobson, characterized negatively as not *abrupt.

continuative (Form of verb etc.) indicating a state, etc. continuing up to the time of speaking. Thus the perfect has a continuative use in e.g. *I have lived here since I was three*.

continuous (1) *See* discrete.

continuous (2) (CONT) = progressive.

contoid A consonant defined phonetically, by the way it is produced, as distinguished from a consonant in a phonological sense, defined by its role in the structure of words and syllables. Thus a syllabic nasal, as in the second syllable of *button* ['bʌtn̩], is a contoid even if, in phonology, it were treated as vocalic.
  Cf. vocoid: both terms were introduced by Pike in the 1940s.

contour A pattern of successive levels of pitch. E.g. in intonation: thus the question *What is it?* will often be marked by a contour in which the pitch falls from the second word onwards (*What `is it?*).

contour tone A tone in some *tone languages, such as Chinese, which is characterized by a movement or potential movement in pitch as opposed to a specific pitch level. Distinguished as such from a *register tone: note, however, that in many tone languages a phonetic contour may be characterized in phonology as a sequence of two or more specific levels (falling = high + low, rising = low + high, and so on).

contraction = fusion. E.g. in accounts of Ancient Greek, where 'contracted verbs' are ones whose stem ends in a vowel which fuses with the vowel of a following suffix.

contradictory (Propositions etc.) of which only one can be true and only one can be false: e.g. 'Mary is married' and 'Mary is single'. Distinguished in logic from **contrary** propositions of which only one can be true though both may be false: e.g. 'Mary is tall' and 'Mary is short'.

Thence of lexical units: e.g. *married* and *single* are specifically **contradictory terms**.

contrast The relation between sounds or forms which have or distinguish different meanings in a specific context. E.g. [t] and [d] contrast at the beginnings of words in German: i.e. words with different meanings, such as *Tank* 'tank' and *Dank* 'thanks', can be distinguished by them. But they do not contrast at the ends of words.

Sounds etc. contrasting in at least some contexts are in **contrastive distribution**: opp. complementary distribution.

contrastive linguistics Any investigation in which the structures of two languages are compared. A **contrastive grammar** establishes point-by-point relations between their respective systems, with the aim e.g. of explaining, and thereby possibly helping teachers to remedy, errors made by speakers of one in learning the other.

contrastive stress 1. Stress as part of a system of phonological contrasts. **2.** A *sentence stress whose function is to draw a contrast: e.g. that of *Our team* LOST (as opposed to winning) or OUR *team lost* (as opposed to someone else's). *Cf.* emphatic (2).

control Relation or principle by which, in a language like English, an element in a larger clause supplies the subject of a non-finite verb subordinate to it. E.g. in *I promised* [*to leave*], the subject of *to leave* is supplied by *I* as the subject of the main clause; in *I asked Mary* [*to leave*], by its object *Mary*.

Mediated in *Principles and Parameters Theory by a null unit *PRO: thus *I promised* [PRO *to leave*], with PRO linked to *I*; *I asked Mary* [PRO *to leave*], where it is linked to *Mary*. The term 'control' has therefore been extended to the interpretation of PRO in general. E.g. in [PRO *to give*] *is better than* [PRO *to receive*] no noun phrases control it; accordingly it has '**arbitrary reference**' and would exhibit '**arbitrary control**'.

'Control Theory' Defined in *Government and Binding Theory as concerned with relations of *control; hence generally with the syntax of *PRO.

control verb A verb which takes a dependent verb whose subject is determined by a relation of *control: e.g. *want* in *I want to see her*. *Cf.* catenative; equi verb.

conventional Having no natural explanation. Thus the meaning of *cat* is purely conventional, in that there is no natural relation between the phonetic form [kat] and any feature of the animals that it denotes. *Cf.* arbitrariness.

conventional implicature An aspect of the meaning of a sentence which reflects that of a specific word but is not part of its *truth conditions. The stock example involves the meaning of *but* in *He was poor but honest*. Plainly this sentence does not mean the same as *He was poor and honest*. But they have the same truth conditions: therefore, if we assume that semantics is limited to an account of such conditions, the meaning of *but*, over and above that of *and*, must be ascribed to an *implicature.

Distinguished as conventional in that, unlike *conversational implicatures, it cannot be explained by general *maxims of conversation.

converb A reduced form of a verb which, unlike full forms, does not distinguish tenses. Used in some languages in the first of a sequence of two clauses: e.g., schematically, *I see* (converb) *it I ran* (full form) 'I saw it and ran away'.

convergence (1) In the obvious sense, e.g. of the speech of different individuals through *accommodation. Especially, therefore, of the historical process by which languages in contact become more similar in structure. E.g. Ancient Greek and Latin converged in antiquity, and Modern Greek and Italian have continued to converge since. On a larger scale convergence results in a 'linguistic area' characterized by a *Sprachbund.

To be distinguished from the sense of 'convergence' in evolutionary biology, by which species independently develop similar characters in similar external conditions.

'convergence' (2) Defined in Chomsky's *minimalist programme as the property of derivations in which related *Logical and *Phonetic Forms are both interpretable, in full, as inputs to performance systems. I.e. of the property by which sentences are grammatical.

conversational implicature Any meaning implied by or understood from the utterance of a sentence which goes beyond what is literally expressed or what may be entailed. E.g. *It is raining* might, in specific contexts, **implicate** 'We can't go for a picnic', 'We had better close the windows', and so on. *Cf.* 'what is said'.

A conversational implicature is **particularized** if, like these, it holds only on specific occasions when a sentence is uttered. It is **generalized** if it holds, in principle, on any occasion. E.g. *I like quite a lot of professors* has the generalized implicature 'I don't like all professors'. *Cf.* conventional implicature; *also* maxims of conversation for the 'Cooperative Principle' from which implicatures arise.

conversational maxims *See* maxims of conversation.

'Conversation Analysis' Treatment of conversation originally developed by sociologists in the early 1970s which concentrates on relations between successive *turns and on the operation of a hypothetical '**turn-taking**' system. This system ensures (according to the hypothesis) that at any moment a specific speaker will 'have the *floor', and that when their turn ends that of the next speaker will follow smoothly without an appreciable overlap, or intervening period of silence, or confusion as to who, in a conversation with several participants, that speaker will be. Hence specific hypotheses about *transition relevance places, constructions or intonations which 'signal' that a turn is ending, specific devices by which one speaker 'selects' the next, etc.

converse terms Lexical units whose meanings are opposed in such a way that sentences in which they appear can be interchangeable if words etc. to which they are syntactically related are distributed differently across a range of similar syntactic roles. E.g. *husband* and *wife*: thus *John is Mary's husband*, where *John* is subject and *Mary* is possessive, implies and is implied by *Mary is John's wife*, where *Mary* is subject and *John* is possessive. Also *sell* and *buy*: compare *John sold a car to Mary; Mary bought a car from John*.
   Converseness is the *sense relation in which such units stand.

conversion A process by which a lexical unit which is primarily of one syntactic class also belongs secondarily to another. E.g. *cook* is a transitive verb in *I am cooking dinner*. In *Dinner is cooking* it is converted, in one account, to an intransitive, with a secondary sense derived from its primary sense in the transitive.
   Often equivalent to *zero derivation: e.g. the noun *cook* is likewise said to be converted from the verb *cook*. But a distinction can be drawn in principle between a single unit in the lexicon which has both a primary and a secondary role in syntax, and the derivation of a different lexical unit by a process like, or of, word-formation.

cooccurrence restriction = selectional restriction.

Cooperative Principle *See* maxims of conversation.

coordinate (Clause etc.) standing in a relation of *coordination.

coordinate bilingualism Bilingualism in which mastery of one language is hypothetically separate in the bilingual's mind from mastery of the other. Opp. compound bilingualism.

coordinate structure constraint Principle by which forms joined by *coordination form an *island with respect to syntactic processes or relations. E.g. one cannot say *What did you see and 'King LEAR', with one element in the coordination questioned (*what*) and the other ('*King Lear*') not.

coordinating conjunction = coordinator.

coordination Relation between two or more separate and syntactically equivalent parts of a sentence: e.g. between the parts enclosed by brackets in [*John*] *and* [*his sister*] *met me*; [*I looked*] *but* [*I could not see them*]; *I bought* [*a blue*] *plus* [*a black*] *handbag*.

Opp. subordination, dependency; *cf*. apposition. A construction relating such parts is a **coordinating** or **coordinative** construction; an element linking them, such as *and*, *but*, or *plus*, is a *coordinator or coordinating conjunction.

coordinative compound = copulative compound.

coordinator A word etc. which links syntactic units standing in a relation of *coordination. E.g. *or* in *You can see me or my secretary* ([[*me*] *or* [*my secretary*]]); also e.g. the *clitic -*que* 'and' in Latin *di omnes deaeque* 'all gods and goddesses' (lit. 'gods all goddesses-and'). Equally called a **coordinating conjunction**; *cf*. subordinator or subordinating conjunction.

'Copenhagen School' *Hjelmslev and his associates, including some by no means in complete agreement with him.

coproduction (of consonants etc.) = coarticulation.

Coptic *Egyptian as written alphabetically from the 4th century AD, after the adoption of Christianity. Progressively replaced by Arabic from the 9th century but surviving in Christian liturgy. The script was derived from the Greek alphabet, with additional letters, for sounds with no Greek equivalent, adapted from the Demotic script, derived ultimately from Hieroglyphic, used previously.

copula The verb 'be' and its equivalent in other languages, seen simply as a link or mark of relationship between one element and another. E.g. *am* is a copula in *I am cold* or *I am a doctor*, where it links the subject (*I*) and the predicative element (*cold, a doctor*). Distinguished from, in particular, the *existential use of 'be', e.g. in *There is a solution* ('A solution exists').

Hence '**copula deletion**', in cases where, in some varieties of English, a form of the verb 'to be' is variably present or absent.

copular Containing or having the character of a *copula. Thus the construction of *They are happy* is a **copular construction**; a **copular verb** is one like *seem* in *They seem happy*, whose syntax is like that of a copula.

Likewise **copulative**.

copulative compound One in which the relation between members is like one of *coordination: e.g. *actor-manager* 'actor and manager', *silly-clever* 'silly and clever'. Also called by the Sanskrit term *dvandva*; also, less usually though more perspicuously, a '**coordinative compound**'.

copying Any process, in syntax especially, in which units or features in one position are duplicated in another.

Common in the 1960s in accounts of *agreement. Thus the affixes or features of e.g. a head noun could be seen as added, by a 'copying rule', e.g. to a modifying adjective. Also, since the beginning of the 21st century, in a reformulation of *movement. Thus, in general, to derive [X [Y]] from [Y X], X may first be copied in its new position: [X [Y X]]; the second X may then be realized as *null. Hence a '**Copying Theory**' of movement as part of Chomsky's *minimalist programme, replacing an earlier account in terms of *traces.

core 1. Any part of a syntactic unit seen as central to it, or more central than others. E.g. the 'core' of a clause is its *nucleus (1); a 'core' *complement (1) of a verb might be one not marked by e.g. a preposition. **2.** (Form etc.) which is a typical or undisputed member of a category: e.g. *sad* is a 'core' adjective. *Cf.* prototype.

coreference The relation between noun phrases etc. which have the same *reference. E.g. in *Mary promised she would come*, *Mary* and *she* are **coreferential** if the promise is that Mary herself will come. Often shown informally by subscript indices: thus *Mary$_i$ promised she$_i$ will come* (coreferential); *Mary$_i$ promised she$_j$ would come* (not coreferential).

core grammar That part of a person's *internalized grammar of a language which, as distinguished by Chomsky in the 1980s, derived directly from *Universal Grammar by the setting of *parameters (2). Opp. periphery (2).

Also called '**core language**': i.e. the core of *I-language. The term dates from the mid-1970s, when its sense was less clear; the boundary between core and periphery, as defined, has proved problematic.

'core vocabulary' Any part of the lexicon of a language judged to be more basic in some respect than others: e.g. as representing concepts for which old words are supposedly less likely to be supplanted by new, for which such replacements supposedly take place at a fixed rate, for which they are supposedly less likely to result from borrowing, and so on.

Cornish *Celtic, similar to Welsh, spoken in Cornwall until the 1800s. Revived in the mid-20th century in an attempt to establish it as a second language.

coronal Articulated with the blade of the tongue raised from its neutral position in the mouth. Hence of any *dental, *alveolar, or *palato-alveolar consonant: defined as a *distinctive feature with that scope in the scheme of Chomsky and Halle, *SPE.

corpus Any systematic collection of speech or writing in a language or variety of a language. Thus, in particular, of large on-line collections, tagged and searchable for research purposes.

Hence '**Corpus Linguistics**', of investigations based on the analysis of corpora; especially by linguists who discount, or seek to disparage, other sources of evidence.

'corpus planning' *See* language planning.

correlation In the ordinary sense; also specifically, in *Trubetzkoy's account of phonological systems, of a set of oppositions characterized by the presence or absence of the same feature. Thus [b] is distinguished from [p] by the presence or absence of voice; likewise [d] from [t], [g] from [k], and so on. Such pairs will accordingly form a correlation 'of voicing'.

correlative (Construction) in which clauses or other syntactic units are linked by a pair of parallel adverbs, pronouns, etc.; e.g. that of *As you sow, so shall you reap*, where the first clause (*as you sow*) is linked to the second (*so shall you reap*) by the parallel elements *as* and *so*.

Also of the linking elements themselves. Thus in the Latin phrase *tam moribus quam doctrina* 'as (in) behaviour so (in) learning', *tam* 'as' and *quam* 'so' are two of a set of correlative adverbs etc., each pairing a form in *t*- with another in *qu*-, that form such constructions.

correption An older term for the shortening of vowels.

correspondence fallacy The assumption that different criteria which are relevant to the analysis of a language will necessarily lead to the same result. E.g. that a set of morphemes identified solely by their *distributions will be the same as one identified by reference to meaning; that, if this is not so, only one of these criteria must be truly relevant; and so on. Identified, named, and attacked by C. E. Bazell in the 1950s.

'correspondence hypothesis' The assumption, rife among psycholinguists for some decades from the 1960s onwards, that structures to be investigated in the minds of speakers will correspond, in some more or less precise way, with those of a language as described independently in grammars.

correspondence theory Concept of truth by which a proposition is true if there is a correspondence between it and a state of the world that it describes. Thus, in a stock example derived from work by the philosopher A. Tarski, the proposition 'Snow is white' is true if and only if snow is in fact white.

corrigible Capable of being corrected: e.g. a form *I today have done it*, which is contrary to a rule for the position of adverbs, can be corrected to *I have done it today*. A test for a *rule (1), or rule in the strict sense, is thus the **corrigibility** of forms that would break it.

Coseriu, Eugenio (1921–2002) Rumanian linguist, finally based in Germany, whose early work, written in Montevideo in the 1950s,

brought an important clarification to the structuralist concept of a
*language system and the explanation of change in language. The
system is an abstraction from the usual patterns of speech in a
community, and it is the *norm which is constituted by these
patterns, not the system, that directly constrains a speaker. The norm
is in turn an abstraction from individual acts of speech on individual
occasions; but, on the basis of these, may over time shift gradually in
such a way that the system itself becomes in part unstable. If so, it will
change to a new system, in which stability is restored.

In later work, Coseriu distinguishes the overall character of a
language (German 'Sprachtypus') as a still more abstract construct. At
the lowest level of abstraction, the norm can change easily; the system
is more resistant, but can undergo saltatory changes in consequence;
the overall character, as an inflecting language, or one with a certain
tendency in word order, is the most resistant but may in the end
change also.

cost The contribution of a *rule (2) to the complexity of a grammar as
measured, or measurable, by an *evaluation procedure.

co-text The relevant text or discourse of which a sentence etc. is part:
e.g. the co-text of *Why wouldst thou be a breeder of sinners? (Hamlet*, III. 1) is
that speech of Hamlet's (*Get thee to a nunnery . . .*), or the dialogue in
that scene between Ophelia and Hamlet, or whatever longer text is
relevant to some specific inquiry. Sometimes defined as part of
*context in a wider sense; sometimes as opposed to it.

countable (Noun) whose syntax is that of ones denoting individuals
that can be counted; thus, in English, a noun such as *sparrow* that
distinguishes singular and plural (*the sparrow, the sparrows*), that can
take a numeral (*three sparrows*) or the indefinite article (*a sparrow*), etc.

Opp. uncountable; alternatively '**count nouns**' (such as *sparrow*) are
opposed to '**non-count**' or '**mass nouns**' (such as *meat*). But the
distinction is not absolute. Many nouns, such as *chicken*, are variously
countable and uncountable: *three chickens* but also, e.g. *the price of
chicken*. Some are intermediate: e.g. *a hundred cattle*, but not *a cattle*.
Many basically of one class may have the syntax of the other on
occasion: e.g. *I'm not going to eat sparrow*.

counter-bleeding Relation between *ordered rules whose order is
designed to avoid an effect of *bleeding; i.e. if one does not want rule
a to remove the whole or part of the input to rule *b*, one orders *a*
after *b*.

counter-example Any example which is taken to show that a
proposed rule etc. is wrong or must be qualified. E.g. examples like
'She was sure that he would never fall in love with herself' (Trollope)
are potentially or arguably counter-examples to a proposed universal

principle by which a reflexive in a finite clause (*he would never fall in love with herself*) cannot have an antecedent (*she*) outside that clause.

counterfactual (*Conditional clause) expressing a condition not in fact met: e.g. *if she had been there* . . . (but she wasn't). *Cf.* remote.

counter-feeding Relation between *ordered rules whose order is designed to avoid an effect of *feeding; i.e. if one does not want the output of rule *a* to become part of the input to rule *b*, one orders *a* after *b*.

'counter-intuitive' (Analysis etc.) variously contrary to a native speaker's feel for their language, or to an experienced linguist's judgement of what is right.

count noun = countable.

covert Not directly identifiable. Hence often = null; also e.g. of any proposed operation on the structure of a sentence that does not affect the form in which it will be realized. A **covert category** is relevant to the grammar of a language but not overtly marked. Thus gender is covert in English but overt e.g. in Spanish.

'covert prestige' The value implicitly attached by members of a speech community to forms or variants which they use quite normally but claim to avoid. Thus, in particular, that of local or non-standard forms which are overtly proscribed but which reflect the solidarity of each member with the others.

   Sometimes contrasted with 'overt prestige', e.g. of the corresponding standard forms.

'covert pronoun' One realized only by a verbal ending, seen as in agreement with it: e.g. in Spanish *Vamos* 'Let's go', the form of the verb ('go-1PL') would be related to a zero pronoun whose properties are in other respects the same as those of the 'overt' *nosotros* 'we'. *Cf.* pro in Government and Binding Theory.

CP A *phrase (2) whose *head (1) is said to be a *complementizer (C).

'cranberry morpheme' One like *cran-* in *cranberry*, which is found in one combination only.

crasis Term in Greek grammar for the *fusion of vowels across a word boundary: from the word for 'mixing'.

creak Slow vibration of the vocal cords, typically at least at the front end. **Creaky voice** is *voice (1) accompanied by creak: often a distinct *voice quality, and also exploited in the phonology of some languages. E.g. a **creaky tone** is a tone distinguished, in part or wholly, by creaky vs. normal voice.

'creativity' In its usual sense. Also used by Chomsky in his early days, specifically of the ability of speakers to produce and understand

sentences they have not heard before. A *generative grammar was
presented as explaining this ability.

Cree *Algonquian language spoken widely across northern Canada,
from the Gulf of St Lawrence to the Rocky Mountains. The different
varieties form a *dialect continuum.

creole Defined, in classic treatments, as a language that has
developed historically from a *pidgin. In theory, accordingly, a pidgin
develops from trade or other contacts; it has no native speakers, its
range of use is limited, and its structure is simplified. Later it becomes
the only form of speech that is common to a community; it is learned
by new speakers and used for all purposes; its structure and
vocabulary are enlarged; and so on.

  Thence, more generally, of any form of speech perceived as having
structural features similar to those of pidgins, or of forms traditionally
described as 'creoles', or known to have arisen historically over a
characteristically short period; whether or not development from a
pidgin is posited or can be demonstrated. E.g. Middle English was a
creole, under a sufficiently loose definition.

'creole continuum' A continuous range of variation, found in
particular in many creole-speaking communities, between the forms
used at the lowest social levels, predominantly those of the variety
called the *basilect, and those used at the highest, predominantly
those of the *acrolect. The phenomenon was first described in these
terms by D. Bickerton in the 1970s, for the English creole in Guyana.

  Also called a '**post-creole continuum**', since it reflects a process of
'decreolization', or progressive assimilation of a creole to a standard
language.

creolization The historical process by which a *creole develops.
Hence e.g. '**abrupt creolization**', where its development is seen as
rapid, and no established *pidgin is its source.

'creoloid' Form of speech with features seen as like those of a
*creole, but not quite meeting whatever definition of a creole, or of
*creolization, may be proposed.

'critical discourse analysis' The study of *discourse in relation to
the structure of a society as perceived e.g. by Marxists; to ideologies
etc. seen as underlying its 'production'; and so on.

'critical period' (of language acquisition) Period of childhood when it
is believed e.g. that perfect mastery of new languages can still develop.

Croce, Benedetto (1866–1952) Italian philosopher, whose treatise
on *Estetica* (1902) develops aesthetics as a science of expression with
which, in a final chapter, general linguistic theory is identified.
Language is 'perpetual creation', like other forms of aesthetic activity:

the mechanisms of grammar, the parts of speech, divisions into words and syllables, and so on belong in contrast to a discipline concerned with nothing more than practical classification.

cross-categorization Assignment of words etc. to classes that intersect. E.g. the noun *despair* is on one dimension uncountable as opposed to countable, and on another abstract as opposed to concrete: by contrast, *butter* is uncountable and concrete, *theory* countable and abstract, *tree* countable and concrete.

crossed dependency Any case in which a dependent *a* is separated from its head *b* by an element *c* whose own relationship, either as dependent or head, is to an element separated from it, in turn, by either *a* or *b*. Dependencies not 'crossed' in that way are 'nested'.

cross-linguistic (Investigation etc.) across languages. Thus any attempt to identify a category in different languages is cross-linguistic; likewise any attempt to establish it as a *linguistic universal, or to develop a typology of categories which involves it.

cross-over principle Principle proposed by P. M. Postal in the 1970s, by which a syntactic process could not move a pronoun etc. across a phrase which has the same reference. E.g. in *I do admire myself* the reflexive (*myself*) has the same referent as *I*: i.e. both refer to the speaker. Hence, if the cross-over principle were to apply, *myself* could not be moved over *I* by a process of *topicalization: *Myself I do admire*.

cross-reference Bloomfield's term for the agreement of a pronoun or verb form with an optional noun phrase that supplies its referent. E.g. in Spanish *Los muchachos cantarán* (lit. 'the boys they-will-sing') the third plural ending of the verb (*-n*) 'cross-refers' to the subject *los muchachos*. Likewise in French *Marie est-elle venue?* (lit. 'Mary is-she come?'), *elle* 'she' cross-refers to *Marie*. For a similar case *see* 'clitic doubling'.

cryptotype Term used by B. L. Whorf in the 1930s for a *covert category revealed only when forms are combined with some specific overt form. One of his examples is a group of verbs with similar meanings (*close, fasten, wrap,* ...) that combine productively with *un-* (*unclose, unfasten, unwrap,* ...).

CS For 'context-sensitive'. Thus CS-grammar or CS-PSG = context-sensitive (phrase structure) grammar.

c-selection Chomsky's term in the mid-1980s for *valency or *argument structure seen as determined by a syntactic category, such as transitive or intransitive, that a verb or other word belongs to. For 'categorial selection': opp. s-selection.

c-structure One of two levels of syntax in *Lexical-Functional Grammar.

cue Psychologists' term for a specific feature seen as an aid to the perception e.g. of some larger structure. Thus intonation is thought of as a cue for the construction of a sentence; a *boundary marker is a cue for e.g. the beginning of a word; one aim of *Conversation Analysis is to identify cues for the conclusion of 'turns'.

'culminative' (Accent) seen as no more than a phonetic peak of prominence on the syllable that carries it. E.g. of the accent in French that falls on the last syllable of a phrase: *la plume de ma tánte*.

cultural transmission Transmission from one generation to the next through membership of a society as opposed to genetic inheritance. One of the set of *design features of language proposed in the 1950s.

cumulation The joint realization of two or more distinct inflectional categories. E.g. case and number are realized cumulatively, or have **cumulative exponents**, in languages like Russian or Latin: Latin *puella-m* 'girl-ACC.SG', *puella-e* 'girl-GEN.SG', and so on.

cuneiform Form of writing first developed for *Sumerian from the beginning of the 3rd millennium BC; later adapted to *Akkadian (from the second half of the 3rd millennium) and later still to other languages of the ancient Near East, including *Elamite, *Hittite, and Old *Persian. Last used in the 1st century AD. The name means 'wedge-shaped', the signs being formed by patterns of triangular marks normally impressed with the flat tip of a stylus in clay.

   The signs were used in various ways, often representing words as wholes and often syllables; they could also serve as *determinatives, indicating either the semantic class or the phonetic form of a word otherwise represented ambiguously. These functions are found in differing degrees in different systems, that of Akkadian being particularly complex, while that devised for Old Persian in the 6th century BC comes nearest to a pure syllabary. Cuneiform signs were also used in the *Ugaritic alphabet.

curly brackets { } *See* braces.

cursive (Script) in which, in writing a word or other sequence of characters, the writing instrument is not in principle raised from the medium. Hence the characters are linked, not separate.

Cushitic Group of genetically related languages, including *Somali and Oromo, spoken in parts of East Africa from the coastal area of Sudan to northern Tanzania. Traditionally and by most still seen as a smaller family within what is now called *Afro-Asiatic.

CV tier = skeletal tier.

cyclic(al) principle Principle in generative grammar by which a set of rules applies first to the smallest constituents which are of a given type or types, then to the next largest such constituents, and so on. Introduced in transformational grammars in the 1960s, when a specific set of *transformations were said to apply to successively larger units of the clause or sentence category 'S'. Transformations not part of this set were accordingly either '**pre-cyclic(al)**' or '**post-cyclic(al)**'.

The same principle was applied to successively larger units in *Generative Phonology.

cyclic node *See* subjacency.

Cyrillic Alphabet devised for Slavic, according to tradition by St Cyril, a missionary from Thessalonica, in the 9th century AD. Used for Russian and other Slavic languages where the Orthodox Church predominates: also for others, including many that are not Slavic, in the former Soviet Union.

Based on contemporary forms of the Greek alphabet. Its relation to *Glagolitic, also used for Slavic from the early Middle Ages and possibly the alphabet in fact devised by St Cyril, is not wholly clear.

Czech West *Slavic, attested in writing from the 13th century, spoken mainly in the Czech Republic. Closely related to *Slovak, with which there is for the most part mutual intelligibility.

D

D = determiner.

DA = Discourse Analysis.

Daco-Romance Branch of *Romance of which *Rumanian is the main representative. From the name of the Roman province of Dacia.

dangling participle A participle which does not depend on any other individual element of a clause: e.g. *walking* in *Walking back, it snowed*. The term is the one by which the construction is traditionally proscribed; alternatively, it is *absolute.

Danish North *Germanic, spoken mainly in Denmark and with official status there and in the Faeroes and Greenland; there are also some speakers across the border with Germany and, through emigration, in North America. A distinct language from the late Middle Ages; a standard form developed from the translation of the Bible in the 16th century.

Dari *See* Persian.

'dark l' One which is accompanied by *velarization: e.g. that of *tell* [tɛɫ] in many forms of English. A 'clear l' is one that is not velarized: e.g. *again* in many forms of English, that of *leave* [liːv].

dash (—) Used to mark the position in a context or environment in which a form appears or a process takes place. E.g. *the* appears before words such as *house*: i.e. in such environments as '— *house*'. Consonants might be voiced between vowels: i.e. in the context 'V—V'.

dative (DAT) *Case whose basic role, or one of whose basic roles, is to distinguish the recipient of something given, transferred, etc.: e.g. in Latin *librum* ('book') *dedit* ('he-gave') *Mariae* ('Mary-DAT') 'He gave a book to Mary'. Also extended to phrases in which this semantic role is marked differently: e.g. *to Mary* would often be described as 'dative' in English, or as marked by *to* in the role of a 'dative' preposition.

dative movement Syntactic process relating e.g. *I lent my copy to Jim*, where *to* is traditionally said to mark the *dative, to *I lent Jim my copy*. Also called '**dative shift**'.

 In the first construction *to Jim* is an *indirect object; also, in most accounts, *Jim* in the second. In an alternative view, the effect of 'dative movement' is to *promote an indirect object to the status of a *direct object: *I lent my copy to Jim* (IO) → *I lent Jim* (DO) *my copy*. It is for that reason, it is claimed, that e.g. it can correspond to the subject of a passive (*Jim was lent my copy*).

dative of advantage Use of the *dative, e.g. in Latin, as a *benefactive. Also of equivalents in other languages: e.g. *for you* in *I did it for you*. A dative 'of disadvantage' is a similar element referring e.g. to someone who suffers rather than benefits.

dative subject A noun etc. which is morphologically in the *dative case, but which syntactically has some of the characteristics of, and is therefore described as being, a subject. E.g., schematically, *cats*-DAT *love milk*-NOM, where the word for 'cats', though dative, is subject e.g. on the grounds that the verb agrees with it (*love*-3PL) and not with the nominative 'milk'.

daughter 1. Any of the later languages that develop separately from a single earlier language. E.g. French and Spanish are 'daughter languages' in relation to Latin. Opp. ancestor language. **2.** Also of *nodes in a *phrase structure tree. Thus a node X is the 'daughter' of node Y if Y immediately dominates (is the 'mother' of) X.

Daughter-Dependency Grammar A precursor in the 1970s of what was to become *Word Grammar.

deadjectival (Process) by which words of other classes are derived from adjectives. Also of the words so derived: e.g. *happiness* (← *happy*) is a deadjectival noun.

dead language One that is no longer the native language of any community. Such languages may remain in use, like *Latin or *Sanskrit, as *second or *learned (e.g. as liturgical) languages.

decidable Capable of demonstration by some formal procedure. Mathematicians' term used in the study of *formal languages: e.g. it is **undecidable** (i.e. there is no guaranteed way of determining) whether a language which is *context-sensitive is also *context-free.

'decision procedure' Used by Chomsky in the 1950s of a procedure which would determine that a given *generative grammar *g* is the best for a given language *l*. Distinguished from a *discovery procedure and an *evaluation procedure.

declaration Defined by J. R. Searle as a *speech act which formally changes some state of affairs. E.g. 'You are fired', said by an employer in appropriate circumstances, makes someone unemployed.

declarative (1) (Sentence, construction) whose primary role is in making statements. Thus *David has come* is a declarative sentence, or 'a declarative', in opposition to the *interrogative *Has David come?* Hence also of subordinate clauses: e.g. in *She said* [*that David had come*] as opposed to the interrogative in *She asked* [*if David has come*].

Sentences whose construction is declarative can in principle be distinguished from statements as *speech acts. E.g. *You must stop at once* has the construction of a declarative; but when uttered it will often constitute an order rather than a statement.

declarative (2) (Model of grammar etc.) in which the well-formedness of an expression is determined by a set of constraints on *representations at a given level, as opposed to a set of rules by which e.g. a representation at one level is derived from that at another. Hence, in particular, of 'constraint-based' models of phonology, as opposed to *Generative Phonology and its immediate successors. *Cf.* Optimality Theory.

declension The inflection of nouns and other words whose categories are similar. Also of a class of nouns etc. which share a characteristic formal pattern of inflection. E.g. a 'third declension' noun in Latin is one of a class whose genitive singular is in -*is*, dative and ablative plural in -*ibus*, and so on.

declination Progressive lowering of pitch, or of successive high pitches in particular, over the course of an utterance. Often equivalent to *downdrift.

decline To inflect, said of nouns and other words traditionally assigned to *declensions. E.g. a noun like Latin *puella* 'girl' declines or is declined in one way, ones like *dominus* 'master' or *civis* 'citizen' in others.

'decoding' Applied loosely to the process of understanding a sentence. Thus, if the term is taken seriously, it would imply that addressees recover in some sense a 'thought' or message that has been 'encoded' by a speaker, through shared knowledge of the 'code' that has been used.

decontextualized (Sentence etc.) abstracted from any context in which it might be uttered. E.g. it is an issue whether a decontextualized form can properly, or safely, be judged either grammatical or ungrammatical.

'decreolization' Historical process by which a *creole is progressively assimilated to a standard language: e.g. the assimilation of English creoles in the West Indies to standard English. Not evidently different, in reality, from processes often affecting regional dialects.

de dicto* vs. *de re Philosophers' distinction between belief in the truth of a proposition (*de dicto* or 'about what is said') and belief about an individual (*de re* 'about a thing'). Thus *I believe his wife is rich* can be seen as expressing either a belief (*de dicto*) in the proposition that he is married to a rich woman or a belief (*de re*) concerning an individual, his wife, that she is rich.

Uses in linguistics reflect or extend this sometimes more and sometimes less faithfully.

deduction Process of reasoning which moves from the general to the particular. E.g. from the general proposition that all trees have leaves and the further proposition that oaks are trees one may draw the **deductive inference** that oaks have leaves. Opp. induction; *see also* hypothetico-deductive method.

In deductive reasoning the conclusion follows logically: contrasted in this respect with *induction; also with *abduction.

deep case = case role. Such roles were at one time represented by case-like elements in *deep structure, with *cases proper, in languages that have them, seen as belonging to *surface structure.

deep structure A representation of the syntax of a sentence distinguished by varying criteria from its *surface structure. E.g. in the surface structure of *Children are hard to please*, the subject is *children* and the infinitive *to please* is the complement of *hard*. But in its deep structure, as it was understood especially in the early 1970s, *is hard* would have as its subject a subordinate sentence in which *children* is the object of *please*: thus, in outline, ₛ[*please children*] *is hard*.

Initially defined by Chomsky in the mid-1960s as the part of the syntactic description of a sentence that 'determines its semantic interpretation'; as such a *phrase marker specified by the *base component of a generative grammar. Later said to determine the semantic representation only in part, and later still, by the mid-1970s, to have no role in determining it. Renamed *D-structure in the late 1970s and as such the second of three levels of syntax in *Government and Binding Theory, until eliminated in Chomsky's *minimalist programme in the 1990s.

DEF = definite.

default (Rule, class, etc.) taken to be operative if no other is specified. Thus a lexicon of English must specify that certain plurals are irregular: *man* → *men*, *child* → *children*. But any other will be assumed to follow the regular pattern: singular → singular + *(e)s*. That rule is therefore the 'default rule' and the class of regular plurals the 'default category'. Likewise, in syntax it might be assumed that all verbs have passives unless, in their lexical entries, it is made clear that they do not; [+ passivizable] would then be the 'default value' of a feature [± passivizable].

Hence, more generally, of whatever obtains unless there is some reason why it should not. E.g. a word or sentence may have a 'default meaning': i.e. that will be its meaning unless, in a specific context in which it is uttered, some other meaning is specifically implied or indicated.

Equivalent, in many uses, to one sense of *unmarked.

defeasible Capable of being cancelled or overridden. E.g. if someone utters the sentence *I have got two eggs*, one might infer, all else being equal, that they have no more than two eggs. In the theory of *maxims of conversation, this is represented by an *implicature that follows from the maxim of quantity. But the inference might be rendered invalid by specific contexts. E.g. the speaker is checking ingredients for a recipe; it calls for two eggs; so, what matters is that there should be at least two eggs, not two only. Alternatively, the speaker might go on to say 'Indeed I may have got a dozen'.

A term in law originally. It is a property of such implicatures that they are defeasible; of *entailments that they are not.

defective (Lexical unit) whose paradigm is incomplete in comparison with others of the major class that it belongs to. E.g. Latin *aio* was a defective verb for 'to say' found only in some tenses and for only some persons.

deferential form = polite form.

'deficit theory' The view once held by some educationalists that 'working-class' children are 'linguistically deprived' or handicapped by a 'language deficit'; hence, it was claimed, they are at a disadvantage in lessons designed for 'middle-class' children who are not so handicapped.

In the theory of B. Bernstein such children had mastered only a '**restricted code**', whose structure is limited in comparison with the '**elaborated code**' of others.

defining (relative clause) = restrictive.

definite Referring to, or characteristically indicating reference to, an identifiable individual or set of individuals. Thus *Mary* or *the woman* is a **definite noun phrase**, referring to a specific person or set of persons that can be identified in context by someone spoken to. Likewise *she* is a **definite pronoun**, *the* in *the woman* or *the girls* a *definite article, and so on. Opp. indefinite: *cf. also* indefinite reference.

definite article A *determiner which characteristically marks a *definite noun phrase: e.g. *the* in *the boy*, French *le* in *le garçon*. Distinguished from a *demonstrative in that it does not, in addition, indicate a referent or referents through *deixis.

definite description Philosophers' term used in effect of any *definite noun phrase, such as *the man over there*, seen as having a common noun as its *head (1).

deflexion Loss of inflections: e.g. in the history of English in the early Middle Ages.

degemination Change or process by which a *geminate is reduced to a single consonant.

degree = grade (1): thus the category of degree in English distinguishes *positive (2), *comparative, and *superlative.

degree of grammaticalness Chomsky's term in the 1950s for the degree to which a form which contravenes a rule of grammar comes close to being grammatical. E.g. *Sincerity admires John*, which was seen as contravening a *selectional restriction, came closer than *Admires John sincerity?*, which contravenes a major rule of word order.

degree-Ø learnability *See* learnability.

deictic centre Whatever time etc. is the foundation for *deixis. Thus the time is normally that of speaking; but in a sentence such as *Then finally, last week, I get a letter,* the *historic present implies a deictic centre in, hence 'shifted to', the past.

deixis ['dʌɪksɪs] The way in which the reference of certain elements in a sentence is determined in relation to a specific speaker and addressee and a specific time and place of utterance. E.g. in *I came yesterday*, the reference of *I* will be to whoever is speaking on some specific occasion, and the time reference of *yesterday* will be to the day before the one on which they are doing so.

Hence **deictic**, of any element or category whose reference is determined **deictically**. Thus *I* and *you* are deictic elements, as opposed to potentially *anaphoric pronouns such as *he* or *she*. So are *here* as opposed to *there* (location in space in relation to a speaker), *now* as opposed to *then* (location in time in relation to the time of speaking), or *come* and *go* (direction of movement basically in relation to a speaker). Tense is similarly a deictic category (present, past, or future in relation to the time of speaking). For further extensions, which start to stretch the sense beyond coherent definition, *see* discourse deixis; social deixis.

The Greek term is from a verb 'to show' or 'to point out'. Applied in antiquity to pronouns, including demonstratives (= 'deictics') such as *this* and *that*. The modern sense has its origin in work by Bühler in the 1930s.

delayed release Term of Chomsky and Halle, *SPE*, for the slow release of a *stop consonant, causing audible turbulence in the air flow. Hence a feature of *affricates: e.g. [tʃ] in *ketchup*. Opp. instantaneous release.

deletion Usually of deletion, by a syntactic or other process, at some level of representation. E.g., by a rule of *Generative Phonology, [t] might optionally be deleted from the phonological representation of *pants* [pants], to derive a phonetic representation [pans].

'**Deletion under identity**' is the deletion of an element in one position when it is identical to one in another position: e.g. by the classic transformational process of *equi NP deletion.

deliberative (Form, construction, inflection) used in considering a decision. Thus *shall* has a deliberative force, or is used deliberatively, in *What shall I do?*; likewise the *subjunctive in Latin *quid agam?* ('What do-SUBJ-1SG').

delicacy Halliday's term for greater or lesser detail in grammatical description. E.g. a distinction between masculine, feminine, and neuter pronouns (*he, she, it*) is made in English only in the third-person singular. It is therefore more delicate than those between singular and plural, or between third person and first or second.

delimitative = demarcative.

delocutive Benveniste's term (French 'délocutif') for a verb derived from the use of a linguistic expression: e.g. French *tutoyer* 'to use *tu* and *toi*'.

demarcative Serving as a *boundary marker. Thus an accent demarcates words if it always falls e.g. on the first syllable after a boundary between them.

demonstrative A word whose basic role is to locate a referent in relation to a speaker, an addressee, or some other person etc. referred to: e.g. *proximal *this* (physically and thence subjectively closer to the speaker) and *distal *that* (physically or subjectively more remote from the speaker). Demonstratives are a classic instance of *deixis.

Demotic (1) *Cursive script, derived ultimately from *Hieroglyphic, used for *Egyptian from the 7th century BC to the 4th century AD.

Demotic (2) Variety of Modern Greek formerly identified as the 'Low' form in a case of *diglossia. Opp. Katharevusa (officially suppressed in the 1980s) as the 'High' form.

demotion The opposite of *promotion. E.g. in the passive *They were seen by everyone,* the subject of the corresponding active, *Everyone saw them,* would be said to be demoted to the role of an agent.

denasalization Change or process by which a sound is no longer *nasal or nasalized.

denominal (Process) by which words of other classes are formed from nouns. Also of the words so formed: e.g. *beautiful* (← *beauty*) is a denominal adjective.

denotation The relation between a lexical unit and the objects etc. it is used to refer to. E.g. *bull* **denotes** (in one account of its meaning) a class of animals, *brown* a property of individuals or objects, etc. The second term in the relation is the **denotatum**.

   Distinguished in theory, though not always necessarily in practice, from both *reference, seen as a relation between a specific expression and e.g. a specific individual, and *sense, defined by Lyons and others as the network of relations between a lexical unit and other such units. *See also* connotation.

dense (network) *See* social network.

dental Articulated with the tip or blade of the tongue against or approximated to the upper teeth: e.g. *t* [t̪] in Italian, where the diacritic (̪) distinguishes dentals from alveolars.

denti-alveolar 1. Articulated at the junction of the upper teeth and the teeth-ridge. **2.** Cover term for *dental and *alveolar.

deontic [dɪˈɒntik] Expressing the presence or absence of an obligation, recommendation, prohibition, etc. E.g. the modal *must* is deontic, or used deontically, in *They told me I must ꜰɪnish it tomorrow*; likewise *ought (to)* in *You ought to take more exercise*, *can* or *can't* in *The children can't play here*, or *may* in *She may if she likes*.

From the participle of a Greek word for 'ought to': opp. epistemic as one of two major categories of *modality.

dependency Any relation in which one element (the **dependent**) is taken to imply the other. Thus a *modifier, such as *big* in *big men*, implies the presence of the element it modifies; a *complement, such as *nothing* in *I saw nothing*, implies that of the element whose construction it 'completes'. Also in fields other than syntax. Thus in the structure of *syllables a consonant as onset or coda would depend on its nucleus: having this role implies, that is, the presence of a nucleus to which it is related. A syllable is likewise unaccented in relation to one that is accented: hence, in a word such as *party*, the unstressed *-ty*, or the vowel in the unstressed syllable ([i]), would depend on the stressed *par-*, or on its vowel [aː].

A dependent is often defined in syntax by its relation to a *head (1). Thus, in the same examples, if the noun is the head of *big men* and the verb of *saw nothing*, it would follow that *big* and *nothing* depend on them. In accounts where dependency is primary, *men* or *saw* would alternatively be a '**governor**'.

Also '**dependence**'; *cf.* subordination.

dependency grammar A *generative grammar by which the structures of sentences are represented by *dependency trees. Thence of grammars in general that treat dependency as primary, whether or not all structures reduce to that form.

Dependency Phonology Model of phonology developed by J. M. Anderson and others from the 1970s. Its name derives from a form of representation in which segments stand in a relation of *dependency within the syllable and other larger and smaller units. E.g. an unstressed vowel depends on a stressed vowel; consonants depend, both within the syllable and within the *rhyme of a syllable, on vowels; within a diphthong one vowel depends on the other. Within vowels and consonants in turn, there are further relations of dependency among feature-like components.

The dependencies form a structure more complex than a *dependency tree. In particular, many consonants are *ambisyllabic: i.e. they depend on both a preceding and a following vowel.

dependency tree A *tree diagram which assigns each minimal unit to a class and shows relations of dependency among them. In the illustration, the successive words are assigned to the classes noun (N), verb (V), and adverb (Adv). The root node labelled V is connected to the two lower nodes labelled N and Adv: that is, both the noun (*boys*) and adverb (*well*) depend, in the analysis assumed, on the verb (*play*).

Compare the *phrase structure tree for the same sentence.

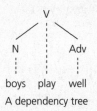

A dependency tree

dependent (Unit etc.) standing in a relation of *dependency. Thus a *subordinate clause is a **dependent clause**, and so on.

dependent marking Marking of syntactic relations on a subordinate or dependent element. E.g. in *their house* the possessive construction is marked by the form of the dependent *their*. Opp. head marking.

deponent (Verb or verb form) in Latin especially, traditionally described as active or intransitive in meaning but with inflections that usually mark a passive. Hence **deponency** in general of (in recent treatments) any case where an inflection characteristic of one *morphosyntactic property realizes exceptionally another property opposed to it.

de re *See* de dicto vs. de re.

derivation **1.** Any series of changes in which a form or structure is altered by successive processes. E.g. the derivation of *cellists* from *cello* might involve the stages ['tʃɛləʊ] → ['tʃɛləʊ + ɪst] (suffixation) → ['tʃɛlɪst] (fusion) → ['tʃɛlɪst + z] (plural formation) → ['tʃɛlɪsts] (devoicing of [z]). **2.** = derivational morphology.

derivational constraint Any rule of grammar interpreted as a restriction on two or more different stages of a *derivation; especially linking stages that do not immediately succeed one another.

Introduced into syntax by G. P. Lakoff in the early 1970s; in Lakoff's account, a *transformation, which was at the time seen as a rule relating two successive stages in the derivation of *surface structures, was a special instance of a derivational constraint, which could relate any such stages whatever.

derivational morphology Branch of *morphology concerned with the derivation of one word in the lexicon from another: e.g. that of *hanger* from *hang*, or of *countess* from *count*. In these examples,

-er and *-ess* are **derivational affixes**, and the processes of which they are part are **derivational formations**.

Traditionally distinguished from *inflectional morphology; also from the formation of *compounds.

derived Resulting from some lexical or syntactic process. E.g. *establishment* is a derived noun (← *establish*); in early transformational grammars a passive was a derived sentence (*I was bowled over by her* ← *She bowled me over*).

derogative = pejorative.

descent Continuity of transmission from an *ancestor language to later languages that have evolved from it. Thus English is hypothetically one of the many **descendants** of an *Indo-European *protolanguage.

descriptive (1) Used in the 1940s and 1950s in opposition to 'historical'. '**Descriptive linguistics**' was therefore another term, especially in the USA, for *synchronic linguistics, and '**descriptivists**' are scholars in the USA who saw that branch as primary. Also opposed to *prescriptive and, rarely at that time but commonly in later attacks on the 'descriptivists', to 'theoretical' or 'explanatory'.

descriptive (2) (modifier, relative clause) = non-restrictive.

descriptive (3) (*Function of language) in describing events in or states of the world. *Cf.* referential; representational.

descriptive adequacy *See* levels of adequacy.

'descriptive order' The relation between processes which are ordered in the description of a language, as opposed to the historical order e.g. of sound changes. *Cf.* ordered rules.

descriptor Used by Quirk *et al.*, *CGE* of a noun combined with proper nouns to form complex names: e.g. *miss* in names like *Miss Schleich* or *road* in names like *Hills Road*.

desiderative (Inflection etc.) indicating a desire to do something. Originally of a set of derived verbs in Latin: e.g. *es-uri-o* ('eat-DESID-1SG') 'I feel hungry'.

designate 1. To distinguish from other members of a set. E.g. in the formulation of phrase structure grammar as a system of *rewrite rules the element S was designated as the only one from which a derivation could begin. **2.** = denote, mean, etc.

design features Concept introduced by C. F. Hockett in the 1960s of a set of key properties of language not shared or not known to be shared, as a set, with systems of communication in any other species. Their number and names have varied from one account to another;

but all have included, as among the most important, the properties of duality (= *double articulation (1)), *arbitrariness, and *productivity.

desinence An older term for an inflectional ending. E.g. *-s* in *books* is the plural desinence.

Det = determiner.

determinative (1) A sign used in writing to resolve an ambiguity in some other sign. A **semantic determinative** is one which indicates the relevant field of meaning, a **phonetic determinative** one which represents some sound or sequence of sounds.

Suppose, e.g. that in a system in which words are represented as wholes, the word for 'hare' is written with a sign <X>. Suppose then that, as in English, the word for 'hair' has the same sound; accordingly it too might be represented by <X>. But <X> is then ambiguous. So, to remove potential confusion, <A> and <B>, which usually represent the words for 'animal' and 'head', are added as semantic determinatives: <AX> 'hare', <BX> 'hair'.

Suppose, alternatively, that the same sign <Y> has been used for both the word for 'hare', which begins as in English with [h], and the word for 'rabbit', which again begins with [r]. To distinguish them, two signs <H> and <R>, each representing other words that begin with these consonants, might be added as phonetic determinatives: <YH> 'hare', <YR> 'rabbit'.

Systems then evolve in which some signs are used only as determinatives.

determinative (2) Huddleston and Pullum's term, in *CGEL*, for a *determiner. *See also* determiner phrase.

determinative compound Any compound whose members are joined in a relation resembling that of a modifier and a head: e.g. *paperback* or *funny face* (both of the subtype called 'possessive' or *bahuvrihi), *blackbird* or *watercress* ('attributive'), *car-crazy*, *punch-drunk*, and so on.

determiner (D) Any of a class of grammatical units characterized by ones that are seen as limiting the potential referent of a noun phrase. Thus, in English, of a class which in most accounts will include the *definite article *the* (limiting reference to individuals etc. that an addressee can identify), *demonstratives such as *this* (limiting reference to individuals standing in a relation to the speaker), with others, such as the *indefinite article *a* and the *possessives *my*, *your*, etc., used in opposition to these. Divided by Quirk *et al*., *CGE* into 'predeterminers' (e.g. *all* in *all those three people*), 'central determiners' (e.g. *those*), and 'postdeterminers' (e.g. *three*).

Extended, by advocates of the *DP-hypothesis, to include pronouns.

determiner phrase (DP) A phrase whose *head (1) is a determiner. Hence especially of units such as *she*, *the girl*, or *Jane*, according to the *DP-hypothesis.

In the account of Huddleston and Pullum, **CGEL*, a '**determinative phrase**' (likewise 'DP') is a unit within a noun phrase seen as headed by a 'determinative': e.g. *almost all the*, with head *the*, in *almost all the people*.

Devanagari Script used for many modern and older languages of India, including *Hindi and *Sanskrit. Developed in an evolved form by the 7th–8th century AD.

Of its 48 characters, 34 represent a consonant followed, unless shown otherwise, by *a*: thus *ka*, *ta*, and so on. Where the same consonant is followed by a vowel other than *a*, a character representing that vowel is added: thus *ki*, for instance, is represented by the character for *ka* plus a character for *i*. Where no vowel follows, a stroke is added instead: thus the character for *ka* plus the stroke represents *k*. The system is typical of *Indian scripts in general. In typologies of writing systems it is described as *alpha-syllabic.

'developmental dysphasia' *See* dysphasia.

'developmental psycholinguistics' *See* psycholinguistics.

deverbal (Process) by which words of other classes are derived from verbs. Also of the words so formed: e.g. *action* and *actor* (← *act*) are deverbal nouns.

'deviant' (Sentence, form, etc.) seen as not conforming to a rule, or to some more general principle or tendency. Often said in practice of one that is perfectly acceptable: e.g., in the 1960s and later, of much poetic usage, whether or not traditionally covered by 'poetic licence'.

devoicing Process or change by which *voice (1) is lost or restricted. Common e.g. at the ends of sentences in French: thus [l] is regularly devoiced in that position in words such as *peuple* 'people', phonetically [pœpl̥].

DF = distinctive feature; likewise **DF-matrix** = distinctive feature matrix.

di- From the Greek word for 'twice'. Thus a **disyllabic** word, or **disyllable**, has two syllables, a *ditransitive verb has two objects, and so on. Opp. mono-, tri-: *cf.* bi- in e.g. 'bivalent'.

diachronic Having to do with changes over time. Thus a diachronic account of a language deals with its history, a diachronic theory deals with the nature of historical change in general, and so on. Opp. synchronic; *see also* panchronic.

diacritic Any mark in writing additional to a letter or other basic element: e.g. the tilde (˜) distinguishing *ñ* from *n* in Spanish; the umlaut (¨) distinguishing *ä ö ü* from *a o u* in German, or, in phonetic transcription, to indicate that a vowel is *centralized.

diacritic feature A feature in *Generative Phonology assigned to units that are exceptions to a rule or follow a rule that is itself exceptional. E.g., in the account of Chomsky and Halle, *SPE*, a form such as *sang* or *rang* was derived from *sing* or *ring* by a rule applying only to words that had a feature explicitly requiring it to do so.

   Features such as this are, in effect, instructions to apply the rule in question. In that sense they 'trigger' the rule, and were also called '**rule features**'.

diaeresis [dʌɪ'ɪərəsɪs] [dʌɪ'ɛrəsɪs] Mark in writing (¨) used to show that successive vowels belong to different syllables: thus Zoë ['zəʊi]. Also to show that a letter is not 'silent': e.g. the *ü* [w] of Spanish *lingüística* 'linguistics'.

diagrammatic Having the property of *iconicity.

dialect Any distinct variety of a language, especially one spoken in a specific part of a country or other geographical area.

   The criterion for distinguishing 'dialects' from 'languages' is taken, in principle, to be that of mutual intelligibility. E.g. speakers of Dutch cannot understand English unless they have learned it, and vice versa; therefore Dutch and English are different languages. But a speaker from Amsterdam can understand one from Antwerp: therefore they speak different dialects of the same language. But (*a*) this is a matter of degree, and (*b*) ordinary usage often contradicts it. E.g. Italian 'dialects' ('dialetti') are so called though many from the north and south are not mutually intelligible. By contrast Danish and Norwegian are called 'languages' though speakers understand each other reasonably well. There are also conventions among linguists themselves: e.g. the 'dialects' of *Indo-European are the original branches of the family: *Germanic, *Italic, etc.

   Cf. accent (2).

dialect atlas An atlas of a geographical region showing the distribution of forms etc. which vary from one dialect of a language to another. This may be shown by points on a map at which e.g. recordings have been made, by drawing *isoglosses, and so on.

dialect continuum A range of dialects distributed geographically across a territory, such that adjacent varieties are mutually intelligible but those at the extremes are not. Thus it is likely that, a century ago, someone who spoke a dialect of rural Devon would not have understood a speaker from Glasgow; but, in intervening areas, each individual shift from dialect to dialect would have been sufficiently minor for communication to be maintained.

The term '**dialect chain**' is used similarly.

dialect geography The study of differences in speech from one place to another within the area in which a language is spoken. Thus including, in particular, the preparation of *dialect atlases.

dialect levelling Historical process by which features found across a range of dialects are extended at the expense of ones whose distribution is more limited.

'dialect mixture' The presence in one form of speech of features seen as reflecting those of two or more historically different dialects.

Usually invoked as a factor which obscures the *Neogrammarian principle of regularity in sound change. E.g. in the Tuscan dialect which forms the basis of standard Italian, intervocalic stops which were voiceless in Latin are voiced in some words (as more generally in dialects to the north) but voiceless in others. If the change had proceeded mechanically they should all be voiced or all be voiceless: that they are not is accordingly attributed to the influence on this dialect of others adjacent to it.

dialectology The study of geographical dialects: e.g., in the preparation of a *dialect atlas, or of **dialect grammars** or **dialect dictionaries** of specific varieties.

dialectometry The quantitative comparison of forms from different dialects, to determine how close one is to another. Developed by the French dialectologist J. Séguy in the 1950s.

diaphone A phonological unit established across accents or dialects: e.g. one which subsumes both the rounded vowel of [pʊt] in the dialect of some British speakers with the unrounded, lower, and more central vowel in that of others.

diastratic (Variation, study of variation) across different classes, or strata, in a society. Opp. diatopic; *cf.* social dialect.

diasystem A phonological or other system established as an abstraction covering dialects whose individual systems differ. Thus the vowels of Scottish and Southern British English differ in that distinctions of quality in one correspond to differences of length etc. in the other. But both might be covered by a diasystem in which series of vowels are distinguished neutrally. *Cf.* diaphone.

diathesis [dʌɪˈaθəsɪs] From the term in Ancient Greek for *voice (2): the sense is that of the role or 'placing' of a subject, e.g. as agent in relation to an active verb, or as patient or 'undergoer' in relation to a passive.

Not usual in English, but available as a term for voice-like categories in general.

diatopic (Variation, study of variation) from one part to another of the area covered by a speech community. Opp. diastratic.

'dictionary word' A word as entered in a dictionary; hence a *citation form or the form used to represent a *lexeme.

diffuse 1. (Speech community) whose extent or identity is not precisely determined e.g. by the acceptance of a common standard. Opp. focused. **2.** The feature opposed to *compact in *Jakobson's system of *distinctive features.

diffusion The gradual spread of words, sound changes, etc. from one person or community to another. Central to the *wave model in historical linguistics: *see also* lexical diffusion.

diglossia The case in which a community uses two distinct forms of the same language, one acquired through education and appropriate to one range of contexts, the other acquired before formal education and appropriate to another. Thus German-speaking Switzerland is described as a **diglossic community**, where the distinct varieties are Standard German and the local forms of Swiss German.

Thence extended to communities in which two different languages are in a similar relationship: e.g. in Paraguay, where the diglossia is between Spanish and *Guaraní. In accounts of diglossia a variety learned formally and used in a range of more formal contexts is the **High** form (often abbreviated **H**), one learned naturally and used in a range of less formal contexts is the **Low** form (**L**). E.g. in Paraguay, Spanish is H and Guaraní is L.

digraph A sequence of two letters corresponding, in application to a given language, to one phoneme: e.g. *sh* in *shin*, representing the single phoneme [ʃ]. *Cf.* compound letter.

diminutive (Word etc.) basically indicating small size; e.g. *piglet* is a diminutive of *pig*, formed with the diminutive suffix *-let*. Opp. augmentative.

Diogenes of Babylon *See* Stoics.

Dionysius Thrax (*c*.170–*c*.90 BC) Scholar in the *Alexandrian tradition, taught by Aristarchus and later established in Rhodes. A short grammar of Greek has come down in his name, and from late antiquity had the same influence in the eastern Roman empire and beyond as those of *Donatus in the west. But it is not clear how much of it he actually wrote. An initial definition of the parts of grammar is known from other testimony to be his. But later sections, dealing especially with the *parts of speech and their *accidents, differ in places from what Dionysius is known from other sources to have said, and are more consistent with a date some four centuries later.

diphthong A vowel whose quality changes perceptibly in one direction within a single syllable: e.g. [aʊ] in *house*, whose articulation changes from relatively open to relatively close and back. Diphthongs are *falling or *rising according to which phase is more prominent.

A distinction might be drawn in principle between a phonetic diphthong and a diphthong in phonology, which would consist of a sequence of two vowel phonemes. Thus the [aʊ] of *house* is phonetically diphthongal, but different phonologists have described it variously as a single phoneme, as a vowel plus another vowel, or as a vowel plus a semivowel. *Cf.* monophthong; triphthong.

diphthongization Change or process by which a *monophthong becomes a *diphthong.

direct 1. Traditionally of the nominative case in e.g. Latin as opposed to the *oblique cases. **2.** The opposite of *inverse.

directional (Phrase, preposition, case) indicating movement to a location. Thus *to New York* is a directional phrase in *We flew to New York*.

directionality Property of any process that applies in one direction rather than another. E.g. a rule determining divisions between syllables might be 'directional' in that forms as represented are scanned from left to right rather than from right to left.

Also of relations between *components (2) of generative grammars. Hence in particular in reference to controversies in the early 1970s, as to whether syntactic representations of a sentence were derived from semantic representations, or the opposite: *cf.* Generative Semantics; Interpretive Semantics.

directive 1. Bloomfieldian term for constructions in which a verb or preposition (the **director**) governs what Bloomfield called an *axis: e.g. those of *visits me*, *from her*, and *while I was there*, where the directors are *visits*, *from*, and *while* and the axes *me*, *her*, and *I was there*. **2.** *Speech act by which speakers direct or elicit action by others. Thus an order; also e.g. a question, since it invites an answer. **3.** = directional.

direct method Method of teaching a language in which learners are exposed to it without translation into or any formal explanation in any language they already know. A reaction to conventional teaching of grammar, once very fashionable.

direct object (DO) An *object traditionally seen as identifying someone or something directly involved in an action or process: e.g. *my books* in *I might leave my books to the library*, where it is distinguished from the *indirect object *to the library*. Hence, in particular, the object typically next to the verb in English, one marked by the accusative case in German, and so on.

director *See* directive (1).

direct speech The direct quotation of something said, thought, etc.: e.g. *Where am I?* is an example of (or is 'in') direct speech in *He asked 'Where am I?'* Opp. indirect speech.

disambiguate To resolve an ambiguity. Thus *Woods are expensive* is ambiguous, since *woods* might refer to stands of trees or a type of golf club. But its meaning will usually be clear in context: i.e. the context 'disambiguates' it.

disconnection model Model proposed for some forms of *aphasia, in which the symptoms hypothetically result from damage to connections between different parts of the brain, concerned e.g. with auditory analysis vs. production of speech.

discontinuous Not realized in an unbroken sequence. E.g. the constituents of *blow it up* are, in most accounts, a *phrasal verb (*blow . . . up*) and its object (*it*): *blow . . . up* is accordingly a **discontinuous constituent**. In some accounts of agreement, a phrase like *those girls* has been said to realize three morphemes: a demonstrative ('that') realized by *th-*, a noun ('girl') realized by *girl*, and a single 'plural' morpheme, realized by *-ose* in the first word and *-s* in the second. 'Plural' would accordingly be a **discontinuous morpheme**.

discourse Any coherent succession of sentences, spoken or (in most usage) written. Thus this entry in the dictionary is an example of discourse; likewise a novel; likewise a speech by a politician or a lecture to students; likewise an interview or any other series of speech events in which successive sentences or utterances hang together. Often equivalent to *text.

Hence, as in usage generally, of a type or style of language: e.g. 'political discourse', 'religious discourse'. More loosely of whatever happens to be the object of 'discourse analysis': thus a way of speaking, a belief or 'practice' seen as underlying discourse, etc.

The French term ('**discours**') was restricted by Benveniste to speech directed by a specific speaker (an 'I') to a specific audience or addressee (a 'you'). Distinguished by him from a narration (e.g. an historical narrative) or 'récit'.

Discourse Analysis Effectively of any analysis of *discourse. Originally applied by (Zellig) Harris, in the 1950s, to an attempt to analyse units larger than words and sentences in the way that they themselves had been analysed. *Cf.* *textlinguistics.

Subsequently of analyses with whatever motive: e.g. from the viewpoint of *pragmatics; in studies of connections between sentences or clauses; of the use of vocabulary in relation to the political or other beliefs of speakers or writers; and so on.

'discourse deixis' All forms of *anaphora and *exophora in discourse: i.e. of relations in fact distinguished from *deixis proper.

discourse marker Any of a variety of units whose function is within a larger *discourse rather than an individual sentence or clause: e.g. *but then* in *But then he might be late* or *well* in *Well what if he is?*

Discourse Representation Theory A formal account of the meaning of a discourse, developed by H. Kamp and others, in which a semantic representation, called a **Discourse Representation Structure**, is derived cumulatively, sentence by sentence, by rules operating on representations of their syntax. Conceived as an idealized model of the way in which people in practice understand passages of connected speech.

'discourse topic' *See* topic.

discovery procedure A mechanical procedure for deriving a grammar of a language from a corpus, or sample, of sentences. Term introduced by Chomsky in the 1950s, with reference to the aims of (Zellig) Harris and other *Post-Bloomfieldians. *Cf.* evaluation procedure.

discrete (Unit etc.) which has an identity sharply distinguished from that of others. E.g. *I love cider* is analysed into the discrete units *I*, *love*, and *cider*; [lʌv] (*love*) is in turn analysed into the discrete units [l], [ʌ], and [v]. Opp. continuous: e.g. it may be disputed whether differences in *intonation reflect distinctions between discrete units, or variation along continuous parameters.

  Cf. non-discrete; fuzzy.

disjunct Used by Quirk *et al.*, **CGE*, of an adverbial such as *perhaps* in *Perhaps he is there* or *honestly* in *Honestly, I can't do it*, seen as an element belonging to the *periphery of its clause and e.g. qualifying, commenting on, or giving authority for the remainder. For the second example compare *honestly* as an *adjunct in *I can't do it honestly*; *see also* conjunct (2); subjunct.

disjunction *Coordination that distinguishes alternatives: e.g. in *She will come by bike or she will take a bus*. A coordinator such as *or* is a **disjunctive conjunction**, a question such as *Will you go or will you stay?* is a **disjunctive question**, and so on.

  A term from logic, where a **disjunctive operator** ($\vee$) is defined as connecting propositions at least one of which is thereby represented as true. Thus $p \vee q$ = 'Either p is true or q is true or both'. Opp. conjunction (2).

disjunctive order Relation between *ordered rules of which only one will apply to a given form. Opp. conjunctive order.

disjunctive pronoun A full as opposed to a reduced or *clitic
pronoun in, or especially in, the Romance languages: e.g. French *moi*
'I, me', Italian *io* 'I'. Opp. conjunctive pronoun.

dislocation *See* left dislocation; right dislocation.

displaced speech Speech referring to objects etc. which are not part
of its immediate setting in space and time. A normal property of
communication in man, but not demonstrated in any other species;
hence **displacement** has been included in accounts of *design
features.

displacement 1. *See* displaced speech. **2.** Otherwise e.g. of any
movement of a tone, accent, word, etc. from its basic or usual
position.

dissective (Verb, form of verb) referring to a state or activity
constant over a period of time. E.g. if someone walks for three hours
then at any moment within that time span they are walking:
therefore *walk*, as a lexical unit, is dissective, as is *walked* in *I walked for
three hours*.

dissimilation Change or process by which two sounds in a sequence
become less like each other. E.g. French *pèlerin* 'pilgrim' is from Latin
peregrin(us) 'foreigner' by, among other things, dissimilation to *l* of the
first of two *r*'s.
    Often sporadic: *see* Grassmann's Law for a more regular instance.

distal (Demonstrative etc.) which basically identifies someone or
something as distanced from, rather than close to, a speaker. E.g. *that*
in *that side of the road* is distal as opposed to *proximal *this* in *this side of
the road*.

distinctive Making a distinction or distinctions between units.
Especially in phonology: thus the phonetic difference between [d] and
[ð] is distinctive in English, since e.g. *den* [dɛn] and *then* [ðɛn] are two
different words. Similar sounds are found in Spanish: e.g. in *dedo*
'finger', phonetically [deðo]. But there the difference is not distinctive,
since no words differ in just that way.
    'Contrastive' is used with the same sense: *see also* opposition.

distinctive feature 1. A phonetic *feature which distinguishes one
phonological unit, especially one *phoneme, from another. Thus
*voice (1) is a distinctive feature in English since e.g. voiced [b] (as in
bit) is a phoneme distinct from voiceless [p] (as in *pit*). **2.** One of a set
of features which hypothetically characterize all such phonological
distinctions in all languages: e.g. voice considered as a *linguistic
universal, instanced in English by voice as a feature of [b] in *bit*, in
German by voice as a feature of [b] in *bitte*, and so on. According to the
hypothesis, not every distinctive feature in this sense is distinctive in

every individual language: thus there are many languages, e.g. in Australia, in which voice is not. But no language will have distinctions that no member of the set covers.

distinctive feature matrix Strictly, a *feature matrix which shows only *distinctive features. Also loosely of any feature matrix.

'distinguisher' *See* semantic marker.

distributed (Consonant) articulated with a maximal degree of stricture extending for a distance along the direction of air flow. A feature in the scheme of Chomsky and Halle, *SPE*, distinguishing e.g. *laminals as [+ distributed] from *apicals as [– distributed].

Distributed Morphology A reformulation in the 1990s of earlier *Item and Arrangement treatments of inflectional morphology. Features such as plural, or [+ Plural], might be represented as such at the level of syntax. But in the course of a derivation they may form or combine into segments, which are associated in a linear order with forms given by a lexicon. Sequences constructed in that way may in turn be subject to rules of phonology.

'Distributed' in that an account of morphology is parcelled out among rules of syntax and phonology and the lexicon. Hence a grammar has no independent morphological component.

distribution The set of contexts within sentences in which a unit or class of units can appear. E.g. the distribution of *hair* in written English is the set of contexts *I combed my —*, *Give me the — spray*, *My — is too long*, etc., in any of which the blank (—) can be filled by it.

The **distribution mode** of a unit was defined by Pike in terms of its distribution in this sense. **Distributionalism** is the doctrine, developed especially by leading *Post-Bloomfieldians, that the formal distribution of units should be studied in abstraction from, and before one goes on to study, their meanings.

distributive 1. Indicating reference to each individual member of a set. E.g. a language might contrast a distributive plural and a collective plural: schematically, *girls*-DISTR *brought present* 'The girls each brought a present' vs. *girls*-COLL *brought present* 'The girls as a group brought a present'. **2.** Indicating that a set of objects etc. are of different types: thus, schematically, *I bought vegetables*-DISTR, where what were bought were e.g. carrots and onions rather than either of these alone.

ditransitive Taking or including two *objects, e.g. the construction of *They taught us arithmetic* or *They taught arithmetic to us*; also the verb *teach*, in taking such a construction. Opp. monotransitive; *cf. also* complex transitive.

divalent = bivalent.

divergence In the ordinary sense: thus in particular of the increasing differentiation of languages as they develop from a common ancestor, as opposed to the *convergence (1) of languages which may be genetically unrelated.

DO = direct object.

domain Usually in a sense reflecting general usage. Thus especially: **1.** Of the extent or range of forms for which some rule etc. applies. E.g. in many languages the word is the domain of *vowel harmony: i.e. it extends to syllables within words, not across word boundaries. **2.** Of cultural or other settings in which different forms of speech may be appropriate: e.g. that of a law court or of a sports commentary, as opposed to that of a family at home, etc.

domal An old term for *retroflex.

dominance The relation in a *phrase structure tree between a node X and any lower node Y that is on a branch originating from X. E.g., in a tree equivalent to a labelled bracketing ₙₚ[ₙ[*books*] ₚₚ[*on the floor*]], the node labelled 'NP' dominates those labelled 'N' and 'PP'. Also, especially in earlier treatments, of the relation between a node labelled 'X' and the entire constituent assigned to that category. Thus, in the same example, the 'NP' node would 'dominate' the whole of *books on the floor*.

Informally as in ordinary uses. E.g. a *head (1) is the dominant unit in a phrase, a stressed syllable dominant in a word, and so on.

Donatus (4th century AD) Roman grammarian, author in particular of a compendium of Latin grammar (the *Ars maior* or 'larger *ars*') and a catechism on the *parts of speech and their *accidents (the *Ars minor* or 'smaller *ars*'), which were to have an immense influence, directly and through their role as a model for other grammars, throughout the medieval and into the modern period.

Dong *See* Kam-Sui.

'donkey sentence' A sentence of the type *Every farmer who owns a donkey beats it*, or *If a farmer owns a donkey he beats it*, seen as problematic in their logical structure through the relation of *anaphora between *it* and *a donkey*. Named after work by P. T. Geach which used these examples.

dorsal Articulated with the convex upper surface of the tongue: e.g. a *velar such as [k] in *cap*, produced with closure of this part of the tongue (the **dorsum**) against the soft palate. Also of a *back vowel such as [uː] in *coop*, in which the dorsum is again raised.

Likewise **dorso-**; *cf.* apical, laminal, radical (3).

'*do*-support' Syntactic process by which *do* is used as a *dummy auxiliary. Thus *do* would be seen as 'supporting' e.g. a negative *I don't know* or the interrogative *Don't they know?*

double accusative Construction, e.g. in Latin, with two nouns both in the *accusative case. Compare what are sometimes described as '**double object**' constructions in English: e.g. both *him* and *my coat* have the form they would have as a direct object in *I lent him my coat*.

double articulation (1) The property of being composed of discrete units at two levels. Thus, at one level, the sentence *You go to sleep* is composed of the words *you*, *go*, *to*, and *sleep*, and, at another level, it or the successive words are composed of the phonological units [j], [uː], [g], etc.

Cf. articulation. Also called '**duality**', and claimed as one of the most important of the *design features that distinguish language from systems of communication in other species. In a leading formulation by Martinet, the articulation of words or other meaningful units is the **primary articulation**, that of phonological units within words the **secondary articulation**.

double articulation (2) Production of a sound at two equal *places of articulation. E.g. [k͡p], in many African languages, is a single consonant produced with partly simultaneous closures of the tongue against the soft palate and of the lower lip against the upper lip.

double bar ($\bar{\bar{X}}$, X″) *See* X-bar syntax.

double-base transformation = generalized transformation.

'double case' *See* case stacking.

double cross (#) Used as a *boundary symbol. In the conventions established in *Generative Phonology, a double ## marks a boundary between words in syntax; a single # a boundary between words that are parts of a larger word; a plus sign (+) a boundary between smaller units, such as stems and affixes. Thus e.g. *large ## wood # pigeon + s*.

double negative Construction in which a single negation is marked by two elements each of which, in the same or another construction, can indicate it independently. E.g. in Spanish: *No he visto nada* (lit. 'not I-have seen nothing') 'I haven't seen anything'. Proscribed in English, on the grounds that sentences like *I haven't seen nothing* ought to mean 'It is not the case (first negative) that I have not seen (second negative) anything'.

Hence '**multiple negation**', when the negatives are three or more: e.g., as again proscribed in English, *I haven't said nothing to nobody*.

double object *See* double accusative.

doublet Two words in a language which are historically from the same source, but with different intervening stages. E.g. *frail* and *fragile* are both from Latin *fragilis*; but *frail* was borrowed into English in the Middle Ages from the form that had developed from it in Old French, while *fragile* was borrowed in the 17th century, directly from Latin as a learned language or via a similar borrowing in contemporary French.

downdrift Gradual lowering of pitch over a sentence or some other unit. Especially in some *tone languages, where successive high tones are progressively lowered, often to a level phonetically below that of low tones earlier in the unit.

Cf. declination. 'Downdrift' is usual when the lowering of pitch is governed by the phonology of a particular language; 'declination' can be used of a purely phonetic effect, due to the progressive lowering of air pressure from the lungs. *Cf. also* downstep.

downgrading Process by which a larger syntactic unit, such as a sentence, has a function like that of a smaller unit, such as a word or phrase. Hence of regular processes of *embedding: e.g. *he was alive* is downgraded to an element of a phrase in *the news that he was alive*. Also of sporadic processes: e.g. the phrasal verb *cut up* is downgraded to the level of a stem in *This meat is un-cut-up-able*.

'downstairs clause' = subordinate clause. Likewise 'downstairs subject' etc. = subject etc. in a subordinate clause.

downstep (ˈ) A phonological unit in some *tone languages which is realized by a lowering of the second of two successive high or mid tones. Thus, in a language with a high and a low tone, this will distinguish three possibilities: (*a*) H L (high followed by low); (*b*) H H (high followed by high without downstep); (*c*) H'H (high followed by high with downstep). The pitch of the tone following the downstep in case (*c*) is intermediate between that of the low tone in case (*a*) and that of the second high tone in case (*b*).

Distinguished from *downdrift in that the pitch is lowered by specific units, whereas in downdrift all high tones are in principle affected equally. Languages with downstep, in particular, are described as having **terraced-level** systems.

downtoner *See* intensifying.

DP-hypothesis An account in which a *noun phrase, as conceived by Chomsky in the 1950s, is seen instead as a phrase whose *head (1) is a *determiner. Thus *the hill* would be headed by *the*, and *Mary* a phrase whose head would be a *null determiner; a pronoun such as *she* would itself belong to a subclass of determiners.

First mooted seriously in the early 1980s; since widely, though not generally, accepted.

drag chain *See* chain shift.

Dravidian Family of languages historically limited to the south of the Indian subcontinent and scattered areas to the north. *Kannada, *Malayalam, *Tamil, and *Telugu all have speakers in the tens of millions.

drift Pattern of change in which the structure of a language shifts in a determinate direction. Described as such by Sapir in the 1920s, with reference to various individual changes in the history of English, interpreted collectively as 'symptoms of larger tendencies at work in the language'. Interpreted in the 1970s, by W. P. Lehmann and others, as reflecting a tendency for languages to conform to a specific structural type: hence for languages which are structurally similar to change similarly.

D-structure Level of syntactic representation in *Government and Binding Theory, more abstract than *S-structure and less abstract than *Logical Form. Developed from what was earlier called *deep structure; hence an initial structure from which structures at other levels were derived.

dual (DU) 1. Term in the category of *number which distinguishes two individuals as opposed to one or to more than two. E.g. in Sanskrit: *pitárau* 'father-NOM.DU' as opposed to singular *pitá* 'father', plural *pitáraḥ* 'more than two fathers'. **2.** *See* inclusive.

duality = double articulation (1).

dubitative (Inflection, particle) indicating a doubt as to the reliability of what is said. E.g., schematically, *I come*-DUBIT 'I might perhaps come'.

dummy A syntactic element which fills a place in a construction that would otherwise be unfilled. Thus, to form an interrogative, the order of a subject and an auxiliary is inverted: *They can ski* → *Can they ski?* But in *They ski* there is no auxiliary: so, in *Do they ski?*, *do* is a dummy that, in effect, supplies one. Similarly in the negative *They don't ski* it supplies an auxiliary to which *n't* is attached (compare *They can't ski*), and in the emphatic *They* DO *ski* one which carries the intonation (compare *They* CAN *ski*). Another dummy in English is the *it* of *It is snowing* or (again of the weather) *It is pouring*. In e.g. *It is falling*, the reference of *it* is to something that falls. But with the 'weather verbs' there is no reference to a 'snower' or a 'pourer'. Therefore *it* is seen as a dummy whose role is to fill the syntactic position of a subject when no other element does so.

Also called a **prop** or **prop-word**.

duration The physical length of sounds etc. as measured on a time scale. Opp. 'length' as a feature in phonology: e.g. the duration of [a] of *sad* is appreciably greater, for many speakers, than that of [ɪ] in *hid*, but in terms of the phonological system they are equally 'short'.

durational (Adverb, adverbial) indicating a period of time: e.g. *all night* in *I sat up all night* is durational, or is an adverbial **of duration**.

durative (*Aspect) indicating a process etc. seen as continuing for an appreciable time. Thus the use of the past tense might be described as durative in *I worked in Paris for five years*. Opp. punctual; *cf.* progressive.

Dutch West *Germanic, spoken in Holland; also in Belgium and the extreme north-east of France, roughly from a line broadly south of Brussels to the North Sea. Related within Germanic to Low *German, but separated from it, with effect on its development and status, by a political boundary that has been constant in the modern period.

dvandva Sanskrit term for a compound in which the relation between members is like that of *coordination: e.g. *fighter-bomber* 'fighter and bomber'. The word means 'pair' or 'couple'; also called a 'copulative compound'.

Dyirbal Australian language of north Queensland; the subject of a grammar in 1972 by R. M. W. Dixon which had a major influence on theories of *ergative languages.

dynamic 1. (Verb) denoting an action, process, etc. as opposed to a state. E.g. *buy* is dynamic; *own*, which denotes a resulting state, is *stative. Also of *aspects: e.g. a verb meaning 'sit' might, in a dynamic form, be used of the action of sitting down. **2.** (Modal, modality) neither *deontic nor *epistemic. Characterized by instances involving properties of individuals referred to: e.g. *can* in the sense of 'be able to', as in *I can speak Spanish*.

dynamic passive One referring to an action or process, as opposed to a 'statal passive'. E.g. *(is) opened* is dynamic in *It is easily opened with a penknife* (what is easy is the action of opening), but statal in *It is already opened* (already in the opened state).

Dynamic Syntax Formal model of a process of left-to-right parsing by which someone hearing a sentence is taken to derive a *semantic representation, as a logical structure of predicates and arguments, from the syntactic properties of the words it includes and the contexts in which they appear. Developed by R. M. Kempson and others in publications from 2001 onwards.

dynamic tone = contour tone.

dys- Greek prefix used in medical terms for malfunctions of one sort or another. Hence in describing speech or other disorders:

'**dysphemia**' (stammering), '**dyssyntaxia**' (errors in syntax), '**dysgraphia**' (difficulty in spelling). etc.

dyslexia Condition in which, for no independent reason, such as lack of education, someone has serious difficulty in reading. Hence **dyslexic**, of someone in that condition.

dysphasia Impaired or less than normal ability to speak. Sometimes of milder cases of *aphasia; also of '**developmental dysphasia**', in which the development of language in a child is delayed or otherwise abnormal, for no independent physical or psychological reason.

Dyula *See* Mande.

E

e General notation for *empty categories.

'early adopter' One of the first people to use e.g. a loan word.

ear-training The training of students of linguistics to identify by ear the full range of sounds that the human vocal tract can produce.

ease of articulation *See* principle of least effort; *cf.* euphony.

East Germanic = Gothic.

'Ebonics' *See* African American Vernacular English.

'echolalia' Mechanical repetition of the words just uttered by another speaker, when symptomatic of a speech or other mental disorder.

echo question A form such as 'You've bought ´WHAT?', partly echoing a statement such as 'I've bought a concrete mixer'.

echo-word A compound whose second member repeats the first with an initial consonant or syllable altered. Widespread in languages of the Indian subcontinent, with the general meaning '. . . and the like': e.g. Hindi *pānī* → *pānī-vānī* 'water and such-like', by a systematic process in which an initial consonant is changed to *v*.

ECM = exceptional case marking.

ECP *See* empty category.

-ed form An English verb form in *-ed*: e.g. *walked*. Also of the past tense in English generally, whether marked by *-ed* or not; *cf. -en* form, for *past participle (2).

edge The boundary of a unit, or a part immediately before or after its boundary. Hence, on the model of writing, 'left edge', 'right edge'.

effected object The *object of a verb which denotes an action etc. that brings things or individuals into existence: e.g. *a book* in *I wrote a book*, where the book would exist as the effect of the speaker writing it. Opp. affected object.

Efik Native to the area of Calabar but used more widely as a literary language in south-east Nigeria. The Cross River languages, of which Efik and Ibibio are the most important, are grouped with many others under *Benue-Congo.

EFL Abbreviation for 'English as a foreign language'.

egocentrism Property of language in being centred on the 'here' and 'now' of the individual 'I' (Latin 'ego') who is speaking. Fundamental, in particular, to *deixis.

egressive (Air stream, *airstream mechanism) in which the direction of flow is outwards. Opp. ingressive.

Egyptian The language of ancient Egypt, progressively replaced by Arabic after the Muslim conquest. A branch of *Afro-Asiatic, related most closely, perhaps, to *Semitic and *Berber.

Written in *Hieroglyphic from the beginning of the 3rd millennium BC; from the middle of the millennium, for ordinary purposes, in *Hieratic; from the 7th century BC, again for ordinary purposes, in *Demotic. Subsequently, from the 4th century AD, in the *Coptic alphabet.

ejective (Consonant) produced on a flow of air initiated by an upward movement of the larynx. Distinguished in phonetic transcription by the diacritic [']; the *airstream mechanism is classed as 'glottalic egressive'.

In the production e.g. of ejective [p'], the lips are closed and the velum raised, as in non-ejective [p]. The vocal cords are also closed and, as the larynx is raised, the air pressure within the mouth is increased. Air then flows outwards when the closure at the lips is released.

'elaborated code' *See* deficit theory.

Elamite Ancient language of south-west Iran, written from the late 3rd millennium BC in a *cuneiform script, largely a syllabary but also including logograms and determiners. It has no certain genetic relation to any other language and is not wholly understood.

E-language Chomsky's term in the mid-1980s for a language conceived as a system of events or utterances or other units external to, or as externalized by, the individual speaker. Applied, in effect, to all conceptions of language other than as *I-language.

elative 1. *Case which basically indicates movement 'out of': e.g. schematically, *ran room*-ELAT 'ran from the room'. **2.** An intensified form of an adjective or adverb. E.g. a *superlative with that sense: *He's the greatest*, meaning 'very, really great'.

electromyography A technique for investigating muscular contractions, e.g. those of the chest muscles and others in the production of speech, by inserting electrodes which register the firing of individual fibres.

electropalatography A technique for recording points of contact between the tongue and the hard palate; hence, in particular, for investigating *coarticulation in this area. The subject is fitted with a thin artificial palate which has an array of electrical contacts. A weak current is passed through the body, so that when the tongue touches any of these contacts a circuit is completed and a signal can be registered. The technique has tended to replace earlier methods of *palatography since the late 1970s.

element 1. A basic or indivisible unit at some level of analysis or representation. Thus the elementary units at the level of syntax are words or, in some accounts, *morphemes: those of phonology are phonemes, or individual features, articulatory *gestures, etc. **2.** A term, position, or role in a construction. E.g. a subject–predicate construction has two elements, subject and predicate; correspondingly, in e.g. *My wife left yesterday* the specific elements are the subject *my wife* and the predicate *left yesterday*. Likewise of syntagmatic structures at other levels: e.g. in phonology the structure of an open syllable, (C)V, has as its elements an optional consonantal onset, '(C)', followed by an obligatory vocalic nucleus, 'V'.

elicit To obtain or draw out from an informant. Thus one might try to elicit from speakers of English, either by asking or by some indirect means of testing, whether they would say or find acceptable a form whose status was uncertain: e.g. in a study of auxiliary verbs, ones like *I didn't use to* or *I didn't ought to*.

elision 1. Process by which a vowel at the end of a word is lost, or **elided**, before another vowel at the beginning of a word that follows. *Cf.* prodelision. **2.** =, in some uses, ellipsis.

ellipsis The omission of one or more elements from a construction, especially when they are supplied by the context. E.g. if A asks *Have you seen my glasses?* B might answer elliptically *I'm afraid I haven't*, with the remainder of the construction (*seen your glasses*) to be understood from the question. Hence 'to ellipt': thus *seen your glasses* would be 'ellipted' in B's answer.

The scope of ellipsis depends in part on how the elements of the sentence are described. Thus in *John* DID one might again say that a part of the construction is missing: cf. *John* DID *see them*. But where the stress is on *John* one might be tempted to argue that there is no ellipsis: JOHN *did*, but not, with a similar expansion, JOHN *did see them*. Instead *did* might be described as a *pro-form which itself forms the entire predicate.

'elsewhere' rule A rule in a *generative grammar that applies whenever the conditions for more specific rules are not met: hence = default rule. The condition implicit in such a rule is likewise an '**elsewhere condition**', and the principle by which it is interpreted the '**elsewhere**' (also *Pāṇini's) **principle**.

ELT Abbreviation for 'English language teaching'.

embedded (Sentence, clause) included in one that is larger: e.g. *who you mean* in *I know [who you mean]*. In early *transformational grammar such units were the subject of **embedding transformations**, by which the structure assigned to one sentence (called the '**constituent sentence**') was inserted into that assigned to another (called the '**matrix sentence**').

Also e.g. in accounts of *code switching. Someone's speech might thus be primarily in a '**matrix language**', but would include parts in an '**embedded language**'.

'embedding problem' The problem, as distinguished by Labov, of pinpointing the linguistic, social, or other conditions under which a change is taking place in a language.

-eme Used in terms for basic linguistic units. Thus *phoneme, for a basic unit of phonology; *morpheme, for a basic unit of morphology; *lexeme, for the basic unit of the lexicon. For others *see* e.g. moneme; morphophoneme; sememe.

Thence, by analogy with the phoneme, to units other than those of speech: e.g. '**chereme**' (from the Greek word for 'hand') for the basic unit of sign language; '**proxeme**' (*see* proxemics) for a distinctive unit of distance etc. between speakers; '**narreme**', for a unit in the literary analysis of narrations.

emergence Process by which a structure, change, etc. is created by the separate behaviour of many individuals. Hence, in one view, in the case of language: e.g. a sound change is a phenomenon emerging from the repeated articulatory movements of many individual speakers; the meaning of a word arises by a process of emergence from its repeated use by individual speakers in individual contexts; a *language system as a whole is a structure generated by innumerable individual acts of speech in a community.

EMG = electromyography.

emic Involving, or having the status of, a unit in *-eme. A term of Pike's in particular: thus an analysis of sounds which aims to establish phonemes is an emic, as opposed to an *etic, analysis.

emotive (Meaning, *function of language) having to do with the feelings of the speaker. *Cf.* affective.

empathy Identification with another. Hence **empathetic deixis** is *deixis, e.g. in *free indirect style, that reflects the viewpoint of someone other than the speaker or writer. Scales reflecting differing degrees of empathy, ranging from the speaker themselves at one end to inanimate objects at the other, play a role e.g. in direct vs. *inverse constructions.

emphasizer Used by Quirk *et al.*, **CGE*, of adverbs or adverbials with a broadly emphasizing role: e.g. *actually* in It *actually worked*; *frankly* in I *frankly detest him*.

emphatic (1) Term for dental consonants, especially in Arabic, in which the body of the tongue is broad and flat in the mouth and with the front part lowered. Thus ṭ in Egyptian Arabic *ṭiin* 'mud' as opposed to non-emphatic *t*, with the front part of the tongue more narrow and pointed. Usually explained by phonologists as an effect of *pharyngealization.

emphatic (2) Marking, or marking among other things, emphasis: thus '**emphatic stress**' (But I ´CAN'T *do it*), emphatic word order, and so on. An '**emphatic pronoun**' is a full form (e.g. *moi* 'I, me' in French) as opposed to a reduced or *clitic form (e.g. *je*).
    'Emphasis' and 'contrast' can in principle be distinguished but, since their realizations tend to be the same, *contrastive especially is often used for both.

'empirical linguistics' A polemical term used by some linguists who wish to argue that their approach to language deals with facts, or specific kinds of data, that others ignore. *Cf.* secular linguistics.

empirical principle Hjelmslev's term for a principle by which accounts of a language system should (*a*) be free of internal contradictions; (*b*) cover the relevant data exhaustively; (*c*) be as simple as possible. The subprinciples have priority in that order: i.e. self-consistency should not be sacrificed to exhaustiveness, nor either self-consistency or exhaustiveness to simplicity.

empiricism Any of a range of doctrines in philosophy which hold that knowledge is derived from sense experience. Traditionally opposed to *nativism.

empty 1. Having or described as having no meaning: e.g. a *dummy. **2.** Having no phonetic or other realization: thus especially an *empty category as posited by Chomsky and others.
    Confusion can be avoided if 'empty' is reserved for sense 1 and 'null' or 'zero' used consistently for sense 2.

'empty category' An element in Chomsky's *Principles and Parameters Theory which occupies a syntactic position but has no phonetic realization: *see* pro, PRO, trace. Seen as subject to a universal principle (the **Empty Category Principle** or **ECP**) resting on Chomsky's definition, in the early 1980s, of *government.
    Strictly an element rather than a category.

empty morph A *morph which does not directly realize a *morpheme (3). E.g. in *children* [tʃɪldrən], a morph [tʃɪld] realizes the morpheme 'child' and a morph [ən], as also in *oxen*, may be said to realize the morpheme 'plural'; the intervening [r] is then an empty morph which is not assigned specifically to either. *Cf.* empty (1).

'empty word' A word seen as 'empty' in that its meaning is *grammatical rather than *lexical. Hence = form word, function word, grammatical word.

enantiosemy A case of *polysemy in which one sense is in some respect the opposite of another. E.g. that of *dust* in *I dusted the mantelpiece*, meaning that something is removed, vs. *I dusted the cake with sugar*, meaning that something is added.

From Greek *enantio-* 'opposite': modelled by G. C. Lepschy on German 'Gegensinn'.

encapsulation The inclusion in the sense of word *a* of that of another word *b* with which *a* could potentially collocate. Usually of cases where the collocation would be pleonastic: e.g. *female wife*, where the sense of *wife* includes that of *female*.

For 'informationally encapsulated' *see* modular.

enclave variety Variety of a language spoken in an area cut off from others where it is spoken. *Cf.* speech island.

enclitic A *clitic attached phonologically to the word which precedes: e.g. Latin *-que* in *arma virumque* (lit. 'arms man-and') 'arms and the man'. *Cf.* proclitic.

'encoding' 1. Representation in the grammar or vocabulary of a language. E.g. English 'encodes' a difference between men and women, in distinguishing *man* and *woman* as lexical units. But it does not encode a difference between e.g. male and female sparrows. Common where what is said to be encoded would reflect the structure of society, or the personal relations among speakers in specific contexts of utterance. E.g. the distinction in French between *tu* and *vous* 'encodes' differences not 'encoded' by similar pronouns in English. **2.** A supposed mental process by which pre-existing thoughts would be encoded as sentences: opp. decoding. Also of any relation of *realization, whether or not in the belief that it is part of such a mental process.

'encyclopaedic knowledge' Knowledge of the world as distinguished from knowledge of the *language system. Thus in many accounts a word like *cat* might have a semantic *feature [+ mammal] or [+ viviparous]: to know that it has this feature and others that distinguish it from other units in the lexicon is to know its meaning in the language. But it would then be a matter of 'encyclopaedic knowledge' that the young of cats are born blind, that the period of gestation in the domestic cat is about 65 days, and so on.

endangered language Any for which there is evidence that it will or might cease to be spoken, soon or in the foreseeable future.

ending Informal term for any *suffix or combination of suffixes at the end of a word. *Cf.* termination.

endocentric Bloomfield's term for a construction in which at least one element is of the same syntactic class as the whole. E.g. that of *meat and fish*, whose role in larger constructions could be filled by either *meat* or *fish*, or of *raw meat*, where it could be filled by *meat*. Restricted, in some later definitions, to cases such as that of *raw meat*, where one element only will meet this criterion. Further extended, in accounts of or reflecting *X-bar syntax, to all *phrases (2), or units seen as having a *head (1), in general.

Opp. exocentric. Also used of compounds: e.g. *blackbird* is endocentric since, to put it in later terminology, it is a *hyponym of *bird*, while *blackcap* (another species of songbird) is not, since it is not a hyponym of *cap*.

endogenous 'Originating inside'. Hence of change whose origin lies within the community whose speech is changing; also e.g. of communication, or a form of communication, among and only among a specific group of people. Opp. exogenous.

endophora [ɛnˈdɒfərə] Sometimes used to subsume *anaphora and *cataphora, seen as relations within ('endo-') what is said or written, as opposed to *exophora.

-en form *See* past participle (2).

English West *Germanic. Old English ('Anglo-Saxon') is attested from the 7th century AD, with an extensive literature before the Norman conquest in the 11th century. After the conquest, Middle English was heavily influenced by French, most noticeably in large and central areas of vocabulary. A standard form, based mainly on eastern dialects spoken in London, developed increasingly from the end of the Middle Ages.

The expansion of English to other continents began in earnest in the 17th century, with the successful colonization of the eastern seaboard of North America. Subsequently spread by colonization both directly from Britain and from the USA and existing colonies, across North America, in Australia and New Zealand, in southern Africa, and elsewhere. Also promoted as a *second language throughout most of the British Empire and in countries similarly occupied by the USA; hence an official language in e.g. India or Nigeria. As a second language it has several regional varieties (Indian English, West African English, Singapore English, etc.); also dominant as an international language, increasingly in forms based on American English, since the mid-20th century.

English for Special Purposes Programme of teaching English for use in specific applications, e.g. in air traffic control.

entailment Relation between propositions one of which necessarily follows from the other: e.g. 'Mary is running' entails, among other things, 'Mary is not standing still'. *Cf.* implication.

Thence of propositions entailed by sentences: thus 'Mary is not standing still' is entailed by *Mary is running*. Distinguished from *implicatures, often similarly described as propositions implicated by sentences, in that entailments are not *defeasible: i.e. they cannot be overridden in a specific context.

environment A context within a word or sentence in which a change or process takes place. E.g. [n] → [m] 'in the environment'— [+ bilabial]: i.e. when a bilabial consonant, such as [b] or [p], follows.

epenthesis [ə'pɛnθəsɪs] Process or change in which successive sounds are separated by an intervening segment. E.g. the [b] of *thimble* developed between an adjacent [m] and [l]: cf. Old English þŷmel. Likewise of processes in morphology or morphophonology: e.g. [ɪ] in *horses* can be described as an **epenthetic vowel** inserted between [s] and [z] in underlying [hɔːs] + [z].

From the Greek for 'insertion'.

EPG = electropalatography, electropalatographic.

epicene ['ɛpɪsiːn] (Noun) used to refer to individuals of either sex. Traditionally of one whose grammatical gender is the same in either case: e.g. French (*la*) *grive* '(the-FEM) male or female thrush'. *Cf.* common gender.

epiglottal Articulated with or, more loosely, in the region of the epiglottis. The epiglottis is a flap of cartilage at the base of the throat whose function is to cover the larynx while swallowing.

epigraphy The study of inscriptions.

epiphenomenon A by-product or secondary phenomenon. Thus in accounts of syntax that became standard in the 1960s it is the individual rules that are primary; constructions, as they have usually been conceived, were by implication secondary or **epiphenomenal**.

episememe Bloomfield's term for the meaning of a construction or other grammatical pattern (in his terms a *tagmeme).

epistemic From a Greek word for 'knowledge, understanding'. Thus the 'epistemic status' of someone using a language might reflect the level of mastery they have of it.

Technically, in particular, of *modals indicating factual necessity, probability, possibility, etc. E.g. *must* is epistemic, or is used epistemically, in *He must surely be there by now*; likewise *may* in *It may have been lost*, or *might* in *The train might be late*. Opp. deontic as one of two major categories of *modality: *see also* alethic.

epistrophe Term in rhetoric for the repetition of a word at the end of successive clauses or sentences: e.g. 'This house is mine; this car is mine; you are mine'.

epithet Variously of an adjective conventionally used of someone or something; or a noun used derogatively: e.g. *heroic* in *our heroic firemen*, or *idiot* in *Some idiot set fire to it*.

From a Greek word for 'applied to': hence the ancient term for *adjectives, originally seen as a subclass of nouns.

eponym An individual name from which a common noun is derived: e.g. that of 'the eponymous' Lord Sandwich as the source for *sandwich*. **Eponymy** is the relation between them.

EPP = extended projection principle.

equals sign (=) Used e.g. to represent the relation of a *clitic to a unit to which it attaches. E.g., in Spanish, *los=veo* 'I can see them', where a masculine pronoun *los* '3PL' is attached as a proclitic to *veo* 'see-1SG'.

equational (Sentence, construction) by which one asserts that two referents are identical: e.g. *Jim's daughter is Harry's wife*, by which one asserts that the daughter of someone called Jim is the same person as the wife of someone called Harry. Thence of other sentences and constructions that are formally similar.

Also called 'equative'; *cf*. ascriptive.

equative 1. (Construction, inflection) by which two individuals etc. are equated with respect to some property: e.g. the *as . . . as* construction in *John is as clever as me*. **2.** (Case) marking a *predicative noun or noun phrase: e.g., schematically, *He is father*-EQUAT 'He is the father'. *Cf*. equational; *also* essive. **3.** = equational.

equilingual *See* bilingual.

equi NP deletion A syntactic operation in early *transformational grammars which deleted one of two identical noun phrases. Thus in most accounts in the 1960s and 1970s a sentence like *I asked Mary to come* was derived from an underlying *I asked Mary [Mary come]* with deletion of the second *Mary*.

Often abbreviated '**equi**': a verb such as *ask* was similarly an '**equi verb**' as opposed to a *raising verb. *Cf*. control; control verb.

equipollent Opposition between phonemes neither of which is *marked in relation to the other: e.g. between English [p] and [t]. Opp. privative (1).

equivalent Technically of e.g. grammars having the same *generative capacity.

equi verb *See* equi NP deletion.

equivocal = ambiguous: opp. univocal.

ERG = ergative (1).

ergative 1. *Case which identifies the *agent in a basic transitive construction when the *patient is *absolutive. The latter identifies the patient with the single argument or valent in an intransitive construction: e.g., schematically, intransitive *collapsed wall*-ABS 'The wall collapsed'; transitive *Bill built wall*-ABS 'Bill built the wall'. The ergative then distinguishes the agent: thus, more fully, *Bill*-ERG *built wall*-ABS. The same terms are extended to other constructions in which an agent is similarly distinguished, but by e.g. word order instead of case. **2.** Also used sporadically, from the early 1960s, of the relation between e.g. *We sank the ship*, where *the ship* is object, and *The ship sank*, where, though now the subject, its semantic relation to *sank* is similar. Hence, in some accounts, *sink* is an '**ergative verb**', as distinct from both a straightforward transitive and a straightforward intransitive.

Sense 2 seems to have arisen, partly at least, from a misunderstanding of sense 1. It could perhaps with benefit be avoided.

'ergative language' One which has an *ergative (1) vs. *absolutive case, or which distinguishes semantic roles, e.g. by word order, in an equivalent way. Languages either partly or wholly of this type are said to illustrate a phenomenon of '**ergativity**'. *Cf.* accusative language; active language.

'erosion' The progressive reduction of the phonetic forms of words by sound change. 'Eroded' words are often replaced: thus a classic study by Gilliéron showed how the forms derived from Latin *apis* 'bee', when reduced by sound changes in French to a monosyllable, were widely replaced by longer forms derived by suffixation (French *abeille* < diminutive *api-culu-s*) or by others.

erotetic [ɛrə'tiːtɪk] From the Greek word for 'to question'; e.g. an **erotetic logic** is a logic of questioning.

error analysis The analysis, for practical but also potentially for scientific ends, of errors made by students learning another language.

Erse = Irish *Gaelic.

Eskimo-Aleut Family of languages whose branches are Aleut, spoken by a minority in the Aleutian and neighbouring islands, and **Eskimo**, spoken over a large area from Greenland to Siberia. The main branches of Eskimo are Yupik, in south and south-west Alaska and across the Bering Strait, and *Inuit.

esophagus = oesophagus.

Esperanto Artificial language first promoted by L. L. Zamenhof in 1887, as a neutral *auxiliary language for people whose native languages were different. It combines elements of various European languages, but with a morphological structure designed to be clear and regular.

essive *Case indicating a state or mode of existence: e.g., schematically, *He cook*-ESS 'He is a cook'; *Cook*-ESS *he good* 'As a cook he is good'.

EST = Extended Standard Theory.

established (Form etc.) accepted as normal in a community. E.g. *courage* is an established word in English; *couragiousness*, though it follows the rules of word-formation and might well be used on occasion, is not.

Estonian Official language of, and spoken mainly in, Estonia. *Finno-Ugric, closely related to *Finnish.

'Estuary English' Coined in the 1980s for a variety perceived as 'classless' and originally typical of the lower Thames valley. Characterized by phonetic features variously shared with, or intermediate between, *Received Pronunciation and the residual urban dialect of London.

état de langue A stage in the history of a language, considered in abstraction from anything earlier or later. From Saussure: also, in translation, 'language state' or 'state of a language'.

ethic (*Dative) used in referring to someone with an interest in or indirectly affected by an action etc. Also '**ethical**': *cf.* dative of advantage.

ethno- From the Greek word for a people or nation. Thus **ethnolinguistics** can have the sense of *anthropological linguistics; **ethnobotany** is concerned with the ways in which specific societies name and classify plants, **ethnopoetics** with their literature, and so on.

ethnography of speaking Term introduced by D. H. Hymes in the early 1960s for the study of the uses and patterns of speaking in a society, as distinct from an account of the *language system. Thus in some communities ritual utterances are a central feature of ceremonial; in others they are not. In some, close friends will tend to greet each other with formal insults; in some, verbosity in speech is appreciated; in some, requests will tend to be made directly rather than indirectly; and so on. The domain of the ethnography of speaking covered features such as these which were seen as falling between the usual scope of linguistics, and that of ethnography in general.
  Cf. communicative competence.

ethnolect Variety of a language spoken by a so-called 'ethnic group'.

'ethnolinguistic vitality' Cover term for various factors, objective
and subjective, seen as determining the ability of a community to
maintain its identity and form of speech in the face of possibly
contrary pressures. These include its size, its perceived status in a
larger society, and so on.

ethnomethodology Movement in sociology that sought to study
social interaction in terms of categories etc. empirically valid for
members of a society, not assumed a priori. Relevant to linguistics as
the source, in the early 1970s, of *Conversation Analysis.

ethology Branch of science concerned with animal behaviour: hence
with, among other things, modes of communication in species other
than man.

etic Not *emic. Thus for Pike an etic account of the sounds of
language would describe them impressionistically as sounds (i.e. as
'phon-etic' units) in advance of an analysis assigning them to
phonemic (i.e. '-emic') units.

Etruscan Ancient language in an area of Italy to the north of Rome,
attested by inscriptions from around 700 BC, until extinguished
by Latin. Not genetically related to any language any better
documented; hence only partly and insecurely understood. Written
in an alphabet derived from that of Greek and itself one source of the
Roman.

'etymological fallacy' The notion that the 'true' meaning of a
word is the one to be expected from its *etymology. E.g. *literature* is
from the word in Latin for a letter of the alphabet (*litera*): therefore, a
pedant might argue, it is incorrect to apply it to compositions
transmitted orally and not written.

etymology The study of the historical relation between a word and
the earlier form or forms from which it has, or has hypothetically,
developed. Thus the etymology of *sheep* relates it, with German *Schaf*
and others, to a reconstructed Common Germanic *skǣpa; that of *street*
relates it, through Old English *strǣt*, to a borrowing into Germanic of
Latin *(via) strata* 'paved road'.
  Loosely described as a study of the 'origins of words'; but if this
expression is taken too literally it can be misleading.

etymon A form at an earlier stage of history or prehistory from
which one or more later forms are derived. E.g. a root *g^wo- is
reconstructed as the Indo-European etymon of English *cow*, French
boeuf 'ox', etc. These are in turn its *reflexes.

euphemism Word etc. used in place of one avoided as e.g. offensive,
indecent, or alarming. E.g. a word for 'girl' used of prostitutes in place
of the specific word for 'prostitute'.

euphony Literally the property of 'sounding well'. But commonly at one time of a principle equivalent to that of 'ease of articulation': thus it was for reasons of 'euphony' that one consonant undergoes *assimilation to another, or that successive syllables are matched in *vowel harmony.

'eurhythmy' Maximal conformity to the rhythmical pattern normal in a given language: defined in *Metrical Phonology in terms of an ideal 'metrical grid' to be approximated as far as possible.

European structuralism *Structural linguistics as developed especially in continental Europe. *Baudouin de Courtenay was an important pioneer, followed in the early 20th century by *Saussure. In the 1920s and 1930s their ideas were developed especially by members of the *Prague School, notably *Trubetzkoy and *Jakobson; from the late 1930s by *Hjelmslev and *Martinet among others; also, though his basic assumptions were in part different, by *Firth. Among later scholars, *Coseriu and, from the 1960s, *Lyons are among those whose ideas, despite many differences, stand clearly in the structuralist tradition.

'Structuralism' in literary studies developed especially in France in the 1960s, inspired largely by readings or misreadings of Saussure.

evaluation procedure A mechanical procedure for comparing two *generative grammars, of the same format and generating the same language, to determine, e.g. by a measure of simplicity, which is the better. Proposed by Chomsky in the 1950s, as a goal for linguistic theory weaker than that of a *discovery procedure.

An **evaluation measure** is a metric employed in such a procedure.

evaluative Indicating a speaker's attitude to some real or potential event etc. Thus an evaluative particle might indicate e.g. surprise: schematically, *He* SURPRISE *didn't* 'Amazingly he didn't'. Likewise the sentence *Why on earth put it in the dustbin?* is likely to be said not as a question which invites an answer, but as an evaluative utterance commenting on what someone has done or proposes to do.

eventive Referring to an event as opposed to a state: e.g. *fell* is eventive in *I fell over*. Opp. stative.

evidential (Particle, inflection) which is one of a set that make clear the source or reliability of the evidence on which a statement is based. Thus a given language might obligatorily distinguish statements based on direct observation from ones based e.g. on inference (*cf.* inferential), or on what someone else has told the speaker (*cf.* quotative), or e.g. on guesswork.

evitative (case) = aversive.

evolution Used both in the biologist's sense and of the development over time of individual languages. Thus 'the evolution of language' refers in one sense to the issue of, as it is traditionally called, 'the origin of language'. In another it refers to the history of languages, without any implication that the principles of evolution, as biologists understand them, will apply.

Ewe Language assigned to the *Kwa family, spoken in south-east Ghana and the south of Togo.

exaptation Introduced by R. Lass in the early 1990s for the development, in the history of a language, of a new semantic role for differences of form that have lost whatever role they may have had earlier. Suppose, e.g. that the distinction of gender is lost in French: *le mur* 'the wall': also '*le*' (now *la*) *maison* 'the house'. Accompanying variations in the forms of adjectives (*grand/grande* 'big') would then have no rationale; but, by a process of exaptation, they might develop a new one, e.g. in distinguishing attributive adjectives ('*le maison grand*' instead of present *la maison grande*) from predicative ('*le maison est grande*' instead of present *la maison est grande*).

exception A form etc. that does not follow a rule applying generally to those of its class: e.g. past tense forms in English generally end in *-ed*: *wait-ed*, *talk-ed*, etc. Forms such as *ran* or *broke*, or *run* and *break* as lexical units, are therefore exceptions to this.

   Cf. regular. As there are degrees of regularity so, conversely, a form may be an exception to a more general rule which covers forms that are themselves exceptions to one still more general.

'exceptional case marking' That of e.g. *her* in *I believe her to be right*. Its form is that of the object in e.g. *I believe her*; therefore, in many accounts, it too is an object. But in that of e.g. *Government and Binding Theory it is not. Instead it is the subject of a subordinate clause (*I believe [her to be right]*); therefore its case marking (realized by *her* instead of *she*) is 'exceptional'.

exclamation *See* exclamative.

exclamation mark (!) Used, in citing an example, to indicate that although it is grammatical, it is not so in the sense that is relevant. E.g. in a discussion of idioms one might write !*The fat was being chewed by the committee for three hours*, meaning that, although a passive is possible in the literal sense, in the sense of the idiom 'chew the fat' it is not.

exclamative (Construction etc.) characteristic of exclamations, as opposed to questions, statements, requests, etc. E.g. in *How wonderful that would be!* or *What a filthy mess!*

   An 'exclamative' sentence can in principle be distinguished from an 'exclamation', defined as a speech act, as an *interrogative can be distinguished from a question, a *declarative (1) from a statement, and so on.

exclusive (First person) specifically excluding reference to an addressee. *See* inclusive.

excrescent Older term used of a consonant etc. historically added to a word. E.g. *-d* is excrescent in *sound* 'noise', which had no *-d* (as in French *son*) before the 15th century.

exhaustive conditional Huddleston and Pullum's term, in *CGEL, for a *conditional clause that covers every possibility: e.g. the clause introduced by *whether* in *I'll do it whether you like it or not*.

exhaustiveness Property of a description, grammar, etc. that covers all the relevant data: *cf.* empirical principle. The crux, of course, lies in the criteria for relevance.

exhortative (Particle etc.) used in enjoining or encouraging an action by a group that includes the speaker: e.g. *let* or *let's* in *Let's go*.

existential (Sentence, construction) indicating what does or does not exist: e.g. the construction with *there* in *There's a wasp in your hair*, *There are no white crocodiles*.

existential quantifier (∃) Operator in logic used in expressions interpreted as asserting existence. E.g. $(\exists x)((boy\,(x))\,\&\,(dance\,(x)))$ 'There exists some x such that x is a boy and x dances': i.e. 'At least one boy dances'.

exocentric Bloomfield's term for a construction in which no element is of the same syntactic class as the whole: e.g. those of *in Washington* or *wrote books*.
  Opp. endocentric. Also used of compounds: e.g. *pickpocket* and *hardback* are exocentric compounds since, to put it in later terms, they are not *hyponyms of either *pick* or *pocket*, or either *hard* or *back*.

exogenous 'Originating outside'; thus of change whose origin lies outside a community under investigation. Opp. endogenous.
  Also, by mechanical substitution of 'exo-' for 'endo-', of communication or forms of communication between members of a community and others outside it.

exophora [ɛk'sɒfərə] The interpretation of a pronoun etc. when it is supplied from 'outside' ('exo-') what is immediately said or written: e.g. of *she* in `SHE*'s coming*, uttered by a speaker who points to the 'she' in question, or for a hearer who can guess who is meant. Opp. anaphora; *also* endophora.

'expanded pidgin' A *pidgin whose form has in time become less simplified but which is still not judged to meet, or to meet sufficiently, the definition of a *creole. Also called an '**extended pidgin**'; *Tok Pisin is one case sometimes so described.

expansion In its ordinary sense: e.g. the 'expansion of English' in the last few centuries. Also specifically, in American structural linguistics, of an operation designed to establish that shorter and longer sequences of words belong to the same class. E.g., in *She came*, *she* can be replaced by the 'expanded' forms *a man*, *the people next door*, *the book which I ordered*, and so on. Accordingly all these are classed as, in the usual term, noun phrases.

experiencer The semantic role of e.g. *I* in *I felt cold* or *Jane* in *Jane saw it*. Seen as one of a set of universal 'cases' or case roles in e.g. *Case Grammar.

experimental psycholinguistics *See* psycholinguistics.

expiratory In or for breathing out. E.g. 'expiratory pressure' is pressure of air being breathed out.

explanatory adequacy *See* levels of adequacy.

expletive From a Latin verb meaning 'to fill out'. Hence e.g. of *dummies or 'prop-words': thus *it* is expletive in *It's obvious that he will*.
   Also, as in ordinary use, of swear words seen as padding which add nothing to the sense. Thence of swear words generally, and of *minor sentences (*Damn and blast!*, *Bugger it!*) that contain them. *Cf.* imprecative.

explicature *'What is said' by a specific utterance in a specific context in which it is uttered, conceived in *Relevance Theory as 'developed from' a *semantic representation in a grammar, as an 'explicit' meaning distinct from whatever may be implicated. Suppose, e.g., that someone says *She's driving too fast and she'll be stopped*. What might be meant specifically is that the person *she* refers to is driving a vehicle at a speed above the legal limit; and in consequence is likely to be stopped by the police. This goes beyond a possible representation in a grammar, which might be 'developed' differently in other contexts. But as an 'explicature' it remains distinct from possible *implicatures: e.g. that the driver is unlikely to make an appointment she is trying to get to.

explicit performative *See* performative.

exponence Any relation between a linguistic unit, structure, etc. and its realization in speech. E.g. the exponents of *stress, as a phonological unit, might be variously the lengthening of a syllable, a difference in vowel quality, a significant pitch movement, and so on. Hence of any relation of *realization by which this is mediated; e.g. in morphology, an affix such as *-en* in *taken* is an exponent of a feature or unit 'past participle'.

expression 1. Any form of words which constitutes a unit of meaning. Rarely an explicit technical term, but *cf.* referring expression; *also* e.g. fixed expression. **2.** Level in *Hjelmslev's theory whose *substance is that of sounds or their equivalent as opposed to that of meaning. Defined formally by its opposition to that of *content.

expressive **1.** Type of *speech act seen as giving expression to a psychological state of the speaker: e.g. an apology, or an expression of thanks or congratulation. **2.** (Meaning, *function of language) having to do with the state of mind of the speaker. *Cf.* affective; emotive; interjection.

extended exponence The realization of a single morphological category in two or more different parts of a word. E.g. in *swollen* the past participle is realized by both a suffix (-*en*) and the vowel [əʊ] in *swoll-*.

'extended pidgin' *See* expanded pidgin.

'extended projection principle' A principle in *Government and Binding Theory, whose substance is that all sentences must have a subject, seen as supplementing the *projection principle.

'Extended Standard Theory' Version of *transformational grammar current in the mid-1970s, distinguished from a preceding *Standard Theory mainly in that *semantic representations of sentences, insofar as they belonged to an account of grammar, were determined either wholly or in part by *surface structures rather than by *deep structures.

extension **1.** In the ordinary sense. Thus **analogical extension** is an extension in the range of words formed in a particular way, seen as by *analogy with those already so formed. '**Extension of meaning**' is the development of a new sense of a lexical unit: thus, in particular, a **figurative extension** which involves a *metaphor or other *figure of speech. It is also used of the widening of an existing sense: *cf.* widening of meaning. **2.** Philosophers' term for the range of individuals etc. to which e.g. a term applies: e.g. the extension of *computer* is the set of all computers. Hence, in particular, an **extensional definition** of a class or set is a specification one by one of its members. Opp., in this sense, intension, intensional.

'extensive' (Verb, complementation) that is not *intensive.

external (1) Not belonging to, or not conceived as directly relevant to, a *language system. Hence the *external history of a language deals with everything except the way its system changes; '**external causes**' of change are factors, such as the influence of another language, seen as lying outside the system of a language whose changes are the object of study; '**external evidence**', e.g. of *psychological reality, is evidence other than that on which an account of a language system is explicitly based.

external (2) Outside or in addition to a syntactic unit. E.g. of a subject seen as an '**external argument**' or '**external complement**': i.e. one outside the *predicate (1) or *verb phrase.

external history The history of a language as the means of communication in a community, as opposed to the *internal history of a language system. E.g. it is part of the external history of English that it was brought to Britain by immigration in the Dark Ages, that it came to be written in a version of the Roman alphabet, that many people spoke both English and French in the Middle Ages, that it was spread to North America in the 17th century, and so on.

'externalized language' = E-language.

external sandhi Processes of phonological modification (*sandhi) that take place at or across word boundaries. Thus, by one common process of external sandhi in English, an initial [s] in words like *steak* is assimilated to an [ʃ] in e.g. *fish steak*.

extraction Any syntactic process by which something is moved from within a clause or other unit to a position outside it. E.g. in *You said* [*who was there*], *who* is an element within the subordinate clause; in *Who did you say* [*was there*]?, it is seen as extracted from that position to become an element in the main clause.

extrametrical (Syllable etc.) seen, originally in *Metrical Phonology, as irrelevant to the definition of a metrical structure. E.g. in Latin, the position of the accent depended on the quantity or weight of the next to last syllable in a word. But that of the final syllable did not matter: therefore, in establishing the structure to which the rule of accentuation applied, the final syllable is 'extrametrical'.

extraposition Construction of e.g. *It's wonderful* [*to see you*], *It amazes me* [*that you have done it so fast*], *It was odd* [*meeting her in New York*]. By implication, the unit enclosed in brackets is 'extraposed' from a formally basic, though often in practice far less usual, position at the beginning: [*To see you*] *is wonderful*, and so on.

   Also of constructions in which an element is detached e.g. from a head noun. Thus the relative clause *who wanted to see you* would be 'extraposed', in some accounts, in *The man is here who wanted to see you*.

extrinsic allophone One which is not *intrinsic.

extrinsic ordering *See* ordered rules.

'eye dialect' Conventional misspellings of words, as e.g. <wuz> for [wəz], intended to suggest non-standard accents.

F

F₀ F_0 = fundamental frequency.

F₁, F₂ F_1, F_2 *See* formant (1).

'face' Developed as a technical term in explaining ways of being polite. If one is ordered about by other people one will, in the ordinary sense, 'lose face': one's self-respect and freedom of action will be diminished. Hence a tendency for people not to give direct orders; instead a request will be put in the form of a question ('Could you come and hold this?'), making clear its slightness and that it is just a request ('Could you perhaps come and hold this for a second?'), and so on. In an account by P. Brown and S. C. Levinson in the late 1970s, face is defined as a basic 'want' of individuals, and analysed into **negative face** (the want that one's freedom of action should not be impeded by others) and **positive face** (the want that one's own wants should be desirable to others also). The basic strategy of politeness is to minimize the threat to an addressee's 'negative face' and enhance their 'positive face' as much as possible.

Hence '**face-threatening act**' (abbreviated **FTA**), of any act of communication which by its nature impinges on the face of someone to whom it is addressed.

factitive (Verb) denoting an action or process that leads to a result. E.g. *kill* or *make*: to kill someone or something is to produce the result that they are dead; to make something or to make someone happy has the result that the thing exists or the person is happy.

factive (Verb etc.) whose use commits a speaker to the truth of a subordinate proposition. E.g. *know* or *realize*: to say *She doesn't know* (or *She hasn't realized*) *that it has stopped raining* is to commit oneself to the truth of 'It has stopped raining'. *Think*, by contrast, is **non-factive**: one makes no such commitment if one says *She thinks it has stopped raining*.

facultative Optional.

'fading' (of meaning) = bleaching.

Faeroese North *Germanic, spoken in the Faeroe Islands in the north Atlantic.

falling **1.** (Diphthong) of which the first part or element is the more prominent: e.g. [ɔɪ] in *boy* as opposed to [jɔː] or [ɪɔː] in *your*. **2.** (*Tone, intonation) in which the pitch falls from relatively high to relatively low. Opp. rising in both senses.

fall–rise Intonational contour in which a fall and following rise are associated with a single position of prominence: e.g. in southern British English, in questions such as *When will dinner be* ˅REAdy?

'false friend' A word in one language which sounds like one in another and may be taken by mistake as having the same meaning. E.g. English *cold* and German *kalt* mean 'cold'; therefore one misunderstands Italian or Spanish *caldo* 'hot' as also meaning 'cold'.

falsetto *Voice quality in which voiced sounds are produced with the vocal cords stretched and therefore thinner. Hence with a higher range of *fundamental frequency, perceived as a higher pitch range.

familiar form Pronoun, form of verb, etc. used in addressing, among others, close friends: e.g. German *du* or French *tu* (familiar second-person singular) as opposed to *Sie* or *vous*. *Cf.* polite form; such oppositions are also described, from the forms in French, as holding between 'T' and 'V' forms.

family A group of languages that have developed from a single ancestor: e.g. *Indo-European, of which English is one of many members.
   Cf. branch; phylum; stock. Some linguists have tried to apply such terms to different levels in a hierarchy, on the analogy of 'genus', 'order', etc. in biology. E.g. Indo-European is a 'family'; any groups above it would be variously or successively 'superfamilies', 'macrofamilies', 'stocks', 'superstocks', or 'phyla'; those below it will be 'subfamilies', in turn divided into 'branches', 'groups', etc. But such distinctions are not established consistently, and generally imply more than we do or can know. A safer alternative is to speak of a family whenever a common origin can be accepted as certain (thus Indo-European or e.g. *Austronesian), and of branches, larger or smaller, within it (e.g. *Indo-Iranian and, within that, *Iranian). When a common origin is speculative or less firmly supported, one may simply talk of a 'conjectural family' (e.g. *Nostratic), a 'proposed family' (e.g. *Austro-Asiatic), or a 'probable family'.

'family resemblance' Wittgenstein's description of the links between different uses of a word. E.g. *point* may be used of the tip of a dagger or a needle, of a point of land sticking into the sea, of a mark on paper made by a point, of a point on a scale, and so on. There is no single property that these and only these have in common, but there are similarities, as among people in a family, that link each of them to the others.
   Taken up by linguists especially in the 1980s; often associated, and occasionally confused, with ideas in *prototype theory.

'family tree' *See* genetic classification; Stammbaum model.

Fanagalo *See* Zulu.

Farsi *See* Persian.

favourite sentence-forms Bloomfield's term for the sentence constructions predominant in a given language: e.g. in English, the constructions of subject and predicate, or of imperatives without subjects. Opposed at the other extreme to those of *minor sentences such as *Ouch!* or *Thank you*.

feature Any property of or assigned to a unit. Originally in phonology, where often restricted to *distinctive features. Thus [iː] in *beat* is phonetically and phonologically a front vowel: that is, it has the feature 'front'. Thence to other types of unit: e.g. in a *componential analysis of word meaning, *woman* has the features 'adult' and 'female': that is, it denotes people who are both adult and female.

Often formulated as a variable. Thus [front] or [± front] represents a variable feature with the values [+ front] (front) and [− front] (not front; i.e. back). Units themselves are often described as **bundles** of features: thus the vowel in *beat* would be constituted as a phonological unit precisely by the bundle of features which distinguish it from others: 'vocalic' (or [+ vocalic]), 'front' (or [+ front]), and so on.

feature matrix A two-dimensional display of the phonetic features characterizing each of a sequence of phonological segments. In the illustration, the features on the left are those proposed by *Jakobson in the 1950s: each has two values, the positive (e.g. vocalic or [+ vocalic]) first, the negative second. In the table the value of each is shown, where applicable, for each of the successive units of *pin*. Thus, in the first column, [p] has a negative value for the feature 'vocalic/non-vocalic' and a positive value for 'consonantal/non-consonantal'; these values are those of every consonant in English except [r] and [l]. In the third row, [p] has the negative value 'diffuse' for the feature 'compact/diffuse', and so on. Where the distinction does not apply the space is blank.

A **distinctive feature matrix** (or **DF-matrix**) is strictly one, like this, displaying *distinctive features only.

	p	i	n
vocalic/non-vocalic	−	+	−
consonantal/non-consonantal	+	−	+
compact/diffuse	−	−	−
grave/acute	+	−	−
nasal/oral	−		+
tense/lax	+		
continuant/interrupted	−		

A feature matrix

feature spreading Term in *Autosegmental Phonology for the extension of a feature, e.g. of tone, to an adjacent element not already associated with such a feature.

feeding The relation between rules which are *ordered in such a way that the application of the earlier rule enlarges the set of forms that the later will apply to. Especially in *Generative Phonology: e.g. a rule by which a front vowel is inserted between two consonants might feed a later rule by which velars are palatalized before a front vowel.

Opp. bleeding; *cf.* counter-feeding, counter-bleeding.

felicity conditions The conditions that a *performative must meet if it is to be appropriate or successful. E.g. the performative 'I pronounce you man and wife' will be effective in marrying people only under the conditions that the person uttering it is qualified to solemnize marriages, that it forms part of a marriage ceremony, that the couple have agreed to marry, and so on.

Introduced by Austin on the model of *truth conditions: elaborated by J. R. Searle for *speech acts generally.

feminine (FEM) *Gender (1) of words characterized as a class by nouns denoting females. Thus French *femme* 'woman' is a feminine noun; in *la femme* 'the woman' *la* 'the-FEM' is the feminine form of the article; in English, by extension, *she* is a feminine pronoun.

field Generally of a network of *paradigmatic relations that units of a language enter into, or of a conceptual or other area that such a network covers. Hence especially of *semantic fields: also e.g. in the distinction by *Pike between a field view of language and a 'particle' or a 'wave' view.

figurative (Sense, use) which is an extension of a basic or literal meaning. E.g. *blossom* has a **figurative sense**, or is used **figuratively**, in *She is really blossoming*, the basic sense being of plants rather than people.

From the traditional concept of *figures of speech. 'Figurative language' refers similarly to a style employing 'figures'.

figure of speech Ancient term for any form of expression in which the normal use of language is manipulated, stretched, or altered for rhetorical effect. E.g. in *metaphor, a word which is normally used with reference to one domain is extended to another; in a figure such as *chiasmus, words are placed in a deliberately striking order.

Many individual figures, such as these, are distinguished in traditional western rhetoric. Some, like metaphor, have been taken over directly into linguistics, e.g. in typologies of semantic change.

Fijian *Austronesian, of the *Polynesian branch; spoken by the indigenous people of Fiji.

'filled pause' A period in which a speaker is uttering a *hesitation form (English [əː], [əmm], etc.).

filler Any unit or class of units seen as occupying a *slot in a construction or similar structure: e.g. *it* fills the object slot (i.e. it has the role or function of object) in *I cooked it*, and is one of a class of pronouns (*her*, *them*, etc.) that is in general one of its fillers.

filter A rule, principle, etc. formulated as an output condition on a grammar or on one component of a grammar. Filters may be very specific (e.g. the proposed **that-*trace filter) or very general. Thus a sentence such as *Mary loves themselves* could be 'filtered out', at whatever level of representation it might otherwise be possible, by a universal principle requiring that an **anaphor, such as *themselves,* must be **bound (2) by an antecedent.

In one account a **lexicon acts as a filter e.g. on productive rules of derivational morphology. Thus a rule might derive both *rationality* from *rational* and, say, *reasonability* from *reasonable*. But *rationality* has an entry in the lexicon and thus passes through the filter. *Reasonability* does not and is excluded.

final 1. In the ordinary sense: e.g. in Portuguese, vowels are lost or reduced in final unstressed syllables. **2.** = purposive. Thus, in Latin grammar, a **final clause** is one translatable by 'in order to': i.e. one which indicates a purpose or 'end' (Latin *finis*).

fingerspelling Representation of written words by hand gestures corresponding to successive letters.

finite clause A clause one of whose elements is a **finite verb: e.g. the subordinate clause in *Accept that it has broken*, as opposed e.g. to the construction with an **infinitive in *Expect it to break*. *Cf.* tensed.

finite state grammar A form of grammar in which sentences are characterized by the transitions of an automaton from one state to another. E.g. for *The man left*, the machine is first in an initial state; in changing to a second state it writes *the*; in changing to a third it writes *man*; in changing to a fourth it writes *left*. A grammar will therefore specify all the sequences of states that the automaton may successively be in, and what word must be written in each transition from each state in a specific sequence to the next. It follows that what can be written at each stage depends solely on the state the automaton is in at that point and the transitions that are possible from it.

Formulated by Chomsky in the 1950s in order to make clear its inadequacy.

finite state Markov process = finite state grammar.

finite verb Traditionally a verb, e.g. in Latin or Greek, inflected for **person and **number. Now more generally of any verb whose form is such that it can stand in a simple declarative sentence: e.g. Latin *veni* ('came-1SG') 'I came'; English *came* in *I came* or *was (standing)* as in *He was standing*. Opp. non-finite, infinitive; *cf.* tensed.

Finnic *See* Finno-Ugric.

Finnish *Finno-Ugric, spoken largely in Finland. The standard language is based mainly on the dialect of the extreme south-west, attested in writing from the early 16th century.

Finno-Ugric Family of languages, generally subsumed with *Samoyedic under Uralic. Traditionally divided into **Ugric**, of which the main representative is *Hungarian, and Finno-Permic: this in turn includes **Finnic** (*Finnish, Estonian, and others in the Baltic region), *Sami (Lappish), Permic (in the region of the Urals), and others in the former Soviet Union.

The term is also used of Uralic as a whole.

'First Grammarian' The anonymous author of the 'First Grammatical Treatise' of Old *Icelandic.

first language The language someone acquires first. Often, therefore, in a sense equivalent to *native language; also of the language mainly used by an individual or a community. *Cf.* second language.

first person (1st, 1) *See* person. For first-person inclusive vs. exclusive *see* inclusive, exclusive.

'First Sound Shift' *See* Grimm's Law.

Firth, John Rupert (1890–1960) From 1944 the first professor of general linguistics in Britain. Distinguished from other theorists of his generation by his insistence that language should be studied as part of a social process. A linguist's data were for him events embedded in specific contexts, and linguistics in general was concerned with the techniques by which they are handled across a spectrum of varying levels of abstraction. Hence, in particular, an emphasis on context at all points, and a profound disagreement with the prevailing view of Saussure and his followers, in which the object of study was an integrated *language system seen as a reality underlying speech.

*Prosodic Phonology was developed by Firth and others from the late 1940s, and reflects the *polysystemic principle, already adopted in the 1930s, by which systems of contrasting elements are established at specific points, within a contextual framework at an appropriate level of abstraction, and not, again, as part of a single overall system independent of the data.

fixed (1) (Accent) whose position is determined by a phonological rule. E.g. Latin had a fixed stress accent, whose position in a word was determined by its syllabic structure. Opp. free (3).

fixed (2) (Order of elements) wholly or largely determined by rules, e.g. that of subject and verb in English: *Jane arrived*, not *Arrived Jane*. Opp. free (4).

A language with '**fixed word order**' is one in which the order both of phrases and of words within phrases is fixed in this sense.

fixed expression Any expression which offers a ready-made way of saying something. E.g. 'nurse back to health' in *He nursed her back to health*: cf. *nursed her into health*, *nursed her out of illness*, or *helped her back to health*, which are not ready-made and which one is much less likely to say.

   Distinctions between 'fixed' or 'set' expressions, *frozen expressions, *idioms, *formulae, etc. are at best variably and hazily drawn.

flap Consonant in which one *articulator strikes the other with a sliding motion: e.g. the *r* of Spanish *pero* [peɾo]. Distinguishable at least in principle from a *tap, in which there is no sliding motion.

flat *Distinctive feature in the scheme proposed by *Jakobson. *Retroflex and *pharyngealized consonants, in particular, are flat; dentals or alveolars with which these contrast are non-flat or *plain.

'flat structure' One represented by a *phrase structure tree with few *branching nodes. Languages said to have 'flat structures' are effectively those called *non-configurational languages.

flectional = inflecting.

Flemish *Dutch spoken in Belgium.

floating quantifier A *quantifier (2) detached from a noun phrase by *quantifier floating.

floating tone A *tone in a tone language which is not associated, at an underlying level of representation, with a syllable or other segment. Posited, especially in some African languages, to explain an effect on neighbouring tones: e.g. in a form with two syllables (σ σ), a pattern of high tone plus falling tone (ó ô) might derive from an underlying pattern of high plus floating high plus low (ó ´ ò).

'floor' Metaphorically in *Conversation Analysis and studies of conversation generally, of an arena in which interaction among speakers is conceived as taking place. Hence '**floor apportionment**', of the division of time, in accordance with a hypothetical 'turn-taking system', among different speakers. Likewise '**yielding the floor**' or '**holding the floor**', respectively for being replaced by another speaker and for continuing to speak.

flout Technically, in pragmatics, of the conscious non-observance of a *maxim of conversation. E.g. A might ask B *How much did you pay for your house?* B replies *What a beautiful tie you are wearing*. In this way B flouts a maxim by which contributions to an interchange should be relevant; but the failure to observe it indicates to A that the question is not one that is going to be answered.

   *Conversational implicatures can thus be distinguished as reflecting a speaker's flouting or observance of a maxim.

focal area An area within a geographical region from which changes in language tend to spread, in accordance with a *wave model, to peripheral areas. Often, therefore, including a capital city such as Paris or London.

focus An element or part of a sentence given prominence by intonational or other means. Usually where there is contrast or emphasis, or a distinction of new vs. *given: e.g. *certainly* in *I ´CERtainly can* or *can* in *I certainly ´CAN*; *was* in the *pseudo-cleft *It `WAS me who did it*, or *me* in *It was `ME who did it*. Other means include, in particular, *clitics or other *particles marking focused elements.

Alternatively in a sense like that of *comment. *See also* focusing.

focused (Speech community) whose membership is transparently determined, e.g. by acceptance of a common standard language. Opp. diffuse (1).

focused interrogative An *interrogative in which questioning is focused on a specific element in the construction. E.g. in *Who is coming?* it is focused on the subject (*who*), in *Whose coat is this?* on a possessive modifier (*whose*), in *How did they do it?* on an adverbial, and so on.

Also called a *wh-interrogative or *open interrogative. Opp. e.g. polar interrogative.

focusing (Adverb, modifier) whose *scope varies. E.g. in *He only visited Mary*, the scope of *only* might be either *Mary* ('Mary was the only person he visited'), or *visited Mary* ('The only thing he did was visit Mary'), or just *visited* (*He only `VIsited Mary*). An adverb or adverbial such as this is called by Quirk *et al.*, *CGE*, a focusing *subjunct.

Hence '**focus**' of the scope distinguished.

folk etymology = popular etymology.

folk taxonomy A taxonomy implicit in the *sense relations between lexical units, as opposed to one developed for scientific purposes. Thus a tomato is, in scientific terms, a fruit. But in the lexicon of English the word *tomato* is a *hyponym not of *fruit* but of *vegetable*: this implies a folk taxonomy which, in that respect at least, is different.

foot A rhythmical unit in speech consisting of one or more syllables grouped together e.g. with respect to their stress pattern. Thus a foot in English is often defined as a stressed syllable plus any following unstressed syllables that intervene before the next stress. Alternatively, if the boundaries of feet can be defined independently, the patterns of stress may be seen as in part determined by them. An important unit, accordingly, in some versions of *Metrical Phonology.

Originally of a rhythmical unit in verse whose type was defined in Ancient Greek or Latin by a pattern of *heavy and *light (traditionally 'long' and 'short') syllables. But the divisions conventionally made in English verse do not coincide with those of the phonological unit. E.g.

the first line of *Paradise Lost* traditionally has five feet each in principle of two syllables. But in a natural reading four syllables might be stressed, and the divisions between phonological feet would, by the definition given, be: *Of* | MAN's | FIRST *diso* | BE*dience and the* | FRUIT.

'footing' The stance or status of an individual in a specific interaction with another or others. E.g. A would have one footing in relation to B when interviewed by B on television, but the footing of each would change if they happen to chat in the studio afterwards.

'foregrounded' The opposite of *backgrounded.

'foreigner talk' Simplified or supposedly simplified forms used by speakers of a language to foreigners presumed to have a poor understanding of it: e.g. *No put there* as a simplification of *Don't put it there*. Historically an important factor in the development of *pidgins.

forensic linguistics Any application of linguistics, phonetics included, in a criminal investigation or judicial process.

form 1. A realization of a combination of units in a language: e.g. *Come away* is as a whole a form, which includes a form *away*, which in turn includes a form *a-*. **2.** A structure of relations among linguistic units, considered in abstraction, as especially in the account of *Hjelmslev, from any corresponding *substance.

formal 1. Based on form rather than meaning. Thus a formal definition of a word class might refer to the *distributions of its members, while a semantic or *notional definition might refer to a type of process, entity, etc. that they denote. **2.** Developed as a mathematical system. Thus a **formal grammar** is a set of rules that precisely specifies a set e.g. of *strings formed by an operation of *concatenation; a **formal language** is a set so specified.

The earliest *generative grammars were formal in both senses. By extension from the second, the term has often been used to mean no more than 'explicit', 'cast in quasi-mathematical notation', etc.

formal / informal style Defined by a relation between aspects of the forms and structures employed and a range of contexts or situations in which they are appropriate. E.g. in the formal style of a scholarly paper or legal document, words will be longer and constructions will be more complex and without *ellipsis: in a casual conversation, the opposite. A broad distinction of degree: details are best referred to the descriptions of specific *registers (1).

*Polite forms or *honorifics are described as 'formal' in a similar sense.

formalization An account or formulation that is *formal (2): especially, in linguistics, of a model of grammar or some part of grammar.

formal semantics Branch of philosophy concerned with the assigning of precise interpretations to expressions in artificial systems of mathematics or logic. Thus especially, in the philosophy of science in the mid-20th century, in accounts of scientific theories, conceived as calculi interpreted with respect to some empirical domain. Thence, in linguistics, of a similar interpretation of languages, on the assumption, due originally to *Montague Grammar in particular, that it is illuminating to represent them, at a sufficient level of abstraction from the phenomena of speech, as systems of the same kind.

formal universal Chomsky's term in the mid-1960s for an abstract condition on the form that, hypothetically, the *generative grammar of any language may take. Thus it might be an abstract condition on rules and representations in phonology that all features should be binary, or, in syntax, that, at a certain level, all rules are *phrase structure rules.

Opp. substantive universal. But as Chomsky's theory developed the distinction became increasingly artificial. E.g. if a format such as that of *X-bar syntax is universal, do 'Specifier (Spec)' or 'Complement (Comp)' represent formal conditions on syntactic rules, or substantive categories or relations?

formant (1) A peak of acoustic energy centred on one point in the range of frequencies covered by the spectrum of a vowel. Vowels have several formants, but the distinctions as perceived between them lie, in particular, in the three lowest. In e.g. [i], the lowest or **first** formant (F_1) is centred on a frequency below 300 Hz, while the **second** (F_2) and **third** are high, around 2,000 and 2,500 Hz. In [a], by contrast, they are spaced more evenly over a marginally narrower range.

Changes in the frequencies of formants can be displayed by a sound *spectrogram. A **formant chart** is a plotting of one formant against another (typically F_1 against F_2). When a vowel is preceded or followed by a consonant, changes in the shape of the vocal tract are reflected by rapid shifts in formant frequencies: the direction of such **formant transitions** is the main acoustic feature distinguishing stops such as [p], [t], and [k].

formant (2) = formative (1).

formation Any specific process by which a unit is formed from one or more other units. E.g. an inflectional formation by which present participles in English are formed by the addition of -ing: sing → singing. Likewise a compound formation by which e.g. *ballpoint* is formed from *ball* and *point*.

formative 1. An *affix or other element within a word which is introduced by a morphological process. E.g. in *destroyers*, -er and -s are formatives introduced by successive processes of suffixation: *destroy* →

destroy + *er* → *destroyer* + *s*. **2.** Also used, e.g. by Chomsky in the mid-1960s, of a minimal unit of syntax equivalent to the *morpheme.

form class Bloomfield's term for a *syntactic category.

Formosan The indigenous languages of Taiwan, which form a branch of *Austronesian.

forms of address Any of the distinct forms that speakers must or will normally use to addressees who are e.g. of different social standing or with whom their personal relationships are different. Thus addressee-controlled *honorifics, *familiar forms vs. *polite forms, forenames or surnames, and so on.

formula A specific form of words used in a specific context: thus especially in ritual (e.g. recital of a Christian creed), or in other ritualized activities (e.g. 'Return to Manchester, please' in buying a train ticket). Thence to other ready-made forms: e.g. those used by oral poets or story-tellers as building blocks in composition, or *fixed expressions generally.
  '**Formulaic discourse**' has a structure built on formulae, especially in stricter senses. Likewise '**formulaic language**', of language or those aspects of language that involve formulae.

form word A word which has *grammatical meaning. E.g. *a* is a form word (or grammatical word or function word) in *a cow*.

fortis (Consonant) articulated, or claimed to be articulated, with higher muscular tension. Traditionally of voiceless consonants as opposed to voiced.
  From Latin *fortis* 'strong'. Opp. lenis: *cf.* tense (2) vs. lax.

fortition Any change or process by which a sound is, or is conceived as being, 'strengthened'; e.g. a sound change by which [t] > [tt], where a longer closure is seen as requiring greater effort of articulation. Opp., and modelled on, lenition.

fossilized (Form, construction) no longer used freely. Thus the *hue* of *hue and cry* is a fossilized form used only in that phrase or, possibly, in allusion to it; a sentence like *The devil take the hindmost!* has a fossilized construction in which subjects, verbs, etc. cannot be freely combined.

'fourth person' Often, though not always, = obviative.

fragment *See* sentence fragment.

frame Any representation of a context, within a sentence etc., in which linguistic units can appear. E.g. adjectives, such as *happy* or *helpful*, are among the units that can fill the blank (—) in the frame *the — people*.
  Originally as a tool in the analysis of distributions: *see* substitution (for substitution frame). Subsequently as a representation in the

lexicon of constructions in which units can be used: *see* Case Grammar (for case frames), subcategorization (for subcategorization frames).

Frame Semantics Treatment of meaning developed by C. J. Fillmore since the 1970s, emphasizing in particular the ways in which words change their meanings with the frame of reference in which they are used. Thus *set* has one meaning in a frame one might distinguish as that of 'tennis', in which it is related variously to those of *game, serve, love,* etc.; but another e.g. in a frame in which one might talk of a complete set of crockery. *Serve* has a meaning in a frame one might describe as 'eating in a restaurant', in relation to *waiter, course,* etc., which again is different from its meaning in the frame of 'tennis'; and so on.

One of many ideas seen as contributing to *Cognitive Linguistics.

Franco-Provençal Philologists' term for the *Romance dialects spoken or once spoken in an area including the west of Switzerland, the Val d'Aosta in north-west Italy, and in adjoining areas of France as far as a point west of Lyons.

free (1) (Form) capable of being uttered on its own: e.g. *unkindly,* which could be uttered on its own in answer to a question like *How did they treat you?*

Hence especially of parts of words that are themselves words: thus, in *unkindly,* the form *kind* is a **free morpheme**. Opp. bound (1): thus *un-* and *-ly* are both bound morphemes, as they do not form words on their own.

free (2) (Pronoun etc.) that is not linked syntactically to an antecedent: e.g. *he* is free in the domain formed by the sentence *I knew he would come.*

Opp. bound (2). The sense is derived from use in logic, where a variable is 'free' if it must be assigned a value for the expression which contains it to be meaningful.

free (3) (Accent) which can fall in principle on any syllable. E.g. Italian has a virtually free stress accent, falling in some words on the final syllable, in others on the penultimate, and so on. Opp. fixed (1).

free (4) (Word order) which is not determined by a rule of syntax: opp. fixed (2). A language with '**free word order**' is accordingly one in which the order of syntactic elements varies according to the context in which someone is speaking, for rhetorical effect, and so on.

Many languages have, to a greater or lesser degree, a **free phrase order**. E.g. in Italian a subject and a verb might be in either order: *Il mio amico* (lit. 'the my friend') *è arrivato* (lit. 'is arrived'), or, with verb first, *È arrivato il mio amico* 'My friend has arrived'. But within these phrases the order of words cannot vary. Other languages, such as Latin or Ancient Greek, have 'free word order' in a stricter sense: i.e. in many constructions words which stand in a close syntactic relation may be separated, e.g. in a specific context or for rhetorical effect, by others to which neither, or only one, relates directly. Thus in Latin an adjective could easily be separated from the noun it modifies, by a preposition or adverb (*paucis post diebus* '(a) few after days'), by a verb, or by a succession of words in various relationships.

free indirect style Style of e.g. literary narrative in which events etc. are presented from the viewpoint of a character as well as that of the narrator. In 'Plainly she was going to ask him tomorrow', the past tense (*was*) and third person pronoun (*him*) are appropriate to the 'present' time of the narration and the 'I' of the narrator: cf., in *indirect speech, *He thought she was going to ask him the day after*. But the adverb of time (*tomorrow*) refers to the future as seen by a character who thinks the other character ('she') will do this: cf., in *direct speech, *He thought 'She is going to ask me tomorrow'*.

From French ('style indirect libre'): *see also* empathy; *cf.* deictic centre.

free relative clause A clause whose structure is or is like that of a *relative clause but whose role in a larger construction is that of a noun phrase; e.g. *whatever she wants* in *Whatever she wants she gets*, or the archaic *who dares* in *Who dares wins*. Also called a **nominal relative clause**.

'free ride' The derivation of a form by means of a rule already posited for some other purpose. Thus a rule was posited, in terms of *Generative Phonology, by which e.g. [dɪˈvʌɪn] (*divine*) was derived from underlying [divīn]: the purpose of this was to explain its alternation with [dɪvɪn] (in *divinity*). But then, by a 'free ride' on the same rule, the [ʌɪ] of e.g. *fine*, which was involved in no alternation, could also be derived from underlying [ī].

The derivation was 'free' in the sense that the measure in the proposed *evaluation procedure was of rules alone. The perceived advantage was that [ʌɪ] could then be eliminated as an element in underlying forms.

free variation The relation between sounds or forms which have similar or partly similar distributions but are not described as being in contrast. E.g. for some speakers of English, a flapped *r* [ɾ] may be in free variation with a continuant [ɹ].

In a strict sense, free variation might be defined as variation which does not correlate with any other variable, e.g. context in a word or sentence, or the style of speech or social background of a speaker. But its use will normally reflect the criteria for contrast in a given investigation. E.g. [driːmd] and [drɛmpt] (both written *dreamed*) might be treated as free variants in a study of morphology, but not in stylistics or sociolinguistics.

French *Romance, spoken mainly in France; also in south Belgium, west Switzerland, and elsewhere through colonization, both as a native language (notably Québecois in Canada) and as a second language, e.g. in Africa. The standard language is in origin the dialect of the Île de France, which includes Paris.

Attested in a form distinct from Latin from the 9th century, and with an extensive literature from the 11th; **Old French** refers to the language of north France and originally of the ruling class in England and in the Crusader and other kingdoms in the Mediterranean, by convention until the mid-14th century.

frequentative (Inflection etc.) indicating frequent repetition: thus, schematically, *She telephone*-FREQ 'She keeps on telephoning'. *Cf.* iterative.

fricative ['frɪkətɪv] Consonant in which the space between *articulators is constricted to the point at which an air flow passes through with audible turbulence. E.g. [f] in *feel* or [v] in *veal* are *labiodental fricatives, with turbulence originating at the point where air flows outwards through a channel constricted by the *close approximation of the lower lip and upper teeth.

frictionless continuant *See* continuant.

Frisian *Germanic language most clearly related, within *West Germanic, to English; spoken mainly in the Dutch province of Friesland, where it is losing speakers to Dutch, and, in different forms, in parts of north-west Germany.

Friulan *Rhaeto-Romance dialect spoken in the extreme north-east of Italy, in an area centred on Udine. Important regionally, with speakers still in six figures.

front (Vowel) articulated with the highest point of the tongue towards the front of the mouth: e.g. [iː] in *seen*. Opp. back; *cf.* central.

Hence [± front] as a *distinctive feature in phonology.

fronting Any syntactic process by which elements are moved to a *marked position at the beginning of a sentence. E.g. the object (*that problem*) is fronted in *That problem I can't solve*; a verb and its complement (*climb that*) in *Climb ˇ*THAT *I* `CAN'T.

frozen expression Often = fixed expression. But it could in principle be restricted e.g. to one which includes a *fossilized word that is normal in that combination only: e.g. *spick and span*, *go berserk*.

FSP = Functional Sentence Perspective.

f-structure One of two levels of syntax in *Lexical-Functional Grammar.

FTA = face-threatening act; *see* face.

Fula African language whose speakers are distributed over much of the northern part of West Africa, from the interior of Senegal and Guinea to northern Cameroon. Major dialects are especially in the west of this range, and in the region of Sokoto and elsewhere in northern Nigeria. Grouped with Wolof and others as *West Atlantic.

full sentence Bloomfield's term for a sentence that is not a *minor sentence: defined as an instance of a *favourite sentence-form.

full stop (.) Used in glosses, typically to distinguish units or categories not realized separately. Thus, in Spanish, *canta-n* 'sing-3.PL' ('They are singing'), where third person and plural are together realized by *-n*. Compare *canta-ba-n* 'sing-IMPF.IND-3.PL', where *-ba-* is distinguished by hyphens as a separate suffix realizing imperfect and indicative.

full word One whose meaning is *lexical rather than *grammatical. Thus, in particular, a **full verb**, such as *come* in *could have come*, as opposed to the *auxiliaries *could* and *have*.

function 1. Used very widely of the part that a unit plays in a larger structure. E.g. in *I met my brother*, the phrase *my brother* has the function or 'role' of *direct object: i.e. it plays the part of direct object in a larger construction of which that is one element. Following the question 'Can you come?', the utterance 'Yes' would function as an answer: i.e. it plays that part in a larger question–answer interchange. The formula 'Let us pray' has a function, with other elements such as kneeling, in a larger ceremony of worship, and so on. *Cf.* functional linguistics; functional syntax; functions of language; Lexical-Functional Grammar; syntactic function. **2.** Other uses reflect a mathematician's sense of functions as dependencies between variables: hence especially, as in other disciplines, (the value of) x may vary '**as a function of**' (that of) y.

functional category Syntactic category whose members are *grammatical words (= function words), as opposed to lexical.

   A **functional head** is a unit which belongs to such a category, seen e.g. in *Principles and Parameters Theory as the *head (1) of a phrase. Thus *that* in *that he came*, described by many as a *complementizer heading a clause as 'complementizer phrase'; tenses as head of a *tense phrase; and so on.

Functional Grammar Model of *functional syntax developed since the late 1970s by S. C. Dik and his followers. Basically an account of clause structure in which functions are distinguished separately on three levels: e.g., in *Bill left yesterday*, *Bill* has the syntactic function of subject and the semantic function of *agent; it might also have the pragmatic function of *theme (1). Semantic functions are associated with *predicates (2) in the lexicon (e.g. agent with *leave*), and the *nucleus (1) of a clause (e.g. that represented by *Bill left*) may also be extended by *satellites (e.g. that represented by *yesterday* in *Bill left yesterday*); syntactic functions are then assigned to its elements; then pragmatic functions. A clear distinction is drawn between the rules by which this functional structure is established, and the 'expression rules' which specify the ways in which it is realized, by order, intonation, cases or prepositions, the voice of the verb, and so on. Of these, the order of elements in particular is determined, as far as the structure of a given language allows, by a universal principle.

functional linguistics Label adopted by various schools of linguists who wish to emphasize the attention given in their theories to the functions of language in general, or to those of specific features in particular textual or other contexts. E.g. the 'functionalism' of the *Prague School, of *Martinet, etc. seen in opposition to forms of *structuralism in which the system of a language is explicitly studied in abstraction from its functions.

functional literacy Literacy as assessed by practical competence in reading and writing, to a level expected in a literate society. Hence '**functionally illiterate**', of someone whose competence is below that level.

Functional Sentence Perspective A model of the *information structure of sentences, developed in the early 1960s by J. Firbas and others in the tradition of the pre-war *Prague School. Parts of a sentence representing *given information are said to have the lowest degree of **communicative dynamism** (or **CD**): i.e. the amount that, in context, they communicate to addressees is the least. These form the **theme**; *cf.* theme (1). Parts representing new information have the highest degree: these form the **rheme**. Parts which have an intermediate degree are sometimes said to form a **transition** between theme and rheme.

Suppose e.g. that A asks 'Who bought it?' B might reply '˘JOHN bought it', with (in this context) *bought it* as theme and *John* as rheme. In languages such as Czech, where the order of elements is more *free (4) than in English, parts with the lowest degree of communicative dynamism tend to come first in the sentence and parts with the highest to come last: schematically, in the same context, *bought-*3SG *it John*. By a general principle this is taken to be, if all else is equal, the natural order.

functional syntax 1. A treatment of syntax in which *syntactic functions, such as subject and object, are primitive or at least central. **2.** A treatment of syntax in which aspects of the construction of sentences are explained by, or related to, the functions that they play in communication.

Some accounts are 'functional' primarily in sense 1, others primarily in sense 2. But there is a widespread implication that, at some deeper level, the senses are the same.

functional yield The number of *minimal pairs distinguished by a given opposition between phonemes. E.g. there is a distinction for some speakers of English between voiceless [ʍ] (in *which, when, whin*) and voiced [w] (in *witch, wen, win*). But pairs such as these are few; therefore its functional yield is low. By contrast, that of [p] vs. [k] is very high.

Also called '**functional load**'. A low value has often been seen as a factor in the loss of oppositions: e.g. the loss, for many other speakers, of [ʍ] vs. [w].

functions of language Any of the kinds of things that can be done in, or through the use of, language. Thus an utterance may give information, show that the speaker is angry, try to get someone to do something, and so on.

Two influential typologies are those of Bühler in the 1930s and Jakobson in 1960. Bühler's distinguishes the *Darstellung* 'representation' function (that of representing states of the world) from the *Ausdruck* 'expression' function (in reflecting states of mind of the speaker) and the *Appell* (lit. 'appeal') function, in being directed towards a hearer. In Jakobson's scheme, these are mirrored in large part by the referential, emotive, and *conative functions, to which are added three others: the *phatic function (of simply maintaining contact between people), the metalingual or *metalinguistic (of elucidating the language itself that is being used), and the *poetic, defined by attention to the form, as such, of what is said. Among later schemes, that of Lyons in the 1970s distinguishes the descriptive function (corresponding to Bühler's representational or Jakobson's referential) from the social and expressive functions, together classed as *interpersonal.

function word One with *grammatical meaning as opposed to *lexical meaning: e.g. *the* and *of* are function words (or grammatical words or form words) in *the top of Everest*.

fundamental frequency The frequency with which e.g. a vibrating string vibrates as a whole. Thus, in speech, the fundamental frequency in the production of a vowel is the frequency, as measured in hertz (Hz) = cycles per second, at which the vocal cords are so vibrating.

fused head Huddleston and Pullum's term, in *CGEL*, for a unit seen as having roles both as a *head (1) of a construction and as one of its *dependents. E.g. *nothing* in *I expected nothing*; compare the separate roles, of *help* as head and *no* as dependent, in *I expected no help*.

In a **fused relative** the same unit has the roles both of a head noun and a relative pronoun. E.g. *what* has both roles in *They gave* *me what is needed;* compare the separate roles of *help* and *which* in *They gave me the help which I needed*. Hence equivalent to a *free relative clause.

fusion Any process by which units etc. that are separate at one *level of representation are realized by a form in which there is no corresponding boundary. Thus in morphology: e.g. *flyer* is made up of *fly* [flʌɪ] and *-er* [ə], but in some varieties of English [ʌɪ] and [ə] are fused to a single long vowel (roughly [flaː]). The morphological units *fly* and *-er* may then be said to have **fused exponents**.

Hence also, in some accounts, of *cumulation.

fusional (Language) in which there is no clear boundary within the word between one morphological unit and another. *Cf.* inflecting.

futhark *See* Runic alphabet.

future *See* tense.

future perfect Form of verb used of a future action or event, seen as prior to some moment of time which is itself still later in the future: thus, in Latin, *venero* 'I will have come' (will have come by e.g. the day after tomorrow) as opposed to the 'simple future' *veniam* 'I will come'. Thence, in English, of forms like *will have come*. *Cf.* perfect.

fuzzy Without definite boundaries. Thus a **fuzzy set** is one whose membership is not determined absolutely; **fuzzy logic** deals in degrees of truth, instead of an absolute distinction between true and false.

G

Ga Language spoken mainly in the coastal area of Ghana, including Accra. Assigned, with *Ewe, to the *Kwa family.

Gaelic *Celtic. Dialects of **Irish Gaelic** (or Erse) are the native language of parts of west Ireland: a standardized form is taught as a national language in schools in the Irish Republic. **Scottish Gaelic** has native speakers in parts of north-west Scotland.

First attested by inscriptions in *Oghams from the early 1st millennium AD, and by texts in **Old Irish** (conventionally from the 7th to the 9th century) in Roman spelling. Carried from Ireland to Scotland by emigration in the Dark Ages.

Galician *Romance, closely related to *Portuguese; an official regional language in north-west Spain.

Gallo-Romance The forms of *Romance (e.g. French) that developed in what is now France.

gap *See* lexical gap; parasitic gap.

gapping The deletion of a verb, with or without other elements, from the middle of the second and any subsequent clauses in a sequence related by *coordination. E.g. in *I liked everything, Jane < > nothing, and her mother < > only some things* gapping, shown here by angled brackets, applies to the single element *liked*; in *I will be giving her some help on Monday and Bill < > on Tuesday* the elements 'gapped' are both the verb and its objects (*will be giving her some help*).
Cf. stripping.

'garden path sentence' One whose beginning suggests that it has a construction which by the end it clearly does not have. The stock example is *The horse raced past the barn fell*: *raced* will be taken at first to be the past tense (cf. *The horse rode past the barn*), but the whole makes sense only if it is a participle (cf. *The horse ridden past the barn fell*).

Gaulish The form of Continental *Celtic spoken in what is now France.

GB = Government and Binding Theory.

Gê *See* South American languages.

Ge'ez South *Semitic: formerly spoken in Ethiopia, Ge'ez is still a language of Christian liturgy.

geminate Doubled: e.g. the consonant in Italian [atːo] 'act' (written *atto*) is analysed as a geminate, in opposition to a single, consonant.

Hence **gemination**, a change or process by which consonants are doubled.

gender (1) Grammatical category dividing nouns into classes basically characterizable by reference to sex. The division is therefore between *masculine (characterized by nouns denoting males) and *feminine (characterized by nouns denoting females), with *neuter as the term for a third class characterized by neither. Also extended, in some modern usage, to categories of *noun class generally.

Often specifically called **grammatical gender**, to distinguish it as a *grammatical category from '**natural gender**' as defined by the *notional categories partly corresponding to it. Thus girls are 'naturally' female, but German *Mädchen* 'girl' is grammatically neuter.

gender (2) General term imported from the social sciences for the sex or sexuality of human beings. Hence 'gender difference', of a difference in speech between men and women; 'language and gender', as a branch of *sociolinguistics dealing with such differences; '**genderlect**', typically defined by features commoner in the speech of one sex than the other; and so on.

General American Accent of the majority of speakers of English in the USA, not specific to or strikingly indicative of a particular region, such as the Southern States or New England.

general grammar = universal grammar.

generalized conversational implicature *See* conversational implicature.

Generalized Phrase Structure Grammar Formal model of syntax developed by G. J. M. Gazdar, and subsequently by others, from the end of the 1970s. Basically a *phrase structure grammar, but with additional devices, in particular the use of *metarules and *slash categories, that removed the need, assumed in most theories of generative grammar at the time, for *transformations. A passive sentence, for example, is characterized by phrase structure rules derived in part, by a higher-level rule, from those that characterize an active; hence there is no need to derive the structure of a passive, by a *transformation, from an active structure assigned to it by a *base component. In an interrogative like *Who can you see?*, *who* is related, by a phrase structure rule, to a phrase that must contain a null noun phrase: [*can you see* ₙₚ[ ]]. This removes the need for a rule by which *who* would undergo *movement from a position it would initially occupy.

Cf. Head-Driven Phrase Structure Grammar. The main applications have been in computational linguistics, where parsing with phrase structure systems is simple and well understood. Usually linked to a system of semantic interpretation, derived from *Montague Grammar, in which semantic rules correspond one-to-one with those of syntax.

'generalized quantifier' Logicians' term for an expression interpreted as representing a set of subsets. Adapted, in *formal semantics, to represent the meaning of noun phrases: e.g. *some people* denotes the set of all subsets of individuals whose members are a subset of people; likewise, e.g. *Matthews* denotes the set of all subsets whose member is Matthews.

A sentence such as *Some people like formal semantics* is true if, in a given situation, a property denoted by the predicate (that of liking formal semantics) holds of, in this case, some people. If noun phrases denote generalized quantifiers, a generalized quantifier can accordingly be represented as a function from a property (such as liking formal semantics) to a truth value (true or false in given circumstances).

generalized transformation A type of rule in early *transformational grammar by which structures assigned independently to different sentences were combined to form a single structure. Thus deriving *coordinate and *embedded sentences.

The sense was that of transformations generalized beyond the special case of a *singulary transformation.

generate *See* generative grammar.

generative capacity The capacity of a given type of *generative grammar both to generate a specific range of *languages and to assign a specific range of structures. Thus the generative capacity of *transformational grammars is greater on both counts than that of *phrase structure grammars.

The set of languages that can be characterized defines the *weak generative capacity; the set of analyses that can be assigned to their sentences the *strong generative capacity.

generative dialectology The application of *Generative Phonology, in the early 1970s, to the description of dialects. Variants of the same form were assigned a common underlying representation in all dialects, with different realizations derived by different phonological rules, by the same rules ordered differently, and so on.

generative grammar **1.** A set of *rules (2) which indicate precisely what can be and cannot be a sentence in a language. Formulated by Chomsky in the 1950s as an abstract device interpreted as **generating**, or producing, a set of *strings or sequences of units: a '**sentence**' was formally a string so generated, and a '**language**' defined as a set of sentences. **2.** Loosely, without the article, of schools or concepts of linguistics based at least historically on the construction of such grammars: thus especially the programme of Chomsky and his followers, the '**generativist**' schools of Chomskyan origin, and so on.

*Phrase structure grammars and *transformational grammars were developed as specific types of generative grammar.

Generative Phonology Any account, in principle, of phonology adopted within *generative grammar. Especially, however, one proposed by Halle at the end of the 1950s, which reached its classic form, in Chomsky and Halle, *SPE, in the late 1960s. At an initial level of representation, the *surface structure of a sentence was a configuration of 'formatives' or *morphemes, each entered from the *lexicon as a single *feature matrix. Such representations were the input to, or were 'interpreted by', an *ordered set of phonological rules, each conceived as an instruction to change, add, delete, or rearrange features in specific contexts. These resulted in *phonetic representations which were in turn feature matrices.

Criticized from the early 1970s, especially for proposing *underlying forms seen as unjustifiably *abstract. Superseded in particular by accounts such as, from the mid-1990s, *Optimality Theory.

Generative Semantics Theory of *transformational grammar developed from the late 1960s to the mid-1970s. The original proposal was that a *base component of a grammar should directly generate *semantic representations of sentences, which would be converted to *surface structures with no intervening level of *deep structure. This was associated in particular with the view that lexical items were units only at the surface level. But in the 1970s it became clear that the proposed semantic representations could not be assigned by rules of grammar independent of the knowledge, beliefs, etc. of individual speakers. Therefore the break with what was later called the *Standard Theory of transformational grammar was in reality far more radical.

Leading proponents included G. P. Lakoff, J. D. McCawley, P. M. Postal, and J. R. Ross. Historically one precursor of what became known, more than a decade later, as *Cognitive Linguistics.

generic (Expression etc.) referring to an entire class of individuals, events, etc., rather than to specific members. Thus *grass snakes* or *the grass snake* has **generic reference** in statements about the species: *Grass snakes eat slugs*, or *The grass snake is not poisonous*. Such sentences are in turn **generic statements**, or express **generic propositions**. In contrast, an expression like *the grass snake* is used non-generically in e.g. *I just saw the grass snake*.

A word like *man* is said to have a 'generic use' in reference to any human being, rather than male human beings in particular. Hence 'male generic' or 'generic masculine'; a word like *duck*, as used of either female ducks or ducks male and female, would analogously be a 'female generic' or 'generic feminine'.

genetic classification The classification of languages according to their presumed development from common ancestors. E.g. French and Spanish are among those classed as *Romance languages, since both have developed from Latin. They are also *Indo-European languages, with the same hypothetical ancestor as many others across

Eurasia. The method of genetic classification is the *comparative method.

Cf. typological classification. Genetic relations are commonly represented by tree diagrams, called '**family trees**'. But the connection with families in the ordinary sense is metaphorical.

Geneva School General name for linguists in Geneva either followers of or associated with *Saussure. The work of C. Bally, on French stylistics in 1909 and later in his *Linguistique générale et linguistique française* (4th edn., 1965), is especially important.

genitive (GEN) *Case whose basic role is to mark nouns or noun phrases which are dependents of another noun. Thus, in German, *Vaters* 'father-GEN' in *Vaters Buch* 'father's book'; or *meines* and *Vaters* ('my-GEN', 'father-GEN') in *das Buch meines Vaters* 'my father's book'. Thence of similar constructions marked by other elements. Thus the construction marked by the *clitic -'s* in English (*Daddy's book* or *the man next door's book*) is also described as genitive; and, in older grammars, the construction with *of* (*the top of the page*).
Cf. possessive.

genre In the traditional sense, of literary genres such as epic poetry. Thence of types of *text, as distinguished by their function or their form, in general.

geographical linguistics = areal linguistics.

'geolinguistics' Variously of quantitative studies of languages, dialects, etc. in a geographical perspective.

Georgian The most important language of the South *Caucasian (Kartvelian) family, spoken mainly in Georgia in the former Soviet Union. Attested by inscriptions from the 5th century AD and by manuscripts from the 8th. Written in an alphabetic script, called 'Mkhedruli', one of two in use in earlier periods: the precise origins of both are uncertain.

German West *Germanic, spoken mainly in Germany and in Austria, and used with others, as an official language in Switzerland and Luxembourg and as a regional form in the Italian Tyrol and elsewhere. Divided historically into two main dialect areas, **Low German**, roughly north of a line from south of Magdeburg to the frontier with Belgium, and **High German**, to the south. The criterion is whether or not forms underwent the so-called '**Second Sound Shift**', by which [t] > [ts], e.g. in the word for 'ten' (standard High German *zehn*), [p] > [pf], e.g. in the word for 'apple' (*Apfel*), and so on.

Old High German is the language of the earliest texts (before the late 11th century). The rise and spread of the modern standard was a gradual process, from the early 16th century, when Luther translated the Bible into his own East Saxon dialect, to the 19th.

Germanic Branch of *Indo-European which includes *German, *Dutch, *English, *Danish, *Norwegian, *Swedish, and others living or extinct. The hypothetical common language, Proto-Germanic, is not directly attested.

Traditionally divided into East Germanic (*Gothic), *North Germanic (Scandinavian), and *West Germanic; but prehistoric relationships are now seen as more complex.

gerund A nominal form of verbs in Latin: e.g. *pugnando* ('fight-GERUND-ABL.SG') 'by fighting'. Hence a term available for verb forms with a noun-like role in other languages: e.g. English *fighting* is traditionally a gerund in *Fighting used to be fun*, as opposed to the *participle, also in *-ing* but with a different syntactic role, in *people fighting*.

gerundive An adjectival form of verbs in Latin: e.g. in *Delenda est Carthago* ('destroy-GERUND-NOM.SG.FEM is Carthage') 'Carthage must be destroyed'.

Gesamtbedeutung An 'overall meaning' seen as covering all the uses of a morphological or other element. E.g. that of a past tense might be described as one of 'distance from the reality of the present': this meaning would then be taken to cover reference to events both distanced in time (*He came last week*) and distanced from what is real or probable (*If he came tomorrow . . .*).

gesture Any voluntary movement of the body which is significant in a specific community or communities: e.g. raising one's hand in the street in casual greeting, moving one's head backwards as a sign of surprise. The study of gestures has sometimes been called *kinesics.

An **articulatory gesture** is a structured movement of the vocal organs which is directed towards a specific articulatory goal: e.g. any pattern of movement that achieves closure of the lips, any that achieves *close approximation of the back of the tongue to the soft palate. In *Articulatory Phonology gestures are the basic phonetic/phonological units and are seen as orchestrated by a **gestural score** derived by rule from representations at a higher level.

Gilliéron, Jules (1854–1926) A pioneer in dialect geography, whose first atlas, of the phonetics of the French-speaking Valais of his native Switzerland, appeared in 1881. Later associated with the phonetician P. Rousselot in the programme that led eventually to the publication, in 1902–10, of the *Atlas linguistique de la France*. The data for this had been obtained on the spot by his co-author, E. Edmont, who had been trained as a very acute observer of sounds.

As a theorist Gilliéron denied that dialects themselves had any objective reality. In monographs based on the atlas, he explored in particular changes in the lexicon, in response e.g. to *homonymic clashes that result from sound change (word X, becoming homonymous with Y, is replaced by Z), or to phonetic *erosion (word

X, having become too short for clear communication, is replaced by Y or extended by an affix). The findings of the atlas have often been cited against the *Neogrammarian regularity principle in sound change. But Gilliéron's own etymological studies seem rather to presuppose it.

given Known to or recoverable by an addressee etc. If parent A asks 'Where are the children?', parent B might answer 'Jane's gone to the hairdresser'. In the sentence uttered by B, the subject *Jane* corresponds to what is given: i.e. Jane is one of the children A has referred to. The remainder, *(ha)s gone to the hairdresser*, corresponds to what is **new**: i.e. what A does not know already.

Usually, as in this account, of given vs. new 'information'. But also of the forms themselves: thus the sentence uttered by B has the *information structure 'given *Jane* + new *(ha)s gone to the hairdresser*'.

Glagolitic One of two alphabets devised specifically for Slavic languages. Once used widely, especially in the western Balkans, but supplanted by *Roman and *Cyrillic under pressure variously from the Roman Catholic and Orthodox Churches.

glide Any audible transition from one sound to another. If described as a transition to a following sound it is an **on-glide**; if described as a transition from a preceding sound it is an **off-glide**.

Extended to sounds which are themselves seen as transitional or which phonetically resemble glides: e.g. *semivowels such as [w] or [j] in *will* [wɪl] or *you* [juː].

'gliding vowel' A *diphthong or *triphthong.

global language *See* international language.

global rule Defined by G. P. Lakoff in the early 1970s as the most general instance of a *derivational constraint.

gloss Any explanation of the meaning of a word or expression. Traditionally of glosses added to texts: e.g. a translation into Old Irish in the margin of a manuscript in Latin. Thence to entries in glossaries or collections of glosses, or in dictionaries.

Hence applied to a partial or complete sketch of the lexical and grammatical units in an example cited. Usually aligned, as in the illustration, beneath successive words, with a translation of the whole in a line following:

multos	per	annos
many-MASC-ACC.PL	through	year-ACC.PL
'for many years'.		

Glosses for a phrase in Latin

glossematics The theory of linguistic structure developed by *Hjelmslev in the 1930s and 1940s.

glossolalia 'Speaking in tongues': i.e. uttering sounds under conditions of religious ecstasy that are believed, wrongly, to be in unknown languages.

glottal (Consonant) articulated with the vocal cords. E.g. the **glottal** ***stop** [ʔ] before initial vowels in most forms of German: *die Arbeit* [diː ʔarbait] 'the work'.
  Hence e.g. *t-glottaling.

glottalic 1. (*Airstream mechanism) in which a flow of air is initiated by, or at least partly by, the larynx. *See* ejective; implosive.
2. (Consonant) = ejective.

'glottalic theory' The hypothesis, advanced by G. Gamkrelidze and others, that the consonants of *Indo-European languages have developed from a system that included *ejectives: thus, for the dental series, the plosives would be [t'] (ejective), [t], and [d], where earlier reconstructions have [d], [t], and [dʰ].

glottalized Produced with a *secondary articulation of the vocal cords: *cf.* glottal reinforcement. Also in the same sense as *ejective. A **glottalized tone** is one realized by *creaky voice.

glottal reinforcement Closure of the vocal cords during or partly anticipating a closure at another place of articulation. Common in southern British English for final, or especially for final, [p], [t], and [k].

glottis The space between the vocal cords. Thus the glottis is closed in the articulation of a *glottal *stop.

glottochronology Method proposed by M. Swadesh in the 1950s, by which he hoped to determine the date at which genetically related languages diverged. He assumed that every language had a **basic vocabulary** (defined in practice by a list of 100 or of 200 concepts) whose members are replaced, by internal change or borrowing, at a constant rate. If that assumption were accepted, one could take a set of languages known to be related, and, by comparing their basic vocabularies, one could determine that some diverged more recently than others. If the rate itself were known, one could also determine the dates at which successive *protolanguages were spoken.
  The method is still trusted by some scholars, especially in disciplines other than linguistics.

glottophagie An attractive term, in French, for the death of a language seen as 'swallowed' by another to which speakers have progressively switched.

GLOW = Generative Linguistics in the Old World, an organization promoting cooperation among Chomsky's followers in Europe, Japan, etc.

gnomic [ˈnəʊmɪk] Used in a timeless statement. E.g. the present tense (*eat*) is gnomic, or has a gnomic use, in *Cows eat grass*. *Cf*. generic.

goal 1. = direct object: e.g. *me* is the goal in *Watch me* or *She kissed me*. Sometimes used with specific commitment to *localism; often, e.g. by Bloomfield and his followers, without. **2.** *Case role, especially of syntactic elements identifying the end or goal of a movement: e.g. that of *(to) Paris* in *They got to Paris* or *They were going to Paris*.

'God's truth' Coined by F. W. Householder in 1952, in reference to linguists who believed they were establishing units, categories, etc. with real existence in a language, as opposed to 'hocus pocus' linguists, who did not.

Goidelic Branch of *Celtic principally represented by Irish and Scottish *Gaelic.

Gothic *Germanic language attested mainly by a partial translation of the Bible dating from the second half of the 4th century AD. Traditionally classed as East Germanic, as opposed to *North Germanic and *West Germanic.

govern *See* dependency; government.

'governing category' Used in *Government and Binding Theory in the 1980s of the smallest domain, as defined by categories labelling nodes in a phrase structure tree, within which a noun phrase is, in the specialized sense developed in that theory, governed. E.g. in *The neighbours said* $_S$[*the children hurt themselves*], the governing category of *themselves* is the subordinate clause (labelled 'S'). By a proposed general principle, *anaphors such as *themselves* must have an *antecedent within their governing category: thus, in this case, the antecedent is *the children*.

government 1. The relation seen as obtaining between a *head (1) and an *object or other complement. Thus, in *I saw her in Bristol*, the object *her* is governed by the verb *saw*; likewise *Bristol* is the complement of, and governed by, the preposition *in*. **2.** A relation between such a head and the *case of an object. E.g. in Latin *in Italiam contendere* 'to hasten into Italy', the preposition *in* governs an accusative (lit. 'in(to) Italy-ACC.SG to-hasten'). **3.** Developed in *Government and Binding Theory into a general principle by which elements were assigned 'cases' by other elements that *c-command them. Always problematic and later superseded by procedures of *checking. I.e. cases are not individually 'assigned', but 'checked' for what in effect is the traditional property of *congruence, against the properties of other units.

Government and Binding Theory Version of Chomsky's *Principles and Parameters Theory named by his followers after

Lectures on Government and Binding (1981). This proposed effectively three levels of syntax, *Logical Form (LF), *D-structure, and *S-structure, related to each other by a single *movement rule (Move α) and related to the lexicon of an individual language by a *projection principle operating at the level of D-structure. The specific constraints of Universal Grammar were the topics of a set of interacting subtheories: *Bounding Theory, *Theta Theory, and so on.

Abbreviated '**GB**'. Developed in detail throughout the 1980s and early 1990s, until reformulated, and thus superseded, by the so-called *minimalist programme.

Government Phonology Theory of phonology developed from the mid-1980s by J. D. Kaye and others. Essentially an account of syllabification based (*a*) on a requirement that successive constituents of a syllable should stand in a defined relationship of 'government'; (*b*) on a theory of the '**charm**' of segments which determines what can enter into that relationship with what. Charm rests on an analysis of phonological features which is specific to this theory; the concept of *government is modelled on that in Chomsky's *Government and Binding Theory.

'Government Theory' Part of *Government and Binding Theory concerned with principles of *government (3).

governor Any element said to 'govern' another, in a relation either of *dependency in general or specifically of *government.

GPSG = Generalized Phrase Structure Grammar.

gradable antonymy Relation of *antonymy in which the opposition is one of degree. E.g. between *large* and *small*: although they are opposites, the same thing may be at once large by one standard and small by another, or larger than 'x' and yet smaller than 'y'. In such a relation one term is often neutral. Thus if one wants to know the size of something one will normally ask 'how large' it is. One will not, except in a specific context or for some specific reason, ask 'how small' it is. In that sense *small* is the *marked term in the opposition, *large* the unmarked.

gradation Usually of *vowel gradation, e.g. or specifically *ablaut.

grade 1. The traditional term (more fully, '**grade of comparison**') for the category in which simple or 'positive' forms of adjectives and adverbs (e.g. *great*) are opposed to *comparatives (e.g. *greater*) and *superlatives (e.g. *greatest*). **2.** *See* ablaut.

gradience A series of instances intermediate between two categories, constructions, etc. E.g. *blackboard* is, by all relevant criteria, a *compound: it has stress on its first element (*bláckboard*), its precise meaning does not follow from those of *black* and *board* individually, and so on. *Fine weather* is equally, by all criteria, not a compound. But many other cases are less clear. *Bond Street* is in meaning as regular as *Trafalgar Square*, but stress is again on the first element. *Able seaman* has stress on its second element, but does not simply mean 'seaman who is able'. *White lie* is likewise not in meaning 'lie which is white'; but it too has stress on its second element and, in addition, *white* might be separately modified (*a very white lie*). So, by such criteria, these form part of a gradience between compounds and non-compounds.

gradual opposition An opposition between extremes with at least one intermediate term: e.g. in the English vowel system, between [ɪ] (close) and [a] (open), with intermediate [ɛ] (mid).

grammar Any systematic account of the structure of a language; the patterns that it describes; the branch of linguistics concerned with such patterns.
    Often restricted to relations among units that have meaning. Hence opp. phonology: e.g. *singing* is a grammatical unit, as are *sing* and *-ing*, while [s] or the syllable [sɪ] are phonological. Also opposed, though again not always, to a dictionary or the *lexicon. E.g. the meanings of *sing* belong to its entry in the lexicon; the role of *-ing* to grammar, where it is described for verbs in general. When limited in these ways, the study of grammar reduces to that of *morphology and *syntax.
    Applied by Chomsky in the 1960s to the knowledge of a language developed in the minds of its speakers. A grammar in the widest sense was thus at once a set of rules etc. said to be *internalized by members of a speech community, and an account, by a linguist, of such a grammar. This internalized grammar is effectively what is later called *I-language.

grammatical 1. Having to do with *grammar: *see* entries following. **2.** Specifically of sentences etc. which conform to the rules of a given language: e.g. *I like tea* is grammatical in English, while *I tea like* is **ungrammatical**. Hence **grammaticality** or **grammaticalness** is variously a property either assigned to sentences by a specific grammar, or of sentences judged to be *acceptable to speakers who hypothetically 'know' its grammar.

grammatical agreement *Agreement determined solely by the grammatical properties of the words or phrases involved. E.g. in *The council has agreed*, the subject is grammatically singular, and the form of the verb (*has*) agrees grammatically with it. Cf. *The council have agreed*, with *notional agreement.

grammatical ambiguity Ambiguity explained by differences in syntax. E.g. *I read the book on the floor* might mean that a book was on the floor and that was the one the speaker read: this would reflect a syntactic construction in which *on the floor* modifies *book*. Alternatively, it might mean that the speaker was on the floor while reading the book: this would reflect a construction in which *on the floor* modifies *read* or *read the book*.

Also 'structural ambiguity'. *Cf.* lexical ambiguity, constructional homonymy.

grammatical case A *case whose main role is to indicate a construction in syntax. Thus *genitive is a grammatical case which typically marks one noun or noun phrase as the dependent of another. Opp. concrete case.

grammatical category A *category of elements with *grammatical meaning, as opposed especially to a *lexical category; also one established in a specific grammar, as opposed to a *notional category.

'grammatical competence' *See* communicative competence.

grammaticalization 1. The property of forming part of the system, thus in the widest sense the grammar, of a language. E.g. many languages distinguish a *dual from a *plural: that is, the conceptual or notional distinction between 'two' and 'three or more' is grammaticalized in these languages. A phonetic process of *declination would likewise be 'grammaticalized' in *tone languages with rules for *downdrift. **2.** The process by which, in the history of a language, a unit with *lexical meaning changes into one with *grammatical meaning. E.g., in Italian *ho mangiato* 'I-have eaten', a form that was in Latin a full verb ('to have, possess') has been grammaticalized as an *auxiliary (*ho*). In *mangerò* 'I will eat', the same form, first combined as an auxiliary with an infinitive (lit. 'to-eat I-have'), has further changed to an inflectional ending (-*ò*).

grammatically conditioned (*Alternation) among forms or processes in different grammatical settings: e.g. between [sɛl] in *sell*, *sell-s*, *sell-ing* and [səʊl] in the past tense or past participle *sol-d*. *Cf.* phonologically conditioned; lexically conditioned.

grammatical meaning Any aspect of meaning described as part of the syntax and morphology of a language as distinct from its *lexicon. Thus especially the meanings of constructions and inflections, or of words when described similarly. Such words include, in particular, ones belonging to *closed rather than *open classes, or those seen as marking a syntactic unit. Thus *he* has a grammatical meaning in opposition to other members of a closed class of personal pronouns; *if* as the marker e.g. of an indirect question in *I asked if they were coming*.

Thence '**grammatical word**' or '**grammatical morpheme**', for units whose meaning is so described. E.g., in *the walls*, both *the* and the plural inflection (-*s*) are distinguished as grammatical units from the lexical unit *wall*.

grammatical morpheme A *morpheme which has *grammatical meaning.

'grammatical relation' Strictly of any relation, or any *syntagmatic relation, in grammar. Often specifically of syntactic relations such as 'subject of' or 'object of'; *cf.* syntactic function, term.

'grammatical role' Used variously of *case roles or of *syntactic functions.

grammatical subject A subject in the usual sense (*subject (1)), as opposed to a *logical subject or *psychological subject. Thus, in *Yesterday I was delayed by fog*, the 'grammatical subject' is *I*: e.g. it is the element with which *was* agrees. But the 'psychological subject' would be *yesterday* (the sentence is about what happened yesterday) and the 'logical subject' would be *fog* (the fog was responsible for what happened).

grammatical word 1. One which has *grammatical meaning: e.g. *to*, seen as marking the infinitive, in *I want to go out*. **2.** One established as a unit of syntax and morphology, as opposed to a *phonological word.

'grammaticized' Huddleston and Pullum's term, in *CGEL*, for a word whose use in a specific syntactic construction does not reflect a meaning assigned to it in a lexicon. Thus *of* is a 'grammaticized' preposition in e.g. *the top of the hill*, as simply marking a relation between *top* and *the hill*.

grammatology The study of the nature, history, etc. of writing systems.

Grantha script *See* Indian scripts.

grapheme A character in writing, considered as an abstract or invariant unit which has varying realizations. E.g. the grapheme <A> subsumes the variants or 'allographs' 'A' (Roman capital), 'a' (Roman minuscule), and so on.

graphic (Medium, *substance) involving written characters. Opp. phonic.

graphology A study of the written forms of languages modelled on *phonology as the study of their sound systems.

Grassmann's Law *Sound law in Indo-European by which an aspirated consonant became unaspirated when it was followed by a vowel which was followed by another aspirated consonant. E.g. in Ancient Greek *té-tʰne:-k-e* 'has died', the first prefix is derived by *reduplication of the first consonant of the root (*tʰne:-*); but, through Grassmann's Law, it is *te-*, with unaspirated *t*, not *tʰe-*.
The change is of the type called *dissimilation.

grave 1. Diacritic (`) originally used to mark low pitch: *see* accent (1).
2. *Distinctive feature of consonants and vowels proposed by
*Jakobson in the 1950s. Characterized acoustically by a relative
concentration of energy in lower frequencies: hence, in particular,
back vowels are grave, also bilabial consonants. Opp. acute; *cf.*
compact.

'gravity model' Geographers' model of the influence of one urban
centre on another, applied by P. J. Trudgill to their influence on
dialects. The degree of influence predicted varies with the effective
distance between them, with the extent to which speech is already
similar, and with the relative sizes of their populations.

Great Vowel Shift A series of changes in late Middle English, by
which close long vowels became diphthongs and other long vowels
shifted one step closer. Thus, in the front series, [aː] > [ɛː], [ɛː] > [eː], [eː]
> [iː], [iː] > [aɪ]; in the back series, [ɔː] > [oː], [oː] > [uː], [uː] > [aʊ]. Often
interpreted as a unitary phenomenon; hence as a classic example of a
*chain shift.

It is in consequence of these and other changes that [eɪ] in *name*
(formerly [aː]) is spelled *a*, or [aɪ] in *shine* (formerly [iː]) spelled *i*. They
are also the main factor in the development of vowel alternations
between long [eɪ] and short [a] (in *sane/sanity*), long [aɪ] and short [ɪ]
(*divine/divinity*), and so on.

Greek *Indo-European, forming a separate branch within the family.
First attested in records of the 15th century BC, written in *Linear B,
and by a rich literature from early in the 1st millennium BC. Spoken
widely, in a *koine* or 'common' language reflecting the Attic dialect of
Athens, after the conquests of Alexander: later the official language
throughout the eastern part of the Roman empire and its Byzantine
successor. Now spoken mainly in Greece and Cyprus, and the national
language of both.

The alphabet was developed around the beginning of the 1st
millennium BC. Derived from a North *Semitic alphabet, but with the
crucial feature that vowels are represented equally with consonants.

'Greek letter variables' (α, β, . . .) Used in *Generative
Phonology as variables over '+' and '−' in phonological features. Thus,
by a rule of assimilation, the value of the feature [± voice] (voiced vs.
voiceless) might be reversed to match that of a segment following: [+
voice] → [− voice] / — [− voice]; [− voice] → [+ voice] / — [+ voice]. Using α
as a variable, we can write the rule in this form: [α voice] → [− α voice] /
— [− α voice]. I.e. whatever value a segment has with respect to voice
(α), that value is reversed (− α) when the next has the reverse value.

Greenberg, Joseph Harold (1915–2001) American linguist, originally
an anthropologist. *See* African languages; Amerind; mass comparison:
also a pioneer of *linguistic universals in the field of word order.

Grenzsignal   *See* boundary marker.

Grice, Herbert Paul (1913–88) Anglo-American philosopher whose
work develops a theory of meaning in terms of the communicative
intentions of speakers. His most substantial contribution was a series
of lectures on 'Logic and Conversation', delivered in 1967, which
proposed a theory of *implicatures and *maxims of conversation
designed to account for discrepancies between the meanings of words
such as *and* or *some* and the roles of corresponding operators in a
system of logic. They were not published fully until the end of his life
(in *Studies in the Way of Words*, 1989), but ideas taken from them have
been influential in linguistics since the early 1970s.

Grimm, Jacob (1785–1863) Germanist, known to the world for the
Märchen collected and published by him and his brother Wilhelm, to
linguistics for his *Deutsche Grammatik* (1819–37) and in particular for
the formulation of *Grimm's Law, based on the insight of *Rask, in
the second edition (1822) of its first volume. At the end of their lives he
and his brother worked together on the *Deutsches Wörterbuch,* published
in parts from 1854 and finally completed over a century later.

Grimm's Law   *Sound law or series of sound laws by which
consonants in *Germanic differ systematically in *manner of
articulation from those of cognate forms in other Indo-European
languages. In a traditional account, 'voiced aspirated' stops (e.g. $*d^h$)
change in Germanic to voiced ([d]); voiced stops ($*d$) change in turn to
voiceless ([t]); voiceless stops ($*t$) change to fricatives ([θ]).
    Called by Germanists the '**First Sound Shift**'. The 'Second Sound
Shift', by which e.g. Germanic $*t > ts$, is peculiar to High *German.

groove fricative = rill fricative.

group   In the ordinary sense. E.g. one may speak of a 'group' of
languages, such as *Khoisan, without implying that they form a
*family. Technically = phrase or word group. Sometimes specifically of
a *phrase (3) that is not a clause.

group genitive   A unit in English such as *someone else's* or *the President
of Italy's* in which -*'s*, historically a genitive suffix, is related
syntactically to a phrase as a whole and not to the specific word to
which it is attached.

group-verb   An idiom in which a verb and words related to it form a
combination with a verb-like meaning. E.g. the *phrasal verb 'to run
over' in *They ran over a dog* or the *prepositional verb 'to stand up to' in
He stood up to everything; also combinations that include nouns, such as
'to take stock of' in *They took stock of their surroundings* or 'to pay
attention to' in *I paid close attention to his argument*.

Guaraní   Spoken throughout Paraguay, and the only language,
though Spanish also has official status, of many of its people.

Paraguayan Guaraní is related to **Classical Guaraní**, now dead but recorded by early Jesuit missionaries, within a branch of *Tupi-Guaraní that extends to neighbouring parts of Brazil, Bolivia, and Argentina.

Gujarati *Indo-Aryan language, spoken mainly in the Indian states of Gujarat, where it has official status, and Maharashtra; also widely, through emigration, in South and East Africa and elsewhere. Written in a script derived from *Devanagari.

Gullah English-based *creole spoken along the coast of Georgia and South Carolina in the USA. The African elements in it were the subject of a pioneering study by a native speaker, L. D. Turner, in 1949.

guṇa Term in *Sanskrit for a unit analysed as the combination of a simple vowel or resonant with a preceding *a*. Thus *i* is a simple vowel; *e* is the *guṇa* form resulting e.g. from a fusion of *a* and *i* across a word boundary. One of three degrees of 'strengthening': *see vṛddhi*.

Gur Family of languages in the Sahel region of West Africa, from south-eastern Mali and northern Ivory Coast across Burkina Faso and the north of Ghana, Togo, and Benin, into north-west Nigeria. Moré, spoken in an area which includes Ouagadougou, is the main indigenous language of Burkina Faso. The family is also called '**Voltaic**'.

Gurmukhi *Indian script developed for *Punjabi.

'guttural' Older term for *velar consonants and others produced in the back part of the vocal tract; no longer used in any technical sense.

Gypsy *See* Romany.

H

H 1. Symbol for a high *tone. **2.** See diglossia.

habitual (Verb, *aspect) indicating something done etc. consistently or habitually. Thus the present tense has a habitual use in e.g. *I exercise the dog on Sundays.*

half-close (Vowel) that is auditorily one-third of the way from *close to *open: thus [e] and [o] in the system of primary *cardinal vowels. Also called **close-mid**.

half-open (Vowel) that is auditorily one-third of the way from *open to *close: thus [ɛ] and [ɔ] in the system of primary *cardinal vowels. Also called **open-mid**.

Halle, Morris (1923–) American linguist, associated first with Jakobson and, from the mid-1950s, with Chomsky. Responsible especially for the development of *Generative Phonology.

Halliday, Michael Alexander Kirkwood (1925–) British linguist who retired in 1987 from a chair in Sydney. Originally a specialist in Chinese, whose earliest general theory was the model of grammar eventually called *Systemic Grammar. In the late 1960s he applied this, in particular, in an analysis of English intonation and in a general account of the dimensions on which sentences are organized. The dimension of 'transitivity' concerns the relations of e.g. actor to action or action to goal; that of 'mood' their broadly *interpersonal function (e.g. as interrogative or declarative); that of 'theme' the relations of *theme to *rheme or *given to new. Halliday's general theory, especially as it emerged in the 1970s, is centred on an all-embracing concept of *function, including both the functions of utterances and texts and those of individual units within their structure, and on the thesis that the nature of language as a semiotic system, and its development in each individual, must be studied in the context of the social roles that individuals play, and the ways in which these develop.

Originally a follower of *Firth. Hence his own theories and followers, especially in the 1960s, were often called '**Neo-Firthian**'.

Hamitic *See* Afro-Asiatic.

hamza Sign in Arabic writing used to represent a *glottal stop.

hanging participle = dangling participle.

Han'gul The Korean alphabet, traditionally ascribed to King Sejong (1419–50). The characters representing consonants and vowels are in part composed of smaller elements, which represent phonetic features such as, in particular, a *place of articulation. These basic characters are then in turn combined into larger units representing syllables. *Han'gul* is the only native alphabet designed for a language in the Far East, and is unique, among systems of writing in normal use, for the phonological insight that informed it.

hapax legomenon ['hapaks lɪ'gɒmənɒn] A lexical unit found only once in the surviving records of a language. Greek 'said once'; often shortened to **hapax**. *Cf.* nonce-word.

haplology *Sporadic change in which successive syllables etc. which are similar in form are reduced to one. E.g. Late Latin *idololatria* 'worship (*-latria*) of idols' was reduced to forms such as French *idolâtrie* (> English *idolatry*).

Harappan script That of the Harappan civilization, flourishing in the Indus valley in the 3rd–2nd millennia BC. Undeciphered and not demonstrably connected to later Indian scripts.

'hard' Used conventionally of *velar plosives in Romance languages: thus 'hard' [k], [g] (spelled *c, g*) as opposed e.g. in Italian to 'soft' [tʃ], [dʒ] (also spelled *c, g*). Also more generally, in languages such as Russian which have palatalized consonants, of those that are not palatalized.

hard palate The roof of the mouth between the back of the ridge behind the teeth and the fleshy part called the *soft palate. *Palatal consonants are articulated in this area.

harmonic Any of a series of tones at higher intervals accompanying the fundamental tone produced by a vibrating body. The frequency of the fundamental tone is the *fundamental frequency, the lowest harmonic the 'first harmonic', and so on.

harmony 1. *See* vowel harmony; consonant harmony. **2.** Of the ranking of forms in *Optimality Theory. Thus, in any *tableau, those ranked higher are 'more harmonic' than those ranked lower.

Harris, James (1709–80) Author of an important philosophical grammar, *Hermes: or, a Philosophical Inquiry Concerning Language and Universal Grammar* (London, 1751). His work is grounded in the philosophy of Aristotle and includes an original analysis of word classes, in which 'substantives' and 'attributives' are opposed as principal parts of speech to 'definitives' and 'conjunctives' as accessories. Substantives include nouns and pronouns; attributives verbs and participles with adjectives and adverbs; definitives are articles with other determiners; conjunctives include both conjunctions and prepositions.

Harris's grammar was widely read and published after his death in both German (1788) and French (1795).

Harris, Zellig Sabbettai (1909–92) The leading theorist of the
*Post-Bloomfieldian school in the USA. In *Methods in Structural Linguistics*
(1951) he set out a series of formal procedures by which, on the basis of
a corpus or sample of actual or potential utterances, a description of a
language, in abstraction from the meanings of its units, could in
principle be obtained in a mechanical and therefore replicable way,
without reference to anything outside the corpus. This was perceived
at the time as a method by which descriptions could be justified
scientifically. In the course of the 1950s Harris developed, in concert
with his pupil Chomsky, ideas which the latter was to make his own:
in particular, those of a *generative grammar and of syntactic
*transformations. But by the end of the decade their paths had
separated, and Harris's later work, which deals especially with syntax,
has had less influence. His thought is summed up in his last two
books, *A Theory of Language and Information* (1991) and, at a more
popular level, *Language and Information* (1988).

'hash mark' (#) *See* double cross.

Hausa *Chadic language, native to northern Nigeria (roughly from
Kaduna northwards and some 200 km east of Kano westwards) and
neighbouring parts of Niger. Also widespread as a second language,
there and elsewhere, and as a lingua franca across West Africa. Written
in Arabic script before the 20th century, now largely in Roman.

Hawaiian *Polynesian, now spoken by a tiny minority of the native
population of the Hawaiian islands.

head (1) A word or other unit which may stand for or is seen as
characterizing a construction of which it is part.
  There have been two main definitions, one narrower and due largely
to Bloomfield, the other wider and now usual, following work by
R. S. Jackendoff in the 1970s. **1.** In the narrower definition, a phrase *p*
has a head *h* if *h* alone can bear any syntactic function that *p* can bear.
E.g. *very cold* can be replaced by *cold* in any construction: *very cold water*
or *cold water*, *I feel very cold* or *I feel cold*. Therefore the adjective is its
head and, by that token, the whole is an 'adjective phrase'. **2.** In the
wider definition, a phrase *p* has a head *h* if *h* is in some sense dominant
within *p*. Hence in particular, in treatments such as that of Huddleston
and Pullum, *CGEL*, a head is seen as determining, or primarily
determining, the syntax of a unit. E.g. the constructions into which *on
the table* can enter are seen as determined by the presence of a
preposition, *on*. Therefore the preposition is its head and, by that
token, it is a 'prepositional phrase'. Similarly, in *I feel cold*, the
predicate *feel cold* is a 'verb phrase' whose construction, as a whole,
with *I* is determined by its having as its head the verb *feel*.
  Cf. dependency, subordination. In early accounts of *X-bar syntax, a
head was a member of a *lexical category, which included that of

prepositions. Extended in the 1980s to *functional heads such as
*complementizers, including many whose realization was then *null.

head (2) The part of an intonation pattern that falls on syllables
preceding the nuclear or *tonic syllable: e.g. in *I didn't see* ˇHER, the
head falls on *I didn't see. Cf.* tail.

Head-Driven Phrase Structure Grammar Formal model of syntax
developed by C. Pollard and I. Sag in the late 1980s. In essence a
variant of *Generalized Phrase Structure Grammar in which the
structure of syntactic units is constrained directly or indirectly by the
properties of lexical units as *heads (1). E.g. the head of *Bill hates silence*
is (in this treatment) *hates*. The lexical properties of *hates* are such that
it combines with a following noun phrase: [*hates silence*]. By a process of
*unification this is in turn a verb phrase, and, since *hates* is a verb in
the third person singular, the phrase as a whole is one which, as a
non-lexical head, combines, again by a process of unification, with
a subject in the third person singular.
  As in other models which extend the role of the *lexicon, there are
either no or few specific rules. As in Generalized Phrase Structure
Grammar, there is no operation, as in earlier or contemporary versions
of *transformational grammar, by which units are moved.

'headline language' The style of newspaper headlines, studied as a
*restricted language. *Cf.* block language.

head marking Marking of syntactic relations on the *head (1) as
opposed to a subordinate or dependent element. E.g. in Semitic
languages such as Hebrew, a *possessive construction is marked by the
form of the head noun (traditionally in the *construct state). Opp.
dependent marking: e.g. in Latin a possessive construction is marked
instead by the genitive case of the noun that depends on the head.

head movement *Movement of a unit from the head position in
phrase A, as defined in *X-bar syntax, specifically into the head
position in a larger phrase B.

Head Parameter A proposed *parameter of *Universal Grammar
whose setting determines, at a sufficient level of abstraction, the order
in which a *head (1) relates to other units within phrases. Thus, in
English, the setting would be 'Head First': hence a head verb or head
preposition precedes a complement; a head determiner, under the
*DP-hypothesis, precedes a noun; a head *complementizer comes at
the beginning of a clause; and so on. For many other languages, such
as Japanese, the setting would instead be 'Head Last'.
  Cf. VO vs. OV languages; centrifugal vs. centripetal.

hearer Strictly, anyone who hears an *utterance, whether addressed
to them (as an *addressee) or not.

heavy (Noun phrase etc.) whose length or complexity affects the positions it can occupy in a sentence. E.g. one can say *I gave John advice* or *I gave advice to John*; but if *John* is replaced by *the man you will remember meeting last week* the second construction is at the very least more likely. One says *I posted a letter to John* rather than *I posted to John a letter*; but the second order is possible e.g. in *I posted to John a letter which was sent here by mistake*.

'**Heavy noun phrase shift**', or more generally '**heavy constituent shift**', is a proposed syntactic process by which 'heavy' elements are moved to a position later in the sentence.

heavy syllable One which counts rhythmically as two units rather than one. E.g. in Latin, one which ended in either a consonant or a long vowel: [lik] in [re'liktus] *relictus* 'left behind', [liː] in [re'liːkʷiː] *relīqui* 'I left behind'. One which ended in a short vowel was **light**: e.g. [li] in ['relikʷiː] *reliqui* 'the rest'. In the last two examples this difference determines, in particular, the different positions of the stress accent.

Called, in the western tradition, '**long**' (= heavy) as opposed to '**short**' (= light). The distinction in terminology between the weight of syllables (heavy vs. light) and the length of vowels (long vs. short) is from the ancient grammarians of Sanskrit.

Hebrew West *Semitic, spoken in antiquity in the interior of Palestine; the language of the Jewish Bible (Old Testament), progressively influenced and replaced by *Aramaic from the 8th century BC. Last attested in the 2nd century AD; thereafter a written and liturgical language, until revived in its modern form, especially from the 1920s, as a prospective official language of Jewish settlers in what is now Israel. Written in a *Semitic alphabet whose modern form ('square Hebrew') can be traced back to the 3rd century AD.

hedge Any linguistic device by which a speaker avoids being compromised by a statement that turns out to be wrong, a request that is not acceptable, and so on. Thus, instead of saying 'This argument is convincing', one might use a hedge and say 'As far as I can see this argument is convincing'; instead of simply giving an order 'Carry it into the kitchen!' one might use an interrogative as a hedge and say 'Could you perhaps carry it into the kitchen?'

height (of vowels) *See* vowel height.

heightened subglottal pressure Posited as a *distinctive feature by Chomsky and Halle, *SPE, where seen as one property of consonants impressionistically called *tense (2).

Hellenistic grammar The study of grammar in the West in the period called 'Hellenistic', conventionally 323–31 BC: the period of the early *Stoics and *Alexandrians, including *Dionysius Thrax.

hendiadys [hɛnˈdʌɪədɪs] Term in rhetoric for two words joined by a coordinator but seen as expressing a single complex idea: e.g. in *These cushions are lovely and soft*, meaning that they are lovely in being soft, not that they are separately lovely cushions and soft cushions. Lit. 'one (Greek *hen*) through (*dia*) two'.

'heritage language' One valued or perceived as part of the history of a community, but now dead or obsolescent. E.g. Welsh in parts of Wales now predominantly English-speaking.

hermeneutics Movement in the philosophy of science, according to which the task of the human sciences is to elucidate the structure of the social institutions underlying behaviour. Thus the aim of linguistics, as one human (and therefore 'hermeneutic') science, is to elucidate the rules of language, seen as rules that constitute such an institution.

From a term that usually means 'interpretation' or 'exegesis'. The movement developed in Germany in the 1960s; its ideas have been applied in linguistics since the 1970s, in opposition especially to those of Chomsky.

hesitation form Any sound used conventionally in a specific community to indicate that one is about to start or to continue speaking: e.g. English [əː] (*er*).

hesternal (Tense, form of verb) used or basically used in referring to events etc. that have taken place on the day before the day of speaking. From Latin *hesternus* 'of yesterday': *cf.* hodiernal.

hetero- From the Greek word for 'other'. E.g. a noun whose inflection follows something other than the regular pattern is traditionally '**heteroclite**'; the head e.g. of a noun phrase is **heterocategorial** if it is itself something other than a noun; **heteroglosses** link speakers using different forms on either side of an *isogloss. Often in implied or explicit opposition to *homo- 'same': e.g. two successive consonants are **heterorganic** (as opposed to *homorganic) if they have different *places of articulation; a word is **heteromorphemic** if it is formed from two (i.e. two different) morphemes; successive sounds are **heterosyllabic** (as opposed to *tautosyllabic) if they belong to different syllables.

'heteronomous' Term proposed by J. K. Chambers and P. J. Trudgill for a form of speech perceived as a dialect of a language 'superposed' or 'imposed' on it. E.g. the form of English spoken in Merseyside is 'heteronomous' in relation to standard English. Derived mechanically in opposition to 'autonomous'.

heteronymy Defined variously in varying opposition to *homonymy. Thus in particular of words with the same meaning, such as *pail* and *bucket*, used by different speakers or in different dialects. Also, however, of *homographs or *homophones, where the homonymy is only in writing or only in speech, and not both.

heuristic General term, e.g. in computing, for a procedure which is designed to solve a problem by exploring the most likely possibilities, as opposed to an **algorithm**, which mechanically examines every alternative.

hiatus [hʌɪ'eɪtəs] A division between vowels belonging to different words or syllables. E.g. [ɔː] and [aʊ] are '**in hiatus**' in a pronunciation of *draw out* as ['drɔː 'aʊt].

hic et nunc Latin for 'here and now'. Hence of a time and place of speaking, e.g. as the centre of *deixis.

hierarchy Any ordering of units or levels on a scale of size, abstraction, or subordination. E.g. a *phrase structure tree assigns a hierarchical structure to sentences; *levels of representation are often seen as forming a hierarchy from phonetics upwards; Jespersen's theory of *ranks (1) proposes a hierarchy of primary, secondary, and tertiary.

Hieratic *Cursive form of *Hieroglyphic used in writing *Egyptian from the 26th century BC. Replaced by *Demotic, for ordinary purposes, from the 7th century BC, but retained for religious texts; hence the name ('priestly').

Hieroglyphic Writing system developed for *Egyptian and used, mainly on or in monuments, from around 3000 BC until the 3rd century AD. Replaced for ordinary purposes by *cursive scripts (*Hieratic, *Demotic) derived from it.

  The signs are basically pictures of objects, people, etc., but function variously as representations of words as wholes (*logograms), as representations of consonants or successions of consonants (*phonograms), and as *determinatives added to phonograms to indicate the semantic class to which the word belongs. These functions are all found in the earliest texts.

high 1. (Tone, intonation) realized at a pitch that is high within a speaker's range. Usually represented by 'H' or by an acute accent. **2.** (Vowel) = close. In the scheme of Chomsky and Halle, *SPE, the feature [+ high] is that of a sound produced by 'raising the body of the tongue above the level that it occupies in the neutral position': hence also of *palatal and *velar consonants.

  Opp. in both senses to *low.

High (H) *See* diglossia.

High German *See* German.

highlighting Introduced by Quirk *et al.*, **CGE*, with reference to any linguistic means by which a phrase etc. is put into focus; e.g. the placing of the *nucleus (3) of an intonation, or the use of a *cleft or *pseudo-cleft construction.

Hindi-Urdu *Indo-Aryan, native to a large area centred on the valley of the upper Ganges, but spoken more widely across the north of the Indian subcontinent. The national language of Pakistan, where called **Urdu** and written in an Arabic script derived through Persian, and one of the national languages of India, where called **Hindi** and written by non-Muslims in *Devanagari. Distinct from other modern Indo-Aryan languages since around AD 1000 and with a literature from the 12th century.

hiragana One of two syllabic systems used in writing *Japanese.

'hissing' Used of dental or alveolar sibilants such as [s] in *hiss*, as opposed to palato-alveolar or 'hushing' sibilants, such as [ʃ] in *hush*.

historical linguistics The study of change in individual languages and in language generally. Distinguished by most schools of *structural linguistics as a branch of the subject concerned with *diachronic relations among language systems, separate from and presupposing the findings of *synchronic or *descriptive linguistics.

historic present A present tense used, especially with an effect of vividness or immediacy, in an account of past events. E.g. 'I was in Oxford Street yesterday and suddenly this man turns on me and grabs me by the arm and . . .'.

history In the ordinary sense in *historical linguistics. Also metaphorically of the stages in a *derivation: e.g. in a *transformational grammar the '**transformational history**' of a form or structure was the series of structures resulting from the transformations that applied to it.

Hittite *Indo-European language attested by *cuneiform texts of the mid-2nd millennium BC, mainly from the capital of the Hittite empire (modern Boğazköy in north central Turkey). The main language of the Anatolian branch.

Hixkaryana *Carib(an) language in the state of Amazonas in Brazil. Famous in the history of *typological classification as the first known *OVS language.

Hjelmslev, Louis (1899–1965) Danish linguist and one of the major exponents of *structural linguistics after *Saussure. His most important theoretical work, *Omkring Sprogteoriens Grundlæggelse* ('On the Foundations of Linguistic Theory'), appeared in 1943: later in English, *Prolegomena to a Theory of Language*, trans. F. J. Whitfield (1953).

Hjelmslev's theory carried Saussure's concept of the linguistic sign to a logical conclusion. The sign itself is represented by a 'sign relation' (or 'sign function') between two 'planes' or levels: one of *expression and one of *content. By the *commutation test, a difference between units at one level must entail a difference at the other. At each level, units are characterized by their *syntagmatic and *paradigmatic relations to other units, and these relations constitute a *form (2), again at each level, independent of its projection onto distinctions of *substance.

Hjelmslev called his theory '**glossematics**' from 1935 onwards.

Hmong-Mien *See* Miao-Yao.

'hocus pocus' Coined by F. W. Householder in 1952 in reference to linguists who did not ascribe any reality to the units, categories, etc. that they established, as opposed to 'God's truth' linguists, who did.

hodiernal (Tense, form of verb) characteristically used to refer to events etc. that have taken place earlier on the day of speaking. From Latin *hodiernus* 'of today': *cf.* hesternal.

Hokan Proposed family of languages spoken or formerly spoken in various parts of western North America, from northern California to Baja California and Sonora; also in the south of Mexico, in parts of Oaxaca. **Yana** was a Hokan language studied by Sapir.

Hokkien *See* Chinese.

holistic (Meaning etc.) of an expression referring to something as a whole. E.g. *the silver* would be understood holistically in *I cleaned the silver*, but *the garden* as non-holistic in *I watered the garden*, unless the water was sprayed everywhere.

holophrase A sentence or utterance consisting of a single word. Especially of single-word utterances by children at an early stage in their development of language: called accordingly the **holophrastic** stage.

homo- From the Greek word for 'same': thus **homonyms** (*cf.* -onym) are identical forms with different meanings, *homonymy is a relation between such forms, and so on. *Cf.* hetero-.

homographs Forms which differ phonetically but are spelled in the same way: e.g. *tear* [tɪə] and *tear* [tɛə]. *Cf.* homophones.

homonymic clash A clash between two homonyms, either of which could be used in similar contexts. A classic example is a posited clash in parts of south-west France between a word *gat* 'cat', derived from Latin *cattus*, and an identical form *gat* 'cock', predicted by regular processes of sound change from Latin *gallus*. In fact the second was replaced by other forms that changed or extended their meaning: *faisan*, historically 'pheasant', *vicaire* 'curate', and others. The explanation, proposed by *Gilliéron, is that these replacements avoided the misunderstandings that the clash would often have caused.

homonymy The relation between words whose forms are the same but whose meanings are different and cannot be connected: e.g. between *pen* 'writing instrument' and *pen* 'enclosure'.

Distinguished from *polysemy in that the meanings cannot be connected: therefore the words are treated as different lexical units. Also distinguished from cases of *conversion: e.g. for either of these homonyms, that of *pen* (noun) to *pen* (verb). Also from *syncretism, which is between forms of the same paradigm. Further distinctions can be drawn between homonymy of words as lexical units (e.g. the two lexical units *pen*) and e.g. identity of *roots or other *morphemes. Also between forms identical in both sound and spelling (such as the two words *pen*) and those that are the same in spelling only (*homographs) or in sound regardless of spelling (*homophones).

Cf. constructional homonymy; grammatical ambiguity.

homophones Forms which are homonyms, at least phonetically. Often therefore of ones spelled differently: e.g. *tier* and *tear* [tɪə].

homorganic (Consonant) which has the same *place of articulation as one which precedes or follows. Especially of a phonological unit that must be so realized: thus a nasal consonant in e.g. Italian is always homorganic with one which follows: [n] before [t] or [d] (*andare* 'to go'), [ŋ] before [k] (*cinque* 'five') or [g], and so on.

honorific (HON) Pronoun, form of verb, etc. used in expressing respect for someone, e.g. of higher social status. **1.** In the characteristic use this is a person referred to. E.g. in a sentence in Japanese meaning 'The professor helped him', the form for 'helped' might be marked to show respect for the professor who is referred to by its subject: this would be a **subject honorific**. In a sentence meaning 'He helped the professor', it might be marked in a different way to show respect for the professor as referred to, in this case, by its object: this would be an **object honorific**. **2.** Also, in some accounts, of *polite forms. Such a form is then distinguished, as an **addressee-controlled honorific**, from subject or object honorifics, which are **referent-controlled**.

hortative = exhortative.

host 1. The form to which e.g. a *clitic attaches. Thus, if *-n't* is a clitic in *He isn't there*, it has the host *is*. **2.** (Language) into which a *loan word is borrowed, as opposed to its *source language.

HPSG = Head-Driven Phrase Structure Grammar.

human Semantic feature of nouns etc. characteristically used in reference to people. Thus *who* is distinguished from *which* as human

([+ human]) vs. non-human ([– human]); *girl* belongs to a class of human nouns. Hence *the girl who came*, rather than *the girl which came*.

Humboldt, Wilhelm von (1767–1835) Prussian statesman and scholar, whose book-length introduction to a study of Kawi (Old *Javanese), published posthumously in 1836, was described by Bloomfield, nearly a century later, as 'the first great book on general linguistics'. In this and other work that dates essentially from the 1820s, Humboldt stressed both the fundamental unity of language in general, and the diversity of the individual languages that were seen as shaping the intellectual life of different nations and societies. This implied a programme of inquiry in which Humboldt made important contributions on three fronts: as a comparativist, whose work on Javanese included the first comparative study of the *Austronesian or Malayo-Polynesian family; as a descriptive linguist, also engaging with Basque among others; and in respect of the distinctions between types (*inflecting, *agglutinating, *incorporating) that inform the grammars of specific languages.

Two particular ideas have been seized on by admirers and followers. One is Humboldt's emphasis on language not as an object or product (Greek *ergon*) but as an activity (*energeia*) constantly renewed in interchanges among speakers. The other, which appears rather rarely in his own work, is that of the '**inner form**' of a specific language, interpreted as the formative principle or principles behind its individual grammar and lexicon. This remained influential in the 20th century, especially in Germany through the work of L. Weisgerber and other 'Neo-Humboldtians'.

Hungarian *Finno-Ugric, spoken in Hungary and by substantial minorities in Romania, Slovakia, and other adjoining countries. Attested from the Middle Ages, with increasing standardization from the 16th century.

The **Ugric** branch of Finno-Ugric includes Hungarian and two languages of the Urals called (after the river) '**Ob-Ugric**'.

humiliative (Form etc.) that speakers use in self-abasement, of themselves, their relatives, and so on: e.g., schematically, *house-*HUMILIATIVE, with the meaning 'my humble dwelling'.

'hushing' Used of palato-alveolar sibilants such as [ʃ] in *hush*, as opposed to dental or alveolar sibilants such as [s] in *hiss*.

'hybrid word' One formed from elements that derive historically from different languages: e.g. *amoral*, with a negative prefix (*a*-) from Greek and the rest from Latin.

hydronym A name for a river, lake, etc.: e.g. *Danube*, *Bin Brook*. *See* -onym.

hypallage [hʌɪˈpalədʒiː] *Figure of speech in which *a* is syntactically related to *b* but belongs more naturally with *c*. Stock examples are of the type *John's drunken speech*, where *drunken* modifies *speech* but it is John who was drunk.

hyper- From a Greek word meaning 'above' or 'over'. Hence e.g. *hypercorrection for 'over-correction'. Opp. hypo- ('under'); hence e.g. *hypernym, coined in opposition to *hyponym (originally 'hyp(o) + *-onym').

hyperbaton [hʌɪˈpəːbətən] Ancient term for any departure from normal word order.

hyperbole The term for 'exaggeration' in the ancient doctrine of *figures of speech.

hypercorrection **1.** The use of an incorrect form by a speaker trying to avoid ones that are stigmatized. E.g. some English speakers have or used to have a dialect with no [h]. But 'dropping an h' is and was stigmatized; so, in trying to avoid the stigma, they might use [h] even when it is not there in the prestige form: e.g. [hɑːmfʊl] for *armful*, where it is **hypercorrect**, as well as for *harmful*. **2.** In sociolinguistics, of the increased use of one form in avoiding another. E.g. a group of speakers do not consistently use [h] in words like *harmful*. But because the lack of [h] is stigmatized, they tend to use it more often than one might predict from other factors, e.g. their position on a scale of social classes or with respect to level of education.

hypernymy The opposite of *hyponymy. E.g. *flower* is a hypernym of *tulip* and of *rose*.

hyphen (-) Used to show divisions within words: e.g. *disappointed* has the morphological structure *dis-appoint-ed*. If an affix or other *bound (1) form can end a word it is cited with a hyphen before it: thus *-ed*. If it can begin a word it is cited with a hyphen after it: thus *dis-*. If it can appear neither at the beginning nor at the end it is cited with hyphens before and after: e.g. in Latin, *-ba-* as a marker of the imperfect (*canta-ba-t* 'was singing').

Also in glosses, e.g. in conjunction with a *full stop.

hypo- From a Greek word meaning 'under'. Hence e.g. *hypotaxis 'ordering under'. Opp. hyper-.

hypocoristic (Word, formation) imitating or reflecting the speech of children: e.g. *tummy*, originally in nursery speech, from *stomach*. Often of formations that have become systematic: e.g. for first names in German (*Stephanie* → *Steffi*, *Fritz* → *Fritzi*, etc.).

hyponymy The relation between two lexical units in which the meaning of the first is included in that of the second. E.g. any tulip and any rose is also a flower: therefore the words *tulip* and *rose* are both **hyponyms**, and together are '**co-hyponyms**', of *flower*.

hypotaxis [hʌɪpə'taksɪs] Greek term for *subordination, applied specifically to subordination of clauses or sentences. Opp. parataxis ('arrangement under' vs. 'arrangement alongside') for their *coordination. E.g. *he came* is **hypotactic** in [*I said* [*he came*]], but paratactic in [[*I promised*] *and* [*he came*]].

hypothetical (conditional) *See* remote.

hypothetico-deductive method Scientific method in which propositions which follow from a general hypothesis are tested against experimental or other data to determine whether the hypothesis is confirmed or is false. Often applied in the 1960s and 1970s to the validation of a *generative grammar. Thus the grammar is a hypothesis about the sentences of a language; from it one predicts that certain forms are grammatical and certain others are not; if these predictions accord with the judgements of speakers the grammar is to that extent confirmed; if not, it must in some respect be wrong.

The value of this method in linguistics is debated, in this and other applications.

hysteron proteron Rhetorical term from Ancient Greek for putting first ('proteron') what should logically be later ('hysteron'): e.g. in a recipe which says that the oven should be preheated to 200°C after it tells you to put the food in.

I Syntactic category posited by Chomsky in the early 1980s, heading a phrase (**IP** or I-phrase) which is effectively a clause minus a *complementizer. E.g. *she married him* would realize an IP within a *CP or complementizer phrase *since she married him*: _{CP}[*since* _{IP}[*she married him*]]. Within it the I would be realized by the tense of the verb (*-ed*).

Short for original 'INFL', itself for 'inflection'. 'T' and 'TP', for 'tense' and *tense phrase, are used similarly.

IA = Item and Arrangement.

iambic (*Foot) consisting of a light syllable followed by a *heavy syllable. Borrowed into *Metrical Phonology from the definition of an iamb in verse.

Ibero-Romance The forms of *Romance, including Spanish, Portuguese, and Catalan, that developed in the Iberian peninsula.
'**Iberian**' refers to a language spoken in antiquity until superseded by Latin.

IC analysis *See* constituency.

Icelandic North *Germanic, attested from the Middle Ages by literature in a form described as Old Norse, at a time when the differentiation of North Germanic into separate languages was still at an early stage. The spelling of Old Norse devised in the mid-12th century, which is set out and justified in the anonymous 'First Grammatical Treatise', is remarkable as an early application of the phonemic method.

iconicity Principle by which semantic relations are reflected in the formal patterns by which they are realized. Thus a *direct object is a *complement of a verb while an *adverbial such as *today* is not: in that sense the semantic relation of verb to object is closer. In the order of words in English, direct objects are also closer to the verbs: *I saw John today* or *Today I saw John*, not *I saw today John*. In this way there is an iconic correspondence between the linear order of elements and their semantic pattern.

The term is from *Peirce's theory of signs, of which 'icons' were one kind. But linguists' usage is now largely independent.

ictus Traditionally of a rhythmical beat in a line of verse: thus in Latin verse a stressed syllable is seen as coinciding or not coinciding with the ictus of the relevant foot.

idealization The process by which, e.g. the elements and rules of a language are established as a system underlying the phenomena of speech. Likewise of the elements so established: e.g. a phoneme seen as an ideal sound which underlies a shifting range of real sounds and real mechanisms by which they are produced.

ideational (Meaning, *function of language) involving the representation of ideas. *Cf.* cognitive meaning; *also* descriptive (3), referential, representational.

identity Loosely, in the social sciences generally, of the property of belonging to, or feeling that one belongs to, a society or a group within a society. E.g. people may be conscious of and value their identity as members of a local community, and may therefore, among other things, maintain a local dialect.

identity operation One which changes nothing. E.g. the plural *sheep*, as in *three sheep*, can be derived by an identity operation from the singular *sheep*, as in *a sheep*. *Cf.* zero morph; *also* rule of referral.

ideogram A character in writing seen as representing an idea in abstraction from words. E.g. in '15', the number itself is represented independently of the relevant word in English (*fifteen*), or in French (*quinze*), and so on.

    Also '**ideograph**': sometimes used, especially in older treatments, for what is now more usually called a *logogram.

ideophone Used by Africanists of a distinct class of forms characterized by phonological structures that tend to be peculiar to them: e.g. by patterns of *sound symbolism, reduplicative structures, or distinct patterns of tones.

    Thence e.g. of *onomatopoeic forms more generally.

idiolect The speech or 'dialect' of a single individual. Hence **idiolectal variation** is variation within a language that is simply between one speaker and another.

idiom A set expression in which two or more words are syntactically related, but with a meaning like that of a single lexical unit: e.g. 'spill the beans' in *Someone has spilled the beans about the bank raid*, or 'put one's foot in it' in *Her husband can never make a speech without putting his foot in it.*

    Not usual, as a technical term, in any other sense. For others current in ordinary usage *cf.* accent (2); dialect.

'idiom chunk' A part of an idiom separated from the rest by a syntactic process. E.g. in *The beans were by then pretty well spilled* (meaning that some secret was out) *the beans* is a detached chunk of the idiom 'spill the beans'.

idiophone *See* interjection.

IE = Indo-European.

iff For 'if and only if'.

Igbo The official language in south-east Nigeria, native to an area from Port Harcourt northwards, including Onitsha, Enugu, and Afikpo. Variously classed, with others in the south of Nigeria, either as Eastern *Kwa or as *Benue-Congo.

I-language Chomsky's term from the mid-1980s for the knowledge of language seen as *internalized (hence in part 'I') as a system in the minds of speakers. *Cf.* grammar; competence.

Opp. E-language or 'externalized language'.

illative (ILL) *Case whose basic role is to indicate movement into something: e.g. schematically, *I walked house*-ILL 'I walked into the house'.

ill-formed Not *well-formed.

illocutionary Applied in the theory of *speech acts to the force that an expression of some specific form will have when it is uttered. E.g. a speaker might stop someone and say 'Please, can you help me?' By virtue of its form (interrogative preceded by *please*) this would have the illocutionary force of a request for assistance.

Cf. locutionary; perlocutionary. In the theory developed by Austin and his successors, the simple act of uttering this sentence is a locutionary act; the illocutionary act is that of uttering it as a request; the perlocutionary act is what is accomplished by uttering it (e.g. the addressee might ignore the request, or might in fact help). But what is 'illocutionary' and what is 'perlocutionary' plainly depends on how much is judged to flow conventionally from the form of an utterance. E.g. if the chairman of a meeting says 'This meeting is now closed', this may be seen as a formula which has the illocutionary force of closing it. But its form is more generally that of a statement, and, as made by the chairman, it might instead be claimed to have that as its perlocutionary effect.

Ilocano *Austronesian language, native to the north-west of Luzon in the Philippines.

'image schema' Used informally by G. P. Lakoff and others of a general concept that structures our perception of the world: e.g. the concept of 'a container', or of 'movement up and down', or of 'a long thin object'. Patterns of *metaphor (2) can be seen as transformations relating one image schema to another.

immanent Inherent. Thus one view of a *language system is that it is a structure immanent, i.e. inherent, in the phenomena studied. Traditionally the opposite of 'transcendent'.

immediate   Used where a relation has no intermediate term. Thus, in accounts of *constituency, the **immediate constituents** of a unit are the smaller units into which it is directly analysed; in a *phrase structure tree, a node A **immediately dominates** another node B if they are connected with no other node intervening.

imparisyllabic   Not *parisyllabic.

imperative (IMP)   (Construction, form of verb) whose primary role is in giving orders. E.g. *Get out!* is an imperative sentence; in Latin, *i* 'go!' is an imperative form of the verb.

Sometimes used simply in the sense of 'order'. E.g. in Latin, a subjunctive such as *eat* 'go-SUBJ-3SG' can be what is traditionally a *third-person imperative ('May such or such a person go'). But, like *declarative and *interrogative, it is in principle a term in grammar, the role of 'order' being one that constructions etc., including ones other than imperative, have in context.

imperfect (IMPF)   Traditional term for forms of a verb that are past *progressive as opposed to *perfect: e.g. Latin *vivebat* ('live-IMPF-3SG') 'was living, was alive', as opposed to *vixit* 'lived, has lived, is no longer alive'. Hence e.g. of forms such as English *was living*.

imperfective (IMPERF)   Not *perfective: i.e. of forms used to refer to actions etc. conceived as extending over a period of time, continuously or at intervals.

Cf. progressive. In a notional analysis of *aspect the progressive in English or the *imperfect in Latin or the Romance languages can be described as imperfective, while the simple past or 'preterite' is perfective. E.g. 'imperfective' *is courting our daughter, was seeing her every weekend*; 'perfective' *met her last weekend*.

impersonal (IMPERS)   (Verb) which does not take a subject: e.g. Latin *oportet* 'ought' in *quid me oportet facere?* 'What should I do?' (lit. 'what-ACC me-ACC ought to-do'). Thence of the construction taken by such a verb, and generally of constructions that are similar. E.g. *It is nice to relax* is impersonal since, although there is a subject (*it*), it is a *dummy which does not refer to a specific individual or 'person'.

The term originates in the description of languages like Latin which have subjects in the strictest sense: *see* subject (1). But it could in principle be extended to any in which some element is similarly distinguished.

impersonal passive   An *impersonal construction in which the verb is passive in form. Thus in German *Es wurde getanzt* 'There was dancing', *wurde getanzt* is passive (lit. 'was danced'); at the same time *es* is a *dummy, as in e.g. *Es schneit* 'It is snowing', which does not refer to something that was being danced.

Also of other impersonal constructions in which the verb can be seen as in some way like a passive. E.g. in Spanish *Se venden casas* 'Houses for sale', the construction with *se* is described as impersonal except that the verb *venden* ('sell-3PL') agrees with *casas* ('house-PL'). Although *venden* is active, its relation to *casas* is taken to be like that of a passive to its subject; so this sentence too is a 'passive impersonal'.

implicate *See* implicature. Distinguished from 'imply' as used of *implication.

implication Relation in logic such that, if *p* is true, then *q* is also true. Commonly written $p \rightarrow q$: e.g. 'girl (x) $\rightarrow$ female (x)' ('If x is a girl then x is female'). **Mutual implication**, written $p \leftrightarrow q$, is the case where each proposition implies the other.

implicational scale Any scale in which a feature associated with a given point implies the presence of those associated with all lower points. E.g. a scale in which points correspond to dialects, such that, at the lowest point, dialect A has undergone a sound change s_1; at the next highest dialect B has, in addition to s_1, undergone s_2; at the next highest dialect C has, in addition to s_1 and s_2, undergone s_3, and so on: i.e. the operation of sound change s_i implies that of all changes s_j, where $j < i$. Also, e.g. in cases of *gradience: thus form A might satisfy one criterion; form B both that and another, form C both those and another, and so on.

*Accessibility scales in syntax reduce to the same model.

implicational universal A *linguistic universal of the form 'if *a* then *b*'. E.g. if a language has phonetically nasal vowels, it also has oral vowels.

implicature Any meaning that a sentence or an utterance may have that goes beyond its meaning as determined, variously in competing theories, by *truth conditions, by its *semantic representation in a grammar, as an *explicature, and so on.

Originally distinguished by Grice, in a study of words corresponding to logical connectives. Thus in Grice's account *Bill came in and undressed* would be true if and only if it was true that Bill came in and it was also true that Bill undressed. It would merely **implicate**, or would normally implicate, that he came in before he undressed and not after. Thence extended to sentences and utterances generally. E.g. *He's had at least three whiskies* could be said to implicate, in an appropriate context, that the 'he' in question should not be allowed to drive home.

Divided by Grice into *conventional implicatures and *conversational implicatures. But often, in practice, of the latter only.

impliciture The meaning of a sentence as extended, in the account of K. Bach, to include in particular what has to be understood when it is uttered in a particular context. E.g. *It is too big* might have the impliciture, in one context, that whatever it is is too big to get through a door; in another, that it is too big for someone to eat; and so on.

Cf. explicature, both seen as a 'pragmatic enrichment' of 'semantics'.

implosive A *stop produced by an *airstream mechanism in which air is initially rarefied above the larynx. In the simplest case, the glottis is closed and a stop is articulated at some place of articulation forward of it; the larynx is then lowered, so that, when the forward closure is released, air is drawn inwards into the space behind it. The mechanism is, on this basis, classed as *glottalic and *ingressive. But the drop in air pressure above the larynx also causes air to pass periodically upwards through the glottis: hence stops of this kind usually have an effect of voicing. A bilabial implosive [ɓ] and dental/alveolar implosive [ɗ] are widespread e.g. in West African languages.

The terms 'implosif' and 'implosion' have a different sense in French. E.g. in *acteur* 'actor' the *c* [k], which ends a syllable, is 'implosive'; the following *t* [t], which begins one, is 'explosive'.

imprecative A sentence, especially a *minor sentence, which includes a swear word or some other form used in abuse. Hence of some, like *Damn you!*, which are indeed, in origin, imprecations. *Cf.* expletive.

impressionistic transcription A *phonetic transcription of speech done by ear without, or as a prelude to, a phonological analysis; alternatively, one done by ear without the aid of instruments.

inalienable possession Possessive relation in which the thing possessed is an inherent part of the possessor: e.g. in *Mary's eyes*, referring to the eyes that are part of Mary's own body. Opp. alienable possession, the two being distinguished in many languages.

inanimate Not *animate.

inceptive = inchoative (1).

inchoative [ɪnˈkəʊətɪv] **1.** (Verb, *aspect) indicating the initiation of some process or action. E.g. Latin *senescere* 'to grow old' or *maturescere* 'to ripen' are traditionally called inchoative verbs, and *-esc-*, by which they are formed from the words for 'old person' and 'ripe', an 'inchoative suffix'. Also called '**inceptive**'. **2.** The construction, in some accounts, of an intransitive such as 'open' in *The door opened*, as opposed to one that is transitive or 'causative', as in *They open the door*.

Constructions like that of *The door opened* seem to attract the abuse of terms traditional in other senses: *cf.* ergative (2); middle.

'incidence' The range of individual forms in which e.g. a particular sound unit is found. Differences of 'incidence' have been distinguished in dialectology from differences in e.g. the system of sound units itself.

inclusion Technically of a relation between sets in which all members of a set A are also members of a set B. If so A is **included** in B; it is **properly included** if, in addition, at least one member of B is not a member of A.

inclusive (Person, pronoun) used in referring to the speaker plus at least one addressee: e.g. Tagalog *kata* 'you and I', *tayo* 'you and I and at least one other'.

An inclusive form used to refer to a single speaker and a single addressee has often been called 'dual'; alternatively it is 'minimal' as distinguished from *augmented. One which refers to either these or more than these is generally called 'first plural inclusive' ('we' including the addressee) in opposition to 'first plural exclusive' ('we' excluding the addressee). But a form referring to both speaker and addressee is logically as much a 'you' form as a 'we' form. Hence an inclusive person (speaker and addressee) may be distinguished equally from both, on the one hand, a first person (speaker but not addressee) and, on the other, a second person (addressee but not speaker). A language may also have a distinction in the second person between a second plural inclusive ('you' plus the speaker) and a second plural exclusive ('you' without the speaker), both opposed to an 'exclusive' first plural.

incompatibility (*Sense relation) among words that are mutually exclusive. E.g. between *black* and *white*: if something is black it cannot be white and if something is white it cannot be black.

incorporation A regular process by which lexical units which are syntactically *complements of verbs can also be realized as elements within the verb itself: e.g., schematically, *hunt-rabbit*-PROG-3SG 'He is hunting rabbits, is rabbit-hunting'. Also of a pattern in which forms appearing only as affixes have meanings which correspond to those of forms appearing only as distinct words. E.g., schematically, *hunt*-RABBIT-PROG-3SG, where 'RABBIT' is a suffix different from, but linked semantically to, a lexical unit also meaning 'rabbit'.

An **incorporating language** is one in which such patterns are systematic: ones of the second type, e.g. in Eskimo, were the earliest known.

'incremental' (morphology) *See* inferential-realizational.

indeclinable (Noun etc.) which, exceptionally for the language in question, does not have distinct inflections.

indefinite Not referring to, or indicating reference to, an identifiable individual or set of individuals. E.g. in *I have to see a student*, the phrase *a student* does not indicate specifically which student the speaker has to see: it is accordingly an **indefinite noun phrase**. By the same token, *a* in *a student* is an **indefinite article**, *someone* in *I have to see someone* is an **indefinite pronoun**, and so on. Opp. definite.

indefinite reference *Reference to a specific individual or set of individuals not necessarily identifiable by an addressee. E.g. if I say to someone 'I have lost a hammer' I myself have a specific hammer in mind; but, to understand me, they do not have to know which it is. Contrast *a hammer* in 'I must buy a hammer', where there is no specific reference, or *the hammer* in 'I have lost the hammer', where the referent is one that the speaker can in turn identify.

independent clause A *clause which forms a sentence on its own: hence often equivalent to *main clause.

'independent motivation' Support for an analysis based on independent, or allegedly independent, evidence. Thus an analysis of a phonological system might be supported by evidence both of sound changes and of the progressive loss of distinctions in aphasia.
   Common in the 1960s and 1970s in the style of argument employed by advocates of transformations. E.g. in *They expected me to leave*, *me* has the form this pronoun has when it is an object: cf. *They saw me*. Therefore, in one analysis, it is on its own the object of *expected*: *They expected me* [*to leave*], not *They expected* [*me to leave*]. In addition, it corresponds to the subject of a passive: *I was expected* [*to leave*]. In that respect it resembles other elements analysed as objects: therefore this evidence might be claimed as 'independent motivation' for treating it as one.

indeterminacy Strictly, perhaps, of cases where a division or distinction cannot be precisely drawn. E.g. in a normal pronunciation of a word like *seeing* there is no way of determining exactly and indisputably where the realization of *see-* ends and that of the ending *-ing* begins. Also, however, of cases where a decision will be made differently by different criteria. Many classic problems, e.g. of *gradience, or in distinguishing *homonymy from *polysemy, involve indeterminacies of both kinds.

indexical Term in philosophy for an expression whose *extension is relative to a specific context, with a specific speaker, addressee, location in space, etc. E.g. *here* is an indexical expression, as in *Mary lives here*. *Cf.* deixis.

Indian languages Those of the Indian subcontinent: specifically of the *Indo-Aryan branch of *Indo-European, covering part of Sri Lanka and most of the area from the Indian states of Maharashtra and Orissa northwards; of the *Dravidian family mainly in south India and north-east Sri Lanka; and of the *Munda family, in scattered parts of

central and eastern India. Among others, English is used widely as a
*second language, and also has native speakers.

Indian scripts Writing systems derived directly or indirectly from
the *Brahmi script, attested in ancient India from the second half of
the 1st millennium BC. Modern forms include *Devanagari, used in
particular for Hindi, and the separate scripts, often with characters of
very different shapes, that have developed for other major *Indo-Aryan
and for the *Dravidian languages: in addition, those of *Tibetan, and
of most languages in South-east Asia, including *Burmese, *Khmer,
*Lao, and *Thai. Earlier forms were used still more widely, in Central
Asia with the spread of Buddhism and e.g. for *Javanese before the
Muslim conquest.

The basic type is *alpha-syllabic, as *Devanagari. The precise
historical links, both within and outside India, are still partly
uncertain: but for those in South-east Asia, the Mon script, attested in
Burma (Myanmar) from the 11th to the 12th century AD, and before it
the Grantha script, used in the coastal area of Tamil Nadu from the
5th century AD, were major intermediaries.

Indic = Indo-Aryan.

indicative (IND) 1. (Form of verb, affix, etc.) which represents an
*unmarked *mood in opposition to a *subjunctive, *imperative, etc.
Hence that, in particular, of unqualified statements: thus Italian
Entra Giovanni ('enter-IND-3SG John') 'John's coming in', as opposed
e.g. to subjunctive *Entri, signore* ('enter-SUBJ-3SG, sir') 'Do come in, sir'.
2. (Sentence) = declarative.

indicator *See* sociolinguistic variable.

indices Commonly of subscripts or superscripts used to show when
phrases have the same or different referents: thus, in *Mary$_i$ said she$_i$
would come*, the expressions *Mary* and *she* are **co-indexed**, with a
subscript i, to distinguish the meaning 'Mary said she (Mary) would
come'; in *Mary$_i$ said she$_j$ would come* two different subscripts i and j
would distinguish instead the meaning 'Mary said she (someone else)
would come'.

'indirect anaphora' A relation between a phrase and some earlier
expression which, though not in a strict sense an antecedent, will
effectively indicate, in the light of people's general knowledge, who or
what it refers to. E.g. people know that bicycles have chains: therefore,
in *I was riding my bicycle but the chain came loose*, the phrase *the chain* will
be understood, all else being equal, as referring to that of the bicycle
referred to by the earlier phrase *the bicycle*. If so there is said to be a
relation of 'indirect anaphora' between them.

indirect object (IO) An object whose semantic role is characteristically that of a recipient, e.g. *to your sister* in *He blew a kiss to your sister*; also, in most accounts, *your sister* in *He blew your sister a kiss*. Opp. direct object.

The relation between these sentences is often described in terms of *dative movement. It is in part because that relation is possible that *to your sister* is distinguished, as an object, from directional phrases such as e.g. *to the seaside* in *He sent his family to the seaside*.

indirect question 1. A question as reported in *indirect speech: e.g. *where he was* in *I asked where he was*. **2.** An utterance with the force of a question which is not in an *interrogative form. E.g. the *declarative *I would like to know his name* might be uttered as an indirect question, with in part the same intention as 'What is his name?'

indirect speech The reporting of something said, thought, etc. with *deixis adapted to the viewpoint of the reporter. E.g. *He said he would bring them* might report a promise, originally 'I will bring them'. But the person who made the promise was someone other than the reporter: hence, in the reporting, original *I* is changed to *he*. Also the promise was earlier than the report; hence, in addition, *will* is changed to *would*. With these adaptations, *he would bring them* is an example of, and is said to be 'in', indirect speech.

Opp. direct speech. E.g. in *He said 'I will bring them'*, the promise is instead reported directly, with the deixis appropriate to when it was made.

indirect speech act A *speech act whose force differs from what is taken to be the literal meaning of the sentence uttered. Thus *Could you close the window?* has the form of an *interrogative; therefore, in some accounts, it is literally a question. The act of uttering it as a request would then be indirect.

Cf. indirect question (2). Other instances were given blended names in the 1970s: *see* queclarative, whimperative.

Indo- 'In India': e.g. *Indo-Aryan. Also in names for groupings of language families which include *Indo-European. Thus **Indo-Semitic** is a conjectural family including Indo-European and *Semitic, **Indo-Uralic** one in which it is lumped with *Uralic. *See also* Indo-Hittite, Indo-Iranian.

Indo-Aryan Branch, within *Indo-European, of *Indo-Iranian: first attested by texts in *Vedic (*Sanskrit) dating from the 2nd millennium BC, and by inscriptions from the first.

The modern Indo-Aryan languages cover most of the north and centre of the Indian subcontinent, with outliers in Sri Lanka (Ceylon) and the Maldives. *Hindi-Urdu and *Bengali are by far the largest; of the remainder, *Marathi, in the south of the main area, *Gujarati in the south-west, *Sindhi to the west, *Punjabi in the north-west,

*Assamese in the east, *Oriya in the south-east, and *Sinhalese in Sri Lanka all have a current literary standard and are linked to major political units. Others, such as *Bhojpuri or *Maithili, also have speakers in the tens of millions.

Across the main area, separate languages have arisen largely by divisions within a geographical continuum. Hence internal branches are not definitively established.

Indo-European Family of languages including, at historically its western limit, most of those spoken in Europe and, at its eastern limit, the major languages of all but the southern part of the Indian subcontinent. Usually divided into eleven main branches: in the order in which they are first attested, *Anatolian (now extinct), *Greek, *Indo-Iranian, *Italic (represented by the modern Romance languages), *Celtic, *Germanic (which includes English), *Armenian, *Tocharian (extinct), *Slavic (Slavonic), *Baltic (represented by Latvian and Lithuanian), and *Albanian. Groupings larger than these are problematic to varying degrees: the safest hypothesis is that of a common *Balto-Slavic.

The *comparative method has its origin in the intensive study of Indo-European, especially in German-speaking universities, from the early 19th century. The size and complexity of the family, in comparison with many others that can be established with the same certainty, reflects in part the early date at which the forms in several branches can be compared.

Indo-Hittite = Indo-European, but seen as dividing initially into two major branches, one including Hittite and the other *Anatolian languages, the other having Sanskrit, Italic, Greek, etc. as sub-branches.

Indo-Iranian Branch of *Indo-European divided in turn into *Indo-Aryan and *Iranian.

Indonesian *See* Malay-Indonesian.

induction Process of reasoning which moves from the particular to the general. E.g. from a series of observations of individual professors, all of whom work very hard, one might draw the **inductive inference** that all professors work very hard.

Opp. deduction: *cf.* abduction.

inessive *Case whose basic role is to indicate position within something: thus, schematically, *I-sit study*-INESS 'I am sitting in a study'.

INF = infinitive.

infection Older term for the influence of one vowel on another, e.g. in *metaphony or *vowel harmony.

infectum Term in Latin grammar for forms of a verb that are not marked as *perfect (2). E.g. Latin *regit* 'rules' or *regebat* 'was ruling' are forms of, and based on the stem (*reg-*) of, the *infectum*; *rexit* 'ruled, has ruled' and *rexerat* 'had ruled', based on the stem *rex-*, are corresponding forms of the *perfectum.

infelicitous (Speech act) not meeting the required *felicity conditions.

inference Any conclusion drawn from a set of propositions, from something someone has said, and so on. This includes things that follow logically: *cf.* implication, entailment. It also includes things that, while not following logically, are implied, in an ordinary sense, e.g. in a specific context: *cf.* e.g. conversational implicature.

inferential (Particle, inflection) indicating that what is said is based on inference and not on direct observation. E.g., schematically, *They* INFERENTIAL *are indoors* 'They must be indoors' (because their door is open, because they are not visible outside, and so on). Opposed to other *evidential elements.

inferential-realizational G. T. Stump's term for a treatment of inflectional morphology in which words are characterized abstractly by a *lexeme and a set of *morphosyntactic features, whose *realization follows in accordance with a set of rules for affixes etc. Opposed especially to treatments seen as '**lexical**' and '**incremental**', in which features are assigned to *morphemes in a lexicon and words derived by adding one such morpheme to another.
    Hence of Stump's own treatment since the 1990s, in opposition to e.g. *Distributed Morphology. *Cf.* Word and Paradigm.

infinitive (INF) A non-*finite form of a verb characteristically used in clauses and in other constructions subordinate to another verb: e.g., in English, the 'bare infinitive' *do* in *I made him do it,* and the infinitive with *to,* as it is usually described, in *I forced him to do it.* An **infinitive clause**, or **infinitival clause**, is one whose verb is in the infinitive form: thus in these examples, if clause boundaries are established after *made* and *forced,* both *him do it* and *him to do it.*
    Originally of forms in e.g. Latin that also regularly headed noun phrases: thus, more marginally in English, *To buy caviar is expensive.*

infix An *affix or *bound (1) morpheme which is inserted within another form. Thus in Latin *rumpo* 'I break' the root is *rup-*: cf. *rup-t-us* 'broken'. The stem *rump-* then consists of the root with, in included position, an infix -*m*-.
    Infixation is the process of inserting an infix; a form is **infixal** if, like *rump-*, it is formed with an infix or, like -*m*-, it is in the position of one.

INFL ['ɪnfʊl] The original notation for the verbal inflection of a clause as represented in *Government and Binding Theory. Later shortened to *I.

inflecting (Language, formation) in which words distinguish grammatical categories whose realizations cannot or cannot easily be separated. E.g. in Russian, nouns distinguish case and number; but a specific case and a specific number are never realized by distinct endings. Likewise verbs distinguish e.g. a perfective from an imperfective, commonly realized by a variation within their stems.

Opp. agglutinating, isolating, in a typology dating from the 19th century.

inflection Any form or change of form which distinguishes different grammatical forms of the same lexical unit. E.g. plural *books* is distinguished from singular *book* by the inflection -*s*, which is by that token a plural inflection.

The term originally meant 'modification' (lit. 'bending'): thus *book* is modified, by the addition of -*s*, to *books*.

inflectional class A class of words or morphemes which have the same inflection or inflections. Thus *sing* is of the same inflectional class as *sink* or *drink*: as *sing* is distinguished from *sang* and *sung*, so *sink* is distinguished from *sank* and *sunk*, and *drink* from *drank* and *drunk*.

Major inflectional classes are often described as *conjugations (of verbs) or *declensions (of nouns).

inflectional morphology Branch of *morphology concerned with *inflections: hence especially with both the semantic and the formal structure of *paradigms. An **inflectional affix** is similarly an affix described as an inflection, a process by which e.g. such an affix is added is an **inflectional formation**, and so on.

Opp. derivational morphology. But the distinction has often been challenged, e.g. in *Lexical Morphology.

informant Any speaker of a language acting as a source for statements that a linguist makes about it. For their own language, linguists are often their own informants; in investigating one that they do not know or that is not theirs, they may work regularly with a single native speaker or group of speakers.

Sometimes replaced by '**consultant**' or '**language consultant**', especially in the USA, where 'informant' has developed the sense of 'informer'.

'informationally encapsulated' *See* modular.

information structure The structure of a sentence or larger unit viewed as a means of communicating information to an addressee. Described in terms of *given vs. new, *theme (1) vs. *rheme, *topic (2) vs. *comment, *focus, etc.

information theory Mathematical theory developed in the 1950s in which the quantity of 'information' carried by a channel of communication is defined in terms of the probability with which specific units may be transmitted. Suppose that messages may consist of any letter of the alphabet in any order: then the probability with which at any stage in the sequence any particular letter will be transmitted is constant. But suppose instead that messages consist of written words in English: then after e.g. initial *f* the probability that *t* or another *f* will follow is very low, that *u* will follow is relatively high, that *r* or *a* will follow even higher. In the second case the quantity of 'information' carried by the channel would be less.

Important in linguistics as a basis for one measure of *redundancy.

-*ing* form A verb form in English such as *sleeping* in *those sleeping*, *We were sleeping*, *I like sleeping*, *Sleeping was impossible*. Often so called because no term inherited from the grammatical tradition, such as *present participle or *gerund, is appropriate to all these uses.

ingressive (Air stream, *airstream mechanism) in which the direction of flow is inwards. Opp. egressive: for specific mechanisms *see* click, implosive.

Ingvaeonic = Anglo-Frisian.

inherent feature One which characterizes a word, etc. in the lexicon as opposed to one assigned to it by a specific construction. E.g. in German a noun is inherently masculine, feminine, or neuter; in specific constructions it will be contingently singular or plural, or nominative singular, accusative singular, and so on.

inheritance Any transfer of properties under an operation. E.g. *inquiry* is a noun derived from *inquire*, by an operation under which it inherits the property of taking a prepositional phrase with *into*: *They inquired* [*into his expenses*], likewise *their inquiry* [*into his expenses*]. Also of the copying of features from a higher to a lower level of constituency. E.g. a sentence is passive; therefore a verb phrase and a verb within it are also passive. For the opposite relation *cf.* percolation.

initial phrase marker Term in *transformational grammar for a phrase structure tree derived by rules of a *base component only, which is then subject to transformations.

initial symbol *See* rewrite rule.

Initial Teaching Alphabet A way of writing English proposed as a compromise between a phonetic transcription and the conventional spelling; devised by J. Pitman and promoted in several schools in Britain in the 1960s and 1970s on the theory that children would learn the spelling more easily if they learned this system first.

initiator Used of whatever initiates a flow of air in the production of speech. Thus in the pulmonic *airstream mechanism an airflow is initiated by the organs that control breathing.

injunctive Term in *Indo-European linguistics for the use of forms based on the stem of the indicative in orders and prohibitions. Attested mainly in *Indo-Iranian.

'innate' Usual in linguistics since the 1960s in the loose sense of 'in part at least determined by genetic inheritance'. Hence, in particular, the '**innateness hypothesis**', with reference to Chomsky's theory of *Universal Grammar.

inner form *See* Humboldt.

innovation Any change by which a language diverges from others historically related to it. E.g. the order of words in *Clearly I have lost* represents an innovation in English as compared with the *verb-second order of Old English and other Germanic languages. When two members of a family share an innovation, that is *prima facie* evidence that they are more closely related than either is to the others.

in pausa At the end of, or before a break in, an utterance. E.g., in many forms of English, a word like *beer* ends in [ɪə] before a consonant or 'in pausa', but has a *linking *r* [r] before a vowel.

instantaneous release Chomsky and Halle's term in **SPE* for the rapid release of a *stop consonant, in which the resulting flow of air is not audibly turbulent. Hence a feature distinguishing e.g. [p] or [t] from *affricates such as German *pf* or *tsch* [tʃ]. Opp. delayed release.

institutionalized = established.

instrumental (1) *Case or *case role of elements indicating an instrument used for some purpose. Thus *with a fork* has an instrumental role in *I dug it with a fork*; also, in accounts following that of *Case Grammar, *a fork* in *A fork would dig it easily* or *I used a fork to dig it.*

instrumental (2) (*Function of language) in achieving some practical end. *Cf.* conative.

instrumentalism Philosophical theory, developed in the late 19th century by J. Dewey, which holds that beliefs, hypotheses, etc. are instruments with which we engage with the world in which we live, and are therefore justified simply to the extent that they are successful and fruitful.

integration Process by which a word etc. borrowed from another language becomes part of the native system. Thus the [ʒ] of *rouge* or *mirage*, both in origin *loan words from French, is not fully integrated into English phonology, since its distribution, within the syllable and in relation to the vowels that it follows, is more restricted than that of [ʃ] (*sh*) and others to which it is most directly opposed. Likewise the words as wholes are not fully integrated, unlike words in [ʃ] such as *push* or *brush*, themselves much earlier borrowings from French, which are.

Integrational Linguistics R. Harris's term for a theory of language grounded in the study of specific utterances in specific contexts in which they are uttered. 'Integrational', therefore, in that languages are not conceived as systems independent of their use in communication.

Hence of work by Harris and his followers generally.

intensifying (Word, intonation, inflection) which in any way adds emphasis to a sentence or some element within it. Thus, schematically, *He did*-INTENS *it* might mean 'He really did it'.

'**Intensifier**' is used by Quirk *et al.*, *CGE, of a class of adverbial elements (in their terms a class of *subjuncts) with an intensifying role that is either positive or negative. The positive ones are **amplifiers** and include, as amplifiers of the strongest degree, **maximizers** such as *completely* or *utterly*; the negative are **downtoners** and include, at the other end of a scale, **minimizers** such as *hardly* or *scarcely*.

intension The properties that define a word or concept. An **intensional definition** of a class will correspondingly specify the properties that something must have to be a member of it. Opp. extension, extensional.

An **intensional logic** is one in which the validity of arguments depends on identity or difference in intension, opposed again to extension.

intensity The physical correlate of perceived loudness, usually measured in decibels.

intensive (Verb) which takes a *predicative adjective or noun phrase: e.g. those of *She is angry*, *He seemed a nice man*. Also of the pattern of *complementation associated with it: thus *angry* and *a nice man* are described as '**intensive complements**'.

Cf. copular, predicative, both of which are used more widely.

interactional sociolinguistics Branch defined by the study of interactions among speakers in face-to-face communication, as reflecting and developing social relationships.

interchangeability The property of language by which the roles of speaker and addressee are interchangeable. Thus any sentence one might utter one would also understand if said by someone else and, in principle, vice versa. Defined as one of the proposed *design features of language.

interdental (Consonant) articulated with the tip of the tongue protruded between the teeth: e.g. in one pronunciation of (*th*) [θ] in *thing*.

interference The influence that knowledge of one language has on the way one speaks another: e.g. in the speech of bilinguals, or as a cause of errors by someone learning a new language.

interfix A morphological element serving simply as a link between other elements. E.g. -*i*- in Latin *particeps* 'participant' or *aquifolia* 'holly', seen as linking two members of a compound (*part-i-ceps*, *aqu-i-folia*).

interjection Traditionally of forms that express 'states of mind' and do not enter into specific syntactic relations with other words: e.g. *Wow*, *Yuk*, *Phew*. Some, such as *phew* [ɸː], are also **idiophones**, with phonetic features peculiar to them.

   A *part of speech in ancient Roman accounts of Latin. Extended by some recent writers to a larger and more indeterminate category of which the traditional interjections are only part.

interlanguage 1. A language, or an artificial system like a language, used as an intermediary, e.g. in translation, between two others. **2.** A system of rules said to develop, in the mind of someone learning a foreign language, which is intermediate between that of their native language and that of the one being learned.

inter-level A *level of description defined as a link between two others: e.g. phonology defined, as by Halliday in the early 1960s, as one linking grammar and phonetics.

internal argument One not external to a *predicate (1) or *verb phrase: thus specifically an object as opposed to a subject.

internal causes Causes of change seen as internal to a language or to the community that speaks it. Thus an internal cause of sound change might be an increase in the *coarticulation of adjacent consonants, or the pressure to maintain an audible difference between vowels; an external cause might be contact with the system of a neighbouring language.

internal history The history of changes in the structure of a language, as opposed to its *external history. E.g. it is part of the internal history of English that rules of word order changed over the early Middle Ages; part of its external history that e.g. Shakespeare wrote in it.

'internalize' Used by Chomsky from the late 1950s for the process of constructing representations in the mind. Thus, in learning a native language, a child was seen as 'internalizing' its grammar. Hence, in Chomsky's terminology in the 1980s, **'internalized language'** or *I-language.

internal reconstruction The attempted *reconstruction of earlier stages of a language on the evidence of that language alone. Thus there are alternations in English between e.g. [ʌɪ] and [ɪ]: *wise* vs. *wisdom*, *vice* vs. *vicious*, etc. On that evidence alone one might argue, first, that either or both vowels must show the effect of sound change, and, secondly, that the most plausible changes would derive *wis(e)* and *vic(e)* from reconstructed *[wiːz], *[viːs].

internal sandhi Processes of phonological modification (*sandhi) found within words, at or across the boundaries of roots or affixes.

internal syntax The relations, rules, etc. that apply within a syntactic unit, as opposed to those into which it enters, as a whole, within larger units.

international language Any used internationally, whether all over the world (hence '**global**') or in one area; whether recognized officially as a language e.g. of diplomacy, or arising simply through bilingual contacts across many countries; whether native in one or more countries, such as English or Spanish, or e.g an international *auxiliary language such as Esperanto; and so on.

International Phonetic Alphabet The system of phonetic transcription developed and promoted by the *International Phonetic Association. Consonants are classified by *place and *manner of articulation, with boxes in the resulting grid filled, where there is no appropriate letter in the Roman alphabet, with special letters partly resembling them. *Secondary articulations, and some manners of articulation not distinguished by the Roman alphabet, are shown by diacritics. The transcription of vowels is according to the *cardinal vowel system.

The increasing adoption of this system is without doubt one of the most important practical achievements of linguistics in the 20th century.

International Phonetic Association Society founded in France in 1886 by Passy and called by this name since 1897. Its original aim was to promote the use of phonetic script in teaching modern European languages, and its journal, *Le Maître Phonétique* ('The Phonetic Teacher'), published articles in the *International Phonetic Alphabet which it devised. In the course of the 20th century its interests have become increasingly academic, with its centre shifted to Britain. Its present journal, the *Journal of the International Phonetic Association*, replaced *Le Maître Phonétique* in 1970.

Passy and his pupil (Daniel) Jones were leading figures for much of its history.

interpersonal (Meaning, *function of language) in developing and maintaining social relations between people. Alternatively, that is said to be the **social function**: the interpersonal then includes both that and the *expressive (affective, emotive) function.

interpretant Peirce's term for the effect that a sign has on someone who interprets or understands it. Hence *pragmatics was originally defined by the relation that signs have to interpretants.

interpretation 1. In ordinary senses, e.g. of the interpretation by one person of what another is saying, or of different interpretations of a sentence that is ambiguous. **2.** Any process in which a representation of a sentence, assigned in accordance with one system of rules or principles, becomes an input to another system. E.g., in *Principles and Parameters Theory, of those envisaged at the interface between internalized 'grammars' and *performance systems; likewise, in any grammar divided into separate *components (2), at the point where rules of one component (e.g. semantic) operate on the output of another (e.g. syntactic). Hence in particular *Interpretive Semantics; *see also* Generative Phonology.

interpreted (Logical calculus, etc.) assigned an interpretation in some system of *formal semantics.

'Interpretive Semantics' Applied in the early 1970s to any model of *transformational grammar in which *semantic representations of sentences were derived from what were seen as purely formal representations of their syntax. Rules deriving them had been said by Chomsky in the 1960s to be 'purely interpretive'. Such models included both the so-called *Standard Theory and the modifications of it leading to the *Extended Standard Theory.

Opp. Generative Semantics.

interrogative (Construction etc.) whose primary role is in asking questions: e.g. that of *Is he here?* as distinguished from the *declarative *He is here*. An **interrogative particle** or **interrogative inflection** is one which marks an interrogative: e.g. in the equivalent sentence in Latin, a *clitic *-ne* (*adestne?* 'be-present-3SG-INTERROG'). An **interrogative pronoun**, **adverb**, etc. is one that represents a focus of questioning: e.g. *who* or *what* in *Who did this?*, *What have they done?*; *where* in *Where are they taking us?*

The terms 'question' and 'interrogative' are often interchanged. E.g. *Is he here?* is a question or is an interrogative sentence or 'an interrogative'. But a distinction can and sometimes must be made. Thus *Can't you shut up?* has the construction of an interrogative, but its usual role would not be as a question but as a request or order. *Cf.* declarative; imperative.

interrogative tag A *tag in the form of an *interrogative: e.g. *has he?* in *He hasn't left, has he?*

interrupted (consonant) = abrupt.

intersection Technically of an operation on sets by which the intersection (or **product**) of sets A and B is the set of all elements, possibly none, which are members of both. *Cf.* union (1).

intertextuality Property of texts specifically linked to other texts: by quotation, as a précis, through allusion, and so on. Thence in a vacuous sense of discourse generally, since any utterance will at least use words in ways like those in which they have been used in others.

intervocalic Appearing between vowels. E.g. [p] is an intervocalic consonant in *kipper* ['kɪpə].

intonation A distinctive pattern of *tones over a stretch of speech in principle longer than a word. Thus there is a difference in intonation between e.g. *That's* `ɪt ('I'm finished') and *That's* ´ɪt? ('Is that all?').

A description of intonation usually has three main aspects. First, the relevant stretches of speech must be identified: in that way sentences or utterances are divided into successive *intonational phrases (or tone groups). Secondly, a syllable or series of syllables within each will be described as maximally prominent: this will be a position in the phrase identified by e.g. a rapid change of pitch. Thirdly, a specific pattern of tones will be distinguished: this might be described as an overall tune or *contour (rising, falling, falling and then rising, etc.) or is alternatively divided into a sequence of smaller units, each with its own pitch level. Descriptions in terms of contours were once usual e.g. in British treatments; the alternative treatment derives historically from American accounts in the 1940s and 1950s, in which patterns of intonation were described as *pitch morphemes composed of successive pitch phonemes.

intonational meaning Meanings associated with intonations, especially as reduced, to the extent that they can be, to systems of discrete units. An **intonational morpheme** is a combination of tones etc. seen as having such a meaning; *cf.* pitch morpheme.

intonational phrase A sequence of units identified as the domain of a pattern of intonation. E.g. in *I'll do it, but I'll need some help* there might be a division between two intonational phrases: *I'll* DO *it*, where the *tonic or most prominent syllable is *do*; *but I'll need some* HELP, where the most prominent syllable is *help*.

Symbolized by an iota (ɪ) in a hierarchy of mora (µ), syllable (σ), and so on. Called alternatively an 'intonation group' or '**tone group**'; *cf. also* breath group.

intransitive Construction in which a verb is related to a single noun or its equivalent: e.g. that of *They vanished*. An **intransitive verb**, or an intransitive sense of a verb, is one that takes such a construction: e.g. *vanish*, or *dry* with the sense it has in *It will dry*. Opp. transitive.

intransitive preposition A word such as *away* in *He walked away*, seen as a preposition which takes no complement. Traditionally classed as an adverb, since, in the ancient account of *parts of speech, prepositions were defined as preposed to a noun or some other element. *Cf.* transitive preposition.

intransitivizer Affix etc. marking a verb as intransitive rather than transitive. E.g., schematically, *Vase shattered*-INTRANS 'The vase shattered'.

intrinsic allophone A variant of a *phoneme which can be explained by the phonetic context, without invoking a specific phonological rule: e.g. one which is an effect of *coarticulation. Opp. extrinsic allophone; but the validity of the distinction depends in part at least on how the relation between phonetics and phonology is in general perceived.

intrinsic ordering *See* ordered rules.

intrinsic pitch The pitch of a vowel in abstraction from the vibration of the vocal cords. Thus [i] has a higher intrinsic pitch, in terms of the underlying resonance of the vocal tract, than [ɑ].

intrusive *r* *See* linking *r*.

intuition Variously of the intuitive grasp that people have or may have of the structure of their own language, and of the intuitive feeling that a linguist may have in investigating it. Likewise 'counter-intuitive'.

Inuit Often = Eskimo. Specifically of a branch of Eskimo within *Eskimo-Aleut, spoken from the Norton Sound in Alaska across the Arctic to Greenland and Labrador.

invariable word One which does not have two or more forms with different grammatical meanings. E.g. *but* or *never*, as compared e.g. with *woman*, which distinguishes singular *woman* and plural *women*.

invariant Not changing. E.g. in the classic theory of the *phoneme the *distinctive features that characterize each unit are invariant; the features with which it is realized in different positions or in different combinations vary. The aim of phonological analysis is accordingly to discover invariants that underlie surface variation.

inverse (Form of verb, affix) indicating, e.g. in Algonquian languages, that of two elements in a clause that differ on some scale of *empathy, it is the one lower on the scale that is the *agent.

Opp. **direct**. Thus, if third-person forms are lower on the scale than first persons, a sentence meaning 'I kissed the sister' will be marked as direct: schematically, with the persons marked respectively by a prefix and a suffix, 1ST-*kissed*-DIR-3RD *sister*. A sentence meaning 'The sister kissed me' will instead be marked as inverse. Thus, with the persons marked in the same way in the same positions, 1ST-*kissed*-INV-3RD *sister*.

inversion Any operation by which the order x + y is changed to y + x. E.g. an interrogative in English (*Is he here?*) is related to a corresponding declarative (*He is here*) by inversion of the subject (*he*) and a verb (in this case *is*).

inverted commas (',') Used variously for things other than individual forms considered in abstraction. Thus for glosses or translations: e.g. French *arbre* 'tree', *Elle vient* 'She is coming'. Also for propositions seen as expressed by sentences: e.g. both French *Elle vient* and English *She is coming* express the proposition 'She is coming'. Also for units represented at a higher level of abstraction: e.g. *coming* is a form of the verb 'to come'. Also of a form as uttered on a specific occasion: thus 'She's coming' would represent an utterance of *She's coming*.

'invisible hand' theory Model of change in language in which change in a given direction emerges, as if directed 'by an invisible hand', from the separate behaviour of individual speakers, directed in itself to strictly individual ends. An application to linguistics by R. Keller of an image in Adam Smith's *The Wealth of Nations*.

IO = indirect object.

iota (ι) *See* intonational phrase.

IP (1) = Item and Process.

IP (2) A *phrase (2) seen as headed by a unit that is typically an auxiliary or inflection (hence I) of a verb, central to *X-bar syntax and its successors from the mid-1980s onwards. Thus the structure of *Bill saw me* might include a *verb phrase headed by a verb with no inflection: $_{VP}[Bill [see me]]$. This would in turn be part of an **IP** headed by the past tense: $_{IP}[PAST [Bill see me]]$.

See tense phrase for the notations 'TP' and 'T', which have often been used equivalently since the 1990s.

IPA = International Phonetic Alphabet, International Phonetic Association.

I-principle Principle in *Neo-Gricean pragmatics by which speakers will be expected to give no more information, all else being equal, than is needed. I stands for informativeness.

First formulated by L. R. Horn, as the **R-principle** (R = relation); both opposed similarly to a *Q-principle. *Cf.* M-principle.

Iranian Branch, within *Indo-European, of *Indo-Iranian, first attested by religious texts in *Avestan and inscriptions in Old Persian from the reign of Darius I (522–486 BC). The modern languages are spoken mainly in a continuous area from eastern Turkey through Iran to Afghanistan and Tajikistan: *Persian, *Pashto, *Kurdish, and *Baluchi are in order of size the most important.

irony Traditionally of a *figure of speech in which one thing is said but the opposite is meant: e.g. 'That's just what I needed!', said as the tool one is using comes apart in one's hands. Usage in pragmatics or linguistics generally tends to reflect this, but others are also current, in literary studies especially.

Iroquoian Family of languages spoken or formerly spoken in parts of eastern North America. The main group were and in part are in the Great Lakes region from Lake Huron eastwards: this includes Mohawk. Others include *Cherokee.

irrealis [ɪreɪˈɑːlɪs] (Affix, form of verb, etc.) used to refer to an event etc. possible or imaginable, as opposed to one that is actually happening or has happened. Opp. realis.
   Had got is thus 'an irrealis' in the *remote or unreal conditional *if you had got there on time*; likewise *were* in *I was hoping you were in town tomorrow*. Especially, as applied to European languages, of a past tense used in this way.

irregular *See* regular.

irreversible binomial A pair of words in a fixed and parallel relation: e.g. (*It is raining*) *cats and dogs*, not *dogs and cats*; (*just a few*) *odds and ends*, not *ends and odds*.

island A syntactic unit whose boundaries form a barrier to specific syntactic relations or processes. For an example *see* coordinate structure constraint: *cf.* complex NP constraint, *wh*-island constraint. An **island constraint** or condition would be any such principle by which an island is defined.

isochrony Principle by which phonological units tend to be equally spaced in time: e.g. syllables in languages that are *syllable-timed, stresses in those that are *stress-timed.

isogloss A line on a map dividing areas whose dialects differ in some specific respect: e.g. between dialects in which a consonant is in principle voiced and those in which the corresponding consonant is voiceless, or those in which a certain thing is normally called *x* and those in which it is normally called *y*.
   Major divisions between dialects are characterized by **bundles of isoglosses**, in which many such lines tend to run together.

isolated opposition An opposition, especially in *Prague School phonology, characterized by a unique pair of features: e.g. in Spanish, between trilled [r] (*rr*) in *perro* 'dog' and flapped [ɾ] (*r*) in *pero* 'but'. Distinguished as such from members of a *correlation.

isolating (Language) in which each grammatical category is represented by a separate word. Opp. agglutinating; inflecting.

Early Chinese is a classic example. E.g. the sentence *wǒ qiě xián zhī yòng* 'I will employ the worthy' is made up of five words, each of which is grammatically indivisible: 'I (*wǒ*) future (*qiě*) worthy (*xián*) them (*zhī*) employ (*yòng*)'.

isomorphism Strictly, a term in mathematics for an exact correspondence between both the elements of two sets and the relations defined by operations on these elements. Hence of linguistic systems: thus a set of oppositions in one language could at an abstract level correspond to, or be 'isomorphic with', one in another, only the forms by which they are realized being different.

Loosely, from the late 1940s, of a general principle by which the structuring of one *level parallels or is made to parallel that of another. E.g. the relation of *morpheme to *allomorph was modelled on that of *phoneme to *allophone; a binary division of the syllable, into *onset and *rhyme, parallels that of the sentence into subject and predicate; semantic features, e.g. in *componential analysis, parallel *distinctive features in phonology. The term was introduced in this sense by J. Kuryłowicz, commenting on the work of Hjelmslev.

isophone An *isogloss where the relevant difference is phonetic or phonological.

Italian *Romance language whose standard form, increasingly dominant since the political unification of Italy in the 19th century, has its ultimate source in the Tuscan dialect of Florence, developed as a literary language from the Middle Ages by Dante and others. Many of the regional varieties called 'dialects' differ from it, in the south especially, to a degree that in other external circumstances would count as a difference between languages; hence their speakers are in effect bilingual.

Attested in a form distinct from Latin from the 10th century AD.

Italic Branch of *Indo-European which includes *Latin; also Oscan and Umbrian, attested by ancient inscriptions respectively from Pompeii and elsewhere in south Italy and from Gubbio in the Appennines.

italics Usual for citing words and other forms in abstraction from their use. E.g. in saying 'I must go home', one utters the sentence *I must go home*, which includes, among others, the word *home*.

Italo-Celtic *See* Celtic.

Item and Arrangement One of three models of morphology distinguished in the 1950s by C. F. Hockett. The 'items' are *morphemes (3); each morpheme is realized by one or more alternating *morphs, and larger units, such as words, consist of 'arrangements' of morphemes, typically (at least) in sequence. E.g. *duchesses* will be represented as a sequence of three morphemes 'duke', whose *allomorph in this context is [dʌtʃ], followed by '-ess', realized by a second morph [ɪs], followed by the plural morpheme, realized by [ɪz].

Contrasted by Hockett with *Item and Process, *Word and Paradigm. *Distributed Morphology is a later development based on similar insight.

Item and Process One of three models of morphology originally distinguished by C. F. Hockett in the 1950s. Contrasted with *Item and Arrangement, *Word and Paradigm.

The term is usually applied to models in which an initially simple element (traditionally the *root (1)) undergoes successive processes of internal change, affixation, etc. E.g. *unsung* [ʌnsʌŋ] might be derived from the root *sing* [sɪŋ] by an internal change of [ɪ] to [ʌ], which forms the participle, followed by the addition of the prefix *un-* [ʌn], which forms a negative.

iterative (Inflection etc.) indicating repetition. E.g., schematically, *They write*-PAST-ITERAT *Wednesday* 'They used to write on Wednesdays'. *Cf.* frequentative.

J

Jacaltec *Mayan language spoken in the interior of southern Guatemala, in an area close to the border with Mexico.

Jakobson, Roman (1896–1982) Structural linguist, Russian in origin, in Brno before the Second World War and a leading member of the *Prague School; in the USA from the 1940s. The driving principle in his work was that of a binary relation: in particular, the opposition of a positive or *marked term to a negative or *unmarked. In the 1930s he pioneered the concept of markedness in morphology, and developed with Trubetzkoy a theory of phonological systems that led, in the 1950s, to a proposal in which any such system is reduced to combinations of at most twelve universal features, each with a positive and a negative value. Through Halle, who was Jakobson's pupil and collaborator, this set of features was incorporated into *Generative Phonology until the late 1960s, when it was replaced by that of Chomsky and Halle, *SPE.

Jakobson's ideas have had a wide influence outside linguistics, through his own work, especially on formal structures in poetry, and his contacts with others, e.g. in the 1940s with the French anthropologist C. Lévi-Strauss. For other aspects of his thought *see* functions of language; *also* compact, for his vowel and consonant triangle.

Japanese Spoken throughout Japan, and by emigration elsewhere. Attested from the 8th century AD in Chinese characters, some used on the basis of meaning and others for their phonetic value; subsequently written in a mixture of Chinese characters (**kanji**) and two forms of *syllabary (*kana*) that evolved from characters used phonetically: **katakana** (lit. 'partial *kana*'), derived by omitting parts of one set of characters, and **hiragana** ('plain *kana*'), derived from cursive forms of another. In normal practice, *kanji* is now used primarily for lexical words; *hiragana* for inflectional endings and words with grammatical meaning; *katakana* for western names and loan words from western languages; with, in addition, Roman letters e.g. for acronyms from western languages.

Ryukyuan, in the Okinawan islands in the south-west, is treated as either a group of dialects of Japanese, or a group of languages related to it. Beyond this, Japanese has no secure genetic relationship in any wider family.

Jaqí *See* Aymará.

jargon In the ordinary sense of technical or pseudo-technical vocabulary. Also of nonsense forms as a symptom in aphasia; hence a type labelled '**jargonaphasia**'.

See also pidgin.

Javanese *Austronesian, spoken in central Java and by colonization elsewhere in Indonesia. Old Javanese (= Kawi '(language of) poetry') is attested by inscriptions from the late 8th century AD and by literature from the 10th; 'Middle Javanese' refers to the period after the Islamic conquest of Java in the late 15th century. Written until the Dutch occupation in a script derived from southern India which survives, with older forms of the language, for learned and ceremonial purposes; now ordinarily replaced by Roman.

jer One of two letters in the *Cyrillic alphabet, one indicating that a preceding consonant is palatalized, the other, no longer in use for Russian, that it is not.

Jespersen, Otto (1860–1943) Danish linguist whose most enduring work is in the theory of grammar and the grammar of English. The theory is set out especially in *The Philosophy of Grammar* (1924), and is founded on the intersecting concepts of *ranks (1) as successive levels of subordination and of *nexus (predication) vs. *junction (1). In *Analytical Syntax* (1938) he developed a linear notation for these and other constructions. His major work on English is the *Modern English Grammar on Historical Principles* (7 vols., 1909–49), as rich throughout in insight as in examples. Before this he had made an important contribution to phonetics, in *Lehrbuch der Phonetik* (1904) and earlier work, including an attempt to develop an *analphabetic notation for speech sounds. He is also remembered for his account of the evolution of languages, in *Progress in Language* (1894) and in the final part of *Language* (1920), in which he argued, against Schleicher especially, that the changes leading e.g. from the older to the modern Indo-European languages should be seen as improvements, not as decay.

Jespersen had a passionate interest in the applications of linguistics, playing a strong role in the movement for an international *auxiliary language and in promoting new methods of teaching foreign languages.

Jones, Daniel (1881–1967) English phonetician, a pupil of Passy and closely involved in the work of the *International Phonetic Association. Jones established the system of *cardinal vowels, and his work on the phonetics of Southern British RP or 'Received Pronunciation', embodied both in his *Outline of English Phonetics* (first published in 1914) and in a widely used pronouncing dictionary, is fundamental. He also made a significant contribution, in the tradition of Sweet, to the theory of the phoneme.

Jones, William (1746–94) Orientalist, working as a lawyer and a judge in Calcutta from 1783. Cited in histories of linguistics for an address in 1786 to the Bengal Asiatic Society, which he founded, in the course of which he remarked as self-evident that Sanskrit, Greek, and Latin, among others, must have descended from a common ancestor.

Judaeo- From the Latin word for 'Jew(ish)'. **Judaeo-Spanish** refers to forms of Spanish spoken in parts of the Ottoman empire by the descendants of Sephardic Jews expelled from Spain by Roman Catholics in the 15th century; **Judaeo-German** = Yiddish.

junction (1) Jespersen's term for constructions that involve subordination (= dependency) without predication: e.g. that of *dreadfully tiresome meetings*, where *dreadfully* is subordinate to *tiresome*, and *tiresome* in turn subordinate to *meetings*. In Jespersen's theory of *ranks (1), *meetings* is the 'primary', *tiresome* the 'secondary', *dreadfully* the 'tertiary'.
  Opp. nexus.

junction (2) = sandhi.

juncture The degree of linkage between successive sounds in speech. Thus, in a stock example, the [t] and [r] of *nitrate* are in *close juncture; hence, in many speakers, the [t] is released as an affricate with the onset of voicing delayed. But the [t] and [r] of *night-rate*, where there is a boundary between two members of a compound, are in *open juncture.
  A **juncture phoneme** is a juncture conceived of as a unit at the level of phonemes. G. L. Trager and other *Post-Bloomfieldians distinguished four such phonemes in English, some of which were to survive as *boundary symbols in *Generative Phonology.

Junggrammatiker *See* Neogrammarians.

jussive (Verb form etc.) used in commands. Thus, in *Let them be freed*, the obsolescent use of *let* has jussive force in English. *Cf.* imperative: it is not clear that both terms are needed.

juxtaposition Relation of sequence between adjacent units. Hence especially where a construction is realized by adjacency alone: thus in many languages the role of a possessive is marked by juxtaposition (schematically 'Peter book' or 'book Peter') without an inflection etc. on either. Also available for a relation in which no specific construction is posited: thus successive sentences, if taken to be the largest unit of grammar, are then, from a grammarian's viewpoint, merely juxtaposed.

K

Kabardian *See* Circassian.

Kadai Family of languages in southern China and the neighbouring part of Vietnam. Grouped with *Tai and *Kam-Sui under 'Tai-Kadai'.

Kam-Sui Family of languages in southern China: Kam (or **Dong**), in adjacent parts of the provinces of Guizhou, Hunan, and Guangxi, is the most important. Grouped with *Tai and *Kadai under 'Tai-Kadai'.

kanji *See* Japanese.

Kannada *Dravidian language, spoken in the Indian state of Karnataka (Mysore). Attested by literary texts from the 9th century AD, and earlier by inscriptions; written in a South *Indian script very close to that of Telugu.

Karen Group of languages spoken mainly in east Myanmar (Burma) at the latitude of the Irrawaddy delta; also in the extreme west of Thailand and southward along the boundary between Thailand and Myanmar. Either a branch of *Tibeto-Burman or a separate branch, alongside Tibeto-Burman, within *Sino-Tibetan.

Kartvelian Family of languages, including *Georgian, spoken to the south of the Caucasus mountains. Also called '**South Caucasian**'.

Kashmiri *Indo-Aryan, spoken in the Vale of Kashmir in the north of India.

Kashubian *See* Polish.

katakana One of two syllabaries used for writing *Japanese.

Katharevusa Variety of Modern Greek formerly opposed to *Demotic (2) as the 'High' form in a relation of *diglossia. Now said, officially, to be suppressed.

'Katz–Postal hypothesis' Principle advanced by J. J. Katz and P. M. Postal in 1964, according to which the *transformations by which a sentence was derived in the current model of transformational grammar had no relevance to its meaning. Translated in Chomsky's *Standard Theory into the principle that meanings are determined by deep structures alone.

Kazakh *See* Turkic.

Kazan' School School of linguists centred on *Baudouin de Courtenay, who taught in Kazan' in Russia from 1875 to 1883, and his pupil M. Kruszewski.

k-command *See* command (2).

kernel sentence Term introduced by Chomsky and (Zellig) Harris in the 1950s for one of an irreducible set of simple sentences, to whose structures the remaining sentences of a language, simple and complex, were related by successive *transformations. Thus the complex sentence *The cake which Harry baked is nice* can be related, by transformations which combine two separate structures, to the kernel sentences *The cake is nice* and *Harry baked the cake*. The simple passive *The tart was bought by Mary* can likewise be related, by a transformation operating on a single structure, to the active kernel sentence *Mary bought the tart*.

The notion of kernel sentences played a central role in Chomsky's theory of *transformational grammar until the mid-1960s, when transformations combining separate sentences were rejected in favour of rules which derived corresponding structures in a *base component.

'key' 1. Used in studies of intonation for a distinction in an intonational unit between relatively narrow variation in pitch and variation which extends higher: e.g. between *I'd be de* `LIGH*ted* said without emotional involvement and with a relatively low pitch at the beginning of `LIGH, and the same said enthusiastically, with a relatively high pitch instead. **2.** Also, in the *ethnography of speaking, of the manner (e.g. hurried or calm) in which speech is delivered.

key word A word or concept characteristic of the thought of a particular community in a particular period. E.g. 'raison' (reason) is a key word of the French Enlightenment; 'rigo(u)r' a key word for American linguists in the 1940s and 1950s.

Khmer The national language of Cambodia (also called 'Cambodian'). A member of the *Mon-Khmer family, attested from at least the 7th century AD, originally in a South *Indian script which has evolved into the present writing system.

Khoisan Group of languages in southern Africa, spoken mainly in the Kalahari region in Namibia and Botswana: those, in particular, of the peoples collectively called Bushman. Two non-Bantu languages of Tanzania have also been included in it.

Kikuyu *Bantu, spoken in Central Province, Kenya.

kinaesthesis The sensation of movements in one's own body. Hence a major element in practical phonetics, in sensing e.g. how a consonant is articulated.

kinesics The study of meaningful gestures and other body movements in communication. Originally of a treatment modelled on American linguistics in the 1950s, with e.g. '**kinemes**' as the smallest gestural units.

kinetic tone = contour tone.

kinship terms Words identifying the relationship of other members of a person's family: e.g. *sister* or *grandson*. A **kinship system** is the system of oppositions among such terms in a given language or culture.

Kiowa-Tanoan A small family of languages in the American South-west, primarily in Mexico and Oklahoma. Conjecturally related to *Uto-Aztecan.

Kirghiz *See* Turkic.

Kiswahili = Swahili.

koiné 1. The form of Greek that became general in the eastern Mediterranean after the conquests of Alexander in the 4th century BC. From a word meaning '(in) common'. **2.** Applied in sociolinguistics to any variety of a language that arises historically in similar or other circumstances, especially through the evening out of differences among dialects. Hence '**koinéization**', of the process by which a koiné, which might later develop into a *standard language, is formed.

Komi The main *Finno-Ugric language in the region of the Urals; also called 'Zyryan'. The branch it belongs to is called 'Permic'.

Kongo *Bantu, spoken north and south of the River Congo, across national borders, from Brazzaville to the sea.

Konkani The southernmost *Indo-Aryan language, historically of Goa and a surrounding area, but also spoken through emigration elsewhere in south India, in parts of the states of Karnataka and Kerala.

Kordofanian A group of languages centred on the Nuba Mountains in the south of Kordofan province, Sudan.

Korean Limited historically to the Korean peninsula, and at best conjecturally related to any other language. Originally written in Chinese characters, which are still not wholly supplanted: more generally, however, and in North Korea especially, in an alphabet (*see* Han'gul) which in its modern form has 24 basic letters.

Krio English-based *creole in Sierra Leone, native in the capital and widespread as a second language.

Kru Family of languages in the south of Liberia and south-west Ivory Coast.

Kurdish *Iranian language spoken in various countries from western Turkey across north-east Iraq to a point to the north-east of the Persian Gulf. There is a major division between north-western and south-eastern dialects, roughly at the level of Mosul.

Kwa Group of languages in West Africa, including *Akan, *Ewe, and *Ga in Ghana and, in accounts formerly at least accepted, Nigerian languages such as *Yoruba and *Igbo.

Kwakiutl *See* Wakashan.

kymograph An early instrument, in use in phonetics until the 1960s, which mechanically recorded e.g. muscular movements or changes of air pressure by traces on smoked paper.

L 1. Symbol for a low *tone. **2.** *See* diglossia.

L₁, L₂ = first language, second language. Especially in discussion of language teaching, where L₂ is the 'target language', or language to be learned.

labelled bracketing Notation in which the constituents of a syntactic or other unit are enclosed in square brackets which are labelled, by subscripts, for the categories to which they belong. Thus in ₙₚ[ₐ[*tall*] ₙ[*men*]], *tall* is assigned to the category 'adjective' (A), *men* to the category 'noun' (N), and the whole is a constituent assigned to the class 'noun phrase' (NP).

The labels for categories are variously written before the opening brackets, as here, or after them: [ₙₚ [ₐ*tall*] [ₙ*men*]]. Occasionally they have been subscripted to both the opening and the closing brackets: ₙₚ[ₐ[*tall*]ₐ ₙ[*men*]ₙ]ₙₚ.

labial 1. Cover term for *bilabial and *labiodental. **2.** = bilabial in cases of *double articulation (2). Thus [g͡b] is a **labial velar**; [j͡b] or [d͡ʒb] a **labial palatal**.

labialization Lip rounding as a *secondary articulation. E.g. [ʃ] in *shoe* is phonetically labialized; in many languages, e.g. in the Caucasus, labialized or 'rounded' velars (kʷ etc.) contrast with non-labialized.

labiodental Articulated with the lower lip against or approximated to the upper teeth: e.g. [f] in *fin* or [v] in *veal*.

labiovelar 1. A velar consonant accompanied by distinctive *labialization: usually written kʷ, gʷ, and so on. **2.** = labial velar.

Labov, William (1927–) A pioneer in sociolinguistics from the mid-1960s, whose early work on class-based variation in the speech of New York and elsewhere led the field, both as a model of research and as the subject of theoretical and other criticism and refinement, into the 1980s. He has consistently advocated the application both of the findings of sociolinguistics and of sociolinguistic models of a speech community to the study of change in languages.

LAD For 'Language Acquisition Device': posited by Chomsky in the 1960s as a device effectively present in the minds of children by which a *grammar of their native language is constructed.

Ladin *See* Rhaeto-Romance.

Ladino = Judaeo-Spanish.

lag *See* voice onset time; *also* progressive assimilation.

LAGB = Linguistics Association of Great Britain.

Lakota *See* Siouan.

lambda operator (λ) Logical operator by which an expression which denotes a set is derived from one which represents a property etc. by which the set is defined. Thus 'λx (clever (x))' is a **lambda expression** denoting the set of all individuals who are clever, derived from a predication 'clever (x)' which includes x as a variable.

The operation is said to 'abstract on' the variable: hence '**lambda abstraction**'. An expression such as 'λx (clever (x)) (Bill)' (an individual Bill is a member of the set of all individuals who are clever) reduces, by what is called '**lambda conversion**', to 'clever (Bill)' (Bill is clever).

laminal Articulated with the *blade of the tongue. A **lamino-alveolar** consonant, such as [t] in *tip*, is articulated with the blade against or approximated to the ridge behind the upper teeth; in a **lamino-dental** the passive articulator would be the teeth themselves. Also called '**laminar**'.

'landing site' Informally, in *Government and Binding Theory, of a position into which some element is, or can be, moved.

langage The phenomenon of language in general: = language (2). Term from French used especially in opposition to *langue* (= language (1) or *language system) and *parole*.

language 1. A language in the ordinary sense: e.g. English or Japanese. Opp. dialect, also as in ordinary usage. **2.** The phenomenon of vocal and written communication among human beings generally, again as in ordinary usage. Thus the subject-matter of linguistics includes both language as a general property of our species (sense 2) and particular languages (sense 1).

'Language' in sense 2 is often extended to cover other forms of communication; hence, in particular, 'animal language' for communicative behaviour in other species. 'A language' in sense 1 is defined more precisely in different ways according to different theories. For some it is a *language system underlying the speech of a community: thus especially a *langue as defined by Saussure. Alternatively, it is a system in the mind of an individual: thus especially *I-language as defined by Chomsky in the mid-1980s. Others have conceived it as the set of sentences potentially observable in a speech community: thus especially a definition by Bloomfield in the 1920s. Alternatively, it is the set of sentences characterized or to be characterized by a *generative grammar: thus Chomsky in the 1950s. A *formal language is accordingly defined, by extension, in a way that is taken to apply not only to so-called *natural languages (2), or languages in the ordinary sense 1, but also to artificial systems in logic, computing, etc.

'language acquisition' Usually, if not qualified e.g. as 'second language acquisition', of the development of language in children. For '**Language Acquisition Device**' *see* LAD.

language change *See* change. Used of change in the structure etc. of a given language, as opposed to '**language shift**', of the replacement in a population of one language by another.

'language consultant' = informant.

language contact Any situation in which members of one *speech community regularly interact through speech with members of another speech community.

'language death' Disappearance of a language, especially where speakers shift progressively to another or others: thus e.g. of many languages in North America or Australia once spoken by people whose descendants now speak only English.

Cf. dead language. But the death of a language may come about in other ways: thus through a growing distinction, as in the case of Latin, between it and its own descendants; or, as with others in North America and elsewhere, by physical extermination of a community.

'language deficit' *See* deficit theory.

language faculty Faculty of the mind, in the traditional sense, controlling language. Used by Chomsky in the 1960s: hence the domain of *Universal Grammar and of *I-language within a *modular theory of the mind in general.

language family *See* family.

Language for Special Purposes Any programme directed towards the teaching of a foreign language for use in some specific context: thus English e.g. for air-to-ground communication with airports.

language isolate A language that cannot to our knowledge be assigned to any larger *family. Basque is a classic example.

language maintenance In the obvious sense, but applied specifically by sociolinguists to cases where a form of speech might be expected to disappear or is officially discouraged. E.g. the maintenance of Welsh in parts of Wales, despite increasing use of English and, in the past, the promotion of English through education. Opp. language shift.

Hence a term in a potentially open-ended typology, of possible developments in the external history of languages, such as '**language revival**', '**language spread**', or '**language renativization**', and of attitudes, such as '**language loyalty**', that might underlie them.

Others, if not already in use, can be invented ad lib: 'dialect maintenance' or 'dialect loyalty', 'ethnolinguistic revitalization' (*cf.* ethnolinguistic vitality), and so on.

'language murder' Emotive term e.g. for the death of a language, variously through the death of its speakers or through the influence of another language which they come to use in its place.

language planning Any conscious attempt, e.g. by a government, to promote one language or one form of a language over another. '**Status planning**' is defined as affecting the role that a language as such has in a society; its standing, prestige, and so on. '**Corpus planning**' is applied in contrast to the manipulation of specific usage: e.g. through codification or the planning of specific vocabulary.

   Cf. language policy. But a distinction between 'policy' and 'planning' may be as elusive in this field as in any other.

language policy In the obvious sense of 'policy regarding language'. E.g. the language policy in France, from the time of Napoleon onwards, was to promote French as a national language, at the expense of other languages and of regional dialects.

language shift *See* language change.

language sign *See* linguistic sign.

'language-specific' (Rules etc.) specific to a particular language: e.g. rules in English for the position of adverbs (*I have often done it,* not *I often have done it*) are, in part at least, peculiar to it. Opposed especially to principles etc. that are hypothetically part of *universal grammar, in that they hold for any language whatever.

'language suicide' Coined in opposition to *language murder, for the process by which a form of speech gradually loses its identity within that of a larger community.

language system The system of a specific language at a specific time, seen in abstraction from its history; from its use on specific occasions and by specific individuals; from other systems of culture, knowledge, etc.

   The scope and status of language systems have been debated, under one name or another, throughout the 20th century. For some they are at best constructs, to be posited to the extent that they are useful. For others they are a real object of description, though conceived in varying ways. *Cf.* language.

language universal = linguistic universal.

langue = language system. French term borrowed from Saussure, for whom 'la langue' was a social reality ('fait social') constraining each speaker. Opposed in that sense to 'langage' (the phenomenon of language in general) and to individual speech performance or *parole.

langue véhiculaire French term for a language used in communication between members of societies whose own languages are different: e.g. French itself in much of West and Central Africa.

Lao Language of the *Tai family, spoken in the valley of the River Mekong, in northern Laos and downstream in both Laos and Thailand into Cambodia. Official in Laos; the script is derived from that of *Khmer (Cambodian).

Lappish *See* Sami.

laryngeal 1. = glottal: thus [h] is sometimes called a laryngeal fricative. **2.** One of a set of three consonants, conventionally h_1, h_2, h_3, established in the *reconstruction of an Indo-European *protolanguage to explain, in particular, what are otherwise aberrant alternations and correspondences of vowels. The '**laryngeal theory**' is the hypothesis, now no longer a subject of serious controversy, that such consonants existed: they are presumed to have been *pharyngeal fricatives or others articulated towards the back of the vocal tract, but the only direct evidence, found after they had been first proposed, is in *Anatolian.

laryngealized Accompanied by *creak: thus a laryngealized vowel is one produced with creaky voice.

laryngoscopy Any of the successive techniques that have been used to study the action of the *vocal cords.

lateral Articulated in such a way that air flows past one or both sides of the tongue. E.g. [l] in *leaf* is a lateral *resonant; Welsh *ll* in e.g. *Llanelli* is a voiceless lateral *fricative ([ɬaˈneɬi]). **Lateral plosion** is the *release of a *plosive consonant by lowering the sides of the tongue: thus distinctively in *affricates in some languages; also of a [t] or [d] in words like *bottle* [bɒtl] or *muddle* [mʌdl].

Latin *Italic, originally the language of Rome, where first attested by inscriptions from before the 3rd century BC; subsequently of the whole of the western part of the Roman empire, and the ancestor of the *Romance languages. A *learned language from the early Middle Ages, linked especially with the Roman branch of Christianity, in whose liturgy it was obligatory until the 1960s.

Written in the *Roman alphabet.

Latinate (Word, construction, style) deriving from, or influenced by, Latin. Hence of a large set of forms in English, many though not all adapted directly from Latin, which have a distinct morphology and morphophonology. E.g. *-ation* in *detestation* is a Latinate suffix: it carries stress (-[ˈeɪʃn]) in a way that reflects its origin in Latin, and is almost always attached to forms, such as *detest*, that are themselves directly or ultimately from Latin.

Latvian *Indo-European, related to Lithuanian within the *Baltic branch. Attested from the 16th century; now spoken by a little more than half the population of Latvia.

law Sometimes in a strict sense, as e.g. of a *sound law. Also, more generally, of laws that may hold only as broad tendencies. *Cf.* linguistic universal; principle; rule.

lax Articulated, or claimed to be articulated, with lesser effort in the muscles of the vocal tract. Opp. tense (2).
   'Lax' and 'tense' are applied both to overall *articulatory settings, and to specific consonants or vowels. E.g. vowels with a broad or *wide posture of the tongue have often been described as 'lax'; also those with a retracted as opposed to *advanced tongue root.

layering Nesting of one unit within another. Hence in various specific cases in syntax: thus phrases or clauses show layering if they have smaller phrases or clauses within them; the structure of a clause is layered if the verb is seen as related e.g. to a direct object at one level of constituency, to an indirect object at a higher level, to a locative adverbial at a third higher level, and so on.

lead *See* voice onset time.

leading tone *See* starred tone.

learnability 1. Identified as a *design feature of language, by which any individual language can, in principle, be acquired equally well by any member of our species. **2.** Property of *formal languages defined by a procedure which is designed to construct a grammar from successive sentences presented to it. A language is **learnable** if, after a sufficient number of sentences have been presented, a grammar can be constructed which does not have to be amended to cope with others. It is said to have '**degree-Ø learnability**' if it is learnable on the basis of input which includes no *embedded sentences: to have '**degree-1 learnability**' if the input need include no sentence with more than one layer of embedding; and so on.
   For sense 2 *cf.* discovery procedure. The mathematical theory of learnability is called '**learnability theory**'.

learned language ['ləːnɪd] One whose only status is as a language taught to an educated élite: e.g. Latin as spoken or written in Europe from the early Middle Ages. **Learned forms** or **learned formations** are characteristically those perceived by speakers as belonging to or derived from a learned language: e.g. English *rictus* 'grin' is a learned form transparently from Latin.

'least effort' *See* principle of least effort.

'lect' Any distinct variety of a language: e.g. a regional dialect ('dia-lect'). Hence 'sociolect' (= social dialect), 'ethnolect' (variety

spoken by an 'ethnic' community), 'genderlect', etc. '**Lectal**' variation
is variation between any such varieties.

left-branching (Structure) in which *dependents successively
precede their *heads. E.g. in *very tightly controlled policy*, *controlled*
depends on and precedes the head noun *policy*, *tightly* in turn depends
on and precedes *controlled*, and *very* depends on and precedes *tightly*.

So called from the configuration of branches in a *phrase structure
tree: e.g. that represented by the bracketing [[[*very tightly*] *controlled*]
policy]. Languages may accordingly be called '**left-branching
languages**' if their constructions are predominantly of this type:
cf. centrifugal vs. centripetal; Head Parameter.

left dislocation The construction of e.g. *This next man, have I got to see
him?* Distinguished from simple *fronting (*This next man have I got to
see?*) by a pronoun (*him*) or other anaphoric element in the normal
position of the dislocated element. *Cf*. right dislocation.

lemmatize To group together varying words or forms of words: e.g.
in preparing a concordance. Hence '**lemma**', as applied originally to
the headword of an entry, often = lexeme (1).

length Phonetic or phonological feature, especially of vowels. E.g. in
Latin the vowel of *rosa* (nominative singular of the word for 'rose') was
short ([rosa]); that of *rosā* (ablative singular of the same word) was
long ([rosaː]). A phonological distinction may be realized, in part or
entirely, by differences other than physical duration. E.g. the 'long'
vowels of Dutch, in words like *laat* 'late' or *leeg* 'empty', differ
systematically in quality and tongue posture from the 'short' vowels of
e.g. *lam* 'lamb' or *lek* 'leak'.

For long vs. short syllables *see* heavy syllable. Phonetically long
consonants tend to be described as *geminate.

lenis ['liːnɪs] (Consonant) articulated, or thought to be articulated,
with lower muscular tension; hence traditionally of voiced consonants
as opposed to voiceless. From Latin *lenis* 'gentle, weak'. Opp. fortis:
cf. lax vs. tense.

lenition Any process by which a sound is, or is conceived as being,
'weakened'. E.g. that by which, in the history of Spanish, a voiced stop
([b] [d] [g]) became a fricative ([β] [ð] [ɣ]) between vowels, seen as one
which reduced the effort of articulation. Opp. fortition.

Lepontic *See* Celtic.

letter Originally of a unit of speech having both a written form and a
phonetic value. Thus, in ancient accounts, the letter (Latin *litera*) was
the smallest unit into which utterances, defined as movements of air
that are representable in writing, were analysed. Now, as in everyday
usage, of a character in writing only, especially in an alphabetic system.

Lëtzebuergesch = Luxembourgish.

level The usual term since the 1940s for a distinct phase in the
description of a language at which specific types of element and the
relations between them are represented or investigated. Thus at the
level of *phonology one studies the sound structure of a language:
words or larger units are represented as configurations of units (such
as phonemes or syllables) that are specific to that level, and
generalizations are stated about relations among them. At the level of
*syntax, sentences are represented as configurations of words or
morphemes standing in specific constructions in relation to other
such units. Each level is treated in at least partial abstraction from the
others. Thus the phonological structure of a word is in general not
relevant to its role in syntax; the precise construction in which a word
stands is equally not relevant, in general, to its phonology.

   Theories of levels, whether of analysis or of representation, have
been an important part of *structural linguistics, especially in the
middle decades of the 20th century. Some distinguished ordered series
of procedures, in which one phase of analysis must precede another:
thus, in particular, that of (Zellig) Harris and other *Post-
Bloomfieldians. Others have presented a hierarchy of supposedly
greater or lesser degrees of abstraction, ranging from *phonetics as
the 'lowest' level to *semantics as the 'highest'. In many of these, levels
have been defined by the different *components (2) of an integrated
generative grammar.

   Cf. plane; stratum. Also used in other senses: e.g. of levels of
formality in writing; of higher and lower levels in a classification.

levelling Any historical process in which less widespread features
tend to be eliminated. Hence *dialect levelling; also of changes e.g. in
morphology in which irregular formations are replaced by regular.

level ordering Grouping of processes into successive blocks, such
that all those of block *a* must apply before any of those of block *b*.
Argued, in particular, for processes of affixation. E.g. *dis-* in *disloyal*
or *-ic* in *graphic* can be assigned to an inner group of affixes: call this
group 'class 1'. But *un-* in *unhappy* or *-ness* in *happiness* are among those
that can be assigned to an outer group: call this 'class 2'. In the model
of level ordering all processes that add a class 1 affix would apply
before any adding a class 2 affix: hence, it would be argued, it is
possible to form words such as *un-dis-loyal* or *graph-ic-ness* (class 2
affixation following class 1 affixation), but there are no words in
dis-un- or *-ness-ic* (class 1 affixation following class 2 affixation).

   Central to, in particular, *Lexical Phonology.

level-skipping Term in e.g. *Tagmemics for a case in which a unit of
one rank in a hierarchy of size-levels functions directly in the
construction of one at least two ranks above. Thus the levels of word

and phrase are 'skipped' if a morpheme is seen as entering directly, as a morpheme, into the structure of a clause.

levels of adequacy Different levels of success that a description of a language or a general theory of language can achieve. In Chomsky's account in the 1960s, a *generative grammar is **observationally adequate** if it generates the sentences of a language correctly, and is **descriptively adequate** if, in addition, it describes their structure correctly. A theory of grammar is **explanatorily adequate** if it explains how speakers can arrive at a descriptively adequate knowledge of their language.

level tone A *tone which is perceived as having the same pitch throughout; hence in phonology = register tone. Opp. contour tone or 'kinetic tone'.

lexeme 1. A word considered as a lexical unit, in abstraction from the specific forms it takes in specific constructions: e.g. the verb 'sing' or 'to sing', in abstraction from the various *word forms *sing, sings, sang, sung, singing*. **2.** Any other unit, e.g. a *morpheme, seen as having *lexical rather than *grammatical meaning.

lexical 1. Assigned to, or involving units assigned to, a *lexicon. Thus a **lexical entry** is an entry in the lexicon; a **lexical item** or **lexical unit** may be any word etc. which has such an entry; rules are **lexically governed** if they apply only to structures including certain lexical units. **2.** Specifically of words etc. which have a lexical as opposed to a *grammatical meaning, or are assigned in syntax to a lexical as opposed to a *grammatical or functional category.

lexical ambiguity Ambiguity explained by reference to lexical meanings: e.g. that of *I saw a bat*, where *a bat* might refer to an animal or, among others, a table tennis bat. *Cf.* grammatical ambiguity.

lexical category A class of units which have *lexical meaning or of words and morphemes generally as entered in a *lexicon: e.g. noun as a category including e.g. *tree* or *sky*.
  Specifically, in *Government and Binding Theory, of the syntactic categories noun (N), adjective (A), verb (V), and preposition (P), as opposed, in applications of *X-bar syntax, to *functional or non-lexical categories such as *complementizer (C), *I, Agr, etc.

lexical decomposition The analysis of word meanings into smaller units which are seen as standing to one another in constructions like those of syntax. E.g. of the meaning of *die* into the units BECOME, NOT, and ALIVE, seen as standing in constructions like those that the words *become, not,* and *alive* would bear in *He became not alive*: [BECOME [NOT ALIVE]].
  Mooted by Chomsky in the 1960s but developed especially by J. D. McCawley and other proponents of *Generative Semantics.

lexical density The percentage of words in a text assigned to *lexical as opposed to *grammatical categories.

lexical diffusion The gradual spread of a phonetic or other change across the vocabulary of a language or across a speech community: e.g. the spread of [k] > [ʃ] (in *chat*, *chanter*, etc.) across north-west France, attested at the beginning of the 20th century by the survey for the *Atlas linguistique de la France*.

In the ideal case, the spread would be simultaneously in both respects. So, at a given moment, (*a*) some words will have changed, or will be used more often in the changed form, while others will not have changed, or will be used less often in a changed form; (*b*) some speakers will use changed forms, or will use changed forms more often, while others will not use them, or will use them less often. This would lead, again in the ideal case, to smooth variation on both dimensions.

Usual in this sense. But the term could also be used of the *diffusion of individual lexical units.

lexical field *See* semantic field.

Lexical-Functional Grammar Model of syntax developed by J. Bresnan and R. Kaplan, subsequently with others, from the end of the 1970s. The original insight was that relations between, for example, an active and a passive can be treated just as well by rules that systematically relate entries in a lexicon (e.g. that of actives such as *take* to passives such as *(be) taken*) as by *transformations that systematically relate the constructions of sentences (e.g. that of active *John took it* to that of passive *It was taken by John*). This idea was married to an account of *predicates and *arguments which, like that of *Relational Grammar, takes syntactic functions or relations (subject, object, etc.) as primitive. In the developed model, sentences are represented in syntax on two levels, those of **c-structure** (i.e. constituency or phrase structure) and **f-structure**, which assigns the corresponding functions. Principles that are handled in terms of phrase structure in Chomsky's *Principles and Parameters Theory (e.g. those of *control or of *command) are then reformulated in terms of functions.

lexical gap A point within a system of *sense relations at which a word might be expected but none exists. Thus in the system of words for a person's relations *parent* and *child* subsume both *father* and *son* (male) and *mother* and *daughter* (female); from this an analysis of the system might predict a similar term subsuming e.g. *uncle* and *aunt*. Then, since there is none, it might be described as having a gap at that point.

'Lexicalist Hypothesis' *See* Strong Lexicalist Hypothesis.

lexicalization **1.** The representation of a *notional distinction in the lexicon of a language. E.g. the distinction between an animal and the meat of an animal is often **lexicalized** in English, as in *pig* vs. *pork* or *deer* vs. *venison*, where it is not lexicalized in French. **2.** The change that a word undergoes when it is no longer derived by a *productive morphological process. E.g. *truth* is lexicalized in modern English, since the formation of nouns in -*th* is not productive, whereas *trueness*, formed with the productive suffix -*ness*, would in this sense not be.

   The term could also be used, in principle, of the processes of change by which e.g. a former suffix would become an independent lexical unit. *Cf.* grammaticalization (2).

lexically conditioned (*Alternation) among forms or processes in the context of different lexical units: e.g. between the vowel change in *ring* → *rang* (past tense of *ring* 'ring a bell etc.') and the suffix in *ringed* (past tense of *ring* 'put a ring on'), or between the plural suffix of *boys* and that of *children*. *Cf.* grammatically conditioned; phonologically conditioned.

lexical meaning Any aspect of meaning that is explained as part of a lexical entry for an individual unit: e.g. that of 'to run' in *He ran away* as opposed to that of 'to walk' in *He walked away*. Hence specifically in application to a **lexical word** or **lexical morpheme** as opposed to one which has *grammatical meaning: thus, in the same examples, of the meanings of the verbs and of the adverb *away* as opposed to those of the past tense or of *he*.

Lexical Morphology View of morphology developed in the USA, especially, within a broadly generative framework. The basic unit is the morpheme; words have a constituency structure of which morphemes are the minimal elements; and, in the extreme version, the entire construction of words, including those aspects that are traditionally called inflectional, belongs to an account of the *lexicon. The belief that this version is correct is the *Strong (or Strict) Lexicalist Hypothesis.

   See also inferential-realizational, for 'lexical' in general application to inflectional morphology.

Lexical Phonology Model of morphology and phonology developed in the 1980s in a partial reaction to classical *Generative Phonology. The derivation of words is separate from, and in the organization of a generative grammar forms a component operating ahead of, their insertion into syntactic constructions: cf., in that respect, the general concept of *Lexical Morphology. Within this component, phonological processes are sensitive to processes of affixation: e.g. in words like *photógraphy* (← *phótograph*), the placing of the accent and the associated distribution of vowel qualities are sensitive to the suffixation of -*y* and

a boundary (*photograph-y*) specifically deriving from it. Processes are
further divided into blocks by the principle of *level ordering. Thus a
morphological process like the suffixation of *-y*, with its attendant
phonological processes, belongs to a set of rules applying, as a group,
before the rules for suffixes such as *-ness*, which do not, among other
things, entail a change of accent; before rules of compounding; before,
in turn, any rules of phonology that reflect the combination of words
in syntax.

lexical redundancy rule Originally a rule in *Generative
Phonology which allowed entries in a *lexicon to be shortened by the
removal of predictable features. Thus a redundancy rule in English
would state that, if a word begins with three successive consonants,
the first can only be *s*. Then, in the entries for words like *string* or
spring, there is no need to set out all the features that distinguish *s*
from other consonants. One need simply indicate that the initial
segment is consonantal; and, since the next two are also consonantal,
the other features follow automatically.
    Later *lexical rules, sometimes also called 'redundancy rules', are an
extension of the same technique.

lexical rule Any rule that expresses a generalization over sets of
entries in a *lexicon. Thus a form of *metarule, though not usually so
presented.
    One widespread application is in *derivational morphology. E.g. if
there are entries in a lexicon for adjectives such as *happy* or *black*, a
lexical rule can state that, if there is an entry for *X*, where *X* is an
adjective, there is also, barring exceptions, an entry for *X* + *-ness*, where
the whole is an abstract noun with a meaning corresponding to it.
Hence *happiness* or *blackness*. Another application is in *Lexical-
Functional Grammar, where syntactic processes deriving e.g. passives
are replaced by lexical rules deriving lexical units that take such
constructions.
    The term was also used by Chomsky in the 1960s of a general
operation inserting lexical units into phrase structure trees.

lexical source language (of a pidgin or creole) = base language.

lexical stress Stress inherent in a lexical unit: *see* word stress.

lexical word One which has, or is seen as having, a lexical as
opposed to a *grammatical meaning: thus, in *this book*, *book* is a lexical
word, *this* a grammatical word.

Lexicase A form of *dependency grammar incorporating elements of
*Case Grammar, developed by S. Starosta from the 1970s.

lexicography The writing of dictionaries, for practical use or for any
other purpose; distinguishable as such from *lexicology.

lexicology Branch of linguistics concerned with the semantic structure of the lexicon: hence e.g. with *semantic fields and *sense relations. Treatments are often inspired by practice in *lexicography, which in turn has sometimes been presented, especially in continental Europe, as an application of it.

lexicon That aspect of a language, or of a linguist's account of a language, that is centred on individual words or similar units. Its scope varies enormously from one theory to another: in some a simple subcomponent of a generative grammar; in others the basis, in itself, for most if not all specific grammatical patterns; in some seen as an unstructured list; in others as an elaborate network of entries related by *lexical rules and by features shared at various levels.

Usually distinguished, as a theoretical concept, from a dictionary, as part of a practical description: hence e.g. a posited *mental lexicon, not 'mental dictionary'. *Cf.* lexicology vs. lexicography.

lexicostatistics The statistical study of vocabulary, especially in comparing languages that are, or may be, historically related. Hence at times applied, in a strict sense misleadingly, to *glottochronology.

lexifier (of a pidgin or creole) = base language.

lexis The vocabulary of a language and the study of vocabulary. Distinguished by Halliday in the early 1960s as involving relations such as *collocations among open classes of words, as opposed to the closed systems of what was to become *Systemic Grammar.

LF = Logical Form.

LFG = Lexical-Functional Grammar.

liaison Term in French grammar for a pattern by which many words end in a consonant when, but only when, they appear before a vowel in certain syntactic contexts. E.g. *les* 'the-PL' has a final [z] when it appears 'in liaison' in *les enfants* 'the children'; it does not when it appears before a consonant in *les chats* 'the cats'. Seen traditionally as a phenomenon of 'tying together'.

'license' To allow. Thus, in particular, to allow as one of a closed set of alternatives; hence, more specifically, to require.

Replacing, therefore, the traditional 'to take'. E.g. in *They visited London* the verb is one that takes or licenses a direct object; in Latin *post meridiem* 'after midday-ACC.SG', the preposition *post* takes or licenses the accusative; and so on.

light syllable One which counts rhythmically as one unit: *see* heavy syllable.

light verb A verb such as *make* in *make a turn* or *take* in *take a look*, whose contribution to the meaning of the whole is less specific than in e.g. *make a table* or *take a sandwich*.

Thence, in the context of Chomsky's *minimalist programme, of a 'v' posited as in general a *null head (1) of a 'vP', of which a 'VP', headed by a lexical verb 'V', will then be a complement.

Linear B *Syllabary used to write a form of Greek (called 'Mycenaean') in the 15th to 13th centuries BC: the subject of a famous decipherment by M. Ventris in 1952. One of two non-pictographic scripts first discovered at the site of Knossos in Crete; the other, Linear A, has not been deciphered.

linearization A syntactic process by which words and phrases are realized in a specific sequence. Thus, at one level, the construction of *white* and *table* in *(a) white table* might be described, without representation of sequence, as identical to that of *blanche* and *table* in its French equivalent *(une) table blanche*. But, by processes of linearization, the adjective and noun would be realized in two different orders.

Hence **linearization rule**, *linear precedence rule, etc. *Cf.* order for 'linear order' vs. 'structural order'.

linear order *See* order. The **Linear Correspondence Axiom** is a principle proposed in the spirit of Chomsky's *minimalist programme by which linear order within phrases, as represented in X-bar syntax, reflects relations defined over those of constituency.

linear precedence rule A rule by which a syntactic element of one type precedes one of another: e.g. in English, by which a subject comes before a verb. *Cf.* linearization.

Lingala *Bantu, and an important lingua franca along the middle Congo and its tributaries (the Sangha and Oubangi) to the north. The name means 'language of the river'; based historically on the language of one small area.

lingua franca Any language used for communication between groups who have no other language in common: e.g. *Swahili in much of East and Central Africa where it is not native. *Cf. langue véhiculaire*, *also* pidgin; in reference to Africa, in particular, these categories are not always easily distinguished.

lingual Articulated with the tongue: usually of a lingual *trill (e.g. Spanish rolled *rr*) as opposed to a *uvular trill.

'linguicism' Prejudice against a language, perceived as analogous to 'racism'.

linguist Usually, in linguistics, of someone who professes or practises the subject.

linguistic area *See Sprachbund*.

'linguistic exogamy' The system obtaining in a society where marriages are always between members of communities with different native languages.

'linguistic insecurity' Term in sociolinguistics for a hypothetical state of mind seen as giving rise to *hypercorrection.

Linguistic Institutes *See* Linguistic Society of America.

linguistic palaeontology The attempt to relate the vocabulary of a prehistoric language, as reconstructed from descendants that are historically attested, to the time and place or other circumstances in which it may have been spoken. E.g. there are cognate words for 'horse' in Greek (*híppos*), Sanskrit (*áśvaḥ*), Latin (*equus*), and other *Indo-European languages. From this and other evidence a stem for 'horse' (**ekʷo-*) is reconstructed for the prehistoric Indo-European *protolanguage. One may then look at archaeological evidence of the distribution and domestication of the horse as part of an attempt to relate the protolanguage to the cultures of prehistoric peoples who may have spoken it.

linguistic relativism *See* Sapir–Whorf hypothesis.

linguistics *See* the Introduction. Effectively of any investigation of language and languages if not clearly belonging to some other discipline, such as philosophy, the study of literature, etc.

Linguistics Association of Great Britain (LAGB) Founded at the end of the 1950s; the *Journal of Linguistics*, published for it, first appeared in 1965. A society concerned especially with *synchronic theories, including their more technical side.

linguistic sign A word, morpheme, or other unit of a language system, seen as the union of an invariant form with an invariant meaning. Thus, in particular, the 'sign' as constituted, in the account of Saussure, by a relation of mutual dependence between a concept that is 'signified' (French *signifié*) and an 'acoustic image' of the form that 'signifies' it (French *signifiant*).

Also called a '**language sign**'. Sign theories, or theories based on such a notion of linguistic signs, are characteristic especially of European *structural linguistics, above all in the half-century from 1920 onwards.

Linguistic Society of America (LSA) Founded late in 1924, and the publisher from 1925 of the quarterly *Language*. The Society's **Linguistic Institutes**, organized each summer in different places, were in earlier years one of the main ways in which students were taught linguistics, and have had a major role in disseminating ideas.

linguistic universal Strictly, a property that all languages have, or a statement that holds for all languages. Thus, trivially, the statement that all languages have elements that are phonetically vowels, or the property of having such elements. Loosely, and more commonly, of properties or statements that hold at least for a majority of languages: hence a subsidiary distinction between *absolute universals and *relative or *statistical universals.

For further distinctions *see* formal universal; implicational universal; substantive universal. *See also* Universal Grammar.

linguistic variable Usually = sociolinguistic variable.

linguo-labial (Consonant) articulated with the blade of the tongue against or approximated to the upper lip.

linking *r* The [r] of e.g. [klɪərɪŋ] (*clearing*) or [klɪər əʊt] (*clear out*), in a variety of English in which there is no [r] in forms such as [klɪəz] (*clears*). Sometimes limited, at least as an obligatory element, to words where there is an *r* in the spelling. Where there is no *r* in the spelling it is often called an '**intrusive *r***': e.g. in [drɔːrɪŋ] (*drawing*) or [kəʊlər ədvəːtɪsmənt] (*Cola advertisement*).

lip rounding *See* labialization; rounded.

liquid Cover term for 'r's and 'l's, especially in languages where their roles in phonology are similar. Used originally of these consonants in Ancient Greek, where both were variable ('wet' or 'fluid') with respect to rules of syllabification and the weight of syllables.

'literal meaning' Variously of the meaning of a sentence or other expression as determined solely by the separate words etc. of which it is composed, or of *what is said, as opposed to what is implied or implicated, in a given context. *Cf.* compositional meaning.

Lithuanian *Indo-European, related to Latvian within the *Baltic branch. Attested from the 16th century; spoken by a large majority of the population of Lithuania.

litotes [lʌɪˈtəʊtiːz] Term in rhetoric for understatement, especially by 'ironic' use of a negative: e.g. 'That wasn't at all a bad dinner', meaning it was a very good one.

l-marked Term in *Government and Binding Theory for a *complement of an 'l', where 'l' is one of the *lexical categories N, A, V, or P.

loan Anything introduced into a language by *borrowing from another language. Hence *loan word: also **loan translation** (= calque),

loan shift (change of meaning under influence from another language),
loan concept or **semantic loan** (concept introduced by borrowing),
loan blend (*blend of which one element is foreign), and so on.

loan word A word imported by *borrowing from another language.
E.g. English *chamber* is one of many loan words introduced from Old
French in the Middle Ages; *karma* a borrowing from Sanskrit in the
19th century; *blitz* one from German in the 1940s.

   Sometimes *adapted directly to fit the sound patterns of the
borrowing language: thus, strikingly, for most English loan words into
Japanese. But often adapted gradually or only in part: e.g. among
educated speakers of British English in the case of perceived
borrowings from French. Hence in many languages there are
phonological elements specific to loan words, or a '**loan word
phonology**' whose patterns can be described as separate from those of
the main body of vocabulary.

LOC = locative.

local (1) (Rule, relation, etc.) restricted to the domain defined by
a single node in a *phrase structure tree. E.g. in *They said he had hurt
himself* the relation of *himself* to *he* is local, since it holds only within
a clause as defined by a node labelled S: *They said* ₛ[*he had hurt himself*].
Cf. bounded; unbounded.

local (2) (*Case) whose primary role is to indicate positions or
movements in space: thus a *locative, *allative, *illative, etc.

localism Theory in which a range of semantic categories, including
*case roles and those reflecting differences in time or duration, are
reduced to concepts of location and movement in space. E.g. an action
like cooking originates in an agent and is directed to whatever is
cooked. So, in *He cooked the vegetables*, there is metaphorically
movement from the subject, with the case role of *agent, to the object,
with the case role of goal or *patient. In *He died in an armchair* the
dying is literally located in space; in *He died on Sunday* it is
metaphorically located in time.

   Localist theories have been developed especially by Hjelmslev in the
1930s and more generally, from the 1970s, by J. Anderson.

locational Indicating location. E.g. 'locational cases' are one subtype
of *local cases, indicating position as opposed to direction etc. of
movement.

locative (LOC) (*Case) whose primary role is in relating a referent to
some point or location in space: e.g., schematically, *Mary lives London-*
LOC 'Mary lives in London', *Peter is office-*LOC 'Peter is at the office'. Often
distinguished from cases which indicate a more specific location: e.g.
an *inessive (indicating position inside something), or a superessive
(indicating position above or on top of something).

Also of prepositions, phrases, etc. Thus *at* is locative, or has a locative use in e.g. *He is at his office*; in the same example, *at his office* is a locative phrase, or locative expression.

locus Place: thus a 'locus of change' is a place where change occurs, 'locus of articulation' = place of articulation, and so on.

locutionary Applied in the theory of *speech acts to the simple act of saying something. E.g. if one says 'I need a drink' one performs the locutionary act of uttering the sentence *I need a drink*. *Cf.* illocutionary; perlocutionary.

logical 1. In, or in some system of, logic: e.g. '&', as defined in the *propositional calculus, is a '**logical connective**'. **2.** Concerned with aspects of meaning representable in such a system. Thus, in particular, the '**logical form**' of a sentence or proposition is an informal representation of its structure in terms related to those of formal logic. Hence Chomsky's *Logical Form which was in origin, in the 1970s, a representation of the semantic structure of a sentence insofar as it was seen as determined by the rules of a grammar.

Logical Form (LF) One of two essential representations of a sentence in Chomsky's theory of grammar since the 1980s. Opp. Phonetic Form (PF).

Defined as an interface between a grammar, or *I-language, and semantic, called e.g. 'conceptual' and 'intentional', *performance systems. Hence directly related, in *Government and Binding Theory, to the level within the grammar of D- (or formerly *deep) structure.

logical positivism *See* positivism.

logical relations Semantic relations among the parts of a sentence as opposed, especially by grammarians of the late 19th and early 20th centuries, to 'grammatical relations' of agreement, government of cases, etc. E.g. in *A majority of criminals is stupid*, *majority* would be 'grammatically' the head noun and *is* would be in *grammatical agreement with it. But 'logically' *a majority of* qualifies *criminals*, like *most* in *most criminals*.

'logical subject' 1. An element seen as a 'subject' in that, like the subject in many basic transitive constructions, it identifies who or what is responsible for an action or process. E.g. *(of) lung cancer* would be the logical subject of *Smokers die of lung cancer*. **2.** Also applied, in transformational grammar in the 1960s, to subjects in *deep structure as opposed to *surface structure.

Opp. grammatical subject; psychological subject.

logogram A character in writing which represents a word as a whole. Distinguished especially from a *phonogram, which represents a sound or group of sounds; also from a *pictogram or an *ideogram, which represent an object or idea independently of words.

logophoric (Pronoun etc.) used in *indirect speech to refer to the person whose speech is being reported: thus, schematically, *Jane said that* LOGOPHORIC *would come* 'Jane said that she (Jane) would come', as opposed to *Jane said that she* (someone else) *would come*.

logosyllabic (Writing system), such as the Mayan, that includes both *logograms and signs for syllables.

Lolo-Burmese Branch of *Tibeto-Burman, branching in turn into a group which includes *Burmese, and a Lolo group of which the most important is **Yi**, in the Chinese province of Sichuan.

'London School' The group of linguists centred on, or felt by commentators to be linked to, *Firth.

long (vowel, consonant) *See* length. For 'long syllable' *see* heavy syllable.

long-distance (*Anaphora) not constrained within a defined syntactic domain. Thus, if we accept the constraints proposed in *Government and Binding Theory, *herself* is an instance of 'long-distance reflexivization' in *Miss Bingley was left to all the satisfaction of having forced him to say what gave no one any pain but herself*. *Cf.* unbounded.

longitudinal (Survey etc.) comparing data obtained from the same or similar individuals at different points in time. E.g. a study of the speech of a group of children as it develops between the ages of two and five, or of a dialect community as it is now compared to how it was a generation ago.

loudness The auditory property of sounds which corresponds in part to their acoustic amplitude or intensity, as measured in decibels.

low **1.** (Tone, intonation) distinguished or realized by a pitch that is relatively low within a speaker's range: usually represented by 'L' or by a grave accent. **2.** (Vowel) = open. In the scheme of Chomsky and Halle, *SPE, the feature [+ low] is that of a sound 'produced by lowering the body of the tongue below the level that it occupies in the neutral position': hence also a feature of *pharyngeal consonants.

Opp. in both senses to *high.

Low (L) *See* diglossia.

lowering Change or process by which a vowel becomes more *open. E.g. that of *hid* is lowered, to the point at which it is identical with that of *head*, in some forms of American English. Opp. raising (1).

Low German *See* German.

LSA = Linguistic Society of America.

Luba *Bantu language spoken widely in eastern Congo (Kasai Occidental, Kasai Oriental, and Katanga provinces).

ludic From the Greek for 'play'. Hence puns and other forms of wordplay represent a 'ludic' use of language.

Luganda *Bantu language, spoken in south-east Uganda between Lake Victoria and Lake Kyogo.

Luo *See* Nilotic.

Luxembourgish West *Germanic, spoken mainly by the native population of Luxembourg, where it is, since the mid-1980s, an official language with French and German.

Lyons, John (1932–) British linguist, originally a Classicist, whose first book, *Structural Semantics* (1963), is a study of part of the vocabulary of Plato. Two later and much longer works, *Introduction to Theoretical Linguistics* (1968) and *Semantics* (2 vols., 1977), have had a profound influence, often on scholars who, having read the first as a textbook, have not appreciated how original it was. A theorist whose work is centred on semantics in a broad sense, Lyons became a leading exponent of *structural linguistics in the late 20th century, notable both for scope of synthesis and for extreme care in detail, especially in distinguishing concepts and in a scrupulous use of terminology. His work on the classification of *sense relations is fundamental.

M

Macedonian South *Slavic, spoken mainly in (the former Yugoslav Republic of) Macedonia. Written in *Cyrillic.

macro- In its ordinary sense, as 'macroeconomics' or 'macromolecule'. Thus '**macrosociolinguistics**' is said to be concerned with larger topics: e.g. when in general speakers use one language in preference to another. '**Microsociolinguistics**' will instead include the study e.g. of specific variations in the speech of specific individuals on specific occasions.

　　Also in names for enlarged or hypothetically enlarged *families of languages: e.g. 'Macro-Arawakan' would consist of *Arawakan plus other groups classed, in one conjecture, with it. *See* family for '**macrofamily**' in general.

macrolinguistics Defined by G. L. Trager in the late 1940s as the study of language in all aspects, as distinct from *microlinguistics, which dealt solely with the formal aspect of language systems.

macron (ˉ) Traditional sign for a long vowel: thus Latin *rēgēs* 'kings' was phonetically [reːɡeːs]. *See also* X-bar syntax.

Madurese *Austronesian, spoken in Madura and other islands off the north-east of Java, and by colonization elsewhere in Indonesia.

main clause A *clause which bears no relation, or no relation other than *coordination, to any other or larger clause. Thus the sentence *I said I wouldn't* is as a whole a single main clause; in *He came but I had to leave* two main clauses are linked in coordination by *but*. Opp. subordinate clause: *cf.* independent clause, superordinate clause.

main verb 1. The verb in a *main clause: e.g. *asked* is the main verb in *They asked why we left*, as opposed to *left* as a subordinate verb, or verb in a *subordinate clause. **2.** One with *lexical meaning as opposed to an *auxiliary.

Maithili An *Indo-Aryan language, with its own literary tradition, spoken north of the Ganges in Bihar and southern Nepal.

'major class features' Cover term in Chomsky and Halle, *SPE*, for distinctive features defined by degrees of *stricture. Opp. 'cavity features', involving *place of articulation, and *manner of articulation features.

major sentence *See* minor sentence.

major word class 1. One which is not part of a larger word class. Thus the *parts of speech were in origin an attempt to establish the major word classes, or major *syntactic categories, of Ancient Greek. **2.** One which is large or *open, or whose members have *lexical rather than *grammatical meaning: e.g. that of nouns as opposed to that of articles.

majuscule Applied in palaeography to large letters, such as capitals, or to scripts in which all letters have the same height. *Cf.* minuscule.

Makua *Bantu language of north central Mozambique.

Malagasy *Austronesian language, spoken throughout Madagascar, where it is an official language.

malapropism Use of a word in error in place of one that sounds like it: e.g. in 'It's a strange receptacle', for 'It's a strange spectacle'. From the character Mrs Malaprop in Sheridan's play *The Rivals*.

Malayalam *Dravidian language spoken in the Indian state of Kerala. Written in a South *Indian script; the language itself is closely related to *Tamil, from which it had diverged before the earliest literary texts, in the 13th century AD.

Malay-Indonesian *Austronesian language, commonly referred to as **Malay**, standardized in an official form both in Indonesia (**Indonesian** or Bahasa Indonesia 'language (of) Indonesia') and in Brunei, Singapore, and Malaysia (Bahasa Malaysia). Native to an area including, in particular, the Malay Peninsula and east Sumatra; hence straddling a major trade route through the Malacca Straits and carried thence from the colonial period, in a pidginized form called 'Bazaar Malay', as a lingua franca elsewhere. A language with a written literature after the adoption of Islam in the 15th century: formerly in the Arabic, now generally in the Roman alphabet.

Malayo-Polynesian = Austronesian; alternatively, the largest group within Austronesian, covering all except *Formosan.

Maltese *Semitic; basically a variety of Arabic but heavily influenced, in vocabulary and grammar, by Italian and Sicilian. Written in the Roman alphabet and a literary language independent, through religion, of Classical *Arabic.

mand An utterance by which a speaker tries to get an addressee to do something: thus a command, demand, request, etc.

Mandarin *See* Chinese.

mandative (Construction etc.) indicating something required or requested. Thus *that you be there* is a mandative clause, distinguished by an uninflected or *subjunctive form of the verb, in e.g. *It is essential that you be there*.

Mande Family of languages in West Africa, centred on the west of Guinea and adjoining parts of Mali, Ivory Coast, Liberia, and Sierra Leone. **Bambara**, **Maninka**, and **Dyula** are closely related members, spoken in the north of this area.

manifestation = exponence. The **manifestation mode** of a linguistic unit was defined by Pike in terms of the varying *etic units that may realize it.

Maninka *See* Mande.

manner (Adverb, adverbial) of a type which characteristically qualifies the sense of a verb: e.g. *well* is a manner adverb or adverb of manner in *He wrote it well*; *with care* is a similar adverbial in *He wrote it with care*.
  For 'manner' as a term in pragmatics *see* maxims of conversation; M-principle.

manner of articulation Cover term for any factor in the production of a consonant other than its *place of articulation. E.g. both [p] and [b] are *bilabial, but in their manner of articulation one is *voiceless and the other *voiced; both [b] and [m] are also bilabial, but in their manner of articulation one is an *oral stop and the other *nasal; both [tʃ] in *chop* and [ʃ] in *shop* are *palato-alveolar, but in their manner of articulation one is an *affricate and the other a *fricative.

Manx Formerly native in the Isle of Man, between England and Ireland. *Celtic, of the same branch as Irish and Scottish Gaelic.

Maori *Polynesian, once spoken throughout New Zealand, now restricted to an area in the north-east of North Island.

mapping Term in mathematics for a function which associates each member of a set A with a member of another set B. The function is said to map A **into** B; it maps A **onto** B if, in addition, there is no member of B that is not associated with at least one member of A.

Marathi *Indo-Aryan, the official language of the Indian state of Maharashtra. Written in *Devanagari; with other major Indo-Aryan languages, such as *Hindi-Urdu to the north, it was distinct from around AD 1000.

margin Anything not assigned to a nucleus: thus the *periphery (1) of a clause, or the onset and coda of a *syllable. *Cf.* edge.

marginal area One whose dialect is relatively unexposed, in terms of a *wave model, to changes initiated elsewhere; hence often geographically peripheral.

mark Term in *Prague School phonology for a feature seen as present in a *marked member of an opposition but absent in the unmarked.

E.g. in an opposition between [p] and [b], [b] is distinguished by the 'mark' of voicing. Central, in particular, to accounts of *correlations: thus in [p] vs. [b], [t] vs. [d], etc. voice is the 'mark of' a correlation that is thereby one 'of voice'.

marked 1. Having a feature, or the positive value of a feature, as opposed to lacking it or having the negative value. E.g. a nasalized vowel in French is marked, as specifically 'nasal' or [+ nasal], in opposition to an oral vowel, characterized negatively as 'not nasal' or [− nasal]. Likewise, in many accounts, a past tense in English is marked, as [+ past] or as used specifically in referring to past time, while the present is distinguished negatively as 'not specifically past' or [− past]. **2.** Having a feature or a value of a feature which is not that predicted or expected, by some general principle, e.g. from other features. Thus a back vowel which is produced with the lips spread is marked in terms of a general principle by which, unless there is a specific statement to the contrary, back vowels are rounded. **3.** Thence, in general, of any unit, construction, etc. which is in any way a special case, which is more complex or is subject to more restrictions, which is perceived as unusual, or which is simply rarer. E.g. the order of words in ´YOU *I* `WILL *see* ('you though not anyone else') is marked in various senses as opposed to that of *I will see you*.

Opp. unmarked; *cf.* default.

markedness reversal Any shift, over time or e.g. between dialects, in what is marked and what is unmarked. E.g. the construction of *Nor had he vanished*, with the verb in second position, is *marked (3) in Modern English; that of *Then he had vanished* is unmarked. But the former derives from the unmarked order in Old English.

marker Any unit or feature conceived (*a*) as the realization of a unit etc. at a more abstract level of representation, or (*b*) as indicating something to a potential addressee. Thus a 'case marker' or 'tense marker' is an inflection etc. which realizes a *case or a *tense; a *boundary marker indicates a boundary e.g. between words; *the* in *the house* 'marks' the phrase as definite. A *social marker likewise gives an indication of the status of a speaker in society.

Specifically, without qualification, of a unit seen as marking a syntactic construction: e.g. *that* as a subordinator, in e.g. *I told you that they were here*, is in one account a 'marker' of the role of the *that*-clause in relation to *told*. *See also* discourse marker; semantic marker; sociolinguistic variable.

marking convention Term in Chomsky and Halle, **SPE*, for one of a set of general principles seen as specifying the *marked (2) vs. unmarked values of phonological features. Thus, by one such convention, the feature [± nasal] has [+ nasal] as its marked value and

[– nasal] as its unmarked: i.e. a consonant or vowel is implicitly oral (or non-nasal) unless it is stated explicitly to be nasal.

Markov process *See* finite state grammar.

Martinet, André (1908–99) Structural linguist, influenced especially by the ideas and specific theories of the pre-war *Prague School. His earlier work, done partly in New York during and after the Second World War, developed Prague School phonology and, in particular, a structuralist account of sound change as arising, in part, from internal pressures within a phonological system. This was developed most fully in *Économie des changements phonétiques* (1955), published after his return to Europe. Of his later writings, *Éléments de linguistique générale* (1960) is a brief introduction to *structural (or *functional) linguistics which has had a major influence in France and beyond.

Martin of Dacia *See* Modistae.

Marwari *See* Rajasthani.

masculine (MASC) *Gender of words characterized as a class by nouns denoting males. Thus French *garçon* 'boy' is a masculine noun; in *le garçon* 'the boy', *le* 'the-MASC' is a masculine form of the article; in English, by extension, *he* is a masculine pronoun.

'mass comparison' The comparison of sets of languages in terms of similarities of individual units across any subset. Seen by Greenberg and his followers as a method of *genetic classification which validly extends, or even replaces, the *comparative method; certainly one which creates vastly larger groupings.
  Also called '**multilateral comparison**'.

mass noun = uncountable.

'matched guise' Experimental method in which subjects hear separate recordings of the same speaker, using e.g. different accents or different vocabulary. Its purpose is to exclude from the experiment any factor, other than those that are under investigation, which, if different speakers were used, might interfere with subjects' reactions.

mate *See* clausemate.

mathematical linguistics Usually of the theory of grammars as *formal (2) systems. Thus a theorem might relate e.g. the *weak generative capacity of two types of grammar.

matrix 1. (Sentence) into which another is *embedded. Also, in accounts of code switching, of a language described as 'embedding' forms or passages of another language. **2.** A two-dimensional display: thus especially a *feature matrix.

maximal projection Any category in *X-bar syntax which has the highest level of barring. A maximal projection of, e.g. N is an NP or, in an earlier notation, an N″. The sense of 'projection' derives from that of the *projection principle.

maximizer *See* intensifying.

maxims of conversation A set of principles advanced by Grice, as part of his account of *implicatures. Thus, to illustrate, a speaker might say 'Bill has two cars'. This would be true, in a strict sense, even if Bill had e.g. five cars. But by a maxim 'of quantity' speakers are not expected to give less information than is appropriate; therefore it carries the implicature (strictly, the speaker implicates) that Bill has no more than two cars.

The underlying assumption is that communication requires cooperation between speakers and people spoken to. Together, therefore, the maxims are special cases of what Grice in general called the **Cooperative Principle**. By a maxim of **quality**, speakers are not expected to say anything they believe to be false or for which they lack adequate evidence. By the maxim of **quantity**, as above, they are not expected to give either less or more information than is needed. By a maxim of **relation** they are not expected to say things that are irrelevant. By a maxim of **manner** they are expected to be brief and orderly, and to avoid obscurity or ambiguity. In Grice's account, implicatures arise both from speakers observing such maxims, as in the example given, and when they deliberately *flout them. E.g. a speaker might be asked a question and in reply say something quite irrelevant: the person asking the question might then gather that it was thought improper and that no answer will be given.

Cf. I-principle; M-principle; Q-principle.

Mayan Family of languages in Central America, spoken in the Yucatán Peninsula and to the south and west, in large parts of Guatemala and in the Mexican states of Chiapas and Tabasco. **Yucatec**, in the Mexican part of the peninsula and the north of Belize, has the greatest number of speakers.

The Mayan script is found in three manuscripts that survived the Spanish conquest, and in numerous inscriptions from the 3rd century AD onwards. It included both *logograms, often combined on the *rebus principle, and, increasingly as it evolved, both phonetic *determinatives and signs for syllables. Deciphered by the efforts of various scholars from the mid-20th century onwards.

Mbundu *Bantu language spoken in north-west Angola, in the province that includes Luanda.

m-command *See* command (2).

ME = Middle English.

meaning Traditionally of something said to be 'expressed by' a sentence. E.g. *I hate parsnips* would express the thought, judgement, or proposition 'I hate parsnips'. Forms that express something are **meaningful**, ones that do not are **meaningless**. Thence also of the words, constructions, etc. that make up a sentence: e.g. *parsnip* means 'parsnip'.

Modern theories are often elaborations of this. Thus, in one view widespread in linguistics: (*a*) There is a distinction between the meaning of a *sentence, independent of any context, and the meaning that it will have as an *utterance on a particular occasion. (*b*) Sentence meanings are part of the *language system, and form a *level of *semantic representation independent of other levels. (*c*) Representations at that level are derivable from representations at the level of *syntax, given a *lexicon which specifies the meanings of words and a set of semantic *rules (2) associated with constructions. (*d*) The meanings of utterances, as intended by the speaker or as understood by a hearer, follow from separate principles that are in the domain of *pragmatics. In the extreme case, this leads to a division in which pragmatics is concerned with everything that does not fall under a system of *formal semantics.

Other theories may, for a start, reject (*a*). Therefore the meanings of sentences are not part of a language system, though, for some, the meanings of words and individual syntactic constructions are. Others may reject that also: hence, in particular, an account of word meaning based on the uses of words in specific *contexts, both within an utterance and in terms of a *context of situation. In what is again the extreme view, neither words nor sentences can be assigned meanings independently of situations in which they are uttered.

'meaning-changing' Not *meaning-preserving.

meaning postulate A representation of a *sense relation between two lexical units which takes the form of an implication between general propositions that include them. Thus the relation of *hyponymy between *daisy* and *flower* is represented by the meaning postulate 'daisy (x) → flower (x)': 'if x is a daisy x is also a flower'. Likewise the relation between the *converse terms *buy* and *sell* may be represented by a postulate 'buy (x, y, z) ↔ sell (z, y, x)': 'If x buys y from z then z sells y to x, and vice versa'.

'meaning-preserving' (*Rule (2) of syntax) whose application is deemed not to affect the meaning of a sentence: e.g. a rule of transformational grammar by which *I took off my coat* → *I took my coat off*. A rule which does not 'preserve meaning' is '**meaning-changing**': e.g. one, as formulated in the early days of transformational grammar, by which declarative *He is here* → interrogative *Is he here?*

'mean length of utterance' (MLU) Measure proposed, in studies of children's language, of the average number of grammatical units in what are deemed to be separate 'utterances'. Taken to be an index of a child's linguistic development.

measure phrase Any noun phrase indicating quantity, size, distance, etc.: e.g. *a few pounds* in *I've put on a few pounds* or in *a few pounds of apples*.

'mechanism' Bloomfield's term for the view that processes traditionally called mental are purely physical and no different in principle from other workings of the human body. Opp. mentalism, and identified by him with a physicalist view of science generally.

mediae Ancient term for *voiced plosives, such as Latin *b*, seen as 'middle' in relation to a *tenuis or voiceless plosive, such as *p*, and an 'aspirate', such as *ph*.

medial 1. Neither initial nor final. E.g. in *created* stress falls on a medial syllable: [kriː'eɪtɪd]. **2.** (Clause, form of verb) that can only appear as the dependent of another in a system of *clause chaining.

medio-passive (Form etc.) whose role is variously *middle or *passive.

meditative = deliberative.

medium 1. In ordinary senses: e.g. in teaching French as a foreign language, French might or might not be the medium of instruction. **2.** The physical means employed in communication. Thus speech is transmitted through the **phonic medium** or medium of sound, written language through the **graphic medium**, *sign language through the medium of hand and other gestures.

Meillet, Antoine (1866–1936) French Indo-Europeanist, an early pupil of Saussure, whose *Introduction à l'étude comparative des langues indo-européennes* (1st edn. 1912), with works on Armenian and other branches, is still indispensable. Important as an organizer of French linguistics in the first part of the 20th century: also as a general linguist many of whose ideas have later been developed by others. Thus he is the acknowledged source for Bloomfield's and through him many current definitions of the sentence; also for the notion of *grammaticalization (2), identified by him but developed particularly since the early 1980s.

meiosis Figure of speech in which the importance of something is understated. *Cf.* litotes.

Melanesia Group of islands in the south-west Pacific running from New Guinea in the west to Fiji in the east. The languages of New Guinea are mainly grouped as *Papuan, with some in smaller islands to the west and east. The other languages indigenous to Melanesia are *Austronesian, mainly *Oceanic.

meliorative = ameliorative.

mellow Jakobson's term for a *distinctive feature that is the opposite of *strident.

melody units Originally of phonological features assigned in *Autosegmental Phonology to the *segmental tier: *cf.* skeletal tier.

Menomini *Algonquian language of the peninsula between Lake Michigan and Lake Superior, studied in detail by Bloomfield.

mentalism Applied by Bloomfield to the traditional view that the mind is a non-physical entity controlling but distinct from the body; opposed by him to *mechanism or physicalism. Later applied, especially by linguists who attacked Bloomfield and his followers, merely to the view that the mind is a legitimate object of study.

mental lexicon A *lexicon as assumed by many psycholinguists to be represented in the minds of speakers.

mention The use of a word etc. to refer to itself. Opp. **use**: e.g. *cat* is 'mentioned' in *What is the definition of 'cat'?*; it is 'used' in *The cat is in the garden*.

'Merge' Name in generative syntax, since the 1990s, for the operation of joining constituents. Thus a verb *help* would 'merge' with an object *Peter* to form [*help Peter*]; this with an auxiliary *will* to form [*will* [*help Peter*]]; and so on.

merger Change by which two units etc. that were once distinct become one. Especially in phonology: e.g. voiceless [ʍ] in *white* [ʍaɪt] or *which* [ʍɪtʃ] has merged, for many speakers, with voiced [w] in *wight* [waɪt] or *witch* [wɪtʃ]. Opp. split.

Meroitic Ancient language of north Sudan, attested by inscriptions from the early 1st millennium AD. The writing system is derived from that of Egyptian, but virtually alphabetic.

meronymy Relation between lexical units where the objects etc. denoted by one are parts of those denoted by the other: e.g. *sleeve* is a **meronym** of *coat*, *dress*, or *blouse*. Cf. synecdoche.

Meso-American *See* Central American languages.

mesolect Variety of a language intermediate between an *acrolect and a *basilect. From Greek *mesos* 'middle'.

meta- Prefix used in terms for constructs or investigations on a higher plane or of a higher order of abstraction. Thus a *metalanguage is a 'language' of a higher order than its object language; a *metarule is a higher-order rule; a set of metarules can be said to form a **metagrammar**.

Hence for theories about theories. If a grammar is a theory about a language, a theory of grammar is correspondingly a **metatheory**. A study of the character of a science, e.g. linguistics, is a **metascience**. A higher-order explanation of the principles of syntax might be called a 'metasyntax', and so on.

metalanguage A language used to make statements about a language. The language about which they are made is correspondingly the **object language**.

Typically of artificially constructed systems. E.g. in the programme of *generative grammar as conceived by Chomsky in the 1950s, a theory of grammar can be said to specify a formal metalanguage in which rules which form the grammar of a specific object language (English, French, etc.) are written. But languages in the ordinary sense are also used 'metalinguistically'. Thus a Spanish grammar of English uses Spanish, or a variety of Spanish, as a metalanguage for the description of English; in an English grammar written in English, the same language is both metalanguage and object language; if someone says, e.g. that *cough* is pronounced [kɒf] they too are making a 'metalinguistic' statement about that word.

metalinguistic *Function of language in referring to itself; *cf.* metalanguage. Called by Jakobson the '**metalingual**' function.

Negation, for example, is 'metalinguistic' if it concerns the form and not the meaning of an utterance: e.g. in 'I wasn't [hə'rast] (*harássed*), I was ['harəst] (*hárassed*)'; 'I'm not "visually deprived", I'm blind'.

metalinguistics *See* microlinguistics.

metanalysis Change in the position of a word boundary. E.g. *ewt* became *newt* by a shift of the boundary in *an ewt*, *napron* became *apron* by the opposite shift in *a napron*.

metaphony [mɛ'tafəni] Sound change in which one or more phonetic features of a vowel come to match those of a vowel in an adjacent syllable: thence of phonological processes that result from it or are formally similar. *Umlaut is one of the commonest; *see also* vowel harmony.

metaphor 1. *Figure of speech in which a word or expression normally used of one kind of object, action, etc. is extended to another. This may lead to **metaphoric change** in meaning: thus what is now the normal sense of *lousy* is in origin a metaphorical extension from the basic sense 'full of lice'. **2.** Used by G. P. Lakoff in the 1980s of a general pattern in which one domain is systematically conceived and spoken of in terms of another. E.g. terms directly applicable to war, as one domain, are systematically applied to that of courtship: *She was besieged by suitors*, *I have lost count of her conquests*, and so on. *Cf.* image schema.

metaplasm Ancient term for any alteration in the form of a word, e.g. to make it fit a line of verse.

metarule A higher-order rule expressing a generalization over a set of lower-order *rules (2). Central especially to *Generalized Phrase Structure Grammar. For example, a set of phrase structure rules will specify the structure of the verb phrase in active sentences. Another set might specify that of verb phrases in the passive. But there are systematic correspondences between them; accordingly they can be related by a metarule which, in effect, derives the rules for the passive from those for the active.

Cf. rule schema. *Lexical rules are also a form of metarule, often used for similar ends.

metathesis [mɛ'taθəsɪs] Change or process by which the order of successive sounds is changed. E.g. *wasp* derives from a metathesized form, with *s* before *p*, of a word attested in Old English both as *wæsp* and as *wæps* or *wæfs*.

metonymy [mɛ'tɒnɪmi] *Figure of speech in which a word or expression normally or strictly used of one thing is used of something physically or otherwise associated with it: e.g. *the Pentagon* (strictly a building) when used of the military inhabiting it. This may lead to **metonymic change** of meaning: e.g. the sense of *bureau* changed successively from 'cloth used to cover desks', first to 'desk' itself, then to 'agency etc. (working from a desk)'.

Defined in the most general sense as any figure based on 'contiguity': as such often taken to include e.g. *synecdoche: opposed in this sense to *metaphor as a figure based on 'similarity'.

metrical grid *See* Metrical Phonology.

Metrical Phonology Model developed by various scholars from the late 1970s, in which accentuation in English and other languages is explained in terms of a hierarchy of **strong** and **weak** units. In the illustration, the first syllable of *maker* is strong (s), the second weak (w); in addition, *maker* as a whole is strong in relation to *cuckoo clock*. Therefore *ma-* is the most prominent syllable of the phrase. Within *cuckoo clock*, *cuckoo* and *cu-* are in turn strong in relation to *clock* and *-ckoo*. Therefore *cu-* is the next most prominent syllable.

Distinguished from earlier accounts in *Generative Phonology by an insistence that stress is a matter of relative prominence, not a *distinctive feature with absolute values. In early accounts the pattern is shown by a '**metrical grid**', in effect a bar chart representing a sequence of syllables in time on the horizontal dimension and their relative prominence by the height of bars on the vertical dimension.

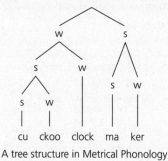

A tree structure in Metrical Phonology

metrics The study of metre in poetry, in part as it reflects the phonological structure of syllables and words in relevant languages.

Miao-Yao Family of languages in south China and the north of Indochina. Hmong or Miao is the largest and belongs to one branch; Mien or Yao is the main member of the other. Also called '**Hmong-Mien**'.

micro- In its ordinary sense, as 'microeconomics' or 'micro-management'. *See* macro-.

microlinguistics The study of *language systems in abstraction from whatever is seen as lying outside them. Coined by G. L. Trager in the late 1940s, and defined as excluding the study of meaning: that belonged instead to a separate field of '**metalinguistics**', seen as relating the formal system of language to other 'cultural systems'. Later redefined by other criteria, e.g. as the study of language systems in distinction from that of *paralanguage.

Micronesia Area in the west Pacific including the Gilbert and Marshall Islands, the Caroline Islands, and the Marianas. The languages are *Austronesian, mostly of the *Oceanic branch.

mid (Vowel) intermediate between *open (or low) and *close (or high). E.g. in the production of [ɛ] in *pet* the position of the lower jaw and the body of the tongue is between those for [a] in *pat* (open, low) and for [ɪ] in *pit* (close, high).

middle Originally of forms of verbs in Ancient Greek whose sense was broadly reflexive: e.g., schematically, *I bought*-MIDDLE *house* 'I bought myself a house'. Called 'middle' because seen as intermediate between active and passive.

   Thence of similar *reflexive forms in other languages. Also of verbs in *intransitive constructions that are understood reflexively: e.g. *shaved* in *I shaved*, meaning 'I shaved myself'. A common application in accounts of English is to an intransitive which bears a passive-like relation to its subject: e.g. *cuts* in *This stone cuts easily*, meaning 'can be cut easily'.

Middle English (ME) Conventional term for the period in the history of English between the Norman conquest (1066) and the accession of Henry VII (1485).

mid-sagittal (Plane) dividing the body into equal left and right halves. Hence the plane on which the vocal tract is represented by a diagram from front to back.

mimesis Imitation: e.g. forms of words are **mimetic** in cases of *onomatopoeia.

Minimal Attachment Principle Principle in psychological theories of speech processing, by which, in parsing a sentence, successive words are construed in ways which lead to minimal additions to already established levels of phrase structure. An explanation, it has been claimed, for the phenomenon of *garden path sentences.

minimal free form A *word as defined by Bloomfield in the 1930s. E.g. *singing* is *free (1) in that it can form an utterance on its own: A. 'What are you doing?' B. 'Singing.' So is *sing*: 'Sing!' As such it is 'minimal' in that it cannot be analysed into smaller units all of which are themselves free.

minimal inclusive An *inclusive form referring to a speaker plus a single addressee. Opp. augmented.

minimalist programme Development of *Principles and Parameters Theory initiated by Chomsky in the early 1990s, with the aim of simplifying *Government and Binding Theory as it had been in the 1980s.

A grammar is seen as relating *Phonetic Forms and *Logical Forms, both defined as interfaces with distinct *performance systems. Both must therefore be in a form that is fully interpretable by such systems; some system of computation must establish relations between them; and the grammar of any individual language must include a lexicon specific to it. Taking these alone as strictly necessary, the object has been to eliminate all other levels of representation, including in particular the earlier remnants of *deep structure and *surface structure, that may not be justified; and to simplify the system of computation, in all other respects, as far as possible.

For specific aspects *see* bare phrase structure, convergence (2), copying, phase (2), spell out. 'Minimalism' has in effect become a cover term for these and other specific revisions of the Principles and Parameters Theory, many at a level of abstraction from the evidence far greater than had previously been achieved, or might have been thought justifiable.

minimal pair A pair of words distinguished by a single phoneme: e.g. *tip* [tɪp] and *pip* [pɪp]. A **pair test** is a test in which speakers of a language are presented with possible minimal pairs and asked whether they are the same forms or different.

minimizer *See* intensifying.

minor rule One restricted to a small class of units: thus especially to a class of *exceptions.

minor sentence Any sentence in whose construction words are limited to specific combinations: e.g. an exclamation like *God help us!*, whose construction, with 'subjunctive' *help*, is restricted in normal use to this and a few other fixed expressions. **Major sentences** are of types which are not so limited, e.g. a declarative like *God helps us*: cf. *Jane helps us*, *Jane rescues us*, *God rescues us*, and so on.

minor word class A word class which is *closed, or whose members are seen as having *grammatical meaning as opposed to lexical meaning. E.g. articles belong to a minor word class, or a minor *syntactic category; prepositions form a minor class in some accounts but a major in others.

minuscule Applied in palaeography to small letters as opposed especially to capitals, and to a script with ascenders and descenders. *Cf.* majuscule.

MIT = Massachusetts Institute of Technology: hence in reference to the school of Chomsky, who has worked there since the 1950s.

mixed language 1. One which could be classed genetically, with equal plausibility, in more than one way. Often in the assertion that no language is in fact mixed in this sense. **2.** One whose vocabulary is historically from one source, but whose grammatical structure is from another. The extreme case is again more hypothetical than demonstrated.

Mixe-Zoquean *See* Central American languages.

'mixing of levels' The use of results obtained in one phase of the analysis of a language as the basis for a phase of analysis held to precede it. Proscribed by many *Post-Bloomfieldians in the 1950s, in the interests of exact method: thus, if phonological analysis precedes grammatical analysis, a phonologist could not, without mixing levels, refer e.g. to word boundaries.

MLU = mean length of utterance.

modal (Particle etc.) indicating *modality: e.g. *possibly* and *probably* might be described as modal adverbs.
  Specifically of a class of **modal verbs** in English, whose uses are typically *deontic or *epistemic. E.g. *can* or *must*: compare deontic *You can come in* (permission) with *You must come in* (obligation); epistemic *She could have arrived already* (possibility) with *She must have arrived already* (necessity). Thence of verbs in other languages, whether a distinct syntactic class or not, whose meanings are similar.

modality Category covering indications either of a kind of *speech act or of the degree of certainty with which something is said. Thus *He left at once* (*declarative) differs in modality from *Leave at once!* (*imperative); *He can't have left* (*epistemic) from *You can't leave now*

(*deontic); *You must leave* (obligation) from *You can leave if you like* (permission); *He has perhaps left* (with a qualifier *perhaps*) from *He has definitely left*.

Cf. mood. Ideally mood might be defined as a grammatical category in specific languages and modality as a *notional category which subsumes it. But it is not clear that, as a notional term, it would be univocal.

modal logic Any system of logic with operators that distinguish *modality. E.g. in which N and P are operators corresponding to necessity and possibility: N *p* 'it is necessary that *p*'; P *p* 'It is possible that *p*'.

modal voice Normal vibration of the vocal cords in the production of speech, as opposed e.g. to *falsetto.

model Often of a general way of conceiving or describing some aspect of one's subject-matter. Thus a model of sound change is a view of how, in general, such change takes place; hence, in addition, a way in which particular changes may be described. A model of syntax is similarly a general view of the relations in which words stand, of the rules that govern these relations, etc.; hence, again, a pattern that may be followed in describing the syntax of particular languages. 'Model', in this sense, is often harmlessly interchangeable with 'theory'.

Also in the sense of e.g. a computer model. Thus a system for *parsing in computational linguistics might be seen as 'modelling', or be presented as a model of, one aspect of the process by which speech is perceived. Distinguished, in this case, from a theory: thus it would not follow, and might not be claimed, that such a model was part of a correct view of perception.

model-theoretic semantics An account of meaning in which sentences are interpreted in terms of a model of, or abstract formal structure representing, an actual or possible state of the world: *cf.* possible world. Usually, at least, an account of *truth conditions; i.e. sentences are interpreted as true or false in such a model.

Cf. Montague Grammar.

modes of signifying *See* Modistae.

modification (1) Type of syntactic construction in which a *head (1) is accompanied by an element typically not required by it. E.g. nouns do not in general require an accompanying adjective: therefore, in *I like white chocolate*, the construction of the object, *white chocolate*, is one in which *white* modifies *chocolate*.

Also called '**attribution**'; the accompanying element (in this example *white*) is a **modifier** (or '**attribute**'). *Cf.* complement, complementation.

modification (2) Morphological process by which a part or parts of a form are altered: e.g. that by which *sing* or *ring* → past tense *sang* or *rang*.

'Modified Occam's razor' *See* Ockham's razor.

modifier *See* modification (1).

Modistae School of grammarians centred on Paris in the second half
of the 13th century. Named after a tripartite theory of 'modes', of
being, of understanding, and of signifying, in terms of which the
different *parts of speech, in the system inherited from antiquity, were
seen as representing reality in different ways. E.g. a verb was conceived
as signifying 'through the mode of' existence independent of specific
substance. The account of parts of speech and of their *accidents, based
in detail on the same underlying philosophy, leads to a theory of syntax
in which different types of construction are distinguished by the
relation between depending and 'terminating' elements. E.g. in the
sentence *John's brother likes tall girls*, the verb (*likes*) would depend on *girls*
in a *transitive construction: in ancient terms, there is a 'crossing over'
to another 'person'. It would also depend on *brother* in an intransitive
construction, both these being constructions 'of acts': i.e. concerned
with processes. *Brother* would then depend on *John's*, again transitively,
and *tall* on *girls*, again intransitively. These would be constructions 'of
persons', concerned with participants, not 'of acts'.

The theory was developed by Martin of Dacia and others in the mid-
13th century, though best known from a systematization by Thomas of
Erfurt some decades later. Abandoned in the 14th century, when its
philosophical basis was destroyed by *nominalism.

modular (Theory) which assumes that the mind is structured into
separate **modules** or components, each governed by its own principles
and operating independently of others. Hence, in linguistics, of any
theory which assumes that *internalized languages are separate from
other cognitive structures, or any model of such languages, e.g. that of
*Government and Binding Theory, which is in turn composed of
smaller modules.

Sometimes applied specifically to a theory proposed by J. A. Fodor in
the 1980s, in which speech processing, to a level of 'logical form', is an
'input' system comparable e.g. to the processing of information from
the eyes. Such input systems are seen as 'informationally
encapsulated', in the sense that processes internal to them have no
direct access to information from the 'central processes' with which,
as wholes, they connect.

modulation Bloomfield's term for grammatical features of stress and
intonation. Hence *She's coming* might be said to have different
modulations in SHE'*s coming* and *She's* COMING. Also used to refer to
differences in *paralanguage.

modus ponens Term in logic for the form of reasoning by which, if
q follows from *p*, and *p* is true, then *q* is also true. ***Modus tollens*** is the
form by which, if *q* follows from *p*, and *q* is false, then *p* is also false.

Latin for 'method of affirming' and 'method of denying'.

Mohawk *See* Iroquoian.

Mon *See* Mon-Khmer.

moneme Martinet's term (French 'monème') for a minimal
*linguistic sign: e.g. French *travaillons* '(we) are working' can be
analysed into monemes *travaill-* 'work' and *-ons* '1PL'. For the general
sense *cf.* morpheme (2). 'Monèmes' are divided into 'lexèmes' such as
travaill- and 'morphèmes' such as *-ons*: *cf.* lexeme (2), morpheme (1).

Mongolian Family of languages spoken mainly in the Mongolian
Republic and an adjacent part of China: the language also called
'Mongolian' is its main member. A proposed branch of *Altaic.
  Classical Mongolian is the language of the Mongols in the Middle
Ages, attested from the 13th century in a script derived ultimately
from the *Semitic alphabet used for *Aramaic.

Mon-Khmer Family of languages in South-east Asia. *Khmer and
*Vietnamese are the most important; **Mon**, though now with far
fewer speakers, was the language of the people dominant in the delta
area of Burma (Myanmar) from, in particular, the 6th to 11th
centuries AD, and was written in one of the earliest *Indian scripts in
the region.
  The family has been grouped with *Munda in a proposed *Austro-
Asiatic.

mono- Prefix from the Greek word for 'alone' or 'single'. Thus a
monosyllabic word, or **monosyllable**, consists of a single syllable;
a **monomorphemic** word or phrase consists of a single morpheme;
a *monotransitive verb takes just one object. Opp. di-/bi-, tri-,
poly-/multi-/pluri-.

monocentric Not *polycentric.

monogenesis Single origin, e.g. of languages. Thus distinguishing
especially the theory that the evolution of language originated in a
single population; also the theory that pidgins and creoles, or
*Atlantic creoles in particular, have derived from a single original by
repeated processes of *relexification. Opp. polygenesis.

monolingual Not *bilingual or *multilingual. Thus, in a strict sense,
having a single native language.

monophthong A vowel which is not part of a *diphthong or
*triphthong: e.g. [a] in *cat* [kat].
  Cf. pure vowel. But a unit may often be described as monophthongal
in phonology when the vowel by which it is realized either is not, or is
not consistently, pure: e.g. that of *more*, realized variously as [ɔː] or [ɔə].

monostratal Having a single *level of representation, e.g. of an
account or model of syntax. Opp. multistratal.

monosystemic Firth's term for analyses which establish single overall systems, e.g. an overall system of consonants, as opposed to one which is *polysystemic, which he advocated.

monotransitive Taking or including a single *object: e.g. of the construction of *He broke a plate*, or of the verb *break*, in taking that construction.

monovalent (Verb) whose *valency has just one element: e.g. the intransitive *die* in *He died*.

Montague Grammar Treatment of syntax and semantics developing work by R. Montague before his death in the early 1970s. Based on the belief that the techniques of *formal semantics, familiar in application to artificial systems of logic, were equally appropriate to languages in the ordinary sense. Hence for any language (*a*) a set of syntactically well-formed expressions had to be specified by a formal system of syntax; (*b*) these expressions had to be assigned interpretations in an appropriate system of logic. In Montague's account, the syntactic categories were those of a *categorial grammar, the form of rules combining categories being, however, essentially unconstrained. In addition, each syntactic rule was associated with a semantic rule that derived the semantic interpretation of its output from the semantic interpretations of its inputs. In later work, both the application of formal semantics and this *rule to rule hypothesis have been associated with more restricted systems of syntax, especially in *Generalized Phrase Structure Grammar.

mood Grammatical category distinguishing *modality. Originally of an inflectional category of verbs in Greek and Latin, opposing in particular *indicative and *subjunctive: thence of other systems of modality marked by verbs, of distinctions in modality between constructions, and so on. 'Modality' and 'mood' are therefore used in the same sense, by different scholars, in some contexts.

mora A unit of syllable weight applicable to languages in which long or *heavy syllables are distinguished from short or light syllables. Different measures have been proposed; but e.g. a syllable ending in a short vowel might have one mora and one which ends in a long vowel or a consonant two morae.

Hence '**moraic**' (for expected 'moric'): e.g. if a syllable has two morae it is '**bimoraic**'; if one, it is '**monomoraic**'. The plural form is sometimes '**more**' in place of 'morae'.

Moré *See* Gur.

morph The smallest sequence of phonological units into which words are divided in an analysis of morphemes. Thus the form [ʌnstrɛtʃt] (*unstretched*) will be divided into the morphs [ʌn], realizing a negative morpheme, [strɛtʃ], realizing the root morpheme 'stretch', and [t], realizing e.g. the past-tense morpheme.

morpheme A unit of grammar smaller than the word. E.g. *distasteful* is composed of morphemes realized by *dis-*, *taste*, and *-ful*.

The term was introduced in the late 19th century, and has had three main senses. **1.** A unit smaller than the word which has *grammatical as opposed to lexical meaning. The original sense, still current in French: opp., in French, 'lexème' (earlier 'sémantème'); *cf.* moneme. **2.** Any configuration of phonological units within a word which has either grammatical or lexical meaning: thus, in *distasteful*, any of the sequences [dɪs], [teɪst], and [fəl] or, in a *basic form, [fʊl]. *Cf.* morph. **3.** An invariant lexical or grammatical unit realized by one or more configurations of phonological units. E.g. [dɪs] in *distasteful* might be seen as one realization of a more abstract 'negative' morpheme also realized e.g. by [ʌn] in *unpleasant*. *Cf.* allomorph.

Sense 1 is virtually obsolete in English-speaking countries, where usage has tended to hover between sense 2 and sense 3.

morpheme-structure rule Used in the 1960s of a form of *lexical redundancy rule by which features were added to *underspecified representations, in the lexicon, of the phonological forms of morphemes. A **morpheme-structure condition** was a *filter that could apply equivalently to representations that were fully specified.

morphemics *Morphology, conceived as a branch of linguistics which takes the morpheme as its basic unit.

morpholexical rule A rule for *allomorphy stated over the lexical entries for individual morphemes, ahead of rules which specify phonological processes.

morphological process Any of the formal processes or operations by which the forms of words are derived from *stems or *roots. E.g. *reran* is derived from the root *run* by two morphological processes, one adding *re-* (*run* → *rerun*), the other changing *u* to *a* (*rerun* → *reran*).

For types of morphological process *see* affix; compound; modification (2); reduplication; subtraction; suppletion.

morphologization Process of *grammaticalization (2) which results specifically in what was formerly a word becoming an element within a word.

morphology The study of the grammatical structure of words and the categories realized by them. Thus a morphological analysis will divide *girls* into *girl* and *-s*, which realizes 'plural'; *singer* into *sing* and *-er*, which marks it as a noun denoting an agent.

A category is '**morphological**' if it is realized within words. Thus **morphological case** is *case as realized by different elements within nouns or words of other classes, as opposed to *case roles realized by

independent words or word order; a **morphological causative** is a
*causative form of a verb as opposed to a causative construction, and
so on.

morphome A pattern or unit in morphology identified by the form
or forms in which it is realized, but corresponding to no single
morphosyntactic property. Thus the *-en* in *taken* can be identified at a
more abstract level with the *u* of *sung*, a regular *-(e)d* in *rolled*, and so on.
But the unit so established has two separate syntactic functions: that
of a past participle, as in *I've taken it*; and a passive participle, as in *It
was taken*. Its identity is thus **morphomic**: in morphology only.

morphoneme = morphophoneme; likewise **morphonemics**,
morphonology = morphophonemics, morphophonology.

morphophoneme Unit posited in the 1930s to account for
alternations in morphology which are *recurrent but not *automatic.
E.g. *knives* or *loaves* has a [v] ([nʌɪv], [ləʊv]) where *knife* or *loaf* has an [f].
The alternation is recurrent, since it is found in more than one word.
But it is not automatic, since it is not found e.g. in *oaf* and *oafs*, both of
which have [f], or in *hive* and *hives*, both of which have [v]. To account
for it, forms such as *knife* and *loaf* are said to end in a morphophoneme
'F', identical to [f] except that, when the plural ending follows, it is
realized by [v]. Thus, in terms of processes, [nʌɪF] + plural → [nʌɪv]-, but
[əʊf] (*oaf*) + plural is unchanged.

Usually written, as here, with a capital letter. But, like phonemes,
morphophonemes can be analysed into features. E.g. 'F' might have
the same phonetic features as [f] plus a *diacritic feature which may
be said to 'trigger' the alternation. The same diacritic feature might
also distinguish a morphophoneme 'S' in *house* (plural [haʊzɪz]) or 'Θ'
in *wreath* (plural [riːðz]).

morphophonemics *See* morphophonology.

morphophonemic script *See* phonemic script.

morphophonology Branch of linguistics concerned with rules or
alternations intermediate between *morphology and *phonology.
Called '**morphophonemics**' by most linguists in the USA, and defined
by C. F. Hockett in the 1950s in a sense that covered the entire relation
between representations of sentences in terms of *morphemes (3) and
their representations in terms of *phonemes. Usual definitions are less
wide: thus, in particular, a morphophonological rule or alternation is
one which (*a*) applies to phonological elements, but (*b*) applies only
under certain morphological conditions. E.g. in *capacious* vs. *capacity*, [eɪ]
(in *cap*[eɪ]*cious*) alternates with [a] (in *cap*[a]*city*). The alternation is not
restricted to this pair of forms: compare *ver*[eɪ]*cious* and *ver*[a]*city*, or
loqu[eɪ]*cious* and *loqu*[a]*city*. Thus (*a*) it concerns the vowels [eɪ] and [a], not
the form *capac-* as a whole. But (*b*) it applies to words with a certain

morphological structure, basically derived from that of Latin. Therefore, in many accounts, it is morphophonological, not simply phonological.

Cf. morphophoneme.

morphosyntactic (Category, feature) distinguishing forms within an inflectional *paradigm. Thus the paradigms of nouns in Latin, Russian, and many other languages have two dimensions, formed by the morphosyntactic categories of number (singular or plural) and case (nominative, accusative, etc.).

Called 'morphosyntactic' from the role such categories play in both morphology and syntax. The term 'category' is traditionally used both of the feature that distinguishes the dimension in general (e.g. number or case) and the specific terms or values (e.g. singular or nominative) along it. Alternatively, the former is a '**morphosyntactic category**', while the latter are specific '**morphosyntactic properties**' (or 'morphosyntactic features'). E.g. Latin *puellam* 'girl-ACC.SG' is characterized by the morphosyntactic properties accusative (ACC) and singular (SG), which are terms respectively in the morphosyntactic categories of case and number. Alternatively, again, a category as a whole may be represented as a variable *feature which has two or more values: e.g. number in Latin as the binary feature [± plural].

morphosyntactic word A representation of a word in terms of its grammatical properties, as opposed to a phonetic or written *word form. E.g. 'the past tense of *run*' or '*run*-PAST' is the morphosyntactic word realized by the word form *ran*.

morphotactics The study of relations of sequence etc. among *morphemes. Thus it is an aspect of the morphotactics of English that e.g. the prefix *un-* (in *unkind* or *unhinge*) comes before the form to which it is added. Usually of the arrangement of morphemes within words, but also of their relations within sentences, if morphemes are taken to be the smallest syntactic units.

morphotonemics *Morphophonology or morphophonemics involving alternations of tones in *tone languages.

'mother' Relation of a *node in a *phrase structure tree to any 'daughter' node that it immediately *dominates.

motherese Form of speech used especially by mothers in talking to very young children: also called 'baby talk', 'caregiver speech', 'caretaker speech'.

'mother-in-law language' *See* avoidance style.

'mother tongue' = native language.

motivation The opposite of *arbitrariness. Thus the relation between form and meaning is **motivated**, or partly motivated, in a case of *onomatopoeia; also e.g. where forms are derived by a semantically regular process of *word-formation. *See also* iconicity.

Motu *Austronesian language in the region of Port Moresby; **Hiri Motu** or '**Police Motu**' is a simplified or pidginized form still spoken widely in Papua New Guinea.

movement Process in generative grammars by which a unit is moved from one position to another within a syntactic structure: thus e.g. *wh*-movement. Formulated in *Principles and Parameters Theory as a principle by which any unit could move anywhere ('**Move**' or, earlier, '**Move α**'), subject to constraints imposed by other general principles, by settings of parameters, etc.

Formulated from the early 1970s as a process that resulted in *traces; reformulated thirty years later in terms of *copying. A movement chain was formed, in *Government and Binding Theory, by the links between a unit that had moved repeatedly and successive traces in the positions it had been in previously.

M-principle Principle in *Neo-Gricean pragmatics by which speakers are expected to use a 'marked' form of words only for good reason. E.g. in I *didn't exactly fail my test*, the expression *didn't exactly fail* is 'marked' in opposition to *passed*; in using it one might accordingly implicate that one's performance was at best not brilliant.

M stands for manner; defined by S. C. Levinson alongside the *Q-principle and *I-principle.

mu (μ) Symbol for a *mora.

multi- From the Latin word for 'many': *cf.* poly-, pluri-.

multilateral comparison = mass comparison.

multilateral opposition One between terms distinguished by more than one feature. Especially of phonemes: e.g. [p] and [s] in English are in a multilateral opposition, since they are distinguished within the consonant system by both place and manner of articulation. Opp. bilateral.

multilingual 1. (Person) having equal control of more than two native languages. **2.** (Community) in which more than two languages are native. Thence loosely, as *bilingual, e.g. of someone who has some command of more than two languages.

multiple negation *See* double negative.

multiplex *See* social network.

multistratal Having a series of *levels of representation. E.g. *Government and Binding Theory in the 1980s assumed a multistratal model of syntax. Opp. monostratal.

multivalued Not *binary. Thus a **multivalued feature** is one whose values are not simply '+' and '−': e.g. that of vowel height if it is seen as involving a *gradual opposition. Likewise a **multivalued logic** is one in which propositions may be other than just true or false.

Munda Family of languages spoken in scattered areas of central and eastern India: a proposed branch of *Austro-Asiatic.

murmured Articulated with breathy voice: i.e. with the vocal cords vibrating but in a position that allows an airflow greater than in *voiced sounds. The *h* in *ahead* is typically murmured: phonetically [ə'fiɛd]. Murmur is distinctive for stops in e.g. Hindi-Urdu, where those called 'voiced aspirates' are murmured [bʱ], [dʱ], etc.

Muskogean A small family of languages native to parts of the southeastern USA, from Texas to Florida. **Choctaw** (Mississippi) is the least endangered.

mutation Generally, of sound changes that lead to alternations between phonemes. Specifically, in Celtic, of grammatically conditioned alternations of consonants, especially at the beginnings of words. E.g. basic [k] in Welsh *cath* 'cat' [kaːθ] → [g] in *y gath* 'the cat' [ə gaːθ]; [ŋh] in *fy nghath i* 'my cat' [ən ŋhaːθ i]; [x] in *ei chath hi* 'her cat' [i xaːθ hi]. These are instances of, respectively, 'soft mutation', 'nasal mutation', and 'spirant mutation'.

mute An old term for an *oral stop. Defined in antiquity as one that could not be uttered without an accompanying vowel: hence, in itself, 'silent'.

mutual knowledge The knowledge that a speaker and addressee are seen as jointly taking for granted at a given point in an interchange. E.g. if A says to B 'Jones is coming', one condition for successful communication is that A and B should share the knowledge of who Jones is: specifically, B knows who A means by 'Jones', A knows that B knows this, B knows that A knows that, and so on. Often in accounts which argue that complete success in communication is possible if but only if all relevant knowledge is shared, in this sense, completely.

Also called 'shared knowledge'; *cf.* background knowledge.

mutually intelligible (Dialects, languages) each of which can be understood, or understood sufficiently for ordinary purposes, by speakers of the other: e.g. Danish and Norwegian or, to a lesser degree, Danish and Swedish. Often seen as a necessary property of *dialects.

Mycenaean Form of Greek attested in the 2nd millennium BC, on the site of Mycenae and elsewhere, by records in *Linear B.

N

N **1.** = noun. **2.** = nasal.

Na-Dené Conjectural family linking *Athabaskan with three other North American languages (in ascending order Eyak, Tlingit, Haida). Proposed by Sapir; the inclusion of Haida in particular is at best doubtful.

Nahuatl *Uto-Aztecan language, spoken in various parts of central Mexico. The language of the Aztecs; important also as a second language before and after the Spanish conquest. Written at the time of the conquest in a script derived from the *Mayan.

narratology The formal analysis of narrative texts, on lines inspired by or seen as similar to European structural linguistics.

narreme *See* -eme.

Narrow Bantu = Bantu.

Narrow Romic *See* Sweet.

narrow transcription A phonetic transcription which is detailed down to the level at which features can be distinguished. Thus a narrow transcription of one pronunciation of *stray* might be expected to indicate that the stop is released by a fricative, that the place of articulation of [s] is slightly backer than in *say*, that in all three consonants the lips are rounded, and so on. Opp. broad transcription.

narrow vowel One in whose production the tongue is bunched towards the centre so that its upper surface is relatively convex in cross-section. A possible factor in distinguishing e.g. [iː] from [ɪ] in English, or in similar distinctions in other northern European languages. Opp. wide vowel.

nasal Produced with lowering of the soft palate, so that air may pass through the nose. Thus [m] and [n] in *man* [man] are nasal *stops or, if not classed as stops, are **nasals**; the vowel of French *saint*, conventionally [ɛ̃], is a **nasal vowel**.
   Opp. oral. The **nasal cavity** is the additional resonating chamber formed by the passages through the nose when the soft palate is lowered.

nasal assimilation Usually of a process by which nasal consonants have the same place of articulation as adjacent oral consonants. E.g. the *n* of *unkind* tends to be either velar ([ŋ]), or to be realized with overlapping [n] and [ŋ], by *assimilation to the velar plosive that follows.

nasalization Change or process by which vowels or consonants become nasal. Thus, in the history of French, the vowel of Latin *unus* 'one' or *manus* 'hand' will have been nasalized, in the context of a following nasal consonant, before, at a later stage, that consonant was lost: thus Modern French *un* (conservatively [œ̃]), *main* ([mɛ̃]).

Also of the lowering of the velum seen as comparable to a *secondary articulation. Thus '**nasalized vowel**' = nasal vowel.

nasal release The *release of a closure by lowering of the soft palate, so that air passes outwards through the nose: e.g. that of the [t] in [bʌtn̩] (*button*). Also called '**nasal plosion**'.

national language One which is a source or sign of identity for a nation. Potentially distinguished from an official language: e.g. until the mid-1980s Luxembourg had two official languages (French and German), but the national language was then, as it is now, Luxembourgish.

native (Form, word, etc.) which is not historically a result of *borrowing. E.g. *cow*, which has cognates in other Germanic languages, is native to English; *beef*, which derives from a form borrowed from Old French, is not.

native language A language that people have acquired naturally as children, as opposed to one learned later, e.g. through formal education. By the same token they are **native speakers**.

nativism The theory that specific properties of the mind are inherited, not acquired. Hence especially, in linguistics, of Chomsky's theory of the development of language in children from genetically inherited principles of *Universal Grammar.

*Empiricism is the philosophical doctrine traditionally opposed to nativism.

nativized 1. (Language) that has become native in a community: e.g. in the development of a *creole from a pidgin. **2.** (Form etc.) that is historically a loan but is no different, nor perceived as different, from those that are native. E.g. *cheer*, from the word for 'face' in Old French, is nativized in English; *rouge* is not.

natural class Any class, of sounds especially, whose members share some property that distinguishes it from others. E.g. in English [m], [n], and [ŋ] form a natural class; [n] and, say, [h] do not.

'**natural gender**' *See* gender (1).

Natural Generative Phonology Model developed by J. B. Hooper and others in the 1970s and early 1980s, in reaction to *Generative Phonology as developed by Halle. Distinguished by a strict division between phonology and *morphophonology, and by attempts to constrain either phonological rules or the forms on which they operate by conditions which exclude *abstract representations. These include a condition by which rules are *ordered only intrinsically.

natural language 1. An imagined or invented system similar to a language except that the relation between forms and meanings is systematic and accords in some way with perceived reality. E.g. one in which, say, all the words for animals would systematically begin with *b*, all those for mammals with *ba*, all those for primates with *bac*, and so on. **2.** A language in the ordinary sense, which is or has been learned and spoken naturally by a community, as opposed to an artificial system resembling language in one or more respects.

Attempts to develop 'languages' which would be natural in sense 1 are characteristic of the *Universal Language Movement from the mid-17th century. But these were not, of course, natural in sense 2. Conversely, languages gratuitously described as natural in sense 2 have *arbitrary relations between forms and meanings, and are thus not natural in sense 1.

Natural Morphology A broad approach to morphology, developed especially in Germany and Austria from the early 1980s, in which both the structural tendencies of languages in general, and the specific processes of change in individual languages, are explained in part by the operation of hypothetically universal laws of *naturalness. Thus it is easier to understand words if their morphological structure is transparent: hence, in particular, if categories are realized by affixes (English *bake-d* or *hen-s*) rather than e.g. by vowel change (English *took* or *men*). In that sense affixation is more natural: hence, in languages generally, it is the commonest process and, as specific languages change, the tendency, all else being equal, is for its scope to increase. E.g. in the history of English, plurals with affixes, like *cows*, have tended to replace ones that are less transparent, like *kine*. By other proposed laws, it is natural e.g. that a plural, which is *marked (1) in opposition to a singular, should be realized by the presence rather than the absence of an affix: plural *hen-s* vs. singular *hen*, not plural *hen* vs. singular *hen-s*. Hence, again, this pattern is found more widely across languages and, again, specific changes will tend towards it.

Laws such as these reduce to a general principle of *iconicity. But one law may conflict with another, and conflicts may be resolved in different ways in different types of language. Moreover, any law may conflict with structures inherent in a specific system. Hence all apply, as above, 'all else being equal'.

naturalness The property of rules, relations, principles, etc. that are in some degree explicable by factors lying outside language or outside the domain of a *language system. Thus a bird name such as *chiffchaff* or *peewit* is natural to the extent that it reflects the song or call of the bird itself; a process by which a velar consonant is palatalized between front vowels is natural in terms of the movements that the tongue must make in articulating it; a principle in syntax by which words linked in meaning also tend to be next to each other is natural in so far as it makes a sentence easier to produce or to understand.

Opp. arbitrariness, in cases like the first especially.

Natural Phonology Theory developed by D. Stampe at the end of
the 1960s, which proposed a universal set of phonetically 'natural'
processes. These were seen as genetically inherited by any child, but
variously confirmed or inhibited as a specific language is acquired.
Cf. Optimality Theory.

Natural Serialization Principle Principle proposed by
T. Vennemann in the 1970s, by which the order of verbs and their
complements, conceived as a relation between an 'operand' and
'operators', tends to be paralleled by that of other elements seen as
standing in a similar relation in other constructions. Thus if, in a
given language, verbs precede their complements that language will
also tend to have prepositions (operands) which precede their own
complements (operators); if verbs follow their complements it will
tend instead to have *postpositions. *Cf.* VO vs. OV languages.

Navajo *Athabaskan language spoken in the American South-west,
in an area from east of the Grand Canyon into north-west New
Mexico: also spelled '**Navaho**'. With speakers in six figures in the late
20th century, it remains the largest indigenous language of North
America.

negative (Sentence, construction, form) whose basic role is in
asserting that something is not the case. E.g. *He is not coming* is a
negative sentence, marked as such by the negative particle *not.* Also
of similar elements or processes within words: e.g. *unhappy* is a
negative adjective, whose sense negates that of *happy.* Opp. affirmative;
positive.

'negative face' *See* face.

negative polarity item A word etc. whose sense is possible in
negative sentences but not or not normally in positive sentences: e.g.
any in the negative *I didn't buy any*, with a sense that it does not have in
the positive (*I bought* ANy). *Cf.* positive polarity item.

'negative politeness' Forms of politenesss seen as enhancing
negative *face.

negative raising The *raising (2) of a negative element. E.g., in
I don't think he's coming, *n't* is part of the main clause: [*I don't think* [*he's
coming*]]. But the sense is like that of *I think he isn't coming*; therefore it is
seen as raised from the subordinate clause. Also called, at one time,
'**negative transportation**'.

'negative transfer' = interference.

negator Any negative element: e.g. *never* in English, *(ne) . . . pas* in
French.

Neo-Bloomfieldians = Post-Bloomfieldians.

'neoclassical' (Compound, formation) involving elements derived from, or resembling those derived from, Ancient Greek or Latin. Especially where both members are *combining forms: e.g. *astronaut*, from *astro-* and *-naut*, or *Slavophile*, from *Slavo-* and *-phile*. Also, however, where this is true of only one member: e.g. *bio-* in *bioscience*.

Neo-Firthians School of linguists following Halliday.

Neogrammarians (German *Junggrammatiker* 'Young Grammarians') School of linguists originating in Leipzig in the 1870s. The tenet for which they are most often cited is the '**Regularity Principle**', according to which changes in sounds, to the extent that they operate mechanically, develop according to laws that admit no exception. Such mechanical changes, whose causes were seen as physical, were contrasted with other forms of change, including *borrowing and change explained by *analogy, whose causes were psychological.

The Regularity Principle was made explicit by A. Leskien in 1876 and by Brugmann in 1878. Neogrammarian ideas in general are best represented by *Paul's *Prinzipien der Sprachgeschichte*, first published in 1880; the movement has been seen by many in the 20th century as the start of scientific linguistics.

Neo-Gricean School of *pragmatics developing in particular the insights underlying Grice's theory of *maxims of conversation. Central concepts include the *I-principle, *M-principle, and *Q-principle.

Neo-Humboldtians School of theorists in Germany, founded between the wars by L. Weisgerber, which developed in particular the concept of a language as a force that shapes the life of, and the perception of reality in, a society or nation. *Cf.* Humboldt.

Neolinguistics Movement in Italy in the first half of the 20th century, led by M. G. Bartoli under the influence of Croce's philosophy of language. Influential mainly in the field of *areal linguistics ('linguistica spaziale'), especially for the insight that, where different words with a similar meaning are distributed across related languages over a large area, those in peripheral regions are likely to be older and those in the centre to be innovations.

neologism Any new word which is introduced into a language, by whatever process. E.g. *Eurocracy*, for the bureaucracy of the European Union, would be a possible neologism in English, either derived from *Eurocrat* or by a direct process of blending.

Nepali *Indo-Aryan, spoken in Nepal, where it is the official language, in Sikkim, and in the north of West Bengal. Written in *Devanagari, in which it is attested from the 13th to the 14th century AD.

nesting The inclusion of one syntactic unit within another. *Cf.* layering; *also* self-embedding.

networks *See* connectionism; social network.

neurolinguistics Branch of neurology or linguistics concerned in principle with processes and structures in the brain associated with the knowledge and use of language. *Cf.* psycholinguistics.

neustic *See* phrastic.

neuter (NEUT) *Gender (1) distinguished as an *unmarked term opposed to the animate genders masculine and feminine. Hence characterized by, or at least tending to include, nouns denoting material substances and inanimate objects. E.g. in German the words for 'water' and the substance 'wood' are among a large subset of such words that are neuter (*das Wasser* 'the-NEUT water', *das Holz* 'the-NEUT wood').

The term is from the Latin word for 'neither': i.e. neither masculine nor feminine.

'neuter verb' *See* active (1).

neutral Usually in the sense of 'intermediate between extremes': hence *neutral vowel. The 'neutral position' of the tongue is its position at rest when it is not being used e.g. in speaking.

neutralizable (Opposition, contrast) that undergoes *neutralization.

neutralization The suppression in one position in a word or syllable of an opposition between phonemes operative in other positions. E.g. [t] in German contrasts with [d] in most positions (*Torf* 'peat' vs. *Dorf* 'village'; *Leiter* 'leader' vs. *leider* 'unfortunately'), but not at the end of a word: despite the spelling, *Hut* 'hat' and *Tod* 'death' end identically ([huːt], [toːt]). In the classic account by Trubetzkoy the opposition is described as neutralized in this position (called the '**position of neutralization**'): the [t] of *Hut* or *Tod* then represents an *archiphoneme, defined by the distinctive features that [t] and [d] have in common. Opp. constant opposition.

Later extended to other cases where a distinction between units is suppressed: thus, in particular, *absolute neutralization. Also e.g. in morphology, for systematic patterns of *syncretism: thus, in German again, the distinctions between cases (nominative, genitive, dative, accusative) are said to be 'neutralized' in the plural.

neutral vowel A vowel such as [ə] in e.g. *fatality* [fəˈtalɪti], which is neither close nor open, neither back nor front, with the lips neither rounded nor spread. Often so called because, in addition, it can be seen as neutralizing differences between other vowels: thus the [ə] of *fatality* corresponds to [eɪ] in *fatal*, that of *ph*[ə]*tography* to [əʊ] in *photograph*, and so on.

new *See* given.

New Guinea *See* Melanesia.

'next-speaker selection' The selection, by what is said by one participant in a conversation, of another participant as the one who is meant to speak next. Thus, if A asks 'Can you come, John?', A intends that a participant called John should reply. *See* Conversation Analysis for the notion of a 'turn-taking' system in which such 'turns' are said to be regulated.

nexus Jespersen's term for any construction involving predication: e.g. the independent nexus in *The door creaks* or the 'dependent' nexus in (*I heard*) *the door creaking*.

   A **nexus substantive** is a noun whose construction is like one of predication: e.g. *analysis* or *happiness* in *their analysis of the problem* (cf. *They analysed the problem*) or *his happiness* (cf. *He is happy*). '**Nexus negation**' has been suggested by Lyons for negation of a predication (e.g. by *(could)n't* in *He couldn't have not seen her*) as opposed to 'predicate negation' or negation of a predicate, as in (*I*) *have not seen her*.

Ngala = Lingala.

NGP = Natural Generative Phonology.

Nguni Group of closely similar languages or dialects of the *Bantu family in the extreme south of its range: they include *Xhosa and *Zulu.

'NICE' properties Acronym originally proposed by R. D. Huddleston for four properties by which *auxiliary verbs in English are distinguished from full verbs. Auxiliaries have negative forms (N): *hadn't*, *can't*, and so on. The order of subject and auxiliary can be inverted (I): *Can he?*, *Had he left?* They can be used in elliptical or 'coded' utterances (C) that can only be understood in context: *he can* (understand 'sing', 'come tomorrow', . . .), *She had*. They can be stressed in emphatic confirmation (E) of a statement: *She* CAN *do it*, *He* HAD *left*.

'Niger-Congo' *See* African languages.

'Nilo-Saharan' *See* African languages.

Nilotic A group of languages in East Africa, from the limits of Arabic and other Semitic and Cushitic languages southwards. **Luo**, spoken mainly in Nyanza Province, Kenya, is the largest.

NLP = Natural Language Processing: i.e. any processing by computer of sentences, texts, etc. in *natural languages (2).

'No Alternation Condition' Proposed in the early 1970s as a constraint which would eliminate the use or misuse of *free rides in Generative Phonology: i.e. a rule would not apply to forms that did not exhibit a relevant alternation.

node Any of the points connected by lines (arcs) in e.g. a *tree diagram.

node admissibility condition Any condition on e.g. *phrase structure trees by which a specific configuration of nodes and arcs is well-formed. Thus a phrase structure rule X → Y + Z can be interpreted as a node admissibility condition by which a well-formed tree can include a node X which immediately dominates (i.e. is connected by arcs to) two successive nodes Y and Z.

noise A sound or component of sounds that is not *periodic (1): thus in speech of, e.g. *fricatives, such as [f] and [s] in *farce*, as opposed to vowels. Also, as generally in models of communication, of extraneous sound that interferes with or obscures a signal.

NOM 1. = nominative. **2.** For 'nominal'. Used especially, as e.g. by Huddleston and Pullum, *CGEL, to label a constituent of a noun phrase that combines or could combine with a *determiner: thus *nice picture* in *a nice picture*, or *pictures of John* in *these pictures of John*. Equivalent therefore to one sense of *noun phrase, except that the heads of such phrases as wholes are taken to be the nouns and not the determiners.

nomen actionis = action noun.

nomen agentis = agent noun.

'nomenclature' A collection of names: thus it is sometimes stressed that a language, or its lexicon, are not a 'mere nomenclature'.

nominal 1. Of or involving nouns (Latin 'nomina'). Thus *child* in *childish* is a **nominal root** or **nominal stem**; *he* and *the party*, seen as noun phrases, are **nominal constituents** of *He loved the party*. In the system of *parts of speech nouns originally included adjectives; likewise, in some modern accounts, these categories share a feature [+ nominal], in opposition to verbs and prepositions, seen as [− nominal]. **2.** Having a syntactic function like that of a noun or noun phrase. E.g. *why he did it* is a **nominal clause**, also called a 'noun clause', as the subject in *Why he did it isn't obvious*.

'nominal aphasia' Aphasia characterized by *anomia: also called 'anomic aphasia'.

nominalism The doctrine in philosophy that *universals are merely names (Latin 'nomina') to which nothing corresponds in reality except the individual entities referred to. William of Ockham, in the early 14th century, was an important advocate, to whom is often ascribed the dictum known as *Ockham's razor.
    Opp. realism.

nominalization Any process by which either a noun or a syntactic unit functioning as a noun phrase is derived from any other kind of unit. E.g. the nouns *sadness* and *government* are nominalizations of the adjective *sad* and the verb *govern*; *their handling of the problem*, in many accounts, of the sentence *They handled the problem*.

nominal relative clause = free relative clause.

nominal sentence One whose predicate is an adjective, noun, etc. with no *copula. Thus, exceptionally in English, *Nothing easier!*

nominative (NOM) *Case whose basic role, or one of whose basic roles, is to indicate a *subject (1) of all classes of verb. Thus, in Latin, *miles portas claudit* ('soldier-NOM gates closes') 'A soldier is closing the gates', where the verb is transitive; *miles venit* ('soldier-NOM has-come') 'A soldier has come', where it is intransitive.

'nominative-accusative language' = accusative language.

non- As a straightforward negative: e.g. **non-distinctive** features are those that are not *distinctive; **non-terminal** nodes in tree diagrams are ones that are not *terminal; **non-canonical** forms are ones that do not conform to a pattern usual, or *canonical, in a language. Also specifically of *unmarked terms in oppositions: e.g. the present *sing* is 'non-past', or [– past], in opposition to past, or [+ past], *sang*.

non-anterior Not *anterior. E.g. vowels are 'non-anterior'; also any consonant whose place of articulation is no further forward than the back of the alveolar ridge: [ʃ], [k], [q], etc.

Non-Catenative Morphology Account of morphology developed by J. J. McCarthy in the early 1980s by analogy with *Autosegmental Phonology. Basically a technique for representing systems such as that of Arabic, in which, e.g. the word for 'book' (Egyptian Arabic [kita:b]) and the word for 'he wrote' [katab] have the same consonantal root (*k . . . t . . . b*) but two different patterns of vowels. In the representation proposed the root is assigned to one tier, analogous to those of Autosegmental Phonology, and the vowel pattern to another; both units will then be realized discontinuously.

nonce-word A word coined on a specific occasion. Thus there is no established word *bananaphobia*; but it might be invented as a nonce-word, e.g. for the condition of some person who refuses to have bananas in the house. Hence of a word attested only once in the textual record of a language or some earlier stage of a language: = *hapax legomenon*.

non-configurational language One that is not *configurational: i.e. one in which the order of individual words is *free (4), and whose sentences have a structure that it is hard or unilluminating to represent by *phrase structure trees. Hence '**non-configurational structure**', of the structure of such sentences or of such a language generally.

non-count (noun) = uncountable.

non-discrete Having no precise bound. Thus a **non-discrete language** is one where the distinction between *grammatical (2) and ungrammatical is conceived explicitly as one of degree; a **non-discrete**

category is one whose membership is similarly not absolute; a **non-discrete grammar** is one which includes such categories, or otherwise characterizes such a language. *Cf.* discrete; fuzzy; gradience.

non-finite (Verb, verb form) which is not *finite: thus an infinitive, participle, or any other form whose role is nominal or adjectival. If a clause has such a form as its central element it is in turn a **non-finite clause.**

non-linear phonology Any school or model of phonology which establishes basic units over a domain larger than that of an individual consonant or vowel. Especially those developed since the 1970s in reaction to the segmental *feature matrices of classic *Generative Phonology.
   See, in particular, Autosegmental Phonology, Metrical Phonology; *also* Prosodic Phonology, Articulatory Phonology.

non-nuclear (argument, valent) *See* nucleus (1).

non-restrictive (Modifier) which does not restrict the reference of a phrase to which or to whose head it relates. In *My father, who is very sorry, can't come*, the noun phrase *my father* will refer to the speaker's father, and will do so regardless of the presence or absence of the relative clause (*who is very sorry*) that follows; therefore *who is very sorry* is a **non-restrictive** (also called an appositional) **relative clause**. The adjective *poor* is likewise non-restrictive in *My poor* `FA*ther can't* ´COME; with or without it, the same person will again be referred to.

'non-sentence' Usually of a sequence of words that is not *grammatical (2): e.g. in the case of English, *Out it put* as compared with grammatical *Put it out*.

non-standard (Form, variety) not *standard. Intended as a neutral alternative to *substandard, that would not imply proscription or disapproval.

'non-verbal communication' Strictly, perhaps, of communication by means other than words. Typically, however, of communication in human beings by non-vocal gestures, and of so-called 'body language' generally, if it is taken to be 'communication'.

'no ordering condition' Proposed constraint, e.g. on *Generative Phonology, that rules should not be *ordered except by the application of general principles.

Nootka *See* Wakashan.

norm A set of patterns in speech which are usual across a community, but are not seen as constrained by a *language system. Thus a front open vowel [a] might be distinguished, in a language system, from a front mid vowel, a back open vowel, and so on. But within the range of phonetic realizations that this implies, a particular quality might be the norm, or the norm e.g in informal speech as opposed to formal, or e.g. for men as opposed to women. A language system might include no rule for the order, say, of verbs and objects. Nevertheless one order might be the norm, or might be the norm except in special circumstances.

The distinction between system and norm is central e.g. to *Coseriu's account of change in language.

'NORM' Acronym for 'Non-mobile, Older, Rural, Male', applied by J. K. Chambers and P. J. Trudgill to the kind of informant traditionally selected in dialect surveys.

normative (Grammar, rule) seeking to establish or prescribe usage: e.g. one which recommends a choice between alternative constructions, or chooses between forms in different dialects, or proposes standardizations in spelling.

Norse *See* Old Norse.

North American languages The indigenous languages of America north of Mexico, now largely extinguished by the use of English especially. Genetically of many different families, some still tentative, and at best conjecturally or speculatively assigned to larger groupings.

The most northerly is *Eskimo-Aleut, from Greenland westwards to Siberia; to its south, across Canada as far as the Rockies and in much of the eastern USA, the majority of languages are or were *Algonquian. In the east of the continent *Iroquoian, centred in the area of Lake Erie, is another established family; also *Muskogean, in parts of an area of much greater fragmentation in the south-east. *Caddoan and *Siouan languages are or again were spoken in the central plains; these are tentatively, but only tentatively, grouped with Iroquoian. To the west, the two most widespread families are *Uto-Aztecan, which extends into parts of northern and central Mexico, and *Athabaskan, in both the states of the American South-west and in western Canada and Alaska. But the South-west is a fragmented area which includes e.g. *Kiowa-Tanoan as one smaller grouping. The Pacific area is in places even more so, with *Salishan and *Wakashan to the north, but languages tentatively classed as *Hokan and *Penutian scattered, with others, in the centre.

North Germanic Division of *Germanic which includes the Germanic languages of Scandinavia (Danish, Norwegian, Swedish), Faeroese, and Icelandic. Traditionally distinguished from East Germanic (*Gothic) and *West Germanic.

Norwegian Either of the two main varieties of *North Germanic spoken in Norway: **Bokmål**, derived from the written form of Danish used before political independence in the early 19th century, and **Nynorsk**, developed after independence on the basis of rural dialects. Bokmål is used more widely, especially in writing; tension between them is not yet resolved.

'Nostratic' Conjectural family of languages whose branches are usually said to include at least *Indo-European, *Afro-Asiatic, *Altaic, *Dravidian, *Kartvelian, and *Uralic. Divers others are added by divers enthusiasts.

From Latin *nostras* 'of our part of the world'. An old conjecture, but despite continuing attempts to give substance to it, still the kind of hypothesis one believes to the extent that one believes in that kind of hypothesis.

notation Any device or convention falling within the ordinary meaning of this term. Thus the representation of *back* as [bak] is an example of phonetic notation; X—Y is the notational convention for 'between X and Y'.

'notational variant' Rarely in any precise sense. Usually of a model of grammar etc. argued to be in some relevant respect essentially the same as another, at least superficially different, model.

notional (Category, distinction) defined by our perception of the world in which acts of speech take place, independently of the structure of a specific language. Thus time is a notional category: for any act of speech, there is a time when the words are uttered, there are other times preceding it and others that are to come. It may be represented, in a particular language, by the *grammatical category of *tense. But time and tense are of a different order; and, although the basic role of tenses is to indicate time, they commonly have other roles as well. Equally, time is commonly indicated in ways other than by tense: e.g. by adverbs such as *today* or *yesterday*.

For similar distinctions between notional and grammatical categories *cf.* e.g. modality and mood; participants vs. persons.

notional agreement *Agreement determined, contrary to a pattern of *grammatical agreement, by the meaning of a word or phrase involved. E.g. in *The council have agreed*, the subject is grammatically singular; therefore, by the rule of grammar that applies in general, the verb might be expected to be *has*. But it refers to a body with several members: therefore *have* (as in *The members have agreed*) is also, notionally rather than grammatically, compatible with it.

notional syllabus Strategy for teaching a language based on and organized by the functions that utterances can have and the notional categories that their elements relate to. E.g. expressions of time might form a single topic, not parts of disparate topics, such as adverbs, tenses, prepositions.

noun (N) One of a class of words characterized by members denoting concrete entities, whose basic role in syntax is in phrases representing *arguments of a verb. E.g. *dog* or *tree*; also words such as *music* or *anger* which, though not denoting concrete entities, have the same or similar roles in syntax. Nouns and verbs have been seen since antiquity as two

'principal' *parts of speech, without which a sentence could not be
*complete. For similar reasons both are widely seen as *universal.

noun class   Usually in reference to systems in which a class to which
a noun is assigned is reflected in the forms that are taken by other
elements syntactically related to it. Thus the system of *gender (1) in
many European languages: e.g. in German *das Mädchen* 'the girl', the
form of the article ('the-NEUT') reflects the membership of *Mädchen* 'girl'
in the class of neuter nouns.

Often synonymous with 'gender' (itself from a word in Latin
meaning, in this context, 'class' or 'kind'). But in many such systems
the number of classes is much larger, and the semantic divisions, to
the extent that semantic principles operate, are not based on sex.

noun classification   1. The classification of nouns, e.g. into *noun
classes distinguished by properties such as gender. **2.** Specifically of
their classification by systems of *classifiers.

noun clause   A clause whose syntactic role is seen as like that of a
noun or noun phrase: thus, in particular, a 'subject clause' such as
what happened in *What happened is unclear*, or 'object clause' such as *that
I would help* in *I said that I would help*.

noun-complement   A *complement of a noun, as opposed to that
of a verb or adjective: e.g. *that they were married* as complement of *news*
in *the news that they were married*.

noun incorporation   *See* incorporation.

noun phrase (NP)   A *phrase (2) seen variously as headed by or having
roles in syntax like those of a noun. Hence, in different treatments: **1.** Of
units such as *a young girl* or *the girl that you knew*, both seen as wholes whose
*head (1) *is girl*. Thence, in Chomsky's in the 1950s, these and any other
units with roles similar or partly similar: thus pronouns, such as *she* or *her*;
also e.g. *noun clauses, such as *she was there* in *Mary said she was there*, or
*free relatives. **2.** Of units such as *young girl* in *a young girl*, seen under the
*DP-hypothesis as headed by *girl*, but as part of a larger unit headed by *a*.

NP = noun phrase.

NP accessibility hierarchy   An *accessibility scale proposed in the
1970s with respect to the formation of *relative clauses. It took for
granted that all languages distinguish subjects (S), direct objects (DO),
indirect objects (IO), and *oblique (2) elements (Obl). The scale can
then be written thus: $S > DO > IO > Obl$. I.e., in some languages,
relative pronouns or their equivalent may only have the role of S. In
others, they may only have the role of S or DO, in others only those of
S, DO, or IO. But in none can they have a role that is lower on the scale
without having all those that are higher.

NP-trace   A *trace left, in terms of *Government and Binding Theory,
when a noun phrase (1) is moved into the position of a subject: e.g. in

Jill seems [*t to be pleased*], where *t* is left by the movement of *Jill*, in what is correspondingly described as '**NP-movement**', from a subordinate to a larger clause.

The process was usually defined more widely, but limited in its effect to movement into subject position.

nth-order approximation An approximation to the sentences of a language that reflects the probabilities with which specific words occur with a specific sequence of *n* words preceding them. Thus in English, taking *n* = 1, *all* can be followed, with a certain degree of probability, by *our*, and *our*, with a similar degree of probability, by *son*. Therefore a first-order approximation to English includes sentences with a subsequence *all our son*. Taking *n* = 2, the probability that *son* can follow *all our* will be zero. Therefore a second-order approximation to English does not include such sentences. As the value of *n* increases, the greater is the approximation to sentences actually acceptable.

n-tuple Any ordered set of *n* elements. Usually enclosed in round or angled brackets: thus, with *n* = 3, the triple (a, b, c) or <a, b, c>.

Nubian Language or family of languages in Sudan and south Egypt, mainly in the region of Lake Nasser, attested by manuscripts of the late 1st and early 2nd millennia AD. Written in an alphabet largely derived from that of *Coptic.

nuclear argument An *argument within a *nucleus (1).
I.e. = argument, unless the definition of either 'nucleus' or 'argument' is such that some arguments are non-nuclear.

nuclear predication = nucleus (1).

nuclear stress *Stress falling on the *nucleus (3) of a unit of intonation. The '**Nuclear Stress Rule**' is a rule of English, according to Chomsky and Halle, **SPE*, by which the normal or default position of the nucleus is on the last word in such a unit.

nucleus (1) A part of a clause consisting, in the usual definition, of a verb plus any elements that are obligatory *arguments or are otherwise within its *valency. E.g. in *I sent it to London on Sunday*, the verb (*sent* or 'to send') is one that requires both a subject and an object (*I*, *it*) and specifically one that allows directional phrases (*to London*). But the remaining element, *on Sunday*, can appear freely and optionally with any verb whatever. Therefore, by this definition, the elements *I*, *sent*, *it*, and *to London* form the nucleus, with *on Sunday* non-nuclear, or forming a *periphery (1) in relation to it.

By another definition, the nucleus in this example might consist of the verb and its obligatory valents alone: *I*, *sent*, *it*. As an optional element, *to London* would then be a **non-nuclear** argument or valent which, with *on Sunday*, would be part of the periphery. In alternative terminology, the nucleus (in either definition) is the '**core**': in that case, 'nucleus' is sometimes reserved for the role filled by the verb, as in turn its central element. Such concepts are central in e.g. *Role and Reference Grammar, where the nucleus is explicitly a unit in the constituency of clauses.

nucleus (2) The central element in a *syllable, usually a vowel or diphthong: e.g. [ʌɪ] in the first syllable (*min-*) of [mʌɪndə] (*minder*). Opp. onset; coda.

nucleus (3) The *tonic syllable in an intonational unit. Thus in BILL *helped* ('Well, certainly Bill did') the nucleus or **nuclear syllable** is *Bill*.

null Having no phonetic or other realization. E.g. a unit such as *children*, in *They like children*, is commonly seen as having a null article, of the same category as the non-null *the* in *They like the children*. *Cf.* empty (2); covert; zero.

null-subject parameter Parameter in Chomsky's *Principles and Parameters Theory distinguishing languages in which verbs must have an overt subject from those in which they need not. English is one in which such a subject is obligatory: *Mary has come*, but not simply *Has come*. But in e.g. Italian it is not needed: *Maria è venuta* 'Mary (lit.) is come' or simply *È venuta* '(She) is come'. Italian is, in that sense, a '**null-subject language**'.

Also (and originally) called the '**pro-drop parameter**'; thus Italian is in the same sense a '**pro-drop language**'. When Chomsky introduced this parameter in the early 1980s, the distinction was seen as linked, in *Universal Grammar, to several others. E.g. Italian, hypothetically by virtue of being a pro-drop language, also has a construction in which a subject follows the verb: *È venuta Maria* (lit.) 'is come Mary'. English, once more, does not: *Mary has come*, but not *Has come Mary*.

number Inflectional category basically distinguishing reference to one individual from reference to more than one. The simplest distinction is between *singular (one) and *plural (any number larger than one): e.g., in English, singular *woman* vs. plural *women*. But many languages also distinguish, in particular, a *dual (two).

Also of a corresponding notional category, that may or may not be represented, or may be only partly represented, by inflections.

numeral One of a set of words or other expressions indicating precise numbers: e.g. *three* or *forty-nine*; also the *ordinal numerals *third* or *forty-ninth*.

numeral classifier *See* classifier.

numerative Another term for a numeral *classifier.

Nyanja *Bantu language, spoken in central and southern Malawi and in parts of neighbouring countries (Zambia, Mozambique, Zimbabwe); also called Chichewa.

Nynorsk *See* Norwegian.

O

O = object.

Obj = object.

object (O) 1. An element in the basic sentence construction of a language such as English which characteristically represents someone or something, other than that represented by the *subject (1), that is involved in an action, process, etc. referred to. E.g. *him* in *I met him*; both *her* and *a flower* (respectively the *indirect object and the *direct object) in *I will give her a flower*; also, on the assumption that it is syntactically the same element, *that I did* in *I said that I did*. **2.** An element seen as standing in a similar relation to a preposition: e.g. *Washington* in *from Washington*. **3.** Any element, in any type of language, which characteristically includes the semantic role of *patient. *Cf.* subject (3): thus, in typological studies, a language may be classified as an *SVO language simply because that is the commonest order, in texts, of agent, verb, and patient.

object clause One which is a *complement (1) of a verb in the position of an object: e.g. *who it was* in *I asked who it was*, or *that I could not come* in *I explained to them that I could not come*.

object complement An adjective, noun, or noun phrase which directly completes the construction of a verb and an object: e.g. *their chairman* in *They elected her their chairman*, or *larger* in *I need them larger*. Also called an '**objective complement**'.

object control Relation of *control in which the subject of a non-finite verb is supplied by the object of a main clause. E.g. in *I asked him to leave*, the subject of *to leave* is supplied by *him* as the object of *asked*.

object honorific *See* honorific (1).

objective *Case which is that of, among others, an object. E.g. *me* is the objective form of the first-person pronoun, as in *Kiss me*. Opp. subjective: these terms are more likely to be used, instead of *nominative and *accusative, when a language has no other contrast of cases.

objective complement = object complement.

objective genitive A noun etc. in the *genitive case, or its equivalent, whose semantic relation to a head noun is like that of an object to a transitive verb. E.g. *my* in *my acquittal*: cf. (*They*) *acquitted me*. Opp. subjective genitive.

object language *See* metalanguage.

object of result A direct object such as *a fence* in *I put up a fence*: i.e. the fence exists as a result of being put up. Also called an 'effected object', as opposed to an *affected object.

object raising *Raising (2) of an object; hence an alternative term for *tough-movement.

obligatory 1. (Element) that cannot be deleted from a syntactic or other structure. E.g. in *She left quickly*, neither the subject (*She*) nor the verb (*left*) can be removed from the construction: cf. *She quickly*, *Left quickly*. Therefore both are obligatory. But *She left* is complete without *quickly*: therefore the adverb is optional. **2.** (*Rule (2)) that must apply wherever it can apply. *Cf.* optional (2).

Obligatory Contour Principle Suggested principle in phonology, originally in application to *tones, by which identical units are not associated independently with two successive positions on a *skeletal tier. Since extended to units of other kinds.

obligatory valent *See* valency.

oblique (/) *See* slash.

oblique 1. (*Case) in e.g. Latin other than the nominative and (where it is distinct) the vocative. In an ancient account the nominative is the 'direct' or 'upright' case (Latin 'casus rectus') and the other cases 'slant off' from it. **2.** Any syntactic element accompanying a verb which is not a subject or object, or the equivalent. E.g. in *I took the painting to London by train*, both *to London* and *by train* are oblique. **3.** Thence extended in some usage to any unit whose syntactic role is marked by a preposition: e.g. *of the cheese* in *some of the cheese*.

observational adequacy *See* levels of adequacy.

'observer's paradox' The problem, faced by sociolinguists in particular, that, in observing or interviewing people to find out about their habits of speech, investigators will, by their own presence and participation, tend to influence the forms that are used. Identified in these terms by Labov in the late 1960s, in the context of a *sociolinguistic interview.

obsolescent Disappearing. E.g. *wireless* used to be an obsolescent form in British English, used at times by older speakers, but very largely replaced by *radio*; Scottish Gaelic is to all appearances an obsolescent language, being replaced more and more by English.

obstruent Consonant produced with an obstruction of the air flow above the larynx. Thus a *stop or an *affricate, in which it is obstructed completely, or a *fricative, in which it is obstructed sufficiently to cause audible turbulence. Opp. approximant; resonant; sonorant.

Ob-Ugric *See* Hungarian.

obviative (OBV) A distinct third-person form used to refer to an individual etc. other than that or those on which reference is already focused in a given sentence or series of sentences. Opp. **proximative, proximate**.

Suppose e.g. that a speaker is already talking about a person *Bill*. For 'he (Bill)' the form used will be proximative (schematically, *he*-PROX). If someone else is then referred to, the form will be obviative. E.g. with subscript *indices to show identity of reference: *Bill$_i$ also asked Charles$_j$ but he$_j$*-OBV *told him$_i$*-PROX *that he$_i$*-PROX *couldn't. He$_j$*-OBV *didn't sound pleased.*

Occitan *Romance language broadly of the southern half of France: the dialects included in it stretch from Gascony and Limousin eastwards, with the exclusion of those assigned to *Franco-Provençal. Now very widely supplanted by French. The term 'Occitan' replaces earlier 'Provençal', now tending to be used of the dialect of Provence specifically.

occlusion = closure.

Oceanic Branch of *Austronesian which includes *Polynesian: also most of the other languages of Micronesia and most of the Austronesian languages of Melanesia.

'Ockham's razor' The philosophical principle that 'entitities should not be multiplied beyond necessity'. Hence the proposal by Grice of a '**Modified Occam's Razor**', by which the senses ascribed to a word, as a basis for *what is said as opposed to what is implicated, should likewise be as few as possible. 'Occam' is a learned spelling of the mediaeval philosopher's home village.

OCP = Obligatory Contour Principle.

OE = Old English; likewise **OF** = Old *French, **OHG** = Old High *German, **ON** = Old Norse, and so on.

OED = *The Oxford English Dictionary*, originally edited by Sir James Murray (1st edn. 1884–1928).

oesophagus Canal through which food is carried from the throat to the stomach. '**Oesophageal voice**' is a substitute for normal *voice (1), in effect a controlled belching, traditionally taught to people whose larynx had been removed by surgery.

off-glide *See* glide.

official language One recognized or approved for use in the administration of a country or some other political unit. E.g. the official languages of the European Union are German, English, French, etc.

OFOM = one form one meaning.

Oghams Alphabet attested by inscriptions in the British Isles from the centuries after the collapse of the Roman empire. The letters are formed by groups of one or more lines inscribed horizontally to the left or right of, or diagonally across, a vertical line or the edge of e.g. a stone. The precise origins both of the system and of its name are uncertain.

Ojibwa *Algonquian language centred in the north of the Great Lakes Region of Canada.

old (information) = given.

Old Church Slavonic The earliest known *Slavic language, attested by texts composed from the 9th century AD; surviving into the modern period in the liturgy of the Orthodox Churches.

Old English (OE) Conventional term for the period in the history of English that ended with the Norman conquest in 1066.

Old French *See* French.

Old High German *See* German.

Old Irish *See* Gaelic.

Old Norse Traditional name for Old *Icelandic, in which there are texts from the 11th century AD.

Omotic Family of languages in the south of Ethiopia, traditionally seen as a branch within *Cushitic.

-on Introduced in *Stratificational Grammar to distinguish the minimal units at each level of representation. At the phonological level, the minimal constituents of phonemes were distinctive features: i.e. 'phonons'. At the morphological level, morphemes were in turn composed of units realized by phonemes: i.e. 'morphons'. At the level of syntax or 'lexology' the minimal unit was the word: i.e. the 'lexon'. In semantics or 'semology' it was in turn the 'semon'.

'one form one meaning' Principle by which forms and meanings tend to correspond one-to-one. Invoked especially in historical morphology: i.e. it is claimed that languages change, or there is pressure on them to change, in ways that maximize conformity to it.

On a strict analysis, this should subsume four subprinciples. (*a*) The same form should not have different meanings in different contexts. E.g. -*s* should not, ideally, mark the plural in *cats* but a form of a verb in *eats*. (*b*) The same meaning should not be carried by different forms.

E.g. if the past participle is marked by -*ed* in *waited*, it should not, ideally, be marked by -*en* in *taken*. (*c*) A single form should not have separate meanings simultaneously. E.g. in Latin, -*m* in *puella-m* 'girl-ACC.SG' should not, ideally, mark both case and number. (*d*) A single meaning should not be carried by two or more forms in succession. E.g. in German *ge-komm-en* '(has) come', the past participle should not, ideally, be marked by both *ge-* and -*en*. But what is usually meant is simply case (*b*): i.e. the principle is invoked to explain the replacement, by *analogy, of (in general) irregular alternants by regular.

one-place (*Predicate (2)) taking only one argument: e.g. the verb 'disappear' in *The butterflies disappeared*, or the adjective, if adjectives are so described, in *The water is cold*.

one-substitution A supposed test for syntactic analysis in English. E.g. in *recent immigrants from Mexico* it is possible to substitute *ones* for *immigrants from Mexico*. Therefore its *constituency might be shown as [*recent* [*immigrants from Mexico*]]. In the same phrase *ones* can also be substituted for *recent immigrants*. Therefore its constituency might alternatively be shown as [[*recent immigrants*] *from Mexico*].

Hence, more generally, a test of substitution of *pro-forms.

on-glide *See* glide.

onomasiology The study of vocabulary from the viewpoint of the things or concepts denoted: e.g. of the words for a group of plants in a specific area, or of words for colours across languages. Originally seen in opposition to *semasiology.

onomastics The study of personal names, e.g. *Mary* or *Smith*. Alternatively, that of both personal names and place-names.

onomatopoeia A word or process of forming words whose phonetic form is perceived as imitating a sound, or sound associated with something, that they denote. E.g. *peewit* or Dutch *kievit* are onomatopoeic words for a lapwing, whose cry they mimic.

onset The part of a syllable, if any, that comes before its vowel or *nucleus (2): e.g. [st] in [sti:m] (*steam*).

ontogeny Biologists' term for the origin and development of an individual organism. The ontogeny of language is therefore its development in children, as opposed to its 'phylogeny', which is its evolution in our species. Thence '**ontogenetic**': opp. phylogenetic.

ontology Branch of philosophy concerned with the nature of existence. The question whether and in what sense a *language system or its elements exist is therefore an ontological question, or concerns the 'ontology of' language.

-onym From the Greek word for 'name', used: **1.** In terms for relations among words: e.g. *antonym 'opposite-name', *hyponym 'under-name'. **2.** In terms invented by analogy with *toponym 'place-name'. Thus hydronym 'water-name', anthroponym 'man-name', phytonym 'plant-name', oronym 'mountain-name', theonym 'god-name', and so on, for scholars who expect their readers to know Greek, ad lib. To study the 'hydronymy', etc. of a region is to study the names of such a type found in it.

opacity The opposite of *transparency. Thus, in syntax, the structure of a clause will be more opaque if, at an underlying level, inflections are represented as *heads (1) of phrases than if, at every level, they are represented as parts or properties of words.

See also referentially opaque. The term 'opacity' was briefly used by Chomsky, at the end of the 1970s, for a principle rapidly reformulated in *Government and Binding Theory.

open approximation A narrowing of the space between *articulators which is not enough to cause a turbulence in the flow of air through the mouth: e.g. in the articulation of both [iː] and [l] in [iːl] (*eel*). Defined as the least of three degrees of *stricture.

open class A class of words or morphemes to which new members can readily be added. E.g. one can list all the determiners in English (*the*, *this*, etc.); therefore that class is 'closed'. But one cannot list all the nouns since, however long an attempted list may be, it will always be possible for speakers to coin new ones or to borrow them from another language. Therefore the class of nouns is open.

open conditional *See* remote.

open interrogative Huddleston and Pullum's term, in *CGEL*, for an *interrogative that has an interrogative pronoun, adjective, etc. as one element in its constuction: e.g. *Who is coming?* or *Which people did you see?* Opp. closed interrogative, e.g. as formed simply by inversion.

Cf. focused interrogative; *wh*-interrogative.

open juncture A degree of linkage between successive sounds characteristic of boundaries between words. Thus in *seal in* [siːl ɪn] there is open juncture between [l] and the following [ɪ]; hence, in most varieties of English, the l is to some degree 'dark' or velarized. In *see Lyn* [siː lɪn] there is open juncture between [l] and the preceding [iː]; hence, in most varieties, it is 'clear' and, in addition, the [iː] may be longer.

Opp. close juncture as the normal degree of linkage within simple words.

open-mid (vowel) = half-open.

open syllable One which ends with a vowel: e.g. the first syllable, [fiː], of *feeling*. Opp. closed syllable.

open transition Linkage between sounds not characterized by *coarticulation. Opp. close transition; *cf.* open vs. close juncture.

open vowel One produced with the mouth wide open, so that the body of the tongue is lowered: e.g. those of *hat* and *heart*. Opp. close: alternatively, open vowels are 'low' and close vowels are 'high'. *See* cardinal vowels.

open vs. pivot *See* pivot (1).

operand Whatever undergoes an operation: e.g. *sing* as the form that undergoes a morphological process by which *sing → sang*.

operant-conditioning Theory of learning developed by B. F. Skinner in the context of *behaviourism, in which specific items of behaviour (called 'operants') were seen as positively or negatively '**reinforced**' (i.e. encouraged or discouraged) by their consequences (e.g. rewards or punishment) for the learner. Progressively abandoned, with behaviourism in general, after the 1950s.

operation Usually of a *process established within a grammar. Thus the rule in English by which plural nouns have the ending *-s* can be formulated, in part, as an operation by which e.g. *cat* (singular noun or root) is changed, by the addition of *-s*, to *cats*. In notation, *cat → cats*.

operator Term in logic and mathematics for a sign which represents an operation: e.g. '+' as a sign for addition. Hence, in linguistics, of syntactic elements seen as corresponding to an operator in some standard system of logic: e.g. *quantifiers (2). Also generally of elements seen as relating others: e.g. in *Jack and Jill*, the conjunction (*and*) as one relating *Jack* and *Jill*; in *Jack loves Jill*, the *predicate (2) or predicator (*love*) as one that relates *Jack* and *Jill* as its arguments.

Sometimes restricted to a particular element. E.g. for Quirk *et al.*, *CGE*, an operator is a first or only *auxiliary, seen as linking a subject (*he* in *He has been seeing her*) to a 'predication' (*been seeing her*).

opposite terms *See* antonymy.

opposition Any *paradigmatic relation between units etc. that are distinct in a given language. E.g. [t] and [d] are distinct phonemes in English; therefore there is an opposition, specifically in this case a *bilateral opposition, between them. At another level *woman* contrasts with, and therefore stands in a direct opposition to, *girl*, or *man*, or *baby*; also, less directly, *cat* or *table*; and so on.

optative (Inflection, construction, etc.) characteristic of wishes: thus, schematically, *She marry-*OPT *me* 'I wish she would marry me'. Ancient Greek distinguished optatives from subjunctives: hence a term in the traditional category of *mood.

Optimality Theory Basically a system in which *constraints (2) are ranked in an ordered series, in a way that determines an 'optimal' realization of any unit. *See* tableau.

A 'theory' in that individual constraints are seen as part of *Universal Grammar, and only their rank as varying from one language to another. E.g. there could be a constraint by which voiced and voiceless stops cannot contrast at the end of words. In German it would have a high rank; therefore such distinctons are neutralized. But the constraint itself is perceived as part of the genetic inheritance of all human beings, including those who will grow up speaking English. In their language, therefore, it will simply be ranked lower, so that the distinctions are in practice retained.

Developed for phonology in the mid-1990s, in opposition to accounts such as that of classic *Generative Phonology, in which forms were derived by ordered processes. A similar account is tempting, however, in any field in which specific constraints, or conflicts among general principles, exist or can be formulated. Hence 'Optimality' accounts of syntax, morphology, pragmatics, or whatever.

optional 1. (Element) that can be deleted from a syntactic or other structure. E.g. the object (*a newspaper*) is optional in the construction of *I was reading a newspaper*: cf. *I was reading*. **2.** (*Rule (2)) that may or may not apply. Thus a grammar might include an optional rule by which e.g. *away* in *I threw away the bottle* might be moved after the object: *I threw the bottle away*.

Opp. obligatory.

optional valent *See* valency.

oracy Educationalists' term, modelled on 'literacy', for ability and skill in spoken language.

oral (Sound) produced with the soft palate (or velum) raised, so that air does not pass through the nose. Opp. nasal: e.g. [t] in *toe* is an **oral stop**, in contrast to the nasal *stop in *no*; the vowel of French *va* 'goes' is an **oral vowel**, in contrast to the nasal vowel of *vin* 'wine'.

The **oral cavity** is the resonating chamber formed by the mouth, as opposed to the pharynx (throat) or to the nasal cavity, formed by the passages through the nose.

orality Used to distinguish the character of a society in which spoken language has the roles associated, in literate societies e.g. in Europe, with writing: thus, in particular, that of having an oral rather than a written literature.

oratio obliqua Latin for *indirect speech. Opp. *oratio recta* = direct speech.

order In the literal sense of sequence: e.g. *Harry* comes before *left* in *Harry left*. Also, in European structural linguistics, of relationship in some abstract structure. Thus *red* comes before *box* in *a red box*, and, in its French translation, *une boîte rouge*, *rouge* 'red' comes after *boîte* 'box'. In that way their '**linear order**' is different. But both *red* and *rouge* are adjectives which modify nouns (*box*, *boîte*); in that way their syntactic relationship or '**structural order**' are the same.

ordered rules Rules in a *generative grammar that must apply in a specified order. E.g. in one account of a plural such as *knives*, a rule by which the final consonant of *knife* is voiced must apply in advance of one by which the ending -*s* would be devoiced. Thus [nʌɪf] + [z] → [naɪvz], whereas, if the order of rules were reversed, it would be changed to [nʌɪfs]: cf., in *cliffs*, [klɪf] + [z] → [klɪfs].

A distinction has been drawn between **extrinsic ordering** and **intrinsic ordering**. In a case of extrinsic ordering a grammar must stipulate explicitly that rule *a* precedes rule *b*. In a case of intrinsic ordering it need not. Thus rule *b* may not in practice be applicable unless rule *a* has applied first. Alternatively, their order may follow from some general principle. Thus, in the case of *knives*, the rule by which [f] is voiced deals with an irregularity, and it is taken to be a general principle that rules for irregularities apply before ones that are more regular.

ordering paradox Any case in *Generative Phonology in which, if rule *a* is *ordered before rule *b*, one set of forms will be derived wrongly and, if *b* is ordered before *a*, another set will be.

ordinal numeral One which indicates an ordered position in a series: e.g. *third* or *twenty-first*. Distinguished from a *cardinal numeral.

ordinary language philosophy Movement in philosophy, centred on Oxford in the 1950s, which sought to analyse the uses of words in ordinary language as a means of resolving or removing problems that were created when they were used as philosophical terms. E.g. *meaning* is a countable noun (*This word has three meanings*, etc.); such nouns characteristically denote self-standing entities (cf. *tree* or *child*); hence, in philosophy, problems arise as to the nature of 'meanings', seen as objects of description existing independently of the forms that 'have' them.

The later work of Wittgenstein is now the most influential in this vein.

Oriya *Indo-Aryan language, spoken in east central India, mainly in Orissa, where it has official status.

oronym A name of a hill or mountain: e.g. *Snowdon. Cf. -onym.

oropharyngeal (Cavity) formed by the mouth ('oro-') and the throat ('pharynge-').

orthoepy Older term used from the 17th century for the study of pronunciation: strictly of correct pronunciation ('ortho-' as in 'orthodoxy').

Oscan *See* Italic.

Ossetic *Iranian language spoken in an area in and to the north of the Caucasus Mountains.

ostension Pointing out. An **ostensive definition** is one which points to individual instances: e.g. of *chair* by pointing out one or more individual chairs, or of *cut* by performing the action of cutting.

OSV language One in which an *object (3), *subject (3), and verb are at least basically or most commonly in that order. Opp. SVO language etc.

'other-initiated' ('repair') *See* repair.

'other-repair' *See* repair.

Oto-Manguean A family of languages in Mexico. Those of a branch called 'Oto-Pamean' are spoken mainly in the state of México; others in or mainly in the state of Oaxaca.

output condition Any condition placed on a structure derived by any system of rules that it has to meet if it is to be an input to another. *Cf.* filter.

Hence in particular, e.g. in the *minimalist programme, of conditions placed on *Logical Forms and *Phonetic Forms by the nature of the performance systems with which they must interface.

overcorrection = hypercorrection.

overdifferentiation The failure, in acquiring a second or foreign language, to suppress distinctions that are made in one's first or native language. Thus [d] and [ð] realize the same phoneme (written *d*) in Spanish; sounds similar to these realize different phonemes in English; therefore, in learning Spanish, a speaker of English may continue to differentiate them.

overextension Extension of a word, rule, etc. beyond its usual domain of application. Especially in reference to the speech of young children: e.g. *doggie* might at first be applied not just to a dog, but to cats and other small animals, a fur hat, etc.

overgeneration The generation by one part of a *generative grammar of forms that are then excluded either by another part or by more general principles. Seen at its simplest in accounts of *derivational morphology and *compounding. E.g. there is a process by which compounds can be formed from an adjective and a noun:

black + leg → *blackleg*. If this applies to any combination it will overgenerate: e.g. *white + wrist* → *whitewrist*. But let it do so: forms like *whitewrist* are then implicitly excluded by a lexicon which will have entries only for the words that actually exist.

overlap In the ordinary sense. E.g. in accounts from the 1940s and 1950s two phonemes are described as **overlapping** if one has among its *allophones at least one sound that is also, possibly in other contexts, an allophone of the other.

over-long Phonological feature of vowels standing in a three-way contrast of duration: e.g. [a] is short, a distinct [aˑ] would be 'long', [aː] would be 'over-long'.

overt Not *null; not *covert.

OV language One in which a verb (V) follows, or basically or usually follows, its object (O): e.g. Japanese. Defined in some typologies by this and a set of associated patterns: *see* VO vs. OV languages.

OVS language One in which an *object (3), verb, and *subject (3) are at least basically or most commonly in that order. Opp. SVO language etc.

oxymoron [ɒksɪˈmɔːrɒn] Term in rhetoric for the deliberate coupling of words that are strictly contradictory: e.g. in *a devout atheist*, or *I am relaxing strenuously*.

oxytone A word, originally one in Ancient Greek, that has an (acute) accent on the last syllable: opp. barytone.

P

P 1. = preposition, postposition. **2.** = predicator, predicate (2). Thus the construction of *I saw him* would have the elements SPO (subject, predicator, object). **3.** *See* patient.

Pahlavi Middle *Persian.

pair test *See* minimal pair.

palaeography The study of ancient documents and forms of writing.

palaeontology *See* linguistic palaeontology.

'Palaeo-Siberian' *See* Siberian languages.

palatal Articulated with the front of the tongue against or approximated to the *hard palate: e.g. the palatal nasal ([ɲ]) in Spanish *niño* ['niɲo] 'child' or French *baigner* [beɲe] 'to bathe'. Often extended to include *palato-alveolars (e.g. [ʃ] in French *chanter* [ʃɑ̃te] 'to sing').

palatalization 1. Change or process resulting in a sound articulated broadly in the *palatal or *palato-alveolar region. E.g. the [tʃ] of Italian *amici* 'friends' [aˈmitʃi] represents the palatalization of an earlier [k] in Latin [aˈmiːkiː]. **2.** *Secondary articulation in which a stop or fricative articulated elsewhere is accompanied by approximation of the tongue towards the hard palate: e.g. in Russian, where 'soft' consonants, such as the [tʲ] of the infinitive ending, are palatalized.

palato-alveolar Articulated with the *blade of the tongue against or approximated to the back of the *alveolar ridge, e.g. English [ʃ] in *ship*.

palatography Any technique for recording contact between the tongue and the roof of the mouth in the articulation of speech sounds. The record is a **palatogram**: e.g. a photograph showing where a substance sprayed on the palate has been wiped off. A record over time is obtained by *electropalatography.

palilalia Speech disorder described as the involuntary repetition of words or larger units.

Pama-Nyungan *See* Australian languages.

'panchronic' (Study, phenomenon) not restricted to specific points in time. Thus, variously, of universal properties of language, of patterns of change recurring across languages, of features of a specific language that are constant over long periods, etc. Opp. diachronic; synchronic.

pandialectal (Feature etc.) found in all dialects.

Pāṇini Ancient Indian grammarian (probably *c*.500 BC), whose rules for *Sanskrit, under the title *Aṣṭādhyāyī* ('eight chapters'), eclipsed the work of his predecessors and became the foundation of linguistics in India. They include a detailed account of morphology and *morphophonology, in which the basic structure of the word is clearly set out, and which was to become a model, in the early 19th century, for the comparative analysis of Indo-European by Western scholars. In the 20th century Pāṇini's descriptive devices, which included the use of *ordered rules and *zero elements, have had a direct influence on Bloomfield and, through him, on generative grammar and *Generative Phonology especially.

Pāṇini's principle The principle in morphology or morphophonology by which less general rules are ordered as exceptions to more general. E.g. rule *a* might derive the plural of a noun *n*, which is more generally a member of an inflectional class *I*. This might then be an exception to rule *b*, which derives the plurals of all other members of *I*, and rule *b* in turn an exception to rule *c*, which derives all other plurals. First found in the work of Pāṇini; *cf.* 'elsewhere' rule.

panlectal (Grammar etc.) embracing all varieties (or 'lects') of a language.

Panoan *See* South American languages.

Papuan Cover term for the indigenous languages of New Guinea, excepting a minority that is *Austronesian; also a few in parts of neighbouring islands. On present knowledge they are of up to 60 families, with no firm reason to believe that they are all genetically related.

para- From the Ancient Greek for 'by the side of': hence e.g. *parataxis 'arrangement alongside'; *paralanguage 'behaviour accompanying language'. Also freely in the jargon for language disorders: *paragrammatism; '**paraphasia**' (wrong choice of words), '**paralexia**' (error in reading), and so on.

paradigm The forms of a given noun, verb, etc. arranged systematically according to their grammatical features. In the illustration, those of the Latin word for 'table' (*mensa*) are arranged in two dimensions, one defined by features of case (nominative, vocative, etc.) and the other by number (singular, plural).

In the teaching tradition, paradigms such as that of *mensa* are learned as models (the original meaning of the Greek word from which 'paradigm' comes) from which a pupil can deduce the

corresponding forms of other words belonging to the same
*inflectional class. In a current account, this is one form of *Word and
Paradigm morphology.

	SG	PL
NOM	mensa	mensae
VOC	mensa	mensae
ACC	mensam	mensās
GEN	mensae	mensārum
DAT	mensae	mensīs
ABL	mensā	mensīs

paradigmatic (Relation) **1.** Specifically between an individual unit
and others that can replace it in a given sequence: e.g. between *cat* and
any other unit (*dog, house*, etc.) that can replace it in the sequence *I saw
the cat*, or between [p] in *spear* [spɪə] and [t] in *steer* [stɪə]. **2.** Generally
between contrasting units, whether or not they so replace each
other: e.g. between *sing* and any other form of 'to sing' (*sings, singing,
sang, sung*).

   Opp. syntagmatic. Distinguished in sense 1 in the 1930s: *cf.*
associative relation.

paradigm economy Principle by which the number of major
*inflectional classes of nouns, verbs, etc. is always smaller than it
would be if the numbers of alternative inflections at individual places
in a paradigm were multiplied together. Thus in Latin there were at
least two endings of the nominative singular, at least two of the
genitive singular, perhaps three of the ablative singular, and so on. So,
if these alternations were independent, the number of inflectional
classes for nouns in general would already be greater than twelve. But
in fact they are interdependent: nouns with ending *-e* in the ablative
can only have ending *-is* in the genitive, and so on. Therefore the
number of *paradigms, in the original sense of models for inflectional
classes, is actually quite small.

   Formulated as an absolute principle, under this name,
by A. Carstairs in the 1980s.

paragoge [parə'gəʊdʒi] The development of an additional sound or
sounds at the end of a word: e.g. the [t] of *pheasant* (compare French
faisan). The loss of sounds in this position is *apocope.

'paragrammatism' A grammatical error in the speech of someone
suffering from *aphasia, seen as an instance of a disorder also called
'paragrammatism'.

paralanguage Any aspect of vocal behaviour which can be seen as
meaningful but is not described as part of the *language system. Thus,
in particular, aspects of voice quality; of the speed, loudness, and

overall pitch of speech; of the use of hesitation; of intonation to the extent that it is not covered by an account of phonology.

By the nature of this definition, the boundaries of paralanguage are (unavoidably) imprecise.

paralinguistics The study of *paralanguage.

Parallel Distributed Processing *See* connectionism.

parallelism The use for stylistic effect of sentences or other units that are parallel in form: e.g. *My wife is gone; my children are drug addicts; my house is falling down; . . . What can I do?* Constructions linking similar members can likewise be called '**parallel constructions**': thus *coordination (*cf.* parataxis) or *correlative constructions.

parameter 1. A limited range of values of some characteristic property. E.g. the realization of a vowel may vary within certain parameters, defined by a range of vowel heights, or of formant frequencies, and so on. **2.** A principle in Chomsky's theory of *Universal Grammar which specifies a finite set of alternatives. E.g. the *null-subject parameter specifies that a language either may or may not allow the subject of a sentence to be null. As a child acquires a language, parameters are said to be 'set' according to experience. E.g. children acquiring English will develop a grammar in which the null-subject parameter is set negatively; hence English speakers will not say e.g. *Are coming* for *They are coming.* But for children learning e.g. Italian it will be set positively; hence Italian speakers can say *Vengono* '(They) are coming'.

parasitic gap A null syntactic element, as seen from a viewpoint such as that of *Government and Binding Theory, which can be null only because it is related to another gap left by an element that has been moved. E.g. the object of *reading* is seen as a null element (∅) in *Which did you mark without reading ∅ properly?* But a null object is not possible when *mark* is followed by its own object (*I marked these without reading properly*). Therefore the 'gap' (∅) is said to be parasitic on a *trace left by *wh-movement: *Which did you mark t . . . ?*

In ordinary terms, *which* is related as direct object to both *mark* and *reading*, or arguably to the whole of *mark without reading properly*. *Cf.*, with coordination, *Which did you mark and not read properly?*

parasynthetic 1. (Compound) one of whose members includes an affix which is related in meaning to the whole: e.g. *red-lipped* = [*red lip*] *-ed* 'having (*-ed*) red lips'. *Cf.* bracketing paradox. **2.** Also, especially in French ('parasynthétique'), of a derived verb formed by the joint addition of both a prefix and a suffix: e.g. *re-juven-ate.*

parataxis 1. The ancient term for *coordination, applied especially to that of clauses or sentences. Opp. hypotaxis. **2.** A syntactic relation between successive units marked only by intonation: e.g. in *I am tired, I am hungry*, said with the same intonation as *I am tired and I am hungry*.

Sense 1 is the original, the term being simply the Greek for 'coordination'. Sense 2 is that of Bloomfield.

Thence **paratactic**, also in both senses.

'paratone' A postulated sequence of units in speech, defined as such by their intonation, thought to constitute a larger unit like a 'paragraph' in writing.

parentese = motherese.

parentheses ( ) *See* round brackets.

parenthesis A syntactic unit which interrupts a larger unit: e.g. in *Bill—let's face it—is too young*, the parenthesis *let's face it* interrupts the clause *Bill is too young*. Defined by Bloomfield and others as a form of *parataxis (2): i.e. the relation of the parenthesis to the unit that encloses it is seen as marked in speech only by the intonation. *Cf.* supplement.

parenthetical verb A verb such as *think* that can be used in a *parenthesis like *He comes, I think, tomorrow*.

parent language An earlier language from which one or more later languages (the 'daughter languages') are immediately descended. *Cf.* ancestor language.

parisyllabic 'Having equal syllables'. Traditionally of those Latin or Greek nouns which have the same number of syllables in all cases in the singular.

parole Defined by Saussure in opposition to *langue* as the system of a language. Hence of the 'executive' aspect of language, comprising both the mental processes involved in acts of speech and the 'psycho-physical' mechanisms by which signs are externalized. Thence of speech in the sense of specific utterances.

paronomasia Play on words of similar sound: e.g. in Pope Gregory's 'Not Angles but angels' (Latin *non Angli sed angeli*). Thence = pun in general.

paronyms Words which are linked by a similarity of form. Hence **paronymic attraction** = popular etymology.

paroxytone A word, originally one in Ancient Greek, which has an (acute) accent on the second syllable from the end. *Cf.* oxytone.

parsing The task of assigning words to *parts of speech with their appropriate *accidents, traditionally set e.g. to pupils learning Latin grammar. Thence generally of the assignment of syntactic structures to sentences, especially by parsing programs, or **parsers**, in computational linguistics or, by analogy, in psychological theories of speech processing.

Part., PART Variously = participle, particle, partitive.

partial assimilation *Assimilation in respect of some but not all features.

partial reduplication *See* reduplication.

partial suppletion *See* suppletion.

'partial synonymy' *See* synonymy.

'participant observation' Research technique, originally in anthropology, in which an investigator becomes or seeks to become an established member of the group of people investigated.

participants 1. Those involved directly in an act, or series of acts, of speech: thus a speaker, a person or persons spoken to, and any others taking part in a conversation etc. **2.** An individual etc. involved in an event or process: e.g. *John hugged Susan* describes an event in which the participants are someone called John and someone called Susan. Thence of the phrases, and the semantic roles of the phrases, by which they are referred to. Thus in this sentence the participants are *John*, with the semantic role of *agent, and *Susan*, with the role of *patient; alternatively, *John* and *Susan* have the '**participant roles**' of agent and patient.

   Cf. person: for sense 2, *actants; also* case role.

participial Of or involving a participle. E.g. *staying with me* is a **participial clause**, or more specifically a **participial relative clause**, in *the people staying with me*; compare the finite relative clause in *the people who are staying with me*.

participial adjective An adjective whose form is that of a participle: e.g. *interested* in *I was interested*, or *interesting* in *a very interesting book*.

participle Term for a *part of speech, originally applied to adjectival forms of verbs in Ancient Greek. Described as a 'sharing' element (Greek *metokhē*) because such forms were inflected systematically both for tense and aspect, seen as a defining property of verbs, and for case, seen as a defining property of nouns. Thence of forms of verbs in other languages whose syntax is at least basically or in part similar: thus, in English of forms such as *visited* in *the cities visited* or *I visited them,* or *visiting* in *the people visiting us* or *They are visiting us.*

   Participles in *-ing* are traditionally distinguished in English grammar from *gerunds, also in *-ing*, on the grounds that participles have a basic role like those of adjectives rather than nouns.

particle Used of divers classes of uninflected words in divers languages. Usually of words that are short, sometimes though not always *clitic, and generally not falling easily under any of the traditional *parts of speech. A typical example is the enclitic *ge* in Ancient Greek, basically a marker of emphasis: *keînós ge* . . . 'THAT (man) . . .', or 'THAT (man) at least . . .'.

Used by e.g. C. F. Hockett in the 1950s of all forms that do not take inflections. Also by Jespersen of all the elements, e.g. in English, traditionally called adverbs, prepositions, conjunctions, and interjections. Thence, specifically in English, of the second element of a *phrasal verb: e.g. *up* in *I picked it up*.

particle movement Posited movement of the 'particle' in a *phrasal verb from its position in e.g. *I will back up Charles* to that of *I will back Charles up*.

particularized conversational implicature *See* conversational implicature.

partitive (PART) (*Case, construction, etc.) by which reference is made to some part of a whole. Thus, schematically, *I ate bread*-PART 'I ate some but not all of the bread'. Hence, more loosely or more generally, of any form or use of a form which can be translated by 'some': e.g. *de* (of) as partitive in French *J'ai mangé du pain* 'I ate some (lit. 'of the') bread'.

parts of speech A system of word classes, developed first for Ancient Greek and for Latin; thence extended, with modifications, to many other languages. The parts of speech canonical in Latin grammars were (in the order e.g. of *Donatus) *noun, *pronoun, *verb, *participle, *conjunction, *preposition, *interjection. The system canonical in Greek grammars included the *article.

The ancient term (Lat. *partes orationis*) means, more precisely, 'parts of the sentence'. A 'part' was thus an element of syntax necessarily or potentially related to other 'parts' (noun to verb, adverb to verb, preposition to noun, and so on).

Pashto *Iranian language, spoken across north-central Afghanistan and in the North-West Frontier province of Pakistan; also the extreme north-east of Iran. Official with Dari (*Persian) in Afghanistan; the writing system is derived from Arabic through Persian.

passive (1) (PASS) (Construction, sentence, etc.) in which a *marked form of a verb has a subject which is characteristically a *patient. Thus *The countryside is destroyed by motorways* is a passive sentence in which the subject, *the countryside*, refers to what is suffering destruction, and the verb has the marked form of a participle (*destroyed*) linked to an auxiliary (*is*).

Also (and more traditionally) of the form of verb in such a construction. E.g. in this example, *destroyed* is a passive participle;

alternatively, *is destroyed* as a whole is the passive corresponding to *destroy* in *Motorways destroy the countryside*.

Opp. active (1).

passive (2) (knowledge, vocabulary) *See* active (2).

passive articulator *See* articulator.

passive participle 1. Any *participle which is *passive (1).
2. Specifically of forms in English such as *painted* in *It is being painted* or *the part already painted*: distinguished as such from a *past participle (2) such as *painted* in *I have painted it*.

Passy, Paul (1859–1940) French phonetician and founder of the *International Phonetic Association.

past *See* tense (1).

past anterior Form of verb used in referring to an event prior to another event itself prior to the time of speaking. *Cf.* past *perfect.

past participle 1. Any *participle which is past in *tense (1).
2. Conventionally of forms such as English *painted* in *has painted*. Distinguished, in some accounts, from the same form as a *passive participle (2); alternatively, both are '*-en* forms', from the ending in e.g. *taken*.

past perfect *See* perfect.

path Any route in e.g. a *tree diagram from one *node to another; any sequence of links between successive stages in a *derivation (1).

patient (P) 1. Noun phrase or the equivalent that identifies an individual etc. undergoing some process or targeted by some action. E.g. *the house* is a patient in *I painted the house*; *Mary* in *I kissed Mary*.
2. Thence of a syntactic role which is characteristically that of a patient. E.g. a direct object in English tends to be a patient, especially a patient rather than an *agent. Therefore direct objects and elements in other languages which are in this respect equivalent to them may be called, in general, patients.

The sense is that of Latin *patiens*, 'suffering' or 'undergoing'. Abbreviated to P especially in cross-linguistic studies, where opp. A for *agent (2); also opp. S (3).

patois Term in French for a specific form of speech within a larger dialect area. Hence especially of a local variety not represented in writing.

patronymic Name derived from that of a father or ancestor: e.g. *Johnson*, originally 'son of John'. Thence of family names generally.

pattern Used in accounts of Arabic and other Semitic languages of a pattern of syllable-forming elements that combine with a consonantal root. E.g. the root *ktb* combines with one pattern, or **pattern morpheme**, in *katab* 'he wrote', with another in *yi-ktib* 'he writes', with another in *kita:b* 'book'. Such languages are said accordingly to have a '**root and pattern**' morphology.

pattern congruity Criterion in phonology which appeals to regularities in patterning. E.g. [tʃ] in *church* might in principle realize two successive consonants or one. But words in English do not generally begin with sequences of stop plus fricative: the putative exceptions are precisely [tʃ] and [dʒ]. So, to regularize the pattern, these too should be seen as realizing single consonants.

paucal Inflection etc. used in referring to a small as opposed to a large number of individuals: e.g. as a term in the category of *number, in opposition to *plural.

Paul, Hermann (1846–1921) Germanist and general linguist, whose *Prinzipien der Sprachgeschichte* ('Principles of Language History'), only one of the massive array of his publications, went through five substantive editions from 1880 to 1920. Its treatment is based on a view of language as a historical or cultural phenomenon, grounded in the psychology of the individual speaker: in a discussion of dialect Paul remarks that, strictly speaking, there are as many languages as there are speakers. The study of language is necessarily historical: apparent exceptions either are not real exceptions or are simply restricted by lack of data. In the processes that lead to change in language, both physical and psychological factors operate. The latter include, in particular, the operation of *analogy, in the learning of word forms by children and as an explanation for morphological change, and in syntax, where it explains the constant production by speakers of new sentences that they have neither said nor heard previously.

   Paul's *Prinzipien* was the most important theoretical work within the *Neogrammarian movement, and the most admired book on general linguistics of its day. Its influence on later theorists, notably Bloomfield, is far greater than is sometimes recognized.

pause Any interval in speaking between words or parts of words, whether of silence (hence '**silent pause**') or 'filled' by a *hesitation form. Thence, in practice, of e.g. the prolongation of a word or part of a word, without pause in a strict sense, if seen as having a similar function.

P-Celtic Branch of *Celtic so called from a sound change by which Indo-European *k^w became *p*. Represented in the modern period by the 'Brythonic' languages (*Welsh, *Breton, *Cornish).

PDP *See* connectionism.

peak (of syllable) = nucleus (2).

Peirce, Charles Sanders (1839–1914) American philosopher, referred to in linguistics for the term 'abduction' and for a threefold typology of signs according to the relation between the signal carrying the sign and the object. The relation is **iconic** if the signal bears a physical resemblance to some aspect of the object: e.g. outside language, a diagram or map, or, in language, an example of *onomatopoeia. It is **indexical** if the signal is directly connected with the object: e.g. smoke as a signal of fire or, it is argued, an *indexical such as *here*. It is **symbolic** if the relation is simply a matter of convention: e.g. a green light as a signal to traffic, or, in language, any word with the property of *arbitrariness.

Peirce and Saussure are seen as the joint founders of a general theory of signs (Peirce's 'semiotic').

pejorative Used to refer to someone or something unfavourably. Thus the earlier sense of *beast* 'large animal' has been virtually replaced by the pejorative sense, e.g. in *The beast hit me*. Also of a change by which a word etc. comes to be used in such a way: e.g. it is possible that *animal* might in the future undergo a similar pejorative change.

Opp. (a)meliorative.

pental (Numeral system) based on five, as opposed to a decimal system based on ten.

'Penthouse Principle' Principle which alleges that any syntactic process applying to subordinate (i.e. lower) clauses can also apply to main (i.e. topmost) clauses.

penultimate Second from the end. E.g. the accent of *computer* [kəmˈpjuːtə] is on the penultimate syllable or vowel, or on the **penult**.

Penutian Hypothetical family of languages, covering many spoken or formerly spoken in various parts of western North America, from central California to the north of British Columbia. **Takelma**, now extinct, was the subject of a classic description by Sapir.

percolation Copying of features typically from a lower to a higher level of constituency. E.g. *which* can be described as lexically 'interrogative'. But in *Which man did she marry?* this feature can be said to percolate upwards to the larger unit *which man*, which as a whole is questioned.

Originally a proposal in morphology. E.g. in *excitement* the suffix, *-ment*, is one that forms nouns; i.e. it has the feature [+ Noun]. From that level this feature percolates to word level. Hence *excitement* itself is also [+ Noun]; i.e. it is a noun. Similarly, the ending *-s* in *horses* has a feature [+ Plural]; by percolation, *horses* as a whole is [+ Plural]. The properties of words are thus seen as determined by affixes; and, in accordance with one definition of a *head (1), words are in general headed by affixes.

*Unification in syntax is, in essence, a similar process.

perfect (PF) **1.** Traditional term for a past tense used of an action etc. considered as a completed whole: opposed e.g. in Latin to *imperfect and *pluperfect. **2.** Thence of any verb form used of actions etc. seen as prior to a specific or implicit moment in time. Thus in *I had worked in Oxford for three years* the form *had worked* is **past perfect**: i.e. working in Oxford was over a period before some moment of time which is itself in the past. In *I have worked in Oxford for three years* or *I have finished already*, the forms *have worked*, *have finished* are similarly **present perfect**: the reference is to working or finishing up to or before the moment of speaking. In *I will have worked there for three years*, or *I will have finished by Friday*, the working or finishing is prior to a moment in the future: hence these are often described as *future perfect.

Also abbreviated 'PERF'; but this might usefully be reserved for *perfective.

perfective (PERF) Verb form etc. used of actions or processes conceived as simple events located at an undivided moment of time. Opp. imperfective; *also* e.g. progressive, durative, habitual, iterative.

Thus, schematically, perfective *go*-PAST-PERF-*I to London* 'I went to London' vs. imperfective *go*-PAST-IMPERF-*I to London* 'I was on my way to London'; perfective *open*-PRES-PERF-*I the parcel* 'I open, have this moment opened the parcel' vs. imperfective *open*-PRES-IMPERF-*I the parcel* 'I am engaged in opening the parcel'. Widespread as an opposition between related verbs in Russian and other Slavic languages: hence central in many general accounts of *aspect.

perfectum Term in Latin grammar for forms of the verb based on, or on the stem of, the tense traditionally called 'past perfect'. *Cf. infectum.*

performance Defined by Chomsky in the 1960s as 'the actual use of language in concrete situations': opp. competence. Hence applied, in *Principles and Parameters Theory, to mental systems seen as interfacing with an internalized *grammar at the separate levels of *Phonetic Form (PF) and *Logical Form (LF). As **performance systems** these are glossed, in one case, as 'articulatory-perceptual'; in the other, as e.g. 'conceptual-intentional'.

A **performance theory**, e.g. of word order, seeks to explain the pattern in which units of specific types are realized, or the prevalence of one pattern over another across languages in general, by the relative ease with which they can be processed in the minds of speakers and hearers in, as originally defined, the 'actual use of language'.

Cf. parole.

performative An utterance by which a speaker does something, as opposed to a *constative, by which a speaker makes a statement which may be true or false. E.g. if one says 'I surrender' that is itself an act of surrender; if one says 'I'll do it tonight' one thereby makes a promise. An **explicit performative** is one in which a specific verb is used to make the nature of the act clear: e.g. 'I promise you I'll do it tonight', or 'I invite you to come tomorrow'. A verb such as *promise* or *invite* is in turn a **performative verb**, or is 'used performatively', in such utterances.

'performative hypothesis' The notion, fashionable in the early 1970s, that every sentence has a *performative verb as part of its underlying syntactic structure. E.g. *Prices slumped* derives from a structure like *I say to you* [*prices slumped*]; *Did prices slump?* from one like *I ask you* [*prices slumped*], and so on.

periodic (1) (Sound) characterized by regular recurrence of an identical wave form. Thence **periodicity**, as the property of such sounds. Opp. aperiodic.

periodic (2) Term in rhetoric for a sentence, passage, or style which includes large numbers of subordinate clauses. A '**period**' is traditionally any complete sentence: thence of such sentences in particular.

periphery 1. The elements of a clause other than its *nucleus (1) or 'core'. E.g. in *I sent it to London last Tuesday* the adverbial *last Tuesday* is a **peripheral** element accompanying the nucleus *I sent it to London*. A peripheral *case or *case role is likewise one associated with peripheral elements. **2.** Those aspects of a grammar which, as distinguished by Chomsky in the 1980s, did not belong to *core grammar.

periphrastic (Form, construction) in which independent words are described as having the same roles as inflections. E.g. *more beautiful* is a periphrastic form of the *comparative, in which the role of *more* is the same as that of *-er* in *prettier*. Likewise the present *perfect *have written* is one of a set of periphrastic forms seen as forming part of the same semantic system as the simple present (*write*) or past (*wrote*).

perispomenon [pɛrɪsˈpəʊmɪnən] The Greek word for the circumflex accent.

perlative *Case whose basic role is to indicate the course of, or a location intermediate in, a movement. Thus, schematically, *walks door*-ᴘᴇʀʟ 'walks through the door'.

perlocutionary Term applied in the theory of *speech acts to the effect brought about by an utterance in the particular circumstances in which it is uttered. *Cf.* locutionary; illocutionary.
    E.g. a wife might say to her husband 'Have you remembered to mend the steps?' The perlocutionary effect might be that perhaps intended, that he goes and mends them. Or it might be that he loses his temper, or simply replies 'Yes, dear'.

permansive (*Tense, *aspect) indicating that a state etc. is persistent or permanent. *Cf.* durative.

permissive (*Mood, *modality) indicating permission. E.g. *can* is permissive in *You can show it to me if you like*; *let* in *They let us leave* is in some accounts a 'permissive' *causative, in opposition to *make* in *They made us leave*.

perseveration Term in psychology for repetition or continuation. A '**perseveration error**' is a slip of the tongue in which a sound etc. in one word is repeated in one that follows: e.g. *cold curkey* for *cold turkey*. **Perseverative coarticulation** is *coarticulation in which the articulation of a preceding unit accompanies or overlaps that of the unit following. E.g. in *boot* the lip rounding of [uː], with raising of the back of the tongue towards the soft palate, may 'persevere' in the articulation of [t]. Hence **perseverative assimilation** = progressive assimilation.

The opposite of anticipation; *cf.* anticipatory.

Persian *Iranian, spoken mainly in Iran, where called Farsi and native to about half the population; also forming a continuum with Dari, spoken mainly in parts of Afghanistan, and Tajiki, centred in Tajikistan. Written in the Arabic alphabet, with minor adaptations.

Modern Persian evolved from Middle Persian after the Muslim conquest of the Sassanid empire in the 7th to 8th centuries AD. **Old Persian** is an earlier form attested by inscriptions of the Achaemenid empire before its conquest by Alexander.

person Grammatical category distinguishing speakers and addressees from each other and from other individuals etc. referred to. Traditionally, a form referring to (or including reference to) the speaker is **first person**: e.g. the pronouns *I* and *we*. One referring to (or including reference to) one or more addressees is **second person**: e.g. *you*. One which involves reference to neither is **third person**: e.g. *he*, *she*, *it*, *they*. Some languages also distinguish *inclusive person, referring to or including reference to both the speaker and the addressee or addressees.

The term is from Latin *persona* 'character in a play' and its sense is therefore like that of *participant (1). But it is helpful to distinguish participants as a *notional category from person as the grammatical category corresponding to it. Thus a specific language may have a form identifying that the speaker is involved in some way in an event referred to: its meaning might thus be represented, in terms of participants, by a feature [+ speaker]. But it might not be opposed directly, within a single system, to other 'persons'.

'personal infinitive' A form, e.g. in Portuguese, which is classed as an infinitive on grounds of syntax but is inflected for *person.

E.g., schematically, *I-heard the neighbours to-shut-*3PL *the door* 'I heard the neighbours shut the door'.

personal pronoun One of a set of pronouns that distinguish *persons: e.g. *I, we, you, he, she, it, they*. Often used of a set distinguishing reference to speakers and addressees only, reference to other participants being indicated by forms whose grammar is different.

person deixis *Deixis depending on the identity of speakers, addressees, and others. E.g. that of *I*: if Bill Bloggs is the speaker it refers to him, if Mary Tonks to her, and so on.

personification Reference to something general or abstract as if it were an individual: e.g. love is personified in *Love conquers all*.

Peters–Ritchie theorem A theorem proved by P. S. Peters and R. W. Ritchie in the late 1960s, establishing that any *formal language that can in general be characterized by a *generative grammar can be generated by a *transformational grammar of a kind that Chomsky's *Standard Theory allowed. At the time this put paid to the hope that the *weak generative capacity of such grammars could be or had been restricted.

PF = Phonetic Form.

PF = perfect.

pharyngeal (Consonant) articulated with the root of the tongue or the epiglottis against or approximated to the back wall of the pharynx. E.g. in Arabic the word for 'eye' (Egyptian Arabic [ʕeːn]) begins with a *voiced pharyngeal *fricative.

pharyngealization *Secondary articulation in which the root of the tongue is drawn back so that the pharynx (throat) is narrowed. The *emphatic consonants in Arabic are described as pharyngealized, though their effect on neighbouring vowels is not like that of the consonants whose primary articulation is *pharyngeal.

phase (1) Used by F. R. Palmer and others for the opposition between *perfect and non-perfect in English. Thus *see* and *saw* (non-perfect) differ in phase from *has seen* (present perfect) and *had seen* (past perfect), while differing in *aspect from *is seeing* and *was seeing*.

phase (2) Applied in Chomsky's *minimalist programme to any stage in the derivation of a sentence at which a *convergence (2) of Logical and Phonetic Forms can be computed independently of the remainder.

I.e. these are forms with their own meanings. The implications are potentially profound or trivial, but that 'phases' in this sense exist appears to follow from the familiar insight that the meanings of sentences are in part *compositional: i.e. are built up in stages from those of smaller units.

phatic (*Function of language) in maintaining or developing relations between speakers. **Phatic communion** was defined by the anthropologist B. Malinowski in the 1920s as 'a type of speech in which ties of union are created by a mere exchange of words'. The phatic function was defined by Jakobson in 1960 in terms of orientation towards the physical and psychological contact between speaker and addressee, as opposed to orientation towards either individually, or towards the state of the world etc.

philology Used in English both of the scholarly study of literary texts (e.g. 'classical philology', 'modern philology') and in the same sense as 'historical linguistics' (*see* comparative philology), or 'linguistics' in general. The **Philological Society** is a linguistic society founded in London in 1842, and its journal, *Transactions of the Philological Society*, is the oldest in the field.

philosophical grammar A study of grammar based on philosophical principles conceived as underlying all languages; *cf.* universal grammar. Applied particularly to a tradition dominant in the 17th and 18th centuries, of which the grammars of *Port Royal and of (James) Harris are outstanding examples.

Phoenician Ancient *Semitic language, originally of what is now Lebanon, spread by trade and migration to Carthage and elsewhere across the Mediterranean. Attested from the 11th century BC, in a *Semitic alphabet believed to be the specific forerunner of that of *Greek.

phonaesthesis = sound symbolism. A **phonaestheme** is a sound or group of sounds, e.g. the sibilants of *hiss, fizz, buzz*, etc., that enters into a pattern of sound symbolism.

phonation The specific action of the *vocal cords in the production of speech. **Phonation types** include in particular *voice (1), in which the vocal cords vibrate, vs. voicelessness, in which they are open; also *creak, *falsetto, *whisper. Normal or 'modal' voice is also distinguished from breathy voice or *murmur; and, in later accounts, from *slack voice and *stiff voice.

   The distinction in singing between 'head voice' and 'chest' (= normal or modal) voice may be wholly or largely one of phonation, but the physiology of head voice is less clear.

phonatory setting An *articulatory setting which involves a persistent feature of *phonation: e.g. persistent creaky voice or falsetto.

phone A speech sound which is identified as the realization of a single *phoneme: e.g. [tʃ], [ɪ], and [p] are phones which realize

successive phonemes in [tʃɪp] (*chip*). *Allophones are different phones
by which an identical phoneme can be realized.

phonematic Of or involving *phonemes or other similar elements.
In *Prosodic Phonology a **phonematic unit** is one associated with a
single position in a linear structure, as opposed to a *prosody, whose
domain is (at least potentially) larger.

phoneme The smallest distinct sound unit in a given language:
e.g.*[tɪp] in English realizes three successive phonemes represented
in spelling by the letters *t*, *i*, and *p*.

Detailed definitions vary from one theory to another. But, in
general, two words are composed of different phonemes only if they
differ phonetically in ways that are found to make a difference in
meaning. Thus in English, [ɪ] and [a] are different phonemes since, for
example, [tɪp] does not mean the same as [tap], nor [pɪt] the same as
[pat]. The individual phonemes are then the smallest units in each
word that distinguish meanings and, in addition, are realized over
distinct time spans. By the second criterion [ɪ] and [a] are single
phonemes since they cannot be analysed into smaller units meeting
the criterion, each with its own distinct time span.

Thence **phonemic**; e.g. a **phonemic transcription** of a word etc. is
its *representation as a sequence or other combination of phonemes.
Also **phonemics**, for the branch of linguistics in which phonemes are
identified.

phonemic script One in which the characters correspond, or tend to
correspond, to *phonemes. Sometimes called 'phonetic': e.g. the
spelling of Welsh is 'phonetic' in the sense that, though the phonemes
of Welsh are not represented unambiguously, the correspondences
between particular letters and particular phonemes is consistent.

Distinguished in principle from a **morphophonemic script**, in
which the letters tend to correspond, as partly in the spelling of
English, to *morphophonemes.

phonetic determinative *See* determinative.

Phonetic Form (PF) One of two essential representations of a
sentence in Chomsky's theory of grammar since the early 1980s. Opp.
*Logical Form (LF).

Defined as an interface with phonetic, or 'articulatory' and
'perceptual', *performance systems. Related in *Government and
Binding Theory to a level of S-structure, as the relic of earlier *surface
structure, and itself described on occasion as a 'surface'
representation.

phonetic naturalness Property of rules in phonology or
*morphophonology that correspond in some degree to phonetic
effects explicable by the movements and structure of the vocal organs.

E.g., in articulating a sequence such as [ata], the voicing of [a] may continue during part of the production of [t]: this can be explained as an effect of *coarticulation. A rule by which a voiceless stop is changed to a voiced stop between vowels is to that extent phonetically natural, or more natural than one by which e.g. it becomes an ejective.

Often, therefore, ascribed to rules that correspond to widely attested sound changes, on the assumption that they have phonetic causes.

phonetic notation Any system of representing sounds in a *phonetic transcription.

phonetic representation A representation of the sound structure of a sentence, seen as one level of representation in Chomsky's theory of grammar in the 1960s and 1970s. Compare *Phonetic Form from the 1980s onwards.

phonetics The study of the nature, production, and perception of sounds of speech, in abstraction from the *phonology of any specific language. Variously divided into **acoustic phonetics**, **articulatory phonetics**, etc. according to the specific aspects investigated.

The relation of phonetics to phonology is problematic. In one view the physical and other mechanisms can and should be studied without reference to their conceivable exploitation in speech. This can lead to the conclusion that phonetics is not part of linguistics. In another view, phonetic distinctions can only be those exploited in one language or another.

phonetic similarity Advanced as one criterion in the identification of *phonemes. Thus the English clear and *dark *l* are sufficiently alike to be treated as variant realizations of the same phoneme; but a non-contrasting [h] and [ŋ], for example, would not be.

phonetic transcription Any written representation of successive speech sounds, in a notation, such as the alphabet of the *International Phonetic Association, designed to be used universally for this purpose. Conventionally enclosed in square brackets: e.g. [sɪˈɡɑː] is a phonetic transcription, in one version of this alphabet in use for English, of *cigar*.

Phonetic transcriptions may show varying degrees of detail: *see* broad transcription; narrow transcription. They have therefore been seen variously as distinct from or equivalent to representations of *phonemes.

phonic (Medium, *substance) consisting of sounds. E.g. speech is opposed as a '**phonic medium**' for language to writing as an orthographic or *graphic medium.

phonogram A symbol in writing which represents a sound or sequence of sounds: opposed especially to a *logogram, which represents a semantic unit.

phonologically conditioned (*Alternation) among forms
appropriate to different phonological contexts: e.g. in English,
between different realizations of the regular plural ending: [ɪz] after [s],
[z], [ʃ], or [ʒ] (e.g. in *horses*); [s] after other consonants if voiceless (e.g. in
cats); [z] after vowels and other consonants if voiced (e.g. in *cows* or
dogs). *Cf.* grammatically conditioned; lexically conditioned.

phonological system The sound system of a language in general.
Specifically, in the terminology of the *Prague School, of a structure of
*oppositions among phonemes defined by the phonetic features that
distinguish them. Hence **vowel system**, of a system formed by vowel
phonemes, **consonant system**, and so on.

In the illustration, six short vowels in Southern British English are
displayed as a system within the **phonological space** defined by the
distinctive features Front ([ɪ], [ɛ], [a]) vs. Back ([ʊ], [ɒ], [ʌ]) on one
dimension, Close ([ɪ], [ʊ]) vs. Mid ([ɛ], [ɒ]) vs. Open ([a], [ʌ]) on the other.

	Front	*Back*
Close	ɪ	ʊ
Mid	ɛ	ɒ
Open	a	ʌ

A vowel system

phonological word A word distinguished as a unit of phonology.
Not necessarily coinciding with a word in syntax: e.g. *I've* in *I've done it*
is a single phonological word, but in syntax it would correspond to
two.

Often seen as one term in a hierarchy that includes as smaller units
the *syllable and the *mora, and as larger units an *intonational
phrase' or '**phonological phrase**', or a '**phonological clause**', in turn
delimited e.g. by intonation.

phonologization Historical process by which a phonetic difference
becomes a difference between *phonemes. Thus a distinction between
*allophones of '*c*' in Latin was phonologized in the history of the
Romance languages: e.g. Latin *cadit* 'falls' > Italian *cade* [kade], but *celat*
'conceals' > *cela* [tʃɛla].

phonology The study of the sound systems of individual languages
and of the nature of such systems generally. Distinguished as such
from *phonetics; other distinctions, between phonology and
*morphophonology, phonology and *morphology, etc., vary among
schools and have not been universally recognized.

In many practical descriptions, and most general discussion until
the 1960s, the central unit of phonology is the *phoneme. Pioneers in
phonological theory, in the first part of the 20th century, include
Trubetzkoy, Sapir, and Jakobson. For other influential general
treatments, approximately in chronological order, *see* Prosodic

Phonology; Generative Phonology; Autosegmental Phonology and Metrical Phonology; Lexical Phonology, Articulatory Phonology; and, from the mid-1990s, Optimality Theory.

phonotactics The relations of sequence etc. in which *phonemes or other phonological units stand. Thus it is an aspect of the phonotactics of English that words can begin with a sequence of consonants such as [str] (*string*) but not e.g. [sfl].

phrasal Involving a *phrase or phrases. Thus *phrasal verbs are *phrases (3) seen as equivalent to single verbs; *of the song* in *the end of the song* is a '**phrasal genitive**'; *more efficient* is a '**phrasal comparative**', and so on. A **phrasal category** (e.g. *noun phrase) is a category of phrases as opposed to one of words or morphemes.

phrasal coordination *Coordination of phrases that cannot be seen as reduced from coordination of sentences. E.g. in *John and my sister met at last*, the coordination of *John* and *my sister* cannot be reduced to a coordination of *John met at last* and *My sister met at last*.

Opp. **sentential coordination**. E.g. *John and my sister were there* can be treated as a reduction of *John was there and my sister was there*.

phrasal verb 1. Any combination of two or more words that is treated as, or as the semantic equivalent of, a verb: e.g. *to take umbrage* might be identified as a phrasal verb, equivalent to a simple verb such as *to bristle*, in *They took umbrage at my suggestion*. Hence = group-verb. **2.** Specifically of a unit in English which is formed from a verb with the addition of a preposition or adverb that can variously precede or follow an object: e.g. *take up* in *I'll take up your offer, He took my offer up*. The second element is usually called a *particle; hence 'particle movement' or 'particle shift' is a syntactic process moving e.g. *up* from (hypothetically) a position before the object to a position after.

A phrasal verb in sense 2 has usually been distinguished from a *prepositional verb by, among other things, the possibility of 'particle movement'.

phrase 1. Any syntactic unit that is not a *clause but has a function as a whole within a larger construction. E.g. in *They like the people in the village*, the subject is a one-word phrase *they*; the object is a phrase *the people in the village*, which includes the smaller phrases *in the village* and *the village*. **2.** The largest syntactic unit seen as having a unit of a specific category as its *head (1). Thus, in the same example, the whole is in one account a phrase whose head is a null *complementizer; *in the village* a phrase whose head is the preposition; *the people in the village* a phrase whose head is either the first *the* or *people*; and so on. **3.** Any syntactic unit which includes more than one word and is not an entire sentence: thus in a similar analysis all and only the units bracketed in *They [liked [the [people [in London]]]]*.

Sense 1 is the oldest and most widespread in grammars. Sense 2 has been central to, in particular, *X-bar syntax. Sense 3 was Bloomfield's, and the apparent source of '**phrase structure**' in e.g. *phrase structure grammar. For specific kinds of phrases, variously in senses 1 and 2 especially, *see* noun phrase, verb phrase, prepositional phrase, etc.

phrase marker The term originally used by Chomsky for the structure assigned to a string of elements by a *phrase structure grammar. Hence equivalent to *phrase structure tree. Abbreviated **P-marker**; *cf.* T-marker.

phrase order *See* word order.

phrase structure grammar Any form of *generative grammar consisting only of *phrase structure rules. Hence any grammar which assigns to sentences a type of structure that can be represented by a single *phrase structure tree.

For varying formulations *see* context-free grammar; context-sensitive grammar; Generalized Phrase Structure Grammar; Head-Driven Phrase Structure Grammar; X-bar syntax; *also* bare phrase structure. In its classic form a *transformational grammar has a phrase structure grammar as its *base component.

phrase structure rule A rule which states that a phrase of a specific category may have one or more constituents, each in turn of a specific category. E.g. a rule S → NP + VP, which was standard in the 1960s, states that a sentence (S) may or must consist of a noun phrase (NP) followed by a verb phrase (VP).

The notation derives from Chomsky's formulation in the 1950s, in which phrase structure rules were conceived as *rewrite rules.

phrase structure tree A *tree diagram which shows the division of a form into successively smaller *constituents and labels each as belonging to one or more categories. In the illustration, a sentence (S) is divided into two constituents: *boys*, which is assigned to the categories noun (N) and noun phrase (NP), and *play well*, which is assigned to the category verb phrase (VP). The latter in turn is divided into *play*, which is a verb (V), and *well*, which is an adverb (Adv).

Tree diagrams are in practice usually represented by a *labelled bracketing. Thus, equivalently, $_S[_{NP}[_N[boys]] _{VP}[_V[play] _{Adv}[well]]]$.

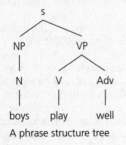

A phrase structure tree

phrastic Term introduced in philosophy by R. M. Hare for whatever in a sentence is neutral between command, statement, etc. E.g. 'your shutting the door in the immediate future' is said to be the phrastic of both *Shut the door* and *You are going to shut the door*. The aspect that differentiates these sentences is the '**neustic**'.

  Cf. proposition for the notion of 'propositional content'.

phylogeny Biologists' term for the evolution of a species or other group of organisms. Theories of the phylogeny of language are similarly theories about what is traditionally called the 'origin of language'. Thence '**phylogenetic**': opp. ontogeny, ontogenetic.

'phylum' A group of language families among which deeper *genetic relationships have been posited. *See* family; *also* stock. Where 'stocks' and 'phyla' are distinguished 'phyla' are usually the larger.

phytonym A name of a plant: e.g. *dandelion*. *Cf.* -onym.

Piaget, Jean (1896–1980) Swiss psychologist, whose studies of the cognitive development of children have had wide influence. These distinguished successively higher levels of intelligence, from the 'sensorimotor' to the 'formal operational', and successive stages in which a child passes from one to another, building on and in part reorganizing what has been learned earlier.

pictogram A symbol in a writing system, or in a precursor of writing, which represents an object etc. by a picture of it; also called a '**pictograph**'. *Cf.* ideogram; logogram.

'picture noun' One such as *picture*, seen by Chomsky in the 1970s as forming a noun phrase with a structure [*pictures* [*of X*]], from which e.g. *who* could be extracted: thus *Who did they take pictures of?*

pidgin A simplified form of speech developed as a medium of trade, or through other extended but limited contact, between groups of speakers who have no other language in common: e.g. the simplified forms of English, French, or Dutch which are assumed to be the origin of *creoles in the West Indies. Distinguished in principle at least from less established forms of similar origin, sometimes described as '**jargons**' or '**pre-pidgins**'.

  Pidginization (*sc.* of a *base language such as English) is the process by which a pidgin is formed; creolization is in turn the process by which they are seen as developing into creoles.

PIE For 'Proto-Indo-European': *see* protolanguage.

pied piping Syntactic process in which a movement of one element is accompanied by that of others related to it. E.g., in *the film which we saw the end of*, *which* is seen as moved from a position as complement of *of*: *the film* [*we saw* [*the end of which*]]. In *the film of which we saw the end*, *of*, by pied piping, moves with it; in *the film the end of which we saw*, the whole of *the end of*.

Pike, Kenneth Lee (1912–2000) American linguist, for much of his career director of the *Summer Institute of Linguistics. His earliest major work is in phonetics and phonology and includes important studies of *tone languages in Central America. In *Language in Relation to a Unified Theory of the Structure of Human Behavior*, published in its definitive form in 1967, Pike described a language as structured on three interpenetrating *levels, of phonology, grammar, and lexicon, and distinguished three 'modes' of any structural unit: the feature mode, defined by its opposition to other units; the manifestation mode, defined by its realization in speech; and the distribution mode, defined by its roles in larger units. In a similar spirit, he has contrasted a 'particle' view of language, which is focused on the individual unit, with a 'wave' view and a 'field' view, focused respectively on linear relations among units in speech and the structure of relations within the overall system.

See Tagmemics for Pike's model of grammar. This has been widely applied to languages studied by members of the Summer Institute of Linguistics.

Pilipino *See* Tagalog.

Pinyin Roman alphabet for Mandarin *Chinese, authorized by the Chinese government since the late 1950s, and increasingly replacing earlier systems of Romanization. Tones are shown by accents: e.g. the name of the system itself is *pīnyīn*, with two level high tones; that of the city traditionally written in English as 'Peking' is *Běijīng*, where the tone on the first syllable is basically a low rise.

pitch The property of sounds as perceived by a hearer that corresponds to the physical property of frequency. Thus a vowel which from the viewpoint of *articulatory phonetics is produced with more rapid vibration of the *vocal cords will, from an *acoustic viewpoint, have a higher *fundamental frequency and, from an *auditory viewpoint, be perceived as having higher pitch.

pitch accent An *accent (1) which is primarily realized by differences of pitch between accented and unaccented syllables. E.g. that of Ancient Greek, where, for instance, the accented syllable of *ánthrō:pos* 'human being' was distinguished by a relatively high pitch; that of *anthrô:pu:* 'of (a) human being' by an initially high pitch which then fell.

See stress for the contrasting term 'stress accent'. *See also* tone; tone language. In the strictest usage a tone language is one in which all syllables are distinguished equally: in languages with an accent one particular syllable, such as the *an-* of *ánthrō:pos*, is prominent. But the distinction is often confused in practice.

pitch morpheme An intonational *tone or contour, seen as a
*morpheme consisting of a sequence of *pitch phonemes. Thus the
sentence *They love me* would consist of four morphemes, the
'segmental' units *they*, *love*, and *me*, and a *suprasegmental morpheme
that, in a notation current in the 1950s, might be the sequence 2 3 1:
mid to low pitch ('2') on *they*, mid to high pitch ('3') on *love*, low pitch
('1') on *me*.

pitch phoneme A phonological unit of pitch in *tone languages; *cf.*
toneme. Also a minimal component, in some analyses of intonation, of
a *pitch morpheme.

pivot 1. Used by M. D. S. Braine in the 1960s, in an analysis of the
speech of very young children. An utterance like 'Me hungry', 'Me
happy', or 'Me banana' was seen as relating a pivot (*me*), which is one
of a small class of words that recur frequently, to a member of an
'open' class (*hungry*, *happy*, *banana*, . . .). **2.** Used by R. M. W. Dixon of a
syntactic element which, like a *subject (1) in e.g. English, can be
related to verbs or predicates in several successive clauses. Thus, in
Mary came to meet us and drive us home, the subject *Mary* is a pivot related
successively to *came*, to the infinitive *to meet us*, and to *drive us home*.

PL = plural.

place (Adverb, adverbial) indicating location. E.g. *in the garden* is an
adverbial of place (or a place or *locative adverbial) in *I was sitting in the
garden*.

place of articulation A position in the mouth by which a
consonant is classified, defined by the point of maximal contact or
near contact between an active and a passive *articulator. In *kick*, for
example, the place of articulation of both consonants is *velar: in
phonetic notation, [kɪk]. That is, the position of maximal contact (in
this instance *closure) is between the back of the tongue and the
velum or soft part of the palate.

   Opp. manner of articulation. For the main places of articulation,
starting from the front of the mouth, *see* bilabial, labiodental, dental,
alveolar, palato-alveolar, retroflex, palatal, velar, uvular, pharyngeal,
glottal.

plain (1) Used in Jakobson's scheme of *distinctive features in the
sense of non-*flat or non-*sharp.

plain (2) Huddleston and Pullum's term, in *CGEL*, for the *positive
(2) grade as opposed to the comparative and superlative.

plane Used by Hjelmslev and others in the sense of *level. Thus, in
particular, the *content plane vs. the *expression plane.

Plato (429–347 BC) Ancient Greek philosopher, one of whose shorter
dialogues, the *Cratylus*, is the earliest discussion in the Western

tradition of the relations between words and things. The main character, Socrates, is represented as disputing first the view that the relations are justified by convention only, and then the view that, interfering factors apart, they are systematic and natural. The main conclusion is that words cannot be taken as a guide to reality. Several other dialogues also deal in passing with problems of language. In particular, a passage in the *Sophist* makes clear the distinction, in the sentence, between what are later called a subject (e.g. *Theaetetus* in *Theaetetus is flying*) and a predicate (*is flying*). Only when both are present—when a subject is identified and something is said about it—can a linguistic expression be seen as true (Theaetetus is indeed flying) or as false.

A central idea in Plato's philosophy is the doctrine of ideal forms (traditionally translated 'ideas') that underlie the world as we perceive it. Thus an ideal 'horse' underlies the varying forms of individual horses, an ideal 'goodness' different concrete forms of goodness, and so on. As one form of *realism this remains influential: e.g. a language is an ideal entity that underlies the varying concrete manifestations of speech.

'Plato's problem' Identified by Chomsky in the 1980s as the problem solved, in his view, by the theory that specific mental structures, such as *Universal Grammar, are genetically inherited. The allusion is to an argument in Plato's *Meno*, for the inheritance of knowledge, through the transmigration of souls, from previous existences.

Plattdeutsch = Low *German.

pleonasm Term in rhetoric for repetition or superfluous expression. Hence, in grammar, a category is sometimes said to be represented **pleonastically** if it is realized by more than one affix, word, etc.

plereme Hjelmslev's term for a unit of *content. A **pleremic** system of writing is accordingly one which represents lexical or grammatical units as opposed to sounds or syllables: e.g. that of Chinese.

From the Greek word for 'full': opp. ceneme, cenemic.

'plexity' *See* social network.

plosive A *stop produced with air flowing outwards from the lungs: e.g. [t] in *tea* or [d] in *do*. Distinguished as such from stops in which the *airstream mechanism is different or more complex, such as *ejectives or *implosives.

'pluperfect' Traditionally of a verb form in Latin whose basic use was as a past *perfect: e.g. *venerat* 'had come', i.e. had come by some moment of time before the moment of speaking. Thence e.g. of forms such as *had come* in English. The ancient term was 'more-than-perfect' (*plusquamperfectum*): opposed to 'perfect' and *imperfect ('not perfect' or 'less than perfect').

plural (PL) Semantic feature of forms used in referring to more than one, or more than some small number of individuals. Often a term in the category of *number: e.g. plural *rooms* ('room-PL') in opposition to *room*, or *-s* itself as a plural ending. But it may also be the meaning of an independent particle, or a derivational affix.

pluralia tantum Latin 'plurals only': i.e. nouns, like *oats* or *trousers*, which appear only in a plural form.

pluralism In its ordinary sense. E.g. a state might follow a policy of '**linguistic pluralism**', as opposed to one of 'assimilation', in maintaining or promoting a diversity of languages among its citizens.

pluri- = poly-, multi-. E.g. '**pluricentric**' = polycentric.

plus sign (+) Used in three main ways: **1.** To mark sequence: e.g. a phrase structure rule as written in the form X → Y + Z says that an X consists or may consist of a Y followed by a Z. **2.** As a symbol for a specific boundary between units. Thus, in one notation, morphemes: [kat + s] (*cats*). *Cf.* double cross (#). **3.** To mark a positive value for a feature: e.g. a front vowel has the feature [+ Front].

P-marker = phrase marker.

'poetic' (*Function of language) defined by Jakobson in terms of orientation towards, or focus on, 'the message for its own sake'. Thus, in ordinary speech, it is by virtue of the poetic function that, e.g. in coordination, one will tend to put shorter phrases first: *I remember especially the wine and the view from the terrace*, rather than, although in terms of other functions they are equivalent, . . . *the view from the terrace and the wine.*

point of articulation = place of articulation.

polar interrogative An *interrogative sentence or construction whose primary use is in asking questions to be answered 'yes' or 'no': e.g. *Are you ready?*
  Also *closed interrogative, 'polar question', 'yes–no question': opp. *wh-interrogative, open interrogative, focused interrogative, *x*-interrogative.

polarity The opposition between positive (e.g. *yes* or *I will come*) and negative (e.g. *no* or *I will not come*). *See* tag for 'reversed polarity'.

'polarity item' *See* negative polarity item; positive polarity item.

Polish West *Slavic; most speakers are in Poland, with the next largest group in the USA. Attested by continuous texts from the 14th century AD, though evidence of names in Polish is found earlier: for most of its recorded history it has been in close contact with forms of German especially.

Cassubian or **Kashubian**, on the Baltic coast, is usually treated as a dialect of Polish, though more strikingly differentiated than others.

polite form A form used to show deference to an addressee: e.g. Japanese *ki-masi-ta* 'come-POLITE-PAST' as opposed to unmarked *ki-ta* 'come-PAST' ('came'). Also e.g. of the pronoun and the verb form in French *vous venez* 'you are coming', when said to one person. But one could alternatively regard the *vous*-forms simply as the unmarked forms of the second person in general, as opposed to marked singular *familiar forms in e.g. *tu viens*.

Often linked, as in Japanese, with a more general system of *honorifics.

poly- Involving many rather than either one or two. Thus a '**polyglossic**' community is like one that is *diglossic except that more than two languages or varieties are involved; a '**polylectal**' grammar is one covering several (dia)lects; **polysyndeton** is *coordination in which several successive members are all linked by conjunctions; a **polysyllabic** word (or **polysyllable**) is one with many, e.g. more than two, syllables.

Alternating in some terms with *multi-; also *pluri-.

polycentric 'Having more than one centre'. E.g. of a language whose standard form is determined, in part independently, in different countries, capital cities, etc.: thus Portuguese, as 'centred' in Portugal and Brazil; or English, as 'centred' in Britain, North America, Australia, and so on. Opp. monocentric.

polygenesis Multiple origin, e.g. of language. Opp. monogenesis.

Polynesian Branch of *Austronesian which includes all the languages of the Polynesian triangle (New Zealand–Hawaii–Easter Island) and a few in Micronesia and Melanesia.

polysemy [pɒˈlɪsɪmi] [pɒlɪˈsiːmi] The case of a single word having two or more related senses. Thus the noun *screen* is **polysemous** [pɒlɪˈsiːməs], since it is used variously of a fire screen, a cinema screen, a television screen, and so on.

Cf. homonymy. The difference, in principle, is that in cases of homonymy the senses are quite unconnected; therefore they are not treated as belonging to the same word. But in many cases it is hard to decide, and in theories of meaning the distinction is not always seen as valid.

'polysynthetic' (Type of language) in which there is a pattern of *incorporation or in which, in general, affixes realize a range of

semantic categories beyond those of *synthetic (1) languages in e.g.
Europe.

polysystemic (Analysis) in which the *system of contrasts
established at each point in a linear or other structure is treated
independently of those established elsewhere. E.g. *though* will realize
one term in a system operative in the structure of subordinate clauses
(*He came though he was late*); others will be realized by *since*, *because*, etc.
In *He came, though* it will realize a term in a quite different system;
compare *however*, *nevertheless*, etc.

  Opp. monosystemic. The principle involved is central to *Prosodic
Phonology, and in *Firth's work generally.

popular etymology The process by which a form is reshaped to
resemble another form, or sequence of forms, already in the language.
E.g. French *beaupré* 'bowsprit' was derived historically by the reshaping
of Dutch *boegspriet*, or a similar loan from another Germanic language,
into a compound apparently formed from *beau* 'beautiful' and *pré*
'meadow'.

  Also called 'folk etymology'; *cf.* paronym for 'paronymic attraction'.

'portmanteau morph' A *morph which is said to realize two or
more successive morphemes. E.g. in French *au théâtre* 'to the theatre',
au is a single morph ([o]) which simultaneously realizes a preposition
(elsewhere *à*) and the definite article (elsewhere *le*).

Port Royal Religious and educational centre in 17th-century France,
whose works on logic and grammar included a learner's manual of
Latin (1st edn., by C. Lancelot, 1644) and a *Grammaire générale et
raisonnée* (by Lancelot and A. Arnauld, 1660) of great influence, in
France and beyond, over the next hundred and more years. A
purportedly universal grammar (hence 'générale'), based on principles
of human reason and thought (hence 'raisonnée'), its technique of
analysis stands in the Post-Renaissance tradition initiated by
*Sanctius, and is sometimes re- or misinterpreted, following a reading
by Chomsky in the 1960s, as drawing distinctions like those then
current between *deep structure and *surface structure. E.g. an
expression such as *an invisible God* ('Dieu invisible') is described in
terms of a proposition or 'judgement' *God is invisible*; a finite verb, such
as *comes*, is analysed, following Aristotle, into a copula (*is*) which links
the subject to a participle (*(in a state of) coming*); a form such as *to* in
I gave it to Jane realizes the same category of case as a dative in e.g. Latin.

Portuguese *Romance, spoken mainly in Brazil and Portugal but
also as a second language, with official status, in Angola, Mozambique,
and other former Portuguese colonies. Historically related to Galician
in north-west Spain; a national language after the independence of
Portugal in the 12th century; carried to Brazil, Africa, and the Far East
by trade and colonization in the 16th. European and Brazilian

Portuguese are now distinct varieties of what is still a common language.

position Used both of position in a literal sense (e.g. *the* is the first word in *The plumber rang*) and of position in an abstract structure established by analysis: e.g. *the plumber* occupies the position of subject in the same sentence. *Cf.* order.

A **positional variant** of a phoneme is its realization in a specific position: e.g. unaspirated [p] in *spin* is a variant of this phoneme in a position after [s]. Likewise 'positional allophone'.

position of neutralization *See* neutralization.

positive **1.** = affirmative: e.g. *I am coming* is a positive sentence, in contrast to the *negative *I am not coming*. **2.** (Adjective or adverb) not marked for a *grade of comparison: e.g. *happy* is positive, in contrast to *happier* or *happiest*.

'positive face' *See* face.

positive polarity item A word etc. whose sense is possible in positive sentences but not, or not normally, in negative sentences: e.g. *pretty* in *It's pretty expensive*, where a simple negation (*It isn't pretty exPENsive*) would be unlikely. *Cf.* negative polarity item.

'positive politeness' Forms of politeness seen as enhancing positive *face.

positivism Philosophical system developed in the 19th century by A. Comte which starts from the assumption that all knowledge is based on positive and observable facts, and therefore, directly or indirectly, on the findings of the physical sciences. Hence, in particular, a system that rejected metaphysics and other a priori speculation.

Logical positivism was a development in Vienna in the 1920s and 1930s whose central doctrine was a 'verification principle', by which the meaning of any statement is the method by which it can be verified through the senses. Hence statements which could not be so verified were strictly meaningless. Positivist ideas were developed in linguistics by Bloomfield especially; they were succeeded, in the Vienna school and, during the 1960s, in linguistics, by a different philosophy of science developed by K. Popper, in which the basic criterion for a scientific statement is not that it should be verifiable but simply that it should have empirical content and, if wrong, should be falsifiable.

possessive (poss) (Case, preposition, etc.) whose basic use, or one of whose basic uses, is to indicate the relation between someone who possesses something and the thing that they possess. E.g. *-'s* marks the **possessive construction** in *Mary's coat*; *my* is a **possessive pronoun** in *my coat*; *Mary's* and *mine* are likewise independent possessives in *That coat is Mary's*, or *That coat is mine*.

Cf. genitive. Where the terms are distinguished it is usually in one of two ways. In the first, 'genitive' is used of a case etc. marking in general a noun which modifies another noun. 'Possessive' is then used when the semantic relation is specifically one of possession. Alternatively, 'genitive' may be used specifically of constructions etc. where the '**possessor**' (*Mary's* etc.) is marked, while, in 'possessive' constructions in other languages, the '**possessed**' element (in Latin, *possessum*) is often marked instead.

possessive compound = bahuvrihi.

'possessor ascension' Syntactic process proposed for some languages by which an element indicating a possessor is moved from a noun phrase into the structure of a clause containing it: e.g. schematically, [*My leg*] *hurt* → *I leg hurt* 'My leg is hurt'.

'possible world' Any state in which the world could be: a proposition, e.g. as expressed by a sentence, may accordingly be true in some 'possible worlds' and false in others.
Cf. truth conditions; model-theoretic semantics.

poss-*ing* construction That of e.g. *John's driving* in *John's driving is terrible*, jointly marked by *possessive -'s* (POSS) and the *-ing* of *driving*. Distinguished from that of e.g. *John driving is terrible*, where *John* is not possessive.

post- After or behind. E.g. a **post-vocalic** consonant is one preceded by a vowel; a *postalveolar has a place of articulation behind that of an alveolar; a **post-lexical** rule applies at a stage in a derivation after lexical units have been introduced.

postalveolar Articulated towards the back of the ridge behind the upper teeth: i.e. with the tongue in a position between that of an *alveolar, as in *too* [tuː], and a *palato-alveolar, as in *chew* [tʃuː].

Post-Bloomfieldians School of linguistic theoreticians dominant in the USA in the 1940s and 1950s: leading members included (Zellig) Harris, C. F. Hockett, and G. L. Trager. They developed ideas derived from Bloomfield's in an extreme form, especially the principle that the *distributions of forms should be analysed independently and in advance of their meanings, and the notion that a description of a language could be justified by following a rigid hierarchy of procedures. Such procedures were later characterized by Chomsky as *discovery procedures.

Chomsky's earliest work was heavily influenced, both in its philosophy and in detail, by Harris and other Post-Bloomfieldians. But after 1960 he derided them as representatives of *structural or *taxonomic linguistics, and within a few years both the school and its direct influence diminished sharply.

'post-creole' Form of speech developed, or thought to have developed, through *decreolization. '**Post-creole continuum**' = creole continuum.

post-cyclic(al) *See* cyclic(al) principle.

postdeterminer Used of an element seen as last in a possible sequence of determiners. E.g. in *those people*, the *determiner is *those*. In *those three people* or *those few people*, it is followed by a postdeterminer *three* or *few*. In *all those three people* it is also preceded by a 'predeterminer' *all*.

   Also, at least potentially, of any determiner that comes after the element it 'determines'.

postmodifier In principle, any modifier that follows its head. Specifically of an element in English which modifies and follows a noun: e.g. *over there* in *the man over there*, or *who watch television* in *children who watch television. Cf.* premodifier.

postposition An element, e.g. in Japanese, related to a noun phrase in the same way as a *preposition, except that it comes after instead of before. Thus, schematically, 'OF' would be a postposition in [*red house*] OF 'of the red house'; likewise 'ON' in [[[*red house*] OF] *roof*] ON 'on the roof of the red house'. Though not usually so treated, the clitic *-'s* could be seen as a postposition in e.g. *my friend's daughter*, *my friend in Washington's daughter*.

   A **postpositional phrase** is likewise the equivalent, with a postposition, of a *prepositional phrase.

post-vocalic Immediately following a vowel. Hence '**post-vocalic** *r*', of the [r], in many dialects of English, at the end of a word, as in *purr*, or before a consonant, as in *hurt*.

potential (Mood, particle, etc.) indicating possibility or ability. E.g., schematically, *You think*-POTENTIAL *that* ... 'You might think that ...'.

power = weak generative capacity. E.g. *context-free grammars are more **powerful** than *finite state grammars since any language that can be generated by a grammar of the latter type can also be generated by one of the former, but not vice versa.

   Also, loosely, of rules. E.g. transformational rules are informally said to be 'more powerful' than phrase structure rules, or to be 'too powerful'. That is, more or too many kinds of operation can be accomplished by them.

PP = prepositional phrase, postpositional phrase.

pragmatic Treated as belonging to *pragmatics. Thus a '**pragmatic presupposition**' is a *presupposition that does not fall under some restricted conception of semantics; **pragmatic ambiguity** is ambiguity that does not have to do with e.g. *truth conditions.

pragmatics A branch of linguistics conceived as dealing, separately from others, with the meanings that a sentence has in a particular context in which it is uttered. Distinguished in that spirit from *semantics, conceived as studying meaning independently of contexts. E.g. *There's a car coming* would have the meaning, out of context, of a statement that a car is coming. But on a specific occasion it might be a warning to a pedestrian not to step onto a road, an expression of hope that people invited to a dinner are at last arriving, and so on. Hence, in particular, pragmatics includes the study of *implicatures as opposed to 'literal meanings' or *truth conditions of sentences.

The term was invented by C. W. Morris in the 1930s, for a branch of *semiotics concerned with the relations of signs to *interpretants. Opposed as such to 'syntax', as concerned with relations of one sign to another, and 'semantics', as concerned with the relations of signs to denotata. Alternatively, in a common reformulation, it is concerned with the relations of signs to 'interpreters'. General in linguistics from the early 1970s onwards, on the initial assumption that a *semantic representation of a sentence, seen as determined by the grammar of a specific language, can be clearly distinguished, e.g. in terms of truth conditions, from further meanings, as determined by principles independent of conventions in particular languages, that it might come to have when it was uttered. From the inevitable critique of that assumption has sprung much of the competing theorizing that has followed.

Prague School School of linguistics centred on the Prague Linguistic Circle. Recognizable as such from the late 1920s: its journal, *Travaux du Cercle Linguistique de Prague*, was published from 1929 until the Second World War. Leading figures included two Russian émigrés, Trubetzkoy (in Vienna) and Jakobson (then in Brno), with Czechs of whom V. Mathesius was the senior.

United among structural linguists by an emphasis on the *function of units: e.g. in phonology, on the role of phonemes in distinguishing and demarcating words; in syntax, on the role of sentence structure in context. Important in the 1930s above all for phonology, where ideas originating in this period are the source for later work especially by Jakobson and Martinet. A functional view of the sentence, fostered by Mathesius, was to lead in the 1950s to the theory of *Functional Sentence Perspective.

Prakrit *See* Sanskrit.

pre- Before in time or position. E.g. a **prevocalic** consonant is one that comes before a vowel; a **preterminal** node in a tree diagram is one that immediately dominates a *terminal node; the **prelinguistic** stage in a child's development is one which precedes the appearance of identifiable linguistic units.

preaspiration The end of *voice (1) in e.g. a vowel before the articulation of a following voiceless consonant. Thus [t] is preaspirated in e.g. [aɑte] (where [ɑ] is a voiceless continuation of [a]) or [ahte]: common e.g. in Scottish Gaelic or Icelandic.

precative Indicating or constituting a direct request. Thus *Please leave the room* is precative in one classification of *modality.

pre-cyclic(al) *See* cyclic(al) principle.

predeterminer Used of an element seen as the first of a possible sequence of determiners. E.g. in *her children* the *determiner is *her*. In *both her children* or *all her children* it is preceded by a predeterminer *both* or *all*. In *all her many children* it is also followed by a 'postdeterminer' *many*.
    Also, at least potentially, of any determiner that comes before the element it 'determines'.

predicate 1. A part of a clause or sentence traditionally seen as representing what is said of, or **predicated of**, the subject. E.g. in *My wife bought a coat in London*, the subject *my wife* refers to someone of whom it is said, in the predicate, that she bought a coat in London. **2.** A verb or other unit which takes a set of *arguments within a sentence. Thus, in the same example, 'buy' is a two-place predicate whose arguments are represented by *my wife* and *a coat*.
    The senses are respectively from ancient and from modern logic. For sense (1) *cf.* verb phrase, but that term often refers to a smaller unit within the predicate, or to one that includes the subject. For sense (2) *cf.* predicator. But that is typically used of the specific word in the construction (e.g. *bought*); moreover it is not used by logicians.

predicate calculus Branch of mathematical logic which deals with expressions containing predicates, arguments, and quantifiers. For quantifiers *see* existential quantifier, universal quantifier; for predicates and arguments *cf.* argument; predicate (2).

Predicate-Internal Subject Hypothesis = VP-Internal Subject Hypothesis.

predicate nominal A *predicative noun or noun phrase: e.g. *a friend* in *She is just a friend*.

predication The relation of either a *predicate (1) to its subject, or of a *predicate (2) to its arguments.

'predication theory' Usually of an account of *predicates (2).

predicative (Adjective etc.) which forms part of a *predicate (1) and has a direct semantic relation to the subject: e.g. *angry* is predicative in *He is angry*; the noun phrase *a fool* is predicative in *He is a fool*.

Predicative adjectives are distinguished from those standing in a relation of *attribution. Thus *angry* is used predicatively in *He is angry*, but is attributive, or is used attributively, in e.g. *angry customers*.

predicator An element in a clause that determines, wholly or in part, the other elements that its construction may or must have. Characteristically a *verb: thus in *I bought a present for Zoë* the verb ('buy') is one that must have both a subject (*I*) and a direct object (*a present*), and allows a *benefactive (*for Zoë*). Also, in many accounts, of *predicative adjectives: e.g. *mad* is the predicator in *She was mad at me*.
   Cf. predicate (2).

predictive (Inflection, particle, etc.) marking a prediction. Thus *is going to* might be described as predictive in *It's going to fall any minute*.

prefix An *affix which comes before the form to which it is joined: e.g. *un-* in *unkind*. **Prefixation** is the process of adding a prefix, and a **prefixal** form is one either derived by prefixation or occupying the position of a prefix. Thus, in the first sense, *unkind* is a 'prefixal negative'.

premodifier In principle, any modifier that precedes its head. Specifically, an element in English which modifies and precedes a noun: e.g. *good* in *good people*, *broken* in *a broken reed*, or *pond* in *pond life*. *Cf.* postmodifier.

prenasalized (Phonological unit) consisting of an *oral consonant briefly preceded by the corresponding *nasal. E.g. in the consonant written 'nd' in Swahili, the soft palate is initially lowered, with the back of the tongue in contact with it. After a brief interval the soft palate is raised: thus, with voicing, [ⁿd]. Prenasalized *stops, such as [ⁿd], are common in sub-Saharan Africa and elsewhere; the term is also applied to phonologically single units in which a nasal briefly precedes a *fricative.

preparatory conditions One kind of *felicity condition that a *speech act has to meet if it is to be appropriate or successful. E.g. if A asks B to open the door the preparatory conditions are (*a*) that B is able to open it, and (*b*) that B is not going to open it of his own accord. Distinguished especially from *sincerity conditions: e.g. it is a sincerity condition, in the same case, that A wants B to open the door.

pre-pidgin *See* pidgin.

prepose To place before: sometimes, therefore, specifically of the *fronting of elements in syntax.

preposition A word or other syntactic element of a class whose members typically come before a noun phrase and which is characterized by ones which basically indicate spatial relations: e.g. *on* in *on the mat*, *behind* in *behind the sofa*, *throughout* in *throughout Asia*. Also *on* in e.g. *on Saturday*, *on receipt*, or *on my honour*, where the temporal and other senses are secondary. Also e.g. *during* in *during August*, although the temporal sense is basic.

One of the *parts of speech, traditionally defined by its position. Hence *postposition, of elements which are similar except that they come after a noun or noun phrase; also 'adposition', as a term which covers both.

prepositional phrase (PP) A phrase consisting of a preposition or sequence of prepositions followed by a noun phrase or the equivalent: e.g. *by Monday*, *out of the kitchen*. In most recent accounts, the preposition is the *head (1) of the phrase, and the noun etc. its *complement or *object.

The precise application of this term depends on what is classed as a preposition and what as the equivalent of a noun phrase. E.g. *after breakfast* is a prepositional phrase; so, in some accounts, are *after eating breakfast*, *since eating breakfast*, or *after I had eaten breakfast*. Alternatively, the last in particular is a clause introduced by *after* in the role of a conjunction.

prepositional verb A unit in English which is formed from a verb and a preposition or two prepositions which directly follow it: thus 'care for' in *I didn't care for the soup*, or 'put up with' in *I put up with it for too long*. Distinguished from *phrasal verbs (2) e.g. because the verb and preposition cannot be separated: *They backed the neighbours up*, with the phrasal verb 'back up', but not *They didn't care the neighbours for*.

preposition stranding Syntactic process by which a preposition in English is left without a following complement: e.g. *to* is stranded in *the address (which) I sent it to*.

The term 'stranding' could, in principle, be used more generally: i.e. preposition stranding would be merely one instance.

prescriptive (1) (Grammar, rule) which aims to 'prescribe' what is judged to be correct rather than to 'describe' actual usage. Hence, in practice, one that may defy usage: e.g. a rule in English by which it is incorrect to say *It's him that will suffer*, with 'accusative' *him*, instead of *It's he that will suffer*, with the 'nominative'.

Opposed to one sense of *descriptive (1).

prescriptive (2) (Inflection etc.) indicating e.g. some arrangement that has been made. Thus, schematically, *sit*-PRESCR-3PL-*here* 'They are to sit here' or, in a question, *sit*-PRESCR-3SG? 'Should I sit?'

present *See* tense (1).

presentational (Construction, particle, etc.) which introduces a topic or new topic of discourse. Thus the construction with *there* has a presentational role in e.g. *There was a man who was following me yesterday*.

Also of forms such as French *voici* in the presentation e.g. of an individual: *Voici mon ami* 'Here is my friend'.

present participle 1. A *participle which is present in *tense.
2. Conventionally of forms such as English *walking* or *running*, or, in English, such forms when they are not *gerunds. *Cf. -ing* form.

present perfect *See* perfect.

presequence Used in *Conversation Analysis for a 'turn', or sequence of 'turns', seen as preliminary to some interchange.
E.g. 'Excuse me' (said to a stranger in the street); 'Morning' (said to a shopkeeper); 'Morning: what can I do for you today?' (said by the shopkeeper in return).

prestige In the ordinary sense, of languages, dialects, forms, etc. E.g. Standard English has greater prestige in England than a Midlands dialect; *aren't I?* or *am I not?* are prestige forms as compared with *ain't I?*
   'Overt' prestige is often contrasted with *covert prestige, by which a form overtly seen as less prestigious is the one in practice used or favoured.

prestopped (*Nasal consonant), as distinguished in some Australian languages, which is preceded briefly by an *oral stop in the same position of articulation.

presupposition Relation between propositions by which *a* presupposes *b* if, for *a* to have a truth-value, *b* must be true. Thus, in one analysis, 'The King of France is bald' is neither true nor false unless the presupposed 'There is a King of France' is true. Term developed in philosophy by P. F. Strawson; thence into linguistics in the late 1960s, where used in ways increasingly closer to its ordinary sense, of sentences and of utterances instancing them. E.g. *I'm sorry John is not here* presupposes 'John is not here'; also that this is known to an addressee or addressees. *I apologize for calling you a communist* presupposes that (in the belief of the speaker or the addressee or both) being a communist is bad, and so on.
   Distinctions were commonly drawn between '**semantic presuppositions**', e.g. of 'The King of France is bald' or of the sentence *The King of France is bald*, and '**pragmatic presuppositions**' which either held in particular contexts or otherwise fell outside a restricted definition of *semantics. In *Generative Semantics the presuppositions of sentences were an important part of their *semantic representations.

preterite = past *tense. Usually used to distinguish the simple past in Modern European languages (e.g. *took*) from periphrastic forms such as the present perfect (e.g. *has taken*) or past imperfect (*was taking*).

pretheoretical (Term etc.) not or not yet defined in a specific theoretical system. E.g. one might refer to the number of languages spoken in Europe, or identify a sentence in a text, using 'language' and 'sentence' in pretheoretical senses which do not rest, or have to rest, on formal explications of what languages or sentences are. A pretheoretical observation is similarly one which is made ahead of any theory which is proposed e.g. to account for it.

prevarication Deviation from what is correct: hence, as a term for a proposed *design feature of language, of the potential for speakers to tell lies; *cf.* displacement.

preverb An element which comes before the root of a verb and forms a lexical unit with it. E.g. *re-* in *remake*, *pre-* in *precook*; Latin *de-* in *desino* 'I desist'; German *ein-* in *einlassen* 'to let in'.

Typically of elements like these that are not straightforward prefixes. Thus *re-* and *pre-* have levels of stress ([ˌriːˈmeɪk], [ˌpriːˈkʊk]) higher than those in e.g. *recall* or *precede*. *De-* in Latin is effectively a preposition (*de* 'down from') forming the first member of a compound. Forms like *ein-* in German are attached to the verb in some constructions and separated from it in others. It is perhaps for this last case that the term is most useful.

prevocalic Immediately before a vowel. E.g. [g] is a prevocalic consonant in *go* [gəʊ].

primary (in syntax) *See* ranks (1).

primary articulation 1. *See* secondary articulation (1). **2.** *See* double articulation (1).

primary cardinal vowels *See* cardinal vowels.

'primary linguistic data' Used by Chomsky in the 1960s of the utterances heard by and of other external sources of information available to a child as a basis for the development of language.

primary stress (ˈ) The main stress in a word, as opposed to any subsidiary or *secondary stress. E.g. in *characteristic* the primary stress is on *-ris-*; there is also a secondary stress on *cha-*: in phonetic notation [ˌkarəktəˈrɪstɪk].

primitive (Unit etc.) from which others are derived but which is itself underived. E.g. words like *fish* or *man* are traditionally primitive words, while *fishy* or *manliness* are derived words. Often = element (1): e.g. the morpheme is the primitive unit, or is a primitive, in many accounts of grammar; a semantic feature is primitive in many accounts of meaning: i.e. neither is derived from simpler elements at the same level of representation.

In formal systems, primitives are a set of undefined terms on the basis of which all other terms are defined.

principal parts A small set of forms within a large *paradigm, chosen in such a way that all the others can be predicted from them.

Thus, in Latin, the principal parts of a verb are traditionally the first-person singular of the present indicative (e.g. *capio* 'I take'), the corresponding infinitive (*capere* 'to take'), the first-person singular of the perfect indicative (*cepi* 'I took'), and the supine (*captum*); from the last one can predict the past and the future participles, from the third all other perfect forms, from the first two all the remainder.

principle Usually of a general principle of language, grammar, etc. which is hypothetically valid for all languages, as opposed to a *rule which is formulated for a particular language. Hence in any theory of *universal grammar specific rules (e.g. a rule for reflexives in English) are reduced to general principles (e.g. a principle applying to reflexives in any language) as far as possible.

principle of least effort Principle by which, it is claimed, speakers do not exert themselves more than is necessary for successful communication. Hence, in particular, a principle of **ease of articulation**: thus if voiceless consonants change to voiced between vowels, the reason, it is argued, is that in articulating the sequence greater effort would be required to alter the posture of the vocal cords. Also invoked e.g. in pragmatics: thus if a speaker says 'I haven't', leaving the rest to be understood from the context, it is because, it is argued, the ellipsis is more economical.

Principles and Parameters Theory The theory of *Universal Grammar in the form developed by Chomsky from the early 1980s onwards. The version current in the 1980s is known as *Government and Binding Theory. But this was progressively reformulated, from the early 1990s, by what was intended to be a simpler form, under the *minimalist programme.

Priscian (5th–6th century AD) Grammarian of Latin, working in Constantinople. Heavily influenced by *Apollonius Dyscolus, whose scholarship he praised. His main work, the *Institutiones Grammaticae* or 'Principles of Grammar', is a large-scale survey of the properties and inflections of the individual *parts of speech followed by two parts (traditionally called the 'Priscianus minor') on syntax. It had a major influence on linguistic thought in medieval Europe.

private verb A verb such as *think* or *see*, which refers to a mental activity or sensation of which an external observer will not be directly aware. Partly distinguished in English by their grammar: e.g. verbs like *see* will normally be used with *can* (*I can see it*) where others might be progressive or simple present (*I am reading it*, *I read it*).

privative 1. (Opposition) between *marked and *unmarked phonemes which are distinguished by the presence or absence of some phonetic feature: e.g. between a voiced consonant or a long vowel, seen as having the feature of *voice (1) or of length, and a voiceless

consonant or a short vowel, seen as lacking it. Opp. equipollent.
2. = negative. Thus a negative prefix *a(n)-* is called 'privative' in
Ancient Greek: e.g. in *an-áxios* 'un-worthy'.

privilege of occurrence Used by Bloomfield and others of the
*distribution of a syntactic unit relative to larger constructions.
E.g. the privilege of occurrence of *him* includes those of following a
preposition like *to* in the construction of a prepositional phrase, of
following a verb like *saw* in that of a verb phrase, and so on.

pro [prəʊ] A phonetically *null element present, according to
*Government and Binding Theory, whenever a finite verb has no
apparent subject. E.g. Italian *Vengono* 'They are coming' has 'pro' as its
subject: pro *vengono*.
    One of a set of so-called *empty categories: called 'little pro' to
distinguish it from *PRO.

PRO [prəʊ] A phonetically *null element posited in *Principles and
Parameters Theory in constructions where a non-finite verb has no
overt subject. E.g. in *She wanted to leave*, PRO is said to be the subject of
to leave: *She wanted* [PRO *to leave*]. Likewise e.g. of *eating* in [PRO *eating
people*] *is wrong. Cf.* control.
    One of a set, originally, of so-called *empty categories: called 'big
PRO' to distinguish it from *pro.

pro- *See* pro-form.

process Any operation established in the grammar of a language by
which a form *a*, as represented at a particular level of description, is
derived from another form *b*, also at that level. Thus, in many
accounts, a representation of a passive sentence is derived by a
*syntactic process, or process at the level of syntax, from that of a
corresponding active. Similarly, the past tense *sang* may be derived, by
a *morphological process, from *sing*.
    Also in general senses. Hence a distinction in particular between
historical processes (in the general sense) e.g. of sound-change and
*synchronic processes (as defined technically) by which phonological
or other units are seen as interchanged within a language system as
established at a specific moment.

proclitic A *clitic attached phonologically to the word which follows:
e.g. *lo* 'it' in Italian *lo faccio* 'I'm doing it' (phonologically [loˈfattʃo]).
Cf. enclitic.

prodelision Process by which a vowel at the beginning of a word is
lost after a vowel at the end of the word preceding. *Cf.* *elision.

'pro-drop' *See* null-subject parameter.

productive (Rule, formation, etc.) which permits new forms to be derived. Thus especially in morphology: e.g. the formation of adjectives in *-able* is productive in that speakers can readily create new ones (*Is it climb-up-able?*, *It's not vacuum-able*, etc.). Opp. unproductive; *see also* semi-productive.

productivity 1. The property of permitting novel combinations of elements. Often referred to as a *design feature of language in general: thus it is possible for any speaker to combine words into a sentence that they have neither spoken nor heard before. **2.** The property, of specific rules etc., of being *productive.

pro-form Any form, such as a *pronoun, that is treated as 'standing for' another form whose meaning can be understood. In *She came*, who *she* refers to will be understood from the context in which it is uttered: in that sense, it 'stands for' a form that would be more explicit (*Jane, the girl in the red dress*, etc.). Similarly, in *Jane wants a red one*, a pro-form *one* 'stands for' a noun (*a red dress*, or *a red car*); in *Jane said so*, a pro-form *so* 'stands for' a form like *that she would come*.

    Generalized from 'pro-noun'. A form such as *so* in *Jane said so*, since it stands for an *embedded sentence, may be described as a **pro-clause** or **pro-sentence**, one 'standing for' a verb phrase a '**pro-VP**', and so on. A form such as *one* in *a red one* would then be correspondingly '**pro-nominal**'.

    Cf. ellipsis.

progressive (PROG) Feature of verbal forms used to refer to actions etc. seen as in progress without necessary time limits. E.g. *am reading* is present progressive in *I am reading your book; was reading* past progressive in *I was reading your book*. More generally, the progressive in English is marked by a construction in which a form of the auxiliary 'be' (*am, was*, etc.) is linked to an *-ing* form.

    Also called '**continuous**'. The distinction between progressive and non-progressive (*I am reading* vs. *I read*) is one of *aspect; *cf.* imperfective as opposed to perfective.

progressive assimilation *Assimilation in which elements are changed to match features of elements that precede them. E.g. the ending *-s* is voiced [z] in words like *sees* [siːz], but in *writes* or *weeps* it is assimilated to the preceding voiceless consonant ([rʌɪts], [wiːps]).

    Opp. regressive assimilation. The sense is that of features, such as voicelessness, being projected forwards or persisting: hence also called 'perseverative', as in corresponding accounts of *coarticulation; also referred to as a 'lag', again in the sense that a feature does not shut off instantly.

prohibitive (Inflection, particle, etc.) indicating a prohibition: e.g. Latin *ne* is prohibitive in *ne metuas* (PROHIB *fear*-PRES.SUBJ-2SG) 'Don't be afraid'. Often described as 'negative imperative'.

'projecting clause' A form of words whose function is to introduce a statement in a subordinate clause that follows. E.g. to lend substance to a claim that crime is falling one might use a formula such as *There is evidence that . . .* or *Research has shown that . . .*

projection of X Phrase headed by an X. E.g. in [*the* [*book on the table*]], if so analysed, the phrases within brackets are headed by a noun (N) and so are projections of N. The largest projection of X is the *maximal projection.

projection principle The principle, as formulated in *Government and Binding Theory, by which the range of syntactic elements with which a lexical unit combines can be 'projected from' a lexicon as restrictions on structures that contain it. E.g. *put* takes an object noun phrase and a locative phrase: *put* [*the book*] [*on the shelf*]. These requirements will be specified by its entry in a lexicon. So, by the projection principle, any syntactic structure in which *put* appears must, at whatever level of representation, include elements that satisfy them.

Just as a lexical unit restricts the structures that can contain it, so a structure itself is possible only if there are lexical units that allow (or *license) it. E.g. the construction with an object and a locative (*put the book on the shelf*) exists precisely because there are verbs such as *put* that take it. Therefore specific constructions do not need to be distinguished independently of entries in the lexicon.

See also extended projection principle.

'projection rules' Rules proposed by J. J. Katz and colleagues in the 1960s by which the *semantic representations of sentences were derived from the representations of words by a repeated process of amalgamation.

prolepsis [prəʊˈliːpsɪs] Any construction in which a phrase etc. is construed with an element earlier than the one to which it is logically related. E.g. *-n't* might be described as proleptic in *I didn't think he would come*; compare *I thought he would not come*.

Usually of Latin or Ancient Greek. E.g. *me* 'me' is a proleptic accusative in *Scis me* ('You-know me-ACC') *in quibus sim gaudiis* ('how happy I am'). *Cf.* raising (2); also 'climbing' in *clitic climbing.

prominent Standing out for whatever reason. Thus especially of syllables that carry an *accent (1), or are *tonic in a pattern of intonation, and may stand out e.g. in their pitch, in their duration, in vowel quality, in loudness, or in any combination of these.

Hence **prominence** as, in general, a cover term for properties by which accentuation, stress, etc. are realized.

promissive Indicating or constituting a promise: thus *will* can be promissive e.g. in *I will certainly help*.

promotion Syntactic process by which the role of an element is changed to one that is seen as higher on some scale or hierarchy of functions. E.g. the role of subject is seen as higher than that of a direct object; *cf.* NP accessibility hierarchy. Accordingly, a change of active to passive will promote a direct object (*this letter* in *Mary wrote this letter*) to the subject position (*this letter* in *This letter was written by Mary*).

Also called '**advancement**'. The opposite process is *demotion or 'retreat'.

pronominal Of or belonging to the class of *pronouns (Latin *pronomina*). Both 'pronoun' and the feature [+ pronominal] were defined in *Government and Binding Theory as *noun phrases, including some pronouns in the usual sense, that cannot have an *antecedent within a specified syntactic domain.

pronominalization The replacement of a noun phrase by a pronoun, conceived as a syntactic process. Thus in *transformational grammars *John hurt himself* was at first seen as derived from *John hurt John*, with the replacement of the second *John* by *himself*. '**Backward pronominalization**' is the case in which the pronoun then stands in a relation of *cataphora.

pronominal verb = reflexive verb.

pronoun (Pron) An element of a class whose members typically form noun phrases whose meaning is minimally specified. E.g. *she* is a pronoun which, of itself, does no more than identify its referent as a single person or thing which is or is classed or conceived as female.

Traditionally said to 'stand for' nouns or noun phrases. E.g. in *She came*, the pronoun stands for any of the more specific expressions *Lucienne*, *Marilyn Monroe*, *the girl in the corner*, etc. Hence defined, partly but not wholly by that criterion, as one of the ancient *parts of speech. *Cf.* pro-form: but N.B. (*a*) that term tends to be used only of elements that are *anaphoric; (*b*) a noun phrase may be anaphoric (e.g. *the idiot* in *I signalled to Bill but the idiot didn't see me*), but not thereby a pronoun.

proparoxytone [prəʊpaˈrɒksɪtəʊn] A word, originally one in Ancient Greek, which has an (acute) accent on the third syllable from the end. *Cf.* oxytone; paroxytone.

proper In a strict or true sense. E.g. a *proper noun is traditionally a 'proper name', or name in the strict sense; proper inclusion is *inclusion in the true sense, as opposed to identity; if by a definition of *constituency each phrase is a constituent of itself, any smaller unit is a 'proper constituent'; if each node in a tree diagram is defined as dominating itself, the relation between it and any genuinely lower node is one of 'proper *dominance'.

proper noun Noun which is the name of a specific individual or of a set of individuals distinguished only by their having that name: e.g.

the name *Mary* as applied to specific girls, or *London* as applied to one or more specific cities. Opp. common noun.

proportional analogy Any pattern in which *a* differs in form and meaning from *b* as *c* differs from *d*: in notation, $a : b = c : d$. The creation of such proportions is one factor in *analogy as a process of language change.

'Proportion' is in origin the Latin word that corresponded to Greek *analogía*.

proportional opposition One which is paralleled by others. E.g. within a *correlation of voicing, an opposition between [t] and [d] is proportional to similar oppositions between [p] and [b], [k] and [g], etc. Opp. isolated opposition.

proposition Whatever is seen as expressed by a sentence which makes a statement. Hence, for example, the same proposition might be said to be expressed by both *I understand French* and, in Italian, *Capisco il francese*. It is a property of propositions that they have truth values. Thus this proposition would have the value 'true' if the speaker did understand French and the value 'false' if the speaker did not.

The '**propositional content**' of a sentence is a part of its meaning seen, in some accounts, as reducible to a proposition. E.g. *The porters had shut the gates*, *The gates had been shut by the porters*, *Had the porters shut the gates?*, *If only the porters had shut the gates!* might be said to have the same propositional content, though in other respects their meanings differ. Likewise '**propositional meaning**', in a sense equivalent e.g. to *logical (2) form.

propositional calculus Branch of mathematical logic in which propositions are treated as unanalysed wholes. E.g. let p be one proposition and q be another: by the definition of an operator &, p & q is true if and only if both p is true and q is true.

Propositions are analysed in the *predicate calculus.

prop-word = dummy.

proscribe To condemn as e.g. contrary to a rule. Thus *prescriptive grammars of English tend to proscribe the use of *like* in *He did it like I did it*, on the grounds that *like* is an adjective and must not be used as if it were a conjunction.

pro-sentence *See* pro-form.

prosodic features Stress, pitch, and length, seen as phonetic features e.g. in the scheme of Chomsky and Halle, *SPE*.

prosodic hierarchy A hierarchy of rhythmical and intonational units formed, in one account, by the successively larger *mora, syllable, *foot, and so on.

Prosodic Phonology Account of phonology developed by Firth and his followers, and distinguished from others by two main features. One is the *polysystemic principle, by which the system of contrasts at one point in a syllabic or other structure is established independently of those obtaining at others. E.g. in a CVC structure (consonant + vowel + consonant), one system is said to operate at the first 'C' position, another at the second. The other is the role of *prosodies in accounting for interdependencies between successive places in a structure. E.g. in a VC structure a single prosodic contrast might be realized by a longer vowel plus a partly voiced consonant (e.g. -ag in *lag*) vs. a shorter vowel with the consonant voiceless (e.g. -*ack* in *lack*). In the final analysis, the linear structure can itself be seen as an aspect of realization: thus the C in a VC structure is there precisely because there are contrasting units wholly or partly realized in that way.

Prosodic Phonology did not develop further after Firth's death in 1960, and later theories of *non-linear phonology were at first conceived independently.

prosody Originally from the Ancient Greek word for a song with an accompaniment. Thence, traditionally, the study of metres in verse; and, in linguistics, of rhythm and intonation in speech: e.g. an intonational *contour, as falling, rising, etc., is a prosodic contour, or is one kind of prosodic unit.

In *Prosodic Phonology, a prosody is an abstract unit which is realized, or potentially realized, at two or more different places in a linear structure. Thus in some dialects of Spanish a final [h] is associated e.g. with a relative lowering of an unstressed back vowel: ['liβrɔh] (*libros*) 'books' vs. ['liβrʊ] (*libro*) 'book'. Hence both features may be said to realize a single prosodic contrast, between say an 'H' prosody, in *libros*, and a 'non-H' prosody, in *libro*.

prospective (*Aspect etc.) indicating something that is about to happen. E.g., schematically, *explode*-PROSP-*it* 'It will explode any second'.

protasis ['prɒtəsɪs] The *conditional clause in a conditional sentence: e.g. *if I had money* in *If I had money, I would buy it*. The term was also the word in Ancient Greek for a premiss.

prothetic [prə'θɛtɪk] (Vowel etc.) that has developed historically at the beginning of a word. E.g. the *e* of *establish* is in origin a prothetic vowel in Old French *establir*, from Latin *stabilire*.

protoform A form reconstructed as belonging to a *protolanguage. *Cf*. etymon.

protolanguage An unattested language from which a group of attested languages are taken to be historically derived. Thus **Proto-Indo-European** is the protolanguage posited as a source for all the *Indo-European languages, **Proto-Germanic** the source for English and the other *Germanic languages, and so on.

prototype theory Theory of word meaning according to which meanings are identified, in part at least, by characteristic instances of whatever class of objects etc. a word denotes. E.g. people think of song-birds, such as a robin, as having more of the central character of a bird than others, such as ducks, falcons, or ostriches. In that sense, a robin or the like is a prototypical instance, or **prototype**, of a bird. But birds are the denotation of *bird*. So, it is argued, the meaning of *bird* should in turn be identified by its prototype: 'robins and the like in the first instance, plus other species that, to varying degrees, share some of their character'.

Prototype theories have often been linked with the view that denotations have no precise limits: e.g. bats are merely still less 'robin-like' than ducks, and so on. A notion of prototypes has also been applied to other aspects of language. E.g. *green* is a 'prototypical' adjective, while *asleep*, with its more restricted syntax, is marginal; the 'prototypical' meaning of the interrogative construction is in asking questions; and so on.

'Proto-World' Conjectural *protolanguage from which, according to some applications of *mass comparison, all later languages have developed.

Provençal *See* Occitan.

pro-verb A *pro-form standing for a verb or verb phrase: e.g. *did so* in *When I was asked to help I did so*, seen as standing for *(I) did help*.

'proxemics' Term invented in the 1950s for the study of the role played in communication by the degree of physical distance between speakers.

proximal (Demonstrative etc.) whose basic role is to identify someone or something as closer to, rather than remote from, the speaker: e.g. *this* in *this side of the street* as opposed to *distal *that* in *that side of the street*.

proximate, proximative (PROX) 1. *See* obviative. **2.** = proximal.

Prt = particle.

'pruning' A process by which specific nodes were eliminated from a *phrase structure tree if, by another process, branches originating from them had been removed or deleted. In vogue especially in the late 1960s.

pseudo- As *pseudo-cleft: i.e. like a cleft but not one. Thus an adjective to which elements such as pronouns can be related has been described as a '**pseudo-adjective**': e.g. *British* in *the British argument that they* (i.e. the British) *are neutral*. The construction of e.g. *John is reading*, where *read* is a verb that can also take an object, has been described as '**pseudo-intransitive**'; a passive like *It has not been sat in*, where *it* does not correspond to an object in the active, as '**pseudo-passive**'; the apparent relative clause in *There is someone who wants to see you* as an example of a '**pseudo-relative clause**', and so on.

pseudo-cleft (Construction) of e.g. *What I want is my supper*: *cf.* cleft. Typically of sentences in which the subject of the copula (*is*) is a free relative clause (*What I want*). But also, in some usage, of others similar in form and function: e.g. *All I want is my supper*, *The reason is that I am hungry*. A '**reversed pseudo-cleft**' is e.g. *My supper is what I want*.

Examples like the first are also described as *wh*-**clefts**.

PSG = phrase structure grammar.

PS-rule = phrase structure rule.

psycholinguistics Any study of language in or from the viewpoint of psychology. Seen in the 1960s as including two main subfields: the empirical study of the development of language in children ('**developmental psycholinguistics**'); and the investigation through experiments of the psychological mechanisms for the production and understanding of speech ('**experimental psycholinguistics**').

Since usual of experimental studies only. The boundary with *neurolinguistics is likely to become increasingly fluid.

'psychological reality' The reality of a grammar etc. as a purported account of structures represented in the mind of a speaker. Often opposed, in discussion of the merits of alternative grammars, to criteria of simplicity, elegance, and internal consistency.

psychological subject An element seen as a 'subject' in that, like many *subjects in the usual sense, it identifies who or what a sentence is about. E.g. *on Monday* in *On Monday it will be my birthday*, seen as a statement about Monday.

Opp. grammatical subject; logical subject. A term from the late 19th century: *cf.* theme (1) *or* topic (2), which have effectively replaced it.

pulmonic (Air stream, *airstream mechanism) in which a flow is initiated by a change in the volume of the lungs. Most normal speech is produced by such an air stream, specifically by a pulmonic egressive air stream, in which air flows outwards as the volume of the lungs is reduced.

punctual (*Aspect) marking an action etc. taking place at an undivided moment of time: e.g. that of *woke* in *I woke up at 5.00 this morning*.

Punic The form of *Phoenician spoken in ancient Carthage; attested by inscriptions in North Africa until late in the Roman Empire.

Punjabi *Indo-Aryan, spoken in the Punjab provinces of Pakistan and India; also through emigration in Britain and elsewhere. Like *Hindi-Urdu, it is written differently by adherents of different religions: by Muslims in an Arabic script derived from that of Persian; by Sikhs in Gurmukhi, developed from other Indian scripts as a vehicle for the Sikh scriptures; by Hindus in Gurmukhi or *Devanagari. A distinct literary language from the 11th century.

pure vowel A vowel with no perceptible change in quality from beginning to end: e.g. the [iː] of *meat* in the pronunciation of some English speakers, as distinct from [ɪi] etc. in others. *Cf.* monophthong.

purism Any movement etc. to protect the supposed 'purity' of a language, e.g. by seeking to remove or prevent the introduction of *loan words, or to prevent the spread of internal changes or stylistic tendencies judged to be 'corruptions'. French attitudes to 'Franglais' illustrate one classic pattern.

'purport' *Hjelmslev's term in English (Danish *mening*) for factors common to the *substance, of content or of expression, in all languages: e.g. in his example, the 'thought' common to English *I do not know*, French *je ne sais pas*, Danish *jeg véd det ikke*, etc.

purposive (Construction etc.) used to indicate an aim or purpose: e.g. *to see my mother* is purposive in *I went home to see my mother*. *Cf.* final (2), telic; but 'purposive' is now more usual.

push chain *See* chain shift.

Putonghua Name in the People's Republic for the official language of China, based on the dialect of Beijing.

Q

Q-Celtic Branch of *Celtic that did not undergo the change by which, in *P-Celtic, Indo-European *k^w became *p*. Represented in the modern period by the 'Goidelic' languages (Irish and Scottish *Gaelic).

Q-principle Principle in *Neo-Gricean pragmatics by which speakers are expected to give as much information, all else being equal, as they can.

Q stands for quantity. *Cf.* I-principle; M-principle.

quadrisyllabic Having four syllables. A word such as *dictatorship* is thus a **quadrisyllable**.

'qualia' Aspects of the meanings of words etc. that distinguish broadly how an entity referred to is built up; how it contrasts with or is grouped with others; what purpose it has; what development etc. it undergoes. Called respectively 'constitutive', 'formal', 'telic', 'agentive'.

Plural of a word in Latin for 'what sort of'. Basically a reformulation by J. Pustejovsky of the four 'causes', or parameters, by which things may be characterized, distinguished by Aristotle.

qualifier The semantic role characteristic of an element that in syntax stands in a relation of *modification (1): e.g. in *heavy furniture* the modifier *heavy* qualifies *furniture*; in *sang sweetly* the modifier *sweetly* qualifies *sang*. Hence also = modifier.

quality **1.** *See* vowel quality. **2.** *See* maxims of conversation. **3.** Ancient term (Latin *qualitas*) for the property of being of one sort rather than another. Thus the traditional 'qualities' or sorts of nouns are *proper nouns, *common nouns, etc.

quantal Characterized by distinct steps as opposed to continuous variation. Applied to the acoustics of speech in work by K. N. Stevens from the early 1970s: thus, in particular, [i] [u] [a] are **quantal vowels**, in whose production precise and distinct acoustic signals, as described by the patterning of *formants (1), can be achieved by variations in the size of the corresponding resonating chambers that are themselves imprecise.

quantified (Noun phrase, pronoun) which includes a *quantifier (2): e.g. *all people, everyone*.

quantifier **1.** Any word or expression which gives a relative or indefinite indication of quantity. E.g. *many* in *many children* or *few* in *the few children who came*: distinguished as such from a *numeral, which gives a precise and absolute indication of quantity, e.g. in *the three children who came*. Applied by Quirk *et al.*, *CGE*, specifically to elements, such as *many* or *few*, that, with numerals, have the position in a noun phrase of a *postdeterminer. **2.** An operator in logic such as the *existential quantifier (∃) and the *universal quantifier (∀). Thence, in linguistics, of a class of *determiners such as *some*, *no*, *all*, or *most*, characterized by ones whose meaning can be represented by expressions containing such an operator. E.g. that of *all* in *All birds fly* can be shown by the universal quantifier in an expression (∀x) (bird (x) → fly (x)) 'For all x, if x is a bird, then x flies'; that of *no* in *No snakes fly* with the existential quantifier in ~(∃x) (snake (x) & fly (x)) 'There exists no x, such that x is a snake and x flies'.

Sense 2 is now more usual, at least in theoretical work. But confusion can arise quite easily. *See also* generalized quantifier.

quantifier floating Proposed syntactic process by which a *quantifier (2) is detached from its phrase. E.g. in *Birds can all fly*, the quantifier *all* is seen as having 'floated' from its position as a determiner in *All birds can fly*.

'quantifier raising' Movement, proposed in *Government and Binding Theory, of an expression with a *quantifier (2) into a position in *Logical Form outside the sentence unit to which it is initially assigned. E.g. of *someone* in *I love someone* to its position in [*someone* [*I love t*]], from which it then 'binds' its *trace (*t*).

quantity 1. Variously of the *length of vowels and of the distinction between *heavy syllables and light syllables, especially with reference to their role in verse in Latin and other older Indo-European languages. **2.** *See* maxims of conversation; Q-principle.

Québécois The form of French spoken in the province of Quebec in Canada.

Quechua(n) Language (Quechua) or family of closely related languages (Quechuan) spoken in large parts of the Andes, from the south of Colombia to the north of Argentina. Widespread over the Inca empire when it was conquered in the 16th century and still the main indigenous language in Ecuador, Peru, and Bolivia. Not securely assigned to any larger family.

'queclarative' Coined in the 1970s for an utterance which has the form of an *interrogative (or 'question') but the force of a statement (or 'declarative'): e.g. 'What use is that?', meaning that it is no use.

question *See* interrogative. A **question marker** is e.g. a particle that distinguishes a sentence as interrogative, a syntactic process which forms an interrogative construction is one of **question formation**, and so on.

question mark (?) Used e.g. to register doubt as to whether a form is grammatical: thus ?*It has been being built for ages* (if the grammarian's judgement is that this is not fully acceptable); ?**It has been being built for ages* (if judged to be even more doubtful).

Quirk, Charles Randolph (1920–) Grammarian of English, founder of the *Survey of English Usage and the leading author, with S. Greenbaum, G. Leech, and J. Svartvik, of two influential grammars, *A Grammar of Contemporary English* (1972) and its successor, *A Comprehensive Grammar of the English Language* (*CGE), in 1985.

quotative (Particle, inflection) indicating that what is said has been heard from someone else and is not based on direct observation: e.g., schematically, *he* QUOT *is rich* 'It is said, I have been told that he is rich'. Opposed to other *evidential elements.

quotes (' ') *See* inverted commas.

R

radical **1.** Of, in, etc. a *root (1). **2.** One of a set of smaller elements, corresponding to semantic categories, into which characters in Chinese writing are analysed and by which they are classified and grouped in dictionaries. **3.** (Sound) articulated with the root or 'radix' of the tongue: i.e. with the back as opposed to the upper surface. Also taken to include sounds articulated with the epiglottis. **4.** In the general sense of 'taken to an extreme'. E.g. **radical pragmatics**, of a treatment of meaning which reduces the role of semantics, seen as separate from *pragmatics, to a minimum.

'radical creole' One thought to have been formed by a process of 'abrupt' *creolization.

raising (1) Change or process by which a vowel is articulated with the tongue closer to the roof of the mouth. Thus, in the history of English, the vowel of *beet* was raised, as part of the *Great Vowel Shift, from [eː] to [iː]. Opp. lowering.

raising (2) A syntactic process by which a noun phrase or other unit is moved from a subordinate clause into the structure of the larger clause that includes it. E.g. in *I believe him to be honest* what is believed is 'He is honest'; therefore, at one level, *him* is claimed to be the subject of a clause marked by the infinitive: *I believe [him to be honest]*. But in other respects *him* has syntactic properties like those that it has as an object, e.g. in the simple sentence *I believe him*. Therefore, in one analysis, the pronoun is seen as raised to that position in the main clause: *I believe him [to be honest]*.

The example given is one of 'raising to object': i.e. of a postulated raising to object position. 'Raising to subject' is posited, for partly similar reasons, in e.g. *He seems to be honest* (from *It seems [he is honest]* or *[He is honest] seems*). The term 'raising' has often been used by linguists who themselves believe that such analyses are wrong, as a convenient label to distinguish the constructions of verbs such as *seem* or *believe*, as *raising verbs, from those said to involve *control.

For similar constructions, or ones often described similarly, *see* negative raising, *tough*-movement; *also* clause union, clitic climbing.

raising verb One which takes a construction for which *raising (2) is or has been posited: e.g. *believe* in *I believe him to be honest*, or *seem* in *He seems to be honest*. Distinguished from, in particular, *control verbs.

Likewise *certain* in *He is certain to fall* can be described as a '**raising adjective**', with a construction derived by 'raising' a subject from its position in *[he fall] is certain*.

Rajasthani A group of *Indo-Aryan languages of which **Marwari**, centred in the Indian state of Rajasthan, is the most important. Also = Marwari specifically.

ranks 1. Jespersen's term for successive levels of subordination or dependency. E.g. in the *junction *very cold water,* *water* has the highest rank and is a **primary**; *cold* has the next highest and is a **secondary**; *very* has the lowest and is a **tertiary**. Jespersen emphasized that the hierarchy of ranks is independent of word classes or *parts of speech. E.g. a substantive (noun) is primary in this example, but in *silk dresses* a substantive is secondary; in *the poor* the adjective *poor* is primary, and so on. The ranks are also distinguished in a predication (Jespersen's *nexus): e.g. *He* (primary) *writes* (secondary) *dreadfully* (tertiary).
2. Halliday's term for successively larger grammatical units. E.g. in *My brother came on Saturday*, the successive words are units of one rank; the successive phrases (in Halliday's account *my brother, came,* and *on Saturday*) are units of the rank above that; above that, in turn, the whole is a clause; above that, it is also a sentence. **Rank-shifting** is the process by which a unit may form part of a larger unit either of its own or of a lower rank: e.g. in *the dance on Saturday, on Saturday* is a rank-shifted phrase which is part of a larger phrase; in *the dance which you promised, which you promised* is similarly a rank-shifted clause. Also called, more specifically, 'downward rank-shifting'.

rapid speech Usually of speech distinguished by phonetic modifications not found or found to a lesser degree in slower or more careful speech. The forms resulting are *allegro forms.

Rask, Rasmus (1787–1832) Danish linguist, the author of several grammars, whose work on the comparative phonology and morphology of European languages stands at the threshold of the development of the comparative grammar of *Indo-European. Notable especially for an early formulation of what was to become known, with less justice, as *Grimm's Law.

rate Used technically of the speed, measured e.g. in syllables per second, with which speech is produced. Also called '**tempo**'.

rationalism The philosophical doctrine that knowledge is based on reason rather than on the experience of the senses: opposed in that sense to *empiricism. Invoked by Chomsky in the 1960s in arguing for specific factors other than the input from sense experience in a child's acquisition of language.

'reading' Used in the 1960s of one way of understanding an ambiguous expression. E.g. *I cooked his goose* has two 'readings', one when understood literally, the other as an idiom.

readjustment rule Any of a series of rules of various sorts introduced into the theory of generative grammar by Chomsky and

Halle, *SPE*. In the account then standard, *surface structures were derived by transformations and were then assigned a phonetic interpretation by rules of phonology. But such structures were not in all respects interpretable directly: e.g. some boundaries between syntactic units did not correspond to those of phonological units. Therefore rules were required to 'readjust' them.

Hence of similar rules posited in *Distributed Morphology.

ready-made (Sentence) seen as a *fixed expression, as opposed to one created freely by speakers on specific occasions. Hence of many more or less ritual utterances: *Have a nice day!*, *Mind your backs!*, *The more the merrier*, and so on.

real Occasionally as the opposite of 'unreal': e.g. *if he comes* is or expresses a 'real' condition, as opposed to the 'unreal' or *remote condition in *if he came*.

realis (Affix etc.) used to distinguish events etc. that have actually happened or are happening as opposed to ones that are possible or imaginable. Formed in general opposition to *irrealis.

realism The doctrine in philosophy that *universals have a real existence, over and above the individual entities that they subsume. *Plato's theory of forms or 'ideas' is characteristic. Distinguished in the Middle Ages from the opposite doctrine of *nominalism.

realistic In its ordinary sense: hence used e.g. of a grammar claimed to satisfy criteria of *psychological reality.

realization The relation between the representation of a form at one *level of abstraction and its representation at another more abstract level. E.g. the word *children* might be represented at one level by the grammatical units 'child' and 'plural'; at a lower or less abstract level, these would be **realized** by the phonetic form ['tʃɪldrən].

reanalysis = restructuring. Used especially of a posited change in syntax by which forms are reassigned to different constituents or to different categories. Thus, in one account, the construction of *I said* [*that he left*], where *that* is a conjunction introducing a subordinate clause, is said to derive from an earlier construction in which *that* was a pronoun to which a subordinate sentence was juxtaposed: *I said that* [*he left*].

reason (Adverbial, clause, conjunction) indicating a reason: e.g. *because* or *because he was happy* in *He smiled because he was happy*.

rebus principle The principle by which, in some systems of writing, symbols representing one or more words are combined to represent another word which is similar in sound. Suppose that English *eye* [ʌɪ] were represented by a single character <eye>, and *deer* [dɪə] by a single character <deer>; then, by the rebus principle, *idea* [ʌɪdɪə] might be represented by the combination <eye><deer>.

'Received Pronunciation' (RP) An accent of English identified by (Daniel) Jones as characteristic of educated speakers in the south of Britain. Still one form of Southern British English: a variety reflecting changes since the period in which Jones described it is sometimes called 'Advanced Received Pronunciation' or '**Advanced RP**'.

recessive (Accent) which falls as early (i.e. as far back in a unit) as possible. Thus, in the structure of the word in Ancient Greek, the accent could in principle fall on any of the last three syllables. In a verb form such as *eléipomen* 'we were leaving' it is 'thrown back' to the earliest position that it is allowed.

recipient Semantic role of a word or phrase which identifies an individual or individuals receiving something: e.g. that of *me* in *They gave me a ticket*, or of *I* in *I received a ticket*.

Usually distinguished as a notional *case role from the *dative as a morphological *case partly corresponding to it.

reciprocal (Pronoun, inflection, etc.) indicating that an action or process is reciprocated by participants. E.g. *each other* is reciprocal, or a reciprocal, in *Mary and Jane like each other*: i.e. Mary likes Jane and Jane likes Mary.

reconstruction The formulation of hypotheses about the form that words or other units had in a period earlier than that in which they are attested. E.g. English *have* and German *hab-* (in *haben*) are derived from the same form in the *protolanguage common to languages of the *Germanic family. Neither it nor any other word of the protolanguage is known from direct evidence. But by inference from the findings of the *comparative method it can be reconstructed as a protoform *Χαß-.

Reconstructed forms are distinguished, as in this illustration, by an asterisk.

recoverability condition A proposed condition on syntactic processes by which, if a unit is deleted, it must still be possible to determine what that unit was. If this is accepted, there could not e.g. be a general rule by which an object is deleted in a sentence such as *I was reading*. For the specific object involved (*a letter, your book, the Koran*, etc.) would not be **recoverable** from subsequent representations of its structure.

rection = government: e.g. of prepositions in Latin governing the accusative or ablative.

recurrent Instanced in more than one unit. Thus the *alternation between [iː] in *obsc*[iː]*ne* and [ɛ] in *obsc*[ɛ]*nity* is a **recurrent alternation** since it is also found e.g. in *serene* and *serenity*.

recursive (*Rule) that can reapply to a form or construction that is itself partly or wholly derived by it. Thus, by a rule of syntax, a noun phrase (NP) can include a modifying prepositional phrase (PP): NP[*the fish* PP[*in the pool*]]. This in turn includes a noun phrase (NP[*the fish* PP[*in* NP[*the pool*]]]); that in turn can include a further prepositional phrase (NP[*the fish* PP[*in* NP[*the pool* PP[*in the garden*]]]]), and so on.

In this construction both 'noun phrase' and 'prepositional phrase' are **recursive categories**. The pattern or phenomenon in general is **recursion**.

recursive language A *formal language for which there is a procedure which will determine, in a finite number of steps, whether or not a given string is a member of it. A **recursively enumerable language** is one for which there is a procedure which can similarly determine that a given string *is* a member, but none which can determine that it is *not* a member.

reduced clause A unit derived from a *finite clause by the omission of a subject and a copula or auxiliary: e.g. *while driving* in *We talked while driving* can be seen as reduced from *while we were driving*. Thence of other units seen as clauses shortened from their full form: e.g. *Bill happy* would for many grammarians be a clause, reduced by the omission of a copula (*to be*), in *She made Bill happy*.

reduced passive An *agentless passive seen as derived by a process of reduction from the structure of a **full passive** with an *agent (3): e.g. *I was rescued* as opposed to *I was rescued by the police*.

reduced vowel A vowel which is shortened or centralized, especially one which is merged with others, by some phonological or morphological process: e.g. the [ə]s of *ph*[ə]*togr*[ə]*phy*, as compared with the corresponding unreduced vowels of *ph*[əʊ]*togr*[ɑː]*ph*.

redundancy The property of having more structure than is minimally necessary. A bridge, for example, needs a certain number of components if it is to stand up. In practice, however, the structure of bridges is redundant; hence, if one component were to fail, the others would still be enough to ensure that it remained standing. Similarly, in languages, a certain number of elements are needed to distinguish each word or sentence from others. But the structures in which these elements are combined are redundant, so that if e.g. an individual element is indistinct the whole may still be correctly understood.

Suppose, by contrast, that every combination of phonemes formed a word and, in addition, every combination of words formed a sentence. Then, if a single phoneme were mispronounced or misheard, an entire sentence could in principle be mistaken for another. But in fact the structures at both levels are highly redundant. E.g. if a word in English begins with [r] only a vowel can follow; if a sentence begins with *the* it cannot be followed by an element that is syntactically a finite verb; if a subject is plural the verb must normally agree with it. In that sense every element is to some degree predictable from those that accompany it, and the dangers of misunderstanding are effectively removed.

redundancy rule *See* lexical redundancy rule.

reduplication 1. A morphological process by which all or part of a form is repeated. E.g. the Latin stem *momord-* (in *momordi* 'I bit') is derived from a root *mord-* by reduplication of the initial consonant and vowel: *mord-* → *mo-mord-*. This is a case of **partial reduplication**; in **complete reduplication** the whole form is repeated. **2.** Any syntactic pattern in which words are repeated: e.g. *very* is reduplicated in *This cake is very very good*. Often systematic: e.g., in Afrikaans, *Die ongeluk* ('the accident') *het hier-hier gebeur* (lit. 'has here-here happened'), meaning 'The accident happened right here'.

reduplicative compound One whose second member is derived by repetition of the whole or part of the first; *cf.* echo-word. Also generally, in Quirk *et al.*, **CGE*, of compounds whose members rhyme: e.g. *walkie-talkie, busy lizzy*.

'Reed and Kellogg diagrams' Representations of the syntactic structure of sentences, named after their formulation by A. Reed and B. Kellogg in the late 19th century and taught in schools in the USA for several generations. A line is drawn with the relations between the main words in the sentence shown above it: thus, in the illustration, subject *men*, verb *ate*, object *cheese*. The roles of words directly or indirectly subordinate to them are shown successively underneath: thus, in the illustration, *the* is subordinate to *men*; *strong* and, in succession, *with* and *onion* to *cheese*.

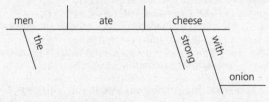

A Reed and Kellogg diagram

reference The relation between a part of an utterance and an individual or set of individuals that it identifies. Thus one might say, on some specific occasion, 'That man is my brother', where the phrase *that man* is used as a **referring expression** whose **referent** is a specific man whose identity one's addressee must either know or be able to determine.

Distinguished by philosophers from *sense (2), and by Lyons especially from *denotation. E.g. *the man* is a phrase that, in such an utterance, is used to refer to a man; the noun *man*, as a lexical unit, denotes a class of individuals that are thereby called 'men', and has a sense distinguished, in a network of *sense relations, from those of *woman, boy, elephant,* etc. But these distinctions are not needed for all purposes, and actual usage, as in many entries in this dictionary, is more fluid.

reference grammar A grammar, in the ordinary sense, designed as a book for reference and not primarily, e.g., for working through in teaching. Quirk *et al.*, *CGE and Huddleston and Pullum, *CGEL are now leading reference grammars for English.

reference tracking Keeping track of the individuals referred to at successive points in a sentence, conversation, etc. E.g. in *Sarah promised Mary that she would see her tomorrow if she had time*, the person spoken to must keep track of who the pronouns *she* and *her* refer to: thus, as it would most likely be meant, . . . *she* (Sarah) *would see her* (Mary) *if she* (Sarah) *had time*.

For relations and categories involved in reference tracking *see especially* anaphora; switch-reference.

referent-controlled honorific *See* honorific.

referential (Meaning, *function of language) involving reference to entities, events, states of affairs, etc. *Cf.* descriptive (3); ideational; representational.

referential indices *See* indices.

referentially opaque (Context) in which one cannot validly draw an inference by replacing one expression with another whose reference is identical. E.g. if Bill's murderer is Jill's brother, it follows from 'John lives next door to Bill's murderer' that John lives next door to Jill's brother, but from 'The police have identified Smith's murderer' it does not follow that the police have identified Jill's brother.

referral *See* rule of referral. Also in obvious senses: e.g. of the act of referring to something.

referring expression *See* reference.

reflectiveness = reflexivity.

reflex A later form which is derived by direct transmission from one postulated or attested earlier. E.g. both English *cow* and French *boeuf* are **reflexes of** the same word in Indo-European (reconstructed in the nominative singular as *$g^w ou$-s*).

reflexive (REFL) (Pronoun) characteristically interpreted as
*anaphoric to an element elsewhere in the sentence. E.g. in *Mary chose*
*her*SELF, *herself* is a reflexive referring to the same person (Mary) as the
subject *Mary*. Also of a suffix etc. indicating that a second participant
in a process or action is the same as the first: schematically, *Mary chose-*
REFL (Mary chose herself) vs. *Mary chose her, Mary chose-*3SG (Mary chose
someone else). *Cf.* middle. Also e.g. of any distinct construction that
includes a reflexive.

reflexive passive An *impersonal passive in e.g. Spanish if analysed
as a reflexive. E.g. *Se venden casas*, analysed as *se* 'themselves' *venden*
'sell-3PL' *casas* 'house-PL' (hence 'Houses for sale').

reflexive verb A verb containing or accompanied by a reflexive
element. Especially one in which the two together are treated as a
lexical unit.
    The latter case is common in descriptions of Romance languages.
E.g. French *s'asseoir* 'sit down' is a reflexive verb in which *asseoir* 'seat,
set down' is obligatorily accompanied by a reflexive (*s(e)* etc.) matching
its subject. The term is not usual in accounts of English: but compare
e.g. the sense of 'kick oneself' in *I could kick myself for forgetting it*.

reflexivity The property of language by which it can be used to talk
about language itself. A proposed *design feature; *cf.* metalanguage,
metalinguistic.

reflexivization A syntactic process, posited in early
*transformational grammars, by which reflexives, where appropriate,
replaced noun phrases. *Cf.* pronominalization.

regimen Used by Jespersen of the element governed by a preposition:
e.g. *Cambridge* in *to Cambridge*.

regional In the obvious sense. Thus a 'regional language' is spoken in
a region within e.g. a larger political unit, 'regional standards' are
forms of speech established as *standard in specific regions, and so on.

register 1. A set of features of speech or writing characteristic of a
particular type of linguistic activity or a particular group when
engaging in it. E.g. journalese is a register different from that in which
sermons are delivered, or in which smutty stories are told. **2.** A feature
of *phonation distinguishing different series of vowels or syllables: e.g.
of 'clear' or normal voice vs. breathy voice or *murmur in several Mon-
Khmer languages. **3.** A set of tones, e.g. in Wu *Chinese, distinguished
as a set by a high or a low pitch range.

register tone *Tone distinguished from others solely by a relative
level of pitch within a speaker's pitch range: e.g. a high tone vs. a low
tone. Opp. contour tone; *cf.* register (3).

regressive assimilation *Assimilation in which elements are changed to match features of elements that follow them. E.g. the [k] of Latin [leːk-s] 'law-NOM.SG' (written *lex*) is voiceless in contact with the suffix -[s] which follows; cf. [leːg-is] (*legis*) 'law-GEN.SG'.

Opp. progressive assimilation. The sense is that of features, such as voicelessness, being thrown back or anticipated: hence also called 'anticipatory', as in corresponding accounts of *coarticulation.

regular (Form) which conforms to a rule whose application is predicted by some general property of a unit. E.g. the unit *table* is a noun; from this it is predicted, by a *default rule, that its plural is in -*s*; therefore *tables*, which is formed according to that rule, is regular or is a regular plural. *Men*, by contrast, is an *exception to the rule and is **irregular**.

Regularity is often relative to specific classes of units. E.g. in Latin, the default rule for the stem of the passive participle was to add -*t*- after the stem or conjugation vowel: *am-a-* 'love', with conjugation vowel -*a*-, → *am-a-t-* 'loved'. Such forms are therefore regular for verbs in general. But for verbs whose conjugation vowel was -*e*- the default rule was to add -*it*- to the root: *mon-e-* 'warn', but *mon-it-* 'warned'. Accordingly such forms were regular for that class in particular.

Regularity Principle *See* Neogrammarians.

reify To treat an abstract concept or construct as if it were something having physical reality. E.g. a 'mental lexicon' seen as represented in the brains of speakers is arguably no more than a **reification** of the concepts underlying the writing of dictionaries.

'reinforcement' *See* operant-conditioning.

related (Languages) which belong to the same *family in a *genetic classification. E.g. English and French are related within *Indo-European. *Cf.* cognate.

relation Any linkage established among elements. Thus, in *sea* [siː], [s] and [iː] are related as onset and nucleus of a *syllable; in *They vanished, they* is related as subject to the verb *vanished*. These are instances of *syntagmatic relations. In the phonology of English, [s] is related as a voiceless consonant to [z] as the corresponding voiced consonant; in its grammar, *they* as plural is related to *he, she*, and *it* as the corresponding singulars. These are instances of *paradigmatic relations. Also of any other linkage: e.g. in some accounts of meaning, a representation of the syntax of a sentence is paired with, i.e. is related to, a *semantic representation.

Formally interchangeable with the concept of an *operation: thus *x* → *y* expresses a relation between *x* and *y*. Often interchanged in practice, especially in specific collocations, with that of a role or *function. E.g. in *They vanished, they* stands in the relation of 'subject of' to *vanished*; alternatively, it has the *syntactic function (or 'grammatical role' etc.) of subject.

relational adjective An adjective derived from a noun whose role is in effect to relate that noun to a noun that it qualifies. E.g. *routière* in French *police routière* 'traffic police': lit. 'police' (*police*) to do with the 'road' (*route*).

Relational Grammar Theory of syntax developed by D. M. Perlmutter, P. M. Postal, and others in the 1970s, in opposition to the account of syntactic functions or relations (subject, object, etc.) proposed by Chomsky in the 1960s. For Chomsky these were derived notions: e.g. a subject was defined as a noun phrase (NP) directly dominated, in a phrase structure tree, by a sentence node (S). In Relational Grammar they were taken as primitive. E.g. in the construction of *Bill visited Mary, Bill* and *Mary* are 'terms' which bear distinct 'term relations' (subject of, direct object of) to the verb. In the corresponding passive (*Mary was visited by Bill*), the object term (*Mary*) is *promoted to subject, and so on.

Many accounts of *functional syntax have their origin, in part, in Relational Grammar. *Arc Pair Grammar, from the late 1970s, was a more direct offshoot.

relational hierarchy Version, in Relational Grammar, of the *NP accessibility hierarchy.

relational noun A noun whose meaning involves a relationship between one entity and another: e.g. *husband* 'man in a relation of marriage to a wife'.

relative chronology One in which events are ordered in time, but without specific dates. E.g. one can deduce from the evidence of Sanskrit that a sound change by which [k] > [tʃ] before front vowels preceded one by which the front vowel [e] > [a]: but both are prehistoric and the times over which they took place are unknown.

relative clause A clause which modifies the head of a noun phrase and typically includes a pronoun or other element whose reference is linked to it. E.g. in *the man who came,* a relative clause *who came* modifies *man*: cf. modification (1). Within this clause, *who* is a **relative pronoun** (traditionally seen as *anaphoric to *man*) which does not have an independent referent.

Thence to clauses with a similar element that are not modifiers: e.g. *who dares* is a *free relative clause in *Who dares wins*. Also to modifying clauses in which a relative pronoun is seen as *null or deleted. Thus *you saw*, or, with a null element, *Ø you saw,* is a relative clause in *That is the man you saw*.

relative pronoun *See* relative clause.

relative superlative A *superlative which indicates pre-eminence within a set, as opposed to an *elative (2). E.g. *tallest* in *the tallest person I know* indicates pre-eminence in height among the specific set of people that the speaker knows.

'relative universal' A property or statement that holds for most languages but not for all. E.g. the property of having phonologically distinct bilabial consonants: though almost every language has them, some do or did not.

   Cf. statistical universal. A *linguistic universal that is genuinely universal is described by contrast as an 'absolute universal'.

relativism *See* Sapir–Whorf hypothesis.

relativization The formation of *relative clauses: specifically, the process by which one element is represented by a relative pronoun or its equivalent. E.g. the subject is **relativized** in *the people who came*; a locative in *the place where we live*.

release The ending of closure in the articulation of a *plosive consonant. In some languages consonants are said to be '**unreleased**' in various positions: i.e. their release is inaudible, either because the air pressure before and behind the closure has been equalized, or because it occurs during the articulation of another consonant that follows. Thus the [k] of French *acteur* is typically 'released' while that of English *actor* is not.

Relevance Theory A theory of the meanings of utterances originally developed in the 1980s by D. Sperber and D. M. S. Wilson. Distinguished from *Neo-Gricean treatments, in particular, by a technical concept of 'relevance', defined as a property inherent in the nature of communication that any utterance, or a proposition that it communicates, cannot but have and be interpreted as having. Relevance in this sense is relative to a set of existing 'assumptions' that constitute the context, or ongoing 'cognitive environment', in which an act of speech takes place, and the 'assumptions' that it adds to this set, though necessarily having relevance, will be relevant to it in varying degrees.

   Equivalent in other ways to treatments that distinguish the meanings of utterances, as the subject of *pragmatics, and the meanings of sentences, and of units within sentences, as determined by the *grammar of a language. Hence, in particular, the role of *explicatures.

relevant Used technically or semi-technically: **1.** Of data or findings taken to bear on some phase or aspect of linguistic analysis. Thus information about sounds is relevant to phonological analysis, but it was long disputed whether, or how far, information about grammar should be. **2.** Of whatever bears on the meaning of an utterance. Thus

if someone says 'Come in!' it may be relevant that they are in their
office, that there has been a knock on the door, etc.: it may not be
relevant that e.g. they have brown eyes or that their carpet is dirty.
The context of an utterance might accordingly be defined as the
features of the total environment that are relevant to its production or
interpretation. **3.** Of an utterance said on a specific occasion. Thus, in
the theory of *maxims of conversation, speakers are expected, by a
maxim of 'relation', to make their contribution to an interchange
relevant rather than irrelevant. *Cf.* Relevance Theory.

'relexification' Process in which the vocabulary of a language is
largely at least replaced, through *borrowing, by that of another
language, without its grammar being affected similarly. In the
extreme case, language A may be described as a 'relexification of'
language B: i.e. the words or morphemes are different, but their
structures are in other respects essentially the same. *Cf.* base language.

The **'relexification hypothesis'** is the theory that *pidgins, e.g. in
West Africa and the West Indies, developed from a single original form
by successive changes of the 'base language'. Thus a pidgin whose
vocabulary was based on French might be 'relexified' to form a new
one based on English, that in turn 'relexified' to form one based on
Dutch, and so on.

'relic form' A form preserved only in the dialect of a specific area.
A **'relic area'** is likewise one in whose dialect such forms have
tended to persist.

remote (*Conditional clause) expressing a condition either not met
or less likely to have been or to be met. E.g. *If Bill had only tried to see
her* ... (implying that he did not); *If she could find a way to get to Paris
in two hours* ... (implying that it is unlikely that she could).

Cf. counterfactual. These and other terms are often used
equivalently: e.g. the condition in *If he had seen her* ... is counterfactual
(= remote, = **unreal**, = **hypothetical**), as opposed to the 'open'
condition in *If he saw her* ... But (a) a condition in the future is always
in a strict sense 'open'; (b) the distinction drawn in languages is often
between remote and non-remote (*If I had seen her I would certainly have
told her, If I saw her I certainly told her*) rather than, in a strict sense,
contrary to vs. possibly in accordance with fact.

renewal of connection Firth's term for the relation re-established,
by statements of *exponence, between an abstract unit, structure, etc.
and the data from which the abstraction has been made.

reordering of rules *See* rule ordering.

'repair' Used in *Conversation Analysis of any instance in which
speakers correct themselves, or correct what other speakers have said,
or query it, or clarify what they or someone else has said, and so on.

A '**repair sequence**' is a *turn, or any part of a 'turn', or any succession of 'turns', by which any of these things is done.

'Repairs' have been variously classed as '**self-repair**' (corrections etc. made by speakers themselves responsible) vs. '**other-repair**' (made by their interlocutors); as '**self-initiated**' (made by a speaker without querying or prompting) vs. '**other-initiated**' (made in response to querying or prompting).

repertoire Used semi-technically e.g. of the range of styles or varieties of a language available to or mastered by a speaker or writer.

replacive A process of morphological *modification (2) treated, in some accounts, as an allomorph of a *morpheme. E.g. in *sang* vs. *sing*, [ɪ] → [a] is a 'replacive' or '**replacive morph**' seen as an allomorph of the morpheme 'past'.

reported speech One utterance as reported by another: e.g. a promise by a speaker to mend something as reported, by a subordinate clause, in a later utterance 'He promised he would mend it'. Strictly including cases of both *indirect speech, as in this example, and *direct speech; often, however, used of indirect speech specifically.

representation The structure assigned to a form at any *level of description or analysis. E.g. a *phonetic transcription is one kind of representation at a phonetic level; a *phrase structure tree is a common form of representation at the level of syntax; a *semantic representation is a description of a sentence or other unit at a separate level of meaning.

representational (*Function of language) in representing or describing events, states of affairs, etc. *Cf.* descriptive; ideational; referential.

representative Type of *speech act by which a speaker represents a state of affairs: thus especially a statement. *Cf.* representational.

resonance The physical effect in which a vibrating body, e.g. the body of air within the vocal tract, selectively reinforces or prolongs a sound produced by the vibration of another, e.g. of the vocal cords. Thus *resonants are speech sounds, or one kind of speech sound, in which the vocal tract above the larynx acts solely as a resonating chamber.

resonant A speech sound in whose production air flows smoothly through the *vocal tract, without audible turbulence. Hence specifically of consonants that are neither *stops nor *fricatives: e.g. [l]. Opp. obstruent; *cf.* approximant, sonorant.

respect 1. In the sense of 'with respect to'. Thus a dative **of respect** indicates e.g. someone with respect to whom a statement holds:

schematically, *You*-DAT ('so far as you are concerned') *that is all*. **2.** In the sense of 'showing respect to': thus pronouns 'of respect' are *honorifics.

REST = Revised Extended Standard Theory.

'restricted code' *See* deficit theory.

restricted language Firth's term for the subset of vocabulary, constructions, etc. used in some very specific situation or for some very specific purpose: e.g. the language of heraldic blazons, or the language used in nautical weather forecasts.

restriction of meaning Change by which the meaning of a word is narrowed by the addition of a feature or features that were not previously part of it: e.g. that by which *deer*, formerly a word for 'animal' in general, came to denote one specific kind of animal. *Cf.* extension.

restrictive (Modifier) which restricts the potential reference of the phrase of which it is part: e.g. *cheap* in *cheap wine* (meaning not wine in general but specifically wine that is cheap). Likewise in *wine that is cheap* the modifying clause *that is cheap* is a **restrictive** *relative clause**.
   Restrictive relative clauses are also called 'defining relative clauses'. Opp. non-restrictive; *also* appositional (2).

restructuring 1. A syntactic or other process by which the structure assigned to a form is changed without change to the form itself. E.g. in *It was made safe, made safe* might be treated as a complex verbal unit (_V[*made safe*]) derived by restructuring from a verb plus a reduced underlying sentence (_V[*made*] _S[*safe*]). Typically of this and similar cases of *clause union. **2.** A change at an underlying level posited in the history of a language. E.g. in phonology, a form might for one generation of speakers have a diphthong or triphthong: thus English [taɪə] (*tyre*). In terms of *Generative Phonology that is both its underlying and its phonetic representation. Then, for a later generation of speakers, its phonetic realization might become progressively monophthongal: phonetic [taː] but, in terms of a general hypothesis developed by Generative Phonologists in the late 1960s, still [taɪə] at the underlying level. Finally, a later generation descended from these, who hear only the phonetic form [taː], might 'restructure' the underlying representation in turn: underlying [taː] = phonetic [taː].
   Also called *reanalysis.

result *See* object of result; resultative.

resultative Used of verbal compounds, e.g. in Chinese, of which the second member indicates a result of what is indicated by the first: schematically, *hit-kill*, *find-possess*, and so on. Also of elements in a clause referring to the result of an action or process: e.g. *solid* in *The lake froze solid*. Also of e.g. an *aspect indicating a result: thus *are destroyed* might be described as resultative in *All my plans are now destroyed*.

Cf. factitive.

resumptive (Pronoun etc.) seen as duplicating the role of a phrase which has the same reference. Common with *clitic pronouns in some Romance languages: e.g. schematically, *Peter him-see-*1SG 'I can see Peter', where *him* 'resumes' *Peter*.

A pronoun such as *he* is also 'resumptive', in a different sense, in e.g. *John's the only one who I don't know if he has had it*.

retracted (Speech sound) in whose production the tongue or part of the tongue is drawn back in contrast to another. E.g. the vowel in *hid* [hɪd] is both retracted and lowered in relation to the *cardinal vowel [i].

'**Retracted Tongue Root**' is the opposite of *Advanced Tongue Root.

retreat *See* promotion.

retroflex Articulated with the tip of the tongue or the underside of the tip against or approximated to the back of the alveolar ridge. Distinctive e.g. in Indian languages such as Hindi-Urdu, where retroflex [ʈ], [ɖ], etc. contrast with dentals.

retrospective anaphora *Anaphora in relation to a unit earlier: i.e. not 'anticipatory'.

reverential = honorific.

reversal of rules *See* rule inversion.

reversed polarity *See* tag.

'**reversed pseudo-cleft**' *See* pseudo-cleft.

reversive (Inflection etc.) indicating the reversal of an action. Thus the prefix *un-* in English has a reversive meaning in *untie*.

Revised Extended Standard Theory Used in the late 1970s to label the version then current of Chomsky's *Extended Standard Theory. Rapidly superseded by *Government and Binding Theory.

rewrite rule A *rule (2) which is interpreted as an instruction to replace one *string of elements with another. Thus, given the string *a b c*, a rule *b → x y* is an instruction to rewrite it as *a x y c*.

In Chomsky's initial formulation a *generative grammar was a series of rewrite rules. A string consisting of an initial symbol S was first successively rewritten by phrase structure rules. E.g. a rule S → NP + VP would be interpreted as an instruction to rewrite S as NP VP; a rule NP → Det + N as an instruction to rewrite that as Det N VP; a rule N → *horse, man,* ... as an instruction to rewrite that in turn as one of

Det *horse* VP, Det *man* VP, and so on. The resulting strings might then be rewritten further, e.g. in a *transformational grammar, by successive transformations.

R-expression Term in *Government and Binding Theory for a noun phrase whose reference is never determined by a relation of *anaphora to an antecedent: e.g. *Bill* as opposed to *he* or *himself*.

RG = Relational Grammar.

Rhaeto-Romance Group of *Romance dialects which includes *Romansch in south-east Switzerland; Ladin, in parts of the South Tyrol in Italy; and Friulan, in the area of Italy bordering Slovenia.

rheme A part of a sentence communicating information relative to whatever is indicated by the *theme (1). E.g. in *The problem is that it is so cold*, the theme might be *the problem*: i.e. that there is a problem is known or anticipated, and the point of the sentence is to explain what it is. The rheme would then be *is that it is so cold*.
　The division between theme and rheme is often seen as one of degree. E.g. in *The problem is that it is so cold at* NIGHT, *the problem* might be maximally thematic, while *at night* (with the intonational stress on *night*) is maximally **rhematic**. The intervening part would then be transitional (or a **transition**) between them.

'Rhenish fan' A transitional area between High *German and Low German or Dutch, defined by the divergence of a series of *isoglosses from an area east of Cologne westwards. A famous finding of dialectology at the close of the 19th century.

rhetoric Traditionally a discipline concerned with the effective use of language, to persuade, give pleasure, and so on. Distinguished from grammar in the ancient Western system of education; from grammar and dialectic or logic as one of three elementary subjects (called in Latin the 'trivium') in a scheme inherited by the Middle Ages. Rhetoric tended, in the nature of things, to overlap grammar, and many topics once claimed for it are now claimed instead for sundry branches of, or on the borders of, linguistics: especially for parts of syntax, pragmatics, stylistics, and sociolinguistics.

rhetorical question Traditional term for a question which does not invite a reply: e.g. *How can I climb that?*, if implying 'I can't climb it'.

rhotacism Replacement by *r*. Thus, in the history of Latin, a single *s*, as in the infinitive suffix *-se*, was generally **rhotacized** between vowels: e.g. **rege-se* 'to rule' > *regere* (cf., with a preceding consonant, *es-se* 'to be').

rhotic ['rɒtɪk] Having an *r*. E.g. dialects spoken in the south-west of England are 'rhotic', since they retain an [r] in words like *tower* or *turn*, which have phonetically no [r] in '**non-rhotic**' dialects. Also as a general term for 'r'-sounds: a class of rhotics will thus include a lingual [r], *uvular [ʀ], *retroflex [ɽ], and so on.

From the Greek name of the letter 'r': thence 'rhoticization' or *rhotacism for the introduction of r or a change resulting in r.

rhyme The nucleus and coda of a *syllable, taken as a unit in opposition to the onset. E.g. [kriːm] (*cream*) has the structure [kr] (onset) plus [iːm] (rhyme).

rhyzotonic (Word) having its accent on the root: e.g. *happiness*, with stress on the root *happy*, as contrasted with arhyzotonic *sensation*, with stress on the suffix *-ation*.

right-branching (Structure) in which *heads successively precede their *dependents. E.g. that of *people living in London*, with the last element *London* represented as dependent on *in*, these in turn as dependent on *living*, and that in turn as dependent on *people*.

From the configuration of branches in a *phrase structure tree: e.g. that represented by the equivalent bracketing [*people* [*living* [*in London*]]]. **Right-branching languages** are those in which such structures predominate: *cf.* centrifugal vs. centripetal; Head Parameter.

right dislocation Construction of e.g. *They are far too tight, these trousers you bought*. As in *left dislocation, the element 'dislocated' (in right dislocation to the end of the sentence) is related to a pronoun (in this example *they*) in its normal position.

'right node raising' The construction of e.g. *I posted and I faxed an answer*, seen as deriving from the coordination of *I posted an answer* and *I faxed an answer*, with fusion of the identical objects into a single phrase whose dominating node, in terms of a *phrase structure tree, is 'raised' to form a new branch: [[*I posted and I faxed*] *an answer*].

rill fricative One in which air flows through a narrowed channel at the centre of the place of articulation: thus a *sibilant such as [s] in *sin* or [ʃ] in *shin*. Also called a 'groove fricative': opp. slit fricative.

rising **1.** (*Diphthong) of which the second part or element is prominent: e.g. [jɛ] or [i̯ɛ] in Italian *viene* (accented *viéne*) 'is coming'. **2.** (*Tone or intonation) in which the pitch rises from relatively low to relatively high.

Opp. falling in both senses.

RNR = right node raising.

role *See* function.

Role and Reference Grammar Approach to syntax so named by W. A. Foley and R. D. Van Valin, who have developed it since the mid-1980s. Broadly *functional in that the treatment of constructions is in principle integrated with an account of their use in communication: distinguished from others especially by an analysis of *layering in clauses in which the verb is the centre and the *nucleus (1), consisting of the verb and all its arguments or valents, forms an inner constituent within an outer constituent that includes its peripheral elements. Influenced in this and other respects by languages whose structure is not like that of English: but, e.g. in English, [*yesterday* $_{nucleus}$[*everybody* $_v$[*played*] *music*] *all morning*].

rolled (Consonant) articulated with a *trill: e.g. the rolled [r], written *rr*, in Spanish *perro* 'dog'.

Roman alphabet First developed in the 7th century BC, on the model of that of *Etruscan. Originally very local; carried from the 1st century BC throughout what became the western Roman Empire, and from the late 15th century AD, by the political expansion of western Europe, worldwide. The original alphabet had 21 letters; in its standard ancient form it had 23, of which two (Y and Z) were introduced in words transparently borrowed from Greek. J, V, and W were not distinguished from I and U until the Middle Ages.

Romance Branch of *Indo-European consisting of the languages that have developed historically from Latin. Originally spoken mainly in the south and west of continental Europe, where *French, *Italian, *Portuguese, and *Spanish are national languages imposed on what was earlier, in large part, a *dialect continuum; thence, through colonization, in the Americas and elsewhere. The family also includes *Rumanian; other important languages and dialects include *Catalan, *Friulan, *Franco-Provençal, *Galician, *Occitan (Provençal), *Romansch, *Sardinian.

Romanian *See* Rumanian.

Romanization The replacement of an earlier writing system with one based on the *Roman alphabet.

Romansch *Rhaeto-Romance dialect with official status in Switzerland; spoken in the canton of Graubünden (Grisons), though losing ground extensively to German.

Romany *Indo-Aryan, with a variety of dialects spoken by populations of Gypsies in Europe and beyond, now mainly concentrated in the Balkans. Local varieties tend to be influenced strongly by other languages in the communities with which Gypsies are in contact.

Romic (Narrow vs. Broad) *See* Sweet.

'roofless' (Dialect) seen as not being 'covered' by a corresponding *standard language. From German *dachlos*: e.g. of forms perceived as dialects of German, spoken outside countries in which German is the national language.

root 1. A form from which words or parts of words are derived and which is not itself derivable from any smaller or simpler form: e.g. *carefully* is derived from *careful* which is in turn derived from the root *care*. Likewise in etymology: e.g. *care* is from an Indo-European root reconstructed as **gar-*. **2.** A node in a **phrase structure tree or other branching structure which no other node dominates.

'root and pattern' (morphology) *See* pattern.

'root compound' One formed without an affix; hence especially, in English, one which does not parallel a verbal construction. E.g. *fish-hook* as opposed to a so-called 'synthetic' compound such as *salmon-fisher*.

'root modality' Any **modality other than **epistemic: thus *can* would be a 'root modal' (whether indicating ability or permission) in *You can do it*.

root transformation One whose application is restricted to **main clauses. Claimed in the late 1970s to be the only kind that could derive structures unlike those derivable by rules of a **base component.

round brackets ( ) Used specifically to show that an element may or may not be present. E.g. a rule $u \rightarrow o$ /—(C) # states that u becomes o before a word boundary (—#), whether or not a consonant (C) intervenes. Likewise in citing examples. Thus *the (sleeping) man* is a conflation of *the sleeping man* and *the man*; *the (*asleep) girl* of **the asleep girl* and *the girl*, with the asterisk showing that the first is ungrammatical.

rounded (Vowel, consonant) produced with rounding of the lips: e.g. [uː] in *you* [juː]. Opp. spread, unrounded, neutral; *cf.* labialization.

RP = Received Pronunciation.

R-principle *See* I-principle.

rule 1. In the ordinary sense: e.g. it is a rule in English, barring specific exceptions, that a modifying adjective comes before a noun that it modifies (*good books*) and not after (*books good*). The main test for a rule is that when it is broken it is clear how the form would be corrected; e.g. in *Girt with many a baron bold* (Gray), the words *baron bold*, in which the adjective comes after the noun by poetic licence, could in principle be corrected to *bold baron*. **2.** Any of the formal expressions that constitute a **generative grammar: e.g. the **phrase structure rule PP → P + NP ('prepositional phrases consist of a preposition followed by a noun'), seen as one of a set that together determine what may and may not be a sentence of the language.

An individual rule in sense 2 is not necessarily in itself a rule in sense 1. Hence, in particular, a distinction drawn by some psycholinguists and sociolinguists at the end of the 1960s, between a **categorical rule**, which if not applied is broken, and a **variable rule**, which may at will be applied or not applied, or applies in *n* per cent of cases, and so on.

rule feature *See* diacritic feature.

'rule inversion' Pattern of language change in which a rule posited at one stage is in effect replaced, at a later stage, by one whose operation is the reverse. E.g., in some dialects of English, [r] was lost when it was not followed by a vowel: thus earlier [biːr] (*beer*) > [bɪə]. Since it remained in words like *beery*, it might be posited that at that stage the basic form of *beer* retained an underlying *r* which was deleted, where appropriate, by a corresponding synchronic rule. But at a later stage it may be argued that such words no longer have an underlying *r*. Hence no rule deletes it; instead it is inserted when, as in words like *beery*, a vowel follows.
    Also called '**rule reversal**'. The change in the underlying form can also be seen as one case of *restructuring.

rule of referral G. T. Stump's term for a rule in morphology by which one form is derived as identical to another. E.g., in English, a rule by which regular participles in *-ed*, such as *opened* in *had opened* or *was opened*, might be derived, by an *identity operation, from forms of the past tense, such as *opened* in *They opened it*.

rule ordering *See* ordered rules. **Rule reordering** is a hypothetical pattern of language change in which the relative order of two or more rules, as posited in the *grammars internalized by one generation of speakers, changes in those posited for a later generation. E.g. rule *a* might at an earlier stage *bleed rule *b*; at a later, *a* might follow *b* instead. So, all else being equal, *b* would then apply more generally.

'rule reversal' = rule inversion.

rule schema Used in the 1960s of any expression in a *generative grammar that formally combined two or more rules under an *abbreviatory convention.

'rules of construal' *See* construe.

'rule to rule hypothesis' Principle by which each rule of syntax is paired with a corresponding rule of semantics. Introduced through *Montague Grammar in particular, and widely assumed in theories of semantics based on the notion of *compositional meaning.

Rumanian *Romance, spoken mainly in Romania and Moldavia. Attested in the *Cyrillic alphabet from the late 15th century; written in the Roman alphabet only since independence in the late 19th century. The standard language is based on that of the former principality of Wallachia, which included Bucharest.

Arumanian, spoken especially in parts of Albania and northern Greece, is one of three other forms of 'Rumanian', in a wide sense, collectively called 'Daco-Romance'.

Rundi *See* Rwanda-Rundi.

Runic alphabet Used for *Germanic languages, especially North Germanic, in what is now Sweden and elsewhere, from the 3rd to the 5th century AD until supplanted, with the spread of Latin Christianity from the early Middle Ages, by the Roman alphabet. Derived from one or other of the alphabets in use in the Mediterranean: whether Greek, Etruscan, or Roman has been long debated. Called '**futhark**' from the successive phonetic values of the first six letters.

Russian *Slavic, related within East Slavic to Ukrainian and Belorussian, from which it has diverged since the late 11th century AD. Written in *Cyrillic; the first language of more than half the population of the former Soviet Union and a second language for many more.

Rwanda-Rundi *Bantu: Rwanda, spoken mainly in the state of Rwanda, and Rundi, spoken mainly in Burundi, can alternatively be classed as different languages each to some degree intelligible to speakers of the other.

S

S 1. = sentence. **2.** = subject. **3.** The single *argument which forms the *valency of the verb in an intransitive construction, as opposed to the *agent (A) and *patient (P) in a transitive.

For S̄ or S′ *see* S-bar.

sagittal (Plane) dividing the body from front to back: often = mid-sagittal.

'salient' = prominent.

Salishan Family of languages, now extinct or moribund, in the north-west USA and British Columbia.

Sami *Finno-Ugric language spoken in northern Norway and adjacent parts of neighbouring countries. Traditionally called 'Lappish'.

Samoyedic Group of languages spoken mainly in Siberia, classed with *Finno-Ugric under Uralic. Only Nenets or Yurak, between the Mezen' and the Yenisei, has speakers in five figures.

Sanctius Latinized name of Francisco Sánchez de las Brozas (1523–1600), professor at Salamanca, whose theoretical work on Latin grammar, *Minerva: seu de causis linguae latinae*, appeared in its definitive form in 1587. In the context of the 16th century, it is remarkable for the space devoted to syntax: of its four books, the second and third deal with nominal and with verbal constructions respectively. For recent commentators, its interest has lain above all in the use of *ellipsis, with other *figures, in relating actual forms and constructions to expanded representations of their logical structure. Sanctius took this much further than earlier grammarians, and his work was an acknowledged source for similar procedures in the grammars of *Port Royal.

sandhi Ancient Indian term for the modification and fusion of sounds at or across the boundaries of grammatical units. E.g. short -*a* + *i*- fused in Sanskrit, both within vowels and across word boundaries, to -*e*-. Introduced into the terminology of 20th-century linguistics by Bloomfield especially.

Sango *See* Ubangi.

Sanskrit *Indo-Aryan language of ancient India, first attested, in the form called *Vedic, by religious chants transmitted orally but thought to date from the 2nd millennium BC. **Classical Sanskrit** is the form which became standard after the middle of the first millennium BC, by which time the spoken language was progressively evolving into vernacular forms (called **Prakrits**). Thereafter a learned language with a rich literature, written and spoken throughout India until the present.

Written in various scripts, now mainly in *Devanagari. The earliest inscriptions in the Indian subcontinent are from the second half of the 1st millennium BC. Western encounters with Sanskrit, from the latter part of the 18th century, were decisive in the recognition of *Indo-European and the development of the *comparative method.

Sapir, Edward (1884–1939) American linguist and anthropologist, trained by Boas and the leading authority in his lifetime on North American languages, many of which he studied directly, at levels ranging from the superficial to the detailed and profound. From 1910 to 1925 the chief ethnologist at the Geological Survey of Canada; subsequently professor at the University of Chicago and at Yale.

Language (1921) develops many ideas that are central to *structural linguistics, and was remarkable, in particular, both for its emphasis on the diversity of languages, for which Sapir drew extensively on his own studies in North America, and for a new and penetrating scheme of *typological classification. In later work he made important contributions to the theory of the phoneme and, though disregarded by his immediate successors, to the descriptive account of word meaning.

Often contrasted with Bloomfield as a *mentalist: i.e. with most others of their generation, he did not share Bloomfield's physicalist or mechanist psychology. A majority of the American linguists who became prominent in the late 1930s and 1940s are Sapir's pupils.

'Sapir–Whorf hypothesis' The notion, currently associated in the English-speaking world with work by the American scholar B. L. Whorf and programmatic statements by Sapir, that the semantic structure of the language which a person speaks either determines or limits the ways in which they are able to form conceptions of the world in which they live.

Also called the hypothesis of '**linguistic relativism**' or, in an extreme form, of '**linguistic determinism**'. The history of this and related ideas is in fact much longer, stretching back through Humboldt and his followers to the 18th century.

Sardinian *Romance language, distinct from Italian. Also called '**Sard**': the main dialect, in central Sardinia, is Logudorese.

satellite An element which belongs to the *periphery of a clause as opposed to its *nucleus. E.g. in *I can't come tomorrow* or *I can't come because I am busy*, a nucleus *I can't come* has as its satellite *tomorrow* or *because I am busy*.

'satəm language' An *Indo-European language belonging to any
branch in which a velar stop, attested in other branches, changed to a
sibilant fricative or affricate. From the word for 'hundred' in *Avestan,
in which this change has taken place: opp. '*centum* language', from the
cognate form in Latin, in which it has not.

Saussure, Ferdinand de (1857–1913) Swiss linguist whose *Cours de
linguistique générale* was published in 1916 after his death on the basis
of notes taken by students at successive courses of lectures. This work
has been much interpreted and reinterpreted, but its most important
single contribution, in the context of the early 20th century, was the
doctrine that the *synchronic study of a particular 'state' of a
language should be separate from, and seen as logically prior to, the
*diachronic study of changes from one state to another. This stands in
sharp contrast to ideas held generally at the end of the 19th century,
and was to become a defining feature of *structural linguistics,
common to all schools. But other ideas have also had a wide influence.
One is an analysis of the phenomenon of language in general (French
'langage') into an 'executive' side ('parole') concerned with the
production, transmission, and reception of speech, and an underlying
*language system ('langue'), seen as having objective reality in a
specific society. Though less accepted in English-speaking countries
(and rejected explicitly e.g. by Firth), this has been central to much
European structuralism, and can be linked with Chomsky's contrast,
in the 1960s, between *competence and *performance. Another basic
doctrine is that the language system ('langue') is no more than a
network of values or functions (French 'valeurs'), in which individual
units are constituted simply by the relations that they bear to other
units. This was to be the germ, in particular, of Hjelmslev's theory of
form and substance. A third idea, again less influential among English-
speaking linguists, is Saussure's concept of the *linguistic sign, formed
by an indissoluble link between a 'signifiant', or phonetic 'signifier',
and a 'signifié' or concept signified. Linguistics itself he then saw as
one branch of a larger science ('sémiologie' or *semiotics) concerned
with systems of signs in general.

'S-bar' (S̄, S′) Symbol introduced by Chomsky in the late 1970s as
an informal label for a clause including its *complementizer. Opp. 'S'
without bar, for a clause minus its complementizer: e.g. *I said*
$_{\bar{s}}[that$ $_{s}[I$ *would come*]].

    Later described more systematically as a phrase headed by the
complementizer.

SC *See* transformation.

scalar Forming, or forming one point on, a scale. E.g. *many* and *few*
are '**scalar expressions**', intermediate on a scale from *none* to *all*.
According to the theory of *maxims of conversation, the use of an
expression lower on such a scale carries the *implicature that, if any

higher expression were used, the proposition would be false: e.g. if one says *Few people came*, one implicates that both 'Many people came' and 'All the people came' are false. Such implicatures have accordingly been called '**scalar implicatures**'.

Likewise a **scalar feature** is a variable feature with at least one intermediate value. E.g. if close, mid, and open vowels were terms in a *gradual opposition, vowel height would be a scalar feature: say [close], with the values [1 close] (= open), [2 close] (= mid), [3 close] (= close).

Scale and Category Grammar *See* Systemic Grammar.

Scandinavian = North *Germanic; also of the languages of Scandinavia in general, including the *Finno-Ugric languages *Finnish and *Sami.

schema Term in psychology for a mental model by which specific experiences etc. are structured. Hence variously in linguistics: thus a child acquiring a language constructs 'schemata' relating to the construction of sentences; in e.g. buying and selling something people speak in accordance with a 'schema' of, or set of expectations regarding, such an interchange; and so on.

See also rule schema; image schema.

schizophasia Quasi-medical term covering rare disorders in the speech of some psychotic patients.

Schleicher, August (1821–68) Indo-Europeanist and theorist of language, whose *Compendium der vergleichenden Grammatik der indogermanischen Sprachen* (1st edn. 1861–2) played a central role, in the decade before the *Neogrammarians, in clarifying aspects of the *comparative method: in particular, the technique of reconstruction based on the postulate of sound laws, and the model of a family tree in which ancestor languages are related to their descendants. As a general linguist, Schleicher identified the method of linguistics with that of the natural sciences, and developed a general view of language as part of the natural history of our species into a specific model in which individual languages were compared to specific organisms, in which they compete with one another, and in which they have a life-cycle of birth, growth, and subsequent decay. This was developed particularly in his reaction to Darwin's *The Origin of Species* (1859), which itself referred to comparative linguistics as a model, and was allied to an interpretation of the typology of languages in which the *inflecting type represented a stage of perfection which resulted from a prehistoric period of growth, followed by a historical decay into the *analytic (1) type that developed in Europe and elsewhere from the classical and other earlier Indo-European languages.

In assessing these ideas one should perhaps note that when Schleicher died he was still in his forties.

scholasticism General term for the schools of philosophy in western Europe in the high Middle Ages. Important in the history of linguistics for the development of *speculative grammar, especially by Petrus Helias in the early 12th century, leading to the work of the *Modistae in the second half of the 13th.

Schuchardt, Hugo (1842–1927) In origin a Romance linguist, who also published extensively on Basque and on many other languages, including pidgins and creoles. In his general ideas, a radical critic of the *Neogrammarians (also of *Saussure), laying emphasis both on the individuality of speakers and on the continuity of usage, both within and across the boundaries of conventional dialects and languages; hence on the diversity of paths by which changes pass from one individual to another, and the existence, at all levels, of mixing of features from different historical sources. These ideas are most accessible in an anthology of his papers (*Hugo Schuchardt-Brevier*) edited in 1922 (by L. Spitzer) for his eightieth birthday.

schwa The mid-central vowel of e.g. the second syllable of *matter*: in phonetic notation [ə] ([matə]). Also spelled 'shwa'.

scope The part of a sentence with which a *quantifier (2), negative, etc. combines in meaning. E.g. in *I didn't say he visited Mary* the scope of -*n't* might be the main clause ('I didn't say it'). But in *I don't think he visited Mary* it might, in one interpretation, be the subordinate clause ('I think he didn't visit Mary').

The term originates in logic, and its use by linguists variously reflects the extent to which they start from language, or start from translations in language of expressions in some logical system.

Scots The variety or varieties of West Germanic spoken in Scotland, especially if presented as a language separate, or having been separate in the past, from English.

'scrambling' Syntactic process by which the order of words or phrases can optionally vary. Originally proposed in transformational grammar by linguists familiar with languages like English, in which their order is largely fixed, as a solution for ones in which it is predominantly free. Now more usual in treating alternative orders within a clause construction: e.g. within the basic 'verb-second' frame in Dutch or German.

scriptio continua Latin for 'continuous writing': i.e. letter by letter without regard, as normally e.g. in early manuscripts, to word boundaries.

S-curve A graph which rises steeply in the middle, but is flatter at the beginning and end. Claimed to be standard e. g. when the progress of *lexical diffusion is plotted vertically against a horizontal time scale. At first few words are affected; hence a flat beginning. Then it rises more and more steeply until, when roughly half the relevant words are affected, it again begins to flatten.

SD *See* transformation.

secondary (in syntax) *See* ranks (1).

secondary articulation (1) A subsidiary articulation of a speech sound accompanying its **primary articulation** elsewhere. The primary articulation is the one with a greater degree of *stricture.

Thus the *sh* of English *ship* or *shoe* is a fricative whose primary articulation is as a *palato-alveolar: in phonetic notation [ʃ]. But for many speakers it is accompanied by a secondary articulation of *labialization or lip rounding.

secondary articulation (2) *See* double articulation (1).

secondary cardinal vowels *See* cardinal vowels.

'secondary response' Bloomfield's term for a statement, especially an ill-informed statement, about language: e.g. 'Working-class children know only a few hundred words'. He then described as a '**tertiary response**' the typical reaction of someone who has made such a statement and is told that it is wrong.

'secondary speech community' A community defined by common use of a *second language (2): e.g. that of speakers of English as an international language.

secondary stress (ˌ) A distinguishable level of *stress on a syllable other than one which carries a *primary stress. E.g. *examination* has a secondary stress on the second syllable ([ɪɡˌzamɪˈneɪʃn]), while *characteristic*, also with five syllables and primary stress on the fourth, has a secondary stress on the first ([ˌkarəktəˈrɪstɪk]).

second-instance sentence Any utterance whose intonation or wording reflects its relationship to a sentence uttered previously: e.g. 'The ˋNEIGHbours left it', in response to, say, 'Someone has left a van in our entrance'.

second language 1. The second language that a person acquires. Thus especially of *bilinguals: e.g. a speaker of Welsh may have learned or begun to learn it, as a first language, before learning English, as a second language. **2.** A language which is not native to a community but has an established role, for certain purposes or at a certain social level, within it. Thus especially in collocations such as 'Teaching English as a Second Language' (TESL).

second-order nominal Lyons's term for a nominal expression which characteristically refers to events, processes, etc. as opposed to physical objects: e.g. *his birth, his decision to leave. Cf.* third-order nominal.

second person (2ND, 2) *See* person.

'Second Sound Shift' *See* German.

'secular linguistics' An approach to linguistics touted by those who practise it as distinct from and superior to that practised by other linguists, in being based on 'real data', on 'actual speech' recorded in social settings, on corpora, on quantitative analysis, etc. *Cf.* empirical linguistics.

segment Any element, at any level of representation, which is described as forming sequences with others. Thus *phonemes are in general segments; also *morphemes. Hence especially in the analysis of sound systems, where consonants and vowels are distinguished as the topic of **segmental phonology** from *suprasegmental tones or units of intonation.

Segmentation is likewise any process, in descriptive analysis or in speech processing, by which a form of representation at one level is divided into a succession of discrete units at another: e.g. one which splits a representation of continuous speech into successive phonemes.

segmental tier Defined in *Autosegmental Phonology as a *tier in phonological representation at which features are associated with single consonants and vowels. E.g. in the representation of *end* a feature of nasality might be associated only with a segment realized by *n*, and a feature 'plosive' only with one realized by *d*.

selection Bloomfield's term for the feature of a construction by which certain individual words or morphemes enter into it. E.g. the construction of *these apples* 'selects' a determiner and a noun, and a plural morpheme in *these* is 'selected' in agreement with one in *apples*.

Thence of 'selection' by rule etc. generally: *cf.* selectional restriction; *also* c-selection, s-selection.

selectional restriction **1.** A restriction on the choice of individual lexical units in construction with other lexical units. E.g. *breathe* will typically 'select' an animate subject (*The girl was still breathing*, *Fish breathe through gills*), not an abstract or an inanimate (*Theories must breathe*, *The table was breathing*). *Cf.* collocation. **2.** A restriction imposed on the potential referents of a phrase etc. related to it: e.g. *pregnant* will typically 'select' a subject referring to someone or some animal that is female.

Sense 1 is that of Chomsky in the 1950s. In the earliest generative grammars such restrictions were seen as subject to rules, called **'selectional rules'**.

selective listening Selective attention to an individual speaker, e.g. in a crowded room where many people are talking.

self-embedding The inclusion of a syntactic unit in another which is of the same class: e.g. one *that*-clause is part of another in *the news* [*that he had said* [*that he was coming*]]. Also specifically of *centre-embedding.

self-initiated ('repair') *See* repair.

'self-repair' *See* repair.

semanteme Adaptation to English of a French term ('sémantème') originally used of a linguistic sign with *lexical meaning, as opposed to a *morpheme ('morphème') with grammatical meaning.

semantic Having to do with *semantics, in whatever way that may be defined. E.g. a **semantic feature** is a *feature by which the meaning of a word is distinguished from that of others; a **semantic component** of a *generative grammar is a distinct set of **semantic rules** that assign representations of meaning to sentences; **semantic criteria** in linguistic analysis are criteria that make reference to meaning, seen as distinct from 'formal criteria', which do not; a **semantic definition**, e.g. of a word class, will refer to types of meaning that characterize it.

semantic change Usually of change in the meanings of words. Types include *extension or *widening of meaning and *restriction of meaning, *ameliorative and *pejorative changes; also *figurative changes which involve a *metaphor or some other of the traditional *figures of speech.

semantic determinative *See* determinative.

semantic extension *See* extension; widening of meaning.

semantic field A distinct part of the lexicon defined by some general term or concept. E.g. in English the semantic field of colour includes words such as *black* and *red* that distinguish colours, or are *hyponyms of the more general term *colour*.

A distinction can usefully be drawn between a **lexical field**, as part of the vocabulary of a specific language at a specific stage in its history, and a **conceptual field**, postulated either as a linguistic universal or established across a range of languages or stages in the history of a language. E.g. a conceptual field of kinship was represented in Latin by a lexical field which is different from any of those representing the same conceptual field in French or the other modern Romance languages.

semanticity The property of language by which words may be used to refer to specific entities in a speaker's physical environment. Distinguished as such in discussions of *design features.

semantic loan *See* loan.

semantic marker Any semantic *feature seen as systematic in a given language: e.g. in words like *man* vs. *boy*, *woman* vs. *girl*, *horse* vs. *foal*, a marker 'Adult' (or [+ Adult]) is systematically opposed to 'Non-adult' (or [– Adult]). In an account by J. J. Katz and J. A. Fodor in the early 1960s, features which were not seen as systematic were '**distinguishers**'.

semantic representation A representation of the meaning of a sentence; thus especially one seen as assigned to it by the rules of a *generative grammar, independently of any context in which it might be uttered. Hence a representation of 'sentence meaning' as opposed to *utterance meaning.

The *Logical Form of a sentence was originally defined in this way in Chomsky's work in the mid-1970s.

semantic restriction *See* restriction of meaning.

semantic role Usually of the roles of nouns etc. in relation to a verb: e.g. in *I can feel it in my chest* the semantic roles of *I*, *it*, and *in my chest* might (in one account) be those of *experiencer, *theme (3), and *locative. *Cf.* case role; theta role.

semantics The study of meaning. Seen by Bréal, in the late 19th century, as an emerging science (French 'sémantique') opposed to phonetics ('phonétique') as a science of sounds: similarly, for Bloomfield in the 1930s, it was a field covering both grammar, as one account of meaningful forms, and the *lexicon. Also seen more narrowly, in a tradition lasting into the 1960s, as the study of meaning in the lexicon alone, including changes in word meaning. Later, in accounts in which the study of distributions was divorced from that of meanings, opposed either to grammar in general; or, within grammar and especially within a *generative grammar from the 1960s onwards, to *syntax specifically. Of the uses current at the beginning of the 21st century, many restrict semantics to the study of meaning in abstraction from the contexts in which words and sentences are uttered: in opposition, therefore, to *pragmatics. Others include pragmatics as one of its branches. In others its scope is in practice very narrow: thus one handbook of 'contemporary semantic theory', in the mid-1990s, deals almost solely with problems in *formal semantics, even the meanings of lexical units being neglected.

'semantic triangle' Model of meaning in which a symbol and the thing it symbolizes are related indirectly via a thought or *concept. Thus, in the accompanying illustration, the word *horse* is related, on one side of a triangle, to the concept 'horse'; this in turn is related, on a second side, to the animal itself; the broken line which forms the third side shows the merely derivative relation between the animal and the word. The form of diagram was introduced by C. K. Ogden and I. A. Richards in the 1920s.

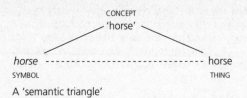

CONCEPT
'horse'

horse - horse
SYMBOL   THING

A 'semantic triangle'

semantic valency The *valency of verbs, or of verbs in particular, in terms of semantic roles or *case roles. Thus *eat* and *see* both take a subject and an object; in that sense they have the same **syntactic valency**. But in *I am eating it* the subject of *eat* is an *agent, while in *I can see it* that of *see* is an *experiencer. Therefore these verbs have different semantic valencies.

semasiology The study of vocabulary starting specifically from forms rather than meanings. Opp. onomasiology.

seme *See* sememe.

semelfactive (Verb, form of verb, etc.) used in reference to an event that happens just once: e.g. the past tense is semelfactive in *He fell over yesterday*, as compared with *was falling* in *He was always falling over*.

sememe Term used by various scholars for a basic unit of meaning. Thus for Bloomfield a sememe was the meaning of a morpheme: e.g. in *the fishes* the plural morpheme *-s* has as its meaning a sememe 'more than one'. Also in European versions of *componential analysis, where the meaning of a lexical unit is a sememe (French 'sémème' or its equivalent) composed of semantic features or **semes** (French 'sèmes').

semi-deponent Traditionally of a class of verbs in Latin whose forms were like those of passives in perfect tenses but like those of actives in others. Hence 'partly *deponent'.

semiology Saussure's term for a prospective science that would study 'the role of signs in social life'; often equivalent to *semiotics.

semiotics A general science of 'signs', of which, according to many scholars in the 20th century, linguistics is part. Thus words and morphemes are 'signs', specifically *linguistic signs. So are traffic lights, or gestures, or Christmas presents, or architectural features like a spire or pointed arch, or anything else that in the broadest sense 'has meaning'.

The notion is due especially to Peirce and Saussure. 'Semiotics' (originally 'semiotic') is the term in the Peircean tradition for what Saussure and the tradition following him call semiology (French 'sémiologie'). Hence Halliday's account in the 1970s of language as 'social semiotic'.

semi-productive (Process, formation) permitting new combinations of elements, but not with complete freedom. Used especially of processes of *word-formation: e.g. it is possible, in principle, to form new nouns like *authoress* from *author* or *deaconess* from *deacon*, but many potential forms, such as *writeress* or *minist(e)ress*, are not used and may not be immediately clear or acceptable.

Semitic Family of languages which includes *Arabic and several others of the Near East and Ethiopia, among them *Amharic, *Tigrinya, and *Hebrew. Others were important or more important in antiquity, especially *Akkadian, *Aramaic, and *Phoenician. Traditionally divided into three main branches: East Semitic (= Akkadian); West Semitic (including Arabic and Aramaic with Phoenician and Hebrew); South Semitic (including Amharic and others in Ethiopia and Eritrea; also ancient and some modern languages in south Arabia).

Seen as a branch of *Afro-Asiatic (formerly 'Hamito-Semitic').

Semitic alphabets Alphabets of a *consonantal type originally developed for *Phoenician and adopted in other *Semitic languages. Thus, among others, that of *Arabic, later adapted widely to non-Semitic languages, among them Persian and thence Urdu, with the spread of Islam.

The earliest alphabet for which we have evidence is that of *Ugaritic, which used *cuneiform characters. Others are divided into **South Semitic** forms, attested mainly in the Arabian peninsula from the early 1st millennium BC, and **North Semitic**, attested in Syria and Palestine from the later 2nd millennium BC. South Semitic is the source of the alphabets now used for *Amharic and other languages of Ethiopia; North Semitic for the remainder, and, from early in the 1st millennium BC, for the Greek alphabet and its Roman and other offshoots. The earliest form attested is that of Phoenician; a related branch, called Canaanite, is found e.g. in early Hebrew inscriptions and survives in the liturgical script of the Samaritans; all other Semitic alphabets, including that of Arabic, derive from the form developed for *Aramaic at the beginning of the 1st millennium BC.

semivowel A unit of sound which is phonetically like a *vowel but whose place in syllable structure is characteristically that of a consonant: e.g. [j] in [jɛs] (*yes*), phonetically a close front vowel, or [w] in [wiː] (*we*), phonetically a close back vowel. *Cf.* glide.

sense 1. A meaning of a lexical unit distinguished, e.g. in a dictionary, from other meanings. Thus *chair* has one sense when it is used to refer to a piece of furniture and another when used to refer to someone chairing a meeting. *Cf.* use for distinct meanings in grammar. **2.** The place of a lexical unit within the semantic system of a language: e.g. that of *chair* is defined by the relations that distinguish it from *furniture*, from *armchair*, from *table*, and so on. **3.** The meaning of an expression as distinct from its *reference. Thus, in a famous example of the philosopher G. Frege, *the morning star* and *the evening star* have the same referent (the planet Venus) but differ in sense.

sense relation Any relation between lexical units within the semantic system of a language; *cf.* sense (2). For types of sense relation *see* antonymy; complementarity; converse terms; hyponymy; incompatibility; meronymy; synonymy.

sensorimotor (Activity etc.) involving coordination of movement with input from the senses. Thus with reference to the lowest and earliest of Piaget's proposed stages of cognitive development.

sentence Usually conceived, explicitly or implicitly, as the largest unit of grammar, or the largest unit over which a rule of grammar can operate. E.g. in the sentence *Come here!* the order of *come* and *here* is subject to rule; but no rule governs a similar relation between it as a whole and any other sentence that might precede or follow it in speech.

Widely distinguished as a unit of the *language system. Thus *Come here!* is a sentence in English in the same sense that *come* is a word in English, and one aim of a grammar of English is to delimit a set of well-formed or *grammatical (2) combinations of words that includes it. Hence, in particular, a distinction between 'sentences' as abstract entities or constructs, whose status is as units defined by a grammar, and *utterances or parts of utterances that correspond to or are instances of them. E.g. in the utterance 'Come here! I love you', 'Come here!' and 'I love you' instantiate, in the speech of a specific person at a specific time, the sentences (conventionally represented in italics) *Come here!* and *I love you.*

Also in two extended senses. **1.** Of any unit structured like a sentence. E.g. in *He said he was coming* the clause *he was coming* is a smaller sentence ('subordinate sentence' or German 'Nebensatz') within a larger. **2.** Of analogous units in formal systems. Thus a *formal 'language' is in mathematical terms any set of *strings, and a 'sentence' is correspondingly any member of such a set. E.g. the 'language' {*ab, abc*} has as its members the 'sentences' *ab* and *abc.* *Cf.* generative grammar.

sentence adverb An adverb whose semantic relation is to a whole sentence or clause, not just to a verb or verb phrase within it: e.g. *obviously* in *Obviously, he didn't do it.* Also called a '**sentential adverb**'.

sentence fragment Usually of a sentence reduced by *ellipsis to an incomplete form: e.g. *My brother*, uttered in answer to a question such as 'Who sent it?'.

sentence grammar A grammar that takes the sentence as its largest unit: i.e. one of the usual kind, as opposed e.g. to a 'discourse grammar' or a 'text grammar' in *textlinguistics.

sentence meaning Usually of meanings ascribed to *sentences in the abstract, as opposed to those of *utterances. *Cf.* semantic representation.

sentence stress Any feature by which a syllable or sequence of syllables within a sentence is made more prominent than the rest. Thus there is a difference in sentence stress between *I left* HER *out*, with emphasis on *her*, and *I left her* OUT. Opp. word stress; *cf.* tonic.

'sentence topic' *See* topic.

'sentence type' Usually of statements, questions, etc. seen as distinguished by *declarative, *interrogative, and other constructions. Thus *He has gone* represents one sentence type, *Has he gone?* another.

sentence word Bloomfield's term for a word which in itself completes a major sentence construction: e.g. Spanish *salgo* 'I am going out' completes the construction of a subject with a predicate.

sentential Of, related to, or consisting of, sentences. **Sentential coordination** is *coordination of, or reduced from that of, sentences: *cf.* phrasal coordination. A **sentential relative clause** is one in which a relative pronoun relates to a predication rather than a noun phrase: e.g. *which was rather silly* in *I said yes, which was rather silly*. A **sentential complement** is a *complement consisting of a sentence or clause: e.g. *I was pleased* as the complement of *said* in *I said I was pleased*. A **sentential adverb** is a *sentence adverb, and so on.

sequence *See* order.

sequence of tenses Pattern in which the tense of the verb in a subordinate clause reflects that of a verb to which it is subordinated. E.g. in *He finished so he could be here tomorrow*, the auxiliary *could* reflects the past tense of *finished*; cf. *He is finishing so he can be here tomorrow*.

sequential bilingualism That of any individual who has acquired one language first and another later. Opp. simultaneous bilingualism.

Serbo-Croat South *Slavic; native, in forms now tending to be perceived as separate, to Bosnia, Croatia, Montenegro, and Serbia. Written since the Middle Ages in precisely matching *Roman and *Cyrillic alphabets, reflecting the division between the Roman Catholic and Greek Orthodox branches of Christianity.

serial construction Used e.g. by Bloomfield as an alternative term for *coordination.

serial verb construction One in which two or more successive verbs are joined together with no connecting particle, clitic, etc.: e.g. in English, that of *go* and *see* in *We'll go see*. Also called **verb serialization**; common or systematic in many languages, e.g. in East

Asia or West Africa, often with tense etc. marked in the first or last of the series only.

series Trubetzkoy's term for a set of consonants which have the same or a phonologically equivalent *place of articulation. E.g. a labial series in English comprises the bilabials [p], [b], and [m] and the labiodentals [f] and [v].

set expression See fixed expression.

setting *See* articulatory setting. Also of the 'setting', in a sense that is generally obvious, of an act of speech in time, in place, in society, etc.
   For setting of parameters see parameter (2).

sg = singular.

shallow structure Used at one stage in the history of *transformational grammars of a level of representation nearer to *surface structure than to *deep structure. Superseded in one of its forms by *S-structure.

'shared knowledge' = mutual knowledge.

sharp *Distinctive feature in the scheme proposed by Jakobson. Palatalized consonants, e.g. in Russian, are sharp: those which are not are non-sharp or *plain (1).

shifter Jakobson's term for words like *I, you,* and others whose interpretation involves *person deixis.

Shona *Bantu, spoken mainly in eastern Zimbabwe; promoted as a lingua franca in the region since the 1920s.

short *See* length. For 'short syllable' *see* heavy syllable.

short-term memory Effectively of the information that is kept in mind at any moment in ongoing psychological processes. Estimated, in the case of language, as a span of roughly seven words: hence, in particular, we have difficulty in understanding a stretch of speech whose structure is not clear within such a limit.

Shoshonean *See* Uto-Aztecan.

shwa = schwa.

Siamese = Thai.

Siberian languages Historically Uralic (*Finno-Ugric, *Samoyedic), *Turkic, *Tungusic (hypothetically grouped with Turkic under *Altaic), plus other groups and languages not genetically related but described collectively as **Palaeo-Siberian**. These include *Chukotko-Kamchatkan. Eskimo is also spoken, in a small area nearest Alaska; also Russian, which increasingly dominates the whole region.

sibilant Fricative characterized by turbulence that produces noise at a high pitch: e.g. [s] and [z] in *sin* and *zip*, or [ʃ] and [ʒ] in *ship* and *rouge* [ruːʒ].

sigma (σ) Usually the symbol for a *syllable.

sigmatic Formed with an *s*: e.g. in Ancient Greek a form such as *élusa* 'I let loose' is a 'sigmatic aorist' (*é-lu-s-a*). From the name for *s* in the Greek alphabet.

sign *See* linguistic sign; semiotics.

signifiant* vs. *signifié Saussure's terms, sometimes rendered into English as 'signifier' and '(the) signified', for the two sides of a *linguistic sign.

signing Communication in a *sign language.

sign language A system of human communication whose character is in general similar to that of a spoken language, except that it is realized through gestures and postures, of the hands, head, lips, etc., instead of sound. Thus the systems used in different societies by the deaf, such as British Sign Language (BSL) or American Sign Language (ASL or Ameslan).

   To be distinguished, as productive systems with their own rules and structures, from gestural transcriptions of languages in the ordinary sense, e.g. in semaphore, or limited systems of hand signals, as used e.g. in directing traffic.

'silent pause' A pause in speaking in which the speaker is silent, as opposed to a pause 'filled' by a *hesitation form.

similative (Compound) of the form ₙ[*x*] ₐ[*y*], with the general meaning 'y like/as (an) x': e.g. *snow-white, ice-cold*.

simple 1. (Clause, sentence) which does not include another: e.g. *I saw him*. Cf. *I saw he had left*, which is *complex; *I saw him but he left*, which is *compound. **2.** (Word) not derived from another or others by a process of *word-formation: e.g. *cook*. Cf. complex *cooker* and compound *cookhouse*.

simple clitic A *clitic whose position, before or after other syntactic elements, is the one that is normal for words with its syntactic role. E.g. in *What's that?*, the reduced form *-'s* is a simple clitic in the same position as the full form *is* in *What is that?* Opp. special clitic.

simple future An inflected or unmarked future as opposed especially to a *periphrastic future or a *marked *future perfect.

simplicity metric *See* evaluation procedure.

simultaneous bilingualism That of any individual who has acquired two languages as native at the same time. Opp. sequential bilingualism.

sincerity conditions One kind of *felicity condition that a *speech act has to meet if it is to be appropriate or successful. E.g. if A tells B that his lecture will be at 10.00 on Monday the sincerity condition is that A should believe that that is when the lecture will be. Distinguished especially from *preparatory conditions.

Sindhi *Indo-Aryan language, spoken in the Sindh province of Pakistan and an adjoining part of India. Written, like *Hindi-Urdu, in *Devanagari by Hindus but by Muslims in an Arabic script derived through Persian.

sine wave A simple wave form, whose shape is specified completely by its frequency and amplitude. Complex wave forms, as of vowels in speech, can be analysed, by the process of 'Fourier analysis', into combinations of two or more different sine waves.

single-base (transformation) = singulary transformation.

'single mother condition' Condition by which, in representations of constituency, a unit cannot belong to two larger units that overlap. E.g., for *I saw him leave*, this would exclude the possibility that, at a single level of representation, *him* can be both the object of *saw* within a larger constituent *I saw him*, and the subject of *leave* within a larger constituent *him leave*.

singular (SG) Term in the category of *number, at least one of whose roles is in referring to one individual as opposed to more than one. E.g. *cat* is singular as opposed to plural *cats*.

singularia tantum Latin 'singulars only': hence occasionally of nouns that only have a singular form.

singulary transformation Term in early *transformational grammar for a transformational rule which operated on a single sentence structure: e.g. one converting the structure of an active sentence into that of a passive. Opp *generalized transformation.

Sinhalese *Indo-Aryan, though influenced by neighbouring *Dravidian languages. Spoken by the majority population in Sri Lanka and an official language with Tamil and English. Attested by inscriptions from the 3rd century BC and by literature from the 9th century AD; the script is primarily from a north Indian form used especially in Buddhist texts.

Sinitic The Chinese branch of *Sino-Tibetan.

Sino-Tibetan Family of languages of which *Chinese and *Tibeto-Burman are two genetically and typologically distinct branches.

Siouan Family of languages in North America, mainly spoken or formerly spoken in the central plains, from southern Canada southwards to the lower Mississippi. Dakotan (or Sioux) forms a *dialect continuum in which e.g. Lakota is one member.

'sister' The relation in a tree diagram between two or more nodes that are connected directly to the same 'parent' node. Thus Dutch and German are sisters, or **sister languages**, within the 'family tree' of Germanic or Indo-European; noun phrase (NP) and verb phrase (VP) are sisters, in the earliest account, in *phrase structure trees.

sister-adjunction Any operation on a *phrase structure tree by which an added element becomes the *sister of an existing unit. E.g. if *horse* has the structure $_N[horse]$, the addition of plural -*s* by sister-adjunction would yield the structure $_N[horse + s]$, where *horse* and -*s* are sisters within N. *Cf.* Chomsky-adjunction.

situation 1. Whatever a clause or sentence is said to be about: thus an event, as described by e.g. *The roof is collapsing*; a state, as described by *She is fast asleep*; an achievement or accomplishment, as described by *I have finished the ironing*; and whatever other types it may be helpful to distinguish. **2.** *See* context of situation.

Situation Semantics Account of meaning developed by J. Barwise and J. Perry in the early 1980s, in terms of the relation between utterances and 'situations' seen as relevant abstractions from states of the world obtaining when they are uttered. An early reaction to *model-theoretic semantics as developed especially in *Montague Grammar.

size-levels = ranks (2); *see* Tagmemics.

skeletal tier A *tier in *Autosegmental Phonology specifying no more than a sequence of structural positions. These are usually the positions of consonants and vowels: hence also '**CV tier**'.
  Features specified on other tiers are linked by *association lines to different parts of this 'skeleton'. By analogy with music, the skeletal tier gives the 'timing'; the *segmental tier, in particular, the specific units that are 'played'. Hence such specific units, again of the segmental tier in particular, are called 'melody' or 'melodic' units.

slack voice Type of *phonation in which the vocal cords vibrate more slowly, with a slightly higher flow of air, than in normal or modal voice. *Cf.* stiff voice.

'slang' Used especially of vocabulary specific e.g. to a particular generation of younger speakers; also, as in ordinary usage, specific to a group or profession (e.g. 'army slang'), to colloquial style, etc.

slant line (/) *See* slash.

slash (/) Used: **1.** To mark a condition under which a rule or operation applies. Thus a rule in phonology 's → z / V—V' means 's is changed to z when it is between vowels'. **2.** Especially in the mid-20th century, to distinguish a representation of phonemes from a phonetic transcription: e.g. English [çuː] (*hue* or *Hugh*) seen as phonemically /hjuː/ or /hjuw/. **3.** As in ordinary usage, in representing alternatives. E.g. *He saw him/himself* conflates the alternatives *He saw him* and *He saw himself*; *I saw him/*himself* conflates *I saw him* (grammatical) and **I saw himself* (ungrammatical).

'slash category' Category assigned in *Generalized Phrase Structure Grammar to a unit seen as including a smaller unit that is null or empty. Named from the original notation: e.g. VP/NP was the category assigned to a verb phrase (VP), such as that of the interrogative *Which will she choose?*, seen as including an empty noun phrase: ᵥₚ[ᵥ[*choose* ₙₚ[   ]]].

Slavic Branch of *Indo-European spoken from across Central Europe eastwards. Divided into three branches: East Slavic, including *Russian and *Ukrainian; West Slavic, including *Polish, *Czech, *Slovak, and *Sorbian; South Slavic, including *Bulgarian, *Macedonian, *Serbo-Croat, and *Slovenian. Closer within Indo-European to Baltic than to other branches: hence *Balto-Slavic.

Slavonic = Slavic.

slip of the tongue Any accidental error in speech: e.g. *chapel harlot* for *apple charlotte*, or *Greek statue* for *Greek statute*. Distinguished as accidental from errors attributable to a speech disorder, or to inadequate command of a language.

slit fricative One in which air flows through a wide slit rather than a narrow channel: e.g. the non-sibilant [θ] in *thin* or [ç] in German [milç] *Milch* 'milk' as opposed to the *sibilants [s] in *sin* or [ʃ] in German [fiʃ] *Fisch* 'fish'. Opp. rill fricative, groove fricative.

sloppy identity Relation in which elements understood in an elliptical construction are not precisely the same, in form or in reference, as those from which they are recovered: e.g. in *I grow my own vegetables and John does too*, between an understood *his own vegetables* and preceding *my own vegetables*.

slot A position or role within a construction or other similar structure. E.g. *it* fills the subject slot in *It blossomed*, *the* the determiner slot in *the girls*.

Slovak West *Slavic, closely related to Czech, though they are not mutually intelligible in all forms. Official in the Slovak Republic.

Slovenian South *Slavic, spoken mainly as the national language in Slovenia.

'sluicing' Term proposed for a syntactic process deleting all but a questioned element in a dependent interrogative: e.g. in *I don't know who*: i.e. *who <she saw>*, *who <is meeting us>*, and so on.

small capitals Used especially for three purposes: **1.** To mark a *tonic or nuclear syllable: e.g. *chea-* in *You* CHEA*ted!*. **2.** To distinguish *lexemes from word forms: e.g. SING is the lexical unit '(to) sing' as distinct from the specific forms *sing* or *sang*. **3.** In abbreviations for specific grammatical categories: e.g. ABL for *ablative.

small clause An object plus an *object complement, if treated as a *reduced clause: e.g. *it excellent* in *I found it excellent*. Also of other reduced clauses.

social (meaning, *function of language) *See* interpersonal.

social context *See* context.

'social deixis' The use of forms which reflect the social status of a speaker in relation either to the addressee or to someone else referred to: *cf.* familiar form; polite form; honorific. Seen by some as falling under an extended concept of *deixis.

social dialect Form of speech associated with a social class or similar group within a society, as opposed to a dialect in the ordinary sense, associated with a geographical place or region.

social encoding *Encoding (1) of distinctions e.g. of status in a society.

social marker Any feature of a person's speech seen as reflecting their status in a society: e.g. in British English, the use of *Mummy* or *Granny* as opposed to *Mum* or *Gran*, or an [ɑː] in words such as *grass* as opposed to a vowel which is shorter and fronter. Called a *marker because such features are seen as potentially indicating social status to an addressee.

A social network

social network A representation of the extent of contact among some set of individuals. Thus, in the illustration, A is shown by a thicker line as in extensive contact with both B and C; also, by a thinner line, as having a lesser degree of contact with D and E. A network is **dense** to the extent that every individual is related to every other: thus, in the illustration, the part linking A, B, C, and D. Contact between individuals is **uniplex** if it is in only one kind of situation: e.g. they might talk to each other only at and in connection with their work. It is **multiplex** if the range of situations is wider: e.g. they also chat at work, they have a drink afterwards, they and their families see each other in the evenings and at weekends. Hence the barbarism 'plexity'.

sociative (case) = comitative.

Société de Linguistique de Paris The senior linguistic society in France, founded formally in 1866; usually referred to simply as the 'Société de Linguistique'. Its annual *Bulletin* has been published since 1869.

socio- In the general sense of 'social': e.g. **sociolect** = social dialect. Also to identify fields of study seen as part of or connected with *sociolinguistics: thus '**sociohistorical**', '**sociophonetics**', etc.

'sociolinguistic interview' The format, in particular, devised by Labov for the study of variation in the speech of individual subjects. Five 'styles' of speech were distinguished, ranging from very formal to very casual, and methods designed to elicit as wide a variation as possible. These included, at one extreme, the reading aloud of word-lists. At the other extreme, subjects would be asked e.g. if they had ever been in danger of death, in the hope that the emotions this aroused would counter or reduce the effect of what Labov called the *observer's paradox.

sociolinguistics Any study of language in relation to society. Originally, from the late 1960s, of studies of variation in language by Labov and his followers. In that sense, sociolinguistics involves the study of correlations between linguistic variables (e.g. the precise phonetic quality of a vowel, or the presence or absence of a certain element in a construction) and non-linguistic variables such as the social class of speakers, their age, sex, etc. Applied more widely, from the end of the 1970s, to any study of language informed by that of societies in general: hence of a range of loosely connected investigations, including forms of *Discourse Analysis and *Conversation Analysis, the identification in a language of distinctions reflecting ideologies or relations of power among those speaking it, linguistic aspects of social psychology, etc.

sociolinguistic variable Any variable investigated by sociolinguists in the tradition of Labov. Thus, in studying [r] after vowels in speakers of English whose usage is not consistent, one might establish a variable, conventionally labelled (r), whose values are + r ([r] present) and − r (no [r]). The incidence of these may then be related to other variables, linguistic or social.

Distinguished by Labov as variously 'stereotypes', defined as subject to comment by speakers and to correction and *hypercorrection; 'markers', defined as varying both with the social class of speakers and with the 'style' in which they were speaking; and 'indicators', defined as varying, as in cases of *change 'from below', with their social class alone.

'soft' Used conventionally for voiced consonants in Welsh (hence 'soft' *mutation), for palatalized reflexes of former velars e.g. in Italian ('soft *g*' [dʒ] vs. 'hard *g*' [g]), for phonologically palatalized consonants such as [tʲ] (ть) in e.g. Russian, and so on.

soft palate The back part of the roof of the mouth, which is soft or fleshy in comparison with the bony or hard palate to the front. Also called the **velum**.

solecism Ancient term for an error in syntax arising from a mismatch between words. E.g. *those page* would be a solecism since plural *those* does not match, or is not 'congruent' with, singular *page*. Opposed in ancient accounts to *barbarism.
  The extension to errors other than of language is modern.

solidarity Hjelmslev's term for a relation in which each term presupposes the other. Thus e.g. the levels of *content and *expression are 'solidary': there cannot be an expression without something that is expressed and there cannot be content that is not that of an expression.
  Also in an ordinary sense: thus feelings of solidarity among speakers are one factor affecting e.g. *forms of address.

solidus (/) *See* slash. 'Solidus' is the traditional term in printing.

Somali *Cushitic, spoken in Somalia, in Djibouti, and in neighbouring parts of Kenya and Ethiopia. The official language of Somalia, written in the Roman alphabet.

Sonagraph Trade name of the earliest sound spectrograph. Hence '**sonagram**' for the displays it produced.

sonant Indo-Europeanists' term for a set of phonological elements, whose reflexes are predominantly *resonants, seen as forming either the nucleus or the margin of a syllable. Thus in reconstructed *nōmn̥ 'name' (> Latin *nomen*), a sonant *n is marginal in the first syllable (nō-) but nuclear or syllabic in the second (in the conventional notation, -mn̥).

Sonoran *See* Uto-Aztecan.

sonorant A speech sound in which air flows smoothly through the vocal tract, without audible turbulence. *Cf*. resonant: both terms are used variously, by different writers, either of vowels and of consonants which meet this definition, or of consonants only. *See also* approximant; opp. obstruent.
  The feature [+ sonorant] was defined by Chomsky and Halle, *SPE* as that of a sound 'produced with a vocal tract configuration in which spontaneous voicing is possible'.

sonority The inherent loudness of a sound. E.g. if pitch, stress, and length are equal, the vowel of *barn* is more sonorous than that of *bean*, and either is more sonorous than the *n* and the *b*. In phonetic accounts of the syllable, the *nucleus (2) (e.g. [ɑː] in *barn*) is represented as a peak of sonority.

Sorbian West *Slavic language, spoken in Germany in the region of Cottbus and Bautzen, towards Poland and the Czech Republic. Also called **Wendish**.

sortal Reflecting or indicating a sort or kind of entity. Thus a system of noun classes might be described as sortal if, e.g. words for animals are in one class, words for plants in another, words for hard inanimate objects in a third, and so on.

Sotho *Bantu; the name is usually applied both to Northern Sotho, in the south and centre of the Transvaal in South Africa, and to Southern Sotho, which has official status in Lesotho.

sound law A phonological *change claimed or assumed to have taken place in all forms that met the relevant conditions: *Grimm's Law is an archetypal example. A term from the 19th century, linked to the programme of the *Neogrammarians.

sound symbolism The use of specific sounds or features of sounds in a partly systematic relation to meanings or categories of meaning. Generally taken to include: **1.** The use of forms traditionally called *onomatopoeic: e.g. *chiffchaff* (warbler whose song alternates a higher and a lower note). **2.** Partial resemblances in form among words whose meanings are similar: e.g. among *slip, slide*, or *slither,* all with initial [sl]. In the second case the correspondence may be partly explicable by the nature of the sounds and meanings involved: e.g. the least sonorous vowel, [i], is often associated, in the vocabulary and in the minds of speakers, with concepts of smallness. But in other cases it is a feature simply of a specific language.

sound system *See* phonological system.

source *Case role of e.g. *the room* in *I left the room* or *from Sydney* in *I hitchhiked from Sydney to Canberra*.

'source feature' Used by Chomsky and Halle, *SPE*, of phonetic features of *voice, *stridency, and *heightened subglottal pressure. The classification of features into source features, *major class features, etc. was said at the time to have 'little theoretical basis'.

source language One from which a translation is made. E.g. if a poem is translated from German into English, German is the source language and English the 'target language'.

Alternatively of the language from which a loan word is borrowed: opp. host language. Thence also in the sense of 'lexifier' or *base language.

South American languages The indigenous languages of effectively three main regions. Those surviving in the south of the continent (roughly present-day Chile and Argentina) belong to a few small families: Araucanian, in south-central Chile and a neighbouring part of Argentina, has the largest number of speakers. Those of the central Andes (roughly from southern Colombia to south of Bolivia) include *Quechua(n), spread originally under the Incas, and *Aymará. Those of the rest of the continent are genetically very diverse, some belonging to small families, others to larger ones distributed at intervals over wide areas. The most important south of the Amazon is *Tupi-Guaraní, of which *Guaraní is, with Spanish, an official language of Paraguay. Gê, or a hypothetical enlargement 'Macro-Gê', is another in the central area of Brazil. To the north and west the most important groupings are Panoan, in the headwaters of the Amazon, *Tucano(an), *Arawak(an), *Carib(an), and *Chibchan; the last group extends into the neighbouring part of Central America.

South Asian languages The languages of the Indian subcontinent: *see* Indian languages.

South Caucasian *See* Kartvelian.

South-east Asian languages Variously classed as *Mon-Khmer, which includes *Khmer (Cambodian) and *Vietnamese; *Tai, which includes *Thai and *Lao; *Tibeto-Burman, which includes *Burmese; also, among the many smaller languages, some belonging to *Austronesian, *Kadai (grouped with Tai as Tai-Kadai), and *Miao-Yao (= Hmong-Mien). The geopolitical area is part of a wider *Sprachbund, from the eastern Himalayas across to southern China, which includes other related languages.

SOV language One in which a *subject (3), *object (3), and verb are at least basically or most commonly in that order. E.g., in the usual account, Latin: thus *Caesar* (S) *bellum* (O) *gessit* (V) 'Caesar waged war'. Opp. SVO language, VSO language, etc.

Spanish *Romance, the official language of Spain and of several countries in Central and South America, from Mexico to Chile and Argentina, that were once part of the Spanish empire. There are also some millions of native speakers in the USA.

Originally the dialect of Castile in north Spain, and a literary language, in poetry and prose, from the Middle Ages; carried southwards as the Moors were progressively driven from the peninsula, and overseas, by missionaries and colonists, after the European discovery of America. The term '**Castilian**' is now used of European Spanish, as opposed to Latin American; also, within Spain, to *Catalan or *Galician.

spatial Indicating or involving location in space. Thus *here* and *there* are opposed in a system of **spatial** *deixis; *under* is a spatial (= locative) preposition in *under the table*.

SPE = *The Sound Pattern of English*, by Chomsky and Halle (1968). The classic account of *Generative Phonology; also the source for one widely disseminated taxonomy of phonetic features.

speaker recognition The recognition of the voice of an individual speaker, either by other people or automatically by a machine.

Spec *See* Specifier.

special clitic One whose position in a sequence of elements is peculiar to it, or to it and to other clitics, and is not that which might be expected from its role in the construction. Thus especially one which appears in second position following *Wackernagel's Law.

Opp. simple clitic. But the possibilities are more complex than this dichotomy implies.

specialization **1.** Narrowing e.g. of word meaning; *cf.* restriction of meaning. **2.** Proposed *design feature of language: speech is 'specialized' in that there is no natural connection between its physical character and its consequences in the behaviour of speakers.

Specified Subject Condition A precursor, in the 1970s, of Chomsky's proposed constraints on *bound (2) elements in *Government and Binding Theory.

Specifier (Spec) The position in *X-bar syntax of a unit that forms an XP with an X´. E.g. that of *large* as, in one analysis, an immediate constituent of a *noun phrase $_{NP}[large _{N'}[houses]]$.

'[Spec, XP]' stands for 'Specifier of an XP'. E.g. a subject is initially in the position [Spec, VP] according to the *VP-Internal Subject Hypothesis.

spectrogram A display of acoustic energy across a range of frequencies. In the form most helpful for the study of speech, changes in the distribution of energy over time are shown on the horizontal dimension; frequency (typically from 1 to 4,000 Hz or cycles per second) on the vertical; and levels of energy, above a set threshold, by a trace that intensifies as they increase.

speculative grammar Style of philosophical grammar in the Middle Ages, in which the structure of language, seen as in essence universal, is explained as mirroring that of reality. 'Speculative' is from Latin *speculum* 'mirror'.

speech act An utterance conceived as an act by which the speaker does something. Originally of *performatives: e.g. by saying 'I name this ship the Queen Elizabeth' a speaker will, in the appropriate

circumstances, perform the act of naming it. Thence of utterances
generally. E.g. in saying 'I will be there tomorrow' one makes a
promise or a prediction: i.e. one performs an act of promising or
predicting. If one says 'Stephen is my brother' the act is that of making
a statement, if 'Is Stephen your brother?' that of asking a question, and
so on.

A theory of speech acts was developed by J. R. Searle at the end of the
1960s, on the basis of work by Austin. It included, among other things,
a division of such acts into *representatives, *directives,
*commissives, *expressives, and *declarations.

speech community Any group of people whose language or use of
language can be taken as a coherent object of study. Speakers of
English in general might be treated as such a community; also e.g.
speakers of a distinct variety that one might call 'Birmingham
English', spoken or usually spoken by part of the population of
Birmingham. So might any other population that meets some test
of coherence, whether large or small, bilingual or monolingual, in
a single place or scattered.

speech error An accidental error in speech: *cf.* slip of the tongue.

speech event Any instance of speech, whether a single utterance,
a conversation, etc. Hence distinctions among types of such events,
according to the people participating in them, the circumstances in
which they take place, etc. *Cf.* speech act.

speech island A small speech community occupying an area
surrounded by speakers of another language.

speech processing General term covering processes posited in the
minds of both speakers (in **speech production**) and hearers (in **speech
recognition**). Thence of superficially equivalent processing by
computers.

speech synthesis Any artificial simulation of speech, e.g. as a
research tool in controlling stimuli for phonetic or psychological
experiments, or in practical applications.

spelling pronunciation A pronunciation of a word which is derived
from or influenced by its spelling. E.g. earlier ['fɒrɪd] *forehead* has been
widely supplanted by the spelling pronunciation ['fɔːhɛd].

'spell out' To supply a *realization: e.g. a specific rule for English
might spell out a plural morpheme in its regular basic form (*-(e)s*).

Hence, in Chomsky's *minimalist programme, a stage in the
derivation of a sentence at which properties that bear only on
Phonetic Form are subject to processes of computation separate from
those that bear on Logical Form.

spirant An older term for a *fricative. **Spirantization** is a historical
process by which a stop consonant becomes a fricative.

split Change by which two distinct units, constructions, etc. develop from what was formerly one. Especially in phonology: e.g. Italian [k] and [tʃ] (in *amico* 'friend' vs. *amici* 'friends') are distinct phonemes which have derived by a split, in Late Latin, from what had been a single phoneme [k] (written *c*). Opp. merger.

split antecedent Two or more units which together supply the antecedent of a single *anaphoric element: e.g. *Roger* and *his wife* as the antecedent(s) of *they* in *Roger told his wife they* (Roger and his wife) *were broke.*

split ergative (Language) in which agents and patients are sometimes distinguished as in an *ergative and sometimes as in an *accusative language. E.g. the 'ergative' pattern is found only when the verb is past or perfect, or the 'accusative' only when the agent and patient are pronouns.

split infinitive A form in English in which *to* and an uninflected verb, together seen as constituting an *infinitive, are separated by e.g. an adverb. Thus *to* and *rid* are 'split' by *systematically* in *to systematically rid this town of layabouts.* Traditionally proscribed under this name.

split intransitive The pattern exemplified in an *active language, in which the single argument or valent of an *intransitive construction is identified under certain conditions with the agent in a transitive construction and under other conditions with the patient.

'split morphology hypothesis' The view, held widely but challenged e.g. within *Lexical Morphology, that inflectional and derivational morphology are in principle separate.

'spontaneous' (Sound change) not explained by the phonetic context or the position in a word in which it takes place: e.g. the merger, in Southern British forms of English, of the vowel of *moor* and *poor* with that of *more* and *pour*. Also described as '**unconditioned**'; but there is no implication, at least in current theories, that such changes may not be explained, or seen as 'conditioned', by other factors.

spoonerism Slip of the tongue in which parts of successive words are interchanged. Classic examples make sense in their turn: e.g. 'our dear old queen' transposed to 'our queer old dean'.

sporadic (Sound change) attested in some forms but not in others: hence an exception, at first sight if no more, to the *Neogrammarian 'Regularity Principle'.

Sprachbund A group of languages, often of different historical origin, which are spoken in the same part of the world and have developed similar structures. Classic examples include the *Balkan languages and those of the Indian subcontinent; those of South-east

Asia or of the Meso-American group of *Central American languages
are other striking instances involving members of several different
families.

The area where such a group of languages is spoken is a **linguistic
area**; the historical process by which they develop similar structures is
that of *convergence (1).

Sprachgefühl A linguist's intuitive feel for a language; *cf.* intuition.

spread (Lips) distended as in a smile: e.g. in the articulation of [i] in
Italian (*dico* or *Dino*). Opp. rounded.

spreading The extension of a phonetic feature intrinsic to one
element to other adjacent elements. Thus in a word like *maim* the
feature 'nasal', intrinsic to the consonants, spreads to the intervening
vowel.

square brackets [ ] Mainly used: **1.** To enclose phonetic
transcriptions: e.g. *fish* is phonetically [fɪʃ]. **2.** To enclose syntactic or
other *constituents: e.g. *went into the garden* can be analysed into the
constituents [*went* [*into* [*the garden*]]]. *Cf.* labelled bracketing. **3.** In
representing phonological or other *features. Thus the vowel in *scream*
has the feature [Front] or [+ Front], among others.

squish J. R. Ross's term for an instance of *gradience.

Sranan English-based creole spoken widely, as a native or second
language, in Suriname and, through emigration, in the Netherlands.

s-selection Chomsky's term in the 1980s for *valency or *argument
structure seen as determined by the meaning of an individual word.
Opp. c-selection.

S-structure The least abstract level of syntactic structure in
*Government and Binding Theory. Derived by successive modifications
from the notion of *surface structure in transformational grammars
of the 1960s and 1970s; effectively jettisoned, with a similar relic of
*deep structure, in Chomsky's *minimalist programme in the 1990s.

stacking Pattern in syntax in which a *head (1) has two or more
dependents standing in a similar relation to it, but at separate levels in
a hierarchy of constituents. E.g. in *a large black dog*, both *large* and *black*
are modifiers of *dog*; but in many accounts *black*, as the nearest, forms
a unit directly with it, which in turn combines as a whole with *large*:
[*a* [*large* [*black dog*]]]. In *the man you saw who kissed me who was here
yesterday*, the relative clauses might be likewise seen as stacked in
their relation to *man*.

Cf. layering. *See also* case stacking.

Stammbaum model The model adopted especially by *Schleicher
in the mid-19th century, in which historical relations among

languages are seen as like those between generations in a family tree (German 'Stammbaum'). Thus *Indo-European is represented as a parent language from which e.g. *Italic developed as one independent daughter language. Latin in turn is one independent daughter of Italic, and the *Romance languages independent daughters of Latin. Contrasted later in the century with the *wave model.

standard (Form, variety) which is learned and accepted as correct across a community or set of communities in which others are also used: e.g. Standard English, as used especially in writing, vs. regional dialects, creoles based on English, etc.

    Standardization is the process, often in part at least deliberate, by which standard forms of a language are established; also of an 'ideology' seen as underlying it. Forms and varieties which are not standard are simply 'non-standard'.

'Standard Average European' B. L. Whorf's term for a group of European languages including English, German, and French, distinguished by a set of common categories of time, space, etc. from many others. An aspect, in effect, of a European *Sprachbund*.

'Standard Theory' Used in the 1970s to distinguish the theory of transformational grammar that Chomsky had proposed in the mid-1960s. Also called the '*Aspects*-theory' or '*Aspects*-model', from Chomsky's *Aspects of the Theory of Syntax* (1965).

    Hence the *Extended Standard Theory and *Revised Extended Standard Theory, seen as remedying in particular the account it had given of the relation between syntax and semantics.

starred form *See* asterisk.

starred tone A tone established, in accounts of intonation current since the 1990s, as the one associated with the most prominent syllable in an *intonational phrase. Symbolized by an asterisk: H* if high, L* if low. Other tones may form a unit with it, e.g. L*H, where an H is in a position described as '**trailing**', or LH*, where that of the L is '**leading**'.

    A phrase in MAN*chester maybe*, where the syllable *Man-* is prominent, might have an intonation represented in part by a starred H* followed by a trailing L, realized over *Manches-*. The intonational unit as a whole would then be completed by initial and final *boundary tones, e.g. both low.

statal = stative. Thus *(was) flattened* is a 'statal passive' if it simply describes the flattened state an object is in, as opposed to a 'dynamic passive' which refers to the action of flattening.

statement *See* declarative.

static tone = register tone: opp. dynamic tone, contour tone.

'statistical universal' = relative universal, but with the added assumption or implication that languages form a population of individuals that can be studied by statistical methods.

stative Referring to a persisting state or situation. E.g. *stand* and *sleep* are stative verbs; *(is) destroyed* is stative if it means 'in the state of having been destroyed'. Opp. dynamic; eventive.

status planning *See* language planning.

stem A form from which a word or series of words is derived by the addition of one or more *affixes. Especially one which is common to all the words that make up a definable part of a paradigm: e.g. French *chanter-* is a 'future stem' or 'stem of' the future, in that it is common to all the forms of the verb that are of this tense (*chanter-ai* '(I) will sing', *chanter-as* '(you) will sing', etc.).

stem compound A *compound formed from elements that are not complete word forms: e.g. Latin *signifer* 'standard bearer', from *sign(i)-* (nominative *signum* 'sign, standard') and *fer-* (cf. *fer-t* 'carries').

stem vowel A vowel which is *thematic (2).

'stereotype' (in Labov's sense) *See* sociolinguistic variable.

stereotype semantics Model of word meanings in which each includes a stereotype of whatever a word denotes. *Cf.* prototype theory.

stiff voice Type of *phonation in which the vocal cords are held more stiffly, with a slightly lower flow of air, than in normal or modal voice. *Cf.* slack voice.

stigmatized (Form etc.) seen as objectionable by some or all members of a speech community. E.g. *ain't*, though widely used, is stigmatized in American English.

stimulus–response model Model of communication in which a stimulus (S) acting on a speaker gives rise to speech as a linguistic response (r); this in turn acts as a linguistic stimulus (s) which in turn gives rise to a response (R), e.g. a visible action, in a hearer. Thus, schematically, $S \rightarrow r \ldots s \rightarrow R$.

   Introduced into linguistics by Bloomfield in the 1920s, on the basis of current theories of *behaviourism, and the foundation for his account of meaning.

'stock' Used by some historical linguists variously of a *family or of a hypothetical grouping of two or more established families into a larger family. In the latter sense sometimes equivalent to and sometimes seen as smaller than a *phylum.

Stoics School of philosophers, founded in Athens *c*.300 BC. The early Stoics divided philosophy into three parts, of which a 'logical' part was in turn divided into the study of the meanings of expressions (what is 'said' or 'signified') and that of the expressions themselves (that which 'signifies'). The work of Chrysippus (280–207 BC) and his pupil Diogenes of Babylon (c.240–152 BC) is particularly important in the development of the system of *parts of speech; also of case, tense, and other semantic categories.

The writings of the early Stoics have not survived, but their ideas are known, in part fragmentarily, from later sources.

stop Consonant in whose articulation a flow of air is temporarily blocked: e.g. [p] and [t] in *pit*. Usually of consonants, such as these, in which the flow is blocked through both the mouth and the nose; but some definitions include those in which it is blocked through the mouth only: thus *nasals such as [m] and [n] in *man*.

stranded (Syntactic unit) left in place when ones accompanying it are seen as having moved or as deleted. E.g. *to* would be stranded, following ellipsis of a verb and possibly other units, in *I don't want to*.

Thus especially through *preposition stranding.

Stratal Uniqueness Law *See* term.

'strategy' Informally in various contexts of a broad way of achieving an end. To use an interrogative as a request ('Can you help me?', 'Could they possibly be kept on the leash?') might thus be said to be one strategy for influencing the actions of an addressee, or one strategy for politeness; a model of language processing will adopt a strategy for e.g. parsing; and so on.

Stratificational Grammar Model of grammar developed by S. M. Lamb from the early 1960s. Forms were represented at each of a series of levels, called '**strata**', of which the lowest dealt with phonetics and the highest with meaning. Each stratum was characterized by one basic unit: e.g. at one level, the phoneme. This was composed of minimal elements labelled by a term in '-on': e.g. 'phonons' were distinctive features of phonemes. Each stratum specified the ways in which its basic unit could be arranged: this constituted a '-tactics', e.g. phonotactics. Finally, each was connected to the next higher or next lower stratum by a relation of realization: e.g. phonemes realized 'morphons', which were the minimal elements of a higher stratum whose basic unit was the morpheme.

Interest in the model had dwindled by the mid-1970s.

stratum A level of *representation, generally (as in *Stratificational Grammar) or within a specific structure. Thus in *Relational Grammar a sentence such as *Mary was seen by Bill* has a structure that distinguishes two strata, one in which *Mary* and *Bill* have the roles they have in the corresponding active, and another in which they have undergone respective *promotion and demotion, to their roles in the passive.

'strength' Used in phonology of any scale or hierarchy in which units are distinguished as stronger or weaker with respect to some phonetic property or properties. Thus stop consonants may be seen as stronger, with respect to the degree of *stricture, than fricatives; voiceless as stronger than voiced; and so on. *Fortition (or strengthening) and *lenition (or weakening) can be defined as processes by which units at one point on such a scale are replaced by others either higher or lower.

stress Phonological feature by which a syllable is heard as more prominent than others. E.g. in *below* the second syllable is stressed [bɪˈləʊ], in *billow* the first [ˈbɪləʊ]. Also of *sentence stress and prominence within larger units generally. Thus in *He did* stress might fall on either word: ʜᴇ *did* 'It was him who did' (stress on *he*), or *He* ᴅɪᴅ.

The phonetic correlates vary: in auditory terms, a difference in length, in perceived loudness, in vowel quality, in pitch, or in a combination of any of these. As a feature of words, *accents (1) are divided generally into **stress accents**, in which the differences reflect or are thought to reflect greater muscular energy in the production of an accented syllable, and *pitch accents. The accent in English, as in *below* and *billow*, is a stress accent.

stress accent *See* stress.

stress group A sequence of syllables of which one bears a *primary stress, seen as a rhythmical unit. *Cf.* foot: e.g. in one analysis, *easy solution* would be divided into the stress groups [ᴇᴀ*sy so*] and [ʟᴜ*tion*].

stress-timed (Language) in which the intervals between stressed syllables in speech are either equal or at least more nearly equal than the intervals between the nucleus of each successive syllable and the next. Thus English, to the extent that, e.g. in a phrase such as *incrédible explanátions*, the relative timing of the two stressed syllables, [krɛ] and [neɪ], will tend, despite the number of intervening unstressed syllables, to equal that in phrases such as *absúrd théories*, where stressed [sə:d] and [θɪə] are adjacent. Opp. syllable-timed.

'strict subcategorization' Introduced by Chomsky in the 1960s for the assignment of a lexical unit to a syntactically defined subclass of its major word class: e.g. that of *make* to the subclass of verbs that can be followed by an object noun phrase.

Cf. c-selection; *also* valency. 'Strict' as opposed to subclassification by *selectional restrictions (1).

stricture Any constriction of part of the vocal tract in the articulation of a speech sound. Degrees of stricture range from closure, in *stops such as [p] in *pea*, through *close approximation, in *fricatives such as [s] in *sea*, to *open approximation, e.g. in vowels.

strident = sibilant. A *distinctive feature in the schemes proposed by Jakobson and by Chomsky and Halle, *SPE*, where characterized acoustically by a higher intensity of noise. Thus [s] in *sin* is strident in opposition to [θ] in *thin*; also, in *SPE*, a labiodental [f] in opposition to a bilabial [ɸ].

string Mathematical term for a linear array of elements. E.g. given the set $A = \{a, b, c\}$, *a, baa, bcbac,* ... are strings 'over' (that is, composed of elements of) *A*. Hence in linguistics in a sense equivalent to 'sequence'.

stripping The reduction of a clause to a single unit by which it differs from an earlier clause to which it is related by *coordination: e.g. in *I sent a letter to her parents and* < > *some flowers* < >: *sc.* 'and I sent some flowers to her parents'. *Cf.* gapping.

strong (1) (Verb, formation, etc.) in Germanic languages distinguished by *ablaut as opposed to suffixing. Thus in English *sing* is a strong verb (past tense *sang*, participle *sung*) while *talk* is a weak verb (past tense and participle *talked*).

strong (2) (syllable etc.) *See* Metrical Phonology.

'strong crossover' Sometimes invoked in excluding the possibility that, e.g. in *Who did she visit?*, both pronouns (*who* and *she*) might be taken as having the same referent. If seen in terms of *wh*-movement this would involve the second of two coreferential elements 'crossing over' the first.

strong generative capacity The range of structures that a specific type of *generative grammar can assign to the sentences of a language. Thus grammars of type A might be capable of generating the same sets of sentences as grammars of type B: in that sense they would have the same *weak generative capacity. But those of type A might be able to assign alternative structures to sentences for which those of type B could assign one structure only. If so then, all else being equal, the strong generative capacity of grammars of type A would be greater.

'Strong Lexicalist Hypothesis' The view that, firstly, there is no distinction in principle between inflectional and derivational morphology and, secondly, they both belong, in a generative grammar, to the lexicon and not to syntax. Distinguished from the '**Weak Lexicalist Hypothesis**', by which derivation belongs to the lexicon but inflection does not.

strongly equivalent (Grammars, types of grammar) having the same *strong generative capacity.

structural ambiguity = grammatical ambiguity.

structural dialectology Treatment developed in the 1950s by U. Weinreich and others, in which dialects were compared within the framework of a common *diasystem. Thus, in their phonology, they could be seen as differing variously in the 'inventory' of units at some point in the system, in general patterns of *distribution of such units, or in the 'incidence' of units in sets of cognate words.

structural linguistics Any school or theory in which language is conceived as a self-contained, self-regulating system, whose elements are defined by their relationship to other elements.

Structuralism originated above all in the posthumous work of Saussure, and by the mid-20th century was not only dominant in linguistics but was having an increasing influence on other disciplines, including anthropology and literary criticism. The term itself was in general use before the Second World War, with reference to a discipline in which the study of a *language system was abstracted from the spoken and written use of languages and from their history: hence a growing divide between structuralism and the older branches of *philology. But since 1960 usage has become in part confused. In particular, Chomsky and his followers identified structural linguistics with the local *Post-Bloomfieldian school to which they were reacting in the USA; since they rejected Post-Bloomfieldian methods, they themselves were not 'structuralists'. But in a wider conception, Chomsky's account of a *generative grammar was clearly structuralist.

See European structuralism for leading scholars in that tradition.

structural order *See* order.

structure Used by Firth and others specifically of *syntagmatic structures. Opp. system.

structure-dependency Principle by which syntactic processes respect the organization of sentences into phrases. The stock illustration is that of inversion in interrogatives in English: e.g. in *The man who was there is coming* it is possible to invert *the man who was there* and *is* (*Is the man who was there coming?*), but not *the man who* and *was* (**Was the man who there is coming?*), since *the man who* does not form a subject phrase.

'Sturtevant's paradox' The paradox by which sound change is regular but creates irregularity while analogical change is irregular but creates regularity. Thus a sound change may give rise to an irregular inflection; an analogical change may replace it with the one that is usual.

Formulated as a paradox by E. H. Sturtevant in the 1940s.

style In the ordinary sense of a style appropriate e.g. to a specific genre of writing or one characteristic of an individual. Thus, in general, whatever is studied under *stylistics.

Quasi-technically, e.g. in the context of a *sociolinguistic interview, of variation in speech described on a scale from maximally formal to maximally colloquial. As such distinguished, in principle, from variation between accents or dialects, or in *register.

stylistics The study of style in language: traditionally, of variations in usage among literary and other texts; now, more generally, of any systematic variation, in either writing or speech, which relates to the type of discourse or its context. Thus there is a style appropriate to public lectures, different from that of casual conversation among friends; the style of prayers in church includes the intonation etc. with which they are recited; and so on.

Hence '**literary stylistics**', as the study of relevant differences, other than in the dialect or language used, among individual writers, periods, or genres.

sub- From the Latin word for 'under'. Hence *subordination 'ordering or ranking under', or *subjacency, of a principle involving elements 'lying under' nodes in a tree structure. Also in the terminology for *local cases: **subessive**, indicating position 'under', **sublative**, indicating movement to a position 'under', and so on.

subapical (Consonant) articulated with the underside of the tongue tip in contact with the top of the mouth: one form of *retroflex articulation, normal in Dravidian languages.

subcategorization The assignment of a lexical item to a subclass of its part of speech, especially with respect to the syntactic elements with which it can combine. *Cf.* strict subcategorization.

In a notation introduced by Chomsky in the 1960s, verbs were assigned to **subcategorization frames** which identified their potential positions in phrase structure trees. Thus a *transitive verb, such as *make*, was assigned a feature [+ —NP]: i.e. it can appear (+) in the frame '—NP', or before a noun phrase.

subfamily *See* family.

subglottal (Air, air pressure) below the vocal cords.

Subj = subject, subjunctive.

subjacency Principle of syntax, as formulated by Chomsky in the late 1970s, by which the movement of a unit was blocked if it crossed the boundaries of two or more designated categories of constituent. Thus, in this account, the reason why one cannot say *Who did you hear the news that he had killed?* is that *who* would have to be moved, by *wh*-movement, across the boundary of both a subordinate sentence [*he had killed <who>*] and a noun phrase [*the news that he had killed <who>*] in which it is included.

Movements were seen as following the *cyclic(al) principle: hence the nodes in a phrase structure tree which dominated the constituents within which they could operate were **cyclic nodes**. Constructions in which, apparently contrary to the principle of subjacency, a unit moved across the boundaries defined by more than one such node were explained as cases of *successive cyclicity.

subject (S) 1. A syntactic element in e.g. English which is traditionally seen as representing someone or something of which something is said or *predicated, and which, in addition, includes the *agent in a basic *transitive construction. E.g. *John* in *John came, John helped me, John was freed, John is my friend,* and so on; also, on the assumption that they have the same syntactic role, *knowing him* in *Knowing him helped me,* or *that he is worried* in *That he is worried is obvious.*

 Thence extended to elements in other types of language that are similar in one or the other respect. **2.** Sometimes, though less usually, of noun phrases etc. serving as a *topic (3) or *pivot (2). **3.** Commonly, especially in typological comparisons of languages, of any syntactic element which characteristically includes forms with the semantic role of agent. E.g. an *ergative case will be said to mark the subject in one type of language, as the *nominative does in another.

subject clause A clause which has the role of subject: e.g. *when it happened* in *When it happened isn't known,* or *that it happened* in *That it happened isn't certain.*

subject complement An adjective or noun or noun phrase which is linked to a subject by a *copula or *copular verb: e.g. *angry* in *She was angry* (with copula *was*), or *traitor* in *He turned traitor* (with copular verb *turned*). *Cf.* predicative.

subject control Relation of *control in which the subject of a non-finite verb is supplied by the subject of a main clause: e.g. in *I wanted to leave* the subject of *to leave* is supplied by that of the main verb, *I.*

subject honorific *See* honorific.

subjective *Case which is that of, among others, a subject: e.g. *I* is the subjective form of the pronoun, as in *I did.* Opp. objective: more usual, instead of *nominative, in describing languages with no other distinction of cases.

subjective genitive Construction in which a noun etc. in the *genitive case, or its equivalent, has a semantic relation to a head noun like that of a subject to a verb. E.g. *John's* in *John's departure*: compare *John departed.* Opp. objective genitive.

subjectivity In the ordinary sense. Also, following Benveniste in the 1950s, of the property of language by which utterances reflect the standpoint of the speaker. Thus, in *deixis, pronouns such as *I* are used by speakers to refer to themselves; a *performative such as *I promise to be there* constitutes an act of promise by the speaker; and so on.

subjectivization Process of change by which words develop a subjective in place of or alongside an objective sense: e.g. *villein,* in the objective sense of 'feudal serf', > *villain,* in the subjective (and in this case *pejorative) sense of someone perceived as base or wicked.

subject-prominent (Language) in which the basic syntactic elements of a sentence are a *subject and a *predicate. Opp. topic-prominent; but whether this division is either exhaustive or revealing depends on how 'subject', in particular, is defined.

subject pronoun A pronoun with the syntactic role of subject. Thus, in *I left*, *I* is a subject pronoun in the appropriate *subjective form.

subject raising *Raising (2) of a subject. Hence, in particular, of the postulated raising of the subject of a subordinate verb to the subject position of a main clause: e.g. *Mary* in *Mary seems to be there* (seen as from an underlying *It seems* [*Mary is there*] or [*Mary is there*] *seems*).

subjunct Used by Quirk *et al.*, *CGE, of a range of adverbials which would include e.g. *morally* in *It is morally wrong*, or *pretty well* in *They pretty well wrecked it*. Said to have 'to a greater or lesser degree, a subordinate role . . . in comparison with other clause elements'. *Cf.* adjunct; conjunct (2); disjunct.

subjunctive (SUBJ) *Mood, especially in European languages, whose central role is to mark a clause as expressing something other than a statement of what is certain. Thus, in Latin, *faciat* (do-SUBJ-3SG) 'Let him/her do (it)' as opposed to *indicative *facit* 'He/she is doing (it)'. Usually with a range of loosely related uses: in particular, the subjunctive is often required in some types of subordinate (= 'subjoined') clause, or in clauses introduced by specific subordinators or subordinating conjunctions.

   Cf. irrealis. Forms such as *be* in *I ask that he be told*, or *were* in *If he were here he would help* are traditionally called 'subjunctive' in English.

subordinate clause A *clause which is a syntactic element within or of a larger clause: e.g. *I like* as the modifier of *people* in the larger clause *I want people I like*, or *what I like* as the complement of *know* in *I know what I like*.

   Opp. independent clause; main clause; superordinate clause: thus a subordinate (or 'lower') clause is an element within the structure of a superordinate (or 'higher') clause. Also called a '**subordinate *sentence**'. The verb of a subordinate clause is a **subordinate verb**, its subject a **subordinate subject**, and so on.

subordinating conjunction = subordinator.

subordination Traditionally in a sense related to that of *dependency; hence in particular of the role of clauses and other syntactic units seen as dependent, as wholes, within the construction of a larger unit. E.g. the object *his brother* is as a whole **subordinate to** *like* in *I like his brother*, as is *what he tells me* in *I like what he tells me*.

   Traditionally opposed to *coordination as *hypotaxis, from the equivalent term in Greek, is opposed to *parataxis. Also, however, in

more restricted senses: e.g., as defined by Bloomfield, as equivalent to
*modification (1).

subordinator A word etc. which marks a clause as *subordinate:
e.g. *after* in *He came [after we left]*, or *that* in *He said [that we had left]*.
Traditionally a '**subordinating conjunction**'; *cf.* coordinator.
   Sometimes restricted to subordinators in *adverbial clauses.
E.g. *after* is a subordinator; *that*, by contrast, is a *complementizer.

substance The projection of a set of abstract relations among units
on to anything concrete corresponding to them. E.g. 'p' in English is
opposed to 'b': that, in the theory of Hjelmslev in particular, is simply
a statement about a difference within an abstract *language system.
But the difference may be realized, in a *phonic medium, by the sound
[p] as opposed to the sound [b] or, in the medium of writing, by the
letter <p> as opposed to the letter <b>. These are accordingly
projections of a relation between units that are in themselves neither
sounds nor letters on to units of, respectively, 'phonic substance' and
'(ortho)graphic substance'. Similarly, 'pin' in English is distinct from
'bin'; that, again in Hjelmslev's theory, is another abstract distinction
in the language system. But it is seen as projected, on to a substance of
'thought', as a distinction between corresponding concepts.
   The abstract relations are those of *form (2); *see also* purport. The
germ of this idea is in the work of Saussure, but Hjelmslev elaborated
and clarified it.

substandard (Form, variety) which is not *standard. Usually of ones
proscribed in relation to a standard: e.g. double negatives, as in *I don't
know nothing*, are proscribed as 'substandard' in English.

substantive ['sʌbstəntɪv] = noun. Originally 'noun substantive', from
Latin *nomen substantivum* (roughly 'independent noun') as opposed to
nomen adiectivum 'noun adjective' (roughly 'dependent noun'). These
were divisions within a class of 'nouns' which was seen in antiquity as
including *adjectives as well as nouns as they are defined nowadays.

substantive universal [səb'stantɪv] Chomsky's term in the 1960s for
any specific category etc. established as part of a general linguistic
theory: thus e.g. a phonetic feature such as voice, a semantic feature
such as abstract vs. concrete, a syntactic category such as noun and
verb. Also of specific rules: thus, in one such theory, of a syntactic rule
by which a sentence in any language must have, as its basic elements,
a subject and a predicate.
   Opp. formal universal.

substitute form = pro-form.

substitution The replacement, in the process of analysing a
language, of one unit or sequence of units by another. Thus, in
establishing its phonemes, one procedure is to interchange sounds to

determine whether the substitution makes a difference of meaning. *Cf.* commutation test.

A **substitution frame** is the rest of a sequence in which substitutions are made. E.g. in the frame *The — have left*, a word such as *men* (*The men have left*) can be replaced by any of *elephants*, *young people*, *workers next door*, and so on.

substratum 1. A language formerly spoken by some population which has influenced their acquisition of a language spoken later. E.g., under the Roman empire, languages such as Gaulish or Iberian were replaced by Latin. But it has often been argued that, in learning Latin, speakers of these languages carried over certain phonetic and other features, and that these are reflected in modern Romance dialects. **2.** A language spoken by some population which has influenced that of a group by which they were dominated. Thus English as a possible influence on the evolution of Anglo-French after the Norman conquest; also any of several West African languages as a factor in the formation of *pidgins spoken in the West Indies.

Cf. adstratum; superstratum.

subtraction Morphological process by which part of a form is deleted. Thus, in one account, French *grand* [grã] 'big' (masculine) is phonetically derived from *grande* [grãd] by the subtraction of the final consonant.

Implicitly distinguished, as a systematic process, from lexical abbreviation or *clipping.

'subtractive bilingualism' The acquisition of a *second language at the expense, or ultimately at the expense, of the first, e.g. that of English by many immigrant communities in North America or Britain. Contrasted, though the facts are hardly so clear-cut, with *additive bilingualism.

'successive cyclicity' Term for cases where, according to *Government and Binding Theory, a syntactic process applies to the same element in two or more cycles as defined under the principle of *subjacency. E.g. in *Who did you say you saw?*, *who* is claimed to move, by *wh*-movement, in two stages: first to the head of the subordinate clause (*who you saw*), then to the head of the main clause.

suction Defined by Chomsky and Halle, *SPE*, as a feature of both *clicks and *implosives, in both of which the *airstream mechanism is ingressive.

suffix An affix that comes after the form to which it is added: e.g. *-ness* in *sadness*. Hence **suffixation**, for the process of adding a suffix. Also **suffixal**: thus *-ness* is in suffixal position, and the formation of nouns in *-ness* a suffixal formation.

sujet parlant Term in French for someone who is speaking. Calqued inappropriately into English as 'speaking subject'.

sulcal Grooved: thus the tongue is in a 'sulcal' position if e.g. the sides are raised but there is a groove in the centre.

Sumerian Ancient language of southern Mesopotamia, not securely related to any other. Written in *cuneiform, which evolved from a set of *pictograms used, in the late 4th millennium BC, for mnemonic labelling, to a full representation of sentences, with both *logograms and syllabic characters, by the late 3rd millennium. Increasingly supplanted by *Akkadian from the early 2nd millennium.

summative Used by Quirk *et al.*, *CGE*, of adverbs or adverbials that introduce a summing up of what precedes: e.g. *all in all* in *So, all in all, it was a success*.

Summer Institute of Linguistics Scholarly organization whose work complements that of the Wycliffe Bible translators. Founded in the USA in 1934 to train missionaries in linguistic fieldwork; *Pike was long its most important member and his theories informed much of its work.

Sundanese *Austronesian; a major language of Java, with several million speakers in the western third of the island.

super- From the Latin word for 'over'. Hence, in the terminology for *local cases, **superessive**, indicating position above or over; **superlative** [suːpəˈleɪtɪv], indicating movement to a position above or over. Likewise *superordinate, in opposition to subordinate; *superfix, for a morphological element realized 'over' others; and so on.

superfamily *See* family.

superfix A morphological element, especially of accent or tone, whose realization is simultaneous with the whole or part of the form to which it is joined. E.g. in *récord* [ˈrɛkɔːd] vs. *recórd* [rɪˈkɔːd], the accentual patterns might be treated as contrasting superfixes ('— and —').

superlative (Construction, inflection, etc.) by which persons, things, etc. are singled out as having some property to the greatest or to an extreme degree. Originally of inflected forms of adjectives or adverbs: e.g. *lousiest* in *It's the lousiest film I've seen* is the superlative form of *lousy*.

    *Positive, *comparative, and superlative are traditionally three terms in the category of 'grade'. Some languages distinguish a superlative, by which individuals are singled out from a specific set, from an *elative (2), whose role is simply that of an intensifier.

superordinate clause A clause seen in relation to a *subordinate clause within it. E.g. *I expect he will come* is a superordinate or 'higher' clause in relation to the subordinate or 'lower' clause *he will come*, which is contained within it. *Cf.* main clause.

superstock *See* family.

superstratum A language spoken by a dominant group which has influenced that of a population subordinate to it. E.g. speakers of English were dominated after the Norman conquest by speakers whose native language was Anglo-French; hence Anglo-French became a superstratum that has influenced the history of English.
   Cf. substratum; adstratum.

supine Term in Latin grammar for a nominal form of a verb with the same stem as the passive participle. Hence available for forms in other languages which are like participles in some respects but different in others.
   The ordinary meaning was that of 'lying on one's back'; the reason for its use in grammar is not clear.

supplement Any syntactic unit related to a unit within a larger sentence, but not a fully integrated element in its structure. Thus *Mary, of course* is **supplementive**, or stands in a relation of **supplementation**, to *my sister* in *My sister—Mary, of course—will be there*. The term 'supplementive' is due to Quirk *et al.*, *CGE, for whom e.g. the adjectival unit *too embarrassed for words* would be supplementive to a clause in *Too embarrassed for words, I rose to my feet*.
   A unit to which a supplement is related is described by Huddleston and Pullum, *CGEL, as an 'anchor'. For related notions *cf.* apposition, non-restrictive relative clause, parataxis (2), parenthesis.

suppletion Morphological process or alternation in which one form wholly replaces another. Thus in *went* either the whole form, or a stem *wen-*, is in a **suppletive** relationship to *go*.
   In **partial suppletion** only a part of the form is replaced. E.g. in *thought* (or *though-t*), the *th-* of *think* is unchanged and only *-ink* is affected.

suprafix = superfix.

supraglottal Above the vocal cords or *glottis. E.g. a plosive such as [t] or [k] is articulated with a 'supraglottal closure'.

suprasegmental (Unit, feature, etc.) whose domain extends over more than one successive minimal element. Thus *stress is a suprasegmental feature whose domain is a syllable, not an individual consonant or vowel within it.

surd An older term for *voiceless.

'surface' Usually in a sense derived from that of *surface structure. Thus a **surface filter** is a *filter that applies to representations of

sentences at that level; likewise treatments may invoke surface
(or 'surface structure') *constraints, conditions, etc.

surface structure A representation of the syntax of a sentence seen
as deriving, by one or more *transformations, from an underlying
*deep structure. Defined by Chomsky in the mid-1960s as the part of
the syntactic description of a sentence that determines its phonetic
representation; therefore a structure in which, in particular, all
syntactic units are in the order of the phonetic forms that realize
them. Later, by the mid-1970s, said to determine the *semantic
representation also, and subsequently replaced by a more abstract
structure renamed, from the late 1970s, S-structure. As such the least
abstract of three levels of syntax in *Government and Binding Theory,
until the early 1990s, when Chomsky's *minimalist programme no
longer took it for granted.
  Cf. Phonetic Form; shallow structure.

Survey of English Dialects By H. Orton and co-workers; based on
fieldwork in the 1950s with findings published from the early 1960s to
the late 1970s.

Survey of English Usage Founded by Quirk in 1960, at University
College London; the repository of a major corpus of educated British
English, written and spoken.

svarabhakti Sanskrit term for *anaptyxis.

SVO language One in which a *subject (3), verb, and *object (3) are
at least basically or most commonly in that order. E.g. English: *They* (S)
helped (V) *us* (O). Opp. SOV language, VSO language, etc.

'Swadesh list' A list of concepts supposedly basic in the vocabulary
of all languages, proposed by M. Swadesh in the 1950s for use in
studies of *glottochronology.

Swahili *Bantu, in origin native to a very small area, spread by
migration along the coast of East Africa and much later, from the 19th
century, as a lingua franca and in pidginized forms, into the interior.
Standard Swahili is based on the dialect of Zanzibar, though not
identical to it: widespread as a second language in Kenya and
Tanzania, where it has official status, in Uganda and into the eastern
Congo; also increasingly, in cities, as a first language.
  Also called '**Kiswahili**', with the noun class prefix appropriate for
names of languages.

Swati *Bantu, spoken in South Africa and in Swaziland; related to
*Xhosa/*Zulu within a group called 'Nguni'.

Swedish North *Germanic, spoken in Sweden and as a minority
language in Finland, where it also has official status. The standard
form dates from the translation of the Bible in the 16th century.

Sweet, Henry (1845–1912) British grammarian, phonetician, and Anglicist, whose contributions to phonetics and to our knowledge of the early history of English are both fundamental. Phonetics was for Sweet 'the indispensable foundation of all language study, whether practical or scientific': his description and classification of vowels, in particular, was brilliant, and his advocacy of transcriptions based on the Roman alphabet, as opposed to *Visible Speech or other *analphabetic systems, was decisive in the period leading to the foundation of the *International Phonetic Association. He distinguished separate systems for *broad and *narrow transcription ('Broad Romic' and 'Narrow Romic'), of which the former was in principle phonological: i.e. it made 'only the practically necessary distinctions of sound in each language', omitting 'all that is superfluous'.

switch-reference (Grammatical system) in which a marker indicates whether a subject or other argument of a following verb has or has not the same referent as that of the verb preceding. E.g. schematically, *John entered*-SAME *sat down*, where SAME indicates 'same referent', means 'John came in and he (John) sat down', while *John entered*-DIFFERENT *sat down*, where DIFFERENT indicates 'different referent', means 'John came in and he (someone other than John) sat down'.

syllabary Writing system in which each character represents a syllable, typically consisting either of a vowel or a consonant plus a vowel: e.g. the 'katakana' and 'hiragana' systems used in writing *Japanese.

Syllabaries are less satisfactory than alphabets for many languages, especially those which have consonants at the end as well as the beginning of syllables. An intermediate *alpha-syllabic type is exemplified by Indian systems such as *Devanagari.

syllabic Forming the *nucleus of a *syllable: e.g. vowels are typically syllabic, and are accordingly said to have the *feature [+ syllabic]. **Syllabic consonants** include e.g. the nasal [ɳ] in [neɪʃɳ] (*nation*), or a syllabic *s* in rapid pronunciations of words like *Manchester* ([mantʃʂtə]).

syllabic script = syllabary.

syllable A phonological unit consisting of a vowel or other unit that can be produced in isolation, either alone or accompanied by one or more less sonorous units. E.g. [bʌn] and [tɪŋ] are successive syllables in *bunting*. The vowel or other central unit forms the nucleus: the illustration, for [bʌn], shows other terms used for other proposed divisions. For types of syllable *see* closed syllable *and* open syllable, heavy syllable (vs. light); *also* Metrical Phonology for strong vs. weak syllables.

Theories of the syllable have been variously based on *distribution or on phonetics. In a distributional theory, syllables are established with the aim of simplifying an account of possible sequences of phonemes, patterns of accentuation, and so on. In a phonetic theory, divisions between syllables reflect the way in which the production of consonants and vowels is or is believed to be organized. These different approaches can lead to an effective distinction, with discrepancies in some cases, between '**phonological syllables**' and '**phonetic syllables**'.

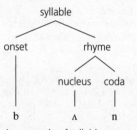

An example of syllable structure

syllable-timed (Language) in which the timing of syllables tends to be equal: e.g. Spanish. Opp. stress-timed.

syllepsis [sɪˈlɛpsɪs] [sɪˈliːpsɪs] Traditionally of constructions in which coordinated elements have different roles in syntax or in semantics. E.g. in *He read me the letter and a warning afterwards*, *read* has its literal sense in relation to *the letter* but a figurative sense in relation to *a warning*. The Greek term means 'taking together'; often conflated with *zeugma.

symbol Restricted in *Peirce's theory of signs to those whose relation to their object is wholly conventional: e.g. the majority of words in any language.

synaeresis [sɪˈnɪərɪsɪs] The contraction of two or more syllables into one: e.g. in English, of [ʌɪ] + [ə] (as in *liar*) into a monosyllable with a triphthong or a single long vowel. The opposite process is 'diaeresis'.

synaesthesia The stimulation of one sense by another: e.g. the association of different colours with the perception of different sounds. Hence one factor in patterns of phonaesthesis or *sound symbolism.

syncategorematic (Word) seen as meaningful only in relation to other elements. E.g., in *boys and girls*, the nouns have meanings that can be described independently of the construction; but *and* has meaning only as a coordinator that links them. *Cf.* grammatical meaning.

synchronic At a single moment in time. A synchronic description of a language is accordingly an account of its structure either at present or at some specific moment in the past, considered in abstraction from its history. Opp. diachronic; *see also* panchronic.

syncope ['sɪŋkəpi] The loss of unstressed vowels in the middle of a word. E.g. in *secretary*, of the vowel in the next to last syllable: thus ['sɛkrətri]. *Cf.* apocope; *also* aphaeresis, aphesis.

syncretism The relation between two or more words in a paradigm that have different *morphosyntactic features but are identical in form. Thus the distinction between a past tense and a past or passive participle is **syncretized** in the paradigms of most verbs in English: past tense *walked* and participle also *walked*; past tense *won* and participle also *won*; and so on. Also of the historical process in which forms become idenitical.

Used especially when the identity is regular across all paradigms. Thus in Latin the distinction between dative and ablative, which was made in the singular in forms such as *puellae* 'girl-DAT.SG' and *puella* 'girl-ABL.SG', was syncretized throughout in the plural: e.g. *puellis* 'girl-DAT.PL/ABL.PL'. *Cf.* neutralization; *see also* case syncretism.

syndeton ['sɪndɪtən] The opposite of *asyndeton. Thus a style, construction, etc. is **syndetic** if clauses are joined by conjunctions.

synecdoche [sɪ'nɛkdəki] *Figure of speech in which an expression denoting a part is used to refer to a whole: also, in the traditional definition, vice versa. Hence a term in typologies of semantic change: e.g. *flower* has by synecdoche the sense 'plant bearing flowers'. Often treated as a special case of *metonymy.

synesis An older term for *notional agreement.

synizesis Phonetic contraction of vowels in successive syllables, into a form not itself distinguished as a phonological unit. E.g., in some forms of English, of the vowels of *see* [si:] and *-ing* [ɪŋ] into what might be transcribed roughly as a long [iː].

synonymy The relation between two lexical units with a shared meaning. '**Absolute**' **synonyms**, if they exist, have meanings identical in all respects and in all contexts. '**Partial**' **synonyms** have meanings identical in some contexts, or identical only e.g. in that replacing one with the other does not change the *truth conditions of a sentence. Thus *paper* is a partial though not an absolute synonym of *article*: compare *I got my paper published*, *I got my article published*.

syntactic category Any class of units distinguished in the syntax of a language. Hence specifically those that label nodes in a *phrase structure tree: sentence (S), noun phrase (NP), verb (V), and so on.

syntactic function A role that a word or other unit fills in relation to other elements in its construction. Thus the construction of *My brother saw her* relates the syntactic roles of subject and predicate, or subject, predicator, and direct object. That of subject is filled by *my brother*, that of e.g. predicate by *saw her*.

syntactic process Any process formulated in accounts of syntax by which one form, structure, or construction is changed into another. E.g. a representation of *Something held me up* might be derived by a syntactic process from that of *Something held up me*; as an active construction that might be changed to a passive (*I was held up by something*); that might in turn be changed, by a further process, to the structure of an interrogative (*Was I held up by something?*).

The usual formulation of syntactic processes is as *transformations.

syntactic valency *See* semantic valency.

syntagm ['sɪntam] = construction (2).

syntagmatic (Relation) between elements that form part of the same form, sequence, construction, etc.: e.g. between *s*, *p*, and *r* in a form such as *spring*, or between a subject and a verb in constructions such as *Bill hunts*.

Defined by Saussure as a relation 'in praesentia': i.e. between units present in the same sequence. Opp. associative; later, from the 1930s, opp. paradigmatic.

syntagmeme *See* Tagmemics.

syntax The study of grammatical relations between words and other units within the sentence.

Usually distinguished from *morphology. E.g. in the phrase *these books,* the relations between the words belongs to syntax: thus *these* modifies or is a determiner of *books*; it comes before it, they agree in respect of number. The internal structure of the words belongs to morphology: thus *books* and *these* are each plural, *books* has the ending -*s*. Also distinguished widely from *semantics. Thus the order of *these* and *books* is seen as belonging to syntax, as does the rule which formally excludes *this books* or *these book*. But anything to do with the meaning of the phrase (that *these* is a deictic element, that it qualifies *books*, that the expression is used to refer to more than one book) belongs to semantics. Distinguished finally, in itself or as part of *grammar, from the *lexicon: thus the role of *these* in relation to *books* belongs to syntax, but the properties of *book* as an individual unit belong to an individual lexical entry.

The term itself is univocal: where detailed definitions vary they reflect varying theories of the structure or nature of language generally.

synthetic (1) (Form, language) in which grammatical distinctions are realized by inflections. Opp. analytic (1): e.g. a possessive construction is realized analytically in Italian (*la casa di Cesare*, lit. 'the house of Caesar'), but was realized synthetically, with a *genitive inflection, in Latin *domus Caesaris* 'house-NOM.SG Caesar-GEN.SG'.

synthetic (2) (Proposition) whose truth depends on a specific state of affairs: e.g. 'Jane has red hair' is true if but only if Jane in fact has red hair. Opp. analytic (2).

'synthetic compound' One derived with an affix; especially, in English, one which parallels a verbal construction. E.g. *earth-mover*, formed with an affix *-er* in parallel to a predicate *moves earth*. Opp. root compound, analytic compound.

Syriac *Aramaic language, first attested in the 1st century AD, and that of the Syrian church, with a rich literature, after the establishment of Christianity in the 4th century. Still in use as a liturgical language.

system Often used, especially by Firth, Halliday, and their followers, to refer to sets of *paradigmatic relations. Opp. structure: e.g. in a word in English with the 'structure' (C)V (zero or more consonants plus vowel), the 'system' that applies or 'operates' at the V position includes [ɑː] (as in *car*), [iː] (as in *see*), and so on.

See Systemic Grammar; system network.

'systematic phonemic' Used by Chomsky and Halle, *SPE*, of the level of *underlying forms in Generative Phonology; the corresponding level of phonetic representation was called '**systematic phonetic**'.

system congruity Conformity to the pattern general or usual in a specific language. Adduced as a factor in explaining directions of language change: *see also* pattern congruity as a criterion in phonology.

Systemic Grammar Model of *functional syntax developed by Halliday from the late 1950s. The basic idea is that any act of communication realizes a set of choices: thus e.g. the utterance of *She went out* realizes, among others, the choice of a declarative structure. Each choice is at a certain level in a hierarchy of *ranks (2): e.g. the choice of declarative is at clause level. It is also related to other choices on a scale of *delicacy or detail: e.g. the choice of interrogative instead of declarative would entail a further choice between *polar interrogative and *wh-interrogative. Each individual set of choices forms a *system: thus polar interrogative and *wh*-interrogative form one system, declarative and interrogative form or are part of another. A grammar will accordingly describe the systems of a language, the relations between them, and the ways in which they are realized, to a level of detail at which all remaining choices are between open sets of lexical units.

Originally called **Scale and Category Grammar**. The 'scale' was that of the successive ranks at which systems operate: e.g. morpheme, word, phrase, and upwards.

system network A network of relations among different *systems of oppositions, in which the applicability of one system depends on the choice of a particular term or terms within another or others. Thus, in the illustration, an opposition in verbs between subjunctive and indicative is shown as depending on the verb being finite, an opposition of tense as depending on it being either finite or a participle, and so on.

Devised in, and central to, *Systemic Grammar.

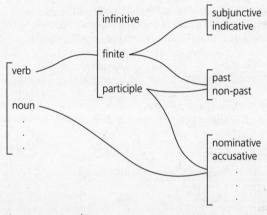

A system network

system sentence Lyons's term for a sentence postulated as a unit in the *language system, as opposed to a 'text sentence' uttered or otherwise instantiated in a text or discourse.

T 1. Cover term for *familiar forms. From the *t* of French *tu*; opp. V from French *vous*. **2.** Abbreviation for 'tense', e.g. as heading a *tense phrase.

t *See* trace.

tableau A tabular representation, in applications of *Optimality Theory, of the mechanism by which optimal realizations are determined.

Constraints are ordered horizontally from left to right. Thus, in the illustration, A is ranked higher than B. Let A stipulate e.g. that a double consonant cannot come between vowels; B, on the contrary, that if a consonant is double in an underlying representation it remains so. Now take two possible alternative realizations of an underlying *etta*. The first shown, [etta], violates A; hence the asterisk in that column and, since A is higher-ranking, it is ruled out. This is shown by an exclamation mark ('!'); and the lower-ranking B, though satisfied, is then marked by shading as irrelevant. In the second row the realization [eta] satisfies A; hence no asterisk. Therefore the lower-ranking B, though violated, is again irrelevant. The optimal outcome, marked by a pointer, is accordingly [eta].

	A	B
[etta]	*!	
☛ [eta]		*

A tableau

taboo word A word known to speakers but avoided in some, most, or all forms or contexts of speech, for reasons of religion, decorum, politeness, etc. Thus in some societies the word for 'death' is taboo, and is accordingly replaced in most forms of speech by a metaphor, *euphemism, or some other figurative or roundabout expression.

'tacit knowledge' Knowledge which people have but of which they are unable to give any account. Thus knowledge of a language (*I-language) as conceived by Chomsky and others following him.

(-)tactic Concerned with the arrangement of units. E.g. *phonotactics is concerned with the possible arrangements of, or '**tactics**' of, phonemes.

tag A reduced form such as *will you?* in *You will be there, will you?* or *hasn't she?* in *Jane has arrived, hasn't she?* These are, more precisely, *interrogative tags or **tag questions**.

Tags in English are usually linked to declaratives (*You will be there, Jane has arrived*), but may also follow e.g. an imperative (*Put it on the table, will you?*). Many show **reversed polarity**: i.e. their *polarity is negative when what precedes is positive, and positive when it is negative. Thus *Jane has arrived, hasn't she?* (positive + negative); *Jane hasn't arrived, has she?* (negative + positive).

Tagalog The official and main language of the Philippines. *Austronesian, of a branch which includes the other indigenous languages of the Philippines: native to south Luzon, which includes Manila, but a second language, in the standard form called **Pilipino**, throughout the other islands.

tagmeme 1. Bloomfield's term for any unit of grammatical patterning: e.g. the 'actor–action' or subject–predicate construction is a tagmeme. **2.** *See* Tagmemics.

Tagmemics Model of *functional syntax developed by Pike, R. E. Longacre, and others from the 1950s. The central concept was the **tagmeme**, defined by the relation between a syntactic 'slot' or function, such as subject or object, and a class of units, such as noun phrase or pronoun, that can 'fill' it. Constructions, or **syntagmemes**, are accordingly characterized by sequences of obligatory and optional tagmemes: e.g. that of *The people were leaving* by one in which there is an obligatory subject slot, filled by the noun phrase, followed by an obligatory predicate slot, filled by a verb phrase. Each syntagmeme is of a specific '**size-level**': thus this example is of a clause-level syntagmeme, while those which would represent the constructions of *the people* and *were leaving* are at phrase level. Size-levels in turn are linked by potentially recursive relations among syntagmemes, functions, and classes. E.g. the structure of *the people* is that of a noun phrase; this can function as subject in a structure which is that of a certain class of clause; that in turn might function e.g. as the object in a larger clause (*They said* [[*the people*] *were leaving*]).

*Pike was the first to develop clearly a model of this type. The earliest version of *Systemic Grammar was to have much in common with it; so too the *Functional Grammar of S. C. Dik and his colleagues.

Tai Family of languages in South-east Asia, spoken extensively in Laos and Thailand (*see* Lao, Thai), in north Burma and Vietnam, and across the borders of these countries with China and India.

Tai-Kadai is a larger grouping, proposed but not securely established, in which Tai is linked with *Kadai and *Kam-Sui.

tail The part of an intonation pattern that falls on syllables following the nuclear or *tonic syllable: e.g. in THEY *could do it*, with tonic *they*, the tail is *could do it*. *Cf.* head (2).

tailless arrow (>, <) Used to represent a change in the history or postulated prehistory of a language: e.g. Old English *hūs* 'house' > modern *house*; likewise *ū*, in this and other forms, > [aʊ].

Tajiki *See* Persian.

Takelma *See* Penutian.

Tamil *Dravidian, spoken in the Indian state of Tamil Nadu and in the north and east of Sri Lanka, and by historical migrations in many other places in the former British Empire. Attested by inscriptions in *Brahmi *c.*200 BC and by literature from soon afterwards; the present South *Indian script has been standard since the late medieval period.

tap A consonant articulated with the shortest possible contact between articulators: e.g. the *t* in *butter* as pronounced by many speakers of American English. *Cf.* flap.

target An ideal sound or articulation which a speaker hypothetically aims at in the production of a phoneme. Central to the account of (Daniel) Jones, and reflected in studies of *coarticulation. Thus the **articulatory target** for [t] in English is an alveolar stop; that of [θ] is an interdental fricative: taken together, these lead to coarticulation in the production of [tθ] in *eighth*.

target language That which one aims to teach, learn, translate into, etc. Opp. source language.

Tatar *See* Turkic.

tatpurusha Term from Sanskrit for a *determinative compound. Named after a representative example: *tatpuruṣa* 'his-man'.

tautology Term in logic for a proposition that cannot but be true: e.g. 'If it is white it is white'. *Cf.* analytic (2).

tautosyllabic Forming part of the same syllable. Thus a phonological *diphthong is analysed into a sequence of two tautosyllabic (opp. 'heterosyllabic') vowels.

'taxonomic linguistics' Term of abuse used by Chomsky in the 1960s, to characterize schools of structural linguistics that, as he saw them, were interested only in procedures for the segmentation and classification of data.

TEFL For 'teaching English as a foreign language'.

'telegraphic speech' Used impressionistically e.g. of the speech of young children, at the stage when they first begin to join words together. Sometimes with the implication that such speech is elliptical: thus, if a child says 'Mummy cup', it might be claimed to stand for e.g. 'Mummy is holding a cup'.

'telementation' Invented by R. Harris to describe the fallacy that communication conveys thoughts from one mind to another.

teleological (Explanation) which appeals to a goal or a result. Thus a teleological explanation for a sound-change might be that it resulted in a greater auditory difference between phonemes, or that it led to a phonological system which was more symmetrical; for a change of syntax that it resulted in a more coherent pattern of word order.

telic ['tɛlɪk] (Aspect, verb) distinguishing events that have an end-point. E.g. *make* is inherently telic, since making something is behaviour with a specific end in view. Thence generally of forms referring to what has ended: e.g. the perfect in *I have read it*, seen as referring to something accomplished, as distinguished from the imperfect in *I was reading it*, as referring to an activity. Also of the type of *situation, thus in this sense an 'accomplishment', referred to.

From a Greek word for 'end'. Originally in the sense of *final = purposive; hence of subordinate clauses with this meaning and the conjunctions with which they are formed.

Telugu *Dravidian, spoken mainly in the Indian state of Andhra Pradesh. Attested by literature from the 11th century AD; the script is very close to that of *Kannada.

template Any structural pattern, at whatever level of abstraction, to which forms are described as conforming. Thus, in *X-bar syntax, phrases of all categories conform to a template in which heads combine successively with other units in defined relations to them; in 'template' or *templatic morphology, a word has a structure formed by slots in fixed positions.

Hence of any specific pattern in any individual language. E.g., in German, main clauses might be said to fit a template in which a finite verb takes second position, with other elements linked to it, e.g. a participle in *ge-* or a preverb such as *auf*, in a position at the end. Thus effectively of any pattern, in grammar or phonology, established as *canonical.

templatic morphology A form of word structure represented by a template in which roots are accompanied by a sequence of slots in fixed positions, filled by mutually exclusive systems of contrasting affixes. Especially of structures like that of the verb in *Athapaskan languages, where many slots can be distinguished. Some languages are seen as having a templatic morphology, others as not having it.

tempo An alternative term for the *rate of speech.

temporal Indicating or involving a time or times. Thus *yesterday* is a **temporal adverb**, and as a deictic element is involved in **temporal *deixis**. *On Tuesdays* or *in April* is likewise a **temporal adverbial**; *when*

I get home is a **temporal clause** in *I will ring when I get home*; in the same clause *when* is a **temporal conjunction**.

tendency A pattern, process, etc. which falls short of a law or rule. E.g. there is a tendency, exemplified to varying degrees in many languages, for a vowel before a nasal consonant to be itself nasalized; but there is no law by which it must be. There is a tendency, e.g. in English, for the longer of two coordinated phrases to come second: *I saw Mary and your friends from New Zealand*, not . . . *your friends from New Zealand and Mary*. But there is no rule of syntax by which the latter is excluded.

tense (1) Inflectional category whose basic role is to indicate the time of an event etc. in relation to the moment of speaking. Divided notionally into **present** (at the moment of speaking), **past** (earlier than the moment of speaking), and **future** (later than the moment of speaking). Thence extended to any forms distinguishing these, whether or not they are inflectional: e.g. English has an inflectional distinction between past (*loved*) and present (*love*), but in addition the auxiliary *will* is often said to mark a future tense (*will love*).

   The division between tense and *aspect is partly fluid. E.g. in *I have done it*, *have* and the past participle (*done*) form a present *perfect: the difference between this and the corresponding non-perfect (*do*) is accordingly one of aspect, or more specifically *phase. But by the same token it identifies the event as prior to the moment of speaking: hence a common change by which a present perfect replaces, e.g. in modern spoken French, a simple past. The boundary with *mood is also fluid. E.g. the past tense in English, though an indication of past time in many basic uses, is also used in e. g. a *remote conditional (*if I saw her* as opposed to *if I see her*) with a role like that of a *subjunctive. It is therefore not surprising that inflections marking aspect, tense, and mood are not always separate, or that the term 'tense' has traditionally been used for distinctions involving all three: thus the 'tenses' of, say, Spanish are the present indicative, present subjunctive, imperfect indicative, etc. Abbreviations such as 'TMA' (for tense–mood–aspect) or 'TM' are now used similarly.

tense (2) Articulated, or claimed to be articulated, with greater effort of the relevant muscles. Opp. lax.

   'Tense' and 'lax' are applied both to overall *articulatory settings and to specific consonants and vowels. E.g. vowels with a narrow posture of the tongue have often been described as 'tense'; also those with an *Advanced Tongue Root.

tensed (Verb, clause) with an inflectional or other indication of *tense (1). *Cf.* finite clause, finite verb; but the terms are not equivalent since e.g. a language may have infinitives which are also inflected for tense.

tense phrase (TP) A *phrase (2) seen, in generative accounts, as headed by a unit characteristically realized by a tense inflection. E.g. *They vanished* as represented, in part, by a structure $_{TP}[\ _T[PAST]\ [they\ vanish]]$, with a head 'T' that would be realized by *-ed*. *Cf.* IP (2).

tension Phonetic feature opposing *tense (2) and *lax, or *fortis and *lenis.

'tenuis' Ancient term for a voiceless, or voiceless unaspirated, stop. From the Latin word for 'slender'.

'term' Name given in *Relational Grammar to elements within the *nucleus (1) of a clause. Such elements bear '**term relations**' (e.g. 'subject of', 'direct object of') to the verb. The '**Stratal Uniqueness Law**' is a principle by which no term relation can be borne by more than one such element on any given *stratum.

terminal node A node in a *tree diagram which is not connected to a lower node. A **terminal string** is, in early formulations of *phrase structure grammar, a string to which no further *rewrite rules apply; hence, in effect, the sequence that can be read off from the bottom of a tree diagram.

termination The ending of a word inflected by suffixes, distinguished from either the *root or a *stem derived from the root. Thus in Italian *-o* is a first-person-singular termination, added e.g. in *mandavo* 'I was sending' to the stem (*mandav(a)-*) of the imperfect indicative.
    Sometimes of a final suffix only. But also, informally, of an inflectional ending as a whole: thus, in this example, *-vo* or *-avo*.

terraced-level (*Tone language) in which successive stretches of speech are distinguished by progressive lowering of the pitch of high tones. Thus, in particular, one with *downstep.

tertiary (in Jespersen's account of syntax) *See* ranks (1).

'tertiary response' *See* secondary response.

TESL For 'teaching English as a *second language'.

TESOL For 'teaching English to speakers of other languages'.

tessitura The pitch range normal in the speech of some specific individual.

tetra- From the Greek word for 'four'. E.g. a **tetrasyllable** is a word with four syllables.

Teutonic An older term for *Germanic.

text Strictly, a written text in the usual sense. Extended by some linguists to cover a coherent stretch of speech, including a conversation or other interchange involving two or more participants, as well as stretches of writing. Hence often equivalent to *discourse, itself extended from similar motives.

textlinguistics The linguistic analysis and description of extended *texts, either written or spoken. Originally in German ('Textlinguistik') and involving, in particular, the concept of a '**text grammar**', or generative grammar for texts, analogous to a grammar generating sentences. *Cf.* Discourse Analysis.

text sentence Lyons's term for a sentence that may be uttered or written as part of a *text, as opposed to a 'system sentence' established as a unit in the *language system.

text-to-speech processing Mechanical synthesis of speech from written input: e.g. in a projected 'reading machine' for blind people.

'textuality' The property by which successive sentences form a coherent *text, as opposed to a random sequence. *Cf.* coherence; *also* cohesion (1).

TG = transformational grammar.

't-glottaling' Pronunciation in English of a *glottal stop [ʔ] in place of intervocalic or final [t].

Thai The official language of Thailand, native to Bangkok and the central third of the country. A member of the *Tai family.

The writing system was developed in or by the late 13th century AD, directly or indirectly from a South *Indian script. But several major sound-changes have intervened, and the relation between spoken and written units is now indirect, with *tones, in particular, distinguished in a variety of different ways.

***that*-clause** A *declarative clause introduced by *that* and serving as the subject, object, or complement of a verb or other element: e.g. *that you will* in *Promise me that you will*, or *that she can*, as complement of the adjective *sure*, in *I am sure that she can*. Distinguished from *relative clauses also beginning with *that* (e.g. in *the man that you saw*).

***that*-trace filter** A rule which excludes e.g. *Who did you say that came*, expressed as a *filter applying to the *complementizer *that* followed by a *trace (*that t came*). Also, since there are parallels in languages other than English, the 'Comp(lementizer)-trace' filter.

thematic 1. Having the role of *theme (1). **2.** (Vowel) which forms a stem to which inflections are added. Especially in accounts of Indo-European languages: e.g. in Ancient Greek the *-e-* and *-o-* of *lú-e-te* 'you are untying' and *lú-o-men* 'we are untying' derive from a thematic vowel *e*/*o* reconstructed as present in some verbs (called 'thematic verbs' and belonging to 'thematic conjugations') but not in others. *Cf.* theme (2): verbs etc. that are not thematic are 'athematic'. **3.** *See* theta roles.

theme 1. A part of a sentence seen as corresponding to what the sentence as a whole, when uttered in a particular context, is about. E.g. *on Sunday* might be the theme (or be thematic) in *On Sunday I have to visit my uncle*: i.e. the sentence as uttered would be about what the speaker is doing on Sunday. *Cf.* topic (2): opp. rheme, e.g. in the theory of *Functional Sentence Perspective. **2.** = stem: the usual term e.g. in French ('thème'), now less usual in English. **3.** Used by Chomsky and his followers from the 1970s for the *case role e.g. of *the rock* in *The rock rolled away* or *I lifted the rock*. Introduced by J. S. Gruber in the 1960s and definable, in such examples, as that of a noun phrase referring to something 'undergoing motion'. Thence, from the outset, of other roles that can loosely be related to this: e.g. that of *I* in *I was there*, as referring to an entity implicitly having moved to a location, of *this car* in *This car is mine*, as referring to one implicitly transferred to the speaker's possession, and so on.

Also, as in ordinary or literary usage, of the theme or *topic (1) of a conversation, text, etc.

theonym A name of a god or goddess: e.g. *Venus, Jehovah. See* -onym.

theory 1. In the usual sense, of any explanatory hypothesis. E.g., in historical linguistics, of the loss of inflections, or the influence of a neighbouring language, as competing explanations for a change in word order. For many linguists *Universal Grammar is a theory in the same sense, that in part explains the acquisition of languages by children. **2.** Thence, more generally, of any abstract characterization of the units, structures, rules, etc. established in the description of individual languages. Thus a theory of the *syllable might specify that syllables have parts defined by binary divisions, have weights distinguished according to *morae, and so on. *Phrase structure grammar is in turn a theory of the structure of sentences, whether or not any explanatory role is claimed for it.

Theories in sense 2 are in particular the domain of what has come to be called '**theoretical linguistics**'.

'theta roles' Term in *Government and Binding Theory for semantic roles such as *agent or *patient: *cf.* case roles. Also written '**θ-roles**': the theta stands for earlier 'thematic', itself derived from *theme (3) for no principled reason.

'Theta Theory' The part of *Government and Binding Theory concerned with the assignment of *theta roles. The most important principle was the '**theta criterion**', which requires that every *argument of a verb should be assigned one and only one such role.

third-order nominal Lyons's term for a nominal expression seen as characteristically referring to an abstract proposition, property, etc.: e.g. *her intelligence* in *I have always admired her intelligence. Cf.* second-order nominal.

third person (3RD, 3) *See* person.

third-person imperative Construction, inflection, etc. used in giving orders or instructions but with the verb in the third person or with a subject traditionally called third person: e.g. the construction, now marginal in English, of *Let no one move*.

Thomas of Erfurt *See* Modistae.

Tibetan Spoken mainly in Tibet; also in Nepal and other adjoining areas. Attested from the 7th century AD, when the writing system, based on an *Indian script, was developed. Classed as *Sino-Tibetan; related within the *Tibeto-Burman branch to many smaller languages of the Himalayan region.

Tibeto-Burman Branch of *Sino-Tibetan distributed over an area from the Himalayas eastwards to north-west Thailand, Laos, and Vietnam. *Burmese has by far the greatest number of speakers: *see also* Tibetan, Karen, Lolo-Burmese.

tier Any of a series of associated levels over which, in models such as that of *Autosegmental Phonology, the phonological representation of a form is distributed. Thus the general structure of words and syllables might be represented at one level: *see* skeletal tier. Specific consonantal and vocalic features might be represented at another, tones or other prosodic features at a third, and so on. *Association lines relate each tier to the others.

Tigrinya South *Semitic language, spoken in northern Ethiopia and Eritrea. Written in a South *Semitic script also used for *Amharic.

tilde (˜) Used in the International Phonetic Alphabet to represent *nasalization: thus French [bɔ̃] (*bon*). A similar symbol, written on the line, is used in logic as one way of representing negation: thus ~ *p* 'It is not the case that *p*'.

timbre The auditory properties of sounds other than those of pitch and loudness: hence sometimes, in phonetics, in the sense of *vowel quality.

time (Adverb, deixis) = temporal.

time depth The distance from the present at which, e.g. two languages that have a common ancestor became separate. Thus, within Indo-European, the time depth for the divergence of any two Romance languages is much less than for either of these and Modern Greek. *Glottochronology was one method designed to establish time depths both relatively and absolutely.

timeless (Proposition etc.) which makes no reference to a specific time or times for which it holds: e.g. 'Iron melts at 1539½° C', as opposed to 'The iron melted (*sc.* at some specific time) in the heat'.

tip The point of the tongue, distinguished as an *articulator from the blade, defined as the upper surface immediately behind it. Hence *apical or apico- ('with the tip') vs. *laminal, lamino- ('with the blade').

TMA *Tense (T), *mood (M), and *aspect (A), especially when marked together. Likewise **TM**, **TA**.

T-marker A representation, in early transformational grammar, of the *transformational history of a sentence. Abbreviation for 'transformation marker'; *cf.* phrase marker.

tmesis ['tmiːsɪs] Construction in which the members of what is elsewhere a compound are separated by other syntactic elements. Originally, in application to e.g. Ancient Greek, of forms involving a verb and a preposition or adverb.

Tocharian Name given to two languages, forming a separate branch of *Indo-European, attested by documents from Chinese Turkestan of the 6th to 8th centuries AD.

token An instance of a unit, as distinct from the unit that is instanced. E.g. in *fluffy* there are three tokens of the letter 'f' and one each of 'l', 'u', and 'y'. Opp. type: thus in the same word six successive letter tokens are instances of four types ('f', 'l', 'u', and 'y').

Tok Pisin Spoken widely in Papua New Guinea. In origin a *pidgin based on English, and now the commonest medium of commerce with, in towns, a growing number of native speakers.

tone A phonetic or phonological unit belonging to a set distinguished or primarily distinguished by levels of or by changes in pitch. E.g. in Ngbaka (spoken mainly in the Central African Republic), *mà* 'magic', *mā* 'I', and *má* 'to me' are distinguished phonologically by a low tone (`), a mid tone (ˉ), and a high tone (´). Used: **1.** As in this example, of units typically associated with a syllable in *tone languages. **2.** Also of units distinguished by variations of pitch in systems of *intonation. E.g. in English, *He's* ´DRUNK (surprised exclamation) is distinguished by a rising tone (´) or by a sequence of a low tone followed by a high tone, from He's `DRUNK (expressing disgust), with a falling tone ( `) or high followed by low.

tone-bearing unit The unit in a *tone language with which a tone is phonologically associated. Typically, though not necessarily, the syllable.

tone group = intonational phrase.

tone language One in which units within words are distinguished phonologically by a distinct *tone or sequence of tones: e.g. Chinese. Typically of those in which tones are assigned to separate syllables; thence, more generally, of ones in which most syllables are so distinguished, or most units of the lexicon, or in which contrasting pitches on accented syllables have some lexical or morphological role. Thus, at the limit, Norwegian is also conventionally called a 'tone language'. *Cf.* pitch accent.

toneme A unit of pitch, especially in *tone languages, treated as or analogously to a *phoneme.

tone sandhi Phonetic or phonological modification of *tones, e.g. in Chinese, in the context of those on preceding or following syllables.

tongue-body (Features etc.) distinguished by the position of the mass of the tongue within the mouth. E.g. front vs. back, *close or high vs. open or low.

tongue height *See* vowel height.

tongue root The part of the tongue opposite the back wall of the throat. Sounds articulated with the tongue root are called 'radical': e.g. a *pharyngeal fricative as opposed to a velar or a uvular, which are *dorsal or articulated with the dorsum.

tonic (Syllable) which is prominent in a pattern of intonation. E.g. in *Peter will finish* any of *Pe-*, *will*, or *fi-* might be tonic: thus, with a tone that falls and then rises in pitch (˅), ˅PE*ter will finish* ('It's Peter who will do it'), *Peter* ˅WILL *finish* ('He's definitely going to'), *Peter will* ˅FI*nish* ('He won't give up before it's done'). In each case the tonic syllable, distinguished by small capitals, carries the main movement of pitch, and may also be longer.

Also called the nucleus (or nuclear syllable): opp. atonic, non-nuclear. A difference in the position of the tonic syllable, as in these examples, is one of **tonicity**.

tonogenesis The historical process by which *tone languages develop from languages without tones. Thus, in one form of tonogenesis, the pitch of a vowel might be lowered before a certain class of consonants; these consonants are later lost, and from then on the pitch distinguishes these syllables from others.

top-down (Procedure) which determines the structure of sentences etc. by working from larger units to smaller. Opp. bottom-up, e.g. as alternative strategies for *parsing systems, or as techniques for analysing an unfamiliar language.

topic 1. Whatever a conversation, text, etc. is about. This might be identified explicitly (e.g. one speaker says 'I want to talk about x') or it might not. **2.** A part of a sentence seen as corresponding to what the sentence as a whole is about: e.g. the topic of *You can now buy clothes at the supermarket* might, in a specific context and with appropriate intonation, be *at the supermarket* ('One thing you can do at the supermarket is buy clothes'). **3.** A specific syntactic element whose role is characteristically that of a topic (2); thus, in English, the phrase which stands first in the construction of *Cheap vodka you should never drink* or *At the supermarket it might be cheaper*.

Topics (1) are sometimes distinguished as '**discourse topics**' as opposed to '**sentence topics**'. For topic (2) *cf.* theme (1). In a language like English, topics (3) and subjects are distinct syntactic elements: _{topic}[*cheap vodka*] _{subject}[*you*] *should never drink*. But in languages of another type, e.g. in Tagalog and others in the Philippines, the term 'topic' is used in preference to 'subject' of an element that has some but not all of the characteristics of a *subject (1) in the traditional European sense. In such cases, in particular, the remainder of the sentence is called the *comment.

topicalization The process of forming a derived construction in which one element is a *topic (3): e.g. that of *Beer I see as a necessity*, with topic *beer*, from that of the 'untopicalized' *I see beer as a necessity*.

'topic-prominent' (Language) in which the basic syntactic elements of a sentence are a *topic (3) and a *comment. Opp. subject-prominent.

toponym A place-name: e.g. *London*.

'total accountability' Principle by which, in an ordered series of *levels, all elements represented at a lower level must be related to elements at higher levels. E.g. each phoneme (at the level of phonology) must be a realization, or part of the realization, of at least one word or morpheme at the level of grammar.

'*tough*-movement' The postulated *raising (2) of an object from an infinitive construction that depends on an adjective such as *tough*. E.g. that of *these conditions* in *These conditions are tough to meet*: compare, with the object unraised, *It is tough to meet these conditions*.

TP = tense phrase.

trace A phonetically *null element seen by Chomsky, from the 1970s onwards, as being left in any position from which a syntactic element has been moved. E.g. in *Mary I really love t*, *t* is the trace left by a movement of *Mary* from its position in *I really love Mary*.

Cf. empty category. Hence a '**Trace Theory**' of movement, in which traces are posited, as opposed to a later account that posits *copying.

trachea Anatomical term for the windpipe.

'trade language' A *pidgin, *lingua franca, or other language, used in commerce among people whose native languages are different.

'trading relation' Used with reference to the balance between different levels of description or different components of a grammar. Thus there are trading relations by which e.g. if the rules of phonology cover less the rules of morphology may in compensation have to cover more, or, by extending the scope of semantics, one may reduce that of syntax.

'traditional grammar' Usually of grammar as it was before the advent of *structural linguistics, conceived as standing in a unified tradition going back to ancient times, with grammar in the 20th century conceived as breaking away from it. Both conceptions are at best qualifiable.

trailing tone *See* starred tone.

transcription Often in the sense of *representation. E.g. a 'phonemic transcription' is a representation of a form as a sequence of phonemes.

transderivational constraint A restriction on a class of syntactic derivations which refers to some factor outside those derivations: e.g. to the possible role of a sentence in *speech acts. Proposed in the context of *Generative Semantics in the early 1970s.

transferred meaning A sense of a word or other unit which is derived by a shift from its basic field of reference to another. E.g. *cold* basically refers to physical temperature; but it has a transferred meaning in *My reception was rather cold* or *She gave me a cold look*. *Cf.* figurative.

transfix A pattern of vowels or consonants seen as a non-continuous affix interleaved with a root or stem that is in turn not continuous: e.g. the *patterns or pattern morphemes in Semitic languages.

transform A sentence, structure, etc. derived by a *transformation: e.g. a passive sentence represented as a 'transform of' an active.

transformation An operation relating one set of structures, especially syntactic structures, to another. Thus, in many accounts, the structures assigned to *declaratives such as *She is here* or *You can help me* have been related by a transformation to those of the corresponding *interrogatives (*Is she here?*, *Can you help me?*).

Transformations were developed by (Zellig) Harris in the 1950s as operations relating one set of forms (e.g. phrases or sentences) to another. Also in parallel by Chomsky as operations on *phrase structure trees deriving other phrase structure trees. In a standard account a **transformational rule** (or **T-rule**) had two parts: a **structural description** or **SD**, which analysed the structures that could undergo the operation into two or more successive elements, and a **structural change** or **SC**, which specified a derived structure resulting from it. Thus the structure assigned to *You can help me* would be divided into three parts: an initial noun phrase (*you*), an auxiliary verb (*can*), and the remainder (*help me*). In the derived structure of the corresponding interrogative the position of the first two would then be reversed: *you can* . . . → *can you* . . . In other cases transformations might or might also involve the deletion of elements, or the addition of new ones, or *restructuring.

transformational grammar (TG) A form of *generative grammar, proposed by Chomsky from the 1950s onwards, of which rules for *transformations formed a distinct component. Hence commonly, in the 1960s and 1970s, of Chomsky's theories, or of the school of linguists that followed them, in general.

In the classic account, which dates from the mid-1960s, the role of transformations was to relate *deep structures to *surface structures. These formed the 'syntactic description' of a sentence, which were then 'interpreted', in the so-called 'Standard Theory' and its successors, by a component whose rules supplied its *semantic representation and *phonetic representation.

For the role they had in the 1950s *see* kernel sentence. By the 1980s the notion of a separate transformational component was already becoming obsolete.

transformational history The sequence of transformations involved in the derivation of a sentence in a *transformational grammar. Represented in the 1950s by a 'transformation marker' or *T-marker.

transition 1. Usually of transitions between successive speech sounds. Thus '**transitional** *formants**' are found e.g. in transitions between stops and vowels; '**transitional probabilities**' concern the probability of one sound, or of one letter, following another. Sometimes in a specific sense like that of *juncture: thus 'close transition', 'open transition'. **2.** *See* rheme.

'Transition Relevance Place' Term in *Conversation Analysis for any point in a speaker's *turn, e.g. the end of a sentence, seen as a natural point at which another participant in a conversation might start speaking, or 'take the floor', instead.

transition zone E.g. between dialects. Hence of a geographical area crossed by *isoglosses, or by many isoglosses rather than few.

transitive (Construction) in which a verb is related to at least two nouns or their equivalent, whose semantic roles are characteristically those of an *agent and a *patient: e.g. that of *She* (agent) *carried him* (patient). A **transitive verb** is one which takes or can take such a construction: thus *carry*, or *carry* in its basic sense.

From Latin *transitivus* 'going across'. The original sense was that of a 'transition' from a 'person' or participant (Latin *persona*) represented by the inflection of the verb to another which is referred to by the object. Opp. intransitive.

transitive preposition A preposition in the traditional sense: i.e. one such as *in* which is followed by a complement (*in Melbourne*). *Cf.* intransitive preposition.

transitivizer An affix etc. by which a transitive verb is derived from an intransitive. E.g., schematically, *cup fell* 'The cup fell over'; *I fell*-TRANS *cup* 'I knocked over the cup'.

'translation' Introduced into French linguistics by L. Tesnière for the process by which a unit that is basically of one syntactic class is transferred to a role that is basically that of another. Thus *cool* is basically an adjective, and *in* and *out* are basically prepositions. But in *the cool of the night* or *the ins and outs* they are 'translated' to the role of nouns. A grammatical element is '**translative**' if it is seen as marking a 'translation': e.g. *the* is translative in both these examples.
  Cf. transposition (2).

transparency 1. The degree to which a form corresponds to a more *abstract representation. E.g. *unhappy* is transparently related to an underlying combination *un + happy*; *illogical* less so to an underlying *in + logical*. **2.** The degree to which the meaning of a form is predictable from its parts: e.g. *undead* is less transparent in meaning than *unkind*.
  Opp. opacity. A **Transparency Principle**, reflecting sense 1, was proposed by D. W. Lightfoot in the late 1970s, as a factor explaining rapid change in syntax. Speakers of each generation were seen as *internalizing a grammar which, as then envisaged, included rules for both *deep (more abstract) and *surface (less abstract) structures of sentences. Over several generations, surface structures might change gradually, through stylistic shifts, contacts with other languages, etc., while deep structures remained constant. But at some stage a required degree of transparency would be lost, and, to restore it, the next generation would restructure them.

transposition 1. Change of sequence: *cf.* metathesis. **2.** Sometimes of processes that change the class of a unit: e.g. the formation of *happiness* is one in which an adjective (*happy*) is 'transposed' to a noun. *Cf.* translation.

tree diagram Any branching diagram in which different branches are connected only at a point of origin, and all are connected, directly or indirectly, to one node which is the origin of the whole: e.g. a 'family tree' which displays the *genetic classification of languages, a *phrase structure tree, a *dependency tree.
  A '**tree**' is technically one type of 'graph' defined in the branch of mathematics called 'graph theory'.

tri- Prefix derived from the Greek word for 'three'. Thus a **trisyllabic** word, or **trisyllable**, is one which has three syllables; a **trigraph**, such as German 'sch' for [ʃ], is a sequence of three letters representing a single phoneme. Opp. mono-, di- or bi-, tetra-, etc.

trial Inflection etc. used in referring to precisely three individuals: *cf*. dual, paucal.

triangular (Vowel system) in which a single open vowel is opposed to closer vowels both front and back. Conventionally displayed on the sides of a triangle, as illustrated e.g. for Spanish.

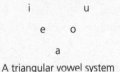

A triangular vowel system

trigger 1. Any factor seen as the immediate cause of change in a language. Thus, in one account, changes in word order in early Middle English were 'triggered by' the reduction of case endings by sound changes. **2.** Any feature etc. whose presence at some stage in a *derivation ensures that a given rule will apply. E.g. in the classic account of *Generative Phonology the rule by which *sing* is changed to *sang* was **triggered by** a *diacritic feature attached to it, for that purpose, by a rule applying earlier.

trigraph *See* tri-.

trill A consonant produced with one articulator held close to another so that a flow of air sets up a regular vibration. E.g. the 'rr' of Spanish *burro* 'donkey' is a lingual trill, with vibration of the tip of the tongue, or specifically a dental trill, articulated in the *dental position of articulation. *Uvular trills, with vibration of the uvula against the back of the tongue, are possible, though not usual, for the 'r' in French.

triphthong A vowel whose quality changes in two successive directions within a single syllable: e.g. [ʌɪə] in many pronunciations of English *tire*, where the quality changes from relatively open to relatively close and front, and then from relatively front to central. *Cf*. diphthong; monophthong.

trivalent (Verb) whose *valency includes three arguments or valents: e.g. *send*, in I *sent her a present*, whose valency includes a subject (*I*) and two objects (*her, a present*).

trochaic (*Foot) consisting of a *heavy syllable followed by a light syllable. Borrowed into *Metrical Phonology from the definition of a trochee in verse.

trope A *figure of speech, especially one involving a *figurative extension of the meaning of a word or other expression.

TRP = Transition Relevance Place.

Trubetzkoy, Nikolai Sergeyevich (1890–1938) Russian linguist, from 1922 Professor of Slavic Philology in Vienna and usually referred to by the Germanized form of his name. A pioneer in structuralist phonology and morphophonology and, with Jakobson, a leading figure in the pre-war *Prague School. His great work, *Grundzüge der Phonologie*, published in 1939 after his death, sets out the foundation for the structuralist theory of the phoneme, of phonological systems and distinctive features, and of phonology generally (English translation, *Principles of Phonology*, 1969).

T-rule *See* transformation.

truncation = clipping.

truth conditions The conditions under which a sentence, or a proposition expressed by it, is true: e.g. *I have red hair* is true under the condition that the speaker has, in fact, red hair. **Truth-conditional semantics** is an account of the truth conditions of sentences, often one in which the meaning of a sentence is equated with them.

Tsonga *Bantu language, spoken in an area divided between southern Mozambique and the Transvaal in South Africa.

Tswana *Bantu language spoken mainly in South Africa and Botswana.

Tucano(an) Family of languages spoken especially in the province of Vaupés in south-east Colombia and across the boundary with Brazil; and to the west across the boundary between Colombia and Ecuador.

tune = contour.

Tungusic Family of languages in east Siberia, including Evenki or Tungus, spoken mainly on Sakhalin Island. A proposed branch of *Altaic.

Tupi-Guaraní Family of languages in South America. **Tupinambá**, now extinct, was spoken along a large part of the coast of Brazil and documented after the Portuguese conquest. Of the other members *Guaraní, centred on Paraguay, is by far the most important; the remainder are scattered across the area to the south of the Amazon, with others classed more generally as **Tupian**.

Turing machine A device, conceived in the abstract by the mathematician A. Turing in the 1930s, capable of performing any finite computation; hence e.g. of producing or processing sentences in any *formal language.

Turkic Family of languages, in part forming what is in effect a *dialect continuum, which extends from the Balkans, across much of Central Asia, into Siberia. *Turkish is the largest; others, roughly in declining order of size, include *Uzbek, *Azerbaijani, Uighur (mainly in the north of Xinjiang in China), Kazakh (mainly in Kazakhstan), Tatar (in the Tatar region of Russia), Turkmen (east of the Caspian mainly in Turkmenistan), Kirghiz (mainly again in Kirghizia); also Yakut, detached from other members in the region of the River Lena in north Siberia.

A proposed branch of *Altaic.

Turkish *Turkic, the official language of Turkey, where it is native to the vast majority; also spoken by minorities in Cyprus and the Balkans, and elsewhere in Europe through immigration. Closely related within Turkic to Azerbaijani, from which it is geographically separated by Armenian, and Turkmen.

Attested from the 13th century AD, and written in Arabic script until the Roman alphabet, supplemented by diacritics, was adopted at the end of the 1920s. As a literary and administrative language Turkish was heavily influenced, especially from the late Middle Ages, by both Arabic and Persian.

Turkmen *See* Turkic.

'turn' A proposed unit of conversation, seen as something said by one speaker and preceded, followed, or both by a 'turn' of some other speaker. Speakers 'take turns', according to the theory of *Conversation Analysis, in a way that is regulated by a specific '**turn-taking**' system.

Hence '**Turn Transition Place**', of a point where turns change, *Transition Relevance Place, etc.

Tuyuca Spoken in the Vaupés valley on the boundary between Colombia and Brazil. Tucano(an), cited in particular for a rich system of *evidentials and as one of the languages, of different families, involved in a system of *linguistic exogamy.

two-place (*Predicate (2)) taking two arguments: e.g. *see* in I *saw Bill* (with arguments I and *Bill*), or *angry* in I *was angry with Bill*. *Cf.* bivalent.

type 1. Any set of languages seen as sharing, to a greater or lesser degree, some structural characteristic or set of characteristics. A language which entirely meets the definition of a type is said to be '**consistent**': thus, in particular, of *VO vs. OV languages. **2.** *See* token.

typological classification The classification of languages into *types (1), especially by sets of similarities seen as logically or otherwise connected. For examples *see* ergative language vs. accusative language; agglutinating, inflecting, isolating; VO vs. OV languages.

Opp. genetic classification.

Tzotzil *Mayan language spoken in an area in the west of the state of Chiapas in Mexico.

Ubangi A group of languages spoken across the Central African Republic and in adjacent parts of Cameroon, Congo, and Sudan. **Sango** is an Ubangi creole based on Ngbandi (from northern Congo), with official status and used increasingly as a second language in the Central African Republic.

UG = Universal Grammar.

Ugaritic Alphabetic script, with *cuneiform symbols, used for the Semitic language of ancient Ugarit (at a site now in north Syria) in the mid- to late second millennium BC. The order of letters is known and corresponds to that of the North *Semitic alphabets first attested a few centuries later.

Ugric Branch of *Finno-Ugric which includes Hungarian.

Uighur *See* Turkic.

Ukrainian East *Slavic, becoming distinct from *Russian by the late 14th century. Written in *Cyrillic; native to a large part of the population of the Ukraine and in the neighbouring part of Poland.

ultimate constituents The smallest units in an analysis of the *constituency of a sentence. Often taken to be *morphemes: thus the ultimate constituents of *The children like eating* might be *the, child, -ren, like, eat,* and *-ing*.

ultimate head A *head (1) in which no smaller head is included. E.g., in *large yellow waterproof boots*, the first adjective, *large*, will be described in one analysis as the modifier of a head *yellow waterproof boots*: [*large* [*yellow waterproof boots*]]. Within this, *yellow* will in turn modify a head, *waterproof boots*, which in turn will be headed by the ultimate head, *boots*: [*large* [*yellow* [*waterproof* [*boots*]]]].

Also called, in earlier accounts, the '**centre**' of such phrases.

Umbrian *See* Italic.

Umgangssprache German for 'colloquial language'.

umlaut Used of various sound changes, especially in Germanic languages, in which a back vowel becomes front in the context of another front vowel. E.g. the front vowel of *feet* (Old English *fēt*) is explained by the fronting of *ō* (Old English *fōt*) before a reconstructed plural suffix *-i* (**fōt-i*). Similar changes in other languages are also called *metaphony.

The umlaut in writing (¨) is used in some phonetic transcriptions for rounded front vowels: thus [ü], as German *ü*, = [y].

unaccusative Used of a verb in an intransitive construction which is seen as taking an underlying object rather than a subject. E.g. *die* or *arrive*: thus, according to what is called the '**unaccusative hypothesis**', *she* is initially an object in *She died* and *She arrived*. Other intransitives are '**unergative**': thus *sleep* is an unergative verb, and *she* is not at an underlying level an object, in *She slept*.

First proposed in *Relational Grammar, and claimed to be the basis for a variety of formal distinctions in various languages. E.g., in Italian, verbs that take the auxiliary 'to be' are claimed to be unaccusative: *È arrivata Maria* (lit. 'is arrived-FEM Mary') 'Mary has arrived'. Those said to be unergative take 'to have': *Ha dormito Maria* (lit. 'has slept Mary') 'Mary has slept'.

unaspirated (*Voiceless *plosive) in which there is no audible delay between the *release of the closure and the onset of *voice in a sound that follows: e.g. the [t] and [p] of Italian *tempo* 'time', in contrast to the *aspirated [tʰ] and [pʰ] in many pronunciations of *tempo* in English.

unbounded (Relation etc.) between syntactic elements that is not subject to a restriction on the complexity of intervening structures. Thus in sentences like *Who has he seen?* the relation between *who* and *seen* is not restricted by the depth at which the verb can be subordinated: *Who does he say he has seen?*, *Who do you think he says he has seen?*, and so on. Opp. bounded; *cf.* local (1).

unconditioned Not *conditioned; *see also* spontaneous.

uncountable (Noun) whose syntax is characteristic of a class whose members do not denote individuals that can be counted. Thus, in English, one that has a singular form with expressions like *less* or *a lot of* (*less meat, a lot of architecture*), that does not take a numeral or the indefinite article, and so on.

Opp. countable; alternatively '**mass nouns**' (such as *meat* or *architecture*) are opposed to '**count nouns**'.

underdetermination Property of the meanings of sentences if considered in abstraction from potential ambiguities in context. Thus, in principle, *You won't die* could mean 'You are immortal'; alternatively, it could mean simply that a course of action will not have dire consequences. A representation of its meaning would be *underspecified (2) to the extent that it did not distinguish these alternatives.

underdifferentiation Failure, in acquiring a second or foreign language, to distinguish units that are not matched by corresponding distinctions in the first or native language. E.g. [t] and [tʰ] are separate consonants in Hindi; in English they are not; therefore an English speaker trying to learn Hindi might perceive them as the same unit and fail to distinguish words that contain them.

underextension Use of a word etc. with less than its usual range of denotation. E.g. a young child might at one stage call the family's own cat 'pussy', but not use the word of cats in general.

undergoer = patient.

underlying (Form, structure, etc.) posited at a more *abstract level of representation. E.g. in the classic account of *Generative Phonology, both [dɪvʌɪn] (*divine*) and [dɪvɪn] (in *divinity*) are assigned an underlying form 'divīn'. At a less abstract level long ī is realized by either [ʌɪ] or [ɪ]. Likewise, in the classic form of *transformational grammar, the *deep structure of a sentence was a representation underlying its *surface structure.

Thence, more generally, of any earlier stage in a derivation.

underspecified In the broad sense of 'not represented fully'. Hence: **1.** Of a representation at any level in which elements are unspecified if they are predictable from others. Thus especially in phonology, of representations that make explicit only features not determined by those of units adjacent to them; or only those whose values are *marked (2), in that they are not seen as predictable by universal principles. **2.** Of a representation of the meaning of a sentence which is neutral in relation to the varying meanings that it might have in specific contexts: *cf.* underdetermination.

Hence '**Underspecification Theory**', of accounts either of phonology or of semantics in which such representations are posited.

'understood' (Words etc.) recoverable in cases of *ellipsis. E.g. in *I won't be going tonight*, the construction might be said to include an understood adverbial of place: *I won't be going* <sc. *to the party*>, <sc. *to the meeting*>, and so on.

unergative *See* unaccusative.

'unfilled pause' An interval of silence in speech: i.e. a *pause not 'filled' by a *hesitation form.

ungrammatical Not *grammatical (2).

unification Process in formal models of syntax by which the set of features that characterize a larger unit is derived from those of its separate constituents. E.g. *these* is a determiner and is plural: thus it has the features [Det, PL]. *Books* is a noun, is plural, and, as a head of a noun phrase, can take a determiner: [N, PL, + Det]. By virtue of these features *these* can combine with *books* to form a larger unit: *these books*. By the process of unification this will in turn have the features [N, PL]: i.e. it is in turn a plural noun phrase.

Cf. percolation. **Unification-based** models, such as *Head-Driven Phrase Structure Grammar, are those in which such a process is central.

uniformitarian principle The assumption that the general properties of language and of processes of change in language have been the same throughout human history and prehistory. Invoked e.g. to exclude *reconstructions positing forms or systems contrary to principles etc. thought to constrain existing languages.

Modelled, tendentiously in one view, on the uniformitarian principle in 19th-century geology.

unilateral One-sided: e.g. in a unilateral dependency *a* depends on *b* but *b* does not depend on *a*. Opp. bilateral (2).

union 1. Technically of an operation on sets by which the union (or **sum**) of sets A and B is the set of all elements which are members of at least one of them. *Cf.* intersection. **2.** *See* clause union.

uniplex *See* social network.

unit Anything that is treated as a whole at some level of analysis or description. Thus in phonology the initial [f] of *fiendish* is a unit; likewise the first syllable [fiːn], seen as a whole in relation to the second syllable [dɪʃ]. In grammar both the root *fiend* and the suffix *-ish* are units; also *fiendish* itself, seen as a whole in potential relation e.g. to a following noun. With such a noun it may in turn form a larger unit, and so on.

universal Traditionally of a general term or concept, e.g. *man* or 'man', and, in one view, of an aspect of reality corresponding to it. *Cf.* nominalism; realism. More usual in linguistics in the sense of *linguistic universal.

universal base hypothesis The notion, common in theories of *transformational grammar from the mid-1960s, that the grammar of every language had a *base component which included the same, or essentially the same, set of syntactic rules. Hence the differences between languages lay in their *surface, not in their underlying or *deep structures.

universal grammar Traditionally of any system of grammatical categories, structures, rules, etc. seen as common to all languages. Thus one in which, e.g., all languages distinguish nouns and verbs, or all languages have rules for *anaphora.

Cf. Universal Grammar as conceived by Chomsky, which has however evolved separately and for different reasons.

Universal Grammar (UG) A set of mental structures seen by Chomsky and his followers as genetically inherited by all human beings, underlying and explaining the development of language in their childhood. Often represented as an idealized initial stage in language acquisition, at which infants are conceived as knowing nothing of particular languages. Such knowledge can then be thought of as developing from it, partly by the setting of *parameters in response to the speech each child will be exposed to; partly, through the same experience, by the addition of rules specific to individual languages, of specific features of the units that will form their lexicon, and so on.

The object in particular, since the early 1980s, of successive versions of *Principles and Parameters Theory.

Universal Language Movement Movement aiming to establish a single written language for scientific or philosophical purposes, important in England in the 17th century, especially in the first decade (1660–) of the Royal Society, and in France and Europe generally from the 17th to the end of the 18th. The motives were different from those which inspired the later development of Esperanto and other international *auxiliary languages.

universal of language *See* linguistic universal.

universal quantifier (∀) Operator in logic used in expressions interpretable as asserting universality. E.g. (∀ x) (human, x → dance, x) 'For all x, if x is human then x dances': i.e. 'All people dance'.

univocal Interpretable in only one way. Opp. ambiguous and, in the philosophical tradition, 'equivocal'.

unmarked Not *marked. E.g. voiceless [t] in German is unmarked ([– voice]) in opposition to voiced [d] ([+ voice]); singular *book* is unmarked ([– plural]) in opposition to plural *books* ([+ plural]); the order of words in *I never did it* is unmarked in opposition to the marked order of *I did it* NEVer.

unordered **1.** (Rules) that are not *ordered rules. **2.** (Form of representation) that does not indicate any sequencing of units.

unproductive (Formation) restricted to a closed set of forms. E.g. the formation of *awake* or *asleep*, with prefix *a-*, cannot be extended to form *adoze, aslumber*, and so on. Opp. productive.

unreal (conditional) *See* remote.

'unreleased' *See* release.

unrestricted rewrite system A system of *rewrite rules, each of the form X → Y, where both X and Y are strings of whatever length. A phrase structure grammar formulated as a rewrite system is by contrast restricted in that (*a*) each rule rewrites one element only, (*b*) the string by which it is rewritten cannot be null.

unrounded (Vowel, consonant) produced either without rounding of the lips or specifically with the lips spread: e.g. the [b] and [ɪ] of *bin*, as opposed to both the [b] and the [ʊ] of *book*.

untensed (Verb, clause) without an inflectional or other indication of *tense (1). Opp. tensed.

unvoiced = voiceless, especially as the result of *devoicing.

'upstairs clause' = superordinate clause. Likewise 'upstairs subject' etc. = subject etc. of a superordinate clause.

upstep Raising of the pitch of a high tone preceded by another high tone. *Cf.* downstep.

ur- German prefix meaning 'original' or 'primitive'. E.g. an 'Ursprache' is a *protolanguage; the 'Urheimat' of the peoples speaking Indo-European is the home territory from which, hypothetically, they migrated across Europe and Asia.

'Ural-Altaic' Conjectural family of languages, of which *Uralic and *Altaic are the proposed branches.

Uralic Family of languages subsuming *Finno-Ugric and *Samoyedic.

'urban dialectology' Usually of sociolinguistic investigations in cities in the broad tradition of Labov and his followers.

Urdu *See* Hindi-Urdu.

usage Traditionally of the way a language is customarily spoken or written, as opposed to the rules laid down by grammarians. Thus, in particular, forms or constructions may be 'justified by usage' even though a rule apparently proscribes them. A grammar which is descriptive rather than *prescriptive will therefore purport to describe usage without prejudice.

use A specific meaning of a grammatical word, inflection, etc. distinguished in a grammar from other meanings. E.g. an *-*ing* form in English has one use in *the men standing up* and another in *Standing up is painful*; the basic use of a past tense is in reference to past time (*He came yesterday*), but its use in a *remote condition is often in reference to the future (*It would be nice if he came tomorrow*).
    Compare a 'sense' (1) of a lexical unit.

use vs. mention *See* mention.

Uto-Aztecan Family of languages either spoken or formerly spoken in various parts of Central America and the western USA. An Aztecan branch includes *Nahuatl with others scattered eastwards to El Salvador and Honduras. Another group (Sonoran) are spoken mainly in north-east Mexico; the northernmost (Shoshonean) includes Comanche and Hopi among others.

utterance Anything spoken on a specific occasion. Often opposed to *sentence: e.g. the words 'Come here!', spoken by a specific speaker at a specific time, form an utterance which would be an instance of a sentence *Come here!*

   Hence **utterance meaning**, as what is meant by an utterance, or is the meaning intended by a speaker, in a specific context on a specific occasion. Distinguished as such from **sentence meaning**, e.g. on the assumption that this is a *Logical Form or *semantic representation determined by a grammar. Differentiated further, in one analysis, into '**utterance-type**' and '**utterance-token**' meanings: the former being characterized by the 'semantics' of the sentence uttered, with the addition of generalized but not particularized *conversational implicatures, seen as belonging to *pragmatics.

uvular Articulated with the back of the tongue against or approximated to the fleshy appendage (or **uvula**) at the back of the soft palate. E.g. the 'r' in French is variously a uvular *trill or, more usually, a uvular fricative.

Uzbek *Turkic language, spoken in Central Asia in an area centred on Tashkent, and with official status in Uzbekistan. Another Turkic language, also called 'Uzbek', is spoken mainly in Afghanistan.

v *See* light verb.

V 1. = verb. **2.** = vowel. **3.** As a cover term for forms such as French *vous*, Dutch *U*, or Spanish *usted(es)*, all polite forms for 'you', as opposed to the corresponding *familiar, or 'T', forms.

V2 order = verb-second order.

valency The range of syntactic elements either required or specifically permitted by a verb or other lexical unit. E.g. the valency of *eat* includes a subject (*I* in *I am eating*) and an object (*cheese* in *I am eating cheese*). An element which is required is an **obligatory valent**; one which is specifically permitted but is not required is an **optional valent**. Thus *eat* must be explicitly associated with an object, since there are other verbs with which an object is not possible; but it is an optional valent since, in e.g. *I am eating*, it can be omitted.

   Cf. argument for 'argument structure'. 'Valency' and '**valence**' are alternative translations of the term in French or German ('valence', 'Valenz'), introduced by L. Tesnière by analogy with the chemistry of atoms. Defined by him as a property of verbs, but soon extended by his followers to adjectives and, in part at least, to other categories.

valency changing (Operation, construction, etc.) involving a change of *valency or *argument structure. E.g. if a *causative verb is derived from a non-causative its valency is enlarged to include a 'causer'; if an active verb or sentence is turned into the passive then, among other things, an agent becomes optional; and so on.

valency dictionary Any listing of lexical units in which *valencies are distinguished.

valency grammar A partial model of grammar, developed especially in Germany in the early 1970s, in which the syntactic and semantic roles of valents are described within a framework of *dependency relations. E.g. in *She saw me* both the subject and the object would depend, as valents, on *saw*; in *She is angry with me* both the subject and *with me* might be described as valents and dependents of *angry*. *Cf.* semantic valency vs. syntactic valency.

value 1. Of a variable: e.g. a *feature such as [Animate] is a variable with the values [+ Animate] (animate) and [– Animate] (inanimate). **2.** = French 'valeur', used by Saussure of the place or function of an element within a network of relations.

variable In the ordinary sense: thus variable *feature, *sociolinguistic variable. For 'variable rules' *see* rule.

variant Usually of the alternative *realizations of a unit: e.g. an aspirated [tʰ] in *top* and unaspirated [t] in *stop* are *conditioned variants of this phoneme.

variety Any form of a language seen as systematically distinct from others: thus the dialect of a specific region (e.g. Cornwall), any more general form distinguished as a whole by speakers (e.g. American English or British English), a *social dialect, one of the forms distinguished in *diglossia, a dialect used in a specific genre of literature, and so on.

variphone Used by (Daniel) Jones for a sound whose pronunciation varies perceptibly in ways independent of phonetic or other context. *Cf.* free variation.

Varro, Marcus Terentius (116–27 BC) Roman polymath, whose work *De lingua latina* ('On the Latin language') is partly extant. Of the books wholly or largely surviving, three are the last of a series on the origins of words, and the remainder the first of a series on what would now be called morphology. A third series, on syntax, is lost. Varro's treatment has flashes of insight, whether his own or from a Greek original, not found in the later grammatical tradition, and his account of the grammatical controversies in his time (*see* analogists vs. anomalists) is widely reflected in histories of linguistics.

Vedic Ancient language of the north-west of the Indian subcontinent, the earliest form of what is later called *Sanskrit. Attested by collections of religious formulae and hymns transmitted orally (the 'Vedas') of which the most archaic linguistically is the Ṛgveda or 'Rigveda', datable to the second millennium BC.

'vehicular language' = *langue véhiculaire*.

velar Articulated with the back of the tongue against or approximated to the soft palate (or velum). E.g. [k] in [kat] (*cat*) is a velar *stop; [x] in some pronunciations of *loch* ([lɒx]) a velar *fricative.

'velaric' (*Airstream mechanism) involving suction of the tongue against the roof of the mouth; hence with the closure of part of the tongue against the velum or soft palate. Used in the production of *clicks. 'Lingual', suggested by J. Laver, would be a more appropriate term.

velarization *Secondary articulation (1) in which the back of the tongue is raised towards the soft palate (velum). E.g. an 'l' at the end of a word is velarized ([ɫ]) in many forms of English.

'velar softening' Process by which e.g the final [k] of *critic* [krɪtɪk] is changed to [s] in *criticism* [krɪtɪsɪzm].

velic closure Raising of the soft palate (velum) so that air cannot pass in or out through the nose. **Velic release** of a stop consonant is release by lowering the velum: e.g. of [t] in [bʌtn̩] (*button*).

velum The soft or fleshy part of the roof of the mouth; = soft palate.

verb (V) One of a class of lexical units whose characteristic syntactic role is as a *predicate (2) or *predicator and which is characteristically that of words denoting actions or processes: e.g. *run, make, melt*. Verbs and nouns were distinguished in antiquity as two 'principal' *parts of speech without which a complete sentence could not be formed; often taken, for similar reasons, to be *substantive universals.

verbal 1. Pertaining to or involving verbs or a verb. Thus *sing-* in *sings* or *singer* is a verbal root or stem; *-s* in *sings* is a verbal ending or suffix; *He sings it* is a verbal as opposed to a *nominal sentence. **2.** Consisting of words: e.g. *he, sings,* and *it* form the **verbal component**, as distinct e.g. from an intonational component, of a sentence or utterance 'He ˘SINGS it'.

verbal noun Typically of forms which derive systematically from verbs but whose syntax is like that of nouns: e.g. *building* in *the reckless building of freeways. Cf.* deverbal.

verb phrase (VP) A *phrase whose *head (1) is a *verb. As conceived in the 1950s the implicit equivalent of a *predicate (1): e.g. *I* $_{\rm VP}$[*will see him tomorrow*]. In other accounts consisting of a verb plus its *complements or *arguments: *I will* $_{\rm VP}$[*see him*] *tomorrow*, or, if the auxiliary is treated differently, *I* $_{\rm VP}$[*will see him*] *tomorrow*; in others a verb alone with accompanying auxiliaries: *I* $_{\rm VP}$[*will see*] *him tomorrow*. Also, in the context of Chomsky's *Principles and Parameters Theory, of a unit that includes the subject: *see* VP-Internal Subject Hypothesis.

　In all cases the verb is seen as the head of the unit. The variation, therefore, is not in the definition, but in its application to different accounts of *constituency and of the categories that constituents are assigned to.

verb raising *Clause union, seen as a process of *raising (2) by which a verb is moved from a subordinate clause.

verb-second order The order of elements e.g. in main clauses in German, in which a verb, either lexical or auxiliary, is in second position: *Vielleicht weisst du das nicht* (lit. 'Perhaps know you that not'), *Das habe ich nicht gesagt* ('That have I not said'), and so on.

verb serialization *See* serial verb construction.

vernacular (Language) native to a given community, as opposed to a learned or other second language: e.g. the native languages of Catholic Europe in the Middle Ages and later, in opposition to Latin. Thence generally of languages that are not standardized, of non-standard varieties of those that are, of forms used locally or characteristic of non-dominant groups or classes.

A '**vernacular form**' is similarly, in the strict sense, a form which belongs to the speech that is native to a community.

Verner's Law The explanation by K. Verner of a set of exceptions to *Grimm's Law in which the Germanic reflex of a Proto-Indo-European voiceless stop was not, as predicted, a voiceless fricative. In words where it was, the accent in Proto-Indo-European, as attested by other languages such as *Vedic, had fallen on the preceding syllable: Gothic *brōþar* (-[θ]-), Vedic *bhrätar-* 'brother'. Where it was not, the accent had fallen elsewhere: Old English *fæder*, Vedic *pitár* 'father'.

The explanation was published in 1876, and played an important role in confirming the *Neogrammarian 'Regularity Principle'.

vertical line (ˈ,ˌ) Used to mark *primary (ˈ) and *secondary (ˌ) stress on the syllable following: e.g. [ˈbʌtə] (*butter*) has stress on the first syllable, [rɪˈbʌt] (*rebut*) has stress on the second. 'ˈ' is also used to represent *downstep in tone languages; also 'ˌ', under a letter, to mark a syllabic consonant.

vetitive = prohibitive.

Vietnamese *Mon-Khmer, native in the lowland areas of Vietnam: sometimes cited as a paradigm instance of an *isolating language. Formerly written in Chinese characters or in characters derived from Chinese; now in a Roman script developed by European missionaries in the 17th century, in which, in particular, tones and associated voice qualities are represented by diacritics.

vigesimal (Numeral system) based on twenty, as opposed to a decimal system based on ten.

Visible Speech System of phonetic notation published by A. M. Bell in the 1860s, in which letter-like characters represent specific positions etc. of the vocal organs.

VO *See* VO vs. OV languages.

vocal cords Parallel folds of mucous membrane in the larynx, running from front to back and capable of being closed or opened, from the back, to varying degrees. In normal breathing they are open; likewise in producing speech sounds that are *voiceless. In the production of *voice they are close together and vibrate as air passes periodically between them. In the production of *ejectives, for example, they are closed completely.

Also called '**vocal folds**'. The space between the vocal cords is the **glottis**.

'vocal fry' = creak.

vocal gesture = articulatory *gesture.

vocalic 1. Consisting of or pertaining to a vowel or vowels.
2. *Distinctive feature in the schemes of Jakobson and of Chomsky and Halle, *SPE*. Voiced vowels and *liquids are [+ vocalic], all others [– vocalic]. *Cf.* consonantal.

vocalized (Text) written in a *consonantal alphabet, to which indications of vowels have been added.

vocal organs Any of the organs involved in the production of speech, from the chest muscles, by which air is expelled or drawn into the lungs, upwards.

vocal tract The passages above the larynx through which air passes in the production of speech: thus, more particularly, the throat, the mouth (or **oral tract**), and the passages in the nose (or **nasal tract**). Also of the oral tract alone.

vocative Form traditionally characterized by use in calling someone or in getting their attention. Thus the archaic *O* of *We beseech thee, O Lord* is a vocative particle; *Bill* has a vocative role in *Bill, where are you?*; in e.g. Latin, nouns with a similar role were in the vocative *case.

vocoid A vowel defined phonetically, by the way it is produced, as distinguished from a vowel in a phonological sense, defined by its role in the structure of words and syllables. Thus, in English, the *semivowels [j] (as in *yes*) and [w] (as in *wed*) are vocoids, though phonologically consonants.
   Cf. contoid: both terms were introduced by Pike in the 1940s.

voice (1) Vibration of the *vocal cords in the production of speech. **Voiced** sounds are those produced with voice or distinguished by a greater element of voice from those classed as **voiceless**. E.g. in the production of [bɪl] (*bill*) the vowel and final consonant are voiced throughout; the initial consonant is distinguished by an earlier *voice onset time from the voiceless [p] of [pɪl] (*pill*).
   Normal or **modal voice** is distinguished, in accounts of *phonation or *voice quality, from *creak or creaky voice, or *falsetto. For 'whispery voice' *see* whisper.

voice (2) Used conventionally from the late Middle Ages for a grammatical category by which forms of verbs are opposed as *active or *passive, or as active, passive, or *middle. Thus in *Everyone admired Margaret* the verb *admired* is in the active voice; in *Margaret was admired by everyone, was admired* or the participle *admired* is in the passive voice.
   Thence of any grammatical opposition in which different verb forms are associated with changes in the syntactic roles of units related to them. Thus in *Everyone admired Margaret, Margaret* is the object; in *Margaret was admired* or *Margaret was admired by everyone* it is instead the subject. Similarly, in an *antipassive, what would otherwise have the

syntactic role marked by the ergative has instead that of the absolutive. Therefore antipassive is a voice just as passive is a voice.

voiced aspirate Used of *murmured consonants in various Indo-Aryan languages. Thus, in the phonology of *Sanskrit, voiceless and voiced stops without aspiration (e.g. *t*, *d*) were opposed to voiceless aspirates (*th*) and voiced aspirates (*dh*).

Thence of a set of reconstructed consonants in Proto-Indo-European, which, in an account disputed but widely accepted, opposed voiceless stops (*t*) to, on the one hand, voiced (*d*) and, on the other, 'voiced aspirate' = murmured (*d^h*).

voice dynamics Features of the production of speech which do not distinguish individual phonological units and which are not those of *voice quality. Thus variation in the rate of speech, in pitch, in loudness, rhythm, and so on.

voiceless Produced without vibration of the vocal cords: e.g. in ['fɪʃə] (*fisher*) the [f] and [ʃ] are voiceless while the vowels are voiced, or produced with *voice (1).

voice onset time (VOT) The timing of an onset of *voice (1) in relation to the *release of a *plosive consonant. Thus in *pea* there tends to be a **lag** or delay between the release of the initial [p] and the onset of voice in the following [iː]; in *bee* there is either no delay or a **lead** in which the onset of voice precedes the release of [b]. The difference in voice onset time is the main factor distinguishing such consonants.

'voiceprint' A printout of the spectrum of a stretch of speech, in a form promoted by its inventors with the claim that it enabled individual speakers to be identified.

voice quality The features that habitually or permanently characterize an individual speaker's voice. Thus, in particular, those involving a fixed *articulatory setting: a nasalized quality, with incomplete raising of the soft palate, a falsetto quality, and so on.

volitive (*Modality) of forms expressing wishes. E.g. that of an explicit wish like *I wish you were here*; also of an *optative inflection. Also called '**volitional**'.

Voltaic = Gur.

VOS language One in which a verb, *object (3), and *subject (3) are at least basically or most commonly in that order. Opp. VSO language, SVO language, etc.

VOT = voice onset time.

VO vs. OV languages Ones in which a verb (V) precedes, or basically or usually precedes, an object (O), opposed to ones in which it follows: e.g. English (VO), Japanese (OV).

Thence of a distinction between *types (1) of languages defined by this and by a number of other structural characteristics seen, especially in work of the late 1970s, as linked to it. E.g. a *consistent language of the VO type would also have prepositions in the sense of *adpositions that precede their complements; a consistent OV language would instead have *postpositions that follow them.

vowel Originally, in ancient accounts of Greek and Latin, of a minimal unit of speech that could be produced on its own and could, on its own, form a syllable: e.g. [iː] in Latin could form the one-syllable word *i* 'go!'. Now, more generally or more precisely, of one that is produced with *open approximation and that characteristically forms the *nucleus (2) of a syllable: e.g. [a] in *bat* [bat], [iː] in *bee* [biː], [ɑː] in *are* [ɑː]. Distinguished as such from *syllabic consonants: e.g. [l] as, uncharacteristically, a nucleus in *battle* ['batl]. Also from *semivowels, e.g. [w] as the onset of a syllable in *we* [wiː], or *approximants.

See vocoid for a proposed distinction between a unit defined in purely phonetic terms and one defined phonologically. *Cf.* vocalic (2) as a distinctive feature [± vocalic] combining with [± consonantal]; also, in some accounts, with [± syllabic].

vowel gradation Differences between vowels which carry morphological contrasts: specifically the system of *ablaut in Indo-European languages.

vowel harmony Agreement among vowels in successive syllables in respect of one or more features. E.g., in Turkish, *köy* 'village' has a front vowel (*ö*) while *son* 'end' has a back vowel; in harmony with these the plural suffix has a front vowel (*e*) in *köyler* (*köy-ler*) 'villages', but a back vowel (*a*) in *sonlar* (*son-lar*) 'ends'.

vowel height One of the main parameters in the classification of vowels. In the system of *cardinal vowels a **close** vowel is described as one produced with the highest point of the tongue as close as possible to the roof of the mouth. An **open** vowel is one produced with the highest point of the tongue as far away as possible from the roof of the mouth; **close-mid** (or **half-close**) and **open-mid** (or **half-open**) represent intermediate points, perceived as auditorily equidistant, between these. Alternatively, close vowels are '**high**', open vowels are '**low**', and a vowel at an intermediate point is '**mid**'.

vowel quadrilateral *See* cardinal vowels.

vowel quality The auditory character of a vowel as determined by the posture of the vocal organs above the larynx. Thus the quality of [a] remains the same, whether it is produced loudly or softly, or with a high pitch or a low pitch. But its quality is different from that of [i], which is produced with the lower jaw and tongue much closer to the roof of the mouth, or that of nasal [ã], in which the passages through the nose are open. *See* formant (1) for acoustic correlates.

VP = verb phrase.

VP-Internal Subject Hypothesis Proposal dating from the 1990s by which, in terms of *X-bar syntax, subjects originate as *Specifiers in *phrases (2) headed by a lexical verb. E.g., in the derivation of *Mary loves me*, an initial $_{VP}$[*Mary* $_{V'}$[$_V$[*love*] *me*]]. This will itself be part of a succession of larger units, headed by tenses etc., into whose structures *Mary* then moves.

'VP-shell' Informally, in the context of Chomsky's *minimalist programme, of any of a number of quasi-verbal phrases, headed by null *light verbs or whatever, seen as enclosing phrases headed by verbs.

vṛddhi Term in Sanskrit grammar for a unit analysed as the combination of a simple vowel or resonant with a preceding double *a*. One of three degrees of 'strengthening': e.g. *i* is simple or unstrengthened; *e* (← *a* + *i*) is the *guṇa form in which it is strengthened by a single *a*; *ai* (← *ā* + *i*) is the *vṛddhi* form resulting from a further strengthening.

VSO language One in which a verb, *subject (3), and *object (3) are at least basically or most commonly in that order. Opp. SVO language etc.

Vulgar Latin The spoken language of the western Roman empire, from which the *Romance languages developed, as opposed to Latin as written in its standardized form. 'Vulgar' simply means 'of the people' (Latin 'vulgus').

Wackernagel's Law Rule of Indo-European syntax, identified by
J. Wackernagel in the 1890s, by which a series of particles and other
clitic elements occupied a position in the clause after the first accented
element. Cf., in Ancient Greek, the position of one word for 'but' in e.g.
nûn dè pôs légeis 'But how do you say now?' (lit. 'now but how you-say?').

Since claimed to be an instance of a wider principle; hence the
second position in a clause or sentence is called the '**Wackernagel
position**'.

Wakashan Family of languages spoken or formerly spoken on the
Pacific coast of North America, in British Columbia and south of the
Canadian border. Nootka and Kwakwala (also called 'Kwakiutl') have
been cited extensively by American scholars from Boas and Sapir
onwards.

'*wanna*-contraction' The reduction in American English of forms
like *want to* or *going to* in *I want to (wanna) do it* or *I'm going to (gonna)
do it*.

Warlpiri Australian language spoken in an area around Yuendumu in
the Northern Territory.

wave model Model proposed by J. Schmidt in the 1870s in which
the historical relations within Indo-European and other families of
languages are seen in terms of the intersection of individual changes,
each originating in a specific group of speakers and spreading to
others with progressively weaker effect. The image is that of the waves
caused by stones dropped into different places in a pool.

German ***Wellentheorie***, proposed in opposition to the
Stammbaumtheorie or *Stammbaum model.

weak **1.** (Verb, formation, etc.) in Germanic languages distinguished
by the addition of suffixes as opposed to *ablaut. Thus, in English, *talk*
is a weak verb (past tense and participle *talk-ed*) while *sing* is a strong
verb (*sang, sung*). **2.** (Syllable etc.) *See* Metrical Phonology. **3.** Also of
reduced forms e.g. of *auxiliaries: thus *-'ve* in *I've finished* or *-'d* in *I'd love
one* are weak forms of *have* and *would*.

weak generative capacity The set of languages, in the *formal
sense, that can be generated by a given type of generative grammar.
Grammars of different types are **weakly equivalent** if the sets of
languages they can generate are the same: e.g. a form of *dependency
grammar was shown in the 1960s to be weakly equivalent to a
*context-free phrase structure grammar. Grammars of type A are more

'**powerful**' than ones of type B if there are languages A can generate but B cannot, and not vice versa. *Cf.* strong generative capacity.

'Weak Lexicalist Hypothesis' *See* Strong Lexicalist Hypothesis.

weakly equivalent (Grammars, types of grammar) that generate the same set of sentences or have the same *weak generative capacity.

'weather verb' A verb such as English *rain* or *snow* which, in its basic sense, is seen as taking no more than a *dummy subject. Thus *it* is a dummy in *It is raining*, while an equivalent verb has no subject in e.g. Italian *Piove* (lit. 'rain-3SG').

weight The property by which *heavy or 'long' syllables are distinguished from light or 'short' syllables, or syllables counting e.g. as two *morae from those counting as one mora.

Wellentheorie *See* wave model.

well-formed In accordance with a given system of rules; hence often = grammatical (2). Opp. ill-formed.

Welsh *Celtic, related within the Brythonic branch to *Breton and *Cornish. Spoken by a minority of the population of Wales, mainly in the north-western counties of Gwynedd and Dyfed; attested by literary texts from the 6th century AD.

Wendish = Sorbian.

'Wernicke's aphasia' A form of *aphasia characterized by fluent but meaningless speech: '**Wernicke's area**' is a part of the brain where lesions have been diagnosed as giving rise to it.

West African languages Historically fragmented: larger genetic relationships have been and are still in dispute. For specific groupings *see* Benue-Congo; Chadic; Gur; Kru; Kwa; Mande; West Atlantic languages.

The administrative and other use of English or French largely coincides with boundaries between former colonies. The distribution of indigenous languages, even when one is dominant in a political unit, for the most part does not.

West Atlantic languages A group of languages spoken mainly along the Atlantic coast of Africa, from Senegal to west Liberia, but also including *Fula. Wolof, spoken in Senegal and Gambia, is another important member. Also called '**Atlantic**'.

West Germanic Conventional division of *Germanic which includes German (both High *German and Low *German), Dutch, and English. Traditionally distinguished from East Germanic (*Gothic) and *North Germanic.

WFR A rule (R) of word-formation (WF): e.g. that by which *happiness* or *sadness* are formed from *happy* and *sad*.

'what is said' Distinguished technically, in theories of *pragmatics, from 'what is implicated'. E.g. what is said by *I am in bed* is that the speaker is in bed; but when this sentence is uttered it might have the *implicature that they would rather not receive a visitor, come out for dinner, etc.

The notion is as problematic as that of 'pragmatics' vs. 'semantics' generally; hence, in particular, accounts that involve *implicitures or *explicatures; or the meanings of *utterance types as opposed to utterance tokens.

***wh*-cleft** *See* pseudo-cleft.

***wh*-form** Any of a class of words in English that typically begin with *wh*-: e.g. *who*, *which*, *why*. Also of phrases that begin with such words: e.g. *which book*, *what people*.

Thence extended, by linguists whose native language is English, to forms that play similar syntactic roles in other languages.

'whimperative' Coined in the 1970s for a sentence that has the form of an *interrogative but the force of an order or instruction: e.g. *Why don't you shut up?*, meaning 'Shut up!'.

***wh*-interrogative** An *interrogative formed with a **wh*-form: e.g. *Who is coming?, What will she do?* Also called a '*wh*-question'; or, to avoid a label specific to English, 'open interrogative'; 'focused interrogative'; '*x*-interrogative'.

***wh*-island constraint** Proposed principle by which a unit in a clause introduced by a **wh*-form cannot bear a direct syntactic relation to a unit outside it. E.g. one does not say *Whose book did he say where he stole?*: the reason, according to this principle, is that *whose book* would be directly related as the object of a verb (*stole*) which is within a clause (*where he stole*) introduced by the *wh*-form *where*. *Cf.*, on the assumption that *how* is not a *wh*-form, *Whose book did he say how he stole?*

Cf. island. Formulated in the late 1960s as a constraint on movement: thus in an underlying *he said [where he stole whose book]*, *whose book* could not be moved from the bracketed clause by **wh*-movement.

whisper Technically of a type of *phonation in which air passes with turbulence through a small opening at the back of the glottis. In whispering, in the ordinary sense, sounds that are normally voiced are produced with whisper instead.

In **whispery voice** the vocal cords are close enough to vibrate but air also passes continuously through them.

***wh*-movement** Proposed movement of **wh*-forms to the beginning of a clause or sentence: e.g. in *Who can you see?*, the movement of *who*

from an underlying position as the object of *see* (*you can see who*). Hence
of this type of construction in general, even when a process of
movement from an underlying position is rejected.

wh-question *See* wh-interrogative.

'wh-raising' Process peculiar to *Government and Binding Theory
by which in e.g. *Who does what?* the second *wh-form (*what*) is moved at
the level of *Logical Form to a position in which, like the first, it is a
unit binding an argument in a larger structure.

'wh-trace' A *trace hypothetically left by *wh-movement: thus the
trace *t* in *Who can you see t?*, seen as derived from *you can see who*.
Distinguished in *Government and Binding Theory from an *NP-trace.

widening of meaning Enlargement of the class of entities that a
word denotes: e.g. the meaning of *bird*, formerly 'young bird', was
extended, in the early history of English, to mean 'bird' in general.
Also called '**extension of meaning**': but extensions that involve the
simple loss of a restriction (like the restriction to birds that are young)
might usefully be distinguished from those by which new senses will
be added.

wide vowel One in whose production the tongue is relaxed and
flattened in cross-section. A possible factor in distinguishing e.g. [ʊ]
from [uː] in English, or in similar distinctions in other Germanic
languages. Opp. narrow vowel.

wish *See* optative; volitive.

Wittgenstein, Ludwig (1889–1951) Austrian philosopher whose
career lay mainly in England. Influential in linguistics especially
through his posthumous *Philosophische Untersuchungen* (English
translation *Philosophical Investigations* (1953)), which, in sharp contrast
to his earlier *Tractatus Logico-Philosophicus* (1921), sought to replace
conventional theories of meaning with a theory based simply on the
ways in which words are, in specific situations, used. Often cited, in
particular, for a passage illustrated with the uses of the word *game*, in
which he shows that a definition of its meaning, in the strict sense of a
set of precise conditions which something must meet to be a game, is
not possible. *Cf.* family resemblance; ordinary language philosophy.

Wolof *See* West Atlantic languages.

word Traditionally the smallest of the units that make up a sentence,
and marked as such in writing. In practice, words are established by
various criteria. They are generally the smallest units that can form an
utterance on their own: in Bloomfield's terminology, they are
*minimal free forms. There are often restrictions on their phonetic
make-up: e.g. words in English cannot begin with [ŋ] (*-ng-*) or [ʒ]. The

position of a stress or other accent is often *fixed (1): i.e. it is determined by the boundaries of words or their syllabic structure. Elements within them show greater *cohesion (2) than larger units: thus *stems and *affixes cannot be separated except by other affixes. Nor does the order of their elements tend to vary. These criteria sometimes conflict, but no other unit shows such near agreement in such different respects.

Distinctions are often drawn: **1.** Between a *phonological word or word as seen from the viewpoint of phonology, and a *grammatical word (2), established by grammatical criteria only; **2.** Between *lexemes as words distinguished in the lexicon (e.g. the verb 'to sing') and the individual *word forms that they subsume (past tense *sang*, present participle *singing*, etc.).

Word and Paradigm One of three models of morphology first distinguished by C. F. Hockett in the 1950s. Usually applied to any account in which the primary focus is on the oppositions between words as wholes within a *paradigm, rather than their internal structure. E.g., in Italian, *cantavo* 'I was singing' is characterized as a whole by its oppositions, as first person, to the second and third persons *cantavi*, *cantava*; as singular, to the plural *cantavamo* 'we were singing'; as imperfect, to the present *canto* 'I am singing'; as indicative, to the subjunctive *cantassi*. Any division of the word into smaller elements (say, *cant-a-v-o*) is then secondary.

Distinguished by Hockett from *Item and Arrangement, *Item and Process. For an alternative typology, in the light of accounts developed later in the 20th century, *see* inferential-realizational.

word class Any class of word established by similarities in syntax or in grammar generally. Often specifically of *major word classes, such as the *parts of speech.

word form The form of a specific word, either phonetic or orthographic. Distinguished as such from the word as a lexical unit or *lexeme: e.g. *ran* or [ran] is one of a set of word forms (*run, runs, ran, running*) each of which is a '**form of**' the lexeme '(to) run'. Also distinguished from a *morphosyntactic word or word as characterized by grammatical categories: e.g. *ran* or [ran] realizes a unit that is morphosyntactically the past tense of '(to) run'; *run* or [rʌn] either one that is morphosyntactically its past participle (in *It has run out*) or one that is present or infinitive (in *They run fast* or *Make them run*).

word-formation 1. The formation of words in general. **2.** Specifically of the formation of words as lexical units, subsuming *compounding and *derivational morphology. **3.** = derivational morphology.

Word Grammar Model of grammar developed in the 1980s by R. A. Hudson. Basically an integrated account of syntax and the lexicon, in which syntactic relations other than coordination are reduced to ordered *dependencies of one word on another. E.g., in *Sensible people ride bicycles*, *sensible* depends on and precedes *people*, *people* depends on and precedes *ride*, *bicycles* depends on and follows *ride*. Dependencies are determined by the interaction of the lexical properties of individual words (e.g. *ride* is a finite or 'tensed' verb, *people* a plural noun) with general rules that state e.g. that finite verbs take a subject, that a subject precedes and depends on a verb, and so on. Similarly *ride*, as an individual word, can take an object, which, by a general rule, will depend on and typically follow it.

One of various models whose origins lie in a reaction against *transformational grammars in the late 1970s. With others, such as *Generalized Phrase Structure Grammar, it proposes a single level of syntactic structure; but no other treatment has rejected the concept of constituency, or developed those of dependency and of a syntax grounded in the lexicon, with such thoroughness.

word-group Two or more words forming a syntactic unit: hence = phrase (3).

'word order' Used widely of the order of elements within the sentence, whether words or, more commonly, phrases. E.g. the 'basic word order' in English is 'SVO': i.e. a subject phrase S, whether one word or many, precedes the verb (V), and an object phrase O, again whether one word or many, follows it. Hence '**free word order**' often means, more strictly, free order of phrases: *see* free (4), as opposed to fixed (2).

word stress *Stress that is intrinsic to a word, as opposed to *sentence stress. The term '**lexical stress**' may be used of stress associated with a unit of the lexicon, as opposed to '**morphological stress**' determined e.g. by a specific affix. E.g. in Italian, an infinitive such as *indicare* 'to point out' has a morphological stress on the syllable before the infinitive suffix: *indic-á-re*. But this overrides a lexical stress on the first syllable of the root: cf. *índic-o* (with stress on *in-*) 'I indicate'.

'world English' Loosely of any form of English, whether native or a second language, spoken outside the territory in which English historically developed.

Wörter und Sachen German 'words and things': name given to a movement in the early 20th century (and to the journal founded by it) which insisted that the etymology of words and their distribution across dialects should be studied in close association with that of the artefacts etc. that they denoted.

WP = Word and Paradigm.

X

X Variable, in *X-bar syntax, ranging over N, V, and other syntactic categories. Hence XP, as a variable ranging over categories of phrase; and so on.

X-bar syntax System of *phrase structure grammar developed by Chomsky and R. S. Jackendoff in the 1970s and incorporated into *Government and Binding Theory in the 1980s.

Basically one in which a sentence is represented by a hierarchy of *phrases (2), each of a category determined by that of a head. Thus the phrase in the illustration has as its *head (1) a preposition (P); and as a whole is correspondingly a preposition(al) phrase (PP). Within phrases all divisions are binary, between the head itself or a constituent that includes it, and other units that are generally of other categories. Thus, in the illustration, *in the middle* is a smaller unit that includes the preposition, and is labelled correspondingly a P´; as such it then stands in a binary relation to *right*. The name of the system reflects an alternative notation in which' equivalently, for the same example, the P´ would be a 'barred P' or 'P̄'; similarly, in the earliest accounts, the PP would have been a 'P̄̄'.

Hence a template for syntactic structure in general. Thus, in what has become the received formulation, every XP must immediately include an X´, which may combine, as shown in the illustration, with a unit in the role of *Specifier (Spec). Any X´ may in turn include one in the role of *Complement (Comp), combining either, as in the illustration, directly with the head X, or with a smaller X´ which will be structured similarly. Heads of any category may be *null; hence, from the mid-1980s onwards, an account of syntax is reduced entirely to this format, with both null and overt units moving, in as many stages as necessary, from smaller XPs into larger.

Reformulated in the *minimalist programme, but in substance no different. *See* bare phrase structure.

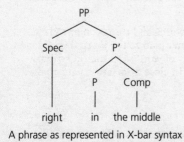

A phrase as represented in X-bar syntax

Xhosa *Bantu language, spoken in Cape Province and Transkei (South Africa) and distinguished by political divisions, within a group called *Nguni, from *Zulu. The name is pronounced in English with initial [k].

x-interrogative Proposed as an alternative to *wh-interrogative. Also called an 'x-question'. *Cf.* open interrogative.

Y

Yana *See* Hokan.

Yawelmani *See* Yokuts.

'yes–no question' One which has a simple positive or negative answer. *Cf.* closed interrogative, polar interrogative.

Yi *See* Lolo-Burmese.

Yiddish West *Germanic, historically a variety of German influenced heavily by Hebrew and spoken by Jewish communities over a wide area of central and eastern Europe; also described for that reason as '**Judaeo-German**'. After the massacre of Jews in the Second World War the largest body of speakers was in the USA.

yod The sound [j], written as *y* e.g. in English *yet* [jɛt]. Hence **yodization** (also '**yoticization**' etc.) is a sound change or other process resulting in [j].

Yokuts Family of languages, spoken or formerly spoken in and around the San Joaquin Valley in California. The sound system (of Yawelmani more specifically) was a subject of repeated reanalysis in the heyday of *Generative Phonology.

Yoruba The official language in south-west Nigeria; spoken over a large area which includes Lagos; also across the border in parts of Benin. Yoruba and others closely related to it are among a large group of languages variously classified either as within *Kwa or as within *Benue-Congo.

yoticization *See* yod.

Young Grammarians *See* Neogrammarians.

Yucatec *See* Mayan.

Yurok Californian language related to *Algonquian within Algic.

zero (Ø) Usually of an element posited at some level of representation but realized as *null. Thus a phrase such as *women*, as in *Women adore him*, is often described, e.g. in accounts that accept the *DP-hypothesis, as having a **zero determiner** (Ø *women*), opposed to those of *the women* or *a woman*. *Relative clauses such as *I saw* in *the men I saw* would similarly have a **zero relative pronoun**: *the men [Ø I saw]*, like *the men [who I saw]*.

Other examples in syntax have included *traces, *PRO, and *pro as so-called 'empty categories'.

zero anaphora Relation in which a phonetically *null element is seen as linked by *anaphora to an antecedent.

Thus, in English, an element such as *he* may be linked by anaphora to a preceding noun phrase: *John says he* (i.e. John) *is coming*. In a similar construction in Spanish there is usually no corresponding element: *Dice Juan que viene* (lit. 'says John that comes'). But in many accounts the subject of *viene* 'comes' would be described as a null element: e.g. in *Government and Binding Theory, a phonetically null *pro. Like *he* in English, this could then be anaphoric to *Juan*: thus, with the relation shown by subscript *indices, *Juan$_i$ dice que pro$_i$ viene*.

zero derivation A process of *word-formation in which there is no change to the form that undergoes it: e.g. that by which the verb *fish*, seen as one lexical unit, is derived from the noun *fish*, seen as another lexical unit. *Cf.* conversion.

zero morph A *null element posited as an *allomorph of a morpheme when no actual allomorph is present. E.g. in (*three*) *sheep* the noun is plural, but, unlike *cats* or *horses*, it has no plural ending. The plural morpheme is accordingly said to be realized by a zero morph: *sheep-Ø*.

zero-valent (Verb etc.) whose *valency or set of *arguments is null. Thus verbs in Italian generally take a subject and e.g. an object, but *piovere* 'to rain' is a zero-valent verb that takes neither: *Piove* (lit. 'rains') 'It is raining'. 'To rain' in English has also been described as zero-valent, on the assumption that the *it* of *It is raining* is a *dummy.

zeugma Traditionally of cases of coordination in which one element would not form a construction on its own. E.g. one cannot say *They said that so what*; therefore there is a zeugma in *They said that [[they were coming] and [so what]]*. Often extended to include *syllepsis.

Zipf's Law Statistical law proposed by G. K. Zipf in the 1940s which relates the frequency (f) with which a word occurs in a text to its rank

(r) in an order of frequency. According to the law, the product $f \times r$ is, or is within limits, constant.

zoonym A word for a kind of animal, e.g. *fox*.

zoosemiotics Term coined in the 1960s for the study of systems of communication in species other than man. The implication is that, with linguistics, this is a branch of *semiotics.

Zulu *Bantu, spoken mainly in northern Natal (South Africa) and distinguished from Xhosa, by political divisions, within a closely related group called *Nguni. **Fanagalo** is a pidginized form of Zulu/Xhosa, used especially in mining regions in South Africa and beyond.

Zuni A genetically unclassified language of New Mexico in the USA.

Zyryan = Komi.

Oxford Paperback Reference

The Concise Oxford Dictionary of English Etymology
T. F. Hoad

A wealth of information about our language and its history, this reference source provides over 17,000 entries on word origins.

'A model of its kind'

Daily Telegraph

A Dictionary of Euphemisms
R. W. Holder

This hugely entertaining collection draws together euphemisms from all aspects of life: work, sexuality, age, money, and politics.

Review of the previous edition
'This ingenious collection is not only very funny but extremely instructive too'

Iris Murdoch

The Oxford Dictionary of Slang
John Ayto

Containing over 10,000 words and phrases, this is the ideal reference for those interested in the more quirky and unofficial words used in the English language.

'hours of happy browsing for language lovers'

Observer

OXFORD

Oxford Paperback Reference

A Dictionary of Psychology
Andrew M. Colman

Over 10,500 authoritative entries make up the most wide-ranging dictionary of psychology available.

'impressive ... certainly to be recommended'
Times Higher Educational Supplement

'Comprehensive, sound, readable, and up-to-date, this is probably the best single-volume dictionary of its kind.'
Library Journal

A Dictionary of Economics
John Black

Fully up-to-date and jargon-free coverage of economics. Over 2,500 terms on all aspects of economic theory and practice.

A Dictionary of Law

An ideal source of legal terminology for systems based on English law. Over 4,000 clear and concise entries.

'The entries are clearly drafted and succinctly written ... Precision for the professional is combined with a layman's enlightenment.'
Times Literary Supplement

OXFORD

Oxford Paperback Reference

The Concise Oxford Companion to English Literature
Margaret Drabble and Jenny Stringer

Based on the best-selling *Oxford Companion to English Literature*, this is an indispensable guide to all aspects of English literature.

Review of the parent volume
'a magisterial and monumental achievement'

Literary Review

The Concise Oxford Companion to Irish Literature
Robert Welch

From the ogam alphabet developed in the 4th century to Roddy Doyle, this is a comprehensive guide to writers, works, topics, folklore, and historical and cultural events.

Review of the parent volume
'Heroic volume ... It surpasses previous exercises of similar nature in the richness of its detail and the ecumenism of its approach.'

Times Literary Supplement

A Dictionary of Shakespeare
Stanley Wells

Compiled by one of the best-known international authorities on the playwright's works, this dictionary offers up-to-date information on all aspects of Shakespeare, both in his own time and in later ages.

OXFORD

Oxford Paperback Reference

The Concise Oxford Dictionary of Quotations
Edited by Elizabeth Knowles

Based on the highly acclaimed *Oxford Dictionary of Quotations*, this
paperback edition maintains its extensive coverage of literary and
historical quotations, and contains completely up-to-date material. A
fascinating read and an essential reference tool.

The Oxford Dictionary of Humorous Quotations
Edited by Ned Sherrin

From the sharply witty to the downright hilarious, this sparkling
collection will appeal to all senses of humour.

Quotations by Subject
Edited by Susan Ratcliffe

A collection of over 7,000 quotations, arranged thematically for easy
look-up. Covers an enormous range of nearly 600 themes from 'The
Internet' to 'Parliament'.

The Concise Oxford Dictionary of Phrase and Fable
Edited by Elizabeth Knowles

Provides a wealth of fascinating and informative detail for over 10,000
phrases and allusions used in English today. Find out about anything
from the 'Trojan horse' to 'ground zero'.

OXFORD

Oxford Paperback Reference

The Concise Oxford Dictionary of Art & Artists
Ian Chilvers

Based on the highly praised *Oxford Dictionary of Art*, over 2,500 up-to-date entries on painting, sculpture, and the graphic arts.

'the best and most inclusive single volume available, immensely useful and very well written'

Marina Vaizey, *Sunday Times*

The Concise Oxford Dictionary of Art Terms
Michael Clarke

Written by the Director of the National Gallery of Scotland, over 1,800 entries cover periods, styles, materials, techniques, and foreign terms.

A Dictionary of Architecture
James Stevens Curl

Over 5,000 entries and 250 illustrations cover all periods of Western architectural history.

'splendid ... you can't have a more concise, entertaining, and informative guide to the words of architecture'

Architectural Review

'excellent, and amazing value for money ... by far the best thing of its kind'

Professor David Walker

OXFORD